COLLECTOR CAR
RESTORATION
BIBLE

PRACTICAL TECHNIQUES FOR PROFESSIONAL RESULTS

Matt Joseph

©2005 KP Books
Published by

kp books
An Imprint of F+W Publications

700 East State Street • Iola, WI 54990-0001
715-445-2214 • 888-457-2873

Our toll-free number to place an order or obtain
a free catalog is (800) 258-0929.

Library of Congress Catalog Number: 2005906833

ISBN: 0-87349-925-5

Designed by Jon Stein
Edited by Brian Earnest

Printed in United States

Dedication

Dedicated to:

Sam Adelman, early old car recycler and supplier of parts, information and wisdom ...

and

Dick Brigham, author, inventor, editor, printer and gentleman ...

and

Bill Cannon, founder of the monthly restoration journal, Skinned Knuckles, and its publisher for more than 35 years, before his recent retirement ...

The first letters of their last names combine to form "ABC," and together they have helped to teach me and to exemplify the ABCs of understanding cars and people and so much more.

Contents

Preface

THE STANDARD GUIDE to Automotive Restoration was first published in 1992 and has been extensively revised, updated and improved in the present edition—called the *Collector Car Restoration Bible*. The enduring popularity of the original Standard Guide encouraged me and KP Books to make the changes necessary to keep it current. The addition of mostly color photography should be a big plus for readers of the new edition.

Like the first issue of *The Standard Guide*, the revised edition is about how to restore old automobiles. Its purpose is to inform owners and restorers about many aspects of car restoration. It is not meant to be comprehensive, and such topics as upholstering, plating and wiring are not specifically discussed here. What is covered are all of the major mechanical systems in old automobiles and all major aspects of restoring old vehicle bodies.

The approach taken is "generic," so the discussion is of general approaches, principles, strategies, and practices—not of particular cars. Each chapter attempts to inform the reader regarding the historical development of the item or system under consideration—how it works, how it developed historically, how it varies on many different cars. With that background, this book attempts to describe the major issues involved in how to repair and/or restore these components and systems.

I hope that the information and photographs in this book will be of interest and use to novice restorers, to intermediate restorers and even to advanced restorers.

A great deal about old car collecting has changed since *The Standard Guide* came out in 1992. The era of many professional restoration shops came to an end. Many of the parts and systems in old cars have become obsolete and it has become increasingly challenging to find the parts, information and services needed to restore old cars.

Once common knowledge of things like carburetors and point-condenser ignition systems has become somewhat obscure and often hard to find. I hope that this book will help fill some of these information voids.

One thing about car collecting has not changed: Most old cars never see the services of professional restoration shops. Instead, owners marshal their skills, talents and resources, or the purchase the skills and talents of others, to accomplish their restoration goals.

Those goals may be very limited—an engine component repair or refinishing a panel—or they sometimes may range to complete body-off-frame restorations. The attempt here is to provide useful information on old vehicle renovation that addresses the wide variety of goals that are possible in old car restoration pursuits.

Old car owners need all of the restoration help that they can get. What they are doing amounts to grass roots preservation of important historical artifacts. This is an enterprise of tremendous importance, but it is also work that is often difficult and/or expensive to do and to commission. Often, it is very satisfying work that results in a tremendous sense of accomplishment. The information in this book is intended to be a useful resource for restorers at many levels in performing and/or commissioning this work. This information is stated regarding a wide range of topics.

This book grew out of a series of lectures on car restoration—"The Mechanical and Physical Restoration of Old Cars" that I delivered at the University of Wisconsin on several occasions and at several campuses from the late 1970s into the 1990s. Those lectures were published in about 30 articles in Skinned Knuckles magazine in the early to mid-1980s. Over the years, numerous students and *Skinned Knuckles* readers suggested that I write a "restoration book." This book is a major revision of that original volume.

There are so many people whom I would like to thank for helping me with this book that the list would be as long as any chapter in it. That would make pretty dull reading and might embarrass some of the people who have contributed to my knowledge of car restoration. Let me single out a few people for thanks, people whose contributions to this effort were both crucial and extraordinary.

Brian Earnest, John Gunnell and Bill Krause at KP Books encouraged me to revise the original book and provided great help and support with every aspect of this project. I greatly appreciate their aid and support.

In particular, John Gunnell was tireless in helping me to locate venues for many of the photos that I needed to illustrate this book. He helped with almost every aspect of it. It would be difficult to adequately thank him for his efforts on my behalf.

Bill and Terry Cannon at Skinned Knuckles magazine have published my restoration articles on a monthly basis for almost 30 years. Without their support and encouragement over those years, this book would not have been contemplated, much less written. The Cannons represent the very best in every aspect of old car collecting. Their magazine, *Skinned Knuckles*, has been an important beacon for that best for more than decades.

By the time that you read this, the ownership of *Skinned Knuckles* magazine will have changed and Bill and Terry Cannon will have gone on to other pursuits. The old car collecting hobby owes the Cannons, Bill, Terry and the late Charlotte Cannon, a tremendous debt for their great magazine and for their dedication and service to our hobby.

My special appreciation goes to five businesses, and their proprietors, for extending terrific resources and tremendous courtesies to me in allowing me to photograph several restoration processes on their premises.

Mark Weaver's Weaver Auto Parts Machine Shop allowed us to photograph numerous aspects of engine and other mechanical, machining and rebuilding processes in their well-equipped shop. Brad, the shop foreman and his staff did everything possible to make this process seamless and easy. This is a terrific automotive machine shop and this book has benefited greatly from having access to the knowledge and equipment at Weaver Auto Parts Machine Shop in Sauk City, Wisconsin.

Bob Lorkowski at L'Cars in Cameron, Wisconsin, gave us free run of his terrific full restoration facility to take photographs and to learn their processes. L'Cars may just be the best restoration shop in the United States and it was a great privilege to be able to learn from the craftsmen there and to photograph their work in progress.

Carl Heideman at Eclectic Motors in Holland, Michigan, shared knowledge and his facilities, while allowing me to photograph the sophisticated equipment, skills and work in his metal fabrication shop. I greatly appreciate his help.

Sammy Ashendorf at Northwestern Auto Supply spent a day with me showing me his impressive operation, one of the truly great storehouses of old car parts, knowledge and services on this continent. It was a pleasure meeting him and working with him.

John Twist, the genial proprietor of University Motors Ltd. in Ada, Michigan allowed me to photograph his British car restoration and service facility and provided useful insights and information for this book. His museum (display cases) of mechanical horrors deserves a book of its own. It is a collection of the disasters that result from mistakes, oversights and stupidity in working on mechanical systems.

Well, by now, it may seem that I have thanked everyone but the kitchen sink. Still, there are a few other people who did a lot to make this book possible. My neighbor, Bob Kaschel, spent many days working with me on photography. I thank him for modeling in several of the photos and for his good humor and for his useful suggestions regarding the photographs that we took.

Nick Steinbrink helped with some of the photography and my wife, Gail, and youngest son, Jared, also worked tirelessly with me on photography.

Finally, I want to express appreciation to my parents, who offered early support for and encouragement to my interest in old car restoration: my father by nurturing my early interest in this activity and supporting it with his great knowledge of automobiles, and my mother for tolerating and even encouraging her two "car guys" more than any male car collectors had a right to expect from any American lady in the 1950s and 1960s.

My thanks to those named above, and to many other friends and acquaintances who have helped to further my understanding of automotive restoration and my enthusiasm for it.

Matt L. Joseph, Prairie du Sac, Wisconsin, July, 2005

Chapter

Restoring Old Cars in Times of Significant Change

Restoration is about dreams, the dreams of taking something old and shabby and making it look and perform more like it did when it was new. Some projects, like the 1941 Chevrolet pickup truck pictured here, are very challenging. This book is about how to confront restoration challenges.

THERE HAS BEEN A QUIET BUT MASSIVE REVOLUTION in automobiles in the last 25 years. Most of it has occurred since Krause Publications' *Standard Guide to Automotive Restoration* first appeared in 1992. That revolution has completely changed most aspects of how automobiles are constructed, repaired and restored. Because the materials, technologies and processes to make new cars have changed, the same factors in repairing them have changed. Inevitably,

this has altered many of the methods and specifics of how we now approach restoration work.

From the earliest days that cars were restored, there has been a continuum in how they were designed and fabricated. Most often, significant changes in these technologies occurred slowly and were slow to take hold.

There were a few rapid, watershed changes, like the adoption of point-condenser ignitions and electric lighting

Seen through the weeds darkly at first, the charm of this old truck is striking. It will take years of dedication, not to mention considerable skill, to realize the dream of restoring it. But all things are possible to those who strive mightily.

The only strategy for restoring a vehicle as deteriorated as this one is complete restoration. Partial restoration is not an option.

These photos show the "first step" on a long journey—removing the ridiculous International hood from this truck. That step reveals some good news – there is an authentic engine in the bay. More good news is that the authentic box for this truck is visible on page 8.

systems in 1912 and 1913, but most important changes in automobiles occurred glacially by comparison. Automatic transmissions required two decades of intensive refinement before they became common and reliable. Alternators replaced generators over a period of several years, while the conversion to acrylic finishes took decades. The pace of automotive change was leisurely.

However, the digital revolution of the last quarter century has swept like a tidal wave over every aspect of automotive production, operation, repair and restoration. This has meant great changes in the basic processes used to manufacture motor vehicles. Accordingly, things like materials, joining techniques and controls have been revolutionized.

The revolution in how cars are made, repaired and maintained carries vast implications for restorers. It creates potential pitfalls, but it also brings with it great opportunities.

Twenty years ago, it was difficult to find an American male who did not understand a point-condenser ignition system well enough to repair and calibrate one. Intimate knowledge of carburetors was, perhaps, less widespread, but still broadly held.

In that period, the auto industry had to scramble to find or coin technicians who could deal with the emerging technologies of computer controlled ignition and fuel injection.

Today, that situation is almost exactly reversed. People who understand and can repair arcane point-condenser ignition systems are becoming rare, since the daily business in our nation's service bays rarely encounters them.

Increasingly, restorers of older cars are discovering that what was once was easy to find or accomplish has become more difficult. This situation calls on restorers for the exercise of their best ingenuity, and for a sense of when to compromise with modernity and when not to.

As some needed skills, parts, processes and materials become increasingly scarce, old car restorers must look to those with common interests for mutual aid. Hot rodders, tuners and tractor restorers, for example, often face the same problems as old car restorers. Today's restorer is more likely to find an obsolete partial-flow, canister-type oil filter cartridge at a farm store than at an auto parts store. The same goes for oddball 6-volt batteries and battery accessories. Knowledge of complex panel forming and tools to perform it are more likely to come from the hot rod sector than from the usual sources of autobody supplies.

Resisting new materials and processes, like powder coating, likely will prove futile in the long run, while resurrecting old processes, like Zinctone°, will prove increasingly difficult and will require great ingenuity and perseverance in finding old formulas and the chemicals to make them work.

In fact, modern automotive restoration problems

This MG TD looks great from a distance because there is no major impact or rust damage visible, and everything looks sound and authentic. The paint is deteriorated, but that is expected in an original car.

will refocus restorers on what was always a central area of dilemma for them, knowing when to compromise and when not to bend, that is, knowing when to quit.

What will never change is the deserved sense of accomplishment that restorers feel when they reach what they have defined as their restoration objectives.

This book is intended to help them to do that.

A Place to Begin

Usually, the hardest part of any complex undertaking is finding a place to begin and the self-assurance to do so. This is true of restoring an automobile or revising a book on how to restore automobiles. Once started, most projects proceed, either in or out of control, to various rewards and/ or catastrophes.

It is the purpose of this book to share with readers the benefits of knowledge resulting from my many rewards and catastrophes in automobile restoration in the last 5 decades.

The *Collector Car Restoration Bible* is organized by automotive systems and topics, because a good first step in attacking any complex task or problem is to break it down into a series of simpler and more manageable component tasks.

The knowledge I have of restoration practices was gained mostly by the expedient of trial-and-error. There were few helpful books on this topic years ago, when I began to gather my experience. In recent years, new communications media, such as videotapes, CDs, DVDs and the Internet have greatly eased making the quest for restoration information and knowledge.

Still, trial-and-error remains very much a part of the restoration learning curve proposition. Often, the amount of error is enormous and costly in time and money. However, as I look back over 5 decades of restoration endeavors, I am amazed at how uncostly some of my errors were.

I remember, for example, a 1923 Pierce Arrow that my father and I worked on in the late 1950s. Pierce had a really nifty system for separating the heads from the blocks of its massive six-cylinder, 24-valve engines. There were two "blind bolts" threaded into the head at each end that rested against the blocks' deck surface. To unseize the heads from their numerous studs, you simply ran these blind bolts down against the blocks, and dislodged the heads. It was a wonderfully simple way to accomplish what otherwise would have been a difficult job. However, this system of head removal placed one heavy premium on any mechanic who used it—to remember to run the blind bolts back up into the head before reinstalling it.

Uh huh, you guessed it. I learned about the installation imperative from watching a huge error. In one of our early restoration efforts, we forgot to run the bolts back into the head when we went to replace it. As we tightened the head nuts there was an ominous cracking sound. I suggested that we stop to find the cause, but I was only in my teens and the gnarled old mechanic who was assisting us that evening acidly responded to my caution, "Aw, it's just the head settlin' in."

Closer inspection reveals local areas of possible rust deterioration, particularly around the running board and fender beading and on the hood louvers.

Of course, it wasn't, but I have often marveled at that gentleman's improbable and impromptu explanation. It was offered so spontaneously and with such commanding authority, as if everyone knew the sound of a "head settlin' in." Finally, the cracking sound reached crescendo levels and, after the gnarled, old mechanic had excused himself from the premises for the unlikely (for him) mission of "spending the evening with the wife"—I think that he sensed a catastrophe was at hand— we found the cause of the sound. Of course, the block was badly cracked and distorted.

In those days, this was a catastrophe, but one of minor dimensions. A call to Sam Adelman, a major old car parts guru in the Northeast in those days, solved our problem. Another block was dispatched from his emporium in Mount Vernon, New York, to us in Bennington, Vermont. The replacement block cost $65, plus $15 for Railway Express. Crating was included in the $65.

The new block had to be cleaned, checked for cracks and deck ground. The cylinders had to be honed and the valves and guides dealt with. Then we had to paint it. The point is, the whole miserable misadventure cost, maybe, $250. Unpleasant, yes, but it was not devastating to our finances.

That same error today would probably run you 25 times what it cost us in the late 1950s. The cost of making mistakes has gone up radically. Forty years ago, if you had a car painted and the paint checked, you were out a few hundred dollars. Today, it amounts to thousands. And mistakes do happen. No one is immune.

A gracious and economical teacher, trial-and-error, assisted my early learning about restoring old cars. However, by now she has become an expensive mistress. Somehow, when she was cheap her capricious nature was masked and she appeared a gracious teacher. Now that she is expensive, her erratic excesses class her as a mistress.

It is my intention in this book to try to help readers avoid what are by now costly mistakes.

Restoration is a vast, varied and ever-changing field. It includes many obscure specialties, and there is a good deal

To really judge the damage to the metal over the cowl, you will need a magnifying glass, and even that won't reveal everything. Some things you only find when you get there.

The wood framing on this MG's door looks good, but only probing it will tell the whole story.

of controversy at every juncture of decision as to which approach is best and/or most efficient.

And things change. New techniques and new technologies come "on line" and change the ways in which we approach restoration problems and procedures in general. Specifically, "best practices" and procedures change as new technologies, processes and materials become available. For example, body paint stripping has gone from brushed-on paint removers to dip stripping, to mineral blasting, and now to plastic media blasting. Several new, successor technologies are on the horizon.

The old truism holds for automobile restoration. The only thing that is constant is change.

Restoration and the Restorer

Restoration is probably the most intimate involvement of human being and automobile that is possible. It can be an almost endless relationship; the only limits on the tasks that you can accomplish will be imposed by your available time, your aptitudes and your resources. For some, just organizing a restoration is a thrill. For most of us, economic constraints and the natures of our enjoyment dictate involvements beyond simple check writing.

I think that the checkbook restorers miss most of the fun and all of the sense of accomplishment that can come from hands-on restoration work. What they know about their cars is limited to what they are told. Worse, they often

exist in a state of perpetual dependency on others to keep their restored cars tidy and functioning.

True restorers are a breed apart. They congregate at meets and at other gatherings. Because there are many kinds of cars and many valid approaches to restoring them, restorers are basically a varied lot with diverse interests and skills.

Still, some general characterizations are possible. Good restorers are set apart by their massive patience, their certain knowledge of many fields, their tenacity in the face of adversity and their innate curiosity. They possess capabilities for incisive research, mastery of impeccable manual skills and good work habits, perfect judgment, and, finally, the uncommon ability to make water run uphill. Theirs is a fraternity of dedication, talent, and accomplishment.

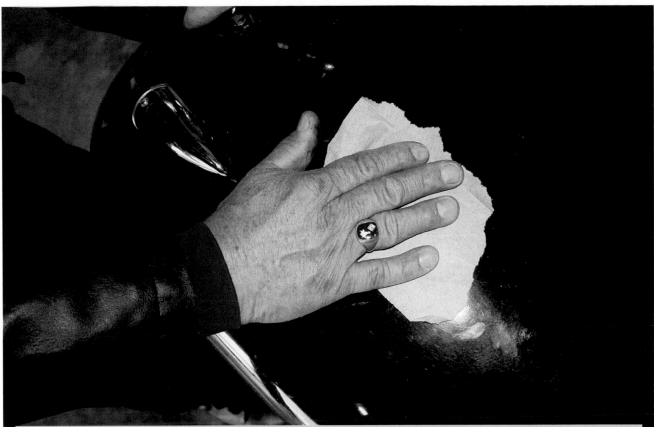

Running your finger tips over the sheet metal with a thin rag or paper towel under them will reveal irregularities that your eyes cannot see. This works because the towel or rag makes it possible to move your fingers over the metal without having the oil and moisture on them create friction against the paint. It's an old bodyman's trick.

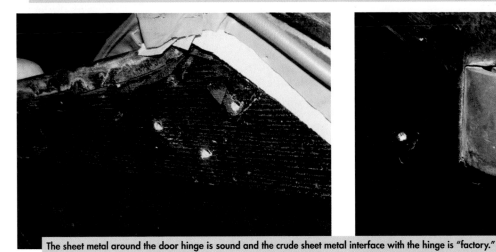

The sheet metal around the door hinge is sound and the crude sheet metal interface with the hinge is "factory."

The Meanings of "To Restore"

Clearly, "restore" means different things to different people. It has also meant different things in different periods. To the neophyte, it usually means to apply shiny paint. For some, a deluxe run through the local car wash is considered tantamount to restoration.

In fact, the definition of restoration is dynamic. It is a different proposition for different cars. Standards of restoration vary over time, from place-to-place and from club to club. Restoration is always a matter of degree. That degree must relate the purpose for owning a car to the work done to improve it. Restorers must be exceedingly clearheaded regarding this point.

Most cars are owned for one or a combination of the following three purposes: fun and driving, competitive showing or investment. The reason(s) for owning an old car dictate which type and what degree of restoration work is called for and rational. Clearly, the three different reasons for owning an old car will suggest different kinds of emphasis in restoration work. Economics may impose additional limits.

Having this car's original identification plate in place is a real plus. So often, they are missing.

Even when the purpose(s) for engaging in restoration work are sorted out, it is hardly obvious what work should be done or how best to accomplish it. In fact, there is no single, exclusive standard of restoration. Some people might like it if restoration simply meant to exactly duplicate original condition. Unfortunately, such a simple approach is not possible. Even if it were, it would rarely be practical or economically feasible.

Take, for example, the business of refinishing a car. It is possible to refinish cars in authentic materials—varnishes, Japanning lacquers, nitrocellulose lacquers, and synthetic enamels. While such authentic finishes have unique and, to me, highly desirable appearances, it is simply not practical to use them on cars that are going to be driven and/or stored in less than ideal conditions. These old finishes are too fragile for cars that are intended to be driven. Some of them are too difficult to apply and to repair to be practical. By today's standards, all of the old finishes oxidize, check, crack, separate and generally deteriorate too quickly. Although these finishes are still available in varying degrees, and can exactly duplicate the original finishes that were applied to most old cars, they are not practical to use for the purposes of most of today's old car owners. For some they are. For most, the durability of modern acrylic and catalyzed acrylic finishes is an economic necessity. The costs of refinishing dictate this choice.

Inevitably, when the purpose(s) for undertaking a restoration is squared with the restoration possibilities, a series of compromises results. These are compromises between some perfect ideal and some affordable, practical reality.

That ideal is to authentically preserve and maintain, and to improve. This ideal can and should become an obsession for every restorer. No action should ever violate it without a good reason. Temporary fixes have their place, but there is no place for damage done in the name of restoration. "Do no harm" is a primary tenet of the Hippocratic Oath, taken by medical doctors, and it should be an article of faith for those who restore cars.

This may sound obvious, but I have seen cases of cars that were destroyed in the processes of restoring them. In fact, restoration damage is very prevalent. Sometimes it results from the work of a quick-buck artist doing a fast job to unload a car. More often, it is the result of ignorance and/or impatience on the part of a well-meaning owner who has gotten in "over his head" trying to restore a car.

I cannot overemphasize the importance of avoiding restoration damage. Nor, can I honestly say that I have not been responsible for doing some of it, myself, over the years. I will always regret those instances.

Authentic restoration means bringing a car back as close as possible to its original condition, with some exceptions. The use of original finishes is technically possible, but in the case of older cars they are far less durable than modern finishes. Some modern finishes, like cross-linked acrylic lacquers and enamels, look very much like the original finishes that were applied in nitrocellulose lacquer and synthetic enamel. However, some of the very modern urethane and polyurethane finishes do not look original on old cars and should be avoided in restoration work.

As the causes of deterioration of old automobiles are reviewed and accounted for—wear, corrosion, impact damage, and the like—restoration damage and maintenance damage often emerge to pose the most serious problems for restorers. I have seen cars taken from restorable condition to scrap condition by well-intentioned owners and their minions. Sometimes, the damage is gross, like pop rivet and Bondo repairs lurking under shiny paint. Sometimes, it is less obvious, like the skillful but improper conversion of Packard touring cars into dual cowl phaetons that occurred at a rapid pace in the 1970s. Sometimes, it is downright subtle and is discovered only after an extended period of ownership.

In this last category, I once owned a '37 Dodge that had been owned by a plumber for 35 years. After he sold it, the car changed hands every couple of months.

The problem that caused love for this car to turn to hate so quickly for those who succeeded the original owner was that he had used the "materials at hand" to maintain his Dodge, converting almost every possible thread on the car to a pipe thread. In some hidden areas he had used modified plumbing fittings for nuts and bolts.

For all I know, after I sold it, it continued to run the buy-sell cycle six times a year. I class this as subtle damage because you had to work on this car to discover the problem.

I suggest that if most restorers of old automobiles would adopt the simple rationale for restoration stated above—to preserve, to maintain and to improve—restoration damage would become rare. If any action taken in restoration does not square with that rationale, then damage is likely to happen. There is often an enormous temptation to do something, sometimes anything, to make an old car look better or run for a while. These are temptations that should be resisted if they do not permanently improve a vehicle. Most restorers would far rather deal with the ravages of time and wear than with the quick and dirty fixes of previous owners, restorers and their mercenaries.

The issue of doing restoration damage poses a simple question: whether a restorer wants to join that nameless, faceless legion of boneheads who have defiled part of our national historic heritage, or the informed elite who are actively preserving our grass-roots history. I strongly suspect that if you have read this far, you are, or aspire to be, part of that elite.

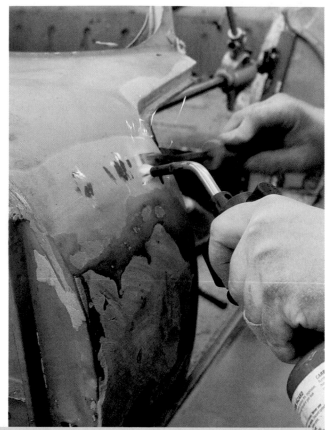

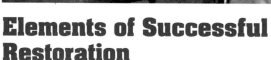
Restoration can involve some very radical procedures. This Jaguar XK-E cowl required the removal of rusted-through metal from its side, so that new metal could be "sectioned" in. Even after abrasive blasting, the extent of the damage was not visible. Only after the lead covering the damaged area was removed did the crude repair that the lead covered become evident.

Elements of Successful Restoration

Once a restorer adopts his or her rationale for restoration, the actual process becomes a small war against wear, corrosion and the sins of previous owners and their operatives. In this war, you will need to employ strategy, tactics, logistics, and timing. Strategy is the grand plan for a restoration. It includes what you want to accomplish and, in broad outline, how you will proceed. Tactics involve the deployment and use of personnel, the details of the sequences in which work to be done, the utilization of outside resources and your specific methods. Logistics involves such things as efficiently and effectively purchasing necessary parts and services. Finally, timing is the element that brings it all together at one time. If these aspects of a restoration plan are not kept under tight control, unnecessary expense and delay will result. That is where most restorations that fail run off the tracks.

Anyone can restore a car given endless amounts of time and a limitless budget. Most of us don't have the luxury of unlimited resources and must work with what we do have. Besides, the challenge of the thing is not just to restore a car by throwing money at it; that takes little talent. The proper object should be to accomplish what must be done at an acceptable level of expense and in a reasonable amount of time.

I have seen restorations reputed to have taken 10 years, or more. Frequently such cars weren't in particularly bad condition when these marathon restorations began. Usually, the element of timing was ignored in these nearly endless endeavors. First, one task was completed, say the body restoration, then its result was laid aside and another task was undertaken, say the powertrain. At any point in this sequence, a delay in one area would stop the whole project, sometimes for weeks or months.

A more serviceable approach is to account for timing at the outset of a project and to attack multiple components in the same time frame. If your restoration timing is worked out properly, the slack caused by a delay in one area will allow you to make offsetting progress in others, as effort and money are shifted to them. Rescheduling, or minor schedule adjustments, will then allow the various aspects of the project to reach completion at about the same time and in line with the original plan.

Or take the matter of logistics. I knew a man who erected a prefab spray booth to paint one car. He was only restoring one car, but he insisted on completing all work on-premises. Since he was a perfectionist and an equipment freak, he erected an expensive spray booth to paint just one car. Certainly, the job of painting his car was accomplished under very good conditions. Logistically, the decision to build a spray booth to paint one car was incredibly inefficient.

Two Basic Restoration Strategies

There are two basic, overall strategies that a restorer can utilize. They are the "ground-up" and "component" approaches. One involves the total restoration of a car at one time. The other proceeds, component by component, with the car being operable between restoration bouts. Making the choice between these two strategies involves such variables as the reason(s) for attempting a restoration, the resources available, and the specific capabilities of the restorer.

If a complete restoration to a very high standard is the objective, the component approach will inevitably be more expensive and will yield a lesser result than an all-at-one-time method. This is because component-by-component restorations involve more time, and their overall results lack the crispness of restorations completed at one time. Inevitably, the first items restored deteriorate by the time that a restoration is finished by this approach.

Another difficulty with the component approach is that what should be restoration often lapses into repair. The difference is that restoration involves the best and most authentic reconditioning that can be done, while repair only contemplates overhaul that will last the expected life span of the repaired vehicle.

Yet, having said all of that, the component approach to restoration definitely has its place. Component-by-component restoration can yield excellent results and it is generally far more susceptible to owner efforts than is total, ground-up restoration. It also reduces the risk of creating a "basket case," that is, a disassembled car with some restored parts and systems. The component approach is economically more forgiving, because it spreads what might otherwise represent an intense and huge financial outlay over a time frame that can include periods of economic recuperation.

Authentic restoration means bringing a car back as close as possible to its original condition, with some exceptions. For example, the use of original finishes is technically possible, but in the case of older cars these finishes will be far less durable than modern finishes. Some modern finishes, like acrylic lacquers and catalyzed enamels, look very much like original finishes that wcre applied in nitrocellulose lacquer and synthetic enamel. However, very modern urethane and polyurethane finishes do not look original on old cars and should not be used.

The choice of one of these two major strategies, the component approach or a total, all-at-one-time restoration, ultimately relates to your purpose(s) for restoring a car, the resources that you can marshal, and the condition of your car. If your purpose is to produce a show car, and you have the requisite money and/or skills, the all-at-one-time approach is probably your ticket. If your main purpose is to have fun owning and driving your old car, and you can tolerate the minor deterioration of components that may occur before you can work all the way through your restoration, then you are best advised to stick with restoring components and systems, one at a time. This is particularly true for postwar cars, because they are more complex than prewar cars, and there is always the chance of getting in over your head with them. It is worth remembering that it is easier to disassemble a car than to reassemble it. That fact, alone, may dictate a component-by-component approach.

In many cases, the choice of an overall restoration strategy will be out of your hands because the condition of your car will dictate the best strategy to use.

The actual strategy underlying the component approach is far simpler than for the all-at-one-time approach. The issues mostly devolve on the sequence in which components will be restored. Say, for example, a car's engine is in need of a complete rebuild. It is logical to go through the clutch and transmission while they are out of the car, and to install an engine wiring harness at the same time. It also makes good sense to paint the engine bay, firewall, inner fenders and suspension components at this time.

The most reasonable sequence, therefore, is to deal first with the deteriorated components that are most likely to degrade badly if they are not attended to. It makes sense to restore the components that become easy to get at when you are restoring those that demand immediate attention. A knocking rod or chronically low oil pressure says, "Deal with me and my environment, before you send out the

With the bad metal removed it is obvious that sectioning was the right approach.

This kind of work requires knowledge and planning, as well as strong manual skills. In the end the sectioning approach will look better than and out perform various stopgap measures, like trying to weld and fill the unsound sheet metal in this area.

chrome plating." While you have the engine out, a shabby wiring harness in the engine bay is likely to whisper, "Hey, fella, what about me? I need loving attention, too. Now's the best time to replace me."

If all of this seems obvious, that is because it simply restates the basic rationale for restoration: to maintain, to preserve, to improve. However, restorers frequently do not deal first with the components that most call for their attention. Instead, they often deal with the components that most *visibly* need attention. Thus, an engine with bad bearings is left on self-destruct mode, while shiny paint is applied to correct a chalking or rub through problem with a car's finish. This may be a more efficient way of raising the presentability and price of a car, but it does not effectively consider the ultimate welfare of the car. The engine will have to be dealt with eventually, and it will probably be increasingly difficult and expensive to do so as damage progresses. That nice paint that was applied undoubtedly will be damaged when the engine is removed and replaced—it almost always is. I am describing a bad strategy that does not

square with my, and I hope your, rationale for restoration. A careful, rational and flexible plan of component restoration can make the technique workable and efficient.

One prejudice that I carry into these matters is to leave operable components alone when this is possible, and to stop at restoring them cosmetically. I am not quite endorsing the "don't-fix-it-if-it-ain't broke" wisdom, but I see no reason to disassemble and rebuild or replace components just because they are old. If maintenance will do the job, try to avoid the mania for throwing overhauls, new old stock (NOS), new old replacement stock (NORS) and reproduction parts at every area of a restoration. It's expensive, and often pointless or counterproductive to the ultimate preservation of a vehicle. Restoration should not be just throwing upgraded parts together.

The "ground-up" approach—when I use this term, I often envision a huge grinder with grated old car coming out of its mesh—places extreme requirements on the restorer for a carefully worked out strategy. We've all heard of someone who disassembled a car and restored it, bit by bit, in his living room. Then he had to tear a wall down to get his car out of his house. Rather a lack of strategic planning there, I think. Any strategy for a ground-up restoration has to account for the availability of time and money to complete the job at hand, and for such basic factors as living in the same place long enough to finish what may be an undertaking of several years duration.

Before such a project is begun, a worst-case scenario has to be formulated for tasks like mechanical work, electrical work, and structural and cosmetic body restoration. Suppliers of parts and services have to be identified and the relevant costs and lead times determined. Only then can the other elements of planning a ground-up restoration— tactics, logistics, and timing—be nailed down. Restoration is one of those areas of endeavor where a few hours spent in initial planning can result in weeks or months saved in completing a project.

I know a man who restores cars and plots his projects' progress, or lack thereof, with pins stuck in a 4-foot-long chart on his garage wall. He creates a timeline chart for

One element of strategy and tactics that you should nail down early in any restoration project is a good place to do your work. The MGs shown will each require an area a minimum of three times their footprint for body-off restorations. That is the minimum. An area five times the size of the car will be more comfortable for this work.

every restoration that he does. Each component or service is represented vertically. His chart plots time horizontally in weeks, from left to right. Each task, performed in-house or out, is begun at a time that is selected to assure completion when it will be needed for some other stage of the vehicle's subassembly or final assembly. The interlocking nature of individual tasks is considered and meshed into the timeline. Suppliers who fall behind are represented by pins to the left of the actual calendar week. Frequently, there are expletives and uncomplimentary suggestions about their ancestry written above their lines.

This elaborate technique for scheduling and coordination may seem overkill, but it sure beats having a car completely restored but unusable because an intake manifold, sent out for porcelainizing, or a water pump that was missing, hopelessly damaged, or consigned to a subcontractor for repair was let go until everything else was done and is therefore not available when a car's restoration is otherwise finished.

It is incumbent on any serious restorer to do a careful inventory of the tasks and subcontracts that his or her contemplated restoration will require. He then can formulate a plan that will produce a uniformly completed project in a reasonable time frame.

When you do this kind of restoration planning, you get a fix on the probable expenditure of time and money needed to complete your project. Many restorations that ultimately fail would never have been attempted if this kind of planning had preceded them. You know how these

failures are announced, "...for sale, reasonable, disassembled for restoration, body in primer, ninety percent complete, easy restoration...."

Chapter 2

Alligator Tactics, Logistics and Timing

A **FRIEND OF MINE WHO COLLECTS AND RESTORES** the strange little cars built by Powell Crosley has a profound sign on one of his garage walls. It's one of those 8-by-10-inch cardboard ditties with jagged edges and a grotesquely unreal wood grain background. There's a cartoonish silhouette of a man amongst alligators on the left side. The text next to it reads: "WHEN YOU'RE UP TO YOUR ASS IN ALLIGATORS, IT IS DIFFICULT TO REMEMBER THAT YOUR PRIMARY OBJECTIVE WAS TO DRAIN THE SWAMP." For anyone involved in restoration endeavors, this must strike a resonant chord.

We've all had "those days."

The plater calls to inform you that an inexperienced forklift operator ran down your radiator shell. He's very sorry. (That one really happened to me. At first I thought that it was a plater's inside joke. It wasn't.) You finally reach the man in New Jersey who said he had the carburetor that you need. Now he says that he doesn't. You think that he sold it to someone else for a few bucks more than you offered him for it. The pistons came in from the coast, but they're the wrong ones. The machine shop called to tell you that the head that you left for Magnafluxing is almost hopelessly cracked. Finally, an "expert" in Kansas writes to tell you that the pictures you sent him indicate that the body you have just finished restoring is 3 years earlier than the chassis that you removed it from and now are restoring. He's sure.

Had enough?

The point of this dismal account of mostly imaginary disasters is that some of the approaches to restoration mentioned in the last chapter—strategy, tactics, logistics,

The insides of doors and hidden areas of battery boxes are the kinds of places where major restoration problems can lurk, waiting to derail your most carefully thought-out restoration plans and strategies.

Days spent inspecting the insides and hidden spaces in an old car and planning a restoration strategy to confront what you find is the key to staying on budget and on schedule in these projects.

and timing—can help you to avoid the kind of cascading disasters detailed above. In Chapter 1 we looked at restoration strategies in some detail. Now we will concentrate on tactics, logistics, and timing.

Certainly the application of these approaches will not eliminate all disasters, but, as with the element of strategy discussed in Chapter 1, the adoption of a restoration plan that includes effective tactics, logistics, and timing will help to minimize the impacts of adversity, on the trail to a good restoration.

In the matter of tactics, the first and most important tactic is the deployment of personnel. This consideration often boils down to what tasks you will do yourself and what jobs you will subcontract to others. Decisions here tend to be critical. Knowing what you cannot do effectively, and how to choose those who can, will often call for very fine points of judgment.

I am a pretty fair "farm welder" with experience in torch, stick, MIG (GMAW) and TIG (GTAW) applications. When it comes to sheet metal and other non-critical welding, I am comfortable doing my own work. But when it comes to critical welds or difficult cast-iron repair, I usually defer to someone else, someone with experience doing this work all day, every day. Knowing when to quit and what not to attempt can be difficult, but necessary.

On the other hand, some people are unnecessarily intimidated by expertise and will not attempt any new procedures, just because they are new. Good tactics involve knowing your limits and working up to them. You also should push those limits as far as possible to increase your competencies.

Now if all of this discussion of tactics has tended to cast the restorer in the role of a "general," it should be remembered that most of the work to be done is definitely at the level of the enlisted "grunt."

The unromantic truth is that vehicle restoration works out to between 60 and 80 percent cleaning things. I know that restoration has been pictured as some sort of endlessly exciting endeavor in which the restorer will travel to the far and exotic coasts of the earth and discourse with quaint and interesting people about complex and engrossing problems that are ultimately resolved with brilliant, scintillating solutions. Bunkum! Most of this work is cleaning; cleaning old lubricants, varnish, carbon, and corrosion. There is precious little romance to be found in any of that. What can be found is some level of efficiency.

All cleaning is the result of abrasive processes. When the abrasion is on a molecular level, the process is usually classed as a chemical process; occasionally an electrolytic or ultrasonic factor is thrown in to enhance the chemistry. When cleaning abrasion is not chemical, it is mechanical. Then its instruments will be things like wire brushes, sandpaper and blast nozzles. In any case, some level of mechanization will reduce the amount of "grunt" work. Such techniques as steam cleaning, dip tank immersion, glass beading, plastic media blasting, reverse plating and the like can greatly reduce the number of hours spent on the dirtiest and most monotonous aspects of restoration.

But remember, when you're out there deploying all of that personnel, most of it may be yourself, and the most exciting things that you are likely to see for several hours at a stretch may be a can of solvent, a putty knife, and a succession of Scotchbrite* pads. The funny thing is, you may find doing this "grunt" work very satisfying. You may also revel in increasing your efficiency at performing it with every job that you do.

Tactic: Deploying Others

In the heyday of dip-stripping auto bodies and frames, two decades ago, many restorers would begin their restorations by having their cars dip-stripped. Then they would progress to subcontracting just about every other job in their restorations. In this approach, they become assemblers of assemblies and subassemblies restored by others. There is probably nothing wrong with this, except

Abrasive blasting is one technology that aids greatly in the seemingly endless job of cleaning small parts. It doesn't work well for light sheet metal parts or for big panels unless you have very highly specialized blasting equipment and supplies, but for cleaning small parts it is just what the restoration doctor ordered.

that it can be needlessly expensive and leads one to a false sense of knowing one's own car.

Sometimes the specialty shops that recondition items like clutches and dashboard instruments have highly specialized skills, tools and equipment, and can do their work better than any generalist could hope to. Most clutches, for example, require precise grinding and balancing equipment and special parts, fixtures and assembly tools. For all but the most primitive clutches, it is probably best to have the work done by those who specialize in it.

Carburetors, on the other hand, will usually yield restoration perfection to a talented and persevering amateur. Special tools and knowledge are necessary to refurbish some carburetors, but most can be rebuilt and/or restored effectively without resorting to sending them out. Having a good kit and illustrated rebuild and calibration instructions in hand is a good first step. If sending a carburetor out means that it will go to a local electrical and ignition shop, be careful. The few such enterprises that have survived have shown an often severe decline in repair capability and quality in recent years, as rebuilding has gone from the mainline of their businesses to a distant sideline. I have seen work come out of these shops that is atrocious. Some of the nationally advertised old car carburetor specialists are competent and fair (Jon Hargrove's "Carburetor Shoppe" is the best among the best), but at least a few of them are wildly overpriced, and show little evidence of providing quality work. Sending assemblies and subassemblies out for restoration is not always the easiest or best tactic. If you do not have pretty good knowledge of the work of the supplier to whom you send a part or assembly for rebuilding, you are doing no better than rolling the dice.

A special warning pertains to old car services and parts

providers that advertise on the Internet, because they merit very special investigation before you entrust any aspect of your restoration to them. It is easy and cheap to put up Web pages these days. It is even easier, and free, to make extravagant promises regarding quality, delivery and cost in ads on these pages. It was always easy to take a photograph of a car, wheel, fender, water pump, etc., reduce it to 2 x 2, and have it look good. Now, with easy-to-use photo editing software like PhotoShop®, it is even easier to make anything look good.

Be warned that much of what is promoted on the Web for old cars is very disappointing. Perhaps worse, there is no policing of items advertised for old cars on the Internet.

Understand that if a party regularly and grossly misrepresents parts or services advertised in mainstay old car hobby publications, like *Old Cars Weekly,* word from unhappy subscriber victims will reach these publications' managements, and sometimes action will be taken. The offender's advertising privileges may be discontinued. The threat of this sanction helps keep most parts and services providers reasonably honest. However, in reality, this enforcement regimen tends to grind slowly. In the end, it has a chance of removing the worst crooks' advertising from the classified columns in these publications. Lesser villains can go on cheating the car restoring public for years, or even decades.

A similar process is at work on the advertising in numerous car club publications, like the Antique Automobile Club of America's *Antique Automobile* or the Veteran Motor Car Club of America's *Bulb Horn,* to name just two of hundreds of highly respected national car club publications.

No such reviewing and sanctioning functions exist for Internet advertisers, beyond the very slow and painfully selective short reach of "the law" in these matters. Once they have paid for a page, the bad guys advertise almost for free and with no fear of being held accountable for their misdeeds. Before you ever give a credit card number to or, heaven forbid, mail a part for reconditioning to a provider whom you have found on the Internet, you are well advised to check out that provider with the proverbial "fine tooth comb."

We live in an age of specialization and experts. This may be comforting, but if a restorer overdoes it, it can be very expensive. If a job doesn't require specialized and expensive tools and equipment, a restorer should consider doing it himself. Even such seemingly unfathomable mechanisms as automatic transmissions can often be rebuilt with little more than common hand tools when you know what you are doing.

For those items that have to be sent out for specialized restoration services, there is the difficult business of choosing good work sources. In some cases, there are so few people who can do a given job that the choice is virtually automatic. In other cases, where you may choose to subcontract fairly common tasks, like plating, refinishing, engine machine shop work or upholstery, there are so many

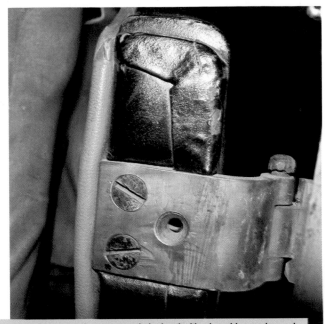

There is just so much about restoration that is different from commercial repair work. In a good restoration, little details, like the rubber gasket under the windshield post and the screws that secure the post of the MG TD, shown here, will have to be brought back to crisp original condition. The hinge pin in the door will have to be replaced to look original. The fuel tank sheet metal and chrome trim end piece will have to be straightened and painted and plated. The minor damage to the wheel will have to be removed and all rust will have to be excised. Restoration is the accumulation of favorable details, and there are so many of them to accumulate that it is often hard to explain this work to people who don't deal with it all day, every day.

potential providers that the choices are often baffling. There is no foolproof way to choose competent and reasonable providers of services, but I do have a short list of suggestions that will increase the odds in your favor when you have to make these kinds of tactical choices. Needless to say, my basis for these suggestions results from the expense of considerable bitter experience.

The first tactical rule in choosing providers of restoration services is to demand to see examples of their actual work *before* you commit your job. Don't take a provider's word for his level of workmanship. Lots of individuals and shops want to get involved in restoration work. It's more interesting than everyday repair, and it reflects great glory on the shops that do it, particularly if they do it well.

Body shops that do fair-to-average commercial repair work will often represent themselves to the unsuspecting as providers of exquisite restoration sheet metal work and refinishing. They will point to examples of their work on the shop floor and then dismiss them with phrases like, "Oh, that's just our commercial work—our restoration work is very different—much better." Don't bet your collector car on it.

My experience suggests that the differences between performing undistinguished versus superb work can be

Damage done by previous owners can be a big issue. The orange lights or reflectors below the authentic tail lights will have to be removed and the areas where they were mounted will require repair.

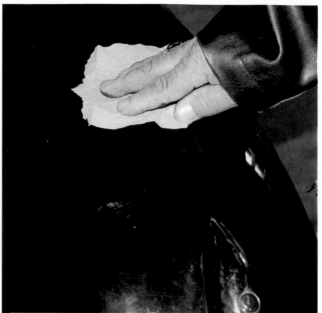

Restoration involves the use of very special and refined approaches to common tasks to produce the highest quality work possible. The rag-or-tissue-under-your-fingertips trick, shown here, will help you make a realistic assessment of the amount of sheet metal bodywork that will be required to restore this car. Feeling the metal with your fingertips through a rag will often answer this question better than your eyes can. Once you eliminate the friction of moisture and oil on your fingers by feeling through a rag, you will be amazed at how sensitive they are to minor variations in sheet metal. Try this little restoration trick. Well planned restoration work involves many such tricks.

very subtle. They generally involve things like good work habits, fine judgments and basic attitudes. It's pretty hard to switch these things "on" and "off" from one job to another. In reality, each shop and each craftsman establishes just one standard of workmanship—no more. If what you are shown is tacky, commercial work, it is probably what you will get on your "restoration" job. Many more people talk good restoration work than actually perform it. There is no magic baseball cap with the word "RESTORATION" embroidered on its bill that confers instant competence on its wearer, or anything approaching perfection on the results of his or her work.

In the last decade, more and more shops have been forced out of general repair work by their own obsolescence in the face of advancing automotive technology—they wouldn't or couldn't keep up with the revolutions in areas like electronics, electronic controls, high strength steel body fabrication and new body fillers and coatings. In many cases, as a last resort, these individuals and shops have hung out shingles reading "Auto Restoration." Don't become a victim of their desperation. These refugee shops from general repair obsolescence often have little understanding of the considerations and/or economics of restoration work. Some of them mean well, but that doesn't salvage the results of their often wretched work on old cars.

With some exceptions, it is good restoration practice to avoid large, commercial repair facilities. They are simply not set up to do restoration work. Usually they lack experience with old cars, don't understand them, and are bound by production schedules that are not conducive to learning this work. For example, many nationally franchised transmission shops will try to repair anything that can be driven, towed, or pushed through their doors. The results are almost uniformly disastrous when old cars are involved.

When you choose subcontractors for specialized work, you need to use common sense. Disgustingly messy and cluttered shops are unsafe and will usually produce poor or inconsistent work. There are exceptions. Obsessively neat and antiseptic shops are sometimes very slow, often overpriced and sometimes just plain incompetent. With very little real work going through them, they have all kinds of time to clean tools and tidy the workspace. Again, there are exceptions.

Any shop that wants to be seriously considered for your work should be able and willing to provide references from satisfied customers. You should ask for these references and check them out. Anyone can find two or three satisfied customers, so try to get a list of 10, and check some of them out.

A basic tactic in commissioning restoration work is to demand a detailed explanation of the work to be done, the price for completing it, the time required and details of any warranties or guaranties on it. Employ this tactic *before* any

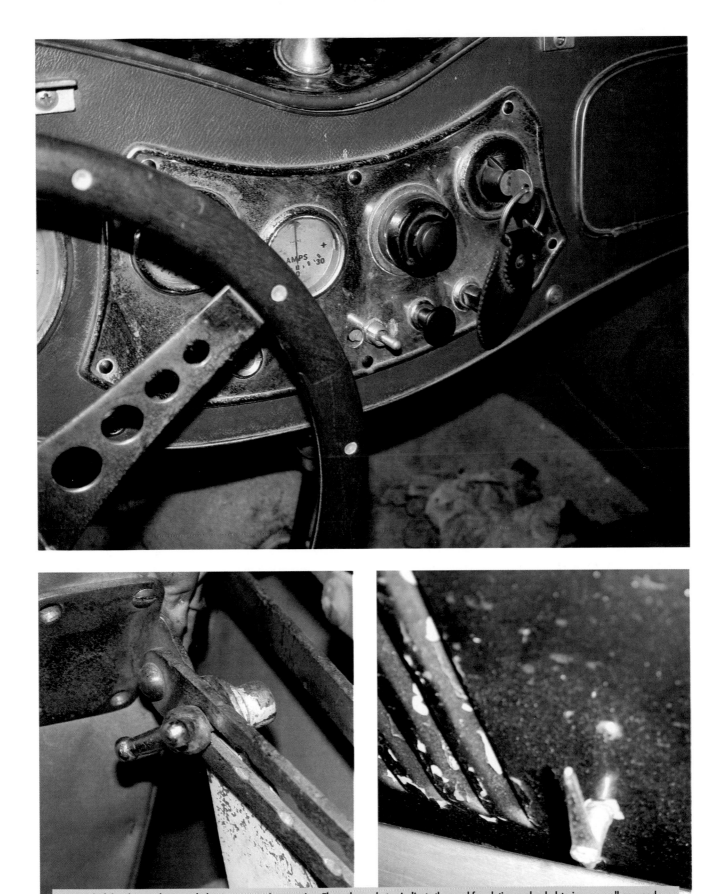

A myriad of details must be attended to in any good restoration. These three photos indicate the need for plating and upholstering, as well as wood sheet metal, plastic, and electrical instrument repair and refurbishing. See how many inauthentic details you can spot just in these photos.

Simple, advanced and rugged, describes this MG TD's steering and double A-arm coil spring suspension. The early rack-and-pinion steering is durable if it gets reasonable maintenance. Rebuilding it is best left to experts.

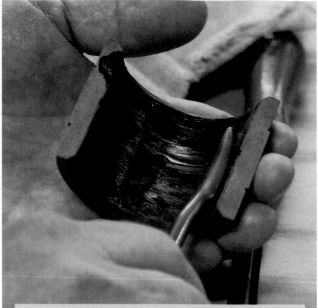

Rod bearings, like this one from a 1933 KB Lincoln, are among the fussiest and most precise components in any old engine. While most of the sizing done on these bearings is done by machine, it is still a good idea to check them for interference and high spots in their working environment, and to make corrections by scraping them lightly by hand if any defects are found.

commitments are made or work commences. If a provider cannot explain the work that he proposes to do on your car, it is time to get suspicious and to look for another provider.

Car restoration is not nuclear physics or brain surgery. Most work can be explained pretty easily. People who cannot explain what they are doing, often—not always—do not know what they are doing. If you don't understand the whole explanation of work to be done, evaluate the part or parts that you do understand on the basis of what you do know. If something seems inconsistent or doesn't make any sense, persevere in demanding explanation(s), until it is clarified. Never let service providers talk you out of quality or authenticity.

When restoration tactics of are considered, the importance of choosing the best subcontractors for specialty work cannot be overemphasized. An incompetent or unreliable provider can mess up everything by butchering or endlessly delaying the repair of a needed component.

A second tactical rule for choosing restoration services involves resisting the temptation to pursue convenience by letting a specialist work in an area that is not his real area of expertise. For example, it may seem convenient to let the transmission people do your engine work, or *vice versa*. This can end in trouble. It is far better to let specialists broaden their skills on their own machinery and time than on yours. The cost of their education, working outside of their specialties, can be greater than wasted money; it can be wrecked parts and disrupted restoration schedules. This is not to say that some shops don't have multiple specialties; many do. Just be sure to restrict the shops that you employ to areas in which they can demonstrate successful previous experience.

Many years ago I was visiting a well-known and highly regarded restoration shop that specializes in body

restoration. I noticed that the workers were assembling the engine for a 1933 KB Lincoln for which they had just completed the body restoration. Since this particular shop had no reputation—good or bad—in mechanical work, I wondered how capable they were in this area. As I looked around, I noticed the rod and main bearings for this engine in a box with a mailing label that indicated the bearing work had been done by a large and very well known machine shop that advertises nationally. This worried me because I had just finished making a new set of rod bearing shells for a man with a KB Lincoln who had sent his bearings to this same shop for re-babbiting. They had been returned to him warped and racked almost beyond repair. We found it easier to make a new set than to try to straighten his.

Sure enough, six weeks later I was making up another set of rod bearings for the body restoration firm that I had visited. The point of this sad story is that the body restoration shop was working well out of and beyond its areas of experience, specialization and competence. It was exercising little or no good judgment in its sourcing. In this bad process, a remarkably incompetent subcontractor had been chosen to do extremely critical work. If you suspect that one of your subcontractors is going to use the services of other sub-subcontractors, check out these ultimate providers yourself, if you can. When you are in a shop that does work for you, be very observant regarding things like the mailing labels on cartons and the advertising calendars on the walls.

This four-cylinder overhead valve engine might have looked complicated in comparison to the four-cylinder side-valve engines that dominated the low price field before it. It may even look complicated compared to some modern engines, where much of what you see in the engine bay is hidden under plastic covers. However, in terms of the number of parts and complexity of operation, this is a very simple engine. Most older engines are relatively simple. That is a benefit to restorers.

Doing It Yourself

As you progress in restoration endeavors, the tactic of performing more and more reconditioning tasks for yourself will probably accompany that progress. You will tend to adopt this tactic because it gets support from both the economics of the situation and from a basic sense of pride in accomplishment. Another reason for doing your own work is the inherent simplicity of most old automobiles. While today's automobiles are estimated to have upwards of 15,000 parts, cars of the 1950s averaged about 5,000 parts, and when you consider the cars built before World War II, all but the most expensive of them are far simpler than that.

For some all but inexplicable reason, people viewing the under-hood area of a well-restored car will often marvel at how "complicated" it looks. Actually, it may not look that "complicated," just shiny and well kept. People often confuse those two attributes.

Devices like carburetors tended to be much simpler,

more purposeful, and better built before the era of emissions controls destroyed this basic integrity and ushered in the age of fuel injection. It was often possible to "eyeball" an old carburetor and to determine the function of each of its parts and circuits. The last carburetors did not enjoy this virtue,

These photos of completed disasters are from the John Twist display case of mechanical horrors, located at University Motors in Ada, Michigan. If it involves MGs, John has seen it all and knows how to fix it.

as the emissions-motivated designs for some of those 175-plus-part Thermo-Quad and Quadra-Jet monstrosities of the 1960s-1980s attests. By now, in the age of fuel injection, it is difficult to eyeball much of anything. You scan for codes and replace parts.

Many different types of work are inherent in any restoration. Some of them require competences beyond special skills and equipment; they call for high levels of basic aptitudes. Most of this becomes possible with experience, but don't expect to do every task in a restoration yourself. Few people can handle everything from mechanical rebuilds to upholstery and painting. More people claim that they do all of the work on a restoration than actually do it.

Some General Tactical Considerations

There must be about 100 general tactical considerations that could be stated regarding approaches to car restoration.

You may not recognize all of these mistakes. The first two photos from the display case show linkage forks and clevis pins, worn almost beyond recognition. The melting damage to the piston in the third parts photo indicates what can happen if you use a six-cylinder ignition chopper wheel in a four-cylinder engine. What was a connecting rod, in the next photo, will never see service again. The next group of parts are of a broken clutch throw-out bearing and several throw-out bearing cradles that did service long after the bearings that they held exited the scene. Restorers often have to deal with the sins of maintenance and repair omission of previous owners.

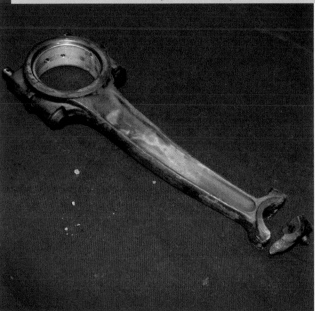

A handful of them are far from obvious but still very important. Here are three of those.

- Evaluate systems and components before you disassemble them. This can be difficult to do when a car is not running, but it often is still possible. It is a mistake to just tear an automobile apart for restoration without any idea of what areas may be malfunctioning. I have seen this done hundreds of times. A new acquisition is dismantled without any consideration of what works and what doesn't. Here's a basic fact: It is far easier to repair and restore things if you know which ones are failing and how. Such knowledge is also a good guide to determining which items should be left alone. If a car is not running when it is acquired, it is

often a worthwhile investment of time to get it running and gain some experience with it on the road before beginning major restoration work.

- Inspect and test each system in a car separately, particularly where systems are closely interrelated. If, for example, a car overheats, it is a bad tactic to simultaneously disassemble and repair or replace: the thermostat, radiator, water pump, ignition system, head gasket(s), and fuel system. You may never pinpoint which system(s) caused the problem. It is, however, a good idea to test and replace or repair, as necessary, the systems listed above, singly, and in roughly the order that they are listed. With that approach, when the problem is located, you will know its origin and you

Casting repair is a very difficult business. Zinc ("pot metal")castings present the worst problems. To get items like these repaired and plated you should allow plenty of lead time.

will avoid the pitfall of inducing other problems that may mask the solution.

• Perhaps the most important rule of procedure is to seek simple solutions to problems. This is appropriate because, for the most part, the vehicles that we are talking about were relatively simple in their designs and constructions. True, complex solutions are more intriguing, but they are usually unnecessary.

I recently worked on a "restored" car that was plagued with violent overheating just after start-up. If the car had been left to stand and cool off for more than a couple of hours after running, its engine would heat up after it was restarted and boil violently very soon thereafter. Then, as it ran, it would cool to normal. Changing thermostats hadn't helped. The radiator, hoses, water pump and block had been either rebuilt or replaced in its restoration. The ignition checked out, and the fuel system was delivering the correct mixture, as measured with infrared equipment at its tailpipe. Exotic theories of hose collapse, cooling system suction leaks and water pump cavitation had been proposed. Appropriate remedies for these obscure problems had been applied without success.

Overheating can be one of the most difficult to solve of the common problems afflicting old cars. In cars, as in human beings, overheating can be a symptom of almost anything that is wrong. Causes can run the gamut from a slipping clutch or coupling to combustion leaks, or from a simple error in ignition timing to an improperly assembled carburetor or dragging brake shoe. Sometimes, overheating results from a combination of two or more causes, which makes it particularly difficult to diagnose.

In the case of this particular car, the cause of the problem turned out to be disarmingly simple. After restoration, its cooling system had been filled with antifreeze containing a highly effective sealing additive. Unfortunately, the new thermostat that had been installed had an extremely small air bleed hole. When the overheating had occurred, this thermostat had been tested and, even though it tested okay, replaced with an identical unit in an effort to cure the problem. It didn't. No one had bothered to save the original thermostat to see if it was somehow different from the new ones that were used to replace it.

This is what was happening: The sealer in the coolant was sealing the air bleed holes in the thermostats that replaced the original unit. Their air bleed holes were so small that this became possible. As the engine cooled off after a run, the heat soak expansion of the coolant drove it out of the head and upper cylinder block areas and into the radiator. Then, as the car continued to cool, the plugged bleed hole air-locked the system and prevented coolant from reentering the head. Since there was no water in the head to transmit heat to the thermostat, and thus open it as the engine's temperature rose, when the car was started the engine overheated and boiled. Eventually, extreme heat and pressure in the cooling system allowed some water vapor to reach the thermostat and open it. This established coolant flow. Then the thermostat would open fully and the engine temperature would decline.

Simply drilling the pin-size bleed hole in the thermostat plate out to 3/32-inch completely cured the problem. I suspect that some of the "mechanics" who had worked on solving this car's overheating problem were dismayed when it turned out that their exotic theories had been totally irrelevant to solving the real problem. I sure hope that the car's owner didn't pay them for all that nonsense. Most problems with old cars yield to simple solutions. It's a good idea to give problems some careful observation, analysis, and logical thought before you flail at them with wrenches and tear down machinery in pursuit of improbable, obscure or exotic causes of problems.

Another example of this was a restored Lincoln Continental that was brought to my shop with an erratic running symptom. The shop that had restored the car had tried everything to cure the problem, from balancing its water pumps to having three different carburetor specialists look at its carburetor, and replacing it twice. The engine had been out three times and everything in the engine and driveline had been professionally balanced. Still the car ran roughly. The owner talked about suing the shop that had restored his car. He told me that my shop was the last step before litigation.

I had the owner raise the Continental's hood, looked at his engine and said, "It's the condensers." He looked at me disbelievingly and said, "In my practice, it is usual to examine the patient thoroughly before rendering a diagnosis."

"*Well, in my* practice," I answered, "I have found it expedient to state the obvious when it is obvious and to avoid running up a customer's bill when that is not necessary. *It's the condensers.* Here, I'll demonstrate...."

Then, I disconnected the condensers that were mounted externally on the side of the engine's distributor and installed a pair of good condensers that I keep in my toolbox. They are fitted with alligator clip connectors for testing purposes.

The Lincoln started easily and purred. It ran perfectly on the road.

Of course, the owner wanted to know how I knew that it was the condensers. That was easy. The rough running was typical of an engine with failed condensers. The ones mounted on this car were beautiful NOS Neihoff units in pristine cosmetic condition. They even sported perfect decals on their barrels. I knew looking at them that they were at least 50 years old. I also knew that electrolytic condensers rarely work after 10 or 15 years, even if they are not in service.

Since everything else on the car had been checked, it made sense that those pretty, 50-year-old condensers were the cause of the problem. As it turned out, I was right. The owner sheepishly admitted that he had purchased the condensers for $60 at a swap meet, "because they looked so nice." He had had them tested on a Sun Machine. They tested out okay. I tested them on my Sun Machine. Again, they passed. Then I tested them on an old, World War I-era discharge-type condenser tester that I keep around to amuse myself and they showed leakage.

Once again, a simple defect had caused the problem.

Logistics and Timing

In restoration work, good logistics, timing and planning usually result in having the whole project come together at about the same time. Proper planning in these areas can save vast amounts of money, time and frustration. Much of this planning involves squaring the resources available with the best sequences in which to proceed. It involves choosing the most appropriate sources of parts and services in terms of cost and availability. For example, if the general strategy for a restoration dictates project completion in 18 months, it is not necessary in the early stages to acquire a second, fully restored steering box if the one on the car can be restored at a considerably lower cost over a period of three months. In fact, if a three-month turnaround for restoring the steering box is a certainty, you would probably do well to schedule its restoration for four or five months before it is actually needed and to allocate the resources that won't be tied up in it someplace else where they are needed.

On the other hand, if you need to replace a cylinder head, and they are scarce, it would be a good logistical move to find one in the early stages of your restoration, so that this crucial item isn't the last thing to hold up completion of your project.

Two elements of logistics and timing that are especially important are to cultivate reliable sources and not to overlook small problems. The basic wisdom in restoration sourcing is that when you find good work at tolerable prices, stay with and cultivate it, and be willing to pay a fair price for it. The temptation to abandon good and proven providers for those who might be a bit cheaper or a tad faster often leads to disaster.

"Multiple sourcing" is a great strategy for large shops with huge volumes of subcontract work. It guarantees them fallback suppliers if their primary suppliers lose their quality edge or go out of business, and it allows them to use competition between suppliers of the same item or service to improve quality, or reduce price, or both. Great stuff if you manage a $3 million-a-year-plus restoration budget. I wouldn't suggest trying this strategy if you restore one car every few years or so. You will find it hard enough to gain the attention and loyalty of the suppliers of services like chrome plating at such a low work volume. When you find good sources, stay with them.

Always remember that seemingly innocuous and simple little things, like dash gauges, can mess up good restoration plan. I once worked on a 1913 Locomobile with an Adlake-Newbold-Westinghouse electrical system. We could never seem to acquire a voltage regulator for this car. For years after the restoration was otherwise completed, we had no charging system and had to avoid night driving and rely on battery charges to keep our Locomobile running. It took 10 years to find a voltage regulator, which turned out to be a beautiful cast-aluminum box, about 3 inches thick and 6-by-8 inches on its sides. It had a neat little window that revealed a dashpot connected by cable to an electromagnet. The cable ran over to a cute little brass arm and moved it to switch various resistances into and out of the generator's field circuit.

A 10-year search for this unit finally yielded an interesting piece of information: The regulator had been built by Adlake for Locomobile and for the Pullman Sleeping Car Company, among others. Pullman cars used these units to regulate the outputs of their axle generators on railway sleeping cars. We finally bought one of these gems from a railroad museum and reworked it from 48 volts to 6. Wonder of wonders, we installed it and it worked.

It's good logistics to sort out most of the small unknowns in restoration propositions early in the game. It's also good timing. In this case, if we had known more about the electrical system in our Locomobile at the start, it might have saved us years of looking for a regulator in the wrong places!

Chapter 3

Good Restorers and Old Engines

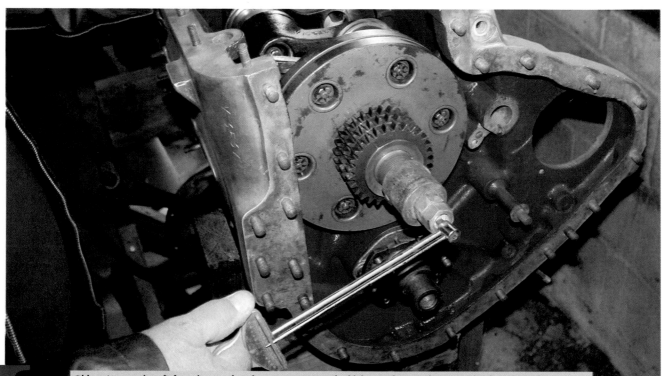

Old engines can benefit from the use of modern equipment to rebuild them. Often, machining can be done that is far more accurate than anything that was available in the repair sector when old engines were new. Despite its massive size and weight, the crankshaft shown in this photograph of a mid-1930s Lincoln engine can be turned with the bearing caps fully tightened with just a few pounds/inch effort.

I WISH TO SAY AT THE OUTSET that I don't personally know the individual whom I am about to describe—the "Good Restorer." He is, in fact, a composite of all of the desirable traits of the best that I have known in the restoration field. I doubt if he or she really exists, but the prototype described here can serve as a model for the rest of us.

"The Good Restorer" has developed impeccable work habits. I say "habits" because his or her good actions have become unconscious reflexes. While some of us occasionally have to remind ourselves that screwdrivers are not cold

chisels and crescent wrenches are not variable metric nut and bolt holders, the "Good Restorer" knows these things instinctively, and acts accordingly. Since most disasters have their origins in small mistakes, good work habits are crucial. Somehow, it is rarely a major lapse of judgment that brings on catastrophe; it's more usually some miserable *little* error, or a string of them. Good habits go a long way to preventing calamities.

For example, several years ago I developed the bad habit of turning sideways to the benches in my shop and working over my lap. This miserable habit meant that when I dropped something, it traveled to the floor, with its impact there related to the distance fallen. Its size and material determined its fracture, bounce or roll. It could be very hard to find the thing or its remains on the floor if it or its pieces were small.

Once I realized that I had acquired this habit, it took me a month and some analysis (No, not the on-the-couch kind of analysis.) to break it. That was possible only when I discovered its cause. The light was better in the directions to which I was turning. I installed lights over the benches and was able to break my bad habit. The reasons for bad habits can be subtle.

The best time to develop good habits is when you are first developing new skills. In refinishing, for example, once you have acquired it, it is very difficult to break the habit of "arcing" or "fanning" a spray gun—the natural tendency is to move it in an arc with respect to that panel that you are painting, rather than parallel to the panel. Fanning a spray gun causes non-uniform finish application. Not arcing a gun requires an unnatural maneuver, because the human body is more or less wired to pivot from single fixed points, like shoulders, elbows and wrists.

It is best to learn new skills right in the first place. Then there are no bad habits to break later, and it is easier to fine-tune your newly acquired skills. The key to all of this is analysis of, and concentration on, what you are doing.

The "Good Restorer" is almost disgustingly well organized and flexible. He makes detailed plans but can always adjust them to emerging reality. He is never caught short by the failure of a supplier or of a service provider. If his chrome plating provider is late, he shifts his effort to another area of his restoration and remains on or ahead of schedule.

The "Good Restorer" cultivates flawless judgment. In the abstract, this is not difficult. When a restoration problem is reviewed at some distance, it is almost always easy to come up with rational and correct solutions to it. But in the heat of dealing with some miserable press-fitted part that won't yield to the persuasions of a decently sized hammer, puller or press, it is always tempting to commission a bigger hammer, heftier puller or more massive press.

This kind of thing can escalate rapidly to the point where a 16-oz. hammer gives way to a 2-lb. persuader and then to an 8-lb. sledge. When that doesn't work, the "gas wrench" (torch) comes out with a large-bore tip. Somewhere in this escalation, it is easy to forget that the part that you are working to free is living in a fragile grey iron casting, or that the casting may not be yielding the part to your increasing applicaations of force because of something that you overlooked, like a concealed pin or a threaded retaining collar.

In these situations, you should try to resist the bigger-hammer or longer-pipe-over-the-wrench-handle temptations, even in the heat generated by frustration mounting towards fury. Such success as I have had in applying rational judgment, rather than overusing brute force, has come from remembering Oliver Cromwell's excellent words to the Theologians: "Gentlemen, I beseech you, from the bowels of the earth, consider the possibility that you may be wrong." It's difficult to believe that Cromwell never worked on old cars.

"The Good Restorer" has struck a balance between acquiring adequate knowledge before attempting something new, and not being intimidated by the lack of perfect knowledge. Just think for a minute how difficult it is to explain with words and diagrams the functioning of the differential drive mechanism in an automobile. If a restorer insisted on understanding how this device works before disassembling his first differential, the job might never get done. Yet when a differential setup is laid bare and is sitting in front of you, its operation can be understood from simple examination. In this case, the understanding process is intuitive.

It is often necessary to take something apart that you don't fully understand. This can produce a queasy feeling and the attendant fear that lots of little springs, levers and assorted other "thingies" are going to jump out of the part or assembly and make its reassembly very difficult. In the cases of a very few devices this may happen, but it's unusual. If you can easily discover the construction details of something before you take it apart, so much the better. It's silly not to be armed with an adequate manual for a procedure, if one is available.

For example, if a torque pattern and values are available, it would be the height of folly to tighten a cylinder head without employing this information. But if this data is not available, it is necessary to improvise torque values and a tightening sequence pattern. Only after a thorough search indicates that this information cannot be found should such "improv" methods be used. In this particular case, torque values can be estimated from the diameter and observed metal specification of the cylinder head's fasteners, while a tightening sequence pattern can be fashioned from the logic of starting in the center of the head and working outwards to its extremes. This may not be perfect, but it is far better than just tightening fasteners willy-nilly to random values. Actually, improvised torque values and sequence patterns are usually necessary for early cars because this kind of repair procedure specification was not generally available from manufacturers before the 1930s.

While it is unrealistic to always insist on perfect knowledge, it is ineffective to be intimidated by the lack of it. Strike a balance that directs a reasonable amount of time and effort to research, but not an all-consuming effort that never allows you to get to the job at hand.

Coupled with a balanced approach to knowledge, "The Good Restorer" has innate curiosity, which always causes him to seek a better way to do every job. This approach is now popularly known as "continuous improvement." Sometimes it involves employing a better material, or a better understanding of the engineering of a thing, or a better manual technique, or a better tool.

Contrary to common rumor, the Japanese did not

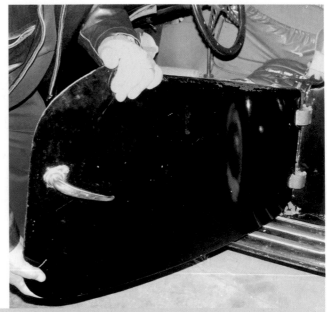

It takes experience and good judgment to evaluate the condition and restoration potential of a door like this wood-framed item. Shown here, MG enthusiast Bob Kaschel is inspecting an MG TD door. Note that he is checking the hinges for looseness by lifting the door and he is checking the structural integrity of the door by applying twisting forces to it.

invent the continuous improvement regimen and teach it to us. It was in place in American manufacturing well before it could have been transferred here from Japan as something new. It is true that Japanese industry, tutored by Americans: Joseph Juran and Dr. W. Edwards Deming, among others, learned that lesson very well and internalized it. Later, their industrial success caused American industry to study their methods and to relearn this approach.

"The Good Restorer" never counts on luck. He never hopes a problem will "fix itself" or will "maybe go away." He knows that the sad truth is that there are few, if any, problems in an automobile that will cure themselves on a long-range basis. If a problem is important enough to worry about, it is important enough to do something proactive about. Luck is something best enjoyed or cursed at a casino. If you hanker for it, buy a lottery ticket or take a trip to Las Vegas, but don't include luck in your restoration plans. If you do, you will be disappointed, routinely.

Small intimations of disaster, that faint whine from a deteriorating bearing, a burning smell, the appearance of the first evidence of rust, etc. should be dealt with at the earliest possible times. Not only will these symptoms not go away of their own accord, the causes underlying them will cause worse and more difficult and expensive damage if you do not deal with them.

For example, if you hear an engine knock or see a leaking seal, there is little or no chance of self-improvement. Disassembly intervention of some sort is required. While we're on this topic, I know of very few products that can be poured, spooned, sprinkled, squeezed, or hammered into any of the filler holes, sumps, orifices, or other entry points of automotive mechanism that will cure any real problem, except on the most short-term basis.

Various cooling system stop-leak concoctions, transmission sealers, friction-reducing nostrums and the like amount to nothing more than automotive snake oils. They will cause little improvement, except in the bank accounts of their sellers. At best, they offer only the most temporary symptomatic relief, and at worst they will not only allow the problems to which they are addressed to fester and worsen, but in many cases they will create entirely new problems of their own. Of course, "The Good Restorer" instinctively knows all of that.

The one exception to this stern dictum may be the use of "top oil" products to slowly remove carbon deposits from the combustion chambers of engines and to improve their valve guide lubrication, thereby reducing valve guide and stem wear and possibly alleviating the symptom of sticking valves.

"The Good Restorer" has an absolute mania for good record keeping. This takes the form of good handwritten and computer produced notes, tags, diagrams, photographs, videotapes, and the like. In the age of digital photography, there is no excuse for not having crisp, clear photos of complex details before things are disassembled. A good photo goes a long way to making it easier to later reassemble things to original configuration. It is also helpful to take detailed photos of original and restored cars that are the same as or similar to the ones on which you work. This increases your odds for maintaining authenticity in your restorations.

I once knew a man who had a voice-activated tape recorder in his shop. It was a neat idea because he could take verbal notes without having to stop working to degrease his hands to write down items of information or to photograph details. However, there were a couple of flaws in this approach. Every time he dropped a wrench or made any other discernible noise, the tape recorder ran for ten seconds. This resulted in many long, annoying gaps in the tapes.

Underdash wiring can be a real rat's nest. This wiring on this 1970s Alfa Romeo is refreshingly tidy and original. When you see splices, "sisters" (parallel wire) and deteriorated insulation, beware. In your restoration plan, allow plenty of time to repair or replace bad wiring.

Another problem was more serious. Some of what he said as he worked was in the nature of spontaneously emitted expletives. His children found some of his shop tapes and had a dandy time with them. Now, he uses a tape recorder that is activated by a foot pedal to record his verbal notes, a nice refinement on his good idea.

"The Good Restorer" understands the importance of very careful inspection before he disassembles and reassembles old cars and their systems. It is amazing how much useful and important information simple visual inspection will yield if it is unhurried by some overpowering desire to get things back together. When I take apart and reassemble something that didn't work, I have often found obvious faults when it was disassembled the second time to find the cause of the problem(s). Often, I have wondered how I could have missed these obvious problems that had caused the malfunctions the first time around.

"The Good Restorer" understands the importance of using proper equipment properly. That usually involves no more investment than walking across a room to get the right type and size wrench, or avoiding the temptation to make Vise-Grips the universal tool.

Most of the special tools shown in post-World War II shop manuals are desirable for doing the work for which they are recommended, but they are not usually absolutely necessary. If a restorer actually had to find all of them to do

Highly developed and practiced manual skills are crucial in restoration work. In the panel fabrication process, shown here, you have to use just the right equipment, tools, materials and skills to get good results. All of this takes concentration, practice, and dedication.

If you concentrate on what you are doing and think about every action that you take in restoration work, you will discover little tricks like blowing out the lids of paint cans before you pour paint. That eliminates one very obvious source of paint contamination. Eventually, these little tricks become habits, and the kind of thinking and logic that underlies them becomes ingrained and automatic.

a job or to restore a car, the job might never get done. Often, they can be approximated with homemade special tools or disregarded entirely. It is counterproductive to insist on using special tools just because a shop manual directs you to do so. It may be more productive to analyze the reasons for using special tools and to come up with alternatives that preserve their underlying concepts, without actually having to find the tools. Still more important is the practice of using very ordinary tools properly and for the purposes that they were intended.

"The Good Restorer" is safety conscious for his person and for his work. He pulls wrenches when possible and avoids pushing them. When working with heavy things or with parts constrained by great pressure, he knows that it is vitally important to provide an escape route for himself, just in case things get out of control. He constantly considers fire hazards, and is downright obsessive about eye, ear, and lung safety. He knows that pliers are not wrenches, screw drivers are not chisels and wrists are not hammers.

Finally, "The Good Restorer" keeps the importance of authenticity uppermost in his mind, as well as the ideal of restoration that was stated in Chapter 1—to preserve, to maintain, and to improve. He realizes that restoration is an extreme exercise in detailing. A perfect restoration is an accumulation of all possible perfect details—many of which may seem insignificant when taken singly. However, when taken together, their resulting totality is the quality of any restoration.

As I said at the outset, I don't claim to know this fellow, "The Good Restorer," but his reflected brilliance has lighted the way for me and I hope for you as well. Outside of his restoration work, I suspect that he is an insufferable fuss-budget who may well routinely kick his cat through his perfect hedge row after a day of working perfectly in his perfectly organized shop. Pity that cat.

Characteristics of Old Engines

To varying degrees and with obvious exceptions, progress in automobile engine design and manufacture over the years has involved greater design sophistication, consistently higher engine RPMs produced, greater compression ratios, and more highly stressed components. This trend continues today in response to the demands for better performance, fuel economy, and emission control. It is made possible by design evolution and by the introduction of new materials and production processes and techniques. Once-exotic overhead-cam and dual overhead-cam engines are now the norm. Items like lubricant impregnated piston skirts and low-tension piston rings have also become commonplace on even the least-expensive modern automobiles.

What this means for restorers is that by comparison to modern engines, older engines tend to be simple, turn at lower speeds and to have less stressed parts. Due to design and materials limitations, old engines tend to produce less local heat in critical areas and to be more over-built in terms of component stress tolerance. Machining tolerances tend to be less critical in many areas in old cars. When you get to the early part of the last century, automobile engines were so over-built that they tended to be amenable to the crude ministrations of blacksmiths and other crude practitioners of the mechanical arts, often the main sources of their repair.

This is not to say that particular components and systems in specific automobiles were not notoriously overstressed. The pioneering front-wheel-drive Cord L-29 of the late 1920s and early 1930s had chronically failure-prone universal joints. Or consider the bearings in Ford's trouble-prone small 12 (Lincoln Zephyr and Continental) built from 1936 to 1948. These engines were so over-stressed, due to a lack of main bearings, and tended to fail so rapidly and repeatedly, that a large percentage of the engines originally fitted in existing examples of these cars have been replaced with various and assorted V-8s made by Ford and by others. But, it is still generally true that older engines tend to run cooler, slower, and with less component stress than modern units.

They also tended to benefit from very adequate engineering, often bordering on over-engineering. Basic component failures and "recalls" are more a fact of modern automobile production than a feature of automotive history. Much of this is caused by the demands made on modern engines for improved emissions, fuel economy and power.

Most restorations involve working with cars that are combinations of authentic original parts, inauthentic parts that were added later, and parts that are borderline in terms of authenticity. All of the hardware of this 1953 Aston-Martin DB2 appears to be authentic, except for the obviously aftermarket steering wheel. Closer examination of the car indicates an obviously incorrect fire extinguisher and inauthentic vinyl upholstery. Items like the window wind have been reproduced but it is nice to have the correct originals. Note the authentic clear plastic directional indicator switch wand at the top of the photo, between the speedometer and instrument cluster. Items like this can be difficult to find or fabricate.

within reason, such improvements, coupled with enormous improvements in lubricants and fuels over the years, make it possible to achieve restored engines that will far outlive many original constructions between rebuilds.

In some cases, these modifications are necessary. The old, soft exhaust valve seats intended for use with leaded fuels will not survive long when unleaded fuels are used. This is particularly true in freshly rebuilt engines. The solution—if you don't intend to saddle a restored car with the requirement of routinely having to add doses of lead replacement additive to its fuel—is to use stainless or hardened valves or hardened valve seat inserts. This topic will be covered in detail later.

In other cases, while not absolutely necessary, engine modernization is highly desirable. For example, modern Teflon/composite valve stem seals will greatly outperform some of the older natural rubber and Neoprene units. In fact, some of them perform so spectacularly that they will actually deprive valve stems and guides of the minimum lubrication necessary to prevent rapid and premature wear.

Accommodating these demands can result in somewhat marginal engineering.

This fact of generally less-stressed engine components in collector car engines has an important payoff for restorers. It is usually possible to make minor improvements in older engines in the course of rebuilding them. This is done by including modern parts and materials in rebuilds. If kept

The people who factory built engines, like this 1934 Lincoln mill, probably had some type of torque limiting wrench that they used for bearing cap installation. However, this equipment was so unusual at that time that no torque specifications were published in the repair sector for critical bolted and nutted assemblies, like rod bearing caps, main bearings caps, and head bolts. You can improve on old repair procedures by figuring out tightening specifications for critical areas of an engine and using a precise torque wrench to apply them.

Care must always be taken when adapting new technologies to old machinery. Engines are integrated entities and must have their systems working in accord. Consider this when adapting some new part or material in your restorations, but do not overlook the enormous potential benefits of using new materials and techniques in restoring older engines.

The technique of knurling valve guides can be both economical and mechanically desirable. It produces a working surface that can be more durable than the original, and at a fraction of the cost to bush or to replace old guides. The use of Teflon packings in steam engine crosshead glans has virtually eliminated the routine repacking of these units. Modern materials have often tripled the life expectancy of older textile clutches and transmission bands. The application of machine shop knacks, like countersinking crankshaft oil holes and block stud holes, or providing more generous crankshaft journal fillet radii than were originally included, has often greatly improved the durability of those crankshafts.

In some cases, I suspect that the use of the new materials and rebuilding procedures enhances restoration only to a degree made necessary by modern conditions. It is doubtful that the cars of the early 1930s, and before, could have been driven at anything like the continuous high speeds that are characteristic of today's roads on the lubricants that were

Although old engines were substantially constructed and carefully engineered, inconsistencies and mistakes did occasionally occur. Whenever you have a highly stressed part, like a camshaft, out of an engine, make the extra effort to check for cracks with the best technology that you have or can buy. This picture shows a dry magnetic particle inspection being performed with a black light. Although the inspection of this four-cylinder camshaft was routine, and there was little expectation of finding crack damage, a surprise was found. The shaft was cracked near one of its bearing journals. A wet magnetic particle inspection is even more sensitive but much messier.

available when they were new.

When these cars were new, poor roads tended to limit their exposure to sustained high-speed operation. There just were not the roads to support it. Or consider what the exclusive use of modern unleaded fuels means for old cars. Now, once-exotic hardened valves and/or hardened valve seats have become a virtual necessity in all restorations.

Usually the only tolerances in older engines that were held to standards approaching modern practices were the bearing specs. Such factors as valve concentricity and cylinder taper were not held to such rigorous dimensional tolerances as are those for today's fast-turning, short-stroke engines. Yet, in rebuilding older engines, I would advise holding the tightest specifications possible. In many cases, the interface of modern parts and old engines requires this. Modern split skirt pistons, for example, will not tolerate the out-of-round and taper that their cast-iron predecessors did.

When we consider rebuilding a pre-World War I engine that was originally equipped with cast-iron pistons, or even a post-World War II General Motors engine fitted with cast-steel pistons, it would be good practice to use modern split-skirt aluminum pistons. This would dictate holding

modern out-of-round and taper limits. Most contemporary automotive machine shops have equipment that makes this a snap to do.

While it is easy to improve on many older tolerances and materials, it is a mistake to assume that the basic engineering of older engines was not sound. It is a mistake born of a certain kind of arrogance, and it is sometimes paid for in the currency of broken and twisted engine parts.

It is one thing to replace an old-fashioned, graphited, braided rope water pump packing with a modern Teflon packing, or to Parkerize a camshaft after a regrind. It is quite another matter to start using exotic items, like sodium filled valves in old engines, with the hope of reducing the running tappet clearances by seventy percent, to make things a bit quieter. Solid valve lifters are inherently noisier than their hydraulic counterparts. Either learn to live with this kind of condition or collect electric cars—they are whisper quiet.

A happy solid tappet is one you can hear telling you that it has adequate clearance. Its signature click is telling you that the valve that it is operating probably isn't burning. Trying to modernize old cars by second guessing the people who engineered them is often a risky proposition.

I knew a man many years ago who restored a 1934

If you do a little checking with good equipment and sometimes do a little repair, you can avoid purchasing new or restored assemblies for every component in a car that you restore. The check-and-repair-when-possible approach to restoration work saves a lot of money, and should produce more satisfaction than just bolting on NOS/NORS reproduction stuff everywhere.

Lincoln phaeton. It was a meticulous restoration by the standards of the time, completed over the course of several years. Somewhere along the way, he decided to balance his engine. When I heard of his plan I wondered about the necessity of balancing an engine that turned as slowly as this one did and that benefited from so many power impulses. I couldn't imagine that any benefit would come from balancing it. It seemed, at best, pointless. Well, in the general category of "he knew just enough to be dangerous," this individual balanced his connecting rods by grinding material from the edges of the parallel surfaces of their I-beam configuration. Apparently, he thought that the rods' strength was contained in their wide central sections. In reality, the central section in a connecting rod is there mostly to keep the parallel side sections separated and contributes little to the strength of the rod beyond this basic service. This fact was vividly illustrated when, on its post-restoration "maiden voyage," the balanced engine in this Lincoln launched three con rods and was degraded to mangled junk. In restoration work, overkill can, indeed, kill.

I keep hearing about exotic improvements that can be made in older engines. Some of them sound OK and have proven out in use. I can buy the idea that a Model A Ford will benefit from the installation of a counterbalanced crankshaft. It makes sense. It works. But when I hear theories that involve halving factory bearing clearances to solve the chronic problem of crankshaft bending in the problematic small Lincoln V-12s, or doubling the pumping capacity of their oil pumps by retrofitting truck oil pumps, I become skeptical.

The people who engineered cars in the past were no dummies. Their outlooks may have been limited by the materials that they had to work with and by the concepts and standards of contemporary engineering, but they didn't often overlook the obvious basics of good practices. To assume that they did and to try to make corrections will usually lead to all kinds of mischief, not to mention inauthentic restorations. The issue of modifications in engine restoration is always a matter of judgment and of balance.

On several occasions I have met people who propound or endorse some of the wilder modifications to old engines. They have seemed a pretty squeaky lot. In most cases, the wildness of their ideas for re-engineering old engines is related to their ignorance of the basic engineering underlying them. By the way, the ideas held by people with cockeyed notions and wares for engine modification are not only described in the classified and text columns of club and hobby publications. Many of them emanate from people who work at automotive parts house counters and in automotive machine shops. Beware.

Some Good News about Older Engines

Now, if you have gotten over any disappointment associated with hearing that the engineering of older engines usually was pretty sound, I have some good news for you.

Older engines were designed with much more consideration for rebuilding than modern mills. For one thing, car bodies were very substantially constructed in the past, and engines had to last longer—not necessarily more miles—than they do today to equal the durability of those bodies. Then too, the old lubricants were vastly inferior to what is commonly available today. For that reason, among others, engines wore more rapidly and had to be repaired more often than they do now.

If we go back before the 1920s, we find that fuels were so inconsistent that it was the recommendation of many automobile manufacturers to remove the cylinder head(s) from their engines at intervals of 6,000 to 10,000 miles for the routine maintenance operation known as "decarbonizing." This meant scraping or wire brushing the accumulated carbon off combustion chambers and piston tops. Can you imagine that sort of maintenance regimen being applied to the engines in today's cars, much less being tolerated by consumers?

Older engines were built to be rebuilt, and then rebuilt again, without any consideration to make them somehow disposable or throwaway units. This meant that adequate material was provided for successive grinding operations on cranks and cylinders, etc. I'm not sure who invented the concept of the disposable or impossible-to-work-on engine, but developments by the 1950s went a long way in that direction.

Take, for example, the "Kettering Engine" that appeared

Shown here are simple electrical checks of a point-condenser distributor. The point circuit continuity is checked with the ohms scale on an old d'Arsonval type meter. Then, the point circuit isolation is determined with a modern digital ohmmeter.

in the late 1940s in the Oldsmobile and Cadillac lines. It is considered the predecessor of the modern, light, fast-turning, push-rod overhead valve, short-stroke engine. It set the direction for the light, over-square, high-speed engines of the later 1950s through the 1990s. It also set the pattern for engines that were not particularly durable to begin with and difficult to repair. A developmental error caused the heads on early versions of these engines to crack easily and extensively. Worse, the rocker arms were not adjustable, and valve rework that took valve stem and actuation part dimensions outside of the limited range of the hydraulic lifters made it necessary to use hard-to-find, nonstandard (over and under length) push rods.

Some years after the Kettering engine debuted, Chrysler introduced its infamous "thin wall" blocks with cylinder bores so close to each other that they could not be bored to the oversizes usually associated with engine rebuilding. At about that time Chrysler also introduced its "Tufftrided" (nitrided) crankshafts, which, while enormously durable, could not be reground or welded-up without taking extraordinary measures. There followed such rebuilding nightmares as camshafts that ran without separate bearings (now modern practice) and even without detachable bearing caps. Then, there were those cylinder heads with integral valve guides. Ugh!

All of these developments, and others in the direction of throwaway components, have made modern engines

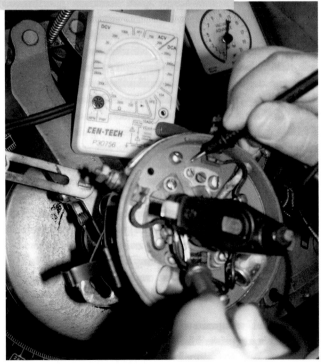

either difficult or uncommonly expensive to rebuild. As cars of the 1970s through the 1990s enter the collector car realm, restorers have had to solve many of these difficult problems.

Many of the subsystems used in post-1970 engines are

Mechanical components like wire wheels and mag wheels are readily available as reproduction parts. Sometimes replacement is necessary when a part is deteriorated to the point of being dangerous, or it becomes prohibitively time consuming or expensive to restore it. However, often you can restore an original part or have it restored. This often saves expense and promotes authenticity. It's a judgment call.

designed with little contemplation of repair or adjustment. After the 1940s, distributor vacuum advance units were built without provision for calibration of their springs and spacers. By the 1960s mechanical fuel pumps often could not be disassembled for the replacement of inexpensive wear parts, like valves and diaphragms. They were crimped together in ways that made disassembly and reassembly difficult or impossible. Simple, functional mechanisms, like manifold heat control valves, gave way to absurdities like exhaust restrictors, allegedly because no one bothered to maintain the old heat control valves anymore. By the 1980s, computer-controlled fuel injection and distributor-less ignition had replaced all of the old hardware for controlling fuel and ignition delivery. Modern automobiles are designed for minimum maintenance and adjustment. Closed loop computer systems, hooked to arrays of sensors, make nearly instantaneous adjustments thousands of times a minute, or more. Most repairs involve the use of bolt-on replacements for malfunctioning parts or systems. This makes repair easy, but often unnecessarily and stupidly expensive.

The point of mentioning all of this is to note that older engines and related subsystems are refreshingly susceptible to rebuilding, but also require periodic calibration and adjustment. The subsystem parts on older cars tended to be much more individually designed for particular applications, and were not generic items designed for "groups" or "families" of engines, as they are today.

It is sometimes hard to find the specific parts and information necessary to rebuild items like old fuel pumps, or to adjust and calibrate devices like voltage regulators. Yet that's often a lot less difficult and less expensive than finding replacement units.

For years, in restoration, there has been a mania abroad in the land for mindlessly throwing new old stock (NOS), new old restored stock (NORS), reproduction, and new

design parts at old engines. People who engage in this kind of "bolt-on-restoration" have missed most of the point of the design of old engines and their accessories. They are supremely repairable.

Sometimes it's comical. I once had a customer argue that he preferred to have me install a 30-plus-year-old NOS rebuilt fuel pump on his car (cost $65 plus installation at the time) to my suggestion that he or I rebuild his existing pump (cost $20 plus installation at the time). It was his car, so we did it his way. The old, rebuilt pump that he had found looked pretty, but only lasted two days in service before its rotted textile diaphragm ruptured and the pump quit pumping. Then it had to be removed and the pump rebuilt.

In recent years, people have come up with all sorts of modern parts and systems to replace old ones. Precise modern, solid state voltage regulators can be slipped into the boxes that originally housed electromechanical voltage regulator mechanisms, and diode and laser-triggered ignition systems with fully computerized advance/retard functions can be fitted into old distributor cases to provide many of the benefits of modern ignition systems. These include accuracy, reliability and adjustability, among other things. Some of this stuff produces functional improvements in performance over what it replaces, and some of it is easier to deal with than it would be to repair or to restore the original items. None of the modern replacement hardware is authentic, and restorers should consider this point carefully before installing any of it.

It is not the point of a good restoration to figure out how many modern systems or parts can be hidden in an apparently authentic engine. The point is to use original parts and systems when it is practical and prudent to do so.

Chapter 4

A General Approach to Engine Rebuilding

There are all kinds of reference books that are useful when you work on old engines. Before the 1930s there weren't many shop manuals for cars. These aftermarket repair manuals are great resources for specifications and repair procedures.

ONDEROUS BOOKS COULD BE, AND HAVE BEEN, written about engine rebuilding. It is not a topic that can be covered exhaustively in a few chapters in a general book on restoration. My purpose here in dealing with this topic is to touch on some of its high points, and to discuss some of the areas where I have seen people get into trouble—not to mention various problems that I have encountered rebuilding old engines over the years.

As for the books, a few stand out in my mind and should be consulted as comprehensive authorities on engine rebuilding techniques and skills. These are *Motor's Auto Engines and Electrical Systems,* various books on this topic by Harold Glenn (published by Chilton) and several pertinent texts published by the American Technical Society. The latter were published from nearly the turn of the 20th century through mid-century and often explain

The shop manuals, owners manual and piece of sales literature shown here can be extremely useful in restoration. Shop manuals contain detailed repair information. Older owners' manuals frequently have similar content. Sales literature can serve as a guide to authentic detail.

Here are two parts books from aftermarket suppliers, Auto-Lite and Delco/Northeast. These types of books are treasure troves of all kinds of good information.

contemporary thinking on the engineering behind various features of auto engines and other automotive mechanisms. This kind of insight can be very useful because it fills the restorer in on the "whys" of some of the engineering that he will encounter.

Other readily available and well-written works are Martin Stockel's *Auto Service and Repair* published by Goodhart-Wilcox and several chapters of a book by that publisher titled *Automobile Encyclopedia*. The latter title was published from the World War II era into recent years. The volumes devoted to engines in Chilton's *Mechanics Handbook* series are also excellent. There are several other books that are useful on this topic, but the ones mentioned above are probably the best.

Some books that should be avoided for instruction in engine rebuilding (but not for bedtime reading) are various

Trade publications can also be useful when they cover a topic that you need to know about. They are also great fun to browse.

The *Hollander* Manuals provide detailed interchange information on what parts and assemblies fit more than one vehicle. They can be lifesavers in helping broaden a search for an obscure part.

newsstand hot rod journals and several obsolete works such as A. L. Dyke's *Encyclopedias*. The latter contain some useful information and much dangerous misinformation. It is sometimes difficult to sort one from the other. Hot rod journals often include useful engine rebuilding tips and techniques, but hold modification rather than authenticity as their priority. That makes them an uncertain source of restoration knowledge. Again, they can make excellent leisure reading.

There are many areas of controversy in engine rebuilding, and it is not my purpose here to attempt to settle many of these. It is generally my policy to take a very conservative approach to rebuilding engines. Where controversy exists, I side with the sure thing—even at the cost of not getting onto the ultimate cutting edge of potential performance and durability.

There has been, for example, a controversy raging over the use of "chromium" piston rings in old engines. Advocates suggest that these modern rings retain their shapes better, provide more predictable sealing pressure, and improve wear resistance. They are also claimed to reduce engine friction.

Opponents of the use of these rings in older engines suggest that the metallurgy of pre-World War II engine block cylinder surfaces is inadequate to withstand the wear inflicted by chromium piston rings. I have heard both sides of this argument for many years. Both can be presented persuasively and with numerous and convincing examples. I suspect that there is nothing wrong with using modern chrome alloy piston rings in some old engines. However, I have heard of and seen old cylinder bores that were literally carved up (presumably) by chromium rings. At this point, I am not sure. Until I am, I will continue to order out cast-iron rings for my prewar restoration work. They are adequately reliable, and break in quickly. I simply won't take the chance on chrome content rings until I am certain that they will not inflict damage on old cylinder surfaces. Cast-iron piston rings are much closer to original equipment on old engines and are the "sure thing" in this case.

On the other hand, the argument that knurling valve guides provides performance and durability equal to or surpassing their replacement, and at much less expense than replacement, have convinced me. As long as the knurling technique is not used unrealistically to reduce unreasonable clearances, this technique tends to produce a desirably hard-running surface for valve stems and improved oil retention. It does this by creating recesses for oil in the guides' working surfaces. This is one modern engine rebuilding technique that I fully endorse and use frequently in my own work.

It is counterproductive to reject all new techniques, materials, and processes just because they are new. It is equally bad policy to adopt all of them without determining their individual merits. A good basic approach is to adopt those that have proven worthy over several years and in the experience of several people, and to avoid those where the "jury is still out."

Not all cockeyed theories of engine rebuilding are new. Some of them have been around for years. My work on the first engine that I ever rebuilt was under the direction of a seasoned, hard-boiled German mechanic. I learned a lot from him about measuring techniques and the need for cleanliness in engine rebuilding.

When that first engine rebuild was finally finished and ready to leave his machine shop, he gave me a present. Or rather, he inflicted a present on me. Without my consent or approval, he poured some of the contents of a rumpled and disreputable looking brown paper bag into the oil sump of my just-completed engine. He explained, reassuringly, that this mysterious stuff would aid the break-in process. I didn't know any better, so I thanked him. I got to thank him again about 15,000 miles down the road when I burned out a rod bearing in that engine. I should have just dropped the pan and gotten rid of his gift before I put that engine back into service.

Somehow, my friend and mentor had overlooked the possibility that the flake graphite he poured into my oil was of a particle size too large for colloidal suspension in the oil. Most of it settled harmlessly to the bottom of the oil pan, where I found it when I had to go in after that rod bearing. Some of the rest of it was quickly trapped in the engine's partial-flow oil filter. Unfortunately, some of the remainder was efficiently centrifuged by the crankshaft until several oil passages from the main bearings to the rod bearings were blocked. That caused my rod bearing failure. Bad ideas come in many disguises and formats, in this case out of a rumpled paper bag offered as a gift by a friend.

Basic Engine Disassembly

Although basic engines may seem simple, I again emphasize the importance of taking careful disassembly notes. Things like the positions of long studs or of studs with curious top-threaded extensions can be very vexing to reestablish at the time of reassembly if you do not know exactly where they belong.

After the accessories have been removed from a basic engine block and head, and the particulars of their proper mounting adequately recorded, and all rotating parts indexed, one to another, it is time to disassemble the basic block.

Engine disassembly can be done quickly and violently, with little regard for the fine points, or it can be done slowly and carefully. If you choose the first route, you will inevitably find that any time saved in this kind of disassembly will be spent tens or hundreds of times over repairing the damage that you may have inflicted. I have seen people apply brutal kinds of force removing cylinder heads when some simple observation, analysis, and preparation would have saved them from the damage that resulted from this violence. Basically, any method of prying or wedging a cylinder head off a block will inflict damage. A cold chisel will do more damage than a .015-inch feeler gauge hammered in sideways. But both of these approaches run an unacceptably high risk of causing harm.

Heads do not seize to blocks or to head gaskets, they seize to studs. If a head is bolted on, rather than secured with studs and nuts, you get a free pass to remove it. In the case of aluminum heads, seizure to studs is electrolytic in nature and achieves a bond that has the tenacity of welding. If the process has occurred over decades, no amount of prying is likely to lift a head off a block in one piece. In fact, any head that cannot be lifted off a block with the compression generated by rotating the crankshaft will need to have the stud-to-head clearance reestablished by undercutting the stud-to-head interface. This can be done relatively easily by acquiring some thin-wall stainless tubing with an i.d. a "smidgeon" larger than the size of the studs. A half-dozen cutting teeth can be ground into the business end of the tubing and a visual stop installed to prevent undercutting into the block's deck surface. Then this cutting tool can be

turned by hand or chucked into a drill motor and run down over each stud to the block deck. With the stud-to-head clearances reestablished, the head can now be removed easily.

In the above example, a little thought and a little fine work can prevent the destruction of an important component.

Another example of violent engine disassembly involves the removal of studs themselves. I have seen people go at this with massive pipe wrenches and with long arm "persuaders" with an abandon that is mortifying. The theory seems to be, "what the—if I break 'em off, I'm gunna replace 'em anyway."

Perhaps, but drilling out broken studs is one of life's most irksome and unrewarding tasks. True, studs should be replaced during an engine rebuild because the torque characteristics of old studs are suspect, at best, but breaking them off sends you into the queasy world of devices like "Easyouts," "wedge-proof screw extractors" and "fluted screw removers," etc. Since this class of tools often fails, escalation to drilling out the broken stud(s) and installing remedial thread inserts is just around the proverbial corner.

Basic engine block work must be done precisely. After accurately tightening the bearing caps on this massive crankshaft, it is still possible to keep it turning with a few ounces of pressure once you get it moving.

The automated cleaning system shown here saves a lot of time and conditions metal castings by relieving stress in them. After scraping the grunge off, parts are secured in a cage in a rotating oven and baked at several hundred degrees for 20-40 minutes. Of course, the lid of the machine is closed during the baking process. Next, the parts are rotated in a shot cabinet for several minutes. The bottom right photo shows the airless shot generating wheels at the bottom of this cabinet. They are driven by a 5-horsepower electric motor!

There is a special surprise reserved for those who succeed in breaking their choice of screw extractor off in a drilled-out stud hole. Break a stud extractor off and you may learn a new dimension of the word "misery." You usually will discover that it was made from a steel alloy that is too hard to drill into. Now you have a situation much worse than the problem that you set out to solve. You can go after it with a diamond grinding tool, or make a trip to the local die shop for an expensive bout on an EDM device that will vaporize your broken screw extractor-in-a-broken-stud.

It's simply easier and far more placid to get studs out in one-piece the first time around. Everyone will be happier that way, except possibly the manufacturers of those screw extractors.

Not to leave you hanging, stud removal can be made relatively easy by cleaning the bases of the studs to be removed, heating them a little with a very mild flame, such as air-propane or air-acetylene, and blowing a good grade of penetrating oil into the threads with shop air pressure. This last step is most important whenever you use penetrating oil. I had always used penetrating oil liberally on the theory that it couldn't hurt and it might even help. I discovered by accident several years ago that when penetrating oil is forced into thread interfaces with shop air pressure (150 PSI in my shop) it becomes very effective and always aids in separating threaded fasteners. That is not the case when it is squirted out of an aerosol can at half a dozen or so pounds pressure. That extra step of hitting it with serious air pressure after you dribble it out of its can is decisive. Its capabilities go from marginal to tiger-like.

When you go after a stud that is stuck in a casting, a stud remover is a far better tool than a pipe wrench. If applications of penetrating oil and a stud remover don't do

the job, there is a very effective arc welding technique for heating and removing studs. It usually works on extreme, hard cases and should be performed by someone who knows how to do it.

What's inside an engine seems simple enough. There aren't very many parts, and most of them tend to be large. It's not at all like a carburetor, with all of those pesky little parts. Well, not quite. A carburetor usually has only one or two of everything. A basic block may have one, two, three, four, five, six, eight, twelve, sixteen, twenty-four or thirty-two of everything, among other scary numbers.

The parts are tumbled in every possible orientation (top) to remove the shot from their nooks and crannies. The last step is to rotate the parts in a jet wash cabinet to remove any remaining residues from them.

This professional magnetic particle inspection table has all of the bells and whistles for finding cracks in ferrous metal.

It is always desirable, and often essential, that everything go back in its original position or hole and in the direction that it was originally facing. Accomplishing this means producing the usual notes, diagrams, and photographs. It also means labeling parts as you remove them. Tags are OK, but they can come off or become illegible. My preference is for scribing, stamping, or punching marks onto parts to indicate their relative positions and installation orientations. A good habit to avoid is that of filing marks onto internal engine parts. A V-shaped file mark is a wonderful place from which a crack can propagate.

Somehow, when you are taking a basic engine block apart, it seems simple, straightforward, and easy to remember its assembly details. This may *seem* true, but six months, or a year, or longer may elapse between disassembly and reassembly. In that time, what once seemed simple, clear and obvious can descend into the realm of generous confusions.

If you accumulate enough of these reassembly questions, instead of listening joyously to the vibrant throb of your restored engine when it is first started, you will get to listen to it very carefully and with considerable trepidation and *angst,* as you wait for some result of mis-assembly related failure to occur. Every sound or vibration that cannot easily

be explained will become suspect. That situation may go on for a long time. It can greatly reduce any enjoyment that you might otherwise get from a finished restoration. It is easier to be certain that you got it right the first time around. That is only possible when you keep good disassembly records as you go along.

It is a good idea to do all marking and indexing with an engine's rotating parts in their top dead center (TDC or UDC) positions. Then, if you adopt a ground rule that all marks will be made in an up position (excepting items that are keyed or items like timing gears, chains and sprockets that may obey their own conventions of adjacent markings), it becomes easy to re-mate things such as the flywheels and crankshafts, flywheels and clutches, etc. in their correct relative positions. Piston tops should be numbered gently with steel numbering stamps, and the numbers should be stamped facing in a consistent direction—say, toward the front of the engine. Connecting rods, rod bearing caps, and main bearing caps should be numbered for sequence and orientation.

Valve lifters, push rods, rocker arms, and valves must be identified as to position. Since it can be difficult to stamp or punch numbers onto valve train parts, these items should be kept in compartment containers that clearly indicate their proper sequences. Even if you don't plan to reuse internal engine parts, it is still good practice to note their positions until you have the replacement parts installed. This can also help you to zero in on problems that may have occurred in the past.

Cleaning Basic Engine Blocks and Heads

Only after everything that can be removed has been taken off a basic block can the block be cleaned effectively. All methods of adequately cleaning blocks will tend to destroy any components left behind. This means that such items as camshaft bearings, casting core plugs (alias, Welch plugs or "freeze" plugs) and the like should be removed to enhance cleaning blocks. These items should always be replaced with new items.

There are several exotic methods of cleaning blocks, heads, and other engine parts. Major engine rebuilders and well-equipped automotive machine shops use such techniques as convection oven baking or molten salt baths, followed by cabinet shot peening, tumbling, and cabinet jet washing. These advanced cleaning techniques are usually used due to the economies of scale that are required in production engine rebuilding. Some custom automotive machine shops still use a hot tanking method to clean large engine parts.

There are special hot and "cold tank" solutions available that are compatible with aluminum components. Some of these use ultrasonic transducers to boost the cleaning process. Never allow any aluminum or zinc alloy part to go into a common hot tank. The damage to it will be severe and possibly irreparable. Special solutions and chemicals are available to clean these alloys.

It is a good idea to avoid the use of abrasive blasting processes on basic engine blocks. Such processes as glass beading, grit blasting, and the like present huge cleanup problems. One stray glass bead or piece of aluminum oxide grit can do enormous damage if it gets into the wrong place in an engine. It isn't worth taking the chance. Some people believe that shooting abrasive blasting media at internal engine surfaces, particularly in the crankcase area, impregnates the pores of the metal with minute grit fragments. They reason that these fragments may be released by contact with hot oil that expands those pores when an engine is put into service. I have never seen any proof that this is true, but I have neither have I seen any that it isn't. Besides, it sounds reasonable that this could happen.

The only blasting process that has any proper application to basic block cleaning is the use of air-generated or airless steel shot. This cleaning technique is promoted as fast, effective, and clean. It is also sometimes alleged that shot-peening stress-relieves engine castings. This last claim may be true but, in practice, shot-peening applications to heavy engine parts are almost never carried out in ways

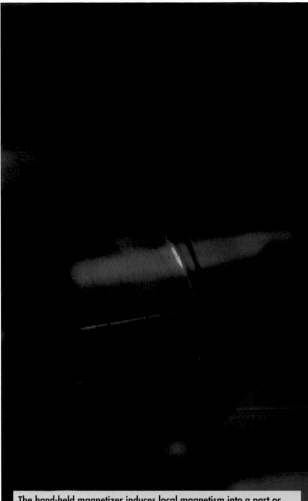

The hand-held magnetizer induces local magnetism into a part or part of a part and causes inspection particles that are spread on it to line up north-and-south along the axis of a crack when the field is oriented at 90 degrees to it. Finding cracks with magnetic particle inspection equipment takes some practice and good observation skills.

that are controlled enough to achieve any predictable stress-relieving results.

One drawback of shot-peening blocks and other heavy engine parts is that the process tends to smear a minutely thin coating of steel on the surfaces of iron parts. This can result in corrosion under the parts' finishes and subsequent paint failure. When you shot-peen engine parts with exposed surfaces that later will be painted, you should always use a conversion coating to etch them, or an etching primer under your engine's paint.

Hot tanking a block is still an acceptable way to clean it. However, this procedure will not remove much rust and it does tend to leave undesirable chemical residues on a block's surface that should be cleaned off before it is painted.

After all machining operations have been completed on a block it should be washed and rinsed with common hand soap and water. This will remove any residual chemicals from the hot tanking or jet washing operation. It also gets rid of any chips, grit and oil residues left behind by machining operations. After administering this "hand bath" to "baby," the working and sealing surfaces of the block should be

A crack indicated by non-fluorescing dry particles looks like this.

This power source, used with the somewhat homemade coil, rod and contacting accessories shown here can be very effective for doing wet or dry magnetic particle inspections. In this case, the "wet" inspection is being performed with an aerosol can of phosphorescing inspection fluid that causes cracks to stand out strongly. A connecting rod is being inspected in several ways and orientations in these photos.

completely dried with compressed air and coated with light oil to prevent rusting prior to reassembly.

Crack Detection and Repair

For a very small cost you can have a Magnaflux® inspection performed on the basic engine block, head, and internal components of any engine that you restore. This step will detect cracks and is absolutely essential to proper engine rebuilding. Most engine cracks will be found in the combustion chambers in the vicinity of the valves. In "L," "T," and "F" head engines this means that they will be in the block, but there are other possibilities. Cracks across the deck of a block, in the bearing saddle areas, or in valve chambers are common. Cracks in upper and lower cylinder areas are less common, but their potential existence makes it worth inspecting these areas.

We do our own Magnaflux® inspections of critical and stressed engine components. Then we take the same parts to the machine shop that we use for a second inspection. Whenever I take the parts from an engine that we are working on to our favorite automotive machine shop, a standing joke is activated. I say something like, "Look here, this engine model has a bad reputation for cracks, better give it a particularly careful going over." And one of the machinists always says something like, "Oh, where do they crack?" To which I always answer, "Everywhere, just everywhere."

The people who sell Magnaflux® crack detection systems also sell a very abbreviated detection process called "Spotcheck®," and a slightly more sophisticated process called "Zyglo®." These systems are generally sold through welding supply shops, but have also been offered and misrepresented through advertising in several old car journals. They are reasonably effective in discerning gross cracks, but their usefulness ends there. They are not a substitute for Magnaflux® or other magnetic particle inspection analyses of blocks, heads, and ferrous internal engine parts. They were never intended for that purpose.

These and some other dye-penetrant, aerosol crack detection systems simply do not exhibit the sensitivity to cracks that is necessary for the purposes of engine rebuilding. The sad fact is that very small cracks in engines can open up and become very large when they are repeatedly heated, cooled and mechanically stressed. Inevitably, there are enough unknowns in rebuilding 20 to 90 year-old engines, without adding the potential of propagating detectable cracks to the list. Magnafluxing® isn't particularly expensive, and it comes as close to being foolproof as any non-destructive testing procedure (NDT) that I know. I recommend it.

Measurement and Inspection of Basic Blocks

Measurement and inspection are critically important in engine rebuilding. This is particularly true of basic engine blocks. Inspection does not end with Magnaflux®. Such matters as the condition of threaded holes and the soundness of manifold mating surfaces are critically important. Part of any inspection process relies on the educated, unaided eye, as, for example, the evaluation of sealing and running surfaces for porosity and pin holing.

Every flat mating surface in an engine should be inspected with a straightedge and thickness gauges. The straightedge should be a hefty piece of stabilized and ground steel, and the thickness gauges should be in good

The penalty for not finding cracks can look like this. Massive failure of major, highly stressed engine components is never pretty.

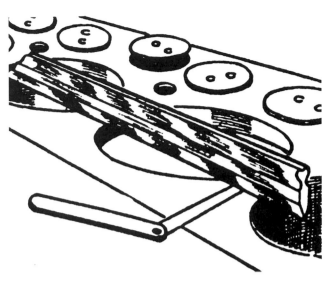

Block decks, heads, and other flat mating surfaces in engines should be checked for flatness with a straight edge and feeler gauge. This provides a simple but effective indication of warping defects.

condition, not chewed up from doing "hot" adjustments on valves. As a general rule, if you can find warping in a head or block of more than .002 inches any 6-inch run, it's time to surface grind that surface. This is true for head and block deck surfaces, as well as for manifold mating surfaces. Of course, if visual inspection reveals porous, rough, or deeply scratched surfaces, then surface grinding is required, even if the ".002 inch in 6 inches" test is passed.

Throughout the inspection and measurement process, remember that old castings can be very capricious in the ways that they choose to distort. Blocks tend to twist, warp and wear in unexpected directions. I have seen examples of wear that seem inexplicable, according to the generally accepted physical laws that would seem to govern such things. I suppose that if all of the variables were known and accounted for, there would be logical explanations, but at the present state of my knowledge, I sometimes just shake my head and think, "...must have happened during a full moon."

You may have to look hard for weird wear patterns and distortions to find them. My basic rule is to make every possible measurement that I can. Assume that the engine you are working on was never inspected, assembled by an incompetent apprentice and maintained by lunatics. Proceed from there and check the alignment of the main bearing saddles for straightness and for squareness against the cylinder bores, the alignment of the camshaft bearing bores, the straightness of the cylinder bores, etc.

Bore straightness is an interesting example of the subtleties of measurement. Cylinder wall wear patterns should tip you off to a crooked cylinder, but they don't always do that for you. If you attempt to surface a cylinder wall with a simple hone, or even with a sophisticated dwell-hone, you will perpetuate any deflection in the cylinder wall from straight. The only way to cure this problem is with a boring bar.

But what on earth could cause a cylinder to be non-perpendicular to the crank centerline and deck? A lot of things could, but this condition, when it is found, is often there because the block left the factory that way. In other words, the inspection and measurement process is not just to account for wear and casting distortion after manufacture, it also has to account for manufacturing error, and there is a surprising amount of that error to be found in older engines.

The business of measuring block dimensions and deviations is not terribly complex or hard to learn, but it does require some experience. The use of feeler (thickness) gauges, micrometers, bore gauges, etc. requires a sense of feel that it takes some time to develop. Conventional measuring tools (vernier scales) are easily capable of measurement to .0001 inch. This level of precision is highly desirable in areas such as bearing clearances. To achieve this level of accuracy requires not only a feel for the measuring instruments that you use, but also the ability to calibrate these devices, and extreme attention to cleanliness. Newer electronic/digital readout instruments are making precise measurements easier to obtain, but it would be a mistake to attempt any precision measurements with any kind of measuring equipment without proper instruction and, at least, some experience.

Another critical aspect of measuring technique involves knowing and understanding measurement terminology, cold. It is surprising how many people engaging in engine rebuilding cannot handle the basic use of the decimal system. They will say, "three thousandths," but write ".0003" (which is really three ten-thousandths). The results can be disastrous.

Terminology confusion goes beyond the use of the decimal system. Take, for example, the conventions surrounding the specification of bearing clearances.

A cylinder bore gauge is the best way to check cylinders for wear, distortion, out-of-round and taper. Always carefully record the measurements that you make and indicate exactly where they were taken. Modern bore gauges are digital and can record the measurements that they take as they go along.

These clearances are specified as the differences between the diameters of bearing bores and the diameters of the shafts that will run in those bores. Yet, some people think that this specification denotes the space on each side of a shaft centered in a bearing. If someone operating under this misconception orders a crankshaft grind or a new set of bearings, and the error is not caught, he is likely to end up with twice the specified running clearance. It sounds ridiculous, but it happens every day. If you have any questions about measurement terminology or convention, don't be embarrassed to ask somebody. Never guess. Errors in this area are always more embarrassing than honest questions.

When dealing with old engine blocks and their innards, try to get the particular data that applies to the engine that you are rebuilding. While most main and rod bearings run in the clearance range of 0.0015 to .0020 inch, some do not. It pays to find the right specifications for any engine that you are working on and to adhere to them throughout the rebuilding process. Splash-lubricated systems, for example, have different bearing clearance requirements than full-pressure systems.

The Repair of Basic Blocks

There are basically three major classes of defect that occur in old engine castings: cracks, rust-throughs and distortions. This is not to say that there are not other possibilities. Burnout defects are occasionally encountered and extraordinary wear, such as bearing spinout damage, can erode the metal of a basic block. But cracks, rust-outs and distortions account for about 90 percent of the block defects that require repair.

Cracks are commonly repaired by drilling the crack ends to stop propagation, and either welding, peening, or pinning and peening. The pinning and peening approach involves drilling either adjacent or overlapping holes in a crack and forcing threaded or tapered pins into the holes. The heads of the pins are then cut off and the stubs peened over with a pneumatic peening hammer. Then the whole inside of the block's or head's water jacket is sealed internally by coating it with ceramic sealant that is flowed through it under pressure and at elevated temperatures. This technique may sound haphazard in my description of it, but it has proven remarkably successful in use for more than 60 years. A crucial aspect of this, or any other crack repair technique, involves pressure testing the finished repair.

Welding cracks in castings is another highly successful repair method, but requires extreme skill to produce reliable results. Cast iron, particularly the gray and nodular castings that sometimes show up in automobile engine blocks, is very difficult to weld. Even when a successful weld bead is achieved, there is a considerable tendency for a parallel crack to develop in the heat-affected zone adjacent to that weld. Specific measures, such as stress-relief peening, preheating, slow heat reduction, and the like are required to circumvent this tendency. I know enough about welding stressed castings to pretty much stay away from it. This is one of those skill areas best left to people who do it all day, every day.

Several specialty-welding shops produce great results welding engine block and head cracks. There are also several companies that specialize in repairing cracked diesel heads for the trucking industry. These providers are a particularly good bet because they routinely deal with castings that are stressed way beyond almost anything ever encountered in old car gasoline engines. Water jacket cracks are susceptible to brazing or silver soldering, but are still best left to people who can accurately assess the movements and stresses of castings under the application of welding heat.

The choice of crack repair technique ultimately depends on the metallurgical composition and design of the block in question and the location of the crack(s). In some cases, the economics of crack repair will dictate replacing a block. This is particularly true of some freeze-cracked blocks, where the cracks, combined with block distortion, can make any repair very expensive.

One thing should be obvious from all of this: Never put an engine together that contains any cracks or suspected cracks. I have seen this done because some misinformed individual has assumed that he could beat the cost of crack repair by pouring some magic potion or powder into his cooling system after the engine was together, and thus cure the problem. Such a cure will be temporary, at best, and the crack will just get bigger after the engine has been bolted together and run a few times. ("Nature always sides with the hidden defect" is my favorite configuration of Murphy's Law.)

I realize that the crack repair fluids and solids that are sold for addition to cooling systems often have confidence-inspiring names and come in some really great-looking packages. Often, these substances have the wonderful appearances of bronze, copper or aluminum flakes. A few of them even look like rejected props from the sci-fi movie, *The Blob*. Whatever the appearance or product name, whether it's high-tech sounding or just folksy, such remedies won't work for long.

I've heard all of the stories about using sodium silicate to make cooling system crack repairs to blocks and heads and I don't believe any of them. The ultimate cost of trying to live with unrepaired cracks is, at best, running problems. At worst it's twisted and ruined parts caused by the dreaded "hydrolock" monster.

Hydrolock occurs when a pressurized cooling system has filled a cylinder with coolant by leaking into it after shutdown. Subsequently, an attempt to start the engine may bring the torque of a 1-horsepower starting motor against a single connecting rod through a 25:1 gear ratio reduction on the flywheel. Since the cylinder has filled with a relatively incompressible fluid, the piston can't move up in its bore.

That's right, something has to give. It will usually be the connecting rod in any cylinder that has its valves closed, has filled with and trapped the coolant coming through the crack and is at some non-perpendicular angle to the crankshaft. Hydrolock is a major disaster.

If you're old enough to be rebuilding engines, you already know Part I of life's sad truth. There's no tooth fairy, just generous parents. Here's Part II—there's no block fixing genie that can be poured out of a bottle or squeezed from a tube.

Rust-throughs in blocks are best handled by welding. High metal-content, high-temperature epoxies are often promoted for this job, but I have never seen much long-term success with them. In the same vein, wet-sleeve engines that require repairs in the sleeve seating and lower sealing areas are best repaired with welding and remachining.

Block distortion and warping is fairly rare and can only be fixed by align-boring bearing saddles and/or reboring cylinder holes. Usually, when this defect occurs, it is only in very minor dimensions and can be corrected easily in a well-equipped automotive machine shop.

Internal block threads often require repair. We have already discussed the desirability of removing all threaded block fasteners intact. When this cannot be done, or when threaded holes have rusted through into an engine's water jacket, it is time to use a rethreading technique.

The best solution is to carefully center drill the damaged fastener to the next thread size and to run a regular tap in, followed by a blind tap. If this cannot be done due to lack of wall material or to the need to maintain a uniform fastener size (for both torquing and appearance considerations), you can use a special turn-down stud with different sizes at its ends or employ one of several thread insert techniques that are available. Although the spring-like Heli-Coil® is probably the best known and most popular such repair, I find threaded sleeve-type rethreading inserts, such as the Slimsert® and the Keensert®, to be more satisfactory. Their most obvious advantage is that they are solid pieces and therefore have sealing capability and strength that Heli-Coils® do not possess. I have also found torque readings in Heli-Coil® repaired threads to be erratic. It should be stressed that if simply "chasing" threads or re-tapping them will do the job, this is far preferable to any of the re-drilling-to-oversize or thread insert repair techniques.

In any thread repair that involves drilling, take extreme care to center the pilot hole that you drill into the old fastener, and keep the new hole parallel to it. If you don't, you will have a real problem; one that may be worse than the one that you set out to solve.

The tops of threaded holes in blocks should be counter bored to the depth of one thread. This prevents a tightened fastener from raising the top thread in a hole above the deck surface and having it interfere with perfect surface mating.

I have one last word of caution about block fasteners and the holes in which they reside: There is no better way to strip threads and warp and distort castings than to try to torque down a fastener that is too long for its hole. Lubricated threads give enormous mechanical advantage, and the fasteners in them can exert fantastic pressures when they are tightened. Take extreme care in disassembly to note any differences in fastener lengths, and to relate them to reassembly in the proper holes. Failure to take this precaution can result in a cracked block casting and/or distortion damage.

Chapter 5

Basic Engine Remachining

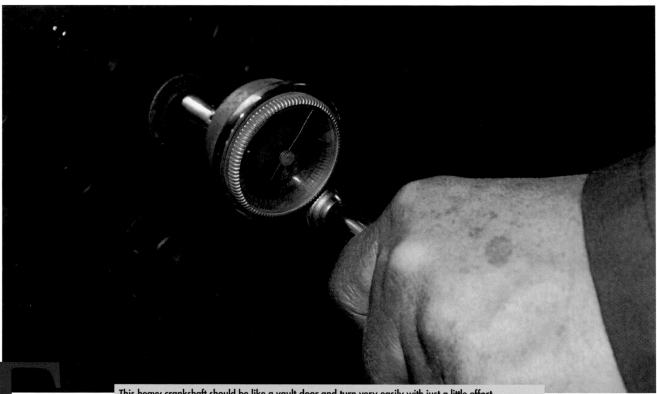

This heavy crankshaft should be like a vault door and turn very easily with just a little effort.

EVERY SO OFTEN, AT AN AUCTION OR SWAP MEET, I SEE some of the crude old tools that were used to do basic engine remachining years ago. Sometimes, from the representations that accompany these devices, it is actually suggested that they could be used today for this purpose.

A few probably can. I have seen 40-year-old boring bars that still do credible work, and some well-maintained align boring devices and crankshaft grinders seem to have lives of their own.

The class of devices that I am worried about includes hand-held crankpin reamers, or the devices that were used to grind rod journals with a crankshaft still in an engine, and that engine in a car! Most of these "gyp" tools were used by service stations, used car lots, and minor repair shops—outfits, which were sometimes involved in major overhauls that they never should have attempted. These, and items like hand-drill operated valve grinders, are about as appropriate to restoration engine remachining as a paint brush would be to refinishing your car.

Automotive machine shop tools have become

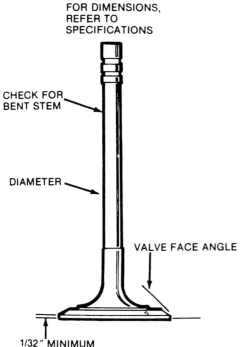

FOR DIMENSIONS, REFER TO SPECIFICATIONS

CHECK FOR BENT STEM

DIAMETER

VALVE FACE ANGLE

1/32" MINIMUM

Engine valves and springs come in many sizes and configurations. Poppet valves are the weakest link in most engines and require extreme care when engines are rebuilt. There aren't too many factors to account for in valve work, but you have to be deadly accurate with the factors that must be accounted for.

very precise and very automated. That offers a definite advantage for today's rebuilders and for their customers. Such precision and automation were not always the case. While most automakers held reasonably close tolerances in their basic manufacturing processes, those tolerances tended to get degraded in the successive ministrations of repair shops. Grotesque practices were once commonplace, like hand filing bearing caps to remove the thickness of a nonexistent shim. In fact, most, if not all of the practices that are presently considered substandard were described in great detail in popular "how-to" books. They were presented in some of these old books and manuals as standard and acceptable shop techniques and practices. Consider such presentations and the methods that they describe obsolete.

Occasionally, you meet an old-time tractor mechanic who can't understand why anyone would bother to repour and remachine a thick shell babbitt bearing when a few swaths with a file and alternately hitting the bearing shell's outside radius with a hammer and compressing it in a vise "will do the same thing" Nix on that, because *it won't accomplish "the same thing,"* or anything else that is likely to work for very long. While it is not necessary to build the precision of a Formula 1 racing engine into the likes of a 1949 Hudson power plant, it is a good idea to use contemporary standards of precision rather than those of 1949 or 1916. I know of no engine failure that occurred because relevant rebuilding specifications were adhered to too precisely or upgraded to greater precision.

The automotive machine shop is simply one place where we can be very happy that they don't "[re]build 'em like they used to." I wouldn't trade a modern wet valve facer for one of the old dry ones, or a new Sunnen rod honing machine for a 1930s vintage bearing sizing machine for all of the washers in the Ford Motor Company's inventory in Dearborn.

Three Basic Systems to Consider

There are three basic systems to account for when considering machine shop operations on conventional engines. These are the valve system, the crankshaft system, and the cylinder/piston system.

The valve system in its simplest form is comprised of a camshaft and its bearings and side-play control system, the tappets (including hydraulic and other self-adjusting types) and tappet bores, the valves and their seats, and assorted valve springs and their retainers, keepers and rotators or other rotating provisions. On overhead valve (OHV) engines that are not overhead cam-type (OHC), you can add push rods and one or more sets of rocker arms and shafts, or studs and bucket rockers to this inventory.

The crankshaft area includes the crankshaft itself, counterweights (integral or attached), the rod and main bearings and an endplay thrust-limiting system. It may also have an attached vibration-damping device and will always include some method of preventing oil leakage past its rear crankcase and timing cover containments. Rod oil scoops (non-pressurized or partially pressurized systems) may also be present.

The cylinder/piston system is comprised of pistons, rings, wrist pins, their retainers and bearings, rods and the cylinder walls, or in some cases, sleeves.

There are other areas and surfaces, such as the timing system and head and block deck surfaces, which may require attention in the machine shop, but the basic division outlined above is a reasonable framework in which to consider the moving, removable parts in an engine.

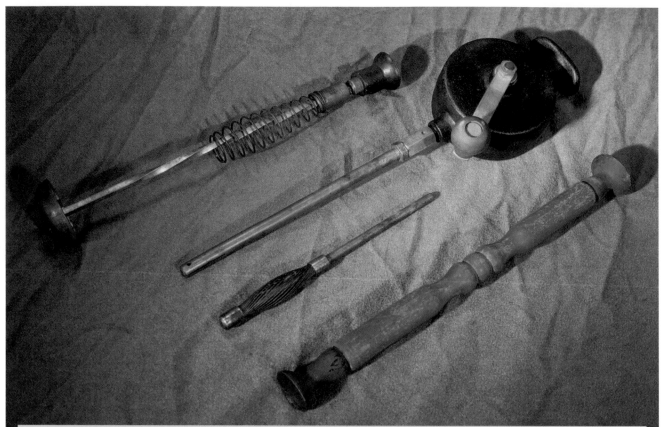

Some of the old tools that were used for valve work just don't meet modern standards. The old style guide cleaner (second from right) is OK for cleaning guides, but the reciprocating hand valve "grinder" and push spiral device (first and second from left) should not be used to lap valves and seats. Valves should be ground on the specially designed machines that have been available for the last sixty plus years for this purpose. The suction cup hand grinder on the right is useful for checking valve/seat contact area with Prussian blue. It should never be used with abrasives to actually lap valves and seats.

The Valve System

The environment in which automotive valves operate is not quite impossible, but it comes close. Valves are far and away the most stressed parts in the average engine. Exhaust valves operate at hellish temperatures, often causing them to run cherry red. They open and slam shut a couple of thousand times for every mile driven in most postwar cars. For every mile that you drive, each valve will travel more than 100 feet in increments of about 1/3 inch. If all of this weren't bad enough, the valves in an automobile engine are constantly surrounded by incredibly hot and corrosive gases and are subject to attacks by nasty squadrons of carbon and other particles that are the byproducts of combustion. Smidgeons of silicon and carbide find their ways into the valve seat area in accompaniment with the incoming air and fuel.

Add to all of this the fact that valve stems are virtually impossible to adequately lubricate where they need it most, and you have a component that has good reasons for being the weakest link in an engine system. Cam lobes are a distant second on the list of engine self-destruct components.

Almost anything that is wrong in a valve train will cause disaster in fairly short order. Burned valves will never cure themselves, and valves that are set too "tight" can be ruined in a matter of a few hours, or in extreme cases, in

a few minutes. Next to engine bearings, valves require the greatest accuracy in engine rebuilding, but they don't always get it. Valve work, whether it is a minor refacing or a more major rework, should be done by people who know exactly what they are doing and who work with equipment that is proven.

In valve work, problems can be encountered that are difficult but never impossible to solve. One of my favorite examples is the set of problems that can be encountered when an engine (early postwar GM V-8s and others) with push rods and hydraulic lifters is rebuilt and there is no provision for adjusting valve clearances. Getting the hydraulic lifters acceptably positioned (centered) can involve grinding the valve stem ends and keepers, shimming the rocker shaft supports, converting to adjustable push rods or rocker arms, etc. Again, this is work for professionals who know their equipment, your situation and all of the available options.

Because there are several valid approaches to valve work, and many different kinds of equipment on which to accomplish the basic machining operations to recondition the components of valve systems, I will deal with just the general considerations.

In the area of valve seats and guides, the main consideration is that valve guides be absolutely straight and uniform in bore, and perfectly concentric to their seats. They must also provide the proper clearance for the valve

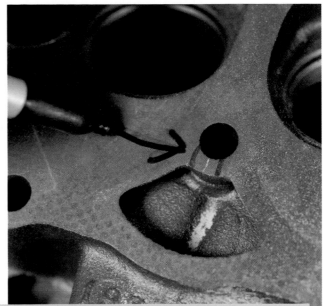

Before you do head work, always check for cracks in the combustion chambers. This check turned up a crack outside of the combustion chambers, but one that had to be repaired, nonetheless.

stems. Guides must be installed at the correct heights and must be correct with regard to undercut. Valve seats must be cut to exactly correct widths. They must meet valve faces at the prescribed angles and be absolutely concentric with respect to their valve guides. Valve faces must sit in their seats in heads or blocks at correct depths and the seats must contact the middles of the valve faces.

Operationally, all of this means that proper valve work cannot be accomplished using grinding equipment to hand lap or machine lap valves and seats, as was common practice many years ago. This was not an accurate enough procedure to produce usable results, because it did not yield an acceptably accurate or smooth finish. The fact that older engines now require modern levels of valve seat or valve face hardness to withstand the use of unleaded fuels makes it mandatory to achieve modern levels of accuracy in this work.

Proper valve work involves the use of precise pilots and accurately faced grinding stones or carbide cutters to produce the necessary three-valve seat angles that provide for proper seat width and position. The old hand-turned metal cutters that were used in conjunction with a final lapping operation produced pretty dismal results. Another type of equipment that should not be used is the old, dry valve facers. These devices tended to heat check valve faces in the grinding process. The quality of some of the valves on the market today is questionable enough without adding the problems caused by using substandard grinding processes.

Not every valve can be saved by refacing it, though some rebuilders seem to try to accomplish this. When you replace valves, you can use exhaust valves of comparable dimensions in intake applications, but not the other way around. Exhaust valves are much more durable and heat resistant than intakes. They have to be.

Since many restorers do not have the equipment or experience to do their own valve work, they have it done by commercial machine shops. It is probably best to leave most decisions about valve work to the machinists who do this work. Still, there are a few areas where owners and restorers should maintain input. On the issue of whether or not use seat inserts, my feeling is that if there is any question about saving a valve seat, (if the seat is marginal in any way), an insert should be installed. At this point, I use seat inserts on almost all exhaust valves.

Valve seat recession can occur when old engines (pre 1973) are run on unleaded gasoline. This is because the metallic additive, lead, that cushioned the impact of valve faces on their seats is no longer added to gasoline.

As an interim measure, valve seat recession can be prevented by using non-lead-based gasoline additives until engines are rebuilt. However, it would be folly not to permanently solve the problem when you rebuild an old engine. Using stainless steel valves, hardening valve faces with a welded or metal sprayed coating, or using hardened seats will do the job. This is an either/or proposition. You do not have to use hard or hard-faced valves and hard seats; either one will solve the recession problem.

This is because valve seat recession is often caused by hard particles that embed in valve faces and grind valve seats away on rotating impact. The tetraethyl lead additive in gasoline cushioned and lubricated this contact. That is no longer the case, so you have to make other provisions for long valve face and seat life.

If you harden a valve, these particles will not embed in it. If you install hard seats, the particles will not grind them away. Of course, all of this applies only to exhaust valves. Intake valves are cooled by the incoming air/fuel mixture and do not require measures to combat the valve seat recession that is a problem when you use unleaded gasoline in older engines.

Proper seat width is another "hot" valve issue. The wider the contact area of a valve face and seat, the more

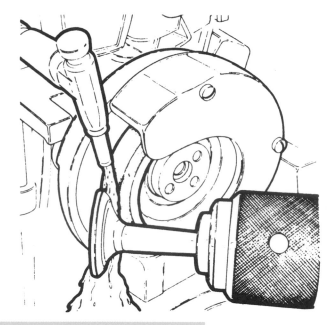

Modern "wet" valve grinding machines are deadly accurate, and they don't heat check the valve faces as the older "dry" machines often did when they ground them.

contact surface area and resulting opportunity there is for heat transfer during valve closure. However, a wide seat contact also increases the chances for particles to lodge between valves and seats and to hold valves slightly open. This not only prevents the contact that promotes valve cooling, it also subjects valves to the transit of high-temperature, high-velocity gases for the duration of the combustion and exhaust cycles in four-cycle engines. These are perfect conditions for burning valves.

Also, as seat width increases, the pounds per square inch of available sealing pressure declines proportionally. This sets valves up for leakage and disables their ability to use high-contact PSI to break up carbon and other particles that may lodge between valve faces and seats. I have found that a seat width of 3/32 inch, or slightly less, is an almost ideal valve seat width specification for most engines, but

you should check particular specifications for any engine that you work on.

Some engines require an interference angle between valve faces and seats. This means that a valve face and seat are ground to slightly different angles, usually by 1 degree. Some machinists will attempt to grind an interference angle into every valve and seat that they do. I tend to use interference angles only where they are specified by engine manufacturers, as this approach requires certain characteristics in the metallurgy of valves and their seats. However, if you are replacing or modifying both valves and seats, you can deviate from manufacturers' original specifications.

One procedure that used to be fairly commonplace, but is now, thank goodness, dying out, is the practice of doing a final check on valves and seats with fine lapping compound. This practice is an interesting study in the persistence of obsolescence. When modern valve facing equipment arrived on the scene 60 or more years ago, automotive machinists did not trust this new equipment, or, perhaps, their use of it. To check the surfaces of freshly ground valves and seats, they would place some very fine grinding compound between a valve and its seat and gently lap the surfaces together. If the grind was correct, they would see the contact area as a continuous dull gray band, uniformly distributed on the polished surfaces of the valve face and seat, "Ah, a good seal!" they might exclaim.

Unfortunately, this practice destroys the dimensional accuracy of grinding procedures and replaces it with a random approximation of that accuracy. It also produces a vastly inferior finish to the one left by good grinding equipment. If there is need or desire to check the contact area of a valve and seat, Prussian blue will do a very adequate job. A final hand lapping might sound to some like a venerable craftsman's approach when, in fact, it is the

Valve seat inserts for exhaust valves are one sure way to provide for the use of unleaded gasoline in older engines that were not designed for this fuel. These seats also can be used to repair badly damaged valve seats when there isn't enough material left in a head or block to grind new seats into it. A modern head machine, like the one shown here, provides precise and reliable results in valve work.

The first step is to bolt the head to the machine bed.

The head is then leveled to the machine and the guide that is being worked on is centered to the cutting device.

A precise cutter is used to cut a press-fit recess into the head for the new seat insert.

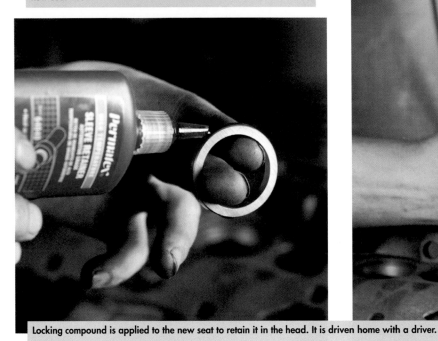

Locking compound is applied to the new seat to retain it in the head. It is driven home with a driver.

mutilation and replacement of an accurate pair of surfaces with ones that are generated by somewhat random factors.

Valve guide wear is probably the main, predictable cause of valve seat failure. Because the hot ends of valve guides receive little or no lubrication, these areas tend to wear to a bell-mouth shape. Eventually, they will fail to provide adequately accurate locating to the closing valves. The result is run-out (too much clearance between valve stems and guides).

This causes rapid deterioration of valve seats. In older engines, valve guides could be replaced easily, and this was standard practice in engine rebuilding. Presently, many engines are being built without removable valve guides. In these engines, excessive guide-to-stem clearance has to be dealt with by knurling guide surfaces, or by using valves with oversize stems and reaming the guide surfaces to the new size.

The knurling process tends to produce very hard valve guide working surfaces and adds the advantage of creating pockets or recesses that retain oil. If guides are still in the range of successful knurling, I prefer knurling to guide replacement. When guide replacement is necessary, it is often possible to find bronze guides, or to have them made. These are far superior to the more usual cast-iron guides and eliminate some of the vulnerability of a potentially weak engine component. With the advent of integral valve guides in engines, there are also bronze and iron guide liners that can be used when guide bores are worn beyond the limits of knurling.

Since the 1950s, the automobile industry has developed

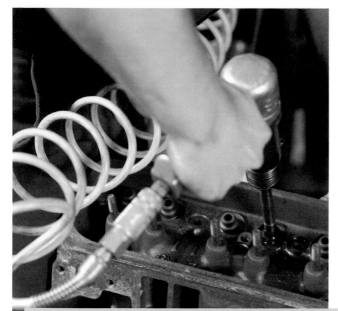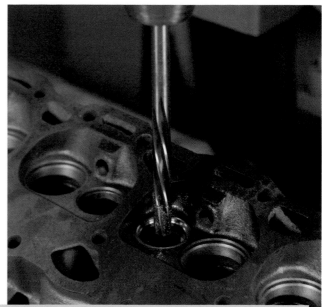

The old guide was driven out with the tool shown here and a new guide is driven into place after the guide bore is reamed to dimension.

increasingly effective valve stem seals. In the old "L" and "T" head (valve-in-block) engines, sealing valve stems was hardly a problem. In fact, the stems' tappet-end downward position in relatively dry valve chambers usually deprived the valves and guides of adequate stem lubrication at their upper ends, near the valve ports, where it is most needed. Often, they had to run more on good will and oil fumes than on real lubricants.

In those days many owners used top oils (also called "upper cylinder lubricants"), so at least some lubrication was provided to the critical upper ends of the valve stems and guides. Using top oil in side-valve engines is still a very good idea.

With the complete conversion of American engines to OHV configuration by the mid-1950s, the problems of dry valve stems disappeared. In these engines the valves are inclined downward and the upper ends of the stems and guides run in a virtual oil bath. Now, the problem became sealing the top ends of valve guides and stems from an overabundant oil supply. Two basic seal types were developed. One is a stem seal which employs O-rings fitted into the upper ends of valve guides for the purpose of sealing the stem-to-guide interface. The other type of stem seal is the bucket, or "umbrella," (a.k.a. "shedder") type, which sits inside valve springs and over the ends of the guides, where they shed most of the oil sprayed by the rocker arms.

Both types of seal prevent excessive oil from traveling down guides, a situation, which would result in high oil consumption and engine smoking. It is relatively easy to retrofit either or both types of seals to early OHV engines that did not have them originally, and it is usually an exceedingly bad idea to do so.

Unless an engine was designed for these seals, their use can deprive the valve stems and guides of adequate lubrication and can cause premature and rapid wear. Some of the modern materials used in bucket seals have far

The installed new guide is now reamed to dimension.

better durability than those in early versions of these items. Teflon insert seals are a great improvement, as are seals made from other materials that do not become brittle and crack. I routinely throw away the bucket seals that come in "complete engine gasket sets" and opt for some of the higher-quality aftermarket versions of this item. The best practice is not to retrofit stem seals to engines that didn't have them, and to upgrade the quality of the seals that you use in engines that did have them.

Another area of the basic valve assembly that requires critical attention is valve springs. Old springs should never be reused without thorough evaluation, and new springs should also be checked before they are installed. Automotive machine shops have equipment for checking the relationship of spring height to various loadings. Valve

An alternative to installing new guides is knurling the old ones to a larger size. The knurler expands guide metal into the bore. Later the knurled guide is reamed to the proper size. Knurled guides retain oil well and wear quite satisfactorily.

Correct valve seat width is critical to valve survival. Modern practice is to grind three angles into a valve seat so that the contact width can be adjusted exactly. Old cars often employed only one angle in their valve seats because the cutters used to machine the seats weren't precise enough to cut a throat and deck angle in addition to the seat angle. Modern carbide cutters, such as the one shown here, give restorers this good option. The drawing shows an old-style valve seat with only one angle.

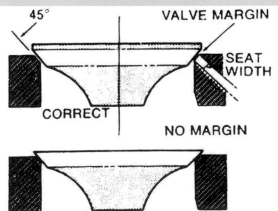

springs must match the compression-pressure-at-height specifications given for them. Special spring seat washers can be used, as necessary, to exactly achieve correct and uniform installed load-at-height specifications.

It is vitally important to check the performance of new valve springs as thoroughly as you would check old ones. The use of overly aggressive springs will pound valves and seats into oblivion in short order. Weaker-than-specified springs will usually cause compression leakage that rapidly worsens as valve faces and seats are eroded by leaking gases. It should be noted that some aftermarket springs do not physically resemble the springs that they replace, and in some cases double springs are used to replace single

Check valve spring installed height:

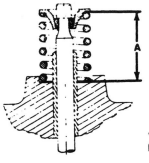

Valve spring installed height (A)

GRIND OUT THIS PORTION

Measure the valve spring installed height (A) with a modified steel rule

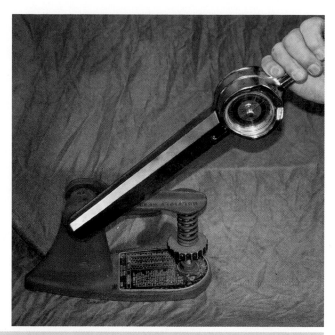

It is very important to check every measurable aspect of valve spring condition. Height, installed height, and compression loading are critical. A weak or overly aggressive valve spring will lead to valve failure in short order. Shown here are several kinds of equipment for checking valve spring specification and performance. Some checks are general, such as indicating squareness with a carpenter's square. Other spring testing equipment is dedicated and very precise, such as spring compression testers that employ torque wrench or hydraulic pressure readings.

springs. This is not a problem, as long as the replacements are engineered to achieve the necessary characteristics for the applications in which they are used.

Other Parts of the Valve System

The other parts of the valve system include the camshaft and anything between it and the valve stems. On "L" and "T" head engines this usually involves a simple tappet or a roller tappet. On OHV engines, the hardware for each valve will include a push rod and rocker arm setup, and for OHC engines the mechanism between valve stem ends and camshafts will include tappets, and sometimes rocker arms. Exotic devices, like roller tappets, are common in cars of the first 40 years of the 20th century. And, of course, there is the ubiquitous push rod/rocker arm system used in some American cars since early in the 20th century, favored by American manufacturers from the 1950s through the turn of this century and still in use in some new vehicles today.

Any part of a valve system is subject to wear, misalignment, and warping. Each component must be checked for these defects. Push rods are very susceptible to bending, and should be checked by rolling them on a flat surface or chucking them in a lathe and replacing them if necessary. Their ends should also be checked for wear.

Tappets should be checked for pitting and scoring on their cam following surfaces and ground, as necessary, to correct these potential defects. Many tappets have small angles ground into their lower surfaces to cause them to rotate as cam lobes contact them. This, in turn, promotes valve rotation and reduces wear by randomizing recurring

contacts. Any original tappet base angle must be duplicated when tappets are resurfaced. Tappet bore clearance must also be checked, and if it is found to be excessive, it should be corrected by the use of oversize tappets or other means. This consideration is particularly critical for engines fitted with hydraulic lifters (tappets), since excessive bore clearance can result in inadequate oil pressure to operate their hydraulic zero-lash systems.

Hydraulic lifters require particular attention. They are built to exceedingly close tolerances and include an engineered factor called "leak-down," which allows them to circulate a little oil internally and prevents them from pumping up beyond correct clearances. However, if this

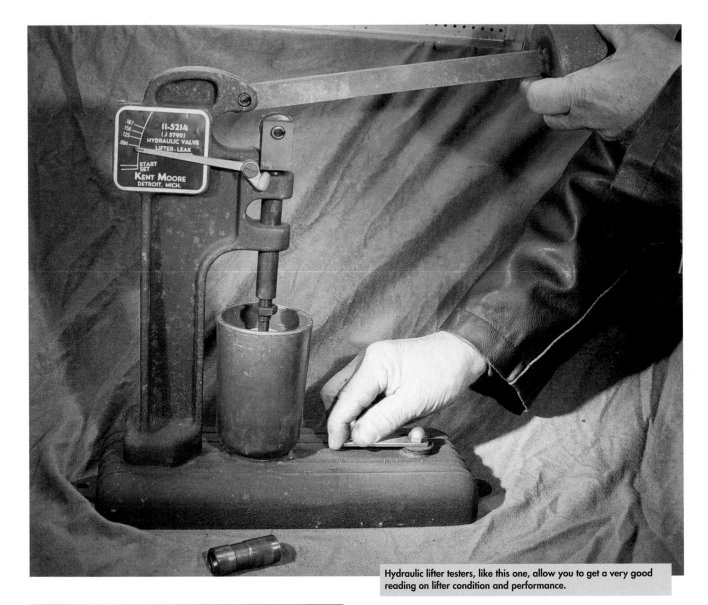

Hydraulic lifter testers, like this one, allow you to get a very good reading on lifter condition and performance.

Hydraulic valve lifters usually work well if they are kept clean. Never mix lifter parts, and always return lifters to their original bores.

desirable leak-down characteristic—which is expressed as plunger-to-bore clearance in lifters—wears beyond very specific limits, the lifters will tend to collapse and will then provide excessive clearance. This critical leak-down factor can be checked with a set of lifter pliers or a leak-down tester in an oil bath. It can also be pretty well ascertained by visual inspection and the measurement of lifter parts.

The main reason for hydraulic lifter failure is the presence of grit, varnish, and sludge. Very small amounts of these contaminants can clog the ball (early style) or disk (late style) valves that are at the heart of hydraulic lifter operation. Unless lifters have been subjected to an excessively contaminated oil supply, they usually can be put back into service after simple disassembly, cleaning, inspection and testing.

It is critical that hydraulic lifters from any engine be returned to the bores from which they were taken and that their internal parts never be mixed. When evaluating an engine prior to disassembly, lifter operation should be an area of particular attention. If a valve cannot be adjusted to run quietly within the adjustment range provided, or will

Old roller tappets, such as those shown here, can be very difficult to rebuild because they are often swaged or welded together and have to be disassembled to replace the needle bearings or bushings on which the rollers run.

not hold an adjustment, the lifter and other parts in the valve train become suspect and should be examined especially carefully during engine disassembly and evaluation. If a camshaft has been replaced or reground, it is absolutely essential that the lifter contact faces be ground or the lifters replaced. Failure to do this will almost invariably cause the camshaft to chip out after an engine is returned to service.

Rocker Arms

Excessive rocker arm and shaft wear is a problem in some engines. That is because these engines were notoriously under-oiled in this area—Buicks of the late 1950s and early 1960s in particular—and their rocker arms and shafts tended to wear severely. Some rocker arms are susceptible to rebushing, while others have to be replaced. In any case, excessive clearance at this point in a valve system is intolerable, as it will lead to erratic valve clearances. A complete automotive machine shop will have a tappet grinder and a device for resurfacing rocker arm pads (valve contacting surfaces).

Ideally, there would be few parts between cam lobes and valves. One of the advantages of OHC engines is that they can achieve this ideal almost completely—that is, those that operate without rocker arms. In engines that interpose items like rocker arms and push rods between tappets and valve stems, it is the rebuilder's objective to keep any unspecified motion, such as rocker arm-to-rocker shaft play, to a minimum.

The problems of reciprocating weight and dimensional change (heat expansion) are somewhat endemic to push rods and rocker arms, and therefore it is never possible to attain the valve accuracy in push rod engines that is inherent in simpler OHC designs. Still, every attempt should be made in that direction. Any worn or bent valve-actuating parts that get by a rebuilder will inevitably cause some level of performance problems.

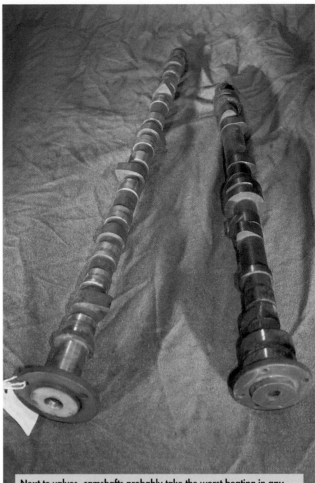

Next to valves, camshafts probably take the worst beating in any engine. Any good rebuild will include camshaft regrinding. Badly damaged cams can be welded up and ground. Cams should always be Parkerized (hardened) before they are put back into service.

The Camshaft

Most camshaft bearings are replaceable. On many recent engines and a few older ones, the camshafts run on integral bearings in the cylinder head. Camshaft bearings run at relatively wide clearances and rarely wear severely. Most cam bearing wear occurs in a narrow area in the direction that valve springs push a cam via pushrods, tappets, etc. However, because any method of adequately cleaning a block or head will destroy the camshaft bearings if they are left in place, they must be removed during a total engine rebuild. Unfortunately, it is not advisable to reinstall old camshaft bearings after their removal because damage is inevitably inflicted on them in the removal process. That mandates replacing thin shell-type bearings. Thick shell bearings should be rebabbitted and align-bored, if there are any questions about their surfaces or soundness.

By the late 1930s, most camshaft bearings were of the thin-shell babbitt type. In these cases, replacements can be installed without any other consideration than checking the bore saddles for alignment, out-of-round and smoothness. However, earlier engines used thick babbitt (thick shell) cam bearing designs that requires align boring new camshaft bearings when old ones are replaced. In cases where damaged camshaft journals have been ground to a smaller diameter to clean them up, new bearings can be selected or poured to fit this reduced diameter. Camshafts do not have to have their journals welded up and ground to their original diameters.

Whatever type of camshaft bearings you install, always make sure that their oil holes line up with the corresponding holes in the bearing saddles. Failure to do this is not uncommon and causes problems quickly, including severe damage to camshafts and blocks. If a cam bearing has two oil holes, both must line up with the holes in its bore. This sounds obvious, but it is sometimes overlooked.

The camshaft itself is one the most neglected components in engine rebuilds. Cam lobes and camshaft bearing journals do wear, and this is not always obvious from visually inspecting them for pitting, grooving, scoring and galling. I consider it essential to regrind cams and tappet bottoms in any serious engine rebuild. This work should be done by a very large general machine shop or by one that specializes in cams.

The grinding process for cams uses master blanks to achieve original and proper lobe profiles. A few shops have historical collections of these blanks and can grind almost any cam from them. Try to find such a shop. In the cases of particularly obscure engines, you may not be able to locate master blanks to guide cam grinding, and all that can be done is to select the best cam lobe on a shaft and grind the others from its format, after repairing any worn or damaged areas on the weaker cam lobes. This is a compromise, but it is far preferable to no grind at all. Any serious wear in cam lobes—this usually occurs in the ramp area—can be repaired by welding, as can damage to camshaft bearing journals.

A final step in reworking camshafts is to surface harden them. Parkerizing (a phosphating surface treatment), Tufftriding˚ (a nitriding treatment) and other more exotic measures are available. These treatment processes will enhance the wear characteristics of lobes and journals. It is not worth reworking a camshaft if you do not have it surface treated after the rework.

In my experience, the cost of camshaft work is not particularly high, but the difference in the quality of an engine restoration result is enormous. A reground camshaft silences all kinds of little vibrations and noises that would otherwise be heard and felt if this work was not done. I would not consider an engine rebuild complete without grinding the cams, any more than I would consider it complete if an old, stretched timing chain was reinstalled.

When working on valves and their actuating mechanisms, it should be realized that there isn't much safety factor or margin built into their design. Mistakes are rarely made without serious consequences, and that variant of Murphy's Law, which states that "Nature always sides with the hidden defect" seems to be in control.

Chapter 6

The Crankshaft
and Bearing Systems

You'll need a few specialized and very accurate tools to install a crankshaft.

THE BASIC CONCEPT OF FRICTION BEARINGS GOES BACK to the beginnings of mechanical times. The specific application of hard metal on soft metal friction bearings was patented in roughly its present form in 1839.

The use of this type of bearing to support crankshafts in reciprocating internal combustion hydrocarbon engines (that is, conventional automobile engines) was an obvious extension of the practices that were applied to pumps, locomotives and stationary engines in the late 19th century. Although various attempts have been made to use alternative bearings (usually anti-friction bearings in a ball or roller configuration) in this application, these alternatives have not met with notable success. In this connection, one thinks of Lozier at the beginning of the automobile era and, more

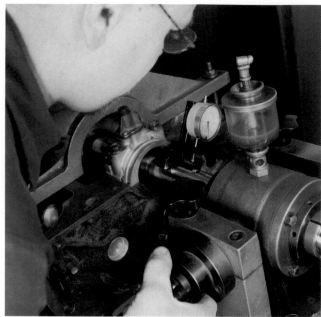

In some older engines it may be necessary to align bore main bearings or camshaft bearings. This is particularly true in the case of engines with thick-shell babbitt bearings in these applications. In other cases, spun-out bearing shells or other kinds of local damage may mandate repair and align-boring. Shown here is the align boring process, in which the boring bar is trued to the crankcase (or head in the case of some overhead cam engines) and calibrated for the size of the bore.

recently, Porsche.

Although conventional hard metal on soft metal bearings sound like an improbable proposition, the fact is that they work. Amazingly, they work remarkably well if their operating conditions do not differ too radically from their design capabilities. However, when these factors do differ significantly, say for example in conditions of oil deprivation or badly contaminated oil, friction bearings do fail, often quickly and violently.

The basic proposition underlying crankshaft and rod bearings is that the crankshaft bearing contact surfaces will be somewhere between hard and extremely hard—the latter in the cases of crankshaft surfaces treated with nitrate

("nitrided") or other surface hardening processes—and that they will run in metallic bearings that are very soft. In fact, these surfaces are so soft that it is possible to leave an impression in them with your fingernail. They can be fabricated from one of several alloys. The choices include alloys containing tin, lead, copper, aluminum, zinc, bronze, etc. Heavy-duty bearings, like those fitted to diesel and high-performance gasoline engines, are often made of aluminum alloys or aluminum-bronze alloys.

Most of the friction bearing alloys used in old car engines fall under the label "babbitt," which encompasses several alloys based primarily in tin and lead. The actual composition of babbitt (named after its American patent

The boring bar is then moved through the areas to be bored and exact, aligned dimensions are bored.

holder, Isaac Babbitt) is both complex and varied, according to application. About four commercial grades of babbitt are presently available to rebuilders, and those involved with this material have nothing but complaints about its contemporary quality. In fact, some bearing shops now compound their own custom bearing metals, particularly babbitt.

Until the mid-1930s, and in a few cases much later, babbitt crankshaft and rod bearings were poured extremely thick in rigid and thick bronze shells. A 1/8-inch thickness of babbitt was not uncommon. After it was poured, the babbitt in these "thick shell" applications was bored to size and surface finished by honing it. On some connecting rods the babbitt was poured directly into the iron or steel rod saddles without a separate bronze shell to contain it. Chevrolet, for example, persisted in this practice in its "stovebolt 6" engines into the 1950s.

For the most part, after World War II, auto manufacturers had converted the bulk of their rod and main bearing applications to the thin shell ("insert" type") design that we still use today. In this construction a relatively thin layer of babbitt is plated over other metals that have been plated or sprayed onto relatively thin and flexible steel backings ("shells"). These bearings typically use copper plating under their babbitt and include a factor called "crush" in their designs.

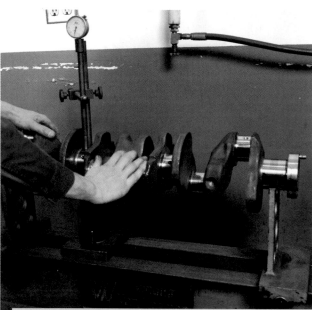

Very minor crankshaft bending and warping are eliminated when crankshafts are ground, but bigger deviations must be corrected in a straightening process. The crankshaft straightening device shown here both gauges and straightens crankshafts. Operating this device takes skill and experience.

Babbitt and Crush Bearings

In bearing terminology, "crush" describes bearing shells that are actually a few thousandths of an inch larger in diameter than their saddle and cap bores. When the caps on crush bearings are tightened down, the protruding ends of the bearing shell halves are crushed into the saddles by some small factor. This forces the bearings into conformity with their saddles and guarantees a high degree of surface contact with the saddles. That crush pressure promotes correct bearing shape by forcing the flexible shells to assume the shapes of the more substantial saddles. It also enhances heat transfer from bearing shells to surrounding crankcase metal, where it can be conducted away by engine oil.

Crush-type insert bearings are more durable and better suited to high-speed operation than thick-shell bearings because their vastly thinner babbitt layers do not trap and retain as much heat as thick-babbitt running surfaces. They also attain better roundness and are more dimensionally stable.

The reason for using babbitt as the outer bearing surface remains the same, whether bearings are the old bronze backed rigid, thick shell construction or modern thin shell, crush-types. The underlying concept is that the soft babbitt surface acts in several specific and desirable ways.

Babbitt surfaces accomplish the following tasks: 1)

A hydraulic ram applies pressure to true the shaft and a well-placed sharp wrap with a hammer and tool sets and stress-relieves the correction that the applied force induces into the shaft.

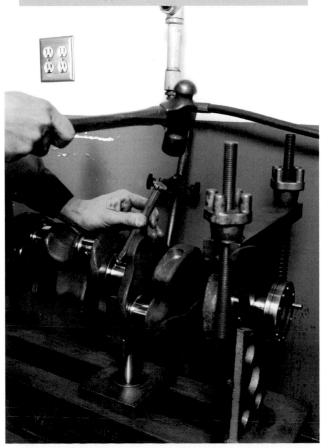

they produce a low-friction running surface; 2) they handle the loads ("radial loading forces") and pounding thrusts to which they are subjected without damage; 3) they transfer heat away from bearing/shaft interfaces; 4) they retain oil in their surfaces, thus maintaining an oil film that protects bearing surfaces from direct metal-to-metal contact with crankshafts; 5) they provide some degree of plastic conformability to crankshaft bearing journals; and 6) they embed a certain amount of small particle contamination that may enter a bearing environment with lubricating oil, preventing it from damaging crankshaft journals.

Bearing Woes

There are more things that babbitt friction bearings have to do, but these are the major ones. When you stop and think that the babbitt bearings in an automobile engine have to survive tens of thousands of miles of high-temperature transit by their crankshafts under very adverse conditions, and that the material involved, babbitt, is soft enough to mark with your fingernail, you gain a certain respect for faithful, hardworking babbitt bearings.

Please remember, these bearings have nothing to do with the icky character of the same surname that is the title subject (George F. Babbitt) of one Sinclair Lewis novel and appears in passing in several others.

The operating requirements of automobile engines are quite varied. Engines must run and start at temperatures as low as minus 30 degrees F. and continue to run at under-hood temperatures that can approach 300 degrees F. Internal temperatures at some critical points in engines can run intermittently as high as 1,750 degrees F. Engines have to operate between a few hundred RPM and several thousand RPM, and all of this takes place under widely changing loads.

These varied and often extreme conditions greatly stress engine parts. A lot of that stress ends up on the rod and main bearings. They will take it until some basic condition of their welfare is breached. Then they may fail rapidly. Because the surfaces of babbitt bearings are slowly consumed by wear, and due to the varied and adverse conditions in which they operate, almost any engine that you may have occasion to rebuild will reveal bearings that are progressing towards failure in one or more ways. Fortunately, that failure usually occurs pretty slowly.

The first step in dealing with engine bearings in a restoration is to determine what sort of failure they were progressing towards, and how quickly they were headed there. Almost all major automotive engine rebuilding textbooks and repair manuals contain sections on bearing failure—morgues, complete with autopsy photographs and captions. It is well worth the effort to compare what you find in an engine with this printed data.

If one particular bearing in an engine is failing due to unevenly distributed thrust, or oil deprivation, or some other discreet factor, it will tell you what to look for and to correct as you proceed—in the above examples, a bent or

Crankshaft grinding must be done very precisely. Shown here is a state-of-the-art crankshaft grinder. In this process the shaft is centered in a lathe for each set of journals and ground wet with a large diameter wheel. The wheel must be dressed for accuracy very often. The setup shown here allows gauging of the main and rod bearing journals while grinding is taking place. If journals cannot be ground to usable dimensions and finishes, they have to be welded up and the new, added material ground to correct dimensions and finishes.

offset rod for the first condition and a plugged oil passage for the second. I emphasize that even if the reason that finally dictated an engine rebuild had nothing to do with its bearings, it still pays to analyze their condition and to correct any problems that your analysis reveals.

Crankshaft Griding

It would be impossible to cover all, or even most, considerations in bearing work here, but there are a few that merit particularly strong attention. The first is that bearing work must be very clean and accurate work. This is one of those jobs where things have to fit very accurately and precisely. The inadvertent inclusion of a particle of grit with a 0.002-inch diameter between a crush bearing and its saddle can do all kinds of damage because it can deform the crush fit in three or four places.

Another critical generality is that bearing work tends to have a set of "rebuilder's standards" for such things as allowable bearing taper, out-of-round, and surface scoring. These should not be confused with restoration standards. For example, undersize replacement bearings for older engines are typically available in undersizes of 0.001 and 0.002 inch, before you get into the standard grind sizes of 0.010, 0.020, 0.030, and 0.040 inch. This is because it is generally considered OK to tolerate 0.0015 or even 0.002

In this sequence we can see how the new crank journal metal appears as the grinding wheel works across the journal the depth as its cut is increased. Note that journal diameter is being measured as grinding progresses. The final dimenion a which the journal cleans up is the largest grind diameter that is usable. All journals on a crank have to be ground to the cleanup dimension of the smallest finished journal.

The polishing belt device shown here is an attachment to the crankshaft grinder. It is used to polish journals that do not need dimensional correction and, in some cases, to put final finishes on freshly ground journals. This finishing operation removes almost no stock from a crankshaft.

inch of out-of-round in a crankshaft before a regrind is mandated. That is, garage practice is to fit a 0.002-inch undersize bearing to a shaft journal that is worn out-of-round by 0.0015 or 0.002 inch.

To all of which I say, when you are restoring an engine, do not tolerate any measurable deviation in out-of-round, taper, or surface finish. The object here is not just to throw an engine together so that it will outlast a rapidly deteriorating car body. That may be a valid repair proposition because it may be dictated by repair economics. The point in restoration is to build an engine that is as permanent as possible and that has no avoidable weak links.

When you restore an engine that doesn't have one of the miracle-hardened crankshafts, the overwhelming

probability is that you will have to grind the shaft. Certainly, if you are doing a total mechanical restoration, and the crankshaft is out of specification or finish, it should be polished or ground. It usually will need grinding because the part of the rod journal that encounters the force transmitted by the rod on combustion strokes will almost always wear more than the other 320 degrees of the shaft. You can just about count on grinding old cranks from cars with any appreciable mileage on them to undersizes.

It is vitally important to check old cranks and blocks for warping and distortion. Blocks and shafts do warp. If the bearing centerline in a block isn't checked, it can come back to haunt a restorer in such obscure ways as failing valve guides, caused by inadequate lubrication, caused by

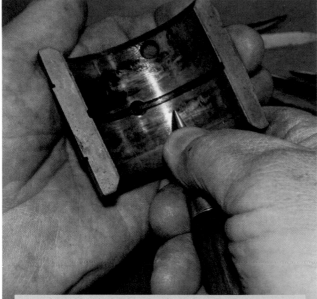

Some of the old thick shell bearings had 1/8 inch of babbitt poured onto bronze shells. Babbitt that thick tends to pound out when it is on the receiving end of large radial loads and thrusts. Thick babbitt also tends to retain heat and fail for that reason. Modern practice is to plate just a few thousandths of an inch of babbitt on crush-insert type bearing shells. Shown here is the operation of hand burnishing (polishing) a bearing surface after it has been scraped to eliminate high spots.

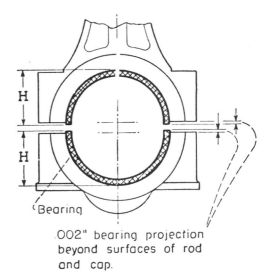

.002" bearing projection beyond surfaces of rod and cap.

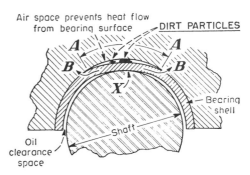

"Insert" or "crush"-type bearings rely on the clamping pressure of the cap against the rod saddle to press them into their proper shapes. This promotes a close contact of the bearing outer surface and saddle, and that helps to transfer heat away from the bearing and to give it its shape. Unfortunately, crush-type bearings will not tolerate any dirt or particles between the bearing shell and saddle. Any contamination there will badly deform this type of bearing when it is tightened into place.

low oil pressure, caused by bearing leakage, caused by a warped crank or block. It's just easier to sort these things out when they are apart and visible, rather than to have to work backwards from seemingly unrelated symptoms of malfunction to their ultimate causes.

If an engine that you are restoring uses modern, thin-shell bearings, its crankshaft can be ground in increments of 0.010 inch to undersizes of up to 0.040 inch. Replacement bearings can usually be found for these grinds. Ordinarily, this will represent enough latitude to repair any shaft wear or damage that is discovered, even if a shaft has been ground an undersize before. In the case of thick shell bearings, you can still grind, as necessary, up to a 0.040 inch undersize on most crankshafts, and even a bit beyond that on the heavier ones, as long as you don't weaken them appreciably or produce unacceptably small bearing surfaces. You can then bore repoured bearings to the new crank journal undersize.

Occasionally, extreme wear or physical damage to a crankshaft is so great that it has to be built up before it is reground. Over the years, several buildup techniques have been tried and have enjoyed popularity. Until recently, the most popular of these was GMAW welding ("Gas Metal Arc Welding," more commonly called "MIG" or "wire" welding). This has proven very satisfactory for all but nitrided crankshafts. Fortunately, nitrided crankshafts are so durable that they rarely require much attention, anyway.

In the last decade, submerged arc crank welding machines have come into use. These provide the very best approach to repairing and building up worn or damaged crankshafts. The superiority of submerged arc repairs is

Crankshafts look rugged, but they are really very delicate. Always store crankshafts standing up to protect them from warping and to protect their bearing journal surfaces from impact and corrosion.

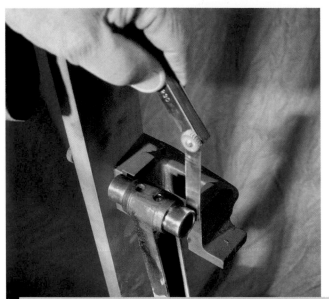

Connecting rods should always be checked in a rod jig for straightness. Forged rods can be straightened in a bending fixture if they are warped, twisted or out of parallel. Cast rods should be replaced if they are out-of-true. Shown here are the old and the automated, modern methods of indicating rod condition, as well as the method of straightening them. Note that in the modern method, the first step is to check the jigging machine and calibrate it as necessary.

The modern method of rod gauging is shown in the top two photos and the photo above. Photos on the middle right and right show show rod straightening.

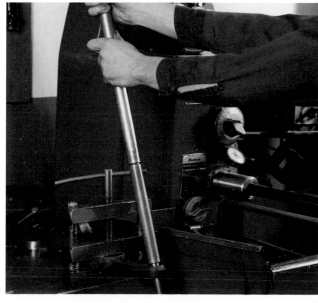

The object of torquing main and rod beatings is to get even and correct securing pressure on them. Be sure to thoroughly lubricate bearing fasteners, including, and especially, the undersides of their heads, and then torque them in a correct pattern and in at least three evenly escalating stages. A high-quality and recently calibrated torque wrench is a real plus in this work.

chiefly seen in the uniformity of the added material and in its lack of any porosity defects.

Crankshaft Polishing

Other repair techniques have been used and still are used to build up shafts. These include metal spray and chrome plating. Both have notable drawbacks and restorers should stick with GMAW and submerged arc welding to build up worn cranks.

There are several common pitfalls that should be avoided in crankshaft grinding. One is the use of oddball equipment. Make sure that your provider of this service is using reasonably modern and well-maintained equipment. There are a lot of pretty shoddy operations doing crank grinding these days.

Make sure that your shaft is ground with wheels that are in good shape and properly dressed. Crank grinding wheels are very expensive and some fast-buck operators who quote terrific prices for this work tend to economize on their wheels. It is also important that your provider have a wheel

or wheels for putting the correct radius on the crankshaft fillets (the right angle journal-to-cheek interfaces). Some crank grinders use small auxiliary wheels for this purpose. In any case, it is not unusual to get a crank back from an "economy grinder" with no radius at all on the fillets. Since sharp fillets are great places for cracks to start and from which to propagate, this defect is bad news for any crank, but particularly for one that is old and stressed.

Another all-too-common pitfall is to order one of the garbage crankshafts that are supplied "ready to install" by unscrupulous mail order purveyors. A friend recently told me that several years ago when he was purchasing some parts at the home office of a very large and well-known auto parts mail order supplier, he was accidentally allowed to see the "inner sanctum," where they "reconditioned" crankshafts. He had accompanied a counterman to the basement of a building to find a part, and he noticed men busily mounting cranks on an ancient shaft grinder and surfacing them with a finishing belt. No attempt was being made to measure them or to grind them accurately to specific dimensions. They were simply trying to make the surfaces of the journals look shiny. When my friend made inquiry regarding this amazing sight, the door that he was looking through was slammed shut, and he was emphatically told, "Don't ask about that."

I have personal knowledge of at least three cranks ordered from this supplier that failed a few thousand miles after their installations. It is best to know the outfit that regrinds your crankshaft and to get one that is fresh and undamaged by poor workmanship or storage. It's amazing but true; a mighty crankshaft will often warp significantly if it is stored on its side for a few days with its bearings unsupported. When you store a crankshaft, stand it up on end and secure it to some vertical feature of the available architecture to prevent it from accidentally being knocked over.

Bearings and Saddles

Main bearing saddles usually require very little attention when you rebuild an engine. They should always be checked for roundness, alignment, and any kind of gross physical damage, but you will rarely encounter problems in this area. Almost any problem that does occur in main bearing saddles can be corrected by align boring the saddles, or by welding them up and align boring them.

Connecting rods are another story. Rods are often afflicted to some degree with two common maladies. One is bending and twisting. The other is saddle elongation. Bent and twisted rods can be repaired by a process of jigging them and applying force to straighten them. Rod saddle elongation is most often a problem in high-speed engines of the 1950s and after. It occurs when saddles stretch out-of-round, and is corrected by milling the parting surfaces of rods and their caps and honing or boring their bores back to perfect roundness.

This process for reconditioning rod bores is a common

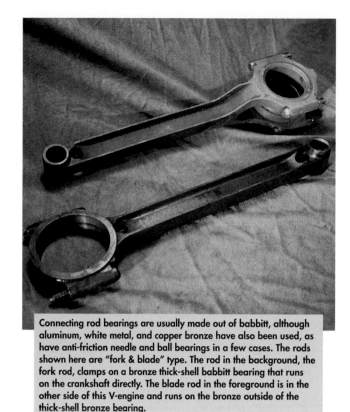

Connecting rod bearings are usually made out of babbitt, although aluminum, white metal, and copper bronze have also been used, as have anti-friction needle and ball bearings in a few cases. The rods shown here are "fork & blade" type. The rod in the background, the fork rod, clamps on a bronze thick-shell babbitt bearing that runs on the crankshaft directly. The blade rod in the foreground is in the other side of this V-engine and runs on the bronze outside of the thick-shell bronze bearing.

operation in most automotive machine shops. In fact, technicians should have an attitude of incredulity when they see rods from an engine that is something over 50 years old with 150,000 miles on it, and the rod saddles are still perfectly round. That doesn't square with their experience with many high speed engines built from the 1950s into the 1990s, but is possible because old engines didn't subject their connecting rods to the levels of stress that are common in modern engines. Those older rods were routinely over-engineered.

Crankshaft Installation

The first and last steps in restoring a crankshaft both involve cleaning. Before a crankshaft is straightened and ground, it should be thoroughly cleaned. You can do this in a hot tank, but there are other, more satisfactory methods (See Chapter 3,"Cleaning Basic Engine Blocks and Heads") that involve oven baking, shot-peening, tumbling, and jet spray washing.

Whatever method you employ to clean a crankshaft, it should be followed by rodding the shaft's oil passages with spiral wire gun brushes and then blowing them clean with compressed air. It is critically important that the oil passages in crankshafts be carefully cleaned, since, over the years, these shafts' rotations will have centrifuged contaminants from the circulating lubricating oil into solid deposits in their passages.

Crankshafts should be cleaned thoroughly before machine shop work is performed on them. Then, when a finished crankshaft is returned from a machine shop, it should again be cleaned meticulously to remove any

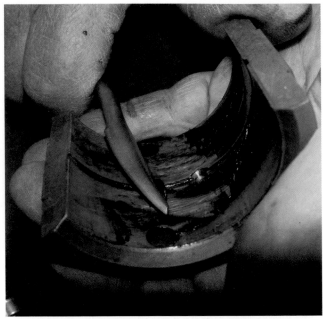

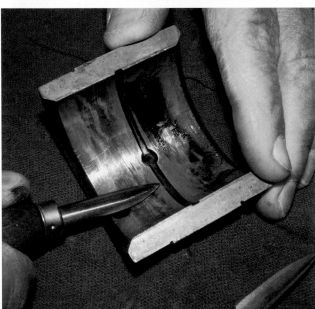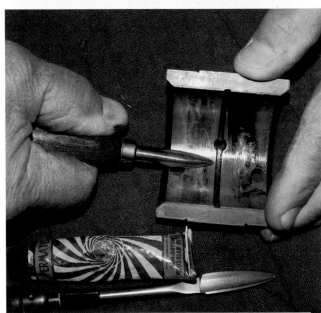

Scraping bearings is an obscure, but useful, technique for removing bearing high spots. Due to the potential for distortion when thick bronze bearing shells are clamped into their saddles, high spots sometimes appear on bearing surfaces. Indicating them with Prussian blue and gently scraping them away will improve bearing contact and avoid local overheating. A scraping tool and three machinist's knives—also useful for bearing scraping—are shown at the top right. Three burnishing tools are also shown. The burnishing tools are used to impress a polished surface into the soft babbitt after it has been scraped.

abrasive residues or chips from machining operations that might foul new bearings. I use Ivory soap and lots of water to rewash crankshafts that I get back from grinding. Then I thoroughly dry them and coat them with a water displacing oil to preserve them until they are installed. Crankcases should receive the same soap and water and drying regimen after they are machined, prior to engine reassembly. Oil or grease should be applied to internal crankcase surfaces after washing and drying to protect them.

Some crankcases were originally painted inside to retard corrosion and to promote oil shedding. The older coatings that were used for this purpose have largely disappeared from the marketplace (Federal Process's Gasoila brand used to list such a varnish-type product), but have been replaced by newer coatings that are sold to engine blueprinting enthusiasts.

It would be impossible to overemphasize the importance of cleanliness when crankshafts are installed. Bearing saddle tops and caps should be blown off with compressed air and then finger wiped to remove any lurking particles. Bearing shells should be carefully wiped down and gently persuaded into their saddles and caps with light hand pressure. A final finger wipe of bearing surfaces should then be performed. Never blow compressed air at bearing surfaces because it can embed particles in them. Be careful not to track lint, threads or fibers from any towel or rag that you use into your work during final cleanups of these areas.

Just before you install a crankshaft, all bearing and shaft

When you torque castellated nuts, it is sometimes necessary to file or grind their bottom surfaces so that they will come into correct readings with the cotter key hole and castellations lined up. This is a fussy business, but it is sometimes necessary. It is best to pre-torque castellated nuts and get the values right, before you try to install them in an engine. After you grind or file a castellated nut, be sure to deburr it, and make certain that all grinding residues and chips are removed from the nut's threads.

working surfaces should be wiped liberally with a good assembly lubricant. I use Lubriplate 105 for this purpose because I have an almost religious faith in it.

After all seals and bearings are in place, the crankshaft should be lowered gently onto its top bearing halves. Then, the caps should be put in place quickly to keep contamination away from the bearings. You should employ every good practice and element of common sense when you tighten main and rod bearings. Anti-seize lubricant should be applied to fastener threads, and spread on the nut or bolt undersides of the fasteners that contact the bearing caps. All parts should be reassembled in the order and orientation

that existed when they were removed. If a bearing cap was out of its numbered position or installed backwards at the time of engine disassembly, it must be reinstalled that way, unless it was dimensionally incorrect or if basic corrective machining was done to install it properly.

An accurate torque wrench must be used to tighten main and rod cap fasteners. Correct figures for torque should be researched or calculated. The object here is not just to get even torque application on fasteners, but to secure them to correct numerical values, as well. Torque should be applied in reasonable alternating sequences and in at least three stages. Inconsistent torque applications can distort

Balancing crankshafts and associated parts is necessary on high speed engines, but is a waste of time on older, slow-turning long-stroke mills. The process involves weighing (and sometimes proportioning) reciprocating parts and putting them and the crankshaft on which they run into balance. Shown here is a modern balancing machine.

crankcases and even cylinder walls. In the latter case, it is a major cause of high oil consumption after engines are rebuilt.

If rod nuts or main bearing cap nuts were restrained by special lock washers or other devices, these must not be reused, but must be replaced with exact duplicates. If castellated nuts were used, it is sometimes necessary to file or grind their bottoms to get cotter key alignment to coincide with correct torque readings. If you file bearing cap fasteners for this purpose, the filing should done away from the engine reassembly area and should be followed by careful de-burring and removal of all chips and grit from these parts before they are returned to the reassembly area. When wired bolts are used, make sure that you understand

the theory and proper practice of aviation fastener wiring before you attempt to recreate this type of fastener restraint.

It is a good idea to run a final Plastigage* check of main and rod bearing clearances, just to be sure. I prefer this approach to taking the chance of scratching the bearings' delicate working surfaces with an inside micrometer, telescope gauge, or bore gauge.

It is also a good idea to spin an installed crankshaft by hand to check for any resistance to its rotation. There must be none. Once you overcome inertial forces, a properly machined crank should travel on its new, lubricated bearings with the inexorability of a bank vault door closing. You should be able to feel this when you rotate it by hand.

The crankshaft position indicator and the electronic console behind it tell the operator where and how much weight to add or subtract. Stock removal, shown below, is the preferred method of adjusting weight, but welding weight onto a shaft is sometimes necessary.

The practice of checking bearing clearances by inserting various lead shim stocks (typically 0.001, 0.0015 and 0.002 inch) between a bearing and shaft until they jam is archaic. Performing this type of check with brass shim stocks adds barbarism to this malpractice. Don't do it.

Final Testing

The reason for a final check of bearing clearances is that new bearings are infrequently mislabeled and a final check is the best way to catch that error before it births catastrophe. It is unnecessary to use Prussian blue to check main bearings and crankshaft journals for contact if your bearings are insert-type, or if they have been align bored and the crankshaft has been checked for straightness and/or ground. However, it is always a good idea to check thick shell rod bearings for shaft contact with Prussian blue, even though their journals have been ground and the bearings sized and finished on a precise honing machine. Every so often, such a check will reveal one or more high spots caused by the rod saddle distortion that can occur when rod caps are tightened onto bearings. Such high spots can be scraped down with a bearing scraper. If you are not thoroughly familiar with the techniques of scraping bearings, do not attempt this work without some instruction and practice—it's easy to do more harm than good.

The final step in installing crankshaft main and rod bearings is to leak test the whole lubrication system. This test accomplishes two desirable tasks. It offers positive proof that the bearing and plumbing work that you have completed is free of obvious errors, and it pre-lubricates the whole engine oiling system for the critical start-up event.

To run this test you will need to find or fabricate a leak detector tank. A tank for this purpose must be clean and it must be capable of withstanding 50 lbs. of pressure. It will need a filler cap into which to pour oil, an input chuck

for compressed air at its top, and a valved output port for pressurized oil at its bottom. It's a good idea to install a filter for the output oil, as well. A pressure gauge on the tester is a nice feature.

In practice, the leak detector is filled with SAE 20 oil and pressurized with air pressure of about 15 PSI over the oil. The tester's oil output is hooked up to the test engine's main oil galley or plumbing with an external adaptor or, if the oil pump has not yet been installed, through the oil pump's

When bearing and crankshaft work is done correctly, it should take very little pressure to turn even a massive crank. It's the same theory that governs opening a fine safe door.

output connection. I prefer the latter connection because relieves you of having to stopper the oil pump pickup. If you pressurize the system through a galley plug, you will have to close off the oil pump pickup to prevent oil from flowing back through the pump and out of the system.

With the engine right-side-up (preferably secured in an engine stand) and the oil pressure from the leak detector valved on, the engine should be slowly turned by its front pulley nut or rear flange with a suitable wrench. Putting a large pan under the crankcase will contain the oil that will drip out of the engine during this test.

Oil leakage should now be observed. At this point, any location where oil leaks will be evident. If a bearing is fitted too loosely or an oil galley connection is leaking, it will show

as a steady squirt, ooze or drip of oil where there shouldn't be one. Half a dozen or so drops per minute should escape from the sides of each rod and main bearing, at the pressure and with the oil viscosity stated above, when the test is run at room temperature. A bearing with too little clearance will drip slowly or not at all.

If a bearing spews out a stream of oil, or if one or more bearings fail to drip at all, there is something wrong that must be investigated and corrected before a rebuilt engine is started. I realize that this is a messy test that wastes a quart or two of oil, but its results are important. Take the time to use a good light source to verify that everything in a pressure lubrication system is working properly. You want to see adequate, but not excessive, flow past the bearings

You can easily run an oil leak test on the lubrication system of any engine that you rebuild. Below is a homemade tester and a professional version on the left. The homemade leak detector was made out of a fire extinguisher shell. Despite this humble origin, it has served admirably for many years. Phosphorescing dye and a black light make leak detection tests very dramatic and much easier to read.

and any other pressurized oiling points.

If you have access to a "black light" or to one of the modern diode lights designed for this type of testing, you can add a fluorescing dye to your test oil and then use the black light to examine the test oil as it exits lubrication points. The light will cause oil drops and seepages to glow and will make your inspection much easier to perform. Such problems as inadequate lubrication of timing chains or gears will become evident in an oil leak test.

Most bearing system failures in recently rebuilt engines could probably have been avoided if oil leak tests had been performed before they were returned to service. This test will pinpoint the causes of lubrication failure before they destroy a rebuilt engine.

Running an oil leak test also pre-lubricates engines so that they are not running "dry" when they are first started. This is a considerable advantage.

After an engine is assembled and started, it is important to monitor its oil pressure as a mother watches her newborn child. Many older cars have external pressure flow and/or relief settings and these should be set to factory specification. Excessively high oil pressure is not desirable because it can damage oil plumbing and seals. Of course, low oil pressure endangers bearings and cylinder walls. Anything that causes a rapid decline in oil pressure, particularly one that is accompanied by pulsations that are visible on an oil pressure gauge, mandates immediate engine shutdown before damage progresses. The cause of this condition must be investigated and remedied before the engine is restarted, because it likely forewarns of a progressing failure in the bearing system.

Watch your oil pressure gauge!

Chapter 7

Basic Engine Remachining: The Piston System

OLDER ENGINES HAVE LESS STRESSED PISTON SYSTEM components than those in modern engines. Contemporary piston systems and the types of equipment available to recondition them are complex and precise. This follows from the fact that modern engines are lighter and run at higher compression pressures and speeds than did their predecessors.

Although the application of modern rebuilding equipment to pistons and piston pins usually represents overkill for old engines, it is a situation that will not harm

Pistons and their associated parts, wrist pins, retainers and rings, do the heavy pushing in an engine. They take quite a beating in this process.

Cylinder block deck surfaces and head surfaces should be checked with a straight edge and feeler gauge to make sure that they are flat enough to seal a head gasket. Resurfacing cylinder heads is a routine automotive machine shop job. The best equipment does this with cutters that shave a few thousandths or more off a head or deck surface. The head is secured to the machine, rotated and leveled to the cutting head.

restoration work, and in most cases this increased accuracy will actually improve the durability, power and smoothness of old engines. However, it is important that the close tolerances that are possible with modern reconditioning equipment not be used *to reduce* some of the critical dimensional tolerances used in older engines. The key to good results is the application of appropriate technology, which involves understanding which tolerances are dictated by engine design and which result from the nature or limitations of the equipment that was once used in rebuilding. This distinction will be evident in the discussion of wrist pin fitting later in this chapter.

The piston system in any conventional automobile engine includes the cylinder walls, or sleeves, the pistons, the piston pins and their bearing surfaces, the pin retainers and the piston rings. Although the dimensional requirements

The surface of the head is cut to flat.

for most of this system (not including the critical pin fit) are not as precise as for systems like engine bearings, they do require a high degree of accuracy and cleanliness when this work is performed. Almost any contemplated rebuild of the "bottom end" of an engine—everything below the head(s), but not including the valves on "L" and "T" head engines—should include consideration of the piston system.

If an engine is being rebuilt due to bearing failure, camshaft failure, or the like, this is a good time to recondition the piston system components. Usually, the bottom end of an engine is rebuilt due to ring failure. This kind of rebuild should always include complete reconditioning of the piston system. The repair practice of simply cleaning pistons, replacing rings, and breaking the glaze on cylinder walls is a traditional repair format that has little or no place in engine restoration work. It may be an economical approach to keeping an aging vehicle on the road for a few more months or years, but it is not a reliable enough approach to be considered for the purposes of restoration work.

On engines with removable heads, the first surfaces encountered in disassembly of a basic block will be the mating surfaces of the block and head(s). These surfaces, and the manifold mating surfaces, should be checked for straightness and resurfaced if deviations from perfect flatness are greater than 0.002 inch in any linear 6-inch run of a head or deck; or more than 0.005 inch for the entire length of the surface in question. On V-type engines, it is necessary to grind the included angle manifold surfaces of the heads when the major head and/or deck surfaces have been ground. This maintains alignment of the intake manifold flanges with their mating surfaces on the installed heads.

The practice of attempting to correct the flatness of and surface defects in heads and manifolds with a large mill file is totally unacceptable. Included angle intake manifolds on V-type engines must be perfectly flat. Straight-6 and

The finished surface looks like this. Any remaining low spots will be immediately obvious to visual inspection.

8 manifolds should be held to no more than 0.012 inch deviation from flat for their entire lengths. In this last case, the possibility of tightening a warped manifold flat against a head or block has to be considered against the probability of weakening the manifold's flanges and cracking or breaking them off if this manhandling approach is used. One option is to build up the manifold flanges with a welding process and then machine them flat.

Frequently, the limits of head warping will be expressed in a phone call from a machine shop that goes something like this: "Hey Mack, the heads that you brought in are warped about 0.006 and 0.008. Do you want us to 'shave' 0.010 off 'em? It'll run ya 30 bucks each." In this case the answer is, "Yes," with the proviso that if 0.010 inch doesn't "clean them up," go to 0.015 inch. On long, flat-head engines

Manifolds and the deck surfaces to which they mate can also be dealt with this way, which is far better than the contemporary practice of belt sanding manifolds to flat, shown below.

with slightly warped heads, those heads are pretty flexible and *may* conform to the block well enough to seal when they are cinched down, but it is better to grind them flat. The exception would be when the head or heads in question have been ground before and there is danger of weakening them with further removal of material, or of producing valve-to-piston interference (OHV and OHC engines), valve-to-head contact ("L," "T," and "F" head engines) or of raising the compression ratio unacceptably by removing more stock. I get nervous in situations where the total removal of stock from a head goes beyond 0.040 inch from the original dimension.

Engine block decks rarely warp significantly, but when they do they should be ground back to flatness. If this is necessary, the stock removal must be considered in conjunction with the amount(s) that may have been removed from the head(s) previously; so as not to go too far.

The Cylinder Walls

To understand the appropriate procedures for reconditioning cylinder walls, it is necessary to describe the nature of the wear to which they are subjected. There are basically three kinds of wear that afflict cylinder walls—two of them are inevitable, while the third is sometimes present. From the first rotation of a new engine, the cylinder walls tend to slowly wear out-of-round in a way that enlarges their dimensions disproportionately at right angles to the crankshaft. This is because their side thrust is in that plane.

They also tend to become tapered with the large end of the taper at the top. This is because greater force is exerted on them there from pistons' power strokes and because upper cylinder areas are somewhat deprived of lubrication due to their distance from oiling system squirts and sloshes, and to the heat of combustion. Actually, most cylinder wear

occurs in the top 2 inches of ring travel, while the bottoms of cylinder walls usually remain relatively unworn. At the very top of a cylinder there will be a ridge that is an unworn section of the cylinder that exists above the top of the top (compression) ring's travel.

A third type of wear that may be present in cylinders is scoring, which almost always results from stuck or broken rings.

As a rebuilding proposition, taper is allowable in amounts of up to 0.010 inch on some engines, and out-of-round is tolerated in small amounts, usually less than 0.005

When you use a ridge reamer (top), be careful not to overdo it and cut below a cylinder's bore size.

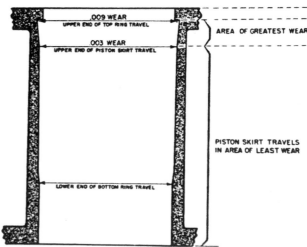

.009 WEAR
UPPER END OF TOP RING TRAVEL

AREA OF GREATEST WEAR

.003 WEAR
UPPER END OF PISTON SKIRT TRAVEL

PISTON SKIRT TRAVELS IN AREA OF LEAST WEAR

LOWER END OF BOTTOM RING TRAVEL

Most cylinder wear occurs at the tops of cylinders and is referred to as "taper." Lower cylinder areas rarely show much measurable wear.

inch on most engines. If these conditions are met, and new or resized pistons with so-called "engineered ring sets" are installed, the results are often serviceable in the short run. In practice, this means that a quick, cheap rebuild uses the above limits and conditions. Cylinders are simply roughed up with a glaze breaker to give them a finish that will retain oil and allow the new rings to seat. While these conditions may be tolerated in the repair field, they are certainly not acceptable in restoration work.

I would suggest that the proper restoration proposition

The two manual (drill motor operated) hones shown here have somewhat different purposes. The one on the left is a sizing hone and has a micrometer adjustment to position the stones for dimensional grinding of cylinders to specific sizes. It can also correct minor out-of-round conditions. The hone on the right is a glaze breaker and is designed to surface cylinders, not to dimension them.

for cylinders is *no taper* and *no out-of-round*. When a collector car's engine is restored, it is a very false economy to do anything but to return the cylinders to perfect roundness and straightness.

The first step in resizing cylinders is to remove the ridge that always forms at their tops. This procedure involves the use of a "ridge reamer," which is a small hand-operated lathe device with a cutter that removes the protruding material on the top 1/2 inch or less of cylinder walls. A ridge reamer must be used prior to piston removal if pistons are to be removed from the top of an engine. This is because it is almost impossible to get a piston and its rings past a cylinder ridge without damaging the piston's ring lands. Be careful not to overuse a ridge reamer, because if you undercut too deeply into a cylinder you may be forced to bore or hone it to a larger oversize than would have otherwise been necessary.

The equipment available for resizing cylinders is varied and highly specialized. Roughly speaking, it falls into two categories: hones (fixed position or floating stones) and boring devices (fixed position cutters). Hones range from drill motor-operated hand tools to sophisticated dwell honing machines. They are considered efficient for resizing cylinders where the taper does not exceed 0.008 to 0.010 inch for the full length of a cylinder. A new generation of

This glaze breaking hone has hundreds of small abrasive stones mounted on wire stems. It surfaces cylinders with almost no measurable stock removal.

dwell honing machines is designed to "dwell" automatically for most of the up-and-down honing cycle in the bottoms of cylinders and then to gradually work its way up to cylinder tops on successive strokes. The actual amount of

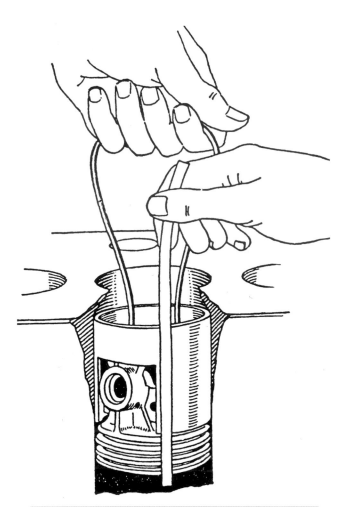

Years ago, piston-to-cylinder clearance was measured with a blade micrometer and a pull scale. This procedure gave a fair indication of piston skirt clearance, but fell far short of modern measuring and specification capabilities.

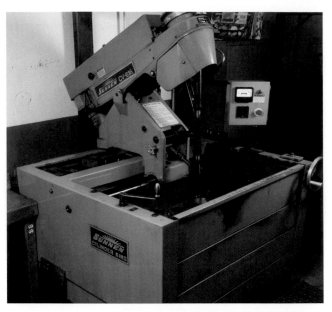

The Sunnen dwell hone shown in these photos is capable of accurately removing several thousandths of an inch of cylinder wall material and removing taper and egg-shaping in the process. In situations where only minor stock removal and surfacing are required to true cylinders and make them usable, honing is a good procedure to choose.

time that a dwell hone spends in any part of a cylinder is determined by the current draw of the motor that runs it or, more recently, by a computer program that uses out-of-round and taper measurements to calculate the hone action that will produce a round, straight cylinder bore with the least number of honing strokes. This type of automation makes it possible to efficiently hone to depths somewhat beyond the 0.008 to 0.010 inch rule-of-thumb standard that prevailed in the past.

Manual "sizing" hones (adjustable fixed stones) that are operated with an electric drill motor are not really efficient, accurate or fast enough to use beyond the above limit. The problem with any type of hone is that if there is any deviation in the centerline of a cylinder with regard to the crankshaft center line (this should always be 90°, but factory error in this area is surprisingly common in older engines), the error will be perpetuated in the honing operation.

Cylinder boring devices differ significantly in type. The newer ones tend to take their positions from crankshaft bearing saddles directly, and not, as the older ones did, from blocks' deck surface(s). Boring relative to crankshaft centerlines is far preferable to boring from block deck(s).

Since boring machines use rigidly positioned cutters to remove stock, they leave surfaces that are not appropriate for piston rings to seat on properly. Therefore, boring is always followed by a honing operation that ideally achieves about a 20-micron finish on the cylinder walls with a crosshatch pattern between 40 and 60 degrees.

Honing is no replacement for boring in situations where a lot of stock has to be removed to correct wear conditions, but it is very usable for removing small amounts of material reasonably accurately. The latest dwell hones are dimensionally controlled and are even more accurate than the one shown here.

If you are dealing with cylinders that have small taper and out-of-round deviations, it is perfectly permissible to use a drill-motor-operated expanding hone to remove these

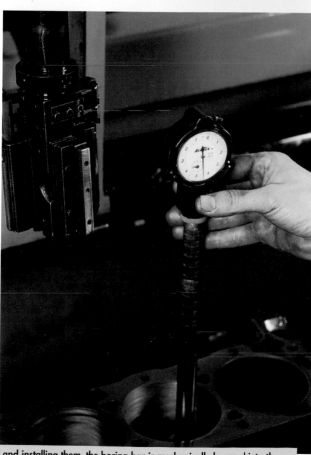

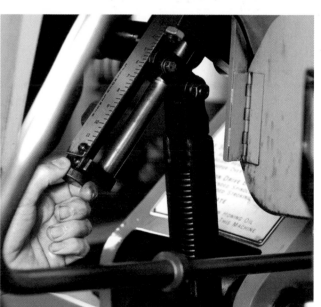

After choosing the right set of four matched cutters for the material being bored and installing them, the boring bar is mechanically lowered into the cylinder and boring commences. Frequent dimension checks with an accurate bore gauge must be performed to measure progress toward a straight and dimensionally correct bore.

They are used at many points because they are necessary, but their residues are deadly to an engine's health, should you be foolish enough to leave them behind in significant quantities. Some years ago, one of the major OEM diesel engine manufacturers sent a directive to its authorized repair facilities stating that in the future, no glass bead process was to be used in any phase of rebuilding their engines. This was because their warranty inspectors had found glass beads embedded in the main bearings of three engines that had been disassembled for inspection because they failed after rebuilding, but while they were still under warranty.

Strictly speaking, glass bead is not an abrasive, but this

After setting the block up on the dwell honing machine, various measurements are made and calibrations set. The hone then automatically moves back and forth in the cylinder in a way that creates the most uniform possible surface. For example, it "dwells" in the bottom of the cylinder where operation of the engine has created a taper condition at the top. This straightens the cylinder wall. The hone knows where to dwell by the load on the motor that drives it—more load indicates a tighter fit and the need for more material removal, thus more honing time is spent in that area.

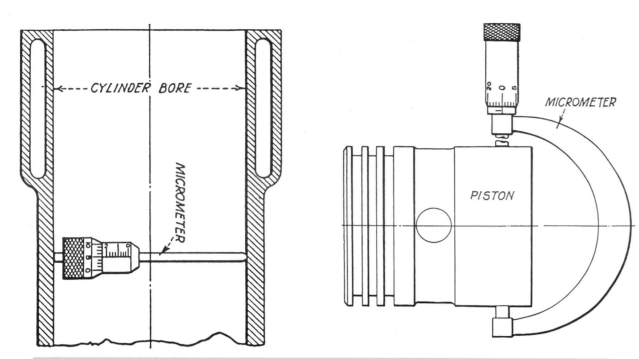

Modern practice is to use measuring instruments to determine the dimensions of pistons and cylinders. Inside micrometers and bore gauges (shown here) can be used, as can micrometers and telescope gauges (also shown here). Pistons are measured with micrometers.

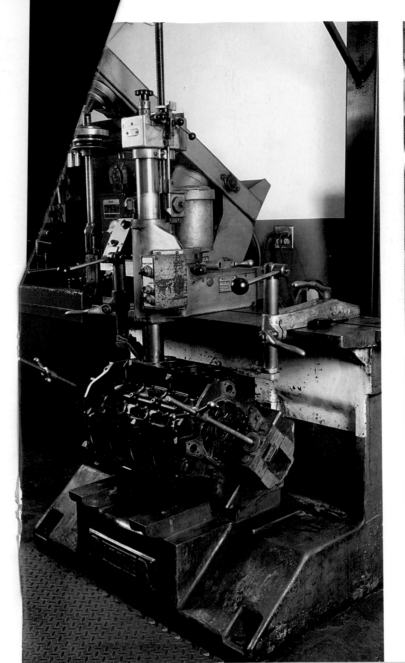

When a lot of stock has to be removed from a cylinder, or when its bore has to be straightened out, honing will not do the job and boring must be employed. The cylinder boring device shown here takes its position off the crankshaft main bearing saddles, not off the block deck. This allows it to straighten out crooked bores, a factory defect that was surprisingly common years ago.

deviations and to leave a proper cylinder surface. Use of this equipment requires at least a 1/2-horsepower drill motor and some practice to achieve the proper final crosshatch pattern. That pattern is important, and depends on drill speed and the speed at which the hone is inserted and withdrawn from a cylinder.

In honing, you begin with fairly rough stones (80 to 150 grit for stock removal and dimensional finishing). This is followed by "medium stones," (250 to 280 grit) used with copious lubrication for the final surfacing. Do not attempt to get a finer finish by wrapping a high grit of abrasive cloth or paper around your honing stones. A 280 finish is as fine as you will ever want to go.

The main trick in manual honing is to spend most of your time at the bottom of a cylinder. This is because that is the area with the least wear and it will require the most stock removal to eliminate taper. As you hone progressively higher in a cylinder, taper is eliminated and the lower, less-worn part of the cylinder acts as a guide for the hone stones as they reach the worn areas of the cylinder near its top.

The honing process should be interrupted frequently for measurement with bore gauges, inside micrometers, or telescope gauges. Honing operations will usually aim at oversizes of 0.010, 0.020, 0.030, or even 0.040 inch. Frequent size checks will insure that you don't go beyond these oversizes before you achieve a final finish.

In practice, boring (not to be confused with being boring) is highly desirable when you need to remove in excess of 0.010 inch of stock. Remember, cylinder/piston clearance is almost always a function of piston size. Cylinder sizes and oversizes tend to be very standard and recognizable figures.

Some engines are constructed with cylinder sleeves. These sleeves are either "dry" (seated against a block's metal for their entire lengths) or "wet" (seated in the block at the top and bottom, but exposed directly to coolant in the water jacket for most of their lengths). Wet sleeves are usually gasketed at their bottoms.

Factory sleeved engines can be treated as non-sleeved engines and normal honing and boring procedures can be applied to them. However, frequently it is easier to replace worn sleeve assemblies with new ones. These are often supplied with fitted pistons, rings, and wrist pins. Occasionally, cylinder damage, usually scoring, is so severe that a dry sleeve must be inserted into a cylinder of an engine that was not built with sleeves originally. This is a specialized job that looks outwardly simple. In reality, it involves a lot of know-how to make it work. Sleeving, which involves boring a cylinder to an oversize and forcing a sleeve into the oversize hole, should be left to shops and individuals that have considerable experience performing this process. Amateur sleeve installations sometimes result in a sleeve(s) working loose in its bore and doing enormous damage to an engine.

Although some older engines sometimes actually left the factory with different sized cylinders in the same block, and although it was not unusual for this situation to be created in rebuilding years ago, it is highly desirable that all cylinders in a restored engine be the same size. Sometimes, a badly scored cylinder requires sleeving, because it is easier and/or better to sleeve one cylinder and bore it to standard size than it would be to bore every other cylinder to an oversize to duplicate the oversize that would be necessary to repair deep scores in one damaged cylinder.

The Importance of Cleanup

There are lots of tricks and shop kinks that are acquired in years of resizing cylinders. Some mechanics swear by kerosene as the ideal lubricant for final honing when they resurface cylinders, while others use engine oil or light machine oil. Opinions vary widely on the exact point at which it is more economical or better to bore than to hone, while the controversy regarding the speed at which a hone should be run can take on the complexity and passion of a theological debate.

One point on which all good mechanics and automotive machinists tend to agree, and which many do not pursue in practice, is the importance of washing parts with soap and water after any honing operation. That's right, the stuff good ol' Mom wanted you to use behind your ears. I have seen people use exotic solvents like methylene chloride, and dangerous ones, like gasoline, to clean up the abrasives and metal debris left behind by boring and honing operations. The fact is that these solvents will not do as good a job as soap and water will. Good old Ivory Soap and a garden hose will float abrasive particles out of the pores of metal in a way that petroleum solvents will not. Wash all engine surfaces liberally after honing because any particles that you leave behind may cause severe wear to rings and cylinders, or worse, they can end up embedded in engine bearings.

While we're on this topic, it should be mentioned that abrasives are necessary evils in engine remachining.

story indicates what a small, stray particle can do if it is left in an engine environment. While I believe that it is both possible and practical to remove glass bead or grinding residues from heads, valves, pistons, etc. to a degree that these contaminants should not be a problem, you should always remember what can happen if you are careless with abrasives or blast particles by failing to remove them from a rebuilt engine. You can't do too good a job removing machine shop residues from engine parts, but try to work in that direction.

Pistons

For some unexplained reason, years ago when pistons were relatively cheap there was all kinds of equipment around to salvage them. Now that they are excruciatingly expensive, it is hard to find a shop that has piston resizing equipment.

All of the various types of equipment available to accomplish piston resizing dealt with the same issue: piston skirts. The long skirts used in older piston designs tend to collapse as a result of contact with cylinder walls in service. For split-skirt pistons, there were nasty expander springs that were installed inside the pistons and stayed there (one hoped) to spread the pistons' skirts. There were other systems that hammer-peened piston skirts back to original dimensions and retempered them. Still others knurled piston skirt faces, to selectively increase their dimensions.

In my opinion, the only piston skirt reconditioning proposition that is valid is knurling, and even this becomes dicey when dealing with cam ground (elliptical) piston skirts. In spite of the expense, when an engine is rebuilt and the pistons have collapsed skirts, or cylinders have been honed more than a few thousandths oversize to regain proper roundness and straightness, the pistons should be replaced. The expense will be considerable because the days of less-than-$35 pistons have mostly succumbed to the days of $60-$350 pistons. Yet, this expense may be justified if it helps a restorer to avoid the uncertainty of delving into the archaic arts of piston resizing. Of course, there are shops that are good at this operation and that can produce good resized pistons at a fraction of the cost of new ones. If you know of such a shop, great. If you don't, I wouldn't spend a lot of time looking for one; the results could be disappointing.

If pistons are dimensionally correct, they can be returned to an engine in which only slight deviations in cylinder format have been corrected. In that case, they should be cleaned, checked for: cracks, ring groove side clearance, ring groove width and depth and pin fit. If they pass these inspections they can be reinstalled.

The best method of manually cleaning pistons is an application of fine glass bead blasting. This will clean them without changing their dimensions appreciably. Piston ring grooves can be cleaned with one of numerous devices made for this purpose, and if they do not clean up within factory ring dimensions, they should be resized for wider rings and fitted with such rings if this is dimensionally possible. If

Ring regrooving tools, such as this one, do a pretty good job of cleaning up piston ring grooves.

not, they must be replaced with new pistons.

Ring side clearance should never exceed .0015 inch, and back clearance should be within your ring manufacturer's specifications.

Many ring sets include a cardboard gauge for measuring this last factor. These measurements are not particularly complex, but they are critical and it is easy to get them wrong. This is yet another reason that when pistons are involved, I tend to forsake my inclination against automatically ordering new parts, and spring for a set of new pistons. A piston, at its widest point, should provide about 0.001 to 0.003 inch clearance to its cylinder. Refer to piston manufacturer's data for an exact figure. Special rings, combined with skirt expansion methods, can be used to fit original pistons to slightly oversized cylinders, but I doubt if it is worth the effort. Most pistons are pretty delicate. Because they are hard-working members of your "engine team," sending in "relievers" (in this case, new pistons) is a reasonable call in the rebuild game. My apologies for that sports analogy.

Not all pistons are created equal. Some outfits that custom make pistons don't really have the engineering depth or sophisticated equipment and processes to properly manufacture them. I have seen some really atrocious pistons from well-known sources; pistons that I wouldn't put in a lawnmower engine. The OEM (Original Equipment Manufacturer) piston companies, like TRW, Perfect Circle, Sealed Power, etc. tend to sell highly engineered pistons that are often less expensive than some of the low-quality stuff sold to old car enthusiasts by specialty outfits.

Balancing pistons is a good idea, up to a point. I have a general suspicion that balancing components in old, low-speed, long-stroke engines is often a fruitless gesture. I have seen people go to enormous lengths to achieve better-than-factory balance in engines where I am sure that it did not make any discernible difference.

Modern practice is to hone, rather than ream, piston pin bosses and rod bushings. Very accurate measuring fixtures are used, so that honing is done to exact dimensions. These dimensions are measured to ten-thousandths of an inch.

subtle; so it is well worth studying that little slip of paper that comes with ring sets. It is called "instructions."

Before installing any new ring set, be sure to check the groove side clearance (never more than 0.0015 inch), ring land depth, and end gap. This last factor is critical, as an engine will overheat, break its rings, score cylinders and even seize up if it has rings installed without adequate ring end gap clearance.

End gap is measured by inserting each ring into its cylinder and pushing it squarely down the bore about half way with an unringed piston. Thickness gauges are then used to measure the gap between its ends. You should file or mill ring ends to provide at least 0.004 inch for each inch of cylinder bore. After dressing ring ends to produce the correct end gap dimension, always debur them.

Manufacturers usually give a specific figure for the crucial ring-end gap dimension and it should be followed rigorously. Rings with diagonal or notched ends also require proper ring end gaps. Just because a few rings in a set check out OK for end gap, do not forgo checking all of the rings in the set. You may find some surprises and, in any case, the potential penalty is too great to take any chances with getting this right. In initial ring installation, be sure that ring ends are placed at 90 degrees to each other to prevent early scoring and rotational lockup.

Fitting Piston Pins

Piston pin fits used to be achieved by reaming rod bushings or piston pin bushings or both, depending on a pin's designed flotation. Strange craftsman phrases like "thumb fit" and "palm fit" emerged to describe the proper feel of a particular fit. Presently, there is honing equipment available for pin fitting, and fits are specified in ten thousandths of an inch. Because honing is much more

accurate than reaming, the pin fits specified when this work is done on honing machines are much tighter than were the old, reamed, "feel" fits. The old reamed bushings and bosses were so rough that they were initially fitted quite tightly and allowed to wear into proper surfaces and fits.

Modern pin fit specifications, for modern pistons, take into account equipment that provides smoother piston boss surfaces and allows fits with even less clearance than was used in the past. Good pin fitting equipment will heat pins and their bushings or bosses to simulate to some degree the temperature in a working engine. I recommend having an automotive machine shop install and burnish new pin bushings, when they are used, and hone fit them to the pins.

I always specify that the pins be fitted "a bit loose" because I am more worried about seizure that can result from too tight a pin fit than by slight looseness. If you go much too loose, a pin will make a hollow, wrapping noise (often described as a "double click") as a piston reverses direction at the top of its power stroke, but it takes a lot of looseness for this to happen, and it is easily diagnosed from the timing and character of its sound. A pin that is fitted too tightly doesn't give any warnings until it deteriorates from overheating, or the piston fails in the boss area or in its skirt. Those failures tend to be sudden, violent and very destructive.

Piston Installation

Piston installation is almost always accomplished from the top of an engine, except in engines with non-removable heads. Bottom installation uses chamfers in cylinder lower ends to enter the rings, but this is a difficult installation and is risky for rings. On a few engines that are designed for bottom end piston installation, the bottom ends of the rods won't clear through the cylinders, seemingly mandating

Final piston pin fitting is done with the pins, rod ends and piston bosses heated to operating temperatures. With all that, the pins should still be checked for a feel fit as a final insurance. A good automotive machinist will know the right feel of a rod rocking on its pin with the pin retaining hardware installed.

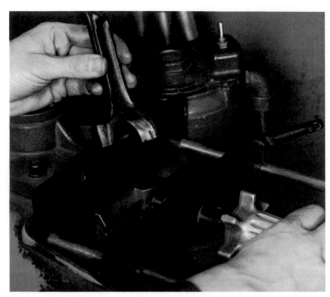
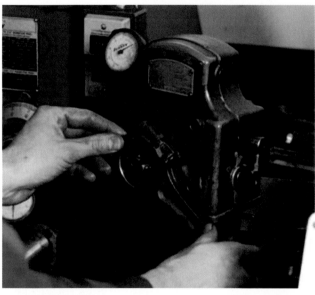

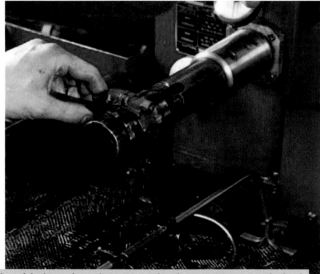

Rod big ends should be reconditioned at the same time that rod pin work is done if the big ends need attention. In this photo sequence, a stretched rod lower saddle is reconditioned by grinding material off the face of the rod and cap mating surfaces. This is done on a very specialized grinding fixture. The rod journal is then cut back to round. Accurate measurement is the key to this procedure.

A good ring expander is a must when you install piston rings. Installing rings with your bare hands, or with a cheap ring expander, like the one shown in the second photograph, is dangerous to rings' health and may open you to a charge of reckless endangerment of a piston ring. You will almost certainly end up with distorted or broken rings if you use this kind of expander.

installation from the bottom. You can beat this dilemma by pushing the rods up from the bottom and then inserting the piston pins with the pistons above the deck. I prefer this installation to installing pistons from the bottom of an engine.

When entering pistons and rings into cylinders, use lots of oil on everything in sight, and use minimum force to push the pistons and rings down through your ring sleeve. A rag taped over the end of a hammer handle makes a nice tamper to push pistons and rings down through an installing sleeve and into cylinders. Always put tightly fitting protectors (plastic or rubber hose lengths) over any protruding rod cap bolts or rod end surfaces so that they won't damage a crankshaft as rods descend into the crankcase during piston installation. The crank throw for each cylinder in which you are installing a piston should be well out of the way.

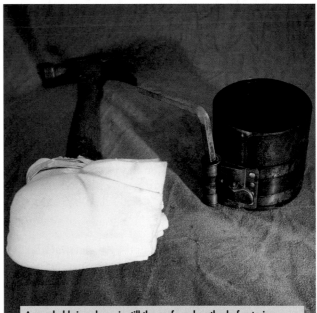

A good old ring sleeve is still the preferred method of entering ringed pistons into cylinders. A hammer handle with a rag taped around and under it looks crude, but works very well for persuading pistons home into their cylinders.

Chapter 8

Engine Lubrication and Cooling Systems

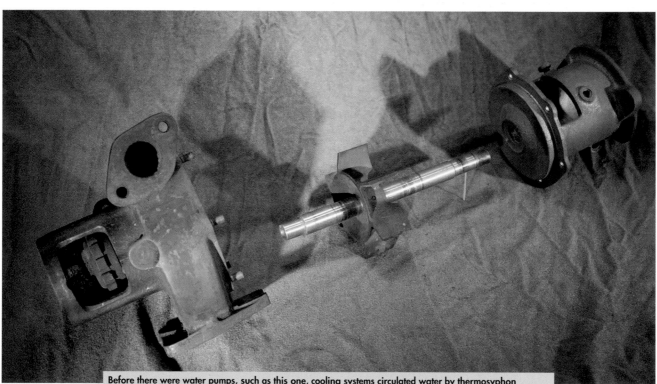

Before there were water pumps, such as this one, cooling systems circulated water by thermosyphon action. It's based on the idea that heat rises, and it was supposed to provide a self-regulating cooling system for automobiles. Model T Fords worked that way. Water pumps, and later, thermostats, were great improvements in automotive cooling systems.

ONE OF THE EARLY PURVEYORS OF PARTS, KNOWLEDGE, and humanity to the old car hobby was a Russian immigrant, Sam Adelman. From the 1930s through the 1960s, Sam ran an exclusive salvage business in Mount Vernon, New York. He humorously referred to his establishment as "The Emporium."

From a set of very old, dilapidated buildings, he catered to the owners of Lincolns, Packards, Pierce-Arrows, Deusenbergs, and Rolls-Royces. Most people who collected these cars in that period knew of Sam, and many were helped by him. As a young man, I was astounded by the knowledge that he had acquired as a result of disassembling hundreds, or perhaps thousands, of classic automobiles. He kept all of this information entirely in his head, without resort to files

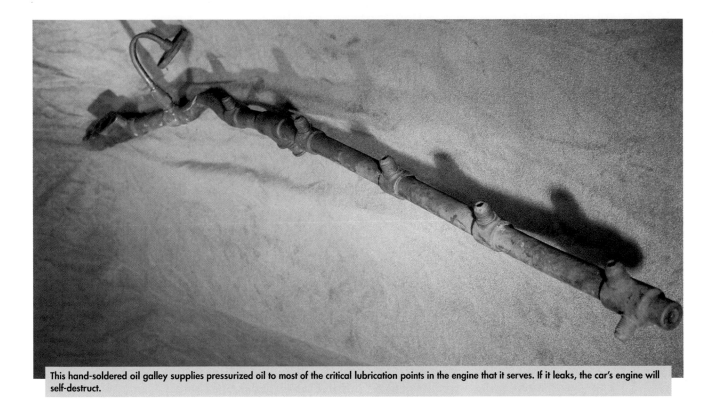

This hand-soldered oil galley supplies pressurized oil to most of the critical lubrication points in the engine that it serves. If it leaks, the car's engine will self-destruct.

or index cards of any kind. Needless to say, computers were not available for such purposes in those days.

It was one of Sam's major beliefs that as long as an engine had an uninterrupted supply of high-grade, clean, relatively cool oil, it would run forever. He impressed this theory on me so completely that it has become an article of faith with me that I call "Sam's Rule." Of course, the impact of Sam's Rule is that if an engine is deprived of this quality of oil supply for any appreciable amount of time, things will begin to fail.

Since most people who restore collector car engines work carefully, it is unusual for them to make big mistakes. For example, major misassembly is rarely a problem. However, in restoration work, small mistakes can be deadly. There are few places that are less tolerant of small mistakes than the lubrication systems of old engines. Many of them were marginal when they were new, so there is little room for error.

I recently heard of a 12-cylinder Lincoln engine that was seriously damaged because one of the solder joints in its oil pickup plumbing failed. The apparent reason for that failure was that some soldering flux had been inadvertently trapped in a joint at the time that the part was manufactured. The resulting failure took almost 50 years to occur, but when it did, major engine damage occurred.

Although modern lubricants are infinitely superior to those available before the 1960s, and have improved steadily since then, they still must be supplied to critical lubrication points in adequate amounts and pressures for engine systems to enjoy long-term survivability. Modern lubricants are wonders of chemical complexity. In addition to basic lubrication, they have been buffered against thinning out and acidification and fortified to prevent oxidation,

foaming, and corrosiveness to degrees undreamed of 40 years ago.

Modern engine oils have levels of detergency that make them capable of cleaning up varnish and harmlessly suspending all kinds of sludge and other garbage—up to a pound in 5 quarts of oil—which older lubricants used to deposit routinely on internal engine surfaces. The huge oil capacities of some older engines—a 1932 Lincoln that I once owned held 12 quarts, plus 2 quarts for the filter—were in large part necessary. This is because the viscosities of the oils that were available when these cars were manufactured were so inherently unstable as to require huge oil reserves in their pans for cooling purposes. Advances in lubricant technology are on the restorer's side, but he must still work to be certain that lubricants are supplied to engines in a clean, cool, and uninterrupted manner.

Oiling systems range from the very simple splash and drip systems of the early automobile age to the more complex pressure, shot, and dry sump systems that had evolved by the 1930s. Many older lubrication systems are marginal, at best. Even with the advantages of modern lubricants, they must perform nearly perfectly to avoid failures of bearings, cam lobes, timing chains or gears and other vulnerable engine components. Always remember Sam's Rule.

The most basic element in working on lubrication systems is to understand them. That may sound obvious, but some of these systems are difficult to puzzle out. The lubrication diagrams in publications like *Motor's Auto Repair Manuals* and shop manuals can be enormously helpful in this regard.

I remember a 1910 Maxwell that I once owned that had a wonderfully simple, but intriguing, oiling system. This car had a two-cylinder, opposed ("pancake") engine. When both cylinders fired or came in on their intake strokes, the incoming pistons momentarily pressurized the crankcase. That pressure pulse was captured by a check valve and conducted to the top of a small, pressure-sealed oil tank that was mounted on the Maxwell's firewall. This tank featured a gasketed screw-on cap and a sight glass for oil level readings. The pressurization conveyed into it from the crankcase sat over the oil in the tank, pressurizing it slightly.

Lubricating oil from this tank was piped to three drip oilers that were located on the dashboard. The drips of slightly pressurized oil were visible through sight glasses, and the intervals between them were adjustable with needle valves. One drip oiler fed a reservoir over the crankcase's rear web that, in turn, fed the rear main bearing through a passage that led to it.

Each of the other oilers was plumbed to a hole midway along, and drilled through the top side of each cylinder—remember, this was a horizontal, opposed engine. The drops of oil flowed to the cylinders and stayed on the sides of the pistons' crowns or skirts until the pistons' movements caused the drops to align with their wrist pins. At that point, the oil would drip into the wrist pins and lubricate their top bearings. (The bottom wrist pin bearings were lubricated by splash.) From there, deflectors directed some of the drip oil down the wrist pins to exit holes at the wrist pin bushings. From there it ran through holes drilled in the rods' pin bosses and into the horizontal troughs formed by the I-beam configured rods. At the rod crankshaft journals, it entered holes drilled into the rod bearings and oiled them.

Since this was not a recirculating system, any oil left over after this "incredible voyage" to the crankshaft fell to the bottom of the crankcase where it was splashed around by the crankshaft and lubricated the front main bearing via an open-top reservoir, the cylinder walls, and the camshafts. Presumably what was left over from all of that was burned when it leaked past the rings or valve guides. It was a wonderfully simple system that pushed any reasonable concept of adequate lubrication to the limits of credulity and of the possible. Still, up to a point, it worked.

Other lubricating designs, such as Franklin's positive displacement shot system, are wonders of uncompromising engineering. Whatever system you are working on, you must understand its theory and its fine points of operation to put it in good clean working order. On engines where the crankshaft is pressurized, the enemy is frequently the centrifuging capability of the crankshaft as it spins out solids that can accumulate and occlude full flow in its passages. All oiling systems require that all passages, galleys, and plumbing be in perfect order, free of dirt and obstructions and tightly and durably connected.

Some older "V" type engines had "fork & blade" or "yoked" connecting rods. This, coupled with the use of very thick babbitt in their bearings, often required as much oil volume at pressure as their small gear pumps were capable of delivering. These rod configurations require enormous amounts of oil for adequate lubrication. Significant decline in the output from their pumps is usually fatal. Modern

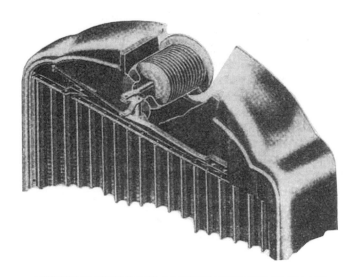

Before the late 1930s, many cars used thermostatically controlled air restriction to regulate engine temperature. The system shown here uses an ether-filled sylphon bellows to control radiator shutters. Hood louvres often were controlled by ether-filled coils.

lubrication systems are less marginal, particularly those that employ rotor-type pumps. It is mandatory to rebuild older oil pumps to factory specifications with regard to side and gear tooth or rotor clearance, and to test them thoroughly before installing them.

Pressure-lubricated engines vary from those that run at very low pressures of 10 to 20 PSI, to those that run as high as 75 PSI. Some older systems are combinations of pressure and splash feeds. Again, every aspect of such systems must be analyzed to determine how it functions, then put into perfect working order. Splash-lubricated bearings depend on simple laws of nature, such as those governing the surface tension of liquids and gravity. About all that can be done for them is to make sure that they are physically intact, absolutely clean and unobstructed, and that they serve bearings that are adjusted to correct clearances. Pressure systems, on the other hand, require all of the above, but also depend on properly functioning pumps, sound plumbing, functioning metering and/or pressure relief valves, and clean pickups and filters (if used). These last items are vitally important, and are sometimes overlooked.

Pressure lubrication systems invariably have some provision(s) for limiting oil pressure to account for bearing wear and for changes that occur in oil viscosity as oil temperatures change. These are either simple or compound spring-loaded pressure relief valves in combination with fixed or adjustable orifices. The orifices usually regulate oil pressure at low engine speeds, and the spring-loaded valves limit oil pressure at higher engine speeds. All parts of regulators must be clean and free to move, but not sloppy. Fixed metering orifice dimensions should never be modified from original. The springs in oil pressure regulators should never be stretched or replaced with other than original specification springs. Later regulator systems reside in oil pumps, while earlier ones were mounted outside of engines to facilitate their adjustment.

When an adjustable oil pressure regulator cannot be adjusted to specified oil pressures within the normal range of manipulations to its spring tension and/or volume orifice, there is a problem that must be found and corrected. Oil pressure regulators must work to produce adequate oil pressure at hot idle and to limit maximum oil pressure to safe levels with cold oil at road speeds. Any problem(s) in this area must be found and fixed, since damage to an engine is almost inevitable if it is not.

Oil pickup devices are either stationary or floating. It is imperative that they not leak, as air entering a lubrication system at this point will raise havoc with proper oil pressure and lubrication. This is because air entering on the vacuum side of an oil pump will foam as it goes through the pump, and this will deprive cylinder walls and bearings of proper lubrication. Always check oil pickups very carefully for cracks, pinholes, joint defects, fit-up anomalies and other problems that could cause air leaks.

Oil filters are either of the partial-flow or full-flow type. Partial-flow filters take a portion of an engine's pumped oil, either oil that is bypassed by the pressure relief valve or oil from a galley, and filter it. Frequently this is no more than 15 to 20 percent of the oil in circulation in a system at any time. While partial filtration helps to cleanse oil, it provides no guarantee against contamination entering and circulating in the pressurized part of a system and damaging bearings. It does lower the odds of that happening. Full-flow systems interpose an oil filter between the oil pump and all lubrication points in a system. These filters almost always have a bypass feature that allows unfiltered oil to flow if they become plugged.

It is imperative that canister-type filters (both full- and partial-flow types) be loaded with the correct filtering elements. Some of the older glued cartridge filters must be changed on a time basis as well as on a mileage schedule because their adhesive seams can deteriorate and cause these filters to rupture.

There was once a great deal of controversy regarding the use of thick (a.k.a. "dense") filter media versus the now common pleated, resinated paper-type filter elements. In some cases, only one type or the other was available for some applications. Few, if any, of the dense-type filters are still manufactured but there are several of them around at swap meets and in the NOS stocks of old car parts dealers. If there is a choice, I would strongly recommend using pleated paper-type filters. They give very adequate particle control (Between a 4 and a 7 micron pass is common, that's 4 to 6 millionths of a meter.) and do not absorb the detergent additives in the oil as readily as do the dense-type filters.

Dirty drain oil may indicate that the oil's additive package is doing its job, suspending contamination. Drain oil that is clear after use does not necessarily suggest the use of a superior oil or filter. It may mean that the inevitable crankcase refuse that hydrocarbon engines produce was deposited somewhere else in the engine because the

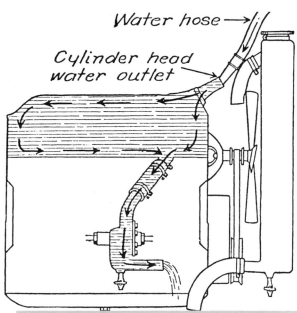

The theory of most cooling systems is simple enough. Water is circulated through an engine's water jacket and picks up heat. It is pumped or thermosyphoned through a radiator and transfers that heat to the air going through the radiator. A radiator fan is usually incorporated in the system to insure airflow through the radiator and around the engine.

detergents and other oil additives that should be emulsifying and suspending it have been filtered out by the oil filter.

Engine Cooling Systems

In the 18th century, Count Rumsford concluded that heat is energy and *vice versa*. Yet even before he came to this then-startling conclusion, tinkerers had been trying to effect an efficient conversion of heat to mechanical energy for centuries. The reciprocating internal combustion hydrocarbon engine that we all know and love (mostly) is the result of more than a century and a half of intensive human effort to get the best possible and practical conversion of heat to energy. It operates within the limits of our design imagination and the limitations of the materials that are available to construct, fuel, lubricate, and cool it—all within the constraints of the economics of the evolved auto industry and its ancillaries in our economy.

In common use, this engine succeeds in converting only 15 to 30 percent of the energy (heat) that is available in the fuel that it burns into useful mechanical energy. Usually its efficiency is closer to the lower limit. One of the things that Rumsford did not realize, and that modern combustion engineers must account for, is the fact that to produce mechanical energy from heat, there must be a "gradient."

Put most concisely, this means that something has to be hotter than something else to extract mechanical motion from heat. In practice, the necessity for this gradient mandates that some considerable proportion of the heat that is generated in any engine design will have to be rejected into the environment purposely for the system to function. This is not the heat of inevitable and necessary friction in an engine. It occurs above and beyond that heat loss.

There are hundreds of cooling system chemicals on the market. Most of them only put off system reconditioning but do not avoid it. It is a good idea to use a high-quality anti-rust water pump lubricant in the cooling systems of older cars with packing style water pumps.

Which brings us to automotive cooling systems. It is difficult to become enthusiastic about a system as seemingly inimical to thermal efficiency as one that is purposely contrived to reject heat from an engine, and to do so efficiently. However, this efficiency is necessary and must be provided for in restoring cooling systems. At a time when engineering journals report on the wonders of adiabatic and LHR (low heat rejection) engine designs and prototypes, as well as hybrid and hydrogen fuel cell powerplants, we must realize that the power plants in our beloved old cars are, for the most part, comparatively inefficient at the business of power production. They need the maximum possible efficiency that their designs make available in the matter of cooling system operation. Okay, the cooling system may well be the most theoretically unlovely part of an automobile, but it still has to work, and work well.

The statistics on automotive cooling systems are impressive, even if the theory of using good mechanical energy to toss all of that heat, willy-nilly, into the environment isn't. Some postwar cooling systems operate under pressures of up to 18 psi and circulate as much as 10,000 gallons of coolant an hour through an engine. Any one of these systems rejects enough engine heat while operating to provide winter warmth for a small house.

Automotive cooling systems must maintain a very narrow range of coolant temperatures, despite widely varying ambient temperatures and incredibly varied engine heat outputs. This is necessary because engines running at water jacket temperatures much below 160 to 200 degrees F tend to produce greatly increased quantities of sludge in their lubricants. Engines running much hotter than 240 to 250 degrees (in highly pressurized systems) will tend toward destructive pre-ignition and boil-over.

Most of the maladies that afflict automotive cooling systems fall into two general categories: leaks and inefficiencies. Every major component in a cooling system is capable of generating leaks or inefficiencies—sometimes both. These include: the block (internally and externally), the hoses and pipes, the radiator, the water pump and the thermostat. The performance of each of these components can deteriorate faster than almost any other component in an engine system. In some cases, the integrity of cooling systems depends on thousands of fragile brass or copper cartridges in a radiator, held together by delicate and fragile solder joints.

In all cases, cooling systems require meticulous restoration and exacting maintenance if they are not to become the proverbial "weak links" in entire engine systems.

In too many cases cooling systems are dealt with by adding chemicals, alone or in combination, to cure defects, or to ward them off shortly before their symptoms become evident. Flushes, sealants, pump lubricants, corrosion inhibitors, etc. are manufactured in thousands of varieties to keep cooling systems operating at high enough levels of integrity and efficiency to keep vehicles on the road. While each of these nostrums may have a place in automotive maintenance, the best restoration policy is prevention, which, in this case, involves the careful evaluation and rebuilding of cooling system components. The importance of cleaning blocks and insuring the soundness of the coolant diverter tubes that lurk in some of them is paramount. The proper installation of core plugs and head gaskets is also critical and is covered under the topic of "Engine Final Assembly" in the next chapter.

Every other part and subsystem in a cooling system

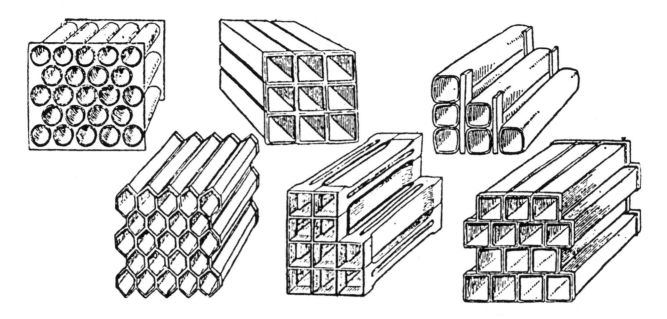

Cartridge core or cellular radiators are built from hundreds or thousands of horizontal copper or brass cartridges that are soldered together at their expanded ends. These radiators have tremendous cooling capacity for their sizes, but have a tendency to leak, and lack a straight path that would allow rodding them like conventional tubular core radiators.

deserves minute attention. Hoses must be in good shape—not old, hard and cracked, or soft and mushy. Bottom hoses frequently have internal springs to prevent collapse during coolant surges. These springs must be replaced when new hoses are installed. Hoses that are very stiff can literally tear an inlet or outlet off a radiator as an engine vibrates on its mounts while its radiator remains stationary. It is sometimes hard to find replacements for old molded hoses and there is a temptation to replace them with modern flex hoses. Usually, the energy stored in the bends necessary to make these hoses fit subjects radiator necks and outlets to unwanted and destructive stress. If you sort through enough bins of the old hoses at truck dealerships, you can usually find something that will work in your application.

Radiator repair has been the subject of many books. Radiator construction has been so varied over the years that it would be impossible to cover it here in any detail. Suffice it to say that radiators from the 1930s on are mostly of the tubular type and it is relatively easy for experienced restorers or radiator repair shops to deal with them. The older, cellular or cartridge type radiator cores are another story, as are recent radiators that are most often constructed with plastic tanks that are O-ring sealed and clamped to tubular aluminum cores.

The latter are so difficult to repair that replacement is usually the best strategy, if it is an option. Restoration of any type of radiator, other than the plastic tank variety, should include thorough cleaning in a radiator hot tank and rodding, if the core is the tubular type and needs it. Before installation, a radiator should be flow tested for capacity at pressure and visually inspected for weak walls and joints. Any defects that are found must be corrected. A marginal radiator will not serve and may mess up other aspects of an

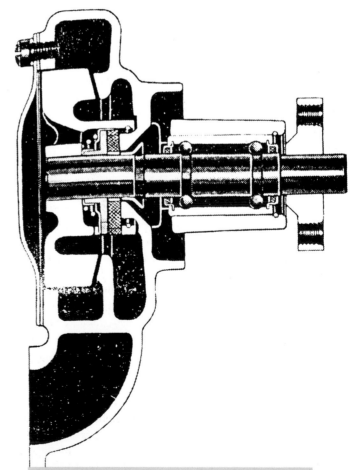

By the mid-1930s, most water pumps looked like this and ran on ball or sleeve bearings with carbon seals. Older pumps were often driven by an engine's timing chains or gears and used stuffing box-type packing systems to seal them.

Water pump packings dry out in service and have to be replaced. You can still buy braided packings, like these, at pump specialty stores. The packings in the foreground are pre-cut and formed. The packing material in the center of the picture is a modern Teflon type. Teflon packings have replaced many of the older packings that were based on asbestos and other natural fibers.

otherwise good restoration.

Sometimes, re-coring (or should I say, "core transplanting") is the only solution. In the case of cartridge type radiators, this work will be very expensive. It is not uncommon to see a tubular core hidden behind a 1/2 inch or so of old cartridge core facings. Even good restorers sometimes do this when they find out what the cost of replacing or extensively repairing an old cartridge core radiator will be.

An often-overlooked aspect of radiator repair is a thorough cleaning of the outside fins or passages. Buildups of external dirt, paint or corrosion can vastly reduce cooling efficiency. When you paint radiator cores and tanks, use the special coatings that are available for this purpose, because they will not interfere unduly with heat transfer. They work because they are very thin and/or very thermally conductive.

Water pumps vary in design from simple front-mounted cavity covers with impellers to magnificent bronze castings with complex seal and bearing arrangements. What they all have in common is perishable bearings, seals and gaskets. Modern pumps use spring loaded graphite or composition seals that rarely give trouble and are not susceptible to periodic adjustment or maintenance. Older pumps used oiled, graphited, braided textile packings that require external lubrication (grease) and some adjustments. On most water pumps of the older variety, I have found that Teflon (generically, "PTFE") packings sometimes can be made to work. Teflon-type packings certainly reduce the

potential for damage to the seal areas on water pump shafts, but some of them tend to ooze out as you tighten glan nuts down on them.

If you replace old textile type packings with similar units, you will find that square packing material almost always works better than the round type. Excessive glan nut pressure will burn and dry out textile packings very quickly. It is important that packings, and the shafts that run in them, get a good initial dose of waterproof lubricant and that they be greased sparingly but regularly if grease cups or fittings are provided. Use a good grade of waterproof grease, such as Lubriplate 1200-2, for this application. Most packing troubles in old water pumps are not caused by simple wear and age. They are initiated by failure to provide adequate lubrication and by over-tightening adjustable packings.

Sometimes, packings spin out because they have been installed incorrectly. The cure for this common malady is to install packing coils counter to the rotation of their pump shafts, and to punch stake the bottoms of packing boxes slightly. It doesn't hurt to level the ends of packings with a razor blade after their correct length and format have been determined, and before they are installed.

If a pump shaft is pitted or galled, no packing will provide a satisfactory seal for very long. Such shaft defects, as well as warped shafts, must be corrected by returning shafts to original condition. Either new shafts will have to be fabricated (use stainless steel, if possible), or the old shafts will have to be trued and plated, welded or metal sprayed and ground back to original dimensions. Sometimes, it is

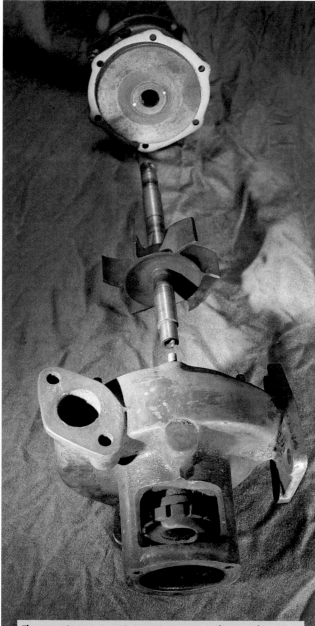

There aren't many parts in most water pumps. The parts that are there have to fit perfectly and must be in top condition if the pump is to do its job without leaking.

cracking because, like seals, they not only have to keep water from leaking out, they also have to prevent air from leaking in on the suction sides of pumps.

By the 1920s most auto manufacturers had adopted some type of automatic mechanical thermostat to regulate coolant temperature by restricting either the water flow in an engine or the air flow around it. Very early automobiles (and some holdouts, like Ford) did not enjoy the benefits of thermostatic temperature regulation. Most of these relied on self-regulating thermo-siphon water circulation, instead of pumped coolant flow.

Before World War II, air restriction systems were preferred by some automakers over coolant restricting thermostats because many motorists persisted in using methanol-based and ethanol-based antifreezes. In certain circumstances these concoctions can freeze in car radiators if coolant flow is restricted. After World War II, the almost complete conversion to ethylene glycol-based antifreezes caused auto manufacturers to uniformly adopt coolant flow restriction thermostats.

Air flow restriction was accomplished with thermostatically controlled radiator shutters and/or hood louvers. These air control devices were operated by ether-filled Sylphon bellows and tended to be quite troublesome. Most problems were caused by bent or poorly lubricated linkage. Restorers should be careful to make sure these parts operate freely. Sylphon bellows thermostats, themselves, often fail due to pinholing and fatigue cracking. There are still companies that repair Sylphon bellows canisters and coils. It is important to specify the desired opening and closing temperatures to anyone who attempts to repair an ether-filled thermostat for you. New Sylphon units are also available for some applications.

Contemporary water flow restriction thermostats use wax pellets to operate their valves and should be tested and replaced if they malfunction. Older water restriction thermostats used ether-filled-bellows activation or, in some rare cases, bimetallic element activation. In most cases, the superior modern pellet types can be substituted. Be sure to always install thermostats with their activation elements facing towards the block and away from the radiator.

Automotive fans are used to pull air through radiators. This is necessary for cooling purposes when a vehicle is stopped or when it is operating at low to moderate speeds. At high speeds, fans are mostly unnecessary because vehicle motion produces enough air flow for cooling purposes except, of course, in air-cooled engines.

At road speeds, cooling fans not only don't do any good, they consume considerable engine power and produce noise and vibration. Enter clutch fans of 1930s origins.

By the 1960s, these devices had become ubiquitous in American automobiles. At about that time, the sophistication of viscous silicone drives and bimetallic calibration had been added to them. Clutch fans are susceptible to internal wear and working fluid leakage. They should be checked for proper operation before engines are disassembled for restoration.

possible to sleeve the seal area of a pitted shaft with one of the special sleeves that are sold by some automotive stores and bearing suppliers. This also solves the problem.

Water pump impellers can rust, erode or cavitate to the point that they are ineffective in moving the necessary volumes of coolant to maintain consistent engine cooling and heat transfer. Postwar, curved vein impellers have to be in perfect shape to work properly, because they are designed to facilitate high-speed pumping and are relatively inefficient at idle speeds. Any wear on them will cause overheating at idle.

Pump bearings are either sleeve or anti-friction types. In either case they have to be in proper alignment and in top condition if pump seals are to function effectively. Water pump castings should be examined for warping and

With an engine stopped and cold, you should feel very little resistance when you turn a clutched fan's blades by hand. After the engine reaches operating temperature and the under-hood temperature reaches the point at which the clutch should engage the fan, turning the blades of the fan by hand, (again, with the engine stopped, of course), you should sense some drag. If there is no drag or if the fan is locked up completely, then the fan clutch is defective. It is difficult to test these fans if they can't be run, so it is best to test them before you take them off engines.

All fan blades should be checked for cracks, deformities, and blade attachment integrity. Since fans spin much faster than crankshaft speed, their integrity must be perfect or they are real hazards. Many fans from the 1930s on have asymmetrical blade arrangements. This design is supposed to break up harmonic vibrations. Whether symmetrical or not, fans must be balanced because their high operating speeds and large diameters mean that small imbalances can result in large radial thrusts that will shake a whole vehicle. The threaded fasteners that hold fan blades to hubs should be replaced routinely with grade 5 or better fasteners. If rivets are used to make this attachment, they should be checked for tightness. Fan hub bearings should be cleaned and lubricated if it is possible to do this.

Some pre World War II water pumps have shafts and hubs that attach directly to fan blade assemblies. These pumps also have sealed bearings that are integral and cannot be separately lubricated or adjusted, short of rebuilding those water pumps. Almost all post-World War II fans are of this construction or electrically driven.

Fan belts must be correctly sized and correctly tensioned. If they run too loose, overheating will result, and if they are over tightened, water pump, generator, alternator, air pump or air conditioning pump bearing failures can result. Old, cracked fan belts should be replaced, and if the old-style link belts are encountered, they should be discarded and replaced with modern one-piece fabric/rubber belts. One of the world's dumbest feelings is sitting by the side of the road with a frayed or broken fan belt.

Coolant recovery systems, or "expansion tanks," date back to the 1920s and must be put into absolutely leak-free condition, as must the plumbing connecting them to radiators. Car heaters also contain coolant. These units should be checked for leaks and for interior and exterior cleanliness during restoration and repaired in much the same ways that radiators are refurbished.

The coolant used in any automobile should be a 50 percent mixture of water and ethylene glycol-based anti-freeze. Propylene glycol antifreezes are advocated by some because they are less abrasive than ethylene glycol antifreezes if they mix with oil and attack engine bearings. This advantage is offset by the fact that propylene glycol anti-freezes have a relatively low flash point (209 degrees F.) and are a definite fire hazard if they seep or leak out of the coolant containment and around an engine compartment.

Since the lime contained in "hard" water has a bad effect on radiators and other cooling system surfaces, it is best to use demineralized water in your coolant mixture. In systems that contain aluminum parts, the use of distilled water is not recommended because this liquid tends to be "mineral hungry" and may have an etching effect on aluminum.

It is also a bad idea to increase the anti-freeze proportion of a coolant mix beyond the recommended 50 percent (minus 34 degrees F. protection). Concentrations above 66 percent will actually cause the freezing point of the mixture to rise. Many commercial antifreezes contain additives to retard corrosion, and some contain water pump lubricant. I always add a water pump lubricant-anti-corrosion additive to antifreeze to protect cooling systems. In practice, this additive is simply water soluble oil that coats the internal surfaces of cooling systems. It is often recommended that sealant be added to coolant to seal very small leaks and voids in pressurized systems. I do not endorse this practice because you should be able to get the system air tight without relying on sealants. The sealants that I have seen on the market all have the potential for reducing cooling efficiency by plugging or coating cooling passages and surfaces.

Cooling system pressure caps operate at specified pressures from as low as 3-5 PSI to as high as 18 PSI. These caps should be tested for sealing and for releasing high pressure on an appropriate tester. Often, these caps are combined with coolant recovery systems. This makes it doubly important to check them for sealing efficiency and release capability. If caps of this type do not release at their specified pressures, you can blow out a radiator core. If they leak or release too early, you may experience boil-over because they are responsible for raising the pressure in the cooling system to a level that will increase the boiling point of the coolant beyond the level set in the system's thermostat.

After a restored vehicle has been started and run for a while, its cooling system should be re-checked. If the system is a pressure system, it should be pumped up and tested for leak-down. On non-pressure systems, it is sometimes possible to apply mild pressure for a leak down test, or you may have to satisfy yourself with physically inspecting for visible leaks or damp spots at vulnerable points. Various phosphorescing black light-activated dyes that dissolve in coolant are available to make cooling system inspection easier and more effective.

The most troublesome cooling system leaks are air leaks on the suction sides of water pumps. These leaks pull air into coolant and cause foaming and bubbling there. This "aeration" acidifies antifreeze solutions, rapidly rusts system components and interferes with cooling by insulating the block and radiator from the coolant. Air is a terrific insulator. The smallest leak that water will work through is very easy for air to pass through, so any small leak that is visible in an inspection must be closed.

A second type of cooling system leak that can cause severe problems involves combustion leakage past head gaskets, blocks or heads. Combustion gases are highly corrosive and tend to acidify coolant to the point that it

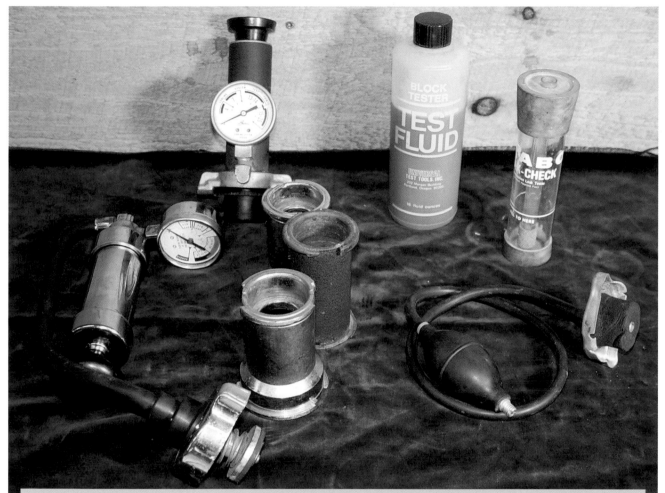

Pressure and leak testing a cooling system is always a good idea. The tester shown in the right rear of this photograph is a monoxide detection system. Air on the top of the radiator is pumped and bubbled through an indicator fluid. If combustion leakage is occurring, carbon monoxide gas in the cooling system will cause the indicator fluid to change color. The testers on the left are cooling system pressure testers. They allow you to pump air pressure into cooling systems to see if they hold or leak. You can also test radiator cap release pressure with this type of tester.

can damage delicate brass, copper or aluminum radiator surfaces and the solder used to join them. Like suction leaks, combustion leaks cause bubbles to enter a cooling system. These insulate heads and/or blocks, thereby making it difficult for them to properly transfer heat to coolant. They also insulate radiator cores, making it difficult for the coolant there to transfer heat from those cores to the air passing through them.

It's a good idea to check for combustion leaks in restored engines with either a bubble or a chemical test. In the bubble test, the top radiator hose, thermostat housing, thermostat, and fan belt are removed. The engine is then run up to normal operating temperature. This will occur quickly with the fan belt removed (or water pump drive coupling removed in the case of engines with direct driven water pumps). The thermostat cavity or top hose outlet is then examined for bubbles. With the water circulating system disabled, there should not be any bubbles visible with an engine idling or accelerating. If there are, a combustion leak or hot spot in the system is indicated and must be located and corrected.

A more sophisticated test for combustion leakage involves bubbling the air on top of a cooling system through a special indicator fluid that will change color in the presence of carbon monoxide. This test does not require that the water pump be disabled or any part of the system dismantled. It also is very sensitive. Several companies market the test unit and fluid for the chemical combustion leakage test under various brand names. For complete results, a monoxide test should be performed with an engine both cold and hot, and at several different speed and load conditions.

Not all overheating problems have their origins in cooling systems. Causes of overheating are frequently found in ignition systems, in fuel delivery and carburetion systems, or in some entirely unlikely areas, such as dragging brakes or a slipping clutch. In many cars, the cooling system is designed with little margin; so minor defects in other systems can cause overheating symptoms. Due to the multiplicity of possible causes for overheating, it is important to restore cooling systems to top-notch condition, so that if overheating symptoms do appear, the cooling system itself can be ruled out as a likely cause.

Chapter 9

Final Engine Assembly Hints, Start-up Procedures and Considerations

EARLIER CHAPTERS IN THIS BOOK have covered the specific assembly of major engine components and subsystems. In this chapter I will discuss some other areas of assembly and look at some general considerations in bolting up old engines.

A general rule is that everything in engine assembly must be right and must make sense. Don't trust anything to luck. If a threaded hole for a head stud or bolt looks weak, it will probably pull out after the head is partially bolted down and the head gasket has been ruined. Please remember, whenever and wherever engines are bolted up, Murphy is there, making sure that his law is enforced.

Core plugs are a particular problem. Some of them are very hard to get at when an engine is in a car, so install them with sealant or Loctite and install them carefully. The bores in the bosses into which core plugs install must be clean and sound. Never attempt to reuse a core plug. It is a very false economy. This is particularly true of the core plugs used at the ends of some engines to seal camshaft oil pressure. Some of these are in or behind bell housing castings. If one of these ever lets go, you have to pull an engine to get at it.

As a point of interest, core plugs are sometimes called "Welch" plugs and occasionally "freeze" plugs. I have no particular objection to calling them Welch plugs because that term probably denotes their inventor, popularizer or an early company that manufactured them. However, calling them freeze plugs implies that they are there to automatically release if the coolant in an engine freezes, and in so doing, to prevent destruction of that engine's castings.

Whoever came up with the concept of calling the plugs in the holes that are used to extract sand in the casting process "freeze plugs" should get a Pulitzer prize for imaginative nonsense. I have never heard of or met anyone who admits to hearing of one of these devices releasing when an engine froze. I have experienced and know many others who have experienced core plug releases at other, usually inconvenient, times.

Various threaded pipe plugs may be used to seal oil and water galleys and their manufacturing drill access holes in engine castings. These should be reinstalled meticulously. Sometimes these plugs can be threaded in far enough to obstruct connecting right-angle passages. This must be avoided. I prefer brass plugs used in conjunction with a Teflon (a.k.a. PTFE or TFE) paste sealant for their threads. A note of caution here, Teflon® sealants are wonderful lubricants, making it very easy to over-tighten any threaded plug that has been sealed with them. If you don't exercise caution here, it is easy to exert enough pressure to crack a casting. This sealant works very well at low tightening torques. Teflon® tapes are messy to use and look unsightly and inauthentic when they protrude on visible threads. Pastes are preferred to them. If you do use tapes, be sure to wrap them counter to the direction of the threads that you are sealing. Otherwise, they may shred and/or separate as you install threaded items that have been wrapped in them.

Main bearing seals should be bolted on if they are that type, or seated in their saddles with a sealant (I prefer high-temperature silicone rubber RTV sealants for this purpose) if they are the one-piece molded type. For the more common rope kind, a good, self-lubricating packing of the right size should be rolled into the groove provided for it with a round bar, or forced in with a special tool. Then its ends should be trimmed almost flush to the saddle but with just a bit of stand-up material beyond it. The ends should be dabbed with a bit of sealant before the bearing cap is installed.

If the upper rear main bearing assembly originally used wooden strips for side sealing, I have found that a fine packing string smeared with silicone rubber will outperform those wooden strips used for this purpose. The string should be pounded into the slots that held the wood strips with a small punch. Those original wooden sealing strips can be hard to find, hard to install and uncertain in sealing.

Timing gears or chains must be installed with their markings correctly oriented or, on some older engines, with the valves set and timed to specification. In the latter case, valve settings replace index markings on chains and gears.

I have dismantled a surprising number of engines in which the valve timing was slightly off. This makes a big difference in performance. Be sure that camshaft endplay is correctly adjusted with shims or by whatever other method is specified. Timing gears or sprockets must be aligned in the same plane, and they must be pre-lubricated with oil or assembly lubricant prior to startup. On most engines the timing cases are the last places to get lubricated by pressure or splash.

Very old oil pans were sealed with simple cork or paper gaskets, but oil pans from the cars of the 1960s, and after, often require a baffling array of stamped and molded gaskets to make them seal. These, and the mercifully simpler gaskets for older pans, should be coated with a good sealant prior to installation. Silicone-rubber RTV compound is ideal for this purpose.

When a pan seal system uses several different pieces of gasketing, it is important to use sealant liberally at their joints. Oil pans should be tightened with a torque wrench and in a reasonable cross-pattern sequence. This will help to prevent gasket distortion and leakage.

Here is a good trick to prevent oil pan leakage. Place the end of a 1 x 2-inch piece of hardwood in a vise with about 6 or 8 inches above the vise jaws. With the pan right-side up, locate the bottoms of the pan bolt hole centers on the piece of hardwood. Then, one-by-one, pound down the metal around the holes until it is flat against the wood. A slightly crowned 16-oz. hammer is perfect for this job. If this is not done, and if the pan metal is distorted (cupped) around its bolt holes from previous overtightening, then a new gasket will tend to squeeze out around the pan securing bolts when they are cinched tight.

The attachment of flywheels is a critical juncture

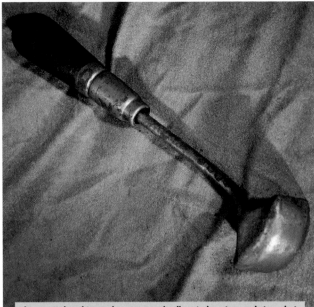

This special tool is used to tamp and roll main bearing seals into their grooves. You can roll them in with any bar if you don't have one of these tools. Small sockets are a good bet for this job.

of engine reassembly. This is because failure to achieve specified and invariably high tightening values on flywheel to crankshaft fasteners can lead to disaster. I was once in a car when the flywheel sheared its fasteners and escaped. It is not an experience that I would like to repeat.

If flywheel fasteners ever do loosen, despite their lock washers, wired heads, cotter keyed nuts, etc., they tend to make a very distinctive thunking noise as you go from throttle to back throttle and *vise versa*. If you hear unexplained "thunks" in those modes of operation, and if you can rule out other causes, like loose U-joints, be aware that the origin of the noises could be a flywheel that is coming loose from its crankshaft flange. This problem must be attended to immediately.

Installing Head Gaskets

Head gaskets can serve for decades if their basic installation was correctly attended to. Most older car engines used copper sheathed asbestos head gaskets, with a few applications of "shim" type steel gaskets showing up by the late 1930s. Modern gaskets are usually of the "composition" type, with "fire ring" protection (steel or tin plated crimp rings) around the cylinders. Some air-cooled engines used solid copper sealing rings and there are a few other obscure gasket types for sealing heads to blocks.

The first step in installing head gaskets is to get the correct gasket. If the old gasket was working without any overheating or leaking problems, the new one should match it for type, and hole-for-hole, binder ring-for-binder ring. If some of the holes in the old gasket are not duplicated in the new one, or vice versa, this may be an acceptable variation of later or earlier design origin. In any case, make sure that you know what the differences are between the gasket that you took out and the one that you are installing. If differences

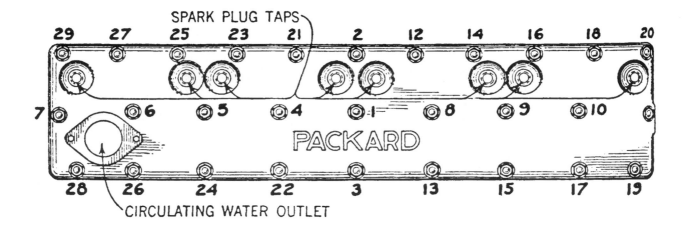

SPARK PLUG TAPS

PACKARD

CIRCULATING WATER OUTLET

Head bolts or nuts should always be torqued to the right lbs.-ft. value in at least three stages. They should also be tightened in the pattern suggested by the engine's manufacturer. If you can't find a pattern for the engine that you are working on, tighten these fasteners in a spiral pattern that radiates from the center of the head outward and that includes all fasteners.

do exist, be sure that you have a plausible explanation for them.

Never attempt to reuse old head gaskets. It's a false economy that never works in the long run. There are wonderfully quaint procedures offered for resealing old gaskets with various compounds, and there is a great deal of folklore about soaking them in various brews in bathtubs with claw feet—and then only during full phases of the moon. If you happen to believe that the Earth is flat, then maybe you will believe that a used head gasket can be resuscitated and clamped true enough to seal. Otherwise spend a few bucks and get a new gasket(s).

Make sure that you install head gaskets right-side-up and correctly end-for-end. Some gasket manufacturers stamp the words "Install This Side Up," or its equivalent, on one side of their head gaskets. It is their custom to do this in small, almost illegible lettering. That does not mean that this instruction is insignificant. Always examine a new head gasket for that fateful phrase, or its equivalent, and abide by it as you would an order from your boss to take a two-week paid vacation.

On engines that do not have alignment pins for gasket installation, it is handy to buy or make a set. These pins sit in the threaded fastener holes of a block and can be drawn out with a special probe tool after a head is in place. On bolted heads, if just cap screws align a gasket, it can end up slightly misaligned. That can interfere with coolant flow and cylinder sealing. Using installation pins helps to avoid this problem. Always be sure that heads and blocks are absolutely flat and clean before head installation. Be certain that there isn't a lurking glass bead or machining chip that will fall out of the head and lodge between it and its gasket when you go to mount it. A very small particle in the wrong place can cause a very big leak in a head gasket.

Heads should be tightened with an accurate torque measuring device, and this should be done in stages and in the prescribed factory pattern. If no pattern is available for the engine that you are working on, use a spiraling sequence that includes all fasteners and radiates from the middle of the head to its ends. It is essential that a good anti-seize compound be used on head fastener threads and fastener head undersides, whether they are nuts on studs or bolts into a block. Head fasteners must be in good condition, not pitted, warped or stretched. Their threads must be in tact, smooth and without burrs. My preference is to replace head fasteners when it is practical to do this.

The penalties for an inconsistently torqued head can be simple coolant leakage, oil leakage, or distortion of a block. The latter can lead to excessive oil consumption. I once knew a man who styled himself "The Human Torque Wrench." He claimed that he could come to within 2 lbs.-ft. on any fastener without the benefit of a torque wrench. Sad to tell, he left a trail of broken and distorted castings in his wake. I hope that none like him shall ever pass this way again.

Some gasket companies that cater to the old car trade supply some really wretched gaskets to replace the original copper sheathed items. These reproductions are typically made out of materials such as Victor's Corbestos*, a fine product when it is used for its intended purpose, which is not to make head gaskets.

Sometimes, reproduction head gaskets are fabricated as copper/asbestos sandwich gaskets, but lack expensive sealing and fire rings for cylinders and/or coolant passages. Often, these gaskets will fail in service. They should be avoided because N.O.S. (New Old Stock) originals in good condition or good reproductions usually can be found for most applications.

Modern fire ring/composition gaskets and older shim gaskets do not need retorquing if they are installed properly. Retorquing may produce a 20 to 30 percent additional compression of gasket material and binder rings. That extra

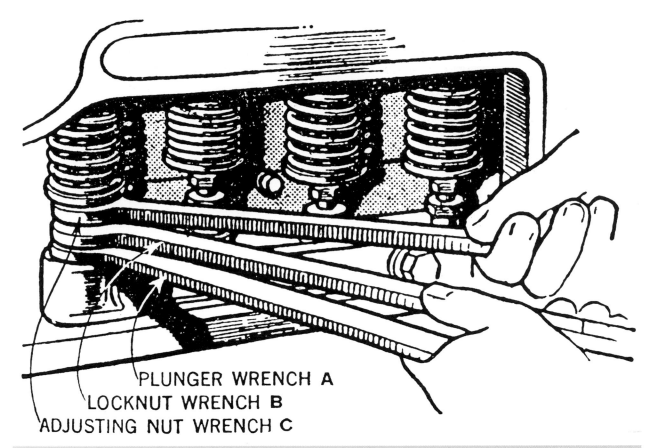

PLUNGER WRENCH **A**
LOCKNUT WRENCH **B**
ADJUSTING NUT WRENCH **C**

This illustration shows the two-wrench and three-wrench manipulations used to adjust the valves in some L-head engines. If ever there was a real need for a third hand, this has to be it. This adjustment is particularly fun when it is performed on a hot, running engine. The lifters are jumping up and down, oil is spraying out of the valve chamber, and you often have to work through a small access panel in a car's inner fender. Fortunately, once valves of this type are adjusted, they usually hold their adjustments for a long time.

torque can endanger the integrity of the fire ring seals. It does not take much over-torquing to fracture these delicate seals.

Without a specific recommendation from your gasket or engine manufacturer, applying sealant to head gaskets will do little good, and may do harm. It is definitely not recommended for shim-type gaskets—these already have an anti-cold flow seizure coating or for modern siliconized composition gaskets. If you are using an NOS shim-type gasket and its lacquer coating is deteriorated, it should be coated with a sprayable high-temperature aluminum paint. This will act to lubricate it.

Some copper/asbestos sandwich gaskets may benefit from applications of sealant and from retorquing (with their engines hot). A lot of failures that are blamed on head gaskets have their real origins in poor installation technique or the use of worn or substandard fasteners.

Roughly the same considerations that apply to head gaskets apply to manifold gaskets. However, it is generally a good idea to use sealer on manifold gaskets, particularly when you have to deal with the one-piece exhaust manifolds that were sometimes used on long engines, such as straight-8s. If manifolds are attached with studs and nuts, it is a nice touch to use brass nuts, as this will give you or your successors a better chance of removing the manifolds at some later date without breaking their studs.

Where heat boxes are used between exhaust and intake manifolds, it is good practice to first tighten the manifolds to the head or block, and then tighten them together. This will produce more satisfactory conformity of manifolds to blocks and will reduce the chances of breaking a flange or cracking a manifold.

Some Other Odds and Ends in Good Engine Assembly Practice

It is undesirable to make final adjustments on valves "cold," unless an engine is constructed in a way that precludes "hot" adjustments. My beloved 1930s Lincolns are configured so that it is necessary to remove their intake and exhaust manifolds to adjust their valves. Clearly, this makes a hot, or "running," adjustment impossible. On most engines it is possible to do a final valve adjustment with the engine hot and running. This is the best way to adjust valves.

Some valves in L-head engines have to be adjusted through inconveniently small access panels in inner fenders. These procedures may require manipulating three wrenches with one hand and a feeler gauge with the other. This is not an easy or task for those without acrobatics backgrounds, but a lot depends on doing it right.

For your preliminary valve clearance settings when assembling an engine, always go a thousandth or so wider than the specified hot setting for valves because valve stems, lifters, and push rods tend to expand as they get hot. This can close up some of the clearances that you allowed in your cold settings. I always tend to stay a bit wide on the final, hot settings, too, because a "happy" valve is one that is adjusted to close fully, and doesn't get held open a crack by expanded linkage, so that it can burn.

Before a rebuilt engine is started, its oil pump should be primed with engine oil by pressurizing it externally, pouring oil into it, packing it, or spinning its gears or rotor with a drill motor. Running the oil leakage test, described in Chapter 6, also works to prelubricate an oiling system. Some people pack oil pumps with Vaseline for this purpose, a decidedly odd practice.

It is also very good practice to fill oil filters or filter canisters with engine oil when they have been emptied and before engines are started. This eliminates the "dry" running time that would otherwise occur while oil pumps fill them. To be absolutely sure of immediate oil pressure, always spin a rebuilt engine with a crank or starter motor and with its plugs removed until you get an indication of oil pressure. Then, and only then, should the sparkplugs be installed and the engine started.

Before mounting clutches on flywheels, secure a dial indicator to a convenient flywheel bolt and check the bell housing for lateral run-out (concentricity) and parallelism. Some older engines have to be shimmed or adjusted with eccentrics to achieve alignment in these regards.

Water pumps that are mounted directly to blocks sometimes have water distribution tubes behind them in those blocks. These should be removed, if possible, before blocks are cleaned and repaired or replaced prior to water pump installation. These tubes are often neglected because they cannot be examined without their removal. Frequently, they rot and their critical function of directing coolant is not performed. This can lead to localized overheating and hard-to-find "hot spots" that cause cooling system boiling.

Take care in tightening flange-type water pumps. They are often machined from relatively low quality castings and break easily if they are tightened unevenly, or if they are held away from blocks by burrs or by rebuilding debris when they are tightened.

Phasing ignition systems, conventional or magneto, can be frustrating. Most magnetos are geared internally, and alignment of their timing marks does not guarantee that they are in the right phase. Distributors have to be put in the correct phase and "dead timed" for initial start up. This involves mounting a distributor so that it engages with its cam gear or oil pump "T" drive with its rotor in the right orientation. In some designs, the oil pump will have to be jogged a little with a long screwdriver before everything engages in the correct manner.

I always start with the crankshaft timing marks at Top Dead Center for the number 1 cylinder (usually designated "TDC" or "UDC") and engage the distributor drive so that the rotor is pointing to the number 1 distributor cap terminal. I then rotate the distributor body to a position where, if the engine were moved in its direction of rotation, the points would open. This is done visually by observing the points and the distributor cam. After this point has been found, roughly, it can be ascertained more precisely by connecting a continuity tester or magneto timing light across the points and moving the distributor body slightly to the exact point where the light goes out. This procedure is no substitute for timing a running engine with a strobe light, but it will always be accurate enough to get an engine started, so that its dynamic timing can be pursued.

Engine Startup

This is the moment that you have been waiting for, for weeks, months, or maybe even years. Will it run? How will it sound? Will all of your efforts pay off?

These are good questions, but there is another equally important consideration. Because the startup for a restored engine may be the most critical period in its normal life, you should ask, "Am I doing anything that will damage this engine?" Remember, when you first turn an engine over with fuel and spark and it begins to run, many of its working surfaces may not fit perfectly. Rings, for example, will not seat completely for several thousand miles. There is the potential in initial engine startup for doing damage that may equal tens of thousands of miles of normal driving wear, or worse.

The first rules of proper engine startup have to do with creating a proper environment. Two main elements are: to have at least one good fire extinguisher handy, and to provide very good ventilation. The great lawgiver, Murphy, makes a point of attending all engine startups—with a vengeance. He delights in things like dripping fuel line connections and leaking manifold gaskets. Be ready for him.

The most critical aspect of a startup is lubrication. It must be immediate and at adequate pressure. To insure this, a reliable oil pressure gauge should be plumbed into the oiling system, in addition to the dashboard gauge or warning light. Engine bearings, cam lobes, timing chains or gears, lifters, etc. should have been coated with assembly lubricant at the times of their installations. The whole oiling system should have been pressurized externally with an oil leak detector.

Finally, the engine should be free spun with its starter or crank until oil pressure registers on the gauges. Only then should you install the sparkplugs and attempt startup. The oil used for startup should be the same grade as the oil that you plan to use in service, or one grade thinner (say 5-30 when 10-30 will be used in regular service). In no case should startup oil be thicker than your intended running oil.

It is imperative that the initial startup of a restored engine be accomplished quickly, and not preceded by

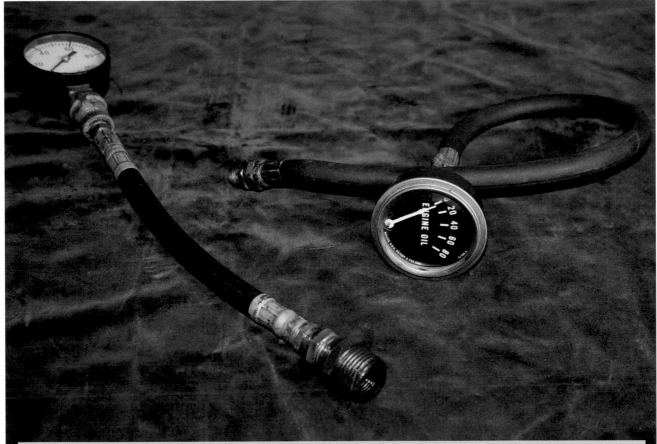

It's a good idea to use an accurate pressure gauge to double-check the oil pressure on an engine when it is first started after restoration. You can usually plumb such a gauge into an engine's oil galley through a drill passage. If this is not possible, it can be piped to pressure via a "T" fitting that is screwed into an engine's oil output tap for its pressure gauge or warning light.

misadventures, such as flooding the carburetor or running the battery down by "grinding" the starter excessively. Extended periods of attempted starting before an actual first start will tend to wash the cylinder walls clean of lubricant with unburned gasoline. Then, scraping damage from unseated rings can occur easily and quickly. To help insure a quick initial startup, use a very good battery in fully charged condition. This is no time to drag an old relic of a battery out of some dark corner of your garage, "just to get the thing started."

Another trick for getting a quick initial startup is to prime the fuel system in whatever way its construction allows. In the cases of air pressure fuel systems, this is done by holding their primer valves open. For engines with priming cups on their cylinder heads, fuel can be induced through these cups. Vacuum tank systems should be filled manually. On gravity systems, all that you can do is make sure that the car is right side up! For systems with fuel pumps, I always suck a little gas past the pump and out of the carburetor feed pipe. For all of these systems, it is a good idea to fill the carburetor float bowl by running a little gas into it from a gravity tank and a rubber hose. I always add half a smidgeon of top oil to the gas used to prime a carburetor for startup, just to get some ring lubrication into action immediately.

The practice of priming an engine by pouring a bit of

gasoline down its carburetor's throat is to be discouraged, unless you know what you are doing and have strong nerves. It is usually safer and more effective to prime a carburetor internally, or by pumping its accelerator pump, if it has one.

Once, many years ago, a friend and I were starting an engine after a lengthy rebuild. Since we were young, ignorant and enthusiastic, we broke every one of the above rules and defied common sense in several other ways. Our final insult to safety and common sense was to have my friend stand poised over the carburetor with a Campbell's Soup can full of gasoline, and pour it liberally down the carburetor as I turned the engine over.

Murphy was there. He must have been. First we succeeded in flooding the engine so that it wouldn't start. Then, when it finally did, it backfired violently and the remains of the gasoline in the can, which were by now burning explosively, left my friend's hand headed for the ceiling of the garage. On the way there the flames ignited a rack of tires. Somehow, he wasn't injured, and we beat the resulting conflagration out with coats and rags—no sissy fire extinguishers for us tough guys. If there hadn't been quite a few people around to help us with damage control, Standard Oil would have been out one three-bay service station. Unfortunately, one of those helpers was the station's manager/franchisee, and my friend and I were required that night to relocate our automotive activities abruptly and forever. We were also required to pay for the damage that we had done to the garage and its contents. From that point on, I began to take safety considerations very personally.

If an engine doesn't start within 10 or so rotations, take the sparkplugs out and check the spark quality, timing, and the availability of gas in the carburetor.

This last check can be made by either pumping the throttle and listening or watching for output from the accelerator pump jets, or, for carburetors without accelerator pumps, watching the carburetor jets for flow while the engine is turned over with its sparkplugs in place. Note: If you watch the jets that way, do so from a safe distance and with full-face protection in place if you have the ignition operative at this point.

Any engine with compression, sparks at roughly the right times and fuel should start and run passably well. It may not run smoothly at this point because too many things like its valve clearance settings, ignition timing and carburetor settings are still only approximate. There also is too much internal engine friction for really smooth operation. At this point, don't try to attend to all of these details at once.

It is critically important that when a fresh engine first fires, it be run at 1200 to 1500 rpm immediately and for about 20 or 30 minutes. This figure applies to engines of the 1930s and after. Earlier engines should be run at lower speeds, but at speeds sufficient to cause their crankshafts to throw oil up onto their cylinder walls. What is *not* recommended is to let a fresh engine sit and idle for half an hour or so at the time of its initial startup. This practice, which was once common in repair shops, may cause substantial damage to cylinder walls because there will not be enough oil thrown up on them by their crankshafts to meet the increased lubrication requirements of rings and cylinder walls that are not broken in. Local overheating and scoring can very easily result.

It is a good idea, during the first 20 or 30 minutes of engine startup, to vary engine speeds up and down a couple of hundred rpm to avoid the premature creation of cylinder top ridges. It is a very bad idea to run an engine after startup with a water hose in its radiator and its radiator drain cock open to "break it in cold." This practice was recommended years ago, along with its sister practice of removing the thermostat during break-in. Both are very bad ideas.

During this initial 20 or 30-minute run of a newly restored engine, it is necessary to keep a close eye on the temperature and oil pressure gauges, and to listen carefully to the engine for any abnormal noises. I always use a mechanic's stethoscope to listen to lifters, timing cases, and to engine bottom ends.

When a newly rebuilt engine has run for half an hour and is thoroughly warm, it is time to set its timing and idle mixture. This will require dropping it back to an idle for a few minutes, but try to keep it to that figure.

After these calibrations have been set, I generally take a car out for a drive for an hour or so. During this drive I keep the speed around 45 mph, or less, and drive very gently. I make a calculated effort to avoid continuous operation at any one speed for more than a few minutes at a time.

Now, and for the first thousand miles, or so, I load the engine gently by accelerating steadily. Then, I go on back-throttle by coasting. Long, downhill coasting is highly recommended. These last two practices tend to suck oil up into the rings, which assists in break-in. It's bad practice to use top oil in gasoline during break-in, or to use synthetic lubricants in crankcases at this time. The superior lubrication that both of these provide will retard the rings' break-in process.

The rest of a good engine break-in regimen mostly involves common sense. Avoid runs at constant speeds for a while, and drive gently. I always change the oil and filter at 1,000 miles, 2,500 miles, and every 2,000-2,500 miles thereafter. At 3,500 miles I begin adding top oil to gasoline, and do so from then on. This is a particularly good practice on side-valve engines, where valve stem and guide lubrication is, at best, marginal.

While all of this may sound finicky, I have had occasion to work on engines that were literally ruined during their break-in periods by driving off at high speed while things were still new and tight. It is astounding how much damage can be inflicted on an old engine if the proper conditions for its break-in period are not observed and respected.

Chapter 10

Old Car Ignition Systems

ALL AUTOMOTIVE IGNITION SYSTEMS WERE THE POINT-CONDENSER type from the 1920s through the 1970s. Some went to that format much earlier, particularly GM, which had introduced this system on its Cadillac Division's 1912 models, along with full electrical systems.

This type of engine ignition system was easy to understand, easy to troubleshoot, simple to repair and responsible for about 90 percent of all engine malfunctions. The substantial reduction in the ratio of mechanics to automobiles that has occurred in recent decades—from about 1:600 to roughly 1:1,400—is largely traceable to the almost universal adoption of more reliable electronic and distributorless electronic ignition systems on cars built after the 1970s. Still, there is a world of sentiment and lore about those old point-condenser ignitions.

Did I tell you about the time I went to a dance and a rival stole the rotor out of my distributor? I made one with a paper clip and some tape. It worked, too. Oh boy, my gal was impressed....

By now, the wonderfully simple point-condenser ignition system has become an oddity in the service sector. Invented by Charles F. "Boss" Kettering at General Motors' DELCO subsidiary in the second decade of the last century, the point-condenser ignition was a vast improvement on what preceded it. Now that it is history, it is mostly of interest to car restorers. That's us.

Ignition systems of the pre-1920 era were often complex and cumbersome. The Model T Ford's system, for example, included a heavy flywheel magneto, four trouble-prone buzzer coils, and a finicky cam-driven timer (distributor). After the Model T, sanity prevailed at Ford for a few years, and the Model A was blessed with a very conventional ignition system. However, that was later abandoned for the needlessly awkward and complicated system found in most Ford products for many years after 1932.

These systems allegedly derived from Henry Ford's aversion to costly distributor drive gears. He preferred to drive his ignition systems directly from their camshafts.

Old point/condenser ignition systems aren't that complex or difficult to understand, but almost any defect in them will cause problems. A visual inspection of the condition of this late-1940s Packard ignition system reveals new parts and good cosmetic condition. Instrumented testing will tell the whole story. Note the shabby primary lead from the distributor to the coil. It is the horizontal wire in the middle right of this photo. It's frayed and gapped insulation could be a problem.

Modern ignition systems are fully electronic and have no distributors, other than timing signal triggers on their camshaft or crankshaft gears.

Other early ignition systems, with generic names like "heat tube," or "make-and-break," or "low tension" and "high tension" magneto were developed and used widely because

This 1930s dual point distributor contains the same basic points and circuits used to the end of the point/condenser igniton era in the 1960s.

the marvelously simple idea of the point-condenser ignition hadn't been developed yet. As I said, the credit for this system—along with some inevitable controversy regarding that credit—goes to Charles Kettering and his Dayton Engineering Laboratories Company (DELCO) subsidiary of GM. With the introduction of this system before World War I, the older electric ignition formats tended to disappear from newly manufactured automobiles.

Most early ignition systems, after the primitive heat tube and make-and-break monstrosities, were magneto based. First, there were the low-tension systems that used individual "trembler" (buzzer) coils to build up the feeble voltage of the timed magneto output. These were followed by "dual-ignition" systems, hybrids that employed high-tension magnetos to supply spark quality voltage without further external buildup, but that also retained a single buzzer coil system for starting.

The dual-ignition employed in these hybrids was made necessary by two factors. Their basic unreliability made duplicate systems desirable for emergencies. Also, there is the fact that magnetos tend to be very inadequate to the low-RPM-high-output requirements of engine starting, while buzzer coil ignitions are fine for starting but have difficulty supplying adequate spark voltage at the shorter between-spark-intervals of the higher engine RPMs that are required to operate cars at road speeds. If you combine these two systems, and switch from battery to magneto after starting, you have something that works reasonably well for both starting and running an automobile. Better still, if one

system fails, you can usually fall back on the other, because the only important shared component of the two systems is their common magneto timer.

Magnetos are self-contained devices that generate, time and distribute either small or large voltage impulses. Those that produce low voltage (low tension) require external induction coil systems to intensify their voltages. The high-tension types have internal induction coils wound onto their armatures or elsewhere, and emit spark quality voltages without resort to external coils. There is nothing terribly mysterious about magneto ignition systems, but the parts in them tend to be highly specialized—magneto points usually don't look like distributor points—and their care, feeding, and adjustment tend to be specialized, as well.

For many years the reigning magneto repair specialist in this country was a man by the name of Louis Volmer. He lived in Longmeadow, Massachusetts until his death in the 1960s and was a disciple of *the* Robert Bosch. Louis was a "crackerjack" magneto mechanic, but he had a way of describing his work that made it, and magnetos themselves, seem incomprehensible. I remember standing in awe, as well as some legitimate fear of life and limb, as Louis—also called "Windinger" because he spoke with a thick German accent and could rewind magneto armatures—presided over three or four rotating, humming magnetos on the test benches in his cellar workshop, each producing from one to six quarter-inch sparks on gap plates.

It was the kind of atmosphere from which one expected Igor, Frankenstein, or at least Bela Lugosi to materialize from thin air at any instant. I liked Louis, but I remember feeling a sense of relief when it was time to leave his magneto enclave. Given the option, I preferred to deal with him by mail.

Years later, I discovered that magnetos were not quite as mysterious as Louis seemed to imply that they were, and that I could often repair them by replacing their bearings, cleaning and adjusting their points, or clarifying the wires and switches that control and feed them. The problems that can stop me on magnetos are: 1) lack of parts, 2) bad windings, or 3) lack of specifications for adjustment. In these cases, it is useful to seek out the aid of a magneto specialist. There are a few to be found in the old car service directories and in club publications. I hasten to add that magnetos are sufficiently unreliable as to make it a good idea to always have a spare on hand for any car that you own that uses one.

Conventional Ignition Systems: The Basic Theory

For the most part, restorers will find themselves working on conventional point-condenser ignition systems because these still represent the majority of all ignitions ever manufactured. There are some small variations here, as for example between single and dual-point systems, but the theory behind these spark producers is engagingly

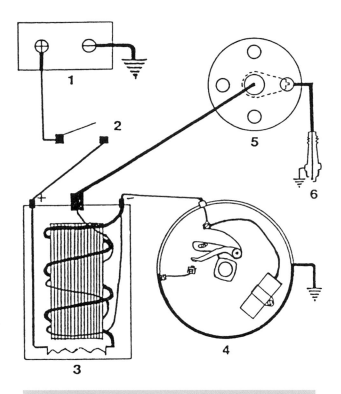

This schematic shows the components and wiring of a point/condenser ignition system. The low tension or primary current is supplied by the battery (1) and flows to an ignition switch (2). When the switch is closed current goes to and through the primary windings on the coil (3) and from there to the primary section of the distributor (4). The arrangement and connections for the points and condenser are shown inside the distributor. Note that the distributor case is grounded. This ultimately grounds the current flowing through the points when they are closed. High-tension voltage, induced into the secondary windings of the coil (3) goes from the coil tower to the center terminal in the distributor cap, which is part of the ignition secondary system (5). Shown in this system are the rotor and cap. From the center terminal of the distributor cap, the high-voltage secondary electricity travels via the rotor to the correct spark plug terminal on the cap and from there by high-tension wires to the individual spark plugs.

Distributors, like this one, contain both primary point and condenser systems and secondary distributor systems. The primary ignition components are mounted under the cap on the distributor plate, and the cap and rotor are the secondary system.

similar and simple, and their hardware is refreshingly uncomplicated. There are, however, some repair strategies and techniques that deserve our notice and attention.

What Kettering and his colleagues at DELCO "discovered," or at least popularized, was the fact that a set of timing points could control the flow of electricity through the primary windings of an induction coil, and thus the resulting secondary spark output of that coil, by making and breaking contact in sequence with each cylinder's need for an ignition spark. This timed low-voltage signal across the coil's primary windings would then induce a voltage rise in a set of secondary windings in the coil case.

The level of the voltage induced into these secondary windings depends on the initial voltage in the primary windings and on the ratio of primary to secondary winding turns. In practice, ignition voltages of 15,000 to 30,000 volts result from a starting point of 6 or 12 volts (Although virtually all point-condenser operated ignition coils run on

6 volts, bypass resistor systems may briefly feed them 12 volts during their engine starting cycles.).

One problem that Kettering and other early ignition researchers encountered was that it was difficult to get their timing points to break off current flow cleanly. In particular, points tended to arc during their opening (break) cycle. The solution to this was the inclusion of a condenser (properly called a capacitor in electrical terminology), wired in parallel to the points. A condenser is nothing more than two conductors of relatively enormous surface area confined in a small physical space. The condenser in an ignition system gives the charge available at the points a place to go when they open and break the circuit. This greatly reduces arcing across the points as they open to initiate the collapse of the primary magnetic field in the coil that induces spark voltages into the coil's secondary windings. This is called a "clean point signal."

That was it. Gone were cumbersome buzzer coils and finicky magnetos. A few simple components did the whole job: a point set, a condenser and a simple induction coil with some wire to connect these components and some insulators to isolate them, as necessary.

Of course, in practice, there were a few other items necessary to make this system work. There had to be a rotor and distributor cap to get the sparks to the correct cylinders and in the right sequence. There had to be wires to conduct spark voltage to the sparkplugs. Later, there had to be one or more systems for advancing and retarding the timing of the spark, with reference to changing engine RPM, or manifold vacuum, or both. Later still, there had to be a method of suppressing the emission of radio frequency signals that could interfere with aviation radar, car radios and home television sets.

Automotive Diagnostic Oscilloscopes

One of the best ways to understand a point-condenser ignition system is to look at a graphic representation of this system on an automotive oscilloscope. During the 1950s, oscilloscopic instrumentation ("ignition scopes") came into use in many repair facilities. These devices made it possible to visually represent the electric action going on in automotive ignition systems. Scopes accomplish this by plotting the voltage in an ignition system (either the low "primary" voltage, or the "secondary" spark voltage) against time, and representing these cycles on a CRT (Cathode Ray Tube). The use of ignition scopes, coupled with knowledge of basic ignition theory, makes it possible for a professional or talented amateur mechanic to tune old ignition systems to performance levels that will, in many cases, exceed what was originally intended in their design.

For example, before the era of scopes, it was accepted practice to run spark plug wires from distributors to sparkplugs with the wires laying parallel for long distances. Often, these wires were confined in conduits that held them in close proximity for 2 or more feet. When ignition scopes became available and ignition systems that were wired this way were displayed on them, it was immediately clear that something called "sympathetic sparking" or "ghost firing" was occurring.

This happens because as a spark plug wire conducts spark voltage to its plug, it builds up an induction field that exceeds the wire's insulation. When the spark voltage ceases, this field collapses. If it does so across an adjacent sparkplug wire for any considerable length, it can induce sparking level voltage into that wire. Given sufficient length exposure, this induced voltage can be high enough (3,000 to 5,000 volts) to fire the plug connected to the adjacent wire.

In practice, this can turn into a six-cylinder ignition system into one firing eight, or perhaps 10, sparks in its two-revolution cycle, instead of the expected six. Of course, if these sympathetic sparks occur at inopportune times—such as during the compression stroke in a cylinder—they can raise havoc with a car's performance and economy by prematurely firing cylinders.

Some cars built in the 1990s had parallel secondary wires, but these were subjected to careful, computer-assisted analysis and positioned so that any sympathetic firing that occurred happened only between wires and at times where and when it did not cause running problems.

Other ignition flaws, such as arcing in distributor caps or points that resonate (bounce) can be diagnosed easily with an ignition scope. In fact, oscilloscopic analysis of ignition systems is the only quick and reliable method of determining whether they are performing optimally. I suggest that any of the considerations in ignition work can and should be checked with a scope *before* an ignition system is "passed," and certainly before one is dismantled.

The basic scope pattern for a functioning ignition plots voltage against time. Time is represented on a left-to-right continuum and voltage increases are shown as upward vertical changes. Any scope pattern of secondary ignition voltage (high voltage as opposed to the voltage in an ignition point circuit) should have the following features—with some possible variation in the actual representation, depending on the vintage and brand of the scope that is used:

- **A SPARK VOLTAGE SPIKE**, indicating how much voltage is used to ionize the air gap between a spark plug's electrodes to initiate a spark.
- **A SPARK LINE**, indicating the lower voltage necessary to maintain the spark for its duration.
- **INTERMEDIATE OSCILLATIONS**, indicating coil/condenser action that dissipates energy after spark firing is completed.
- **POINT CLOSURE**, indicated by a downward line with several small, decreasing oscillations, representing a new buildup of a magnetic field in the coil.
- **A CONTINUING DWELL INTERVAL**, indicated by a straight, slightly upwardly inclined horizontal line, indicating energy flowing into the coil.
- **A POINT OPEN SIGNAL**, that breaks off the dwell line, rising at right angles to it and indicating point opening and the beginning of the next ignition cycle firing event. This signal not only indicates when points are opening but also how they are breaking.

The section of the scope pattern line from the point-close signal to the point-open signal for the next cycle represents the "dwell" section of the pattern and is also a representation of the dwell angle of the points. That is the number of rotational degrees in one firing cycle that the points remain closed. Reference to the accompanying diagram of a basic scope pattern will help you to understand the scope representation of a basic ignition sequence pattern.

Ignition Restoration

It is always a good idea to completely evaluate an ignition system before attempting to repair or restore it. Timing should be checked with a good timing light and, if possible, the system should be "scoped" for its secondary voltage pattern. These two test operations will provide a complete guide to the system's operation, but there are other ways to get the same information. If a scope is not available, it is a good idea to check voltages in the assembled system at every point that it is possible to do this.

Six-volt systems supply full voltage to coils. Their voltage readings should be taken on both sides of a coil and at the ignition points. These readings should then be compared

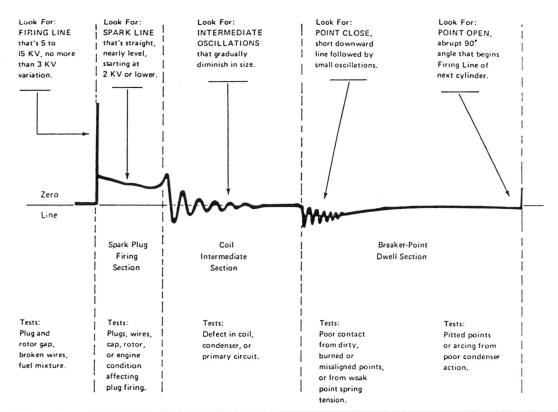

Look For:
FIRING LINE
that's 5 to
15 KV, no more
than 3 KV
variation.

Look For:
SPARK LINE
that's straight,
nearly level,
starting at
2 KV or lower.

Look For:
**INTERMEDIATE
OSCILLATIONS**
that gradually
diminish in size.

Look For:
POINT CLOSE,
short downward
line followed by
small oscillations.

Look For:
POINT OPEN,
abrupt 90°
angle that begins
Firing Line of
next cylinder.

Zero
Line

Spark Plug
Firing
Section

Coil
Intermediate
Section

Breaker-Point
Dwell Section

Tests:
Plug and
rotor gap,
broken wires,
fuel mixture.

Tests:
Plugs, wires,
cap, rotor,
or engine
condition
affecting
plug firing.

Tests:
Defect in coil,
condenser, or
primary circuit.

Tests:
Poor contact
from dirty,
burned or
misaligned points,
or from weak
point spring
tension.

Tests:
Pitted points
or arcing from
poor condenser
action.

The basic secondary point/condenser ignition system scope pattern and an oscilloscopic representation of the first part of one cylinder's secondary firing sequence are shown here. There may be minor differences in how different ignition scopes represent these patterns, but most will be pretty close to the one shown here. For the basic ignition pattern, additional formats, like all cylinders spread out, stacked cylinders (raster), and all cylinders superimposed, are also available on many scopes. Some scopes also include a display format for primary ignition electrical action.

with the specifications given by the system's manufacturer. In general, voltage drops of more than a few tenths of a volt are suspect. On 12-volt ignition systems, there will be either an external block resistor or primary resistance wire ("bypass resistor") that will increase resistance with rising engine compartment temperature, or (very rarely) a resistor in the coil case. In any 12-volt ignition system, the actual voltage delivered to the coil windings for normal operation will be about 6 to 8 volts, and this should be verified. Failure of the resistance circuit to limit coil voltage to 6 volts in a 12-volt system will result in overheating, followed by the rapid deterioration of the points or coil or both.

The most troublesome part in any conventional ignition system is probably its condenser(s). Happily, condensers are also about the cheapest parts in a point-condenser ignition system. Condensers fail unpredictably and are very susceptible to failures that are related to age, use, and exposure to moisture. They can be superficially checked for leakage with an ohmmeter, but any meaningful test must involve loading and unloading them, to check their capacitance and leakage under substantial loads.

Coils also can be inspected for insulation breakdown and discontinuity with an ohmmeter, as can plug wires and distributor caps and rotors. It is far better to do all of this checking with an ignition scope under actual running conditions, or to get someone who has one and knows how to use it to do this for you. This last point needs emphasis. Using older scopes requires knowledge of ignition theory

that goes beyond just knowing how to hook them up.

I am told by the sales people who sold some of the later, computerized instruments for point-condenser era automotive ignition diagnostics that they could be run by idiots—and often were. Just because someone has equipment for ignition analysis does not mean that he knows how to use it. Some of the worst work comes out of shops with the best equipment. Ignition scope analysis is no exception.

When you have gathered sufficient information regarding the operation of an ignition system, it is time to separate it into its component parts and to deal with them separately. Let's look at these component parts individually.

The Coil

Malfunctions in coils are best identified under operating conditions with a scope or with a console unit that can simulate high-demand operating conditions in a coil test. Coils rarely fail suddenly; they usually succumb to partial shorts and "opens" before completely giving up their ghosts. Coils can be statically tested with an ohmmeter. Specific values vary for different coils, but generally you will be looking for very little resistance across a coil's primary (low-voltage) terminals and several thousand ohms from the primaries to its secondary (high-voltage) terminals. An ohmmeter can also be used to spot the sites of arcing around a coil's high-tension tower.

That is what can be determined with an ohmmeter

A period test console, like this 1960s Sun 920 unit, is very useful for gathering a lot of information quickly and accurately. It has a terrific ignition scope and an accurate dwell/tachometer and vacuum gauge. It also has a meter the measures cylinder lead-down, an advance timing light, an ohmmeter and circuits for measuring coil leakage and capacitance. If you every see one of these in good condition at a reasonable price, you won't regret buying it.

about a coil's condition, but it is no substitute for scope analysis and, in the long run, will tell you little of value about a coil's long-range prospects for survival. Obvious physical defects in coils, such as burned high-tension connectors or cracks in towers, will need to be corrected by replacing them or by repairing these cracks. This is best accomplished by grooving them and filling in the groves with a high-dielectric epoxy. Replacement is the best bet, unless you are dealing with a very rare coil that is difficult or very expensive to replace.

Primary Wiring

It is essential that coils and distributors get the full voltage on which they were designed to operate. All switches, primary wiring, and resistance units in that wiring should be checked with a voltmeter. In practice, this means taking readings at the coil positive terminal (often designated as the "ign." or "bat." terminal), at the coil's distributor terminal (almost always marked with a minus sign on negative ground systems) and at the points. These readings vary from system to system, but must be in the correct range, as stated in an appropriate shop or general

Coil tower spark leakage is a fairly common problem in old coils. In the case of very rare coils, repairs with special high dialectric epoxy are sometimes possible.

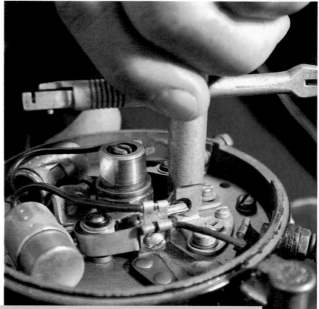

A point-adjusting tool is very handy for aligning ignition points when this is necessary. Although this tool has a fixture for bending the movable point, it is almost always a bad idea to bend anything but the fixed point.

repair manual. If there is no resistance wire or block resistor and the coil does not have internal resistance provisions, these readings should be near actual battery voltage, but that is a very unusual ignition design.

Ignition Points

The physical condition and adjustment of ignition points is critical. This includes: point alignment, rubbing block condition, contact surface condition, dwell adjustment, spring tension, bearing condition, ground quality, and synchronization in the cases of dual-point systems. Let's look at these individually. Remember, those little devils that we call "points" and their accomplices, condensers, account for the majority of the problems that stop old engines.

When points are installed, they should be aligned. This involves bending the fixed point—almost never the movable or "arm" point—with a special point adjusting tool until the point faces meet squarely and in the same plane. If this is not done, rapid point wear will result, and proper point gap adjustment will be lost quickly. Point cams and rubbing blocks should also be checked for wear and lubricated with a smear of point cam grease. Dabs of this special grease should be applied to the recesses in the fiber rubbing blocks that face towards the direction of cam rotation on the moving points. Be careful to use grease that is designed for this purpose, and to use it sparingly.

Some point systems have lubricating wheels or pads that contact distributor cams and deposit lubricant there. These may also need replacement or sparing lubrication.

The leaf spring tension that closes points is adjustable. If it is too light, the points will tend to bounce and give very poor performance. If this tension is too great, rapid rubbing block wear will result and possibly cause distributor cam damage. Almost all points operate at between 19 and 22 oz.

This push-pull spring tension gauge is used to check the closing pressure on the movable point in a point set. Low pressure can cause point bounce that may cause erratic spark. Pressure that is too high will cause rapid rubbing block wear and possibly damage to the distributor cam. This is an easy test to perform, and well worth the effort. Other tests on distributor testers and oscilloscopes can be used to reveal the same conditions.

of spring pressure, measured from the contact end of the movable point.

Properly functioning point contacts will be a dull gray in appearance. If point contact surfaces are burned and black, it probably indicates that grease or oil fumes have come up in from the lower distributor regions and been incinerated on them. If they are severely pitted, revealing a pit-and-crater configuration, it indicates that their ignition condenser is incorrectly sized. There is a cute little rule for correcting this defect, but since ignition condensers that

Setting points with a thickness ("feeler") gauge is the old way to do the job. Newer ways, like using an automotive oscilloscope or employing a dwell meter yield more accurate results. However, if points are new or filed flat, you can use a thickness gauge to set them. The gauge should give you just a faint feel of drag as you pull it through the points with the rubbing block on a high point of the cam. It takes some practice to get the technique of this measurement right. Note that these points are being adjusted with an eccentric screw and locking screws (visible in front of the feeler gauge). Other types of adjustment involve slots, gear wheels, threaded adjusters and many other configurations.

are identified in microfarads are necessary to apply this rule usefully, the rule—the "minus-minus-minus" rule—is more of a curiosity than anything useful these days.

If you can find automotive condensers that are labeled for capacitance, the pertinent rule states that if the negative point (first minus) is missing material (second minus) then the condenser in its circuit lacks capacitance (third minus). If you change any one of these conditions (for example, the positive point loses material or the negative point accumulates material) then the result is opposite and the condenser has too much capacitance. If you change any two conditions, the result is the same.

The movable ignition point pivots on a bushing that can be checked for looseness by applying finger pressure to its sides and checking its lateral motion. A drop of light oil on this bushing at the time of point set installation should preserve it for the duration of the electrical life of the points' contact surfaces.

Point adjustment is given either as an electrical fact, "degrees of dwell" (also called "cam angle") or as a physical approximation of that fact, called "gap." It is always better to set point dwell with an accurate dwell meter than to gap points with a thickness gauge, gap gauge, or dial indicator. The dwell angle for a given application is the number of degrees in one distributor cam segment that the points remain closed. Assuming a correct operating voltage, this is the main operative fact in coil saturation. Gapping points by physical means only approximates "dwell" and is an inferior way to adjust them. For pre-World War II engines, specifications for dwell settings are often not available, so point gap settings must be used. If this latter method is employed, then the best way to set points is with a dial indicator, but a thickness gauge will work if you have the right feel for it.

Unfortunately, cheap, uncalibratable dwell meters abounded in the land years ago and remain to haunt us. It is a sad reality of life that you cannot purchase a good, new dwell meter for $29.95, unless you intend to marry one of the offspring of its manufacturer. Digital dwell meters are very accurate and often very hard to use. They tend to scan rather than to average indicated dwell readings. This means that if there is any dwell variation, a digital gauge may produce a bewildering array of different readings. If these readings vary by more than two or three integers, it is probably an indication of significant dwell variation, but there can be other causes.

Such variations may indicate an electrical fault, or possibly point bounce, or distributor cam wear, or even a slightly bent distributor shaft.

Distributor cam wear is usually evident from physical inspection, but it is a good idea to check for it by comparing the specified gap measurement for a set of points with the actual gap that produces the correct dwell angle reading. If these two measurements differ substantially, you are probably dealing with a worn distributor cam.

When gap data is used to set ignition points, and a range of gap is given, points should be set to the widest opening in that range. This is because as point-rubbing blocks wear, their gap will decrease towards the lower figure in the range.

An often-overlooked aspect of point operation that is essential to good performance is the grounding of the fixed point. This is often provided for by a "pigtail" wire in the distributor that grounds the point subassembly or fixed point to the distributor plate. Sometimes a second pigtail wire carries the plate grounding to the distributor body. These pigtails should be checked for physical condition and with an ohmmeter to insure that there is virtually no

Dwell meters like these are the best way to adjust points if you have the specifications for a dwell setting. The meter on the left uses a pointer (D'Arsonval meter), and the one on the right employs a digital readout.

The condensers shown here are shaped differently from the originals, but they fit in the space provided and have the right microfarad rating for this application.

measurable resistance in a point ground circuit.

The positive point circuit should be checked to make sure that it has low resistance throughout and complete isolation of its components and wiring.

Some distributors employ dual-points in conjunction with either single or dual-coils. When dual-points are used, it is essential that they are synchronized. On some engines, this can be done with a timing light and the markings provided on the flywheel or vibration damper for this purpose. On other engines, a special point synchronizing degree wheel tool or a stroboscopic distributor tester must be used to properly synchronize dual-points.

Condensers

Early automotive condensers were oil-filled units. Modern condensers are not. The oil-filled type had many small plates separated by an oil-insulating medium. Later "electrolytic" condensers use two layers of foil separated by non-conducting goo and wrapped tightly in a jellyroll configuration in a can. In either case, failure occurs when one layer of the condenser penetrates its insulating medium and touches the next layer. Sometimes, this doesn't involve actual contact but a very low resistance barrier between two layers. Both of these situations produce a condition called "leakage," and result in some level of condenser malfunction. The other common reason for condenser failure is a discontinuity in the input wiring to a condenser.

Most ignition condensers are calibrated to about .26 Mfd. (of capacitance), but some use other values. Older condensers were not that standardized. There are also many different mounting configurations for condensers, so substitution has to be worked out carefully to account for electrical characteristics and physical fit. For example, good

old, flat Northeast condensers, used in some 1920s DELCO distributors, are almost impossible to find, and there is no modern automotive condenser that will fit inside those distributors in the narrow spaces that were provided for the original units. Usual restoration practice in this case has been to mount modern electrolytic or heavy-duty oil-filled condensers outside of these distributors.

There are inexpensive condenser testers on the market, but they can only test leakage at very small loads. They do not simulate actual operating conditions. A good condenser tester loads a condenser with substantial current and then unloads it. These testers are usually part of larger tune-up consoles, but some freestanding units are available.

The simplest way to test a condenser, if specialized equipment is not available, is to disconnect its isolated lead and temporarily wire in a condenser that is known to be in good condition. If this substitution improves performance, then the original condenser is defective. The substitute condenser that you use for this test does not have to be the correct unit in electrical characteristic or configuration. An incorrectly sized condenser will perform adequately for the short duration of this test. Over long periods, it would cause a progressive metal transfer from one ignition point to the other, so be sure to replace the test condenser with a correctly sized unit if your test indicates the need for a new condenser.

Other Parts of the Distributor Low Tension System

The initial timing check of an engine that I recommended you perform before any ignition system

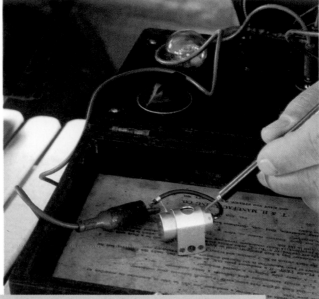

Old console ignition testers can be used to test condensers for leakage and capacity, but an old "discharge" testers will produce a much more rigorous and better test of condenser condition. The discharge tester uses either a neon bulb or actual discharge to test the capacity of a condenser. Discharging a condenser with a screwdriver after charging with the discharge tester is shown below.

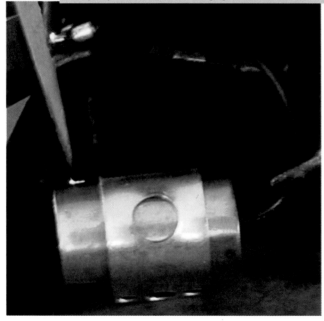

disassembly will disclose any timing variation. This variation appears as a floating or moving timing mark when a timing light is aimed at the timing pointer and marks. Such movement can occur due to looseness or "slop" anywhere in the distributor drive system. Worn camshaft timing gears or worn sprockets and/or stretched chains or belts can cause it, as can very worn distributor/camshaft drive gears. A more usual cause, however, is a worn distributor plate bearing and/or a malfunctioning centrifugal advance system.

Most post-World War II distributors have two timing control systems to match their spark generation to the load and speed realities of engine operation. Centrifugal advance systems go back to the 1920s, and before. They use governor-type weights to advance ignition timing with increasing engine speed. These devices vary in design but are usually housed right under distributor plates.

Generally, they employ two pivoting weights and two matched or differing restraining springs. As a distributor shaft spins, the weights move against their springs and advance a sleeve ("distributor stub shaft") that carries the distributor cam around the distributor main shaft. The cam is thus advanced, and this, in turn, advances the spark timing in relation to crankshaft rotation and engine piston movement. It does this by advancing both the cam that operates the ignition points and the rotor attached to it that distributes secondary voltage to the sparkplugs.

In most distributors that have this type of centrifugal advance system parts are marginally lubricated, and the weight pivot points and base plate bearing surfaces are prone to wear that introduces bind or slack into the system. Advance springs are even more vulnerable, as they can easily stretch and lose the ability to hold cams tightly in their unadvanced position.

The key to diagnosing all of this is that, if an engine is stopped, you can move its distributor rotor forward without it being immediately and crisply pulled back to the farthest point at which it will rest, there is wear or looseness somewhere in its drive system, and probably in the advance system. Before you make this check, be sure that the distributor rotor sits tightly on its shaft, as looseness there will give false indications of drive sloppiness or slack.

The repair of distributor advance systems requires the installation of new parts or, if they are not available, bushing and machining the old ones. While timing variation of a degree or two is marginally tolerable in many engines, if the flutter is more than that, its cause(s) must be found and the underlying faults repaired. Be sure to lubricate the moving parts in centrifugal advance systems when distributors are apart for service. Light machine oil, applied sparingly, is the best lubricant. This should also be an item of routine maintenance. It is accomplished by oiling the felt wicks at

Making a final check of all resistances in a distributor's primary ignition section—isolation and continuity—is always a good idea before you assemble it. A good digital ohmmeter, above, will also let you watch a condenser "load up" on an ohms test.

the tops of distributor stub shafts, (under their rotors) or oiling advance mechanisms through holes provided in the plates of many distributors for that purpose.

Most post-World War II automobiles have vacuum advance units in addition to their centrifugal advance systems. These units are round, flat, cadmium-plated devices that are mounted on the sides of distributors and that act to match spark advance to engine load, read from manifold vacuum. They operate on engine vacuum that is piped to them from carburetors. This vacuum is applied against spring-loaded diaphragms to pull main distributor plates in the direction that advances timing. The pulling is done by small arms that extend from the centers of the diaphragms into the distributor cases and attach to the plates that carry points and condensers. There are small bushings where the arms join the plates.

There are three main considerations in working with vacuum advance units: the integrity of their diaphragms, the condition of their bearings (that allow distributor plates to rotate) and, in some cases, the calibration of the springs that restrain diaphragm movement. There are also some oddball variations on this system, such as one used

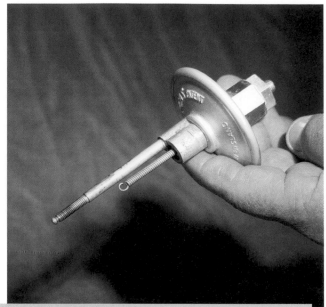

Most centrifugal advance systems and vacuum advance units look something like the ones shown here. The weights pivot out as distributor shaft speed increases and drive the distributor stubshaft to advance the point timing cam and distributor rotor. This advances the ignition spark. All parts in a centrifugal advance system have to be snug but free to work well. This means tight bushings and unstretched springs. Always keep centrifugal advance systems well lubricated when you install them, and maintain this lubrication in service. Note the two different springs in this unit are for low speed and higher speed control. The vacuum unit shown here pulls the distributor plate around on bearings to advance ignition timing as manifold vacuum increases. Again, the bearing parts of this system must be free and the vacuum diaphragm must not leak.

These old point synchronizing tools are surprisingly accurate, and will synchronize points to within about a half degree. They are particularly useful when distributors that cannot be mounted on a distributor tester have to be synchronized.

by Chevrolet that allowed the vacuum advance system to rotate the whole distributor, not just its internal plate. Such variations are not often encountered and are easy to figure out when they are.

The simplest way to check the operation of a vacuum advance system in a gross sense is to attach a small hose to the vacuum advance unit's port and to pull vacuum on it. This should produce visible movement of the distributor plate. If it does not, it is likely that the plate bearing is frozen or the advance unit diaphragm is ruptured. If the diaphragm is ruptured, you will be able to suck air through it. If it is not, no air will pass by it and your problem is excessive resistance to movement in the distributor plate bearing.

These bearings fail by either freezing or wearing out. If a plate bearing is frozen, cleaning and lubrication will often correct the problem, since congealed or dirty lubricant is usually its cause. If it is worn out, it will tend to become very sloppy and can be moved in several directions with finger pressure. Such a condition will provide erratic advance, and possibly dwell variation.

The last distributors manufactured before fully electronic ignitions arrived tended to have plate bearings that used nylon bushings instead of the older practice of using ball bearings. While ball bearings sometimes froze, they rarely wore to the point of sloppiness. The late-type plastic bearings frequently wore loose.

If the problem with a vacuum advance system is in the rubber diaphragm in its advance unit, the whole unit probably will have to be replaced. These diaphragms are made from neoprene or natural rubber and succumb to a combination of age, heat, fumes, and cyclical failure. They can be a real toothache of a problem because some of the more obscure ones have become awfully difficult to find. None are constructed in ways that allow easy rebuilding. Often, new old stock (NOS) units will fail shortly after installation because the diaphragm material has dried up and become so brittle that the normal flexing imposed by service ruptures it.

I have accumulated many hours trying to find these units for cars that I have worked on. The only hope that I can offer is that my efforts have always been rewarded with success. Sometimes, as in the case of locating some early Lucas vacuum advance units, success has been painfully expensive. In recent years, a service has been advertised for opening old advance units and replacing their diaphragms with new material. I have not tried this service, but it sounds like a workable idea.

Some vacuum advance units can be calibrated. This is usually accomplished by removing a threaded plug at their vacuum inlet ports and adding or subtracting small calibration spacers to increase or decrease the tension on their calibration springs. On most advance units that have this feature, adjustments can be accomplished with a vacuum gauge and metered vacuum on a distributor testing machine. In some cases, vacuum advance units can be calibrated with an advance timing light and metered vacuum. The former method is preferable.

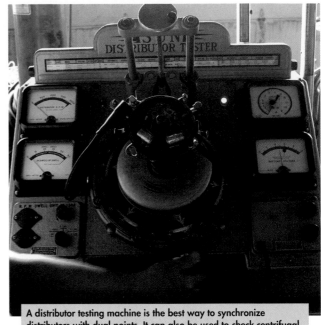

A distributor testing machine is the best way to synchronize distributors with dual points. It can also be used to check centrifugal and vacuum advance systems with great accuracy.

A few cars, notably Ford products built after World War II, use "vacuum brake" devices that operate on such small increments of vacuum (literally tenths of an inch of mercury) that manometers (viscous barometer devices) must be used to calibrate them.

If you do not have the knowledge or equipment to calibrate vacuum units, it is best to leave their restoration to those who do. If you are dealing with the completely sealed, non-calibratable type, simple replacement of a defective unit is the only way to get it right.

Another possible cause of timing flutter is a damaged distributor main shaft, or loose main shaft bearings, or both. Main shaft warping is best checked on a scope with a superimposed pattern, or on a distributor tester. Distributor bearings or bushings can be inspected visually and by feel. Bad distributor bushings can cause very serious problems beyond simple ignition malfunction. At the extreme, they can cause a distributor shaft to seize and strip its camshaft drive gears. It is essential that these bearings be inspected, lubricated, and adjusted for endplay. Loose, sloppy or rough running bearings or bushings must be replaced.

The High-Tension System

All electrical ignition systems for engines of more than one cylinder have some method of distributing and conveying spark quality voltage from a coil or coils to sparkplugs. Commonly, this will involve wires from the coil(s) to a distributing device. This device will include some form of rotor(s) and cap(s) and will have insulated leads to the sparkplugs. While the placement and configuration of high-tension systems varies greatly, the considerations in inspecting and repairing them are pretty standard.

High-tension ignition wire is either cored with conductive metals, like copper, tinned copper or stainless

Spark leakage and arcing can occur on surfaces like coil towers and distributor caps. Feeling around this cap with ohmmeter probes revealed electrical continuity where there shouldn't have been any. A dye penetrant inspection of another, similar cap shows a reason for the conductivity—the plug wire towers are all cracked, and the cracks have filled with carbon. This makes perfect tracks for electrical leakage.

steel, or it is cored with a high-resistance conductive material like carbon-impregnated glass fibers. Non-metallic conductors are used to promote radio frequency suppression and for reasons of manufacturing economy. They are found mostly in cars of the 1960s and after. This type of wire should not be used in older cars because the other parts of their secondary ignition systems are not designed for the higher resistances inherent in it. Some carbon/fiberglass ignition wire has a monel metal shield for radio frequency suppression. Although it is often mistaken for it, this is not metal conductor wire, since it is grounded and is not used to convey spark voltage. This type of shielded wire should not be used in older systems. Nor should modern 7mm wires be substituted for original 9mm secondary conductors.

All old ignition secondary wire has thick insulation because it carries very high voltage that tends to leak, particularly as its insulation ages and deteriorates. This deterioration is greatly accelerated by the fact that as high-tension wires conduct spark voltages, they also produce a "corona" that promotes the formation of ozone. Ozone causes the rapid deterioration of rubber and synthetic rubber insulation. The best high-tension ignition wires are either insulated with silicone rubber, or with natural rubber sheathed in a synthetic shield, like Hyphalon˙. Both types resist the attack of ozone. In recent decades, silicone rubber shielding has replaced other secondary wire insulation

materials in modern cars that do not employ coil-over-plug ignition systems.

For early cars that used high-tension wire with textile (cambric) insulation, modern spark plug wire with a rubber/synthetic layer of insulation under an authentic appearing textile sheath is available. The sheath used to cover this wire usually includes a mildew retardant. This greatly prolongs its life. High-tension wiring must have tight, clean terminal connections. My preference is for soldering these connections, when possible.

Distributor caps and rotors are prone to the same kinds of attack and deterioration that afflict secondary wires, and also to the formation of carbon tracks that promote arcing. These parts should be cleaned with a good electrical solvent and inspected for cracks and pitting of their conductors and insulators. This is particularly important for rotor and cap brushes (contactors) that rub against metal or carbon contacts or tracks. Wiping contact or track designs were common in older single distributor cap/rotor systems designed for dual-ignition. Pits in distributor caps and rotors can be filed and filled with a high-dielectric epoxy. These parts can also be coated with a dielectric lacquer or enamel to fill surface porosities.

Sparkplugs

Automotive sparkplugs vary greatly in type and construction. Generally, they must be correct for their applications, clean, undamaged, and correctly gapped. There is also the issue of quality.

Over the years, a lot of junk plugs have been sold. Swap meets abound with such "off-brands" as the infamous

Clean all secondary ignition contacts with an electrical solvent and a wire brush. The round brush shown in above right photo is used to clean out the distributor cap and coil high-tension terminals.

"Leonard Air Cooled Plug" and the like (Did you ever see a sparkplug that wasn't air cooled?). Some of these, like the Leonard, look great, but are almost useless when you attempt to use them as sparkplugs. Older plugs tended to be rebuildable. They employed packings that could dry out and shrink, creating combustion leaks around their porcelain insulators. Modern plugs are not rebuildable, but are much more durable than the older, rebuildable plugs.

The porcelain insulators on sparkplugs are also very susceptible to cracking. This kind of damage will destroy engine performance. Modern resistor plugs, platinum plugs and air gap plugs are unnecessary in older applications and represent overkill. Stick with standard brand sparkplugs in recommended types and heat ranges.

The gap adjustment for sparkplugs is critical. Engine manufacturers' recommendations should be adhered to rigorously. It is very easy to accidentally break the porcelain insulator in a sparkplug by prying against the center electrode when you gap a plug. Avoid this common mistake.

Final Thoughts on Ignition Restoration

I have stressed the importance of scope testing in this discussion of ignition system restoration because this was the best practice in the repair sector in the last years of OEM point-condenser ignition systems. It remains the best approach to analyzing these ignition systems for restoration purposes. While it is theoretically possible to gather the same information from other tests, this alternative is time consuming and often difficult to perform. A good ignition scope test will not only test older point-condenser ignition systems but will also work with many more modern capacitive discharge and solid-state systems. Very

modern, fully computerized ignition systems require highly specialized scopes and scan tools.

Since a properly functioning ignition system is absolutely essential to good automobile performance, restoration efforts directed toward ignition systems definitely should include a final scope test. This will locate most potential minor problems before they become serious enough to detract from engine performance. If you don't want to invest the time and money involved in purchasing and learning to operate this equipment, seek out the aid of someone who has the necessary equipment and skills.

Chapter 11

Starting and Generating Systems

EXCEPT FOR CARBURETION, STARTING AND GENERATING systems probably encompass more complex variation and detail than any other systems in old automobiles. Like carburetion, theoretical understanding of these electrical system components requires mastery of a substantial body of scientific and engineering material, with some quaint ideas and practices thrown in. It's the sort of stuff that can make your head hurt if you aren't accustomed to it.

While in some cases starting and generating systems can pose very difficult problems for restorers, a great deal of testing and repair can be accomplished without a sophisticated understanding of the theoretical and engineering considerations underlying electrical system operation and components. This is definitely a restoration area where you can clean things up, lubricate them and do some basic testing. Then, if things work, you can declare victory and go on to another challenge without troubling yourself unduly about how or why the item that you just restored functions.

Some years ago I came into possession of a more-or-less complete set of generator and starter test and repair tools—it resulted from a complex trade involving a Hillman, a Zenith Trans-Oceanic radio, and the repair of an ignition switch. For that I got an armature lathe, a growler, testing meters, a commutator undercutting and regrooving tool, special pullers, lots of assorted parts, etc. There were many items for which I never did quite figure out uses.

The whole mess completely occupied the cargo area of my van. Well, in the year after this great acquisition, I had occasion to use my newly acquired capability two or three times, and that was only after I offered starter and

This old generator is pretty straightforward and easy to repair, if you have the parts, knowledge and equipment necessary to do this kind of work.

generator service at cut-rate prices to everyone I knew. Gradually, the paraphernalia was moved into an unheated storage area to join such other nonessential items as my brake arc grinder, my 400,000 BTU gas-fired tempering furnace and an absolutely hideous vase owned by my late maternal grandmother and unmercifully converted into a lamp. Believe me, only a grandmother could love that vase.

On two or three occasions I did use some of that

This venerable armature lathe and commutator grooving device was one of the pieces of equipment that I acquired in my "great" electrical service tools trade.

Careful note taking, sketching, etc. are important when you rebuild any unfamiliar generator (shown here) or starter.

electrical repair stuff. Each involved the kind of situation where three manuals were open at once and confusion abounded. Eventually, I determined that I could, with great effort, successfully test and repair starters, generators, and regulators. Having met that challenge, I had very little continuing desire to engage in my newfound proficiency. For one thing, there is so much variation in these units that to understand each one, and then to apply the correct tests and repair procedures to it is almost impossible on an occasional basis.

It wouldn't be so bad to work on just shunt wound units, or just interpole devices, or only bucking coil generators, etc. But when you have to sort between a seemingly endless variety of equipment types, specifications, and test and repair procedures, you quickly conclude that any serious work on generating systems, and to a lesser degree on starting systems, should be left to those who do this work all day, every day. A second, more practical problem with homespun electrical component repair is that proper repair requires specialized parts, like brushes, springs, and insulators. These parts, in most cases, have been obsolete for years and they now reside mostly in the parts shelving, cabinets, and drawers of a few remaining large automotive electrical repair specialty shops or have to be fabricated from other parts that reside in these places.

Basic Starter and Generator Theory

The general theory that governs the operation of starting motors and generators has to do with the movement of electrons through conductors and with the number of electrons (amps), the pressure at which they are moved (volts), and the tendency of the conductor that they move in

The first step in generator rebuilding is to remove the cover band and see what lies underneath.

to resist their movement (resistance measured in ohms). It also has to do with the phenomenon that occurs when there is movement of a conductor relative to a magnetic field, or vice versa. Such movement induces electron flow in the second conductor when the lines of force of the magnetic field generated by the first conductor are cut by the second conductor.

In the cases of generators, the electron flows that are induced into their conductor(s) ultimately become generated current. In the cases of starters, the magnetic fields are produced in arrangements that allow the attraction and repulsion characteristics of these magnets to force mechanical rotation of shafts carrying one of the magnet

In this case there was massive corrosion of the aluminum brush holder/end assembly. A little wire brushing cleaned it up.

clusters (armatures).

If you understood all of that before you read it here, I hope that it is still be perfectly clear to you. If you didn't, I doubt if what I wrote in the preceding paragraph put you in the picture. Sorry. The problem is that the theory of these things is somewhat complex and has the layered characteristics of an onion. I just described the nugget of the thing. It gets greatly more complex after that.

That nugget ordains that the use of wound armatures that can be rotated on bearings through the fields of other stationary magnets makes it possible to convert mechanical energy into electrical energy (a generator) or the other way around (a starter motor). It is the arrangement of the magnetic and conducting elements and the nature of the connections between them that creates most of the variations in starters and generators.

Common Physical Elements in Conventional Generators and Starters

Outwardly, starters and conventional generators (as opposed to alternators) are remarkably similar in appearance. Of course, starters end in some sort of drive arrangement and generators end in a pulley, sprocket, or gear drive. In both units, the field coils, armatures, brushes, and bearings are very similar, as are the outer casings.

This similarity is so great that over the years, several manufacturers have combined both units into a "starter-generator" device (a.k.a. "starter-genny") that uses one rotating element and case, instead of two. The object of producing these combined units has been to save weight, space and expense. In these regards they have not been notably successful, and reliability has often suffered. Modern integrated starter-generator units used for economy on vehicles called "gasoline-electric hybrids," such as several Honda models, are considerably different from and more sophisticated than the old starter-gennys and are very reliable. There is nothing wrong with this concept.

There is also similarity in the things that can go wrong with the armatures and field coils of starters and generators. Perhaps the most vulnerable parts in both units are the bearings. These are particularly vulnerable in starters, due to the great forces imposed on these high torque motors.

It should be remembered that a large part of the genius in the invention of the electric "self-starter" had nothing to do with the practical considerations of how to wind a sufficiently high-torque motor to start a gasoline engine, or how to couple and uncouple it from that engine. While these questions were always crucial, a more important aspect of the development of the self-starter involved overcoming the then prevalent concepts of the acceptable performance limits and standards for the integrity of electric motors.

What Charles Kettering and the other inventors of self-starting devices came to understand was that to produce an acceptably light and small starting motor, they had to disregard the known standards for electric motor cooling and bearing support. They came to understand that the motors that they were developing for starting gasoline automobile engines had to run for only a matter of seconds, and did not have to have the integrity and resulting mass of motors that were used in continuous service.

Had they followed the normal rules of utility motor construction, they would have ended up with starting motors half as heavy as the engines they were designed to start. That would have made electric starting impractical.

It is interesting to note that Kettering's development of the electric self-starter was influenced by his earlier work for the National Cash Register Company, where he had developed the electric cash register. This invention depended on small, high-torque motors to open cash register drawers—essentially an intermittent-duty motor application. While this conceptual breakthrough, the light, intermittent-duty motor, gave us usable electric starting systems for automobiles, it also gave us motors that were much overstressed and very prone to many types of failure, particularly bearing failure.

The bearings in generators, and particularly those in starters, must receive meticulous attention in restoration. Whether ball or sleeve bearings are encountered, they must be checked for wear, stress and corrosion damage and replaced if defects are found. If they are sound, these bearings should be cleaned, properly lubricated with an appropriate grease and reinstalled. Their installations must be such that they are retained securely and cannot spin out. Where bearings have spun out of their retainers, it may be necessary to weld and remachine their retainer areas. A Loctite product, "Quick Metal," can be used to fill the gaps from spun-out bearings, up to about 0.005 inch, and will retain new bearings. I've used this product for about two decades and my initial skepticism about it has turned into

You sometimes have to improvise in this work. The first attempt to remove this generator's water pump drive coupling with a battery terminal puller ended in failure, and a heavier-duty harmonic balancer puller was "pressed" into service. That worked.

complete approval. It works. Other epoxy and anaerobic fillers are available from other manufacturers for similar purposes.

Many of the older ball bearing starter motors and generators, and all of the sleeve bearing applications, have provisions for periodic lubrication. This should be performed according to the recommended schedule with non-detergent oil of about SAE 20 viscosity. Many electric motor shops sell special motor bearing oils for ball and sleeve bearings. These are particularly appropriate for these applications because they do not leave the residues that some engine oils tend to. Never over-oil a starter or generator. That will cause as much trouble as failing to lubricate it.

Although post-assembly maintenance lubrication of starter motors and generators will have to be performed with oil, they should be lubricated initially, at the time of assembly, with light grease designed for ball bearings or Oilite-type bushings. It is important to remember that bearing deterioration in starters and generators will inevitably (and sometimes very quickly) lead to the destruction of other parts, like armatures or field coils. Bearing problems are usually easily discovered by checking for excessive play in armature bearings, or by listening

for unusual howls, moans, or screeches when generators and starters are working. Any bearing problems that are observed should be attended to immediately, before more serious damage occurs. Certainly, when a car is undergoing restoration, its starter and generator should be disassembled

On old electrical equipment, you often run into all kinds of odd fittings, threads, and fastener configurations. The shiny cover plate was easy to remove but the threaded bearing retainer looked like it would be trouble. First it was softened with some penetrating oil. Then the outer bearing retainer was removed, and the spacers and lubricating felt washer under the outside retaining plate were noted for position. Then it was back to trying to remove the inner bearing retainer by gently hitting it with a punch. It soon became clear that this approach would not work without damaging this part, so a wrench tool was made from an old piece of pipe to remove it. That approach worked.

When you disassemble starters and generators, it is important to mark their bodies and end plates so that you can get them back together the same way they came apart.

The aluminum brush holder section of this generator had become seized to its iron body. The first attempt to separate these two parts was with a small hammer and a block of wood. Gentle strikes were used around the circumference of the brush holder/end plate assembly to avoid cocking it and breaking it. This approach was not successful.

and maintained.

A second element common to starters and conventional generators is a brush/commutator setup. Most operational problems that don't have their origins in bearings are found here. In addition to the friction of the brushes against commutator segments, and wear of both, there is always an element of arcing and the possibility of abrasive contamination. For both starters and generators, the brushes are used to switch the rotating magnetic or conducting elements in and out of the working circuits. In starters, this is done to configure the attracting and repelling forces of the stationary and rotating magnets to rotate the armature with the greatest force. In the case of generators, the brushes switch the armature conductors to provide direct current.

The brushes, themselves, can be made out of many materials, but a high percentage of carbon is common to almost all of them. To work properly, brushes have to be positioned so that they can move in and out to bear against their commutators without excessive sideways deflection. This in-and-out movement accommodates irregularities in the commutator contact segments and may occur in sleeve-like holders, or whole brush holders may pivot to provide brush contact with commutators. In either case, spring arrangements will provide the necessary pressure.

Wear or deformation of brush holders, pivot points, or tensioning springs eventually will lead to a lack of pressure and/or misalignment. This will cause arcing and overall malfunction. Brushes should be replaced if they have worn

to anywhere near half of their original length. Brush holders that are deformed in any way should also be replaced. Brush springs should be checked with a spring pressure gauge or by dimension, and must be replaced if they deviate from manufacturers' specifications.

Before they are reconditioned, armatures should be cleaned in a perchloride vapor bath or with special electrical solvents that are designed for this job. All carbon, oil, and grease should be removed from them and the condition of their insulators and insulating varnish should be checked and repaired as necessary.

Worn, arced out or dirty commutators will tend to deteriorate quickly and should be turned and regrooved if they are even slightly damaged or dirty. This will prevent major arcing damage from occurring. Turning commutators to dress their contacting surfaces can be accomplished on a conventional lathe or on a special commutator cutting device. In either case, remove as little material as is necessary to clean a commutator, and don't undercut its inboard shoulder where bars connect commutator segments to armature coils. These connections should be electrically tested, and physically inspected, as well. Particularly note any solder that has been thrown off this shoulder area because it indicates local armature overheating and likely problems with the bar connectors.

The insulating material (mica on older generators, plastic on newer ones) that separates the segments of generator commutators must be undercut by about 1/32 inch from the copper segment surfaces. While this is not absolutely necessary on more recent starters, undercutting is almost always desirable for older starters and is a must for generators. Sometimes, people attempt to perform this operation crudely, with a hacksaw blade or other "blunt

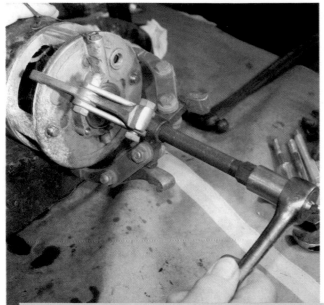

A threaded puller was then tried, and it did separate these two assemblies. A brass hammer was used to apply shock to the brush holder/end plate assembly as pressure was applied with the puller. A small air impact wrench would also have provided shock for this purpose. Success at last. Patience has its rewards.

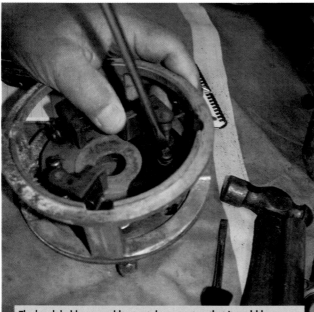

The brush holder assembly was taken apart so that it could be cleaned properly. The fiber parts in these assemblies will not survive the chemical and abrasive assaults that are needed to clean the metal parts.

FINGER RAISES BRUSH WHEN PAPER IS SLID FORWARD
FINGER HOLDS BRUSH DOWN WHEN PAPER IS PULLED OUT

SANDED SIDE OF SANDPAPER

USE STRIP OF SAND PAPER ¾ X 8 IN

PULL PAPER AROUND COMMUTATOR SO THAT EDGE OF BRUSH IS NOT SANDED OFF

When you install new brushes and/or turn a starter or generator commutator down to true or dress it, always use a strip of sandpaper to conform the brushes and commutator.

instrument." It is always best that commutator undercutting be done with a jigged tool so that the straightness, width, depth, and uniformity of the undercuts can be accurately controlled. All of this suggests that this is work for an automotive electric specialist or for a motor shop with the proper equipment.

After a commutator has been cleaned up and regrooved, it is good practice to conform new brushes to it. If this is not done, there will be very little contact between the flat brush ends and the rounded commutator segments until considerable wear has occurred.

This lack of contact will promote arcing and can quickly

ruin the work that you have just done. The usual way to conform brushes to a commutator is to wrap a strip of triple-aught (000) silica or flint sandpaper around the commutator and run it against the brushes for several rotations. Then, use an air gun to blow out all abrasive residues and other sanding debris. Never use emery cloth or aluminum oxide abrasive paper for this purpose, as the aluminum oxide abrasive that is used in these products will embed in the brushes and cause arcing and rapid deterioration.

While it is tempting to lubricate moving brush holders or brush slides, avoid this temptation. Oil and grease are the deadly enemies of commutators, brushes, and insulated

The little item in my associate's right hand in this picture is part of the third brush adjusting assembly. You will have to know where and how all the little parts go to reassemble a unit like this one. The best idea is to take lots of photos and notes and to draw diagrams.

In generator and starter work, you will often have to use a small screw or arbor press to remove bearings from shafts. In this photograph, the armature is below the bearing holder platform on a press, and screw pressure is being applied to the drive end of the armature to remove the bearing from it.

coils, and must be used sparingly in generator and starter environments, specifically, only on bearings. "Sparingly" also applies to lubricating the end bearings and front bearings of generators and starters. Sliding brushes usually do not bind in their holders because there is enough graphite in their composition to lubricate them. Spring pivot-type brush holders are designed not to need lubrication at their pivot points.

Reassembling generators and starters is pretty straightforward. It is essential that end plates be reassembled in the same orientations to motor or generator bodies in which they were at the time of their disassembly. This should be easy, because you should have marked or diagrammed these components before you took them apart. The major assembly problem that you are likely to encounter is keeping brushes away from commutators, so that they can be slipped past them to seat the armature shafts in their end bearings. I have often wished that I could sprout a third shoulder, elbow, arm and hand for this purpose. These extra items might come in handy at cocktail parties, as well.

On many starters and generators, getting the commutator past the brushes is most easily accomplished by keeping the brush springs off the brush holders while you slip the end of the armature into its end plate bearing. Then, you can push the springs into place through the outer ends of their holders after end bearings are seated. You can usually wire pivoting brush holders out of the way, or disable their springs, to facilitate armature installation. In other cases special sleeve or other holding tools may aid in assembly.

Electrical Tests and Procedures—Starters

The simplest on-car test of any starting system involves ascertaining that the battery is producing and delivering ample starting current and voltage, that the switching and engaging devices (solenoids and Bendix or other starter drives) are working properly and that the engine to be started can, in fact, be turned over without extraordinary effort.

There are lots of little parts in an old generator, so it pays to work on these items in an orderly way.

Any time you have an armature out of a generator or starter, you should turn the commutator down just enough to get a true, smooth surface. Remove as little material as is needed to do this job. Then, smooth the commutator with a backed-strip of sandpaper after it has been trued with a lathe tool, and wash and blow away all abrasive residues.

The terminals and conductors that carry battery energy to starter motors have to be in clean and sound condition. They should be checked with an inductive amperage draw meter to prove that they are delivering sufficient current to a starter motor. If all of these conditions prevail, and a starter still will not turn an engine over at a reasonable rate

of speed, it is in need of restoration or repair.

In these cases, starters should be removed and disassembled, and their parts should be cleaned with an electrical solvent. Armatures, field coils, and brushes should be wiped with very light applications of a solvent designed specifically for this purpose. They should never be *immersed*

Commutator continuity and shorting can be easily checked with a test light.

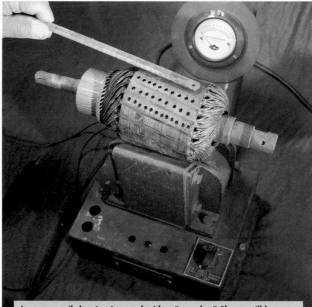

Armature coil shorting is tested with a "growler." Shorts will be indicated by the metal strip—a hacksaw blade in this case— vibrating when a shorted armature coil is encountered and tested.

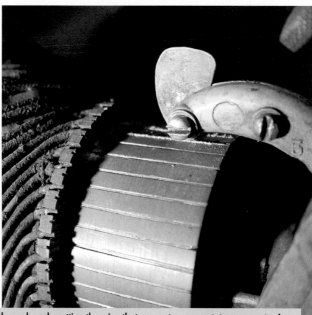

A portable commutator grooving tool, like the one pictured here, will do credible work undercutting the mica that separates commutator segments. A motorized cutting tool does an even better job.

in any solvent as this will damage them. In no case should a petroleum-based solvent be used on any insulated internal part of a starter or generator.

Field coils should be visually inspected and tested with an ohmmeter for isolation from starter frames. They should also be tested for continuity and resistance. This is done by taking ohmmeter readings from the solenoid input terminals to the field brushes. This resistance should be negligible.

Starter motor armatures should be checked for two faults: shorts and grounding. Shorts are checked with specialized pieces of equipment called "growlers." If you don't have one, take your armature to an automotive

electric or electric motor repair shop and they can run this test in about a minute. Armature grounding can be tested by touching one lead of an ohmmeter to any part of an armature's laminated steel core and the other lead to its commutator segments, one-by-one. There must be no continuity here.

Finally, check commutator segments for continuity with the connector bars that go from them into the armature coils. An ohmmeter should show good continuity here. Be sure to apply light finger pressure to the connector bars while running this test, to detect any discontinuities resulting from looseness. If an armature is shorted or grounded, it will have to be repaired or replaced. Commutator-to-connector

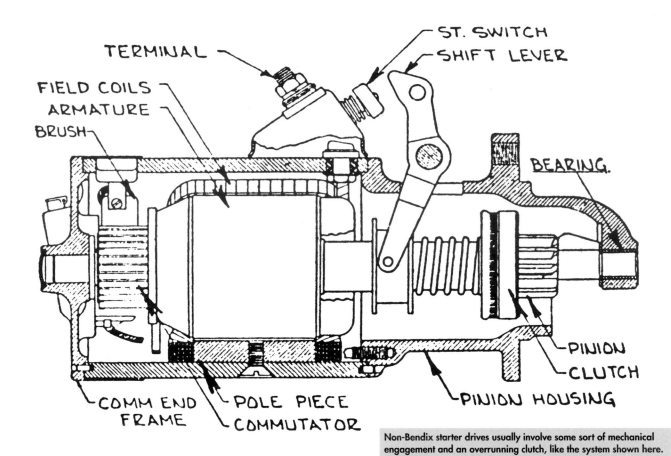

TERMINAL

ST. SWITCH
SHIFT LEVER

FIELD COILS
ARMATURE
BRUSH

BEARING

COMM END FRAME
POLE PIECE
COMMUTATOR

PINION
CLUTCH
PINION HOUSING

Non-Bendix starter drives usually involve some sort of mechanical engagement and an overrunning clutch, like the system shown here. In this case, a toe pedal in the car sequentially engages the drive and closes the starter motor's switch. It's simple and it works.

The Bendix drive is the "Old Faithful" of starter drives. It's simple, compact, and works amazingly well.

Electrical Tests and Procedures—Generators

Electrical testing of conventional generators is more difficult than for starters, due to the wide variety of circuits and windings used in generators. The disassembly and cleaning procedures are about the same as those for starters. As with starters, the field coils must be tested for continuity and for isolation from the generator's frame. The connecting terminals and insulated brush holder must also be checked for isolation from the frame. Testing generator internal field coil insulation is also a good idea, but this requires a good ammeter to determine field coil current draw for comparison to factory specifications. Armature tests for generators are basically the same as those outlined above for starter motors, except that the growler test for shorts may be misleading for some generator armatures that utilize special winding patterns.

Any refurbished generator definitely should be output tested on a test bench. The old folk test of "motoring" generators as a final test should never be seriously confused with proper output tests. Generator reassembly follows the same basic procedures as those outlined for starter motors.

bar defects can often be repaired easily by resoldering. Any time that a starter is reconditioned, it should be checked on appropriate bench equipment to determine its torque output capability.

Usually, when a starter is disassembled for reconditioning without any history of malfunction, it can be reassembled with little more than cleaning, lubrication, and brush and spring replacement.

A starter current draw test is performed with an inductive ammeter, like those shown here. You hold the ammeter against a straight portion of the hot battery cable and see how much current the starter draws. That will tell you if "juice" is getting to the starter, or if too little is getting there, or if too much is being drawn. These inexpensive meters are not particularly accurate, but they still provide useful information.

Starter Engagement Systems

There are two basic methods used in old cars to couple and uncouple starter motors from the engines that they start. One involves a physical or magnetic (either by solenoid or field coil) engagement of the motor gear with engine flywheel teeth. In this configuration, an overrunning (one-way) clutch is used to couple the motor's drive gear to its shaft. When an engine starts, the starter gear is run backwards on the clutch because once an engine starts running its large diameter flywheel drives the much smaller diameter starter drive gear faster than the starter motor can turn it and thus reverses its direction.

In this setup, final uncoupling of the two units occurs when they are physically released or magnetically released by the operator taking his foot off the starter pedal or allowing the starter key switch or button to return to its unconnected position.

The other common method of engaging starters is via an inertial device known as a "Bendix." Bendix drives are engaged by the forces of inertia (their engagers spin out but not with the shafts that drive them). They are easily understood from inspection, or from a good set of pictures of their sequential operation. Explaining how they work

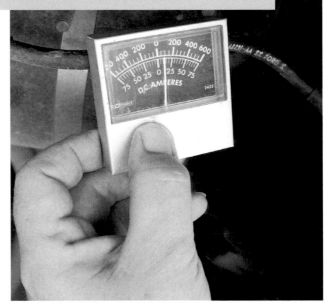

with words is likely to be as successful as trying to explain with only words how to tie a shoelace.

Overrunning clutch starter drives usually work until the starter end bearings fail, their gear teeth break, the overrunning clutch rollers seize or fail to hold, or the shifting fork bends or breaks. They can also fail due to broken cushion springs, or, of course, defective engagement solenoids. It is a good idea to replace any worn drive parts, and to pay particular attention to end bearings—a place

Some restorers are using little custom solid state voltage regulators, such as the one shown here, to improve on the performance and durability of third brush and vibrating point regulated generating systems. You can hide one of these little electronic masterpieces in a generator frame or in a voltage regulator box, and "only your mechanic will know for sure"—except that your ammeter should show much better than factory voltage regulation taking place.

where troubles often begin with these units. Overrunning clutch drives, sometimes called "positive engagement" drives, are usually activated by solenoids mounted directly on the tops of starter motors. These solenoids both engage the starter drive and switch on current to the starter motor. In much older cars these devices often are engaged directly with mechanical linkage from a starter pedal, or, more recently, by a lever activated by the magnetism in one of the field coils (late model Fords).

Bendix-engaged starter drives use massive springs to transmit some of the starting torque and to ease the shock of engagement. These "Bendix springs" are often deformed by that shock and become sources of malfunction. Other problems with this type of drive are wear on engagement gears or of the large threads that drive them into contact with flywheel gears. And, of course, end bearings are vulnerable, as are the drive latch teeth. Physical inspection of a Bendix will quickly show any worn or defective parts. These must be replaced.

Another wrinkle in starter drives is the use of gear cluster reduction motors—particularly on large displacement engine applications. These miserable starters were created primarily to save space or money, or both. Their gears used to be fabricated from aluminum (in modern practice they are steel) and they fail with an amazing regularity. Chrysler used these units extensively in the days of their high-compression/big-displacement engines. You can expect the older gear reduction starters to deliver about half of the working life, or less, of direct drive units. Also in the miserable idea department was a spate of GM starters that for many years required starter motors to be shimmed

against their bell housings for alignment with flywheel ring gears. Whenever shims are removed from this type of starter motor to bell housing interface, make sure that they are reinstalled, or that a proper measuring and installation procedure for starter alignment is followed. The reason that GM used these shims was that their multiple bell housing casting suppliers were unable to maintain a standard depth specification on the housings that they supplied. As "they" say, "go figger."

Generator Regulation Circuits

Starters and generators amaze me. When these devices first appeared on the scene, they both used control systems that were complex and cumbersome. Many starters used physical engagement systems, and generators used magnetically activated regulators that inserted resistances into their field coil circuits. As time went by, most manufacturers adopted simple Bendix drives for their starters and simple third brush and cut out regulation for their generators. These systems were easy to understand, easy to repair, and comparatively inexpensive to construct. Yet, by the late 1930s, the original complex systems were coming back, albeit in improved forms. Of course, today's alternator systems use deadly accurate solid-state regulation and many starters are engaged through main engine computers for "one-touch" starts.

The old electro-mechanical voltage regulators fitted to most cars from the 1930s into the 1970s were among the most finicky devices ever put on automobiles. The older third brush-regulated generators of the 1920s and 1930s did not have "regulators" as such, and achieved self-regulation of voltage and current by energizing their field coils directly from an adjustable third brush. The effect is self-regulation because electrical engineers arranged things so that internal magnetic phenomenon in these generators caused voltage output to fall off with increases in shaft speed, after a specific charging rate was reached. It wasn't a very sensitive or accurate system of regulation—people used to drive on long trips with their headlights on during the day to prevent battery overcharging—but it did work, sort of…. It was also easy to increase or decrease charging rates by adjusting the third brush's position on its armature, relative to the other brushes.

Of course, third brush regulation was only usable with relatively simple electrical systems, and better voltage regulation was necessitated by the increasing array of electrical doodads that became standard and optional on automobiles after the late 1930s.

One part of the old, third-brush systems that was common to later "voltage regulator" equipped systems was the use of a set of cutout points. This was simply a magnetically driven set of contact points that closed when increasing engine speed and generator voltage output reached a predetermined level—a level higher than battery

The two-unit (left) and three-unit (right) vibrating point voltage regulators in this photograph are about average for cars from the late 1930s through the early 1960s. The two-unit device is for small electrical systems and has only voltage regulation. The three-unit regulator is a heavier-duty unit, and will support more electrical accessories on its system. It has both voltage and current regulation capabilities.

voltage. When generator voltage output fell below that level, at low engine RPMs, the points opened and disconnected the generator from the system. This prevented the flow of current from the battery to ground through the generator's brushes. At an idle, or when an engine was turned off, the points remained open and prevented electrical backflow. Cutout devices remained essential elements of the later vibrating point regulators, and have a solid-state analog in the diodes in modern alternators.

The theory of vibrating point regulators is simple enough. The repair and adjustment procedures that pertain to them can be maddeningly complex and varied. Avoiding the variations for the moment, the basic theory is this: In automotive generators, several conductors are energized by rotating them through two or more magnetic fields. This is the basis of any practical automotive electrical generating system. While it is possible to use permanent magnets to supply the necessary magnetic fields (generators now can do just this by employing special, high tech magnets) such magnets would have to have been very large and heavy, given the magnetic materials available in the past. New materials have changed this proposition.

Generator electromagnets are energized by the flow of electrons through coils of wire wrapped around their iron pole shoes. The more electricity that is carried through

these "field" windings, the more output there will be from the conductors on the armatures that are passed through their magnetic fields.

Voltage regulators control the amount of current that flows through generator field coils. They thereby control the level of magnetism in the field coils, and thus the voltage generated in the armature. A voltage regulator does not directly control generator output. It indirectly controls that output by regulating that portion of the output that is passed back through the field coils. By doing this, of course, it achieves control of the overall output.

In addition to the cutout and voltage regulating features that I have described, a voltage regulator may have an additional section, a current regulator. Both of the voltage regulating and current regulating units in a voltage regulator use magnetically controlled points (often called "vibrating points) that open and close contacts. Those contacts control circuits that insert resistance into or remove it from a generator's field circuit.

When resistance is inserted into these circuits it diminishes the strength of the magnetic field surrounding the armature, thus controlling generator output. Both coils, the voltage and the current regulator sections, work by cycling or vibrating, and they never work at the same time. This is because when a generator is meeting large

Temperature is very important in setting voltage regulators. This clip-on thermal correction gauge actually indicates what voltage outputs should be at specific regulator operating temperatures.

current demands, its voltage output will be low and the voltage regulator contacts will not be working. When the current demands are not so large, the current relay will not be working, but voltage output will increase and the voltage points and coil will activate to control it.

Voltage regulators are almost impossible to repair if the nature of their problems involves burned coils, badly burned points, broken or distorted springs, or burned-out resistance units. Otherwise, it is possible to clean and adjust them. To do this, you must know what you are doing in general, and specifically, the particular specifications that apply to the unit that you are working on.

Regulator adjustment is accomplished in some cases by adjusting screws and in others by bending point positioning arms. These adjustments control the spring tension on or the distances between regulator contacting elements. Regulator contacts can be dressed lightly with special point files to clean their contacting surfaces. They should then be cleaned with an electrical contact solvent to remove metal filing and carbon residues and adjusted to proper dimensional specifications.

The temperature of a regulator is one of the major specifications of adjustment on many of these units. The condition of a car's battery is always a factor in making these adjustments. A lot of mechanics and tinkerers will go into voltage regulators (it's easy to find them and to get their covers off) with a screwdriver and a set of needle nose pliers and bend and adjust things randomly until they seem to improve performance. This approach may work in the very short run to increase or decrease a charging rate, but in the long run it will almost always fail.

My experience has been that unless the time is taken to fully adjust all aspects of a regulator to factory specifications of point air gap and dimension, and of gauge measured output, an almost endless series of subsequent adjustments

will have to be undertaken. These are usually indicated by the frequent discovery of a boiling or dead battery.

If you have the equipment, manuals, and understanding to work on voltage regulators, or if you are working with a regulator that is hard to find or expensive, by all means either have it adjusted or make the adjustments yourself. In the cases of common regulators, I usually opt to buy a replacement when one fails. I always save the old regulator for some future date when I may not have easy access to a replacement unit. By now, I have quite a shelf full of the things.

If you go the route of just cleaning and adjusting, you will need a good set of meters, a variable resistor, a clip-on thermometer, a tang bending tool, and feeler gauges. The specific information contained in a *Chilton's* or *Motor's* manual that covers the year of manufacture for the system that you are working on will provide adequate step-by-step adjusting procedure data. Try refurbishing a couple of junk regulators, and decide if the cost of a new regulator, usually in the range of $25 to $75, isn't worth the investment.

"A" and "B" Circuit Charging Systems

Of the many internal differences in voltage regulator designs, the distinction between the "A" and "B" circuits is the one with which anyone working on generating systems must be familiar. Understanding and accounting for this distinction is necessary before you can do preliminary on-car tests to determine whether it is a voltage regulator or a generator that is not working when a charging system ceases to function properly. It is also necessary to know "A" circuits from "B" circuits to reconnect generators and voltage regulators any time either, or both, has been disconnected from its wiring for any reason.

The "A" circuit was used on Delco Remy and Autolite "standard duty" systems, which amounts to almost all of the passenger car systems produced by these manufacturers. In the "A" circuit, the field coils are grounded through the regulator. The "B" circuit was sometimes used by Ford, especially on some "heavy-duty" Autolite applications, and to a lesser degree on heavy-duty Delco Remy applications. It grounds the field internally in the generator.

There are two ways to tell "A" from "B" circuits, aside from the safe assumption that Delco and Autolite car systems will be "A" and Ford applications will be "B." One way is to disconnect the field wire (marked "F" or "FLD") from the generator field terminal and connect a voltmeter from the generator field terminal to ground. With the engine running at moderate speed, an "A" circuit system will give you a voltage reading, but a "B" circuit setup won't. When running this test, be sure to protect the disconnected field wire from contacting ground (it can ruin the regulator if it grounds). The other way to distinguish "A" from "B" charging circuits is to examine the generator brush connections. If the field coil lead in a generator is connected to its insulated brush, you are dealing with an "A" circuit. If it is connected to the grounded brush, you have a "B" circuit.

Armed with this wonderful distinction between the two common grounding systems for field coils, you are now ready to perform an important on-car test, and to install new, repaired or restored voltage regulators and generators in old cars. First the test. When a charging system fails to provide an adequate charging rate, it is important to determine whether it is the regulator or the generator that is not working.

On "A" circuit systems (This pertains only to single contact regulator systems and not to the double contact units used on some air conditioned cars in and after the late 1950's.) make sure that the regulator base is grounded and connect a jumper wire from the regulator field terminal to a good ground. Some older regulators have a ground terminal. If this is the case, make your jumper connection from the regulator field terminal to this ground terminal. Now, run the engine at about 1500 RPM and check for a charge. If the ammeter indicates charging, or if the headlights brighten as engine speed is increased from 1000 to 1500 RPM, the problem is probably in your regulator.

What this test does is to take the regulator out of the charging system and allow the field coils to get full energy. With the regulator eliminated, if the charging rate is adequate, then the fault is probably in the regulator. Remember, when you run this test, the generator is running unregulated. Avoid running the engine faster than 1500 RPM, as you can burn out any circuit or device that is connected to it, as well as the generator, itself. Never attempt to drive a car with the regulator bypassed.

To apply the test described above to "B," or Ford circuits, connect a jumper wire from the "A" or "ARM" terminal on the generator to the "F" or "FLD" terminal on the generator. Again, what this accomplishes for these internally grounded systems is to eliminate the voltage regulator from the circuit. Keeping in mind the above cautions about engine speed, a charge indicates that the regulator is the problem and the absence of a charge indicates that the generator is probably at fault. Of course, in either "A" or "B" circuit tests, remember that the regulator to generator wiring may be defective and should be checked prior to removing either of these components for further testing. These tests also require that the battery in the circuit is capable of accepting a charge.

There is one other system that requires a special hookup for this isolation test. This is the Delco Remy double-contact regulator system. It was used on air-conditioned cars as early as the 1950s, and is basically an "A" grounding system. If you encounter it, don't ground the generator or regulator field terminals, since instant damage to the voltage regulator will result. The isolation and testing of this system requires special procedures that will not be covered here.

Polarizing Generators

The second important use of the "A" and "B" circuit distinction is in "polarizing" generators and/or regulators after they have been disconnected from their wiring. Polarizing is not optional; it must be done before a car is started when the generator or regulator has been disconnected from its partner. If you do not do it, there is a 50 percent chance that the system will not work and that if it is run long enough in this condition, damage will occur to the generator or regulator.

To polarize the "A" circuit (externally grounded), reconnect all leads to the generator and regulator and momentarily touch (flash) a jumper wire between the "GEN" or "ARM" terminal and the regulator's "BAT" terminal. To polarize the "B" circuit (internally grounded), disconnect the lead from the field ("F" or "FLD") terminal of the regulator and flash it across the connected "BAT" terminal of that regulator. On double contact "A" circuit (Delco Remy) systems, used on some air-conditioned cars, you should disconnect the field lead from the regulator and ground it. Then flash a jumper from the "BAT" terminal to the "GEN" or "ARM" terminal. Polarizing conforms the residual magnetism in the generator pole shoes to the battery system hook up.

If all of this sounds cumbersome and detailed, that's because it is. After years of fooling around with this stuff, I still need a diagram on the fender about half of the time when I have to deal with it. The whole situation reminds me of Stevie Wonder's brilliant observation: "...When you believe in things that you don't understand, you get into trouble."

Chapter 12

The Truth About Carburetors: Understanding Basic Carburetor Principles

I**N THE LAST THIRTY YEARS, FUEL INJECTION HAS GONE** from being an obscure and very expensive fuel delivery system, used mostly on expensive and exotic cars, to being the standard system in all modern automobiles. The carburetor, alternately cussed at and beloved by old car collectors and tinkerers, is extinct from the world of new vehicles. Fairly soon, the press will announce that the carburetor has exited use in motorcycles, chain saws and lawn care gear, and gone on to join the immortal ranks of key strike typewriters, bathtubs with legs and passenger pigeons. This passing will be viewed as automotive progress by the general public.

Carburetors were, without doubt, the most unfairly maligned components in automobiles. For the most part, they performed their functions faithfully and reliably, seldom needing repair or adjustment. However, for almost a hundred years, a succession of unskilled but well-meaning individuals, and collectivities of individuals (called service organizations), have tampered the poor things into malfunction and motorist misery.

It has never ceased to amaze me that when I saw a car broken down by the side of the road in the age when carburetors reigned, its hood was invariably raised and someone was mucking around with its carburetor. Frequently, this individual was totally without mechanical knowledge, ability or even aptitude, but this never stopped him from molesting a carburetor. In this degrading process, every adjustment was boldly turned or bent out

of calibration. Every attaching screw was savagely over-tightened, and other liberties were taken and indignities inflicted that are frankly too indecent and gross to describe in detail in a book designed for consumption by the general car collecting/restoring public.

None of this is to say that carburetors sometimes don't fail, or that they are not legitimate objects of repair and adjustment. It is just to note that in my experience; carburetors are "rebuilt" about three times for every time that they actually need it and adjusted out of calibration about every third time that the hoods over them are raised.

Barring defects in a carburetor's environment—bad intake valves or contaminated gasoline, for example—a properly set-up carburetor will function flawlessly for tens of thousands of miles and for years of service. I have no idea from whence the bad reputation of carburetors comes, but I suspect that their vulnerability to unnecessary and harmful tinkering stems largely from the fact that they are usually easy to get at and look like they could cause problems.

It is critically important that carburetors on collector cars are clean, that all of their systems are functional and that the integrity of their parts and the calibration of their adjustments are perfect. Then, for goodness sake, leave the poor things alone to do their job. This job is basically a simple one—to meter and atomize gasoline into an automobile's induction system in the correct concentrations for a variety of running conditions.

Early carburetors performed this function in very

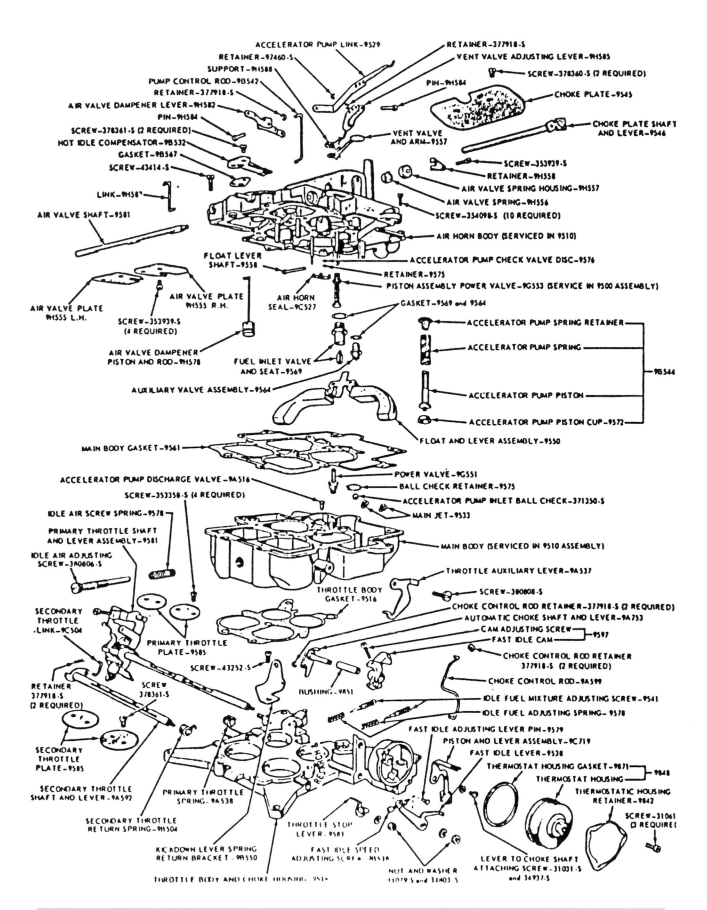

Some of the carburetors built after the mid-1950s got very complicated. The one shown in this parts illustration is a Holley 4160 model used by Chrysler. (Daimler-Chrysler Corp. illustration)

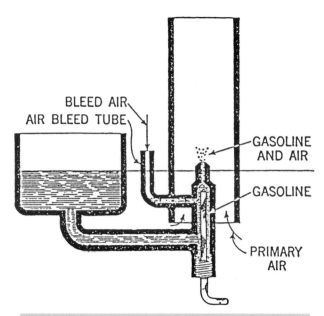

This "basic carburetor" illustrates the most important principles of carburetion. It would need some refinements to work well enough to feed fuel to an automobile engine. Note that this is an "updraft" carburetor, as the air is sucked up into it from its bottom, exiting its top, on its way into an engine.

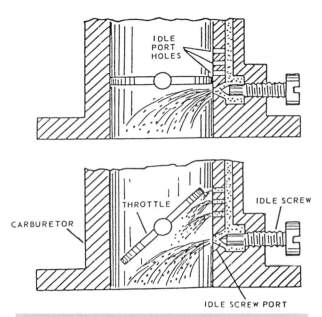

This illustration shows how a carburetor's throttle butterfly uncovers successive idle and low speed jet ports as an engine is speeded up from an idle. Further opening the butterfly will disable the idle and low speed discharge jets and convert them to air bleeds for the carburetor's main discharge jet(s).

simple, but usually inadequate, ways. Some of these were little more than crude wick systems or simple jets in straight tubes. The old carbureting wick devices were not like the delicate wicking items in kerosene lanterns. They were more like the business ends of mops in gas tanks, with short wicks, resembling 2-inch hemp rope, leading to intake manifolds.

By 1900, these crude systems had given way to relatively modern jet-in-venturi systems that had provisions for chokes, and even for multiple metering systems to match fuel delivery to engine requirements in different modes of operation. From then until the recent past, carburetors became more complex and more responsive to engine needs. Multiple barrels were added, and early updraft carburetors had, by the 1930s, mostly given way to downdraft devices.

After the early 1970s, carburetors became increasingly complex and cumbersome as first emission and then fuel economy standards were mandated by the federal government and began to have an impact on automobile engine design and calibration. By the 1980s, increasingly stringent standards, and the availability of small, reliable and relatively inexpensive computer controls, had moved the thrust of fuel delivery design to fuel injection. Now, hybrid, pseudo-carburetors—appearing under such catchy names as "throttle body injection"—preserved some of the outward physical aspects of carburetors in a world dominated by port fuel injection. The invention of the two-way catalytic converter, followed by the three-way catalyst device, sealed the fate of carburetors and their throttle body cousins. They simply lacked the variability and precision to feed these modern emissions control devices.

There is no doubt that fuel injection systems perform the fuel delivery job better than carburetors and cost no more to build. For that reason, they now reign supreme in

automotive fuel delivery. By now, the automobiling public has come to regard carburetors as part of the quaint past that includes wooden spoked wheels and deflector vent windows. (Personal note: I think that I can make peace with fuel injection and steel and mag wheels, but I will never stop lamenting the loss of deflector vent windows.)

The Basic Principles of Carburetion

The basic principles of carburetion, and much of the hardware that supports it, are pretty easy to understand. While a detailed understanding of the underlying principles of carburetion is not necessary to restore carburetors, it is helpful in analyzing some of their hardware.

The basic proposition of carburetion is to mix a liquid (gasoline) with a gas (air, actually a mixture of gasses) in a variety of ratios between roughly 1:12 and 1:18, by weight, with 16.7:1 being the ideal mixture for most driving conditions. This mixing of air and fuel ideally involves complete atomization of the gasoline into a fine mist but, in reality, usually falls short of this ideal when engines are cold. A carburetor's metering function is particularly impressive when you consider that the mix ratio of the volume of gasoline-to-air is on the order of 1:9,000.

The basic principles that describe this mixing function in the device that we call a "carburetor" were elaborated by a Swiss and modeled by an Italian in the 19th and 18th centuries, respectively. The Italian, G. B. Venturi, sometimes gets more of the credit than he deserves when, in fact, the "Bernoulli effect" provides most of the theoretical basis for carburetion.

Bernoulli's principal deals the dynamic fluidic

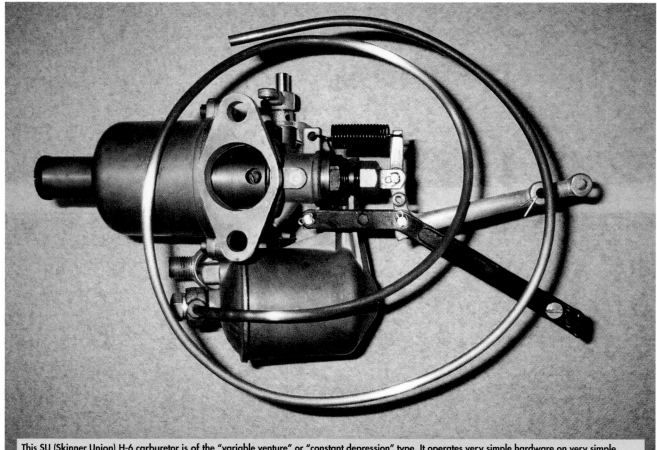

This SU (Skinner Union) H-6 carburetor is of the "variable venture" or "constant depression" type. It operates very simple hardware on very simple principles. Restorers should not be afraid to tackle carburetors like this one that differ from the mainstream.

relationship of the velocity and pressure of liquids or gases as they flow over surfaces. It provides the theoretical basis for the design of airfoils (like airplane wings). Although, presumably, the phenomenon of aerodynamic lift existed before it was described by Bernoulli's equations, just as the effects of gravity presumably were felt before Newton's epochal discoveries in that realm. Although I never took high school physics, I have always suspected the validity of the often-heard statement, "Newton invented gravity."

Simply stated, Bernoulli's principle and Venturi's effect suggest that when a fluid (gas or liquid) flowing through a tube encounters a region of diminishing cross-sectional area, its velocity will increase and its pressure will be reduced. If another fluid at atmospheric pressure is ported into this area of reduced pressure, the fluid at atmospheric pressure will flow into the area of reduced pressure. This explains how perfume atomizers, carburetors, and automatic shutoff gasoline nozzles work, when they work.

For our purposes, the impact of this theoretical framework suggests that if a small jet, or nozzle containing gasoline at a level slightly below its tip, is inserted into an air stream that has been accelerated by being pulled through a tube with a smooth and gradual restriction, gasoline will be pulled from the jet and atomized into the flowing air stream. For the maximum effect, the jet must be placed in, or just beyond, the location of reduced cross-sectional area and (thus) reduced pressure. The whole thing works something

like that perfume atomizer, but more efficiently.

It is, by the way, certain that neither Venturi nor Bernoulli had the any inkling that their theoretical explorations would ever have anything to do with the development of engines for self-propelled vehicles. In fact, they were both long extinct before their theories were applied to automotive engineering. I am, however, certain that both of them would have lamented the passing of deflector vent windows if they had lived into the latter part of the 20th century.

The Practice of Carburetion

In practice, carburetors consist of some sort of "float" device, one, or more, venturi tubes, discharge jets, air bleeds, enrichment and economizer devices, choking devices and throttle plate systems. Let's try to sort out all of that hardware.

Gasoline is supplied to a carburetor by gravity, air pressure, or pump pressure. A float-activated valve in the carburetor's fuel reserve bowl controls the amount of gasoline admitted to the carburetor and holds it at a specific level in the float chamber by closing a needle or disc valve when the gasoline attempts to rise above that level. From the float chamber, the gasoline travels, via one or more circuits, to a point of discharge in the carburetor throat. In practice, two or more discharge points are used, and the choice between them is made on the basis of the position of the throttle plate—a moving plate, located near the carburetor's base (downdraft type), which restricts air flow through the carburetor and, thus, controls engine speed.

The destination and distribution of the gasoline to be discharged can also be determined by a system of internal metering rods or other metering devices. The float level is always set to keep gasoline just below the level of the tip of the main discharge jet(s), so that it cannot continue to flow out of the jet(s) and into the engine's intake manifold (or air intake in the case of updraft carburetors) after the engine has been stopped and the air flow and suction created by the downward travel of its pistons ceases.

The path to the discharge jet(s) is usually restricted by a main or auxiliary metering jet that acts to limit the amount of gasoline that can reach the discharge jet(s). When I refer to "jets," I am speaking of small-calibrated holes that restrict (meter) the flow of gasoline in a carburetor.

What has been described above represents the main operating features of a basic carburetor. It would work, in theory, but in practice it would not accommodate the variety of operating conditions—variables like temperature, speed, load, etc.—that are common to engines in the real world.

Let's consider some of the systems in a carburetor that deal with these variables. Not all carburetors use all of these systems, and there are many obscure control systems that I will not detail here. What follows is a description of most of the important modifications to a basic carburetor, those that you might expect to encounter in any carburetor from a collector car that you will restore.

MULTIPLE BARRELS AND MULTIPLE CARB-URETORS: One way to increase carburetor capacity, and to tailor air/fuel mixture to engine needs, is to add more carburetor barrels to an engine induction system. These barrels can differ in size, so that smaller barrels provide for low-speed operation and larger ones only come into play during acceleration or high-speed operation. You can also link several carburetors together, so that specific barrels in each correspond to and feed air/fuel mixture to one or more cylinders in an engine. While multiple carburetors may increase engine responsiveness and efficiency, such a setup inevitably creates complexity and may produce calibration problems.

Early updraft carburetors usually had only one barrel for all cylinders. Later, downdraft carburetors frequently had two or four barrels. By the 1950s, it was common for high- performance V-8 engines to have three two-barrel carburetors, or even two four-barrel units. In both of these situations, there is a substantial problem keeping everything synchronized so that carburetor valves and circuits open up and close at the optimum times in their sequences.

SECOND VENTURIS: Another feature found on some carburetors, particularly high-performance carburetors, is a second venturi suspended around a discharge jet inside the main venturi in the throat of a carburetor. This greatly increases the local vacuum applied to the gasoline extracted from the discharge jet. More important, the speed of the air/fuel mixture entering an engine is also increased. There were even a few triple venturi carburetors.

MIXTURE HEATING DEVICES: One of the problems with the "basic carburetor," described above, is its tendency to ice up. This occurs because as the gasoline entering its venturi system is transformed from a liquid to a vaporized state, it has to give up heat and the resulting mixture's temperature drops. Condensation from the moisture in the incoming air tends to occur as it is cooled, and ice can form. Various systems have been developed for heating the bases of carburetors with engine coolant or exhaust gases—one or the other of these is common to most carburetion systems.

It is also common to use a manifold heat stove to heat the incoming combustion air fed to cold engines. Water-jacketed intake manifolds and exhaust-stove-heated intake manifolds are also present on some engines to help defeat tendencies towards carburetor icing and to promote atomization of the fuel. Some of these systems are non-regulated, or regulated only in the gross sense that they can be turned "on" or "off." Other heating systems, like some manifold heat boxes (a.k.a. "heat riser valves"), are often controlled by bimetallic springs that sense engine temperature and engine speed (based on exhaust volume and pressure). These systems are inherently troublesome because they operate in the very corrosive environment of heated exhaust gases. They need frequent maintenance and repair and should be put back into "as new" condition when an engine is restored.

COLD STARTING SYSTEMS; THE CHOKE: Almost all engines have some arrangement for radically increasing the fuel-to-air ratio for cold starting. Such a system is generally known as a "choke," even though this term is a misnomer for a whole class of such systems. Almost all American cars use a butterfly valve-type choke, placed near the carburetor's air inlet, above the fuel discharge jet(s). By closing this valve partially, or completely, for cold starting, increased suction is created in the carburetor's throat, and a relatively "richer" (more gasoline) gasoline-to-air mixture is created and sucked into the engine than would have been the case if the choke were open and more air could enter at less vacuum.

This type of choke can be controlled automatically by a thermostatic bimetallic coil and ported vacuum, or manually with a driver-operated control. Often, a choke butterfly will incorporate a spring-loaded feature which allows it to be pushed partially open automatically by the air rushing by it, as soon as an engine begins to run, and before an operator would be able to open the choke manually. On automatic choke systems, a combination of engine vacuum and/or airflow automatically provides this initial choke opening. Complete opening of automatic chokes is provided for by a temperature-responsive bimetallic spring, which may be electrically heated to hasten full choke opening.

Most variable venturi carburetors (also called "constant depression," "constant vacuum" or "choke-type"), such as S.U. (Skinner Union), manipulate their main metering jet for starting enrichment purposes. They do not have conventional butterfly chokes.

THROTTLE: All carburetors provide speed control by restricting airflow into induction systems. This is done with butterfly valves located downstream from venturi and main metering jet(s), or by some exotic tumbler system. When a throttle butterfly is used, as is usually the case, it is controlled by a cable or linkage rods that go to a hand and/or foot control, or both. It is interesting to note that this method of controlling engine speed is one of the main inefficiencies that are inherent in gasoline engines. Diesels, for all of their faults, at least avoid the expedient of controlling engine speed by the strangulation of their induction systems.

AIR BLEEDS AND ANTI-PERCOLATION CIRCUITS: These are small passages that open into the carburetor throat and allow air to mix with gasoline, or gases to escape from the gasoline, before the fuel reaches its discharge locations. Air bleeds enhance atomization, while anti-percolation ports prevent gasoline from bubbling excessively while in a carburetor's internal passages.

FLOAT VENT: This is a baffled vent that allows atmospheric pressure into the float chamber to prevent vacuum or pressure from forming as gasoline enters and is evacuated from a float chamber. On early carburetors float chambers were usually vented directly into the atmosphere, sometimes via small mesh filters. After the early 1930s, it was discovered that if a float chamber was vented into the top of the carburetor barrel, just below the air cleaner, a compensating pressure was effectively applied to the gasoline in the float chamber. This made up for any increase in carburetor vacuum due to air cleaner clogging, and helped to maintain correct air/fuel ratios.

DASHPOTS AND FAST IDLE CAMS: Carburetors, after the early 1930s, used a variety of systems to hold a fast idle when the choke was partially or completely closed. This is necessary to keep a choked engine running. On very early cars, this function was usually provided by a hand throttle, but with the disappearance of hand throttles and the advent of automatic chokes, one or more cam devices was incorporated into carburetor design to provide specified throttle openings when a choke was partially or fully closed.

Another linkage system was used to open chokes when throttles were opened widely while the choke was still closed. On some cars, built after the mid-1950s, vacuum-operated dashpots and solenoid-operated throttle stops performed these functions.

INTERNAL CARBURETOR CIRCUITRY AND ARCHITECTURE: The most complex aspect of almost any carburetor is the internal circuitry that acts to change the metering of fuel to meet engine needs. (The obvious exception to this is constant depression carburetors, which avoid most such circuitry.) The variety and complexity of this type of control system can be mind-boggling. Its main features include a system that switches fuel feed from an idle port to a low speed system, and then to the main discharge or cruising circuit(s). These changes are usually accomplished by uncovering successively larger ports as

the throttle butterfly plate is opened. Ultimately, a high-speed circuit(s) begins to operate and disables the first two systems by converting them to air bleeds for the main discharge system.

In addition to this basic circuitry, most carburetors have either vacuum or linkage-operated metering rods that allow more or less fuel to pass through the metering jets, depending on engine requirements at a given time and the need for economy or power in a given situation. Some of these systems do not even use physical metering devices, but depend on the principles of hydraulics and fluidics to achieve their switching functions. The basic condition to which these metering systems respond is the need for a relatively lean mixture at cruising speeds, compared to idle and low speeds, and the need for substantial air/fuel enrichment when heavy acceleration is demanded. Such terms as "economizer valve" or "acceleration circuits" are often employed to describe the features of this kind of system.

ACCELERATION PUMP OR WELL: Most carburetors employ some sort of system to provide an extra shot of gasoline, instantly, when the throttle is opened rapidly. For this purpose, early carburetors tended to use wells filled with gasoline that were rapidly drawn empty when throttle butterflies were suddenly opened. Later carburetors, of the downdraft type, tended to use little pumps with check valves and separate discharge jets to put extra squirts of fuel into engines. These pump systems are also useful for starting cold engines because a couple of down strokes on the accelerator pedal will cause discharges of raw gasoline into intake manifolds, which aids in starting by priming engines. Too many such strokes will, of course, flood engines before they can start.

IDLE MIXTURE SCREWS: Until almost the end of the age of carburetors, all carburetors featured accessible idle mixture screws for each low speed (primary) barrel. These were used to set air/fuel ratios at idle speeds. Idle mixture screws reside at the bases of carburetors and are recognizable because they are usually brass or brass colored and have springs on their shanks and serrations around their heads. They are among the most misunderstood of all carburetor parts. They regulate air/fuel mixtures entering carburetor barrels for idling purposes only. Usually, they will lean the idle mixture when they are screwed in and enrich it when they are screwed out. Idle mixture screws have no effect on the running mixture supplied by high-speed discharge jet(s).

I emphasize this because many people attempt to set a carburetor's running mixture by adjusting its idle mixture screws and, of course, fail to achieve that end. To further confuse things, a few carburetors use idle mixture screws that control the air flow into idle circuits and, in this case, turning these screws in enriches mixtures and turning them out leans them—the opposite of the other, more common, adjustment format. You have to know with which type you are working.

The hardware comprising carburetor systems,

described above, is most of what is likely to be found inside, and hung outside, the majority of carburetors that a restorer will encounter. There is a whole range of other stuff that has been used over the years, and if you come across any of it, you should try to understand what it is and what it is supposed to do. *Chilton* and *Motor's* manuals from the 1930s through the 1980s do pretty good jobs describing the details of the various carburetor systems used in the cars for the years that they cover. Shop manuals are another good source of repair information. For very early cars, owners' manuals are often the best sources of operating descriptions, adjustment specifications and repair procedures for carburetors. Finally, major carburetor companies like Stromberg, Zenith, Marvel, Carter B&B, Holly, Schebler, Rayfield, etc. used to publish parts and service books that contain a wealth of information that is useful in carburetor repair and calibration.

Restoring Carburetors: The Preliminaries

There are some important preliminaries before you undertake carburetor disassembly. The first is to make sure that you have enough information about the carburetor that you are working on to effect a reasonable rebuild. You should try to know what malfunctions that could be traceable to the carburetor, if any, were occurring in the car on which it was mounted. For example, if the car tended to stall whenever it rounded a corner, you should look for a fault in the float system. While there is a good chance that a complete cleaning, inspection and adjustment will cure most carburetor running problems, it is always better to identify those problems beforehand, and then look for their specific causes and remedy them in your rebuilding effort.

A second important preliminary is to have a good carburetor kit in hand before attempting disassembly. A good kit will include all of the gaskets and many of the wear parts that you will need to reassemble a carburetor. The most prominent of these will be bowl and base gaskets, ball checks, accelerator pump plungers, metering rods, seats and springs (if used), float valves and various other wear and sealing parts applicable to the carburetor on which you are working. Some older kits were much more complete than the later "zip" or "jiffy" kits. However, kits that have sat around for decades often contain parts that have dried out beyond usefulness.

All kits include some form of instructions and diagrams for assembly and calibration. In some cases, these instructions are pretty general, and pretty skimpy on the exact details of assembly and calibration of any particular carburetor in the "family" that they cover. In these cases, you will do better with one of the other information sources mentioned above.

Some older carburetors require kits that are no longer available, and you may have to secure the parts that you need for them from open stock and by cutting your own gaskets. In some cases, reproduction carburetor kits are available from carburetor and marque specialists. These can be located by checking relevant advertising in major old car publications, marque publications, and various old car business and supplier directories. Some of these kits, like those from Jon Hardgrove's "The Carburetor Shoppe" in Eldon, Missouri, are complete and of uniformly high quality. Unfortunately, many of the reproduction kits from other suppliers are no more than a bunch of period and reproduction parts thrown into plastic bags and sold at excruciatingly high prices.

It is usually easier to take something apart than to put it back together—and carburetors may be the best example of this rule. Make sure that before you disassemble any carburetor, you have adequate pictures or keep good enough notes and sketches to put it back together correctly. Since some former rebuilder may have misassembled the thing, it is best to be guided by manuals and the logic of its operation, as well as by disassembly notes and sketches. After a while, you will get pretty good at knowing how carbs fit together.

A final preliminary to carburetor rebuilding is to make sure that you have at hand any special tools or instruments that will be required for disassembly, reassembly and calibration. Many carbs require special tools and instruments to rebuild them. While some improvisation often is possible here, there are limits to what can reasonably be accomplished with a pair of needle nose pliers and a bent screwdriver. I have often seen delicate parts, like jets, ruined by rough handling in previous rebuilds. If you don't have the necessary tools to rebuild a carburetor, send it to someone who does. I receive butchered carburetors for rebuilding many times a year and it can be a very expensive proposition to rectify previous mistakes.

Carburetor Restoration: Disassembly

If you are rebuilding a carburetor that is particularly grimy and varnish-coated on the outside, it is a good idea to do what you can to clean up its exterior with a petroleum-based solvent before you disassemble it. Then remove external linkage and cam parts and lay them out in a logical sequence. There will be lots of little parts by the time that your disassembly is completed, so be sure to work on a clean, uncluttered surface, and avoid working on a surface that will allow little parts to roll around on their way to the floor.

Some linkage parts cannot be removed before major castings like the carb base, intermediate section, and top are separated. Pay attention to how these linkage parts assemble because they will have to be reengaged before the carburetor castings are reassembled and tightened together.

The float(s) will usually come out of its chamber easily, but note how it is retained, and see if what you find is logical or the result of previous misassembly. In the disassembly process, anything that can be unscrewed should be removed

DOME

PISTON

FLOAT
Bowl
&
COVER

BODY

As you disassemble a carburetor, you should lay its parts out in an orderly manner. This helps to keep things simple during reassembly. Note that the disassembled parts shown here have been organized by type and function.

carefully with the appropriate wrench or screwdriver. When you work on slotted jets, remember that they will mar or distort easily if your tool slips or if excessive force is applied to them. Pay particular attention to which removable parts have gaskets, copper sealing rings, O-rings or other gasket provisions under them, and determine if those that do not, should. Generally, parts with tapered shanks or parts that fit into and against tapered seats will require no gasketing, but parts with flat flange sealing areas will.

It is a good idea to keep all internal gaskets segregated with the parts from which they were removed and to take notes as to which parts require gasketing. The concept of using the parts and gaskets in a rebuild kit until they are all gone, hoping that this will put everything in the right place, is a charming but not a very effective way to ensure success in carburetor restoration. Most old rebuild kits are pretty general in content coverage, and will contain some parts and gaskets that you do not need for your particular application, or lack things that you do need, or both.

One of the most difficult disassembly propositions, even for an experienced carburetor technician, is knowing when to stop. For example, some carburetors have external copper, lead, or brass friction plugs that must be removed for proper internal cleaning. Others have pressed-in jets that must not be removed unless replacements are available. If you understand the internal circuitry in a carburetor, this will help you to know what lurks behind various pressed-

in and threaded parts, and whether they must be removed, or even can be removed, for more thorough cleaning after disassembly. One certainty is that all plastic or fiber parts have to come out of carburetors prior to cleaning them in carburetor solvent. Any good carburetor solvent will quickly destroy these parts.

When you disassemble a carburetor, it is important that you keep its body right-side-up until all removable parts have been taken out of it. Many carburetors have two or more check balls that are different sizes. These tend to reside in wells, where they may be hard to see. If they are not removed with tweezers or a magnet, they can end up on the floor before you can note their proper locations. Then you get to wonder how many there were and in which wells they go. The kit or book diagram that you are using may help in these cases, but just as likely, it will not. As I said, kits and their diagrams tend to be pretty general, and may deviate significantly from what you are working on, even though they are supposed to cover it.

Springs and screw-in jets with similar appearances can also cause confusion at the time of carburetor reassembly. Usually, the jets, tubes and other screw-in parts in a carburetor have different-sized threads that preclude misassembly, but don't count on it. Springs must be identified by the number of coils in them, so that they can be replaced with new springs from a kit, or reinstalled in the correct locations.

Very small parts should be put in mesh containers before they are chemically cleaned in carburetor solvent.

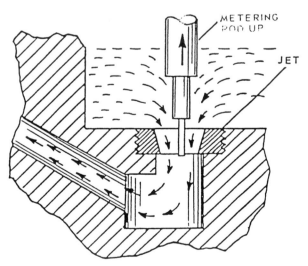

METERING ROD UP

JET

As the metering rod, shown here, works in-and-out of the orifice below it, it restricts and opens the flow of fuel and thus controls running mixture. Metering rods can be controlled by mechanical, electrical or vacuum features, or combinations of two or three of these.

An area of particular concern inside carburetors is the metering rods (if used). Metering rods must be free of wear, absolutely straight, and free of burrs. Their seats must be smooth, round, and unworn. Any linkage or springs involved in their movement must be free and capable of completely smooth operation. All metering rod adjustments must be made correctly and precisely.

Carburetor float level is a critical setting. Be sure that you understand the method of measuring the float level for each different carburetor on which you work. Typically, setting a float involves a measurement from the top of the float to the top of the carburetor bowl or lid surface. Sometimes, that measurement includes the thickness of the bowl gasket, other times it does not. Be sure that you know which way it is measured for the unit that you are calibrating. Float settings are achieved either by turning an external screw or by bending an internal arm and/or tang. Be careful not to exert pressure on the float valve when making any adjustment. If the float adjustment is a bending adjustment, support the float arm, while bending it or any tang that is attached to it.

When you find a screw plug in the side of a float chamber, this is the gasoline level sight line for the proper float setting. Thank the carburetor manufacturer for providing this final positive check of float level setting, and curse other manufacturers for omitting it. Remember that float settings are critical to a carburetor's proper air/fuel mixture in all modes of engine operation. These levels are sometimes given in 32nds or even 64ths of an inch. They are that critical. In a few carburetors, multiple floats are used. They are almost always set to different levels.

How long you dunk dirty carburetor parts in carburetor cleaner depends mostly on their condition, and on the condition and temperature of the cleaner. After immersion, parts should be rinsed and re-rinsed in clean water.

Carburetor Rebuilding: Cleaning the Parts

There used to be several commercial carburetor-cleaning solvents on the market, like Delco, Bendix Speedclean, Bendix Metalclean, Thyme, and Gunk. With the passing of carburetors, most of these products have disappeared. At the present, time Gunk makes a usable immersion cleaner that can be ordered through some parts houses. It is a "hydroseal" formulation.

This means that layers of volatile chemicals reside below an inch or so of water on the top of the concoction. The water acts as a seal to keep the volatile solvents and detergents below it from escaping from the solution. Most carburetor cleaners have "boosters" available to replenish their active ingredients when they are depleted, and all of them require the periodic addition of water to keep their volatiles sealed in. The best carburetor cleaning products have, as one of their top layers, a sealant that will coat and seal the pores of aluminum and pot metal (die cast zinc) parts.

The time required to clean a carburetor in solvent will depend on the cleaner that is used, its temperature, its age and the condition of the carburetor parts that are being cleaned. Overexposure can, in some cases, produce etching and cavitation, so watch out. Never let a carburetor part stick out of cleaning solvent, or even into its water layer. If you do, the part may be etched at the interface of the water and the top layer of the cleaning solution's active ingredients. This could destroy the part! Agitating parts in carburetor cleaner will speed the cleaning action, but it will also tend to release volatiles from the solution and cause premature ageing of the cleaner. Never throw a bunch of small parts

After chemically cleaning the parts of this carburetor, they still look grungy. Carburetor cleaner will not remove the rust and oxides that tend to attack the outside surfaces of carburetors.

into a big cleaner drum, as they will be difficult to retrieve. Always confine small parts in metal mesh containers.

ALWAYS WEAR EYE AND HAND PROTECTION WHEN WORKING WITH CARBURETOR CLEANERS. They are very caustic and will burn your skin, or destroy your eyesight in a second, if you substitute bravado for common sense.

When the carburetor that you are working on is in the "soup" (solvent), let things take their course and don't try to rush the process. Some stubborn stains can require overnight, or even longer, to remove. With sufficient time, any good carburetor solvent should remove all carbon and varnish from the inside and outside of a carburetor. No carburetor cleaner will remove rust or other corrosion products, so don't wait for that to happen.

If you want to avoid the hazards and disposal problems associated with caustic hydroseal-type carburetor cleaners, I recommend using a citrus-based solvent in an ultrasonic cleaning system. This is far more pleasant to use than the old cleaners and the costs are within reach if you plan to do several carburetors. The results can be very good. This is how I have been cleaning carburetors "since the beginning of this millennium."

When your carburetor castings and associated parts have been completely cleaned by solvent action, they should be double-rinsed in clean water and blown dry with compressed air. Be sure to blow out every internal passage at least twice. You will probably need straight and right angle blowgun tips to accomplish this.

Not to harp on this point, but, again, **PLEASE WEAR GOOD EYE PROTECTION WHEN USING A COMPRESSED AIR BLOWGUN ON A CARBURETOR.** Many of the passages that you will be blowing out make connections that may cause the air to exit them right into your face, even though you are applying the air at right angles to the area that you are facing. If you were to succeed in blowing an internal passage of a carburetor out so that its contents exited into your face, you would be exposing yourself to a blast of particles and harsh chemical residues traveling at speeds up to 100 mph. You can imagine what chance your unprotected eyes would have against this assault. No carburetor repair is worth the risk of serious eye injury. Don't put yourself in the position of risking one for the other.

After thorough immersion or ultrasonic cleaning, a carburetor should be internally clean. Its outside may not look great, but the working parts of the carburetor should be clean. If the carb is cast in brass or bronze, it will probably look pretty good. If it is aluminum or pot metal, it may look good or it may have areas showing white chalky deposits. If it is cast iron, it may still show rust deposits. Some restorers will now use a light application of fine glass beads to remove chalky deposits or rust and get down to sound metal. They will follow this blast application with a clear epoxy sealant, a zinc tincture coating, or dichromate plating of the major carburetor castings and visible linkage pieces.

For the sake of appearance, I usually bead blast and clear coat carburetor castings. If you decide to do this, be sure to carefully mask the carburetor castings so that the glass beads are kept out of their internal areas. If a bead lodges there, and later enters an engine's induction system, it can do enormous damage. After blasting is complete and

This carburetor's major castings were abrasively blasted with very fine glass bead media to remove surface deposits and get down to clean metal after chemical cleaning.

the masking provisions have been removed, blow out all internal passages one more time, just to be sure that they are clear of beads and debris.

If you don't have blast cleaning equipment, scrubbing with a very fine stainless wire brush, followed by a brass wire brush, will get most of the chalky oxides off pot metal and aluminum parts and make them look pretty good.

Carburetor Restoration: Repair and Reassembly

At this point, all worn parts should be replaced or repaired, and the carburetor reassembled. A carburetor repair kit usually contains most of the parts that will require replacement. Accelerator pump and economizer valve seals should be replaced routinely in carburetor rebuilding and restoration. Usually, carburetor kits contain whole plunger assemblies to replace these seals. Float needle valves should always be replaced in a carburetor rebuild or restoration. In some cases, Viton-tipped float needle valves are available to replace needles that originally had brass, aluminum or stainless steel sealing surfaces. These soft-tipped needle valves are always a better bet than the solid metal kind.

If a float is the soldered brass type, it should be checked for leaks by placing it in a pan of boiling water and submerging it. Then look for bubbles. If you find any escaping from inside the float, it should be boiled until all liquids and gasses are expelled. It should then be allowed to cool completely before it is resealed by carefully soldering the points from which bubbles were observed to exit the

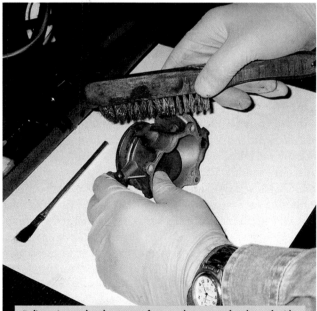

Delicate internal carburetor surfaces and parts can be cleaned with a brass brush if an ultrasonic cleaner is not available. Nothing hard, sharp, or abrasive should be used on these surfaces.

float. It should then be rechecked for leaks. You can tell when all gasoline has been expelled from a float by shaking it and listening for sloshing sounds. It is important that float resoldering be done in a way that adds little or no weight to the float.

Throttle and choke shaft bearing surfaces should be checked for clearance. If either is found to be sloppy, a new, oversize shaft must fitted, or the carburetor body will have

To insure that ball checks seat properly, it is sometimes a good idea to take the old ball that you removed and tap it gently against its seat with a hollow tip punch and hammer. Then, remove the ball and install its new replacement. Tapping the old ball shapes the seat for the new one.

to be bushed and reamed so that its shafts fit with no more than .002 inch clearance between them and their bearing surfaces. When you replace or refit butterfly valves mounted to flat or to split shafts, always close the butterfly plate(s) gently with firm finger pressure before you secure the attaching screws. This seats the butterfly plate(s) squarely in the carb throat bore(s). The butterfly attaching screws should be secured with a good thread-locking compound. It also is a good idea to spread or "stake" the protruding threads of these screws, so that there is no possibility of their vibrating loose and entering an engine's induction system, where they could do enormous harm.

Small internal carburetor parts should have been cleaned in the same solvent as the major parts and castings and blown dry. If you have access to an ultrasonic cleaner, this is certainly a premium way to do a final cleansing of small carburetor parts. If not, use a very fine-bristled brass brush on them. Jet orifices can be rodded with a broom straw or soft copper bell wire, but should never be probed with anything hard or sharp. Threaded parts should be gently screwed into their proper holes and tightened so that their seats contact and deform very slightly, or their gaskets are compressed and seal. They should never be over-tightened, as they can easily be distorted. This is particularly true of screw-in jets.

Make sure that the jets that you install have the right sizing numbers for your application. It is surprising how often incorrect jets are installed by previous owners, rebuilders or repairers. Make sure that all carburetor restoration is done in a clean work environment—almost "medically clean"—because even a human hair in the wrong place can mess up a carburetor's operation. Lots of small parts may be used in carburetors, so you should adopt an organized approach to this work, to help you get things back where they belong.

When installing carburetor ring gaskets, pump or economizer valve leathers or bowl gaskets, it is a good practice to soak them in a dish of kerosene for about an hour prior to their installations. Pump leathers should then be slightly flared with a round tool just prior to installation. Carburetor bowls and bowl covers should be checked for flatness and their mating surfaces should be cleaned with a fine bristled brass brush. Warped covers or damaged bowl sealing surfaces will have to be repaired to achieve satisfactory seals. The final attachment of a carb cover and base can only occur after every internal part, and in some cases some linkage parts, are in place. If you screw a bowl cover down and later have to go back in, you will have to use a new bowl cover gasket, or you will have external fuel leaks. It is best to be sure that everything necessary is in place *before* you tighten down a bowl cover.

About half of the pre-1970 carburetors out there seem

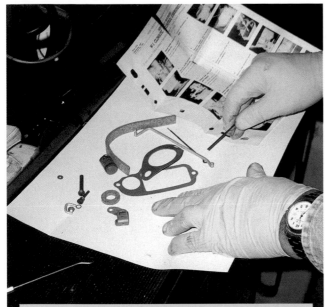

Before you install new, nonmetallic gaskets and seals in a carburetor, they should be soaked in kerosene or penetrating oil for half an hour. This helps them to comply to the surfaces that they will be clamped between.

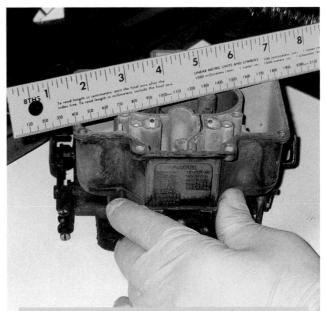

Warped bowl covers are a real problem on many old carburetors. When you rebuild a carburetor, always check the flatness of its major sealing surfaces, and make necessary repairs and adjustments.

to have warped covers. This often occurs because cover attaching screws have previously been over-tightened or tightened unevenly. If you begin with a cover that is warped, and you don't straighten it, you will have dangerous and unsightly gasoline leakage very soon after you put the carburetor back into service.

Warped bowl covers can be gently hammered straight and filed until their sealing surfaces are flat enough to seal. If you have to hammer them, use a very small brass hammer and back the casting up with a flat piece of hard wood. Heating a warped bowl cover in an oven to about 350 degrees F. for 30 minutes will make it easier to straighten it. Whether you heat it or not, it is very easy to crack or break old carburetor bowl covers in the act of straightening them. Go easy.

Soaking a bowl cover gasket in kerosene before installation swells it and helps it to conform to sealing surfaces, and thus achieve a working seal.

Finally, tightening carburetor sections together must be done in stages, and in a pattern that works across the carburetor in a reasonable sequence. Be sure to lubricate the cover screws on their threads and under their heads. If lock washers were used under these fasteners originally, they should be replaced with new ones. Initial or subsequent over-tightening of cover screws will not cure leaks for long, but ultimately will make them worse. It is best to use a torque-indicating screwdriver for cover tightening, and to start with very low values. Final tightening values should be no more than 12 to 24 oz./inch. You can always tighten things up more later, but once you have warped a carb bowl cover you have a much more serious problem than looseness. Some carburetor tops have attaching screws that are pretty well hidden in their throats, or that come up from below. It is important to not to miss these in any tightening sequence that you adopt.

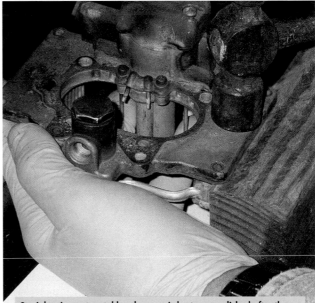

Straightening pot metal bowl covers is best accomplished after they have been oven heated to 350 degrees Fahrenheit for about half an hour. It is then possible to "persuade" the covers straight with a small hammer or other source of pressure.

Calibration and Adjustment

The final calibration and adjustment of a rebuilt carburetor is very important. It will not suffice to simply set things the way that they were before a rebuild. They may have been wrong.

Almost all of the adjustments that you will encounter are given dimensionally or physically. Some require special jigs and tools, but some are very generic measurements or physical directions; for example, "turn the mixture screws out three-quarters a turn from flush for initial setting," or "place the accelerator pump link in the middle lever hole."

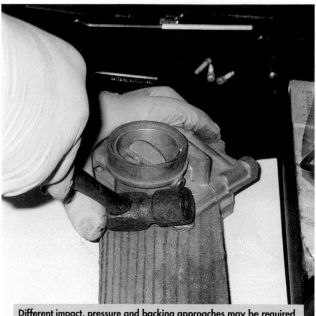

Different impact, pressure and backing approaches may be required to accomplish the desired straightening.

Final flattening of this bowl cover was accomplished by carefully filing it. If you use this procedure, as you file, look for low spots and address them, but be sure to maintain overall cover flatness.

Many carburetor calibration jigs can be fabricated from things like cardboard or bent wire. Some general-purpose tools are available for procedures like float level settings. Some settings, however, like the famous Carter pump-travel-setting, require the use of correct factory tools. Unfortunately, when this situation is encountered, guessing or trial-and-error will usually fail to provide an appropriate adjustment. It is better to locate someone who has the right tool.

On later carburetors, adjustments are frequently effected by the expedient of bending linkage pieces. If you find that a great deal of bending seems to be indicated, go back and check your directions and assembly—there is probably a mistake lying in wait to laugh at you after you have bent some poor linkage rod beyond the possibility of rehabilitation. I speak from bitter experience.

When you bench rebuild a carburetor, calibrations sometimes do not work when they are set "by the book." These calibrations are given only as starting points, and are used as initial settings when a carburetor has been disassembled and is rebuilt. Such settings as choke, idle mixture, choke unloader, and the like, may require further running adjustments on a warm engine. A good manual and some experience will give you the method, sequence and values for making running adjustments after a restored carburetor is installed.

A good final check of carburetor flange sealing is to assemble the cover to the bowl section without a gasket, and see if you can get a .002 inch feeler gauge through the interface at any point. If you can't, the cover should seal.

Chapter 13

Fuel Containment and Delivery Systems

Old fuel pumps and their parts are just unreliable enough so that you should always carry a spare and know how to install it or to repair the one on your collector car on the road.

IT'S REALLY QUITE EXTRAORDINARY WHEN YOU THINK about it. Gasoline, which fuels most automobiles, contains more BTUs of energy than dynamite, by weight or by volume. It is relatively easy to ignite when it is mixed with air, and burns violently, even at atmospheric pressure.

When it is subjected to higher pressures, or wicked, it can burn explosively.

Yet, for all of the potential hazards in the storage and delivery of gasoline in automobiles, relatively few mishaps occur. This, despite the fact that the vast majority of

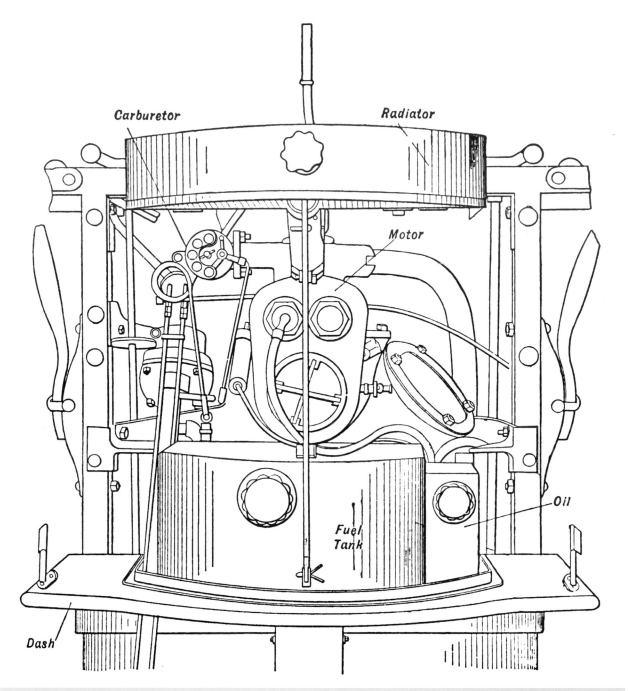

The first practical fuel delivery systems were gravity driven. They worked, but they delivered very little fuel pressure and often required dangerous and inconvenient fuel tank locations, like under the cowl!

automobile operators, and even technicians, have little or no respect for gasoline and its hazards.

In the very early days of motoring, when the mighty Standard Oil Co. of New Jersey was a monopoly that dealt primarily in lamp oil, gasoline was a by-product of the refining process and existed mostly in paint stores for various obscure purposes. Hiram Percy Maxim, an early American automobile innovator, recounts that after purchasing gasoline at a paint store several times for his automotive experiments, he was regarded with suspicion by the stores proprietor. That gent finally warned Maxim that anyone who fooled around with gasoline regularly would

ultimately blow himself up. This was before the turn of the 20th century.

At that time it would have astounded any reasonable person to learn that within 20 years gasoline would be dispensed and purchased routinely, and in such gross quantities that supplying it became the basis of one of the largest and richest industries in the world. The hazards associated with this substance would have made such a scenario incomprehensible to most people in 1900. Keep that in mind the next time you hear a discussion of how dangerous hydrogen is as the automobile fuel of the future.

The delivery of fuel to automobile engines has evolved

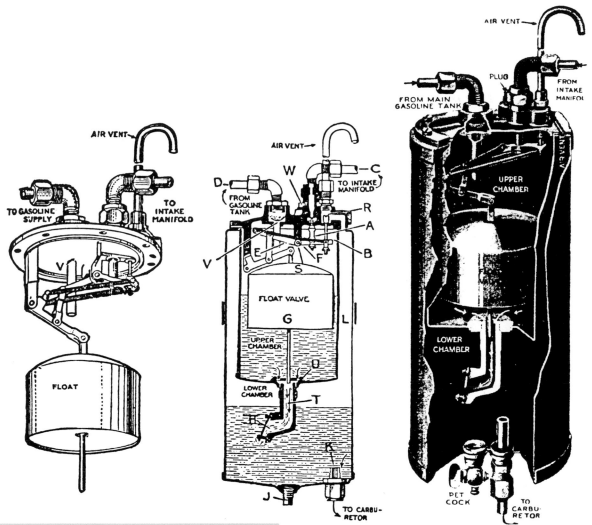

In the 1920s, vacuum tank fuel delivery systems were widely used. These combined an element of danger with a very bad reputation for reliability. Some restorers like to replace these units with hidden electric fuel pumps.

greatly over the years. Many storage configurations and delivery systems have been tried and abandoned. Still, there are certain common elements to all of them, such as a basic gas tank, plumbing and some sort of differential pressure system (pump, gravity or wick) to convey gasoline from fuel tanks to engines.

In part, the nature of a delivery system will dictate the type of tank that is used and its location in an automobile. In one extreme fuel system, a few early motorcars placed the fuel tank above the car and conveyed fuel to the engine via a wick. More practical early systems used gravity, but this made it necessary to locate the gas tank under the drivers or passengers seats or high in the cowl; clearly hazardous locations. Later, it was found that if the entire gas tank was sealed and pressurized, gasoline could be forced through fuel lines to a carburetor. This system worked, but added the hazard of pressurized gasoline to the inconvenience of having to manually pump up the tank when starting a car after an interval of idleness (and inevitable air pressure leakage). There was also the nuisance of having to manually re-pressurize the system after filling it and the

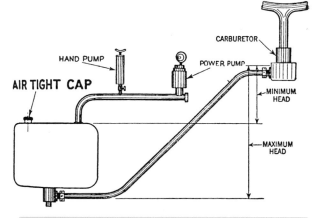

Pressure-over-fuel feed systems allowed location of fuel tanks at the backs of cars, but they were still dangerous, and very difficult to maintain.

service nightmare of having to maintain the integrity of a pressurized system.

Then, in the 1920s, the vacuum tank became ubiquitous on medium-priced and expensive motor cars. This finicky device valved engine manifold vacuum into an auxiliary fuel tank that was mounted on the cowl of a car. Vacuum there sucked gasoline from the main tank into the auxiliary tank. From there it ran by gravity to the carburetor.

In principle it was a good idea, but in fact it involved the hazard of storage of as much as 2 gallons of gasoline on the cowl, dangerously near both hot engine parts and passengers. The system was also prone to numerous gremlins, like vacuum leaks and valving failures. Vacuum tank fuel systems required very well-balanced carburetor float systems because their final gravity feed to carburetors provided only miniscule fuel pressure to open their inlet valves and raise their floats.

By the late 1920s, camshaft-driven mechanical fuel pumps began to appear on American cars, and these remained the standard of fuel delivery systems into the 1970s. Today, mechanical fuel pumps have disappeared and been replaced by submersible electric fuel pumps that feed fuel injectors via "common fuel rails." At this point, not many cars are being restored that have electric fuel pumps feeding carburetors or fuel injection systems, but restorers can expect to encounter any of the variations in fuel delivery systems noted above.

The Gas Tank

Gasoline tanks were almost always made out of steel with welded or crimped and soldered seams until the advent of plastic tanks a decade and a half ago. If they are located under car seats or in their cowls (gravity systems), they are protected from most road hazards. If they are located at a car's rear (pressure, vacuum tank, and pump systems), they are very vulnerable to things that go "thump" from underneath. In any location, they are vulnerable to attack by corrosion from inside and outside. Corrosion and leaking seams are the main defects that restorers will find in gas tanks.

Corrosion damage is most prevalent at the bottoms of tanks because that is where water condensation settles and where corrosive elements in the environment, like road salt, attack them. On pressurized systems it is common to find pin holes almost anywhere in the tanks. Loose tank baffles are also a common result of internal tank corrosion.

If the integrity of a fuel tank is breached, it must be repaired. Some damage is susceptible to soldering repairs, as, for example, damage to the connection of a tank filler neck and its main body, or leakage around crimped side seams, or to top seams around the exit pipe and fuel gage unit plates. These joints are either riveted, crimped, or pressure welded for structural strength. When they develop leaks their integrity usually can be reestablished by soldering them.

The easiest way to find all of the leaks in a gas tank is to wash it out, seal its openings, and put from 3 to 5 lbs. of air pressure in it. Then submerge it in water—one surface at a time—and any leaks will be indicated by escaping air bubbles. Never run this test near a source of ignition and wear full face and body protection when you do it. *Unless a tank has been completely cleaned with steam or by submersion in a hot tank, and completely filled with water or inert gas, it is extremely hazardous to solder it, particularly with an open flame.* This is because as a fuel tank is heated, volatiles trapped in the pores of its metal can be released by the heat. If these areas are heated up beyond their flash points, the results can be disastrous. Even an electrically driven rotary wire brush can provide a source of ignition for these fumes, and should not be used for fuel tank work unless special precautions are observed.

The best preparation for soldering a fuel tank is to clean it thoroughly with chemicals. Then, use a metal bristled hand brush to clean the areas that will be soldered. Then, blow them dry with compressed air, and prepare them for soldering with a non-acid flux. During the tinning and soldering operations the tank should be filled with water or an inert gas, such as CO_2 or argon. The area to be resealed should be tinned and soldered with a 40/60 or 50/50 tin/lead solder. Fuel tank soldering should be done with large soldering coppers (at least 1 1/2 lbs.). The furnace used to heat the coppers should be kept well away from the tank. This is work best done outside.

The first step, tinning, involves applying solder to the metal in the repair area after it has been fluxed and heated with a soldering copper, and then wiping it with steel wool or a rag. This removes excess solder and flux. Solder can then be flowed into the repair area using coppers to heat it. This type of repair will work well for leaking sweated and crimped joints, but should not be used to try to repair large open tears or rust-outs.

If it takes more than sweating a small patch onto a tank to seal it, welding will be required. Be sure that when you weld or solder gas tanks you have adequate ventilation in your work area and that all possible precautions are taken against igniting latent fumes in the tank. As I noted, I prefer to do this work outside when the weather permits it.

Welding patches on gas tanks is dangerous work. Over the years, a lot of people have failed to reach the full promises of their personhoods because they were unaware of the hazards of gas tank repair or failed to heed them. In many cases, these were people who tended to talk when they should have been listening, but their loss is felt, nonetheless. Don't join them. When you heat a seemingly clean gas tank to welding temperatures, it may emit flammable fumes that the welding or brazing process can ignite. An explosion could follow.

Before you attempt fuel tank welding repairs, you should steam clean or hot tank the fuel tank and rinse it with water. Then, you should fill it with water or inert gas and treat it thereafter like a live bomb. The key to welding or brazing tanks is to almost completely fill them with water or inert gas, leaving only the area where you are working clear of the water, if that is what you use to neutralize its dangers. This approach deprives the heated area of the oxygen that could support combustion. Even with these precautions, it is necessary to wear full face protection and body protection when you weld old gas tanks. You get the point. This is an inherently dangerous repair process.

Soldering fuel tanks is a dangerous business. Large soldering coppers, like these, are preferred for this work. The furnace that you heat the coppers in should be about 50 feet away from the tank that you are working on, and this work should be done outside, never in a building, unless special ventilation is provided.

I know that there are people out there who have been soldering and welding gas tanks for years with little regard for the above cautions. As with many hazardous activities, you can get away with this one until the conditions are just right, until your assigned cosmic tumblers click. In the case of gas tank explosions, the penalty is extreme. Don't fool around with welding or soldering gas tanks. If you have any doubts, find a welding shop to do it for you that knows the work.

You can frequently accomplish gas tank dent removal by filling a tank with water and applying 5 to 10 lbs. of air pressure to the sealed tank. This will pop out many large ,creaseless dents. More stubborn dents that are locked into the tank's sheet metal by creases will have to be forced out with prying tools through the available entry holes in the tank, such as the filler neck and sending unit openings.

Restorers should also be concerned with corrosion that has not yet perforated a gas tank. Almost all steel tanks were tinned or plated at the time of manufacture. As long as this barrier to corrosion remains in tact there are no problems. When it breaks down, pinholing, followed by rust-out, will occur. When you look inside a tank through its filler neck or sending unit opening, you can see if corrosion has started, and how far it has advanced. If it hasn't gone too far, you can slow it down by routinely adding commonly available alcohol (methanol or ethanol) gasoline dryers to your fuel. This causes the small quantities of water that may be present in a tank to combine with the alcohol and the gasoline. That prevents the water from promoting further corrosion.

Fuel tanks should first be inspected by feeling their questionable surfaces and then by looking inside them. A simple flashlight will go a long way and light from fiber optic devices and flexible units should give you a good inside view. You can clean as tanks by hot tanking them or by filling them with a buffered, diluted acid solution, and rocking them back and forth on a saw horse or log. This is a messy and somewhat hazardous operation.

If a more permanent and certain solution is desired, the use of one of the commercially available PVC/zinc chromate gas tank sloshing compounds may be appropriate. These are polyvinyl chloride (PVC) based compounds with zinc chromate rust inhibitors. They are widely advertised in old car specialty publications and if they are applied correctly they really do work. The idea behind these "sloshing compounds" is to coat the inside of a gas tank in a way that seals it and protects it from further deterioration. The PVC remains somewhat resilient after it cures, so the sloshing treatment amounts to installing a bladder in a gas tank.

Non-hardening sloshing compounds are applied by pouring them into a gas tank and sloshing them around until all surfaces have been coated. The excess is then drained out of the tank and the tank is air dried until the compound cures to a thin bladder-like coating, adhering to all inside surfaces of the tank. These compounds are absolutely impervious to gasoline and have terrific adhesion to tank metal, even if it is slightly rusty at the time of applying them.

Some of the early sloshing compounds were somewhat soluble in some alcohols, and tanks sloshed with these compounds must not be exposed to too much alcohol. If you run into a fuel tank that was treated with sloshing compound in the 1970s, it is suspect for this problem and should not be fueled with high-alcohol content fuels.

Later, sloshing compounds were formulated in ways that avoid this problem. Keep this in mind when adding gasoline dryer to your car, purchasing a gasohol concoction or purchasing gas tank sloshing compound. Be sure to use only sloshing compounds that are compatible with alcohol additives in fuels.

I must admit that when I first heard of sloshing compounds, I was skeptical. It all sounded like one of those "pie in the sky" quick fixes that you pour in and later get to scrape out when it doesn't work. Later, I found out that some of these coatings are certified by the CAB or FAA for use in aircraft fuel tanks. Instant credibility! You don't park a stalled single-engine airplane by the side of the road when its fuel system fails in flight. In the 25 years that I have been using sloshing compounds, I have had only one failure, and that was my own fault, due to improper application.

Although the sellers of sloshing compounds sometimes claim that you don't have to clean a gas tank thoroughly before applying their products, the truth is that you should. This can be accomplished by taking the tank that you are going to treat to a radiator shop and having it boiled out in caustic radiator solvent. Steam cleaning or an overnight dip in the hot tank at an automotive machine shop will accomplish about the same thing. You can also get a tank clean for sloshing by taking it to a "dip strip" outfit (if you can find one) and having it cleaned in their immersion tanks.

If you want to clean and etch a fuel tank yourself, this can be done with a solution of 20-degree inhibited hydrochloric acid (denoted chemically as "HCL," and frequently called "muriatic" acid) diluted with water in a starting ratio of one part acid to five parts water. To this brew you add some liquid soap, such as dishwashing soap or detergent. Now, pour this solution into the tank you are cleaning and allow it to stand, or gently agitate it, for from 15 minutes to half an hour. The initial 1:5 mix of acid to water is followed by one that is 1:10, again with the addition of some liquid soap. The tank is then thoroughly rinsed with water. It will take at least 15 minutes with a garden hose pushing clean water through the tank to affect a complete rinse.

Then, a gallon of methanol or isopropyl alcohol should be sloshed around in the tank to remove all residues of the water rinse. You should then drain the tank and allow it to dry in a warm environment, such as sunlight, for several hours.

Throughout the cleaning and etching procedure described above you have to wear face and body protection to prevent the possibility of acid burns. Gauntlet-style rubber gloves are a must. If you choose to agitate the tank that you are etching, one good way to accomplish this is to balance it on a sawhorse and gently rock it back and forth.

Once the tank has been thoroughly dried, the sloshing compound should be poured into it, sloshed around onto every internal surface, and drained. Most of the sloshing compound that you pour in will drain back out and can be used on other tanks if it doesn't look too badly contaminated.

It is important that the tank is cool when it is sloshed and that it is dried in a cool place and left open to drain out the excess compound at its lowest drain point. Do not place the tank in direct sunlight to speed up the drying/curing process, as this can cause air blisters between the tank's metal and the cured sloshing compound. These blisters will eventually rupture and allow gasoline to run outside of the bladder containment, where it can leak out of the tank.

If you fail to drain the sloshed tank thoroughly, you will get a thick clot of sloshing compound deposited at its bottom. This lump will skin over, but it will never cure completely. It is good practice to apply two or three thin coats of sloshing compound to a tank. These should be applied at least two days apart to allow each layer to dry and to thoroughly cure.

A few tanks, like those used by Chrysler on some postwar models, have internal gasoline filters and pickup lines that cannot be removed without cutting them apart. Clearly, if the pickup unit in a tank cannot be removed, or masked by working through an access opening (without cutting into the tank), sloshing compound cannot be used because it will plug the pickup. Of course, any tank that is sloshed must have its gas gauge sending unit removed. Any dent removal, soldering, brazing, or welding must be completed before a tank is sloshed.

Gas tank exteriors should be cleaned to bare metal, primed with an etching-type primer and painted with a good enamel. Any high-quality engine enamel or hardened acrylic enamel will give the tank a tough and attractive finish, as will a urethane or polyurethane paint. If a tank is secured to a chassis with metal straps, these should be lined with composition cork or synthetic rubber strips to prevent chafing and rub-through of the tank's surface coating. Tanks are very prone to rusting under their securing straps, so providing non-metallic buffers is a good idea.

However, isolating a tank this way may deprive it of critical chassis grounding. Always be sure that any gas tank that you install is grounded to the chassis. It is good practice to provide redundant grounds to accomplish this. I usually secure two grounding wires to the tops of tanks at their removable sending unit/fuel standpipe plate and then attach the other ends of these ground wires to good chassis or platform grounds.

Any rubber hoses that connect a fuel tank to its gas filler or to a tank vent must be checked for deterioration and clamped securely in place to prevent leakage. Drain cocks and other fittings and connections should be adequately tightened. A good gasoline-resistant sealer like Permatex #1 should be used on their threads. Gasoline leaks are extremely hazardous because gasoline fumes are heavier than air and will pool on a floor and traverse it. If they seep and roll far enough to find a source of ignition, the result probably will be catastrophic. Keep this in mind when you make any connection that will contain gasoline.

Fuel Lines, Fittings, and Filters

Unless you are working on a very early automobile that used copper fuel lines and must be restored with them for the sake of appearance, it is a good idea to use modern double-flared brake lines for fuel system plumbing. The best practice is to purchase your line material in the correct diameter in the bulk 25- or 50-footcoils that are readily available at most auto parts stores in diameters from 3/16 to 3/8 inch. Then, bend the lines that you need to the right shapes and cut them to length. Fuel line terminations vary greatly. Compression fittings should be avoided, and if flared ends are used, they should be made with a double-flaring tool.

Copper lines are a bad idea because when they are subjected to vibration they have a tendency to work harden and crack, and fuel lines do vibrate as a car goes down the road. Single flaring does not produce an adequate seal for fuel, and should be avoided. The best bet is a double-flared mild steel line with as few couplings as possible and good attachment to the chassis to limit vibration travel. Always avoid letting a fuel line or brake line rest against a metal edge chassis feature because over time and mileage it can vibrate through a mild steel line like a knife.

Because most engines after the early 1930s are mounted on flexible rubber cushioning mounts, they are able to rock and vibrate independently of their chasses. This means that the final connection between an engine-mounted fuel pump and its chassis fuel line should be by a flexible hose that allows for this movement. Various kinds of reinforced rubber and plastic have been used to make flexible fuel lines, and it is important that you use a good quality flexible line for this application. The old flex lines, and the new ones that are used to replace them, must be able to sustain both suction and flexing without collapsing. When high-pressure flexible fuel lines are used on the pressure sides of fuel pumps, they must be in perfect condition. These should be replaced as a matter of routine in restoration work.

Vapor Lock

Fuel lines that run in an engine compartment are susceptible to the dreaded vapor lock. This is a condition that occurs when gasoline in a fuel delivery system boils. This starves the engine, resulting in sputtering and stalling. The usual reason for gas boiling in fuel lines is not so much that the ambient under-hood temperature is sufficient to cause it, but that radiant heat from an exhaust manifold is overheating a gas line, filter or fuel pump bowl. The easiest fix is to locate gas lines and filters away from surfaces in the engine that radiate high heat, insofar as this is possible. When the geography of an engine compartment makes this impossible, some heat shielding will usually cure the problem.

Modern gasoline fuels have relatively high Reed Vapor Pressure (RVP) numbers compared to the fuels that were available several years ago. This is because with today's submersible fuel pumps and fuel injection, fuels are subjected to such high delivery pressures that vapor lock is not a problem. However, the high volatility of today's fuels is a very real problem for old car owners and restorers who work on systems that subject fuel to suction, on the downsides of their fuel pumps, and to relatively low pressures upside of them.

Many old-time Ford V-8 drivers and dabblers tell stories of cutting grapefruits in half and stuffing the hemispheres over the glass fuel filter bowls on the tops of early Ford V-8 fuel pumps to stymie vapor lock. It is alleged that this cure worked by shielding and cooling. These good influence s were produced by the entropy from evaporation of moisture through the grapefruit hemispheres' skins. While this sounds both quaint and authentic, modern practice tries to avoid this degree of authenticity in restoration work.

In recent years vapor lock problems have become increasingly worse as refiners have forced more and more "high ends" into their products. Such gasoline components as butane tend to boil out of gasoline at relatively low temperatures and raise havoc with carbureted engine performance, particularly on cars equipped with vacuum tanks. Since modern fuel systems maintain relatively high fuel pressure (about 30 lbs.) in their fuel rails, vapor lock is not a problem, and refiners have not been noticeably concerned with the vapor pressures of their products.

Fortunately, the federal government keeps track of this problem as a pollution issue, and the Environmental Protection Agency has propounded standards to control the volatility of the gasoline that is sold. Keep all of this in mind when you replace fuel lines and filters and can easily reroute them for better protection from radiated engine heat.

Fuel filters are constructed from materials ranging from sintered bronze and ceramic to expanded, resonated paper. Older systems frequently made do with sediment bowls containing fine brass gauze screens on fuel pumps. Except for this last type, fuel filters are meant to be replaced and cannot be cleaned effectively. Attempts to blow out sintered bronze and expanded paper filters will prove fruitless. It is equally fruitless to attempt to check the condition of a fuel filter by blowing compressed air through it, though I have seen this tried many times. Air can be blown easily through barriers that would never allow gasoline to pass.

The only meaningful way to test a fuel filter is to let its fuel delivery system try to force fuel through it. If it can't do this easily, replace the filter. On older systems that depend on a gauze screen and sediment bowl for fuel filtration, it's a good idea to add a modern resonated paper filter. Such filters are compact and effective and will do a much better filtering job than the gauze type. If you decide to add one of these, your related decision of where to locate it should take into account the possibility of vapor lock in the filter's case if it is overheated by radiant heat. You should also consider the aesthetics of the situation. Always locate add-on filters on the pressure sides of fuel pumps, never on the suction sides.

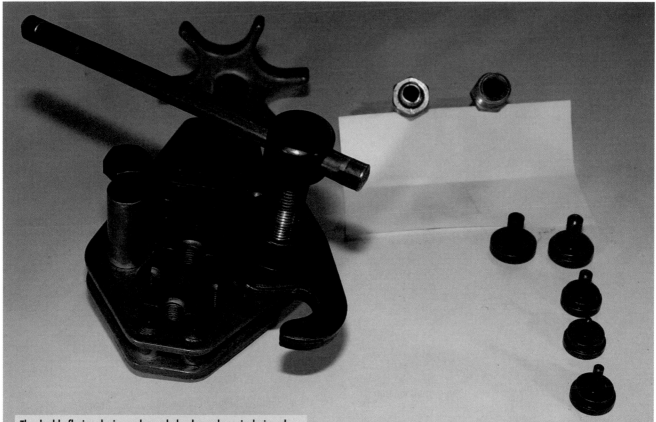

The double flaring device and mandrels, shown here, is designed for brake line work, but it's your best bet for making gas line terminations that use the double flare style fitting. The mandrel is inserted to make the first half-flare and then removed. Then, the tool's anvil is forced down to fold the half-flared lip back against itself for a double flare.

Fuel Delivery Systems

The earliest practical fuel delivery systems were based on gravity. Beyond keeping fuel lines tight and in clean condition, and carburetor floats and needles in top condition, there isn't much that needs special attention in these gravity systems, since constant gravity is one of the immutable givens in any situation on this earth. Operators of cars equipped with gravity systems will quickly discover that fuel tanks should be kept at least one quarter full at all times, if they intend to ascend hills.

Pressure systems that force air pressure into gas tanks are simple in concept, but may require extensive repair and maintenance. Every part in these systems has to be capable of containing air pressure. This includes fuel gauges, filler caps, fuel tanks, and all of the plumbing to engines and air pressure components. These systems usually rely on hand pumps to generate initial pressure, and on small engine-driven piston pumps to maintain that pressure. Blow-offs keep the air pressure from exceeding a few pounds. Those who own cars with this type of system are generally condemned to spending considerable time, usually at incredibly inconvenient moments, finding and repairing leaks. Whenever a car with an air pressurized fuel system is shut off, it is a very good idea to manually bleed the pressure out of the system at the hand pump, if it has a provision for

doing this, or at the filler cap, if it doesn't.

The tribulations of the owners of air-pressurized fuel system-equipped cars may be easily matched or exceeded by those with cars that employ the notorious vacuum tank devices to deliver fuel. About 90 percent of these systems were built by Stewart-Warner. At the time of their manufacture they were considered to be quite an advance in fuel system design.

"That was then, this is now." Aside from the natural

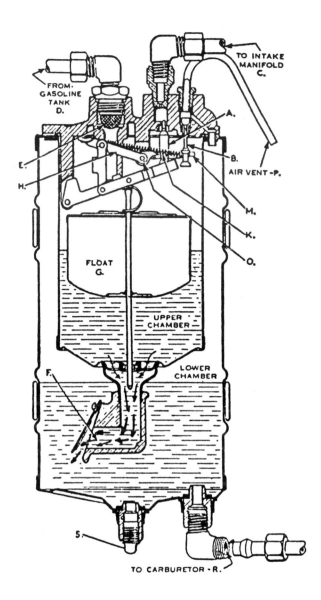

No doubt about it, vacuum tanks are finicky. The flapper valve below the inside tank can be a particular problem; it often sticks or leaks.

deterioration and wear that occurs in these devices, a whole new range of problems is posed by contemporary fuels, with lots of high fractions and volatile gases among their components, and a resulting tendency to vapor lock. There are so many things that can go wrong with vacuum tanks that I hesitate to select the leading causes of their malfunctions for fear of omissions.

The spring-loaded, float-operated valving devices on early vacuum tanks are the sources of many of the problems with them. These fussy-looking items valve vacuum to small tanks inside main vacuum tanks, drawing fuel into them from rear-mounted fuel storage tanks. Incoming fuel raises floats in the inner tanks, and when they are full, the floats shut off the vacuum and release the fuel in the inner tanks so that it flows into the outer tanks, closing the valve between them. Then, float valving reapplies engine vacuum to the inner tanks and repeats the cycle. Strangely, the fussy-looking float-valving systems are not usually the sources of vacuum tank problems. Things aren't always what they seem.

However, the innocuous looking flapper valves on the discharge ports between the inner and outer tanks can cause plenty of trouble. They must not stick to their seats— where they like to bind—and they must be able to seal against their seats effectively. If these valves are the cause of problems, their faces should be lapped onto their seats with a very fine abrasive. The inner tanks, themselves, are very prone to pinholing and internal leakage. If this is a problem, they should be checked and resealed by soldering. As well, every threaded connection and the top tank gaskets have to be perfect for vacuum tanks to work. Any accumulation of varnish or corrosion on vacuum tank valve mechanisms can cause malfunctions. See why vacuum tanks are so beloved by restorers?

When a vacuum tank is restored, my preference is for etching the inner and outer tanks and having them retinned by someone with a tin pot. Almost any other coating will cause problems later. In fact, problems later is what restoring vacuum tanks seems to be all about. Don't feel badly if you restore one and find it failing every so often after that. If the flapper valve sticks or the top gasket leaks about every third time that you want to use a car equipped with one of these systems, you have arrived at the average for these units. Meticulous attention to the fine points *may* produce a vacuum tank that is *almost* reliable.

Camshaft-Driven Mechanical Fuel Pumps

From the 1930s on, mechanical fuel pumps have

dominated fuel delivery system design in this country. At first, most of these pumps were manufactured by the AC division of General Motors. Later, there were other manufacturers. The earliest fuel pumps were pretty simple and tended to incorporate pullrod or pushrod actuation with a straightforward diaphragm pump. By the mid-1930s, compound pumps with secondary vacuum booster diaphragms began to appear. The purpose of the second pumping diaphragm was to provide adequate vacuum for windshield wipers during periods of low manifold vacuum (acceleration and low speed operation). By the 1950s, many pumps included a second, passive diaphragm in the fuel section to help damp out the pulsations that are inherent in any diaphragm pump.

Unfortunately, as fuel pumps became more complex and sophisticated, it also became more difficult to repair them. Early pumps tended to have their valving retained by large hex fittings that were easy to remove and to replace. Later designs utilized pressed in valving with flimsy retainers that are often hard to remove and difficult to resecure, particularly if they have been staked into pumps crudely in a previous repair(s). By the time you get to some of the compound pumps, the valving and rebound springing can be pretty complex and difficult to assemble, because there can be a lot of it.

Finally, in the march to make fuel pumps more difficult to repair, ultimate success was achieved with the development of the sealed (crimped together) disposable fuel pumps of the 1970s and after. These maddening units will fail for want of a 50-cent diaphragm or a 25-cent valve, and there is little that can be done to repair them.

I know, I know.... The labor to repair them would cost more than replacement, so this is the best economic approach. It's progress. Somehow that sounds good in the abstract, but can be a bit too theoretical when you have to pop for a $30-$75 fuel pump that could have been repaired with less than a buck's worth of parts and half an hour of labor, *if* you could get into the thing.

Mechanical fuel pump restoration is similar in many ways to carburetor restoration. The parts tend to be made out of the same materials and such procedures as cleaning and flange straightening are basically the same for both of these fuel system components. Please refer to Chapter 12 on carburetor restoration for this background.

Aside from the obvious need for tight, leakproof connections and assemblies, there are several special considerations in fuel pump repair. The first is testing. Fuel pumps can be tested easily on a car by checking their output pressures, input suction and delivery volumes. Output pressure is tested with a low pressure gauge with an engine running for several seconds on the gasoline in its carburetor bowel. The gauge is held at about the level of the carburetor and connected to the carburetor input line fitting. From 3 to 7 PSI is about average for most pumps output pressures, but check the specifications given by manufacturers for exact values.

Unfortunately, just because a pump can generate adequate pressure does not mean that it can also produce adequate fuel volume. Sometimes, a fuel or air bubble trapped between the layers of an old diaphragm will fill the pumping cavity, causing a pump to produce inadequate fuel volume, while maintaining adequate output pressure. An air leak on the vacuum side of a pump can cause the same result. To check pump delivery, run a hose from the pump's output line into a container with the end of the hose submerged in the pumped gasoline. The pump should produce roughly a quart per minute at 500 RPM, and there should not be any air bubbles in the delivered fuel. Bubbles indicate an air leak somewhere in the pump, or in its supply hoses and lines. The vacuum side of the pump should indicate about 10 inches of Hg (mercury) at that RPM. If a fuel pump is equipped with a booster vacuum section (compound type), it should generate about 8 inches of Hg from that section.

One of the laments that restorers experience with fuel pumps involves "N.O.S." units. Frequently, when these pumps, or pumps that were rebuilt long ago, are put into service, they fail very quickly thereafter. This happens because their diaphragm material has hardened. Although an old diaphragm may work for a short while, it will soon crack and leak.

The older diaphragm materials were made from layers of tarred canvas textile. Later diaphragms were made leakproof by impregnating or surfacing them with rubber or primitive rubber substitutes. Post World War II practice was to use textile-reinforced synthetics like Neoprene. This was a vast improvement. The best diaphragm material that I know of for use today is Nitrile reinforced with Nylon. This material is almost completely impervious to gasoline fuel or anything in it, and seems to resist hardening wonderfully. It is readily available in several thicknesses from any good gasket and packing supply house. In any case, if you are contemplating the use of an N.O.S. pump, or an older rebuild, consider making a new diaphragm for it before you install that pump in a car.

Disassembly and Reassembly of Mechanical Fuel Pumps

Before disassembling a fuel pump, always mark its major parts for phase, so that they can be reinstalled in the right orientation to each other. Barring such unusual problems as cracked or broken castings, almost all problems will be found in the mechanical linkage, inlet and outlet valves, diaphragm(s), or push or pull rod(s) and their seal(s). Any pump restoration should deal with all of these areas.

Mechanical linkage and actuating and tensioning springs should be checked for corrosion, distortion and breakage. Pivot points must be tight. If they are not, rebushing them is necessary. Pump cam followers have to be smooth and flat in the planes of the cams, and if push rods are used, they have to be straight and undamaged by pitting

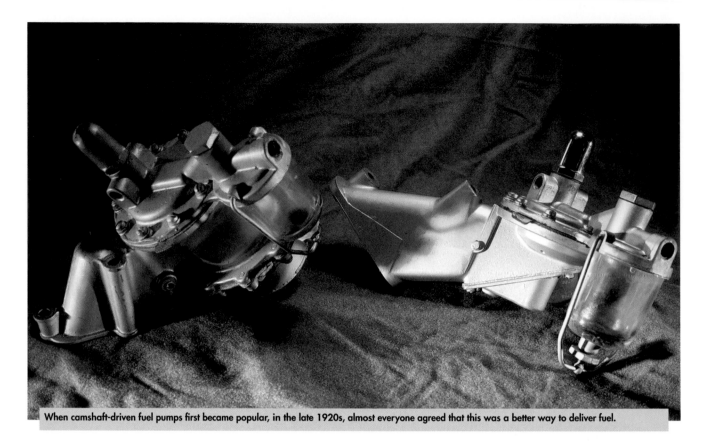

When camshaft-driven fuel pumps first became popular, in the late 1920s, almost everyone agreed that this was a better way to deliver fuel.

or wear. Fuel pump valves have to be flat and smooth. It is always a good idea to replace them and their springs if these valves have been removed. Some valve seats are replaceable and others have to be lapped in the pump. In either case, it is a good idea to recondition the valves and their seats, and to check their performance with mild air pressure and suction. Valves are often held in place by staking the pump body over their retaining parts. Do this carefully, but securely. The push or pull rod seal in a fuel pump is important and should be replaced in any rebuild. Any good kit will contain new push or pull rod seals. The installation of these seals can be difficult. Check the illustration of proper and improper installation in the instructions that accompany your rebuild kit.

Of course, main diaphragms and pulsation diaphragms (if so equipped) cause most of the problems in fuel pumps. Most of the older diaphragms have flanges nutted to their push and/or pull rods and are easy to replace. You simply buy or cut a new diaphragm piece and reattach the flanges. Be sure to save or duplicate any fiber spacers or cushions included in the diaphragm and flange assembly originally. Use a good thread-locking compound to lock the nut threads, and deform the nut slightly to prevent loosening. Go easy on this because someone, someday, will have to rebuild the pump again, and he will need threads that are usable. Where the diaphragm and flanges are secured to push or pull rods by swaging, it is usually possible to grind or to file enough of the swage away to allow for disassembly and subsequent reassembly and re-swaging. Sometimes swaged pull rods can be threaded and reassembled with a nut or a screw instead of the original swage.

For the most part, cam-driven fuel pumps are reliable. When they fail, it is usually because little items, like their valves, valve springs or seats have deteriorated. The valve parts shown here look OK but it is a good idea to replace parts like this when you have a fuel pump apart.

This, of course, makes subsequent rebuilding easier. Whatever the method of securing a fuel pump's diaphragm and flanges to its push and/or pull rod is, it is a good idea to use just a smear of silicone rubber RTV compound to seal this joint.

Final assembly of mechanical pumps is relatively easy. Make sure that the valves are installed correctly—there is

Most automotive vacuum gauges, like this one, have a pressure side that indicates fuel pump pressure. It is the inner circle of calibrations on the gauge shown here. This is a good test to run on any fuel pump, but even if a pump delivers adequate pressure, be sure to check it for delivery volume. That can still be substandard and cause running problems.

Old fuel pump diaphragms are made from layered textile materials and get very hard as they age. Diaphragms cut from the Nylon reinforced Nitrile material, shown here, will last almost forever in fuel pump service. You can buy this material from most packing and gasket supply houses.

an inescapable logic to their positions vis a vis the pumping action. Lubricate all linkage pivot points, and be sure to put a dab of grease on the cam follower or push rod end. Give pump diaphragm flanges a final tightening that is both even and sequenced across their diameters.

About the only thing that you can do wrong in installing a fuel pump is to get its cam follower on the wrong side of the cam. This sounds innocent, but the results can be disastrous. Be sure that you know which side of the follower goes against the cam, and that it is seated there. Installation is much easier if an engine is turned over until the flat side of the cam drive lobe is positioned against the cam follower during installation. Tighten the pump body to the crankcase securely and evenly against a fresh cork or composition gasket.

Electric Fuel Pumps

Electric fuel pumps were born partly in the fight against vapor lock and start-up starvation due to percolation. That sorry sequence occurs when an engine compartment heat

soaks after a car engine is shut down and air no longer flows through it to remove heat from the under-hood area. The high under-hood temperature that results causes the gasoline in carburetor bowls to percolate (boil), so when you go to start the car there is no fuel in its carburetor. Then, it takes many engine rotations with the starter to get gas to displace the air in the system.

However, electric pumps start when keys are turned and do not require starter-driven engine rotation to supply fuel pressure and to force air out of fuel delivery systems. The pumping sections of most electric pumps are similar to those in mechanical pumps. The difference is that in most designs an electromagnet and spring or a motor are used to move them. This drive is activated by a set of contact points that sense the position of the diaphragm and, thus, the need for another pump stroke to maintain proper fuel line pressure.

Most of the trouble with electric fuel pumps is not diaphragm or valve related; it is caused by pitting of their contact points. In some cases, these points can be dressed, while in other cases they have to be replaced. A few submersible electric pumps were used in the past, but this design is mostly a recent application and involves rotary turbine/impeller type pumps.

A small number of British cars, such as Jaguar and Rolls-Royce, used rotary electric impeller-type fuel pumps that allowed the crisp ticking of their dashboard clocks to be heard over what would otherwise have been the din created by fuel pump operation. That's what the manufacturers of these fuel pumps claimed, anyway. These wonderful pumps delivered fuel with very little pulsation but, sadly, with very little reliability as well.

It is not unusual for the owners of old cars to replace

You'll need open stock parts like these, or a kit, to rebuild any fuel pump.

This is about what an average fuel pump will look like when its parts are all separated and laid out. Compound fuel pumps that boost vacuum to windshield wipers have about twice as many parts. The valving and diaphragm section, also shown here, is the key to any fuel pump.

vacuum tanks and mechanical fuel pumps with electric units. This helps to eliminate vapor lock and percolation-related problems, but it also can have some drawbacks. In the case of vacuum tanks, because the final feed to carburetors is by gravity, floats are designed for operation by very low fuel pressures. On the other hand, most electric pumps deliver 6+ psi. Often, this is too much pressure for carburetor float systems designed to operate with vacuum tanks, so the float valves leak.

Even on cars equipped with conventional mechanical fuel pumps, replacement electric pumps frequently deliver twice the pressure for which the original fuel systems were

The valves in this pump had to be removed with a punch and some gentle tapping. When new valves are installed, they should be staked into their receiving holes to supplement the press fit. If you choose to use threadlocking compound to secure valve cages into their pump receptacles, be sure to use only the mildest compound available, or you will have great difficulty removing the cages at a later date without endangering the fuel pump casting.

When you install a new diaphragm on a fuel pump pull rod, put a little dab of silicone rubber on the area where the pull rod goes through the diaphragm material. This will help to seal it. Some pull rods are swaged to their diaphragms, while other use threaded fasteners. Either way, be sure that when you replace a fuel pump's diaphragm material you secure it to its pull rod with a connection that will not fail in service.

designed. Whenever an electric pump is used to replace an original non-electric delivery system, a pressure regulator should be added to the system to bring fuel delivery pressure into the range of what was originally provided for in the carburetor float valve design. One well-known brand of inexpensive electric fuel pumps has an adjustable pressure regulator built into it, but this regulator is between useless and worthless. If you use that pump, add another adjustable pressure regulator to your fuel delivery system.

Fuel Gauges

The earliest fuel gauges were foolproof. They were dead accurate, completely reliable, and cheap to construct. They did lack a certain elegance, not to mention convenience. They were, of course, strips of wood resembling halves of yardsticks with fuel level calibrations marked on them. One only had to remove a car's front seat, fuel tank cover panel and tank cap to measure fuel level. Then, the stick "gauge" was submerged into the gasoline in the tank. It instantly registered the fuel's exact level with no foolin' around. OK, this procedure missed the fine points of safety and convenience, but it was accurate.

By the teen years of the last century, various mechanical gauges based on shellacked cork or soldered brass floats had come into use. In practice, fuel level indications were transmitted through gearing and linkage onto the faces of rotary gauges. Usually, these gauges were mounted directly

If you can't remove a valve seat from a pump body, or if it is only slightly eroded, you can often face it with the flat end of a wooden dowel and some very fine valve grinding compound. You do this in a drill press. I have used toothpaste on a dowel to polish brass fuel pump seats. Fine lapping compounds, like those shown here, will also work well in this application.

on fuel tanks and had to be read at the backs of cars. In the case of the Ford model "A," a float system in a cowl-mounted fuel tank was read from a dashboard gauge. For a few years in the mid-1920s, Lincolns and some other cars actually carried the mechanical motion of gas tank floats by cable linkage up to their dashboards where it was registered on geared rotary gauges.

By the late 1920s, many cars were using the King-Seeley hydrostatic gauge setup. This troublesome device used differential air pressures conducted from fuel tanks, via capillary tubing, to viscous tube indicator glasses in gauges on their dashboards. These systems are a nightmare to maintain because their delicate capillary tubing is prone to damage and the various soldered and cemented joints in these systems are frequently in a failure mode. The indicator fluid—many different fluids were used, with acetylene tetrabromide being the best of them—is frequently quite corrosive and is also susceptible to contamination damage, evaporation and coagulation.

Electric fuel gauges are usually driven magnetically (selsen type) or by a heater and bimetallic element. There are a few oddball designs out there, like the King-Seeley bimetallic heater-interrupter system that was used by Ford, Hudson, Nash and a few others just before and just after World War II.

Common heater and magnetic type electric fuel gauges use gas tank floats linked by pivots and arms to wound resistance coils and contacts that rub across them. This amounts to a rheostat that increases or decreases resistance as the float moves from "full" to "empty." In the magnetic-type indicators (AC), the resistance in tank sending units increases as tanks are filled and floats rise. Single wires connect the dash gauges to the sending units. Two balancing coils mounted at 90 degrees to each other in these gauges pull indicator needles toward "full" and "empty," respectively. The coils are connected in series and grounded through the tank

This electric fuel pump can be inconspicuously installed in a frame rail, or elsewhere, to either assist or to replace a mechanical fuel pump. This particular pump has a pressure regulator built into its top. Be careful not to let too much pressure get at a carburetor float when you install an electric fuel pump as a replacement or helper in an old system. Many carburetor needle valves cannot take higher fuel pressures than those for which they were designed.

rheostats, with the coils on the "full" sides having greater internal resistance than the coils on the "empty" sides. As the resistance in these circuits increases, the coils on the "full" side will produce proportionally greater attraction for the needles.

A variation on the magnetic system that was used by Autolite employed permanently energized magnetic coils on the "empty" sides and potentially stronger magnetic coils on the "full" sides. In this system, an increase in the fuel levels in tanks produces a corresponding reduction in the resistances in the tank rheostats, and thus a stronger attraction toward "full" on the gauges.

The heater-type gauge, associated with Autolite and others, used heater coils and bimetallic elements to indicate fuel levels. In this system, when tanks are full, the gauge wires are effectively grounded, and the heaters in the gauges receive full system voltage. This, in turn, heats the bimetallic elements in the gauges and deflects the needles linked to them to the maximum degree, indicating "full."

Less fuel in tanks means more grounding resistance and, therefore, less heat and less deflection of the bimetallic elements and, thus, lower gauge readings. Heater-type gauges usually have secondary heaters that are designed to correct for ambient temperatures that occur on very hot or

very cold days and that would otherwise distort fuel gauge readings.

Beyond carefully cleaning tank rheostat contacts and resistance coils and dealing with any mechanical or electrical defects in the dash gauge units, none of these electric systems are particularly susceptible to rebuilding.

Sending unit coil failure is a frequent problem, as is float failure. Heat-type fuel gauge systems can be tested. The simplest way to accomplish this is to substitute a good tank sending unit for the one in the tank and determine by moving its float manually if the system fault lies in the sending unit, the gauge or the connecting wiring. In all systems, grounding the sending unit and gas tank to the chassis is critical.

You might wonder why tank-mounted rheostat devices don't trigger fuel tank explosions. There are several answers to that question and most of them are reassuring. Sending unit design includes providing two wiper contacts to run over the in-tank rheostat coils. This double-contact design prevents arcing that could ignite a tank fire because as one contactor is moving between coil wire segments, the other arm is firmly on the next segment. A second reason that electric fuel tank sending units do not initiate the ignition for explosions is that they live in segregated areas in tanks

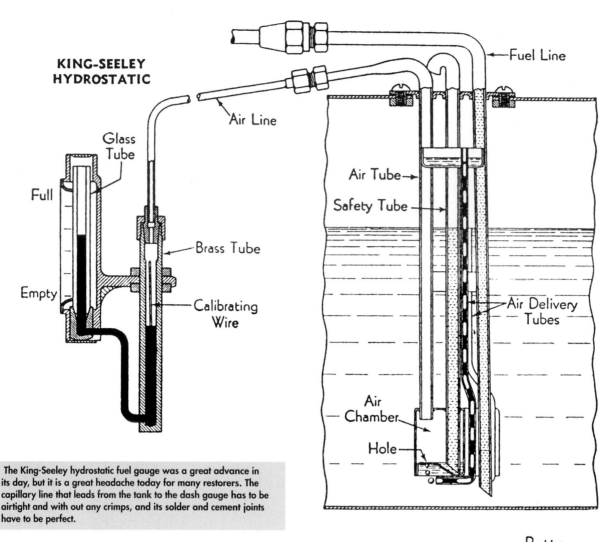

KING-SEELEY HYDROSTATIC

Air Line

Fuel Line

Glass Tube

Full

Empty

Brass Tube

Calibrating Wire

Air Tube

Safety Tube

Air Delivery Tubes

Air Chamber

Hole

The King-Seeley hydrostatic fuel gauge was a great advance in its day, but it is a great headache today for many restorers. The capillary line that leads from the tank to the dash gauge has to be airtight and with out any crimps, and its solder and cement joints have to be perfect.

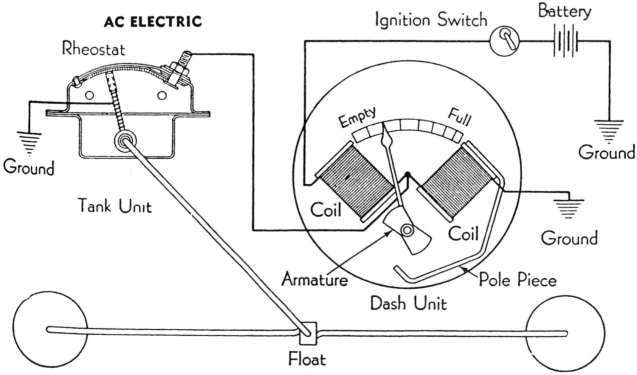

AC ELECTRIC

Rheostat

Ignition Switch

Battery

Ground

Tank Unit

Empty

Full

Ground

Coil

Coil

Armature

Pole Piece

Ground

Dash Unit

Float

Electric fuel gauges are simple and reliable. They indicate on the basis of rheostat varied voltage that moves a bimetallic or a magnetic needle drive.

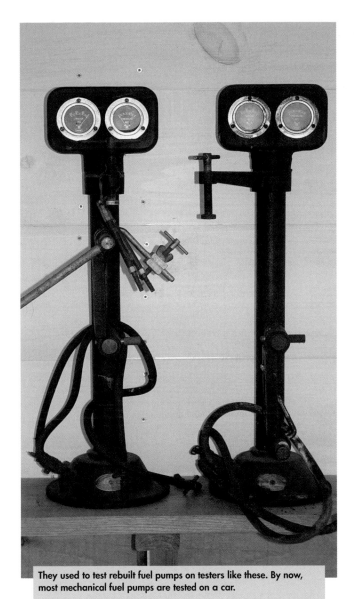

They used to test rebuilt fuel pumps on testers like these. By now, most mechanical fuel pumps are tested on a car.

This compound fuel pump has been rebuilt and detailed to look as good as I hope its performance will be.

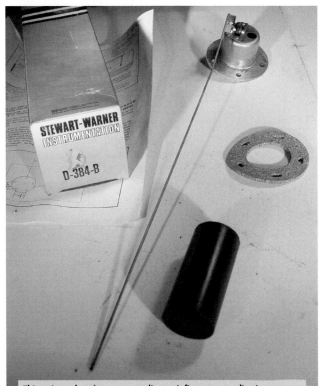

This universal replacement sending unit fits many applications. The float is slid on the drive arm and the arm is bent to duplicate an original sending unit. Then, the float is secured to the arm. The reason that the rheostats in gas gauge sending units don't cause fuel tank explosions is that they are designed with overlapping rheostat contacts that can't spark, and also, because the mixture in a fuel tank is supposed to be too rich to ignite. Fuel tank sending rheostats are located in areas purposely kept fuel rich for that reason.

where the air-fuel mixture is too rich to ignite with a spark.

The third consideration in this matter is less reassuring. Sometimes, fuel tank sending units do initiate fuel ignition, but this is very rare. It can happen with old, gummed-up units in tanks that are almost completely empty. The result is a blown-up tank. I have seen the results of this rare sequence. It is very scary, but usually not fatal to occupants of the cars where it has happened.

Chapter 14

Clutches and Transmissions

John Twist, the amiable and knowledgeable proprietor of University Motors in Ada, Michigan, uses this cut-away transmission as a teaching tool in courses that he instructs on rebuilding vintage MGs. You won't find the power flow color coded like this on any transmission that you disassemble, but with a little study and thought you can dope out how most units work.

IN THE BEGINNING OF THE AGE OF SELF-PROPELLED vehicles, it looked as if there wouldn't be any need for clutches or transmissions. That was just as well because there weren't any units "on the shelf" waiting to be adapted to automotive use. The reason that there was no need to couple and uncouple self-propelled vehicle engines from some cumbersome variable ratio gearing device was that steam and electricity provided motive power for most of the earliest automobiles.

In both cases, with some small allowances for rotary momentum, the "torque curves" of these propulsion units are virtually flat. Take steam, for example; the combustion is external to the engine, and engine speed has no effect on the pressure of the steam being applied to the engine's pistons. If you have, say, 100 PSI of steam supplied to a particular steam engine, the horsepower will be a function of that

The main cluster shaft of a manual transmission looks like this. Just remember that there are a lot of little parts contained in it and it is easier to take apart than to reassemble.

pressure and of the dimensions, valving and efficiency of that engine—with some allowance for friction, momentum, and other minor losses. The same applies to electricity as a source of motive power. Supply a certain level of energy and you will generate a corresponding amount of torque. This is true if the motor is turning over at 1 RMP or 1000 RPM—with some allowance for momentum.

Alas, the reciprocating internal combustion engine has a distinctly unflat torque curve. In fact, its torque curve is so "peaky" that there is only a narrow band of RPMs at which its power can be tapped for the business of driving a motor vehicle. Whereas a gearbox is a fine point on steam cars, used for the somewhat esoteric purpose of limiting engine speeds to reduce wear, for internal combustion powered automobiles it is a necessity.

While the device (transmission) used to perform the function of changing drive ratios may appear in widely varying forms, its purpose is always the same: to mate an engine to driving wheels at a rotational speed that falls within the range in which the engine produces sufficient torque to power the vehicle.

The variety of automotive mechanisms used over the years to gear and to couple and uncouple gearing devices is monumental. The human ingenuity applied to the design of this hardware is astounding.

Several different clutch configurations and materials have enjoyed popularity. Clutch configurations have varied from cones to multiple wet and dry discs to single and compound disc systems. Early clutches used such available friction facing materials as leather, cork inserts and woven compositions of textile.

The simplicity and compactness of the modern

A neat, orderly work area and approach greatly help in transmission work.

clutch was not possible until major advances in friction facing materials had occurred in the 1920s. By the 1930s, manufacturers like Borg and Beck and Long had pretty much standardized the format and materials of the modern clutch. After that, the evolution of clutches continued to involve improvements in materials, most recently replacing asbestos fiber compositions with safer materials based on aramid fibers. This allowed the production of ever lighter and more durable clutches. A few auto manufacturers, like Hudson, persisted in producing cars with distinctive clutches. In Hudson's case this meant using archaic facing

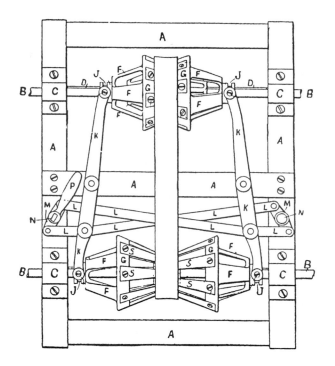

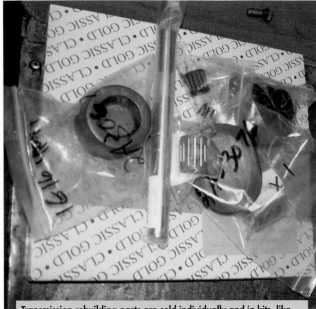

Transmission rebuilding parts are sold individually and in kits, like the one shown here.

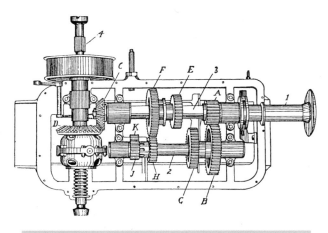

Over the years many different configurations and formats for clutches and transmissions have been used on automobiles. The first illustration shows a variable pulley-and-belt system that is remarkably similar in principle and layout to the cutting edge CVT (continuously variable transmission) systems that are available on some modern cars. If you thought that transaxles arrived in the 1960s or 1970s from Europe or Japan, have a look at this early 20th century transaxle unit that was used in a rear-wheel drive automobile. Note that this is a sliding gear design.

Keep parts together and stored carefully while you are waiting for those replacement parts or kits.

materials like cork, long after they were obsolete. As well, some experimentation with configurations like diaphragm springing and carbon release bearings continued.

Early transmissions tended to divide between planetary gear (epicyclical) systems and sliding gear types. With the exception of the Model T Ford—Henry Ford could be a stubborn man—planetary systems had pretty much given way to sliding gear units by the end of the first decade of the 20th century. By the 1930s, constant mesh, synchronized gearing began to appear on American cars. In the years after World War II, synchromesh-type systems became standard, and synchronization was applied to all gears, not just the top two ratios.

The other major thrust in automotive gearing devices

was the development of the hydraulically operated planetary transmission—"automatic transmission"—just before and after World War II. Over the years, automatic transmissions became the most popular shifters. Their reign is now being challenged by several different forms of CVTs (Continuously Variable Transmissions), pioneered by Van Doorne in Holland on the DAF automobile. Later CVTs were used by Subaru on its Justy model and are presently offered by Honda, Saturn, Audi and others. New forms of CVTs that do not rely on pusher and puller chains are in development for the near future.

These are the main trends in clutch and transmission design. There were also some wonderful "oddball" designs, like Metz's and Cartercar's intriguing applications of

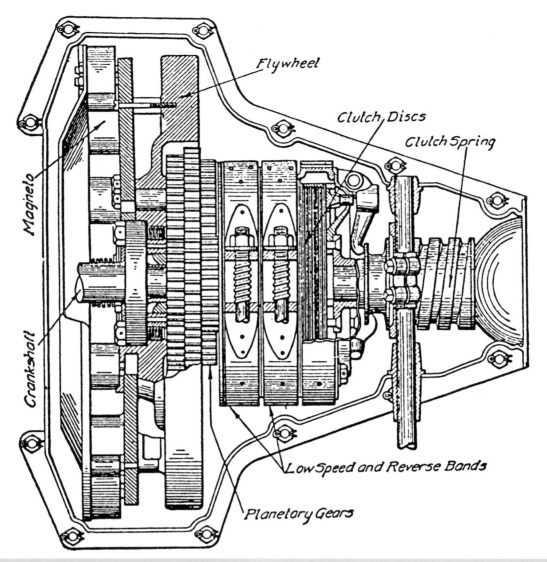

Flywheel

Clutch Discs

Clutch Spring

Magneto

Crankshaft

Low Speed and Reverse Bands

Planetary Gears

Henry Ford's epicyclic (planetary) gear transmission wasn't the latest item in transmission design in 1908 when the Model T was introduced, and it was certainly a dinosaur in 1927, when the venerable T was discontinued. However, for all of the quirks of its design, it was a compact and reasonably rugged gearing device for its time. It was certainly no more difficult to operate than the sliding gear transmissions that were its contemporaries in the early days of the Model T. Maybe Henry got the last laugh. With some exceptions, modern automatic transmissions get their gearing through epicyclic gearsets. However, the addition of torque converters and hydraulically controlled shifts is really what made Henry's beloved planetary gear clusters work.

friction transmissions, the fabulous Owen Magnetic's Entz drive or the early mechanically controlled planetary transmission used on the mid-1930s Reo Royale. Some hybrid transmissions, like Chrysler's Vacamatic or the European Cotal and Wilson preselector controls, predicted parts of the future. BMW and Audi continue that trend with an electronically controlled, hydraulically operated, more-or-less conventional clutched and automatic gearboxes that are more-or-less conventional constant mesh-type transmissions. BMW calls it SMG for Sequential Manual Gearbox. The variations are intriguing and almost endless.

The majority of collector cars are equipped with clutch/constant mesh gear change units, or with hydraulic/epicyclical automatics. Even within these two system headings there is enormous variation in design and fabrication. Many of the automatically shifted units of both types are enormously complex. That is one reason that clutch and transmission rebuilding is generally best left to

specialists, but restorers should know how to remove and replace these units, how to diagnose their maladies and how to provide for their maintenance. The thrust of this chapter on clutches and transmissions will be towards these points.

Operation of the Conventional Three-Element Clutch

Almost all friction clutches operate by squeezing a part or parts attached to the transmission between parts attached to the engine flywheel. This squeezing is effected by spring pressure. When a clutch is fully released (pedal out), the pressure is great enough to produce an almost total lockup of its members. When a clutch is uncoupled ("disengaged," or pedal down) the activating springs are compressed

CLUTCHES AND TRANSMISSIONS

191

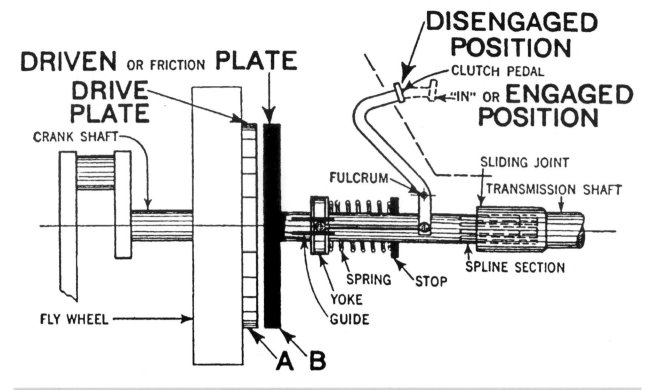

DRIVEN OR FRICTION **PLATE**

DRIVE PLATE

CRANK SHAFT

FLY WHEEL

A B

FULCRUM

SPRING STOP

YOKE

GUIDE

DISENGAGED POSITION

CLUTCH PEDAL

"IN" OR **ENGAGED POSITION**

SLIDING JOINT

TRANSMISSION SHAFT

SPLINE SECTION

This schematic illustrates the action of a simple clutch. The "driven plate" or clutch "disc," which is splined to the transmission shaft ("input shaft"), is squeezed by a spring or springs between an engine's flywheel and the clutch "plate" ("intermediate pressure plate"). The latter is in a housing that is bolted to the flywheel. When the foot pedal is depressed and the clutch is "disengaged," linkage operates a "release" ("throw-out") bearing. This bearing then presses on pivoting fingers that withdraw the clutch's pressure plate from the flywheel and clutch disc. The clutch disc can now spin free of the flywheel and engine. This allows the transmission shaft to which the clutch disc is splined to spin free of the engine as well.

through the application of foot pressure applied through various linkage pieces or hydraulic lines and cylinders. This uncouples the engine from its transmission by allowing the parts of the clutch assembly attached to the engine to spin free of the part or parts attached to the transmission.

In practice, a housing containing the pressure plate is bolted to an engine's flywheel, with a disc between the flywheel and pressure plate. This pressure plate is sometimes called the "intermediate pressure plate." The disc is completely free of attachment to the flywheel or pressure plate, except that when the pressure plate assembly is bolted up, the clutch spring or springs force it toward the flywheel and it squeezes the clutch disc between the flywheel and pressure plate, thereby locking it up for driving purposes. The clutch disc rides on splines on the transmission input shaft. When the flywheel and clutch assembly turn with the clutch disc squeezed between them, the disc rotates and turns the transmission input shaft with it.

When the clutch is disengaged, its linkage withdraws the pressure plate a very small distance from the flywheel. This is usually done through levers that pivot in the clutch housing and move the pressure plate back that very small distance away from the flywheel.

As the spring pressure on the pressure plate is mitigated by these levers moving it, the clutch disc begins to slip. When the pressure plate has been moved back a half inch or so, the flywheel and clutch pressure plate will have no contact with the clutch disc and the engine will spin independently

of the disc and transmission input shaft to which it is splined. When the clutch is partially released, the disc will drag on the pressure plate and flywheel, producing partial clutch engagement. This condition is used in breaking the momentum of a stationary vehicle.

The variations on the basic clutch, described above, mostly involve the use of multiple friction units. Instead of one pressure plate, there can be two or more used to squeeze two or more driving discs. In some clutches 10 or more interleafed discs and plates are used to achieve smooth engagement, and/or release, of large amounts of engine torque. Limitations of available friction facings used in early clutches mandated the use of clutch arrangements with large amounts of friction surface. In almost all cases, the basic sandwich of driving and driven members described above is used.

Clutches in General

Conventional three-element clutches are small, relatively inexpensive, and very efficient units. Still, they can cause more problems than would seem possible. For one thing, you usually can't see them operate or malfunction. Clutch work is very exacting work and an assembly misstep, or improperly placed greasy thumbprint, can ruin a whole job. I have seen more clutch failure after the installations of new and rebuilt units than of any other single major system in a car. When you get into wet clutches and multiple disc units, the potential problems become even worse than those with simple clutches.

I generally go through a clutch completely any time that I have it out for any reason. Clutches are the objects of repair when they grab, judder, or slip. These maladies usually result from wear or distortion of the driven and driving parts of a clutch, but there are other possibilities, such as binding linkage or friction surface glazing due to misuse or leaking oil seals.

One of the realities of clutch malfunction is that defects always get worse, and usually do so rapidly. For example, a leaking rear main bearing seal that sprays just a little oil onto an upper bell housing will cause clutch problems beyond what one might expect. When the oil drips down and gets onto the clutch facings it will cause them to slip. If they slip, they will glaze to a point that causes juddering and further slipping. Further slipping will cause further overheating and warping, scoring or heat checking of the three elements in the unit. So it goes; any defect that causes a clutch to slip or judder will quickly create other damage that will quickly render the clutch inoperative.

It's human nature to wait for improvement and hope and pray that mysterious knocks, wraps and other symptoms of problems in an automobile will go away. If they do, the remissions are temporary at best. In the case of clutches, there will probably be no remissions, and if repairs are not made soon after the onset of symptoms and/or problems, further damage will occur. A juddering or slipping clutch has no good place to go without repair.

Clutch Removal

Removing a clutch is usually not difficult, but if the clutch is a big one, or couples to a one-piece transmission and bell housing, the job can be a clumsy business. It is important to accomplish it carefully, precisely, and with a high degree of advance planning. Failure to plan clutch removal can result in stupidly watching a transmission dangle from its input shaft as it destroys the clutch disc and possibly that transmission input shaft.

The removal of most clutches requires removing a transmission and bell housing from engines. A few can be removed with the bell housing in place through an access plate on the top or bottom.

In either case, the first order of business is to remove the transmission or transmission/bell housing unit. To do this, the clutch operating linkage is removed in the simplest possible way. Some clutch linkage is complex, like Chrysler's old "over-center" compensating linkage. In such cases, do not throw the linkage out of adjustment when you remove it because the special jigs required to readjust it are no longer available and you will spend a long time trying to get it right. New, thicker clutch facings will mandate some adjustments in these cases but at least you will have preserved a place to start if you don't disturb the original adjustments when you disassemble clutch linkage. Minor adjustment of complex linkage is much easier than having

to start from scratch with it.

Clutch release forks usually can be removed with a transmission in place. When this is not the case, they will come out with the transmission when it is removed.

After removing clutch operating linkage, the next step is to unbolt one of the driveshaft U-joints and remove the drive shaft. Be sure to mark the relative positions of the U-joint flanges, yokes, or splines so that they can be reassembled in the same phase that they were in when they were taken apart. Now, position a good transmission jack under the transmission and adjust its tilt to cradle the transmission firmly. Strap the transmission securely to the jack and raise the jack to just contact the bottom of the transmission.

At this point, if you are removing a transmission from a bell housing, remove the two uppermost attaching bolts and install two guide pins. These pins can be purchased, or fabricated, easily by sawing the heads off two unhardened bolts that are the same size and thread as the transmission attaching bolts. The pins should have no more threads than can be screwed into the transmission bolt holes, and it is best to saw screw slots into their beheaded ends so that their installation and removal can be accomplished with a screwdriver.

Your guide pins should be about 4 or 5 inches long. Install them in the bolt holes at the top of the transmission. Then, remove the other fasteners that secure the transmission to its bell housing. The transmission can now be slid back on the guide pins with the jack supporting its weight. If the transmission and bell housing are one piece, use the same procedure, with the guide pins on either side near the top of the bell housing and threaded into the back of the engine block. The use of guide pins virtually eliminates the chance of having a transmission slip off your jack and hang on its input shaft.

Sometimes, a transmission or a transmission/bell housing gets frozen on an assembly rim or on locating pins that project from the surface to which it mates. In these cases it is difficult to separate the two assemblies. If you encounter this situation, some prying force can be applied to the side of the transmission, but avoid trying to wedge anything into the sticking joint. It's tempting, but don't do it. In extreme cases, I have had great success in separating transmissions and transmission/bell housings from their mating members with a little rearward pull applied to the transmission case with a cable-come-along. The come-along is attached between the transmission case and rear axle and tightened a bit. A few smart raps with a brass hammer in the area of seizure will usually do the trick. A little heat may help, too. Remember that the area of separation is always a locating surface, and on wet clutches it is also a gasket surface. Treat it with respect.

Some older bell housings were assembled to their engines with shims, or used cam screws to achieve alignment of transmission input shafts with crankshafts. If there are any shims in a unit that you are disassembling, be sure to note their thickness and location so that they can be reassembled as they were when they were taken apart. This will save you a lot of time and fuss later. Cam screws should be left alone.

When you remove a transmission and bell housing, the throw-out bearing—and in some cases the clutch release fork—will come with it. You now will have access to the clutch.

Before you do anything else, note that there is a brown-gray dust covering the clutch housing and parts of the clutch. This stuff likely contain asbestos fibers and is potentially deadly. Try to avoid inhaling or touching it. It is best to dampen it with water and wipe it away. Avoid vacuuming it with a shop vacuum cleaner, as its harmful fibers may go through a vacuum's filter and into the air that you and others are breathing. There are special vacuum cleaners available for this purpose. NEVER blow this stuff around with compressed air. For reference, the hooked asbestos fibers implicated in a host of lung cancers, emphysema and several other potentially deadly maladies are one seventy-five millionth of an inch long. There is no really safe way to deal with this stuff, but wetting it down is probably the best that you can do. That will somewhat mitigate the hazards.

You are now ready to remove the clutch from the flywheel. Since the existing balance of the rotating crankshaft system may have been achieved by balancing the crankshaft, flywheel and clutch together, it is good practice to reinstall everything in the position that it was in at the time of disassembly. Of course, this will be impossible if a new or rebuilt clutch unit is being substituted for the one that was in service. If you are not going to rebuild and reuse the original clutch, it is best to rebalance the crankshaft system with the new clutch mounted. In any case, mark the clutch housing relative to the flywheel for reassembly. I always bring an engine to top dead center (TDC) and number stamp mark the clutch housing, the flywheel and the crankshaft flange at their 12 o'clock positions. This makes reassembly easy, with no special positioning provisions to remember. Use number stamps rather than punch marks for this lineup indication because mechanics are likely to have used punch marks previously for this purpose, and adding more punch marks may only confuse the issue.

Removing a clutch from a flywheel will require removing the clutch housing-to-flywheel fasteners. This must be done half-a-turn at a time, and working across the housing on each fastener. Any other procedure will apply the clutch springs unevenly against the pressure plate and very possibly bend the clutch housing flange.

When all clutch fasteners have been loosened to the finger tight stage, you can remove them the rest of the way without worrying about this. At this point, a clutch aligning arbor or other rod of the correct diameter should be inserted through the clutch disc hub and into crankshaft pilot bearing end so that when the clutch housing fasteners are taken out of the flywheel the clutch disc doesn't drop out. You can then finish undoing the housing fasteners and remove the housing and clutch disc. Be sure to note whether the disc hub is facing forward or backward with respect to the flywheel. In a very few cases there is no difference, but in most others the disc will only install one way. There are some cases where it will seem to install either way, but will not work properly when it is backwards. It is better to note its correct installation position at this point than to have to experiment with it later.

Clutch Inspection and Diagnosis

The environment in which a clutch operates often causes it to fail. Be sure to check the engine rear main bearing seal and the transmission input seal, if so equipped, for oil leakage. It is pointless to replace a clutch if there is any possibility of it becoming oil soaked again, soon after replacement.

Clutch discs should be checked for wear (thickness) and replaced if they are beyond manufacturers' recommended limits. If you don't have and can't find these specifications, you should strongly consider replacement of an old clutch disc with a rebuilt unit, or relining the origial disc, when the disc's friction surfaces are worn to within 1/10 inch of the attaching rivet heads. This pertains if there are no other problems with a disc. If it is glazed, oil soaked, or heat checked, or if there is any evidence of warping, it should be replaced. If the torsion springs clustered around a clutch's hub are loose or broken, or if the splines are sloppy on the transmission input shaft, hub replacement is necessary.

The only clutch defect that does not require replacement is mild friction surface glazing from normal wear. This condition can sometimes be cured by block sanding to break the glaze with 240-grit open-coat sandpaper. If you choose this approach, remember that you are sanding asbestos when you sand the disc and that there are considerable health hazards involved.

The iron friction surfaces of clutch systems—flywheel faces and intermediate pressure plate surfaces—are also susceptible to a whole inventory of defects. Most of these, warping, glazing, superficial cracks, hard spots and scoring, can be dealt with by grinding. In the case of the pressure plate or plates, this procedure is performed during the rebuilding process. If you commission this work, or use an exchange clutch unit, you will still have to deal with the flywheel surface.

Flywheels should always be ground when clutch work is done, and that grinding is best done on a special flywheel grinding machine. If reasonable grinding does not remove all defects, the flywheel will have to be replaced. Never install a flywheel with a crack or cracks in its clutch facing area. If cracks cannot be ground out at a reasonable depth, replace the flywheel. Flywheels with cracks are dangerous, and besides, the metal in the area of the crack is likely to be harder than the surrounding material and will quickly cause clutch judder in the resurfaced unit, if you are foolish enough to try to use it.

The clutch/pressure plate assembly can often be adjusted if it has finger actuation as opposed to actuation by a diaphragm spring. Beyond this, work on clutches requires

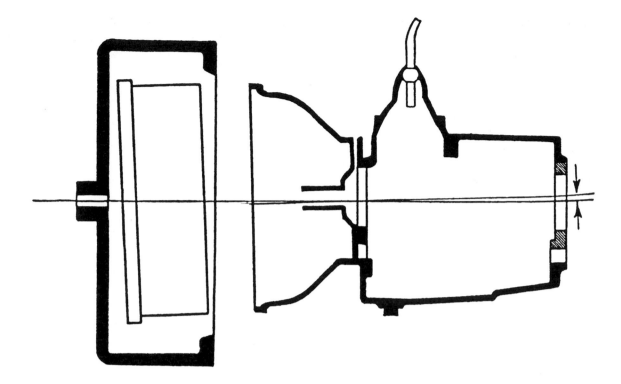

Inspection of this graphic will indicate one of several possibilities for clutch misalignment. The one shown here is flywheel misalignment, but it could as easily be bell housing or transmission misalignment. No matter what the cause of misalignment in a clutch/transmission system is, the result will always be the same, rapid clutch failure.

specialized fixtures, measuring devices and parts. While it is possible for generalists to repair these units, I vastly prefer enlisting the aid of clutch specialists. Many major industrial cities have one or more clutch specialty houses. Often, these concerns deal with both automotive and industrial clutches. These people can reface your disc(s) with appropriate materials and evaluate the overall setup and condition of your clutch. The older houses often have specification books for clutches that reach back into the early 20th century.

Armed with this knowledge, they are able to replace springs, cups, pins, levers, and other parts that will bring your repaired clutch back to its original tolerances and loading figures. Since many manufacturers did not change their clutches over periods of several years, there are still many exchange units available in rebuilder stocks for older cars. Check this out before you have a clutch rebuilt because an exchange will probably be less expensive than custom rebuilding.

A note of caution is in order regarding exchange clutches. It is not unusual for several clutch applications to share common housings. This means that you can get an exchange housing that bolts to your flywheel but that has the wrong number of clutch springs or the wrong specification springs, or incorrect lever ratios. When you install an exchange clutch, make sure that the number of springs matches that in your original clutch. If you have any doubts about this, take your clutch to a clutch house and have its loading measured. To retain this option, never take a core credit for your old clutch on an exchange clutch until the new unit is in place and performing properly. Then you

can return your core and get credit for it.

Another problem with exchange clutches is that some of them are rebuilt late at night at Joe's Saloon, Bar-B-Que, and Automotive Component Rebuilding Facility. They must be, because I have seen exchange clutches that are as bad as some of the carburetors that they do at Joe's. I haven't tried Joe's Bar-B-Que, because I just haven't gotten that hungry yet.

Always eyeball any exchange or rebuilt clutch that you are going to install and be particularly careful to note that its fingers are adjusted correctly. This means that they should all be at the same altitude, measured from the housings' top, flywheel face, or whatever other measurement method is specified for the particular clutch on which you are working. On some older clutches, spring tension on the pressure plate can be adjusted for each spring. It is good practice to leave this adjustment alone unless you are going to rebuild the clutch completely yourself, and understand the method for setting and equalizing spring pressure.

For a clutch to operate properly, the transmission input shaft that supports the clutch disc must run true. In practice, this means that it must be checked for straightness. The pilot bearing that supports it in the crankshaft and the transmission bearing that supports its rear end must both be in good condition. Always remove and service or replace pilot bushings when doing clutch work. If a pilot bearing is a ball bearing design, it should be inspected, carefully cleaned and lightly lubricated before reinstallation. The splines on the transmission input shaft must be unworn and free of burrs, distortion and other defects. They must mate with the clutch disc hub freely and smoothly. The thinnest wipe of

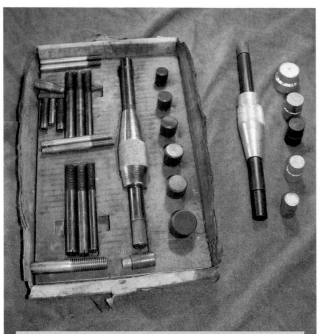

The use of guide pins and an aligning arbor tool, like those shown here, will greatly aid in the safety and ease of clutch removal and reattachment. A set of guide pins of different sizes is shown to the left of the aligning arbor tool and its pilots in the box. A separate aligning tool and its pilots are shown to the right of the boxed clutch tool kit. The sliding arbor clutch centering tools, shown here, use pilot ends that slide firmly into flywheel pilot bearing bores and sliding arbors to center clutch discs to flywheels before clutch housings are bolted down to them. This makes it possible for transmission input shafts to enter their clutch disc splines and pilot bearings. Without this kind of alignment, clutch installation is impossible. If you have a spare transmission input shaft, it can be used to align the clutch instead of an aligning tool.

high-temperature grease on these splines will help a clutch to operate smoothly. More grease than that thinnest wipe will cause problems by getting on friction components.

One way to check for misalignment is with a dial indicator attached to and centered on the clutch housing. Indications from the bell housing surface that mates to the transmission will allow you to check for lateral and in-and-out deviations from concentricity and variations in depth.

Sometimes, clutch problems can originate in problems in the attachment of a flywheel to a crankshaft. Dirt on this interface, or a warped flange or bent flywheel, or any burrs will cause malfunction. It is always a good idea to check the flywheel flange for horizontal run-out with a dial indicator after a crankshaft has been ground and installed. It is also good practice to use a dial indicator to check the back face of the clutch housing for run-out. If run-out is found there, it indicates a warped clutch housing.

The inspection and diagnosis of clutches will be more fruitful if you know about any problem(s) with a unit beforehand. Then, you can try to remedy it in your rebuilding or restoration process. Simply rebuilding a clutch blindly in the hope that a problem will somehow be eliminated will often prove futile, one of those proverbial shots in the dark. Problems involving clutch plate warping and distortion of related components must be tracked down specifically and corrected.

Clutch Installation

The installation of simple clutches is not particularly difficult, but it has to be done carefully to avoid ruining the job. It is essential that clutch facings, pressure plates, and flywheel surfaces be kept clean of all oil and grease. It is a good idea to spray them with a non-petroleum-based, evaporating cleaner (a good aerosol brake cleaner is perfect for the job) and then to wipe them down and blow them off prior to assembly. This will remove any minor traces of oil or grease that may have accidentally gotten on them when they were handled prior to installation. Any grit left from grinding or deglazing must also be removed at this point. Wearing latex or Nitrile gloves when you do clutch work is an excellent idea.

The first order of business in installing a clutch is to install the pilot bearing in the end of the crankshaft if the old one has been removed during crankshaft reconditioning. Pilot bearing spin-out is fairly common among clutch maladies, so make sure that your pilot bearing fits snugly into its bore. Stake it in with a punch if necessary. Treatment with one of the less-aggressive anaerobic retaining compounds (from Loctite, FelPro, etc.) will help with steel backed bushings and bearings, but is of questionable value with the more common Oilite (sintered bronze) type. Ball bearing-type pilot bearings require a sparing application of high temperature grease in their ball/race areas. Bushing-type pilot bearings should have their bores lightly coated with a high-temperature grease. This is also a good time to lightly grease the throw-out bearings and to install them on their transmission input shaft sleeves.

These sleeves and the grease recesses in the bearing carriers that ride on them should be lightly greased. All of these areas must be greased for clutches to work smoothly, but most of them rotate and can throw grease off onto clutch friction surfaces if it is applied to them in excess. It is essential that grease applied to these areas is kept to a thin layer. In this application, I usually paint grease on with a solder tinning brush.

At this point, a clutch-aligning arbor with the correct pilot adapter should be inserted through the clutch disc and into the pilot bearing. Be sure that the disc hub is facing the same way that it was at the time of disassembly. Matching the index markings that you made at the time of disassembly, bring the pressure plate and clutch housing up to the flywheel. Secure the clutch housing loosely to the flywheel with a few symmetrically placed fasteners. Be sure to use the original or graded fasteners and be sure that they are free of cracks and that their threads are in good condition.

Clutch fasteners can break or come undone in service, causing real hazards. Worn or stretched fasteners are dangerous, so replace old fasteners with new ones if you have any doubts about their integrity. Whatever system was used to retain the clutch housing-to-flywheel fastener heads—bend-tabs, wire, cotter keys, lock washers, star washers, etc.—must be reinstalled and in good condition,

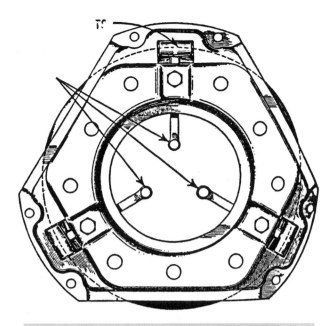

The three (more for some clutches) actuating fingers shown in this graphic have to contact the clutch release bearing at exactly the same time for a clutch to work properly. If one finger hits before or after the others, the clutch will judder. Always check this factor with a thickness ("feeler") gauge before you put a clutch back into service.

or replaced. This is no place to economize by reusing old lock washers.

After all of a clutch's fasteners have been tightened finger tight, they should be snugged down half-a-turn-at-a-time and in a pattern that works across the clutch housing. Then, they should be tightened evenly to the correct torque. The clutch aligning tool can now be withdrawn from the pilot bearing and clutch disc's splined hub.

If the clutch that you are working on has a bell housing that separates from its transmission, it should be installed and a dial indicator should be set up on the flywheel to check for concentricity and parallelism of the bell housing/transmission mating surface and of the clutch and flywheel. Some bell housings have eccentric locating cams that can be used to achieve concentricity. Sometimes shims will have to be used to achieve parallelism. This may all sound finicky, but it is not all that unusual to find misalignment in bell housings. If a clutch was in trouble before a rebuild and no other cause of the malfunction has been found, alignment is a good candidate.

Using the guide pins that were employed for clutch removal, the transmission should now be installed with a transmission jack. With some smaller transmissions, it is possible to wrestle a tranny up and into place without a jack, but don't try this with heavy transmissions. In any case, avoid letting the weight of a transmission hang off its input shaft—guide pins should be used to preclude this possibility—or you may bend the shaft. As the splines on your transmission shaft begin to encounter the splines in the clutch disc hub, turn the transmission's output shaft with the transmission in high gear so that the splines can engage easily. Never use the attaching bolts to force a

transmission into its final position. If a transmission does not slide easily into final position, something is wrong and must be corrected.

Finish attaching your transmission to its bell housing or the transmission/bell housing to the engine and install the throw-out fork with a bit of lubrication on its pivot point. The clutch linkage can now be reinstalled and the final adjustments of free play and pedal height made. Always be sure to leave the specified amount of free play in a clutch, or throw out bearing failure will soon result. In the absence of a specification, I always leave at least 1 inch pedal free travel before the clutch spring or levers are engaged by the linkage. Of course, if there is no free play at all, the clutch linings will slip and overheat, causing clutch failure in short order.

Other Considerations

Throughout clutch removal and installation procedures, a car will have to be elevated a foot or more from the ground. If this work is not done on a lift, very secure wheel stands or jack stands should be used. Be sure that any car that you work on is secure, because some of the loosening and tightening operations in this work will tend to push it laterally.

The above description of clutch work pertains to the simplest forms of clutches that had their origins before the 1920s, became common in the 1930s and are still in use today. There were many other types of clutches and some of them can be pretty hairy to work on. It is always necessary to have data on repair and adjustment to recondition the more complex clutches. There are certain logical propositions that should also be taken for guidance.

For example, all clutches need to have even springing and, if actuation levers are used, some method of equalizing spring pressure is necessary. All propositions in clutch work come from the simple logic of what clutches do, but some of the materials and configurations used in clutches can be difficult to dope out. If you work on complex clutches, be sure that you completely understand how they operate before you disassemble them.

The "Good News" and the "Bad News" About Transmissions

The good news about transmissions is that many of them are capable of going 200,000 miles, or more, without repair, as long as the minimum amenities of maintenance are observed. The bad news is that some of them are inherently trouble prone—particularly early automatics—and bad maintenance can cause even the best of them to fail before their times.

In the normal course of owning old cars, you are likely to have to rebuild five or 10 engines for every transmission that

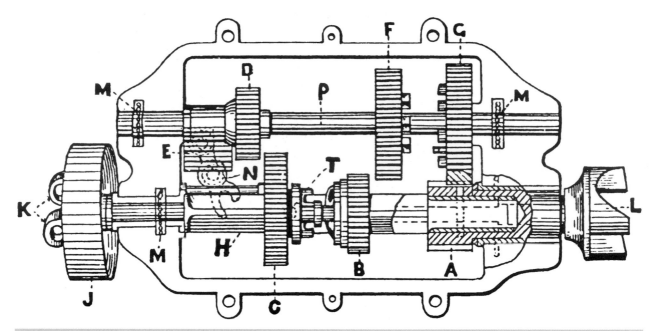

The earliest geared automobile transmissions were sliding gear types. The teeth of the gears in these units were slid in and out of engagement on square or splined shafts. These transmissions had to have large, rugged gears, due to the wear and tear of engagement on their teeth.

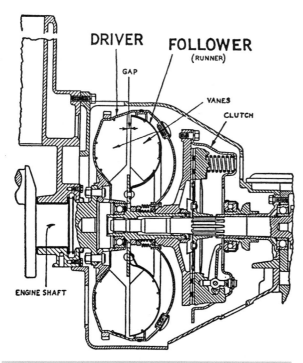

By the late 1930s, fluid couplings were developed by Chrysler and others. The unit shown here is coupled to a conventional clutch and a conventional, semi-automatic hydraulically shifted, synchronized transmission. This semi-automatic two-speed unit had to be clutched into first gear when a car was first put into motion, but then shifted up and down automatically.

you have to take apart. Frequently, transmission problems, like broken detente springs on standard transmissions, will yield to repair with very little deep disassembly. Even some of the more complex automatics often can be repaired with minimum disassembly.

Take, for example, the notorious Buick Dynaflow "no reverse" syndrome that has afflicted many Buicks made from 1948 to 1964. The problem was caused by broken reverse band holding struts and the fix could be made by simply removing pans, filters, and valve bodies, and installing aftermarket strut kits.

When you do have to go into a transmission, you may find what seem to be handfulls of little parts that come apart far more easily than they go back together. This does not pertain to early sliding gear transmissions, but to modern automatics and modern synchronized three-, four-, five- and six-speed units. These are marvels of complexity, and of the tendency to assemble a lot of little parts into small spaces.

I think that my most unpleasant transmission rebuilding experience was with a Subaru 360 (the so-called "Japanese Beetle"). It had a five-speed synchronized transmission that was assembled in a casting that parted as halves of the engine's crankcase. The whole integrated engine/transaxle unit was about the size of a hat box. Items like that little Subaru monster's transaxle should make anyone a fan of a relatively simple Ford or Chevrolet three-speed.

Some automatics are nightmarish in their complexity, and I don't claim competence in their diagnosis or repair. Early Hydramatics fall into this category, as do Packard Ultramatics. Of early the automatics, Chrysler's first Torqueflite units are my favorites and they are among the easiest automatics to work on. They are also so well designed and constructed that they need about half of the attention that some of the more complex band shifted units require.

It is interesting to note that when workshop manuals came into common use to supplant owners' manuals as sources of repair information—this was in the late 1920s and early 1930s for many automakers—they usually had

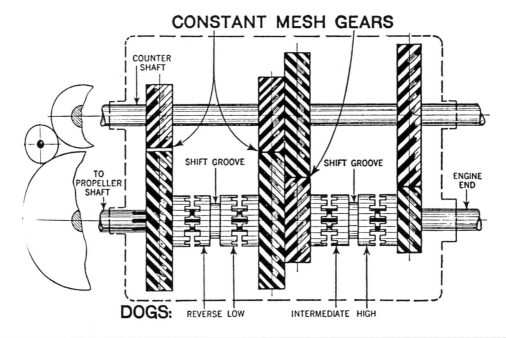

CONSTANT MESH GEARS

COUNTER SHAFT

TO PROPELLER SHAFT

SHIFT GROOVE

SHIFT GROOVE

ENGINE END

DOGS: REVERSE LOW INTERMEDIATE HIGH

Constant mesh transmissions replaced the sliding gear types. In the constant mesh units, the driving and driven gears are all always in mesh. Power is directed to the desired gear set by couplers that lock them to the appropriate shafts.

relatively brief sections devoted to transmission fault diagnosis, removal and repair. These sections were about the same length as the chapters on wheels and tires or suspensions. With the advent of synchronized gearing, and the attendant complexity of these systems, the transmission sections of shop manuals grew to equal the sections devoted to electrical data. Then, when General Motors introduced hydraulically controlled automatic planetary gearing in the late 1930s (Hydramatic), the transmission sections of the shop manuals that covered these cars grew to nearly half of the bulk of the manuals, or had to be issued as separate volumes. From then on it was a good bet that any shop manual covering cars with automatic transmissions would devote half of its content to this topic, and that half of the special tools that were recommended for servicing these cars would pertain to their automatic transmissions.

The development of the hydraulically controlled automatic transmission after World War II was one of the automotive wonders of the age. Europeans, with their Cotal and Wilson units, had nothing that came close in convenience or reliability. Car producers like Rolls-Royce and Mercedes-Benz used American automatics from manufacturers like General Motors and Borg Warner because there was nothing produced in Europe to match them. It was only in the 1990s that several Japanese and European companies came up with world-class automatic transmissions. Now, the Koreans are hot on their heels.

One of the reasons that the development of the automatic transmission was so long in coming and spreading is that the manufacturing technology involved necessitates levels of precision that are well beyond the tolerances of most other systems in automobiles. Automatic transmissions require the mass production of components that in some cases have to be held to specifications of dimension and

finish that are as tight as those for jet aircraft engines. For all of that, as late as the World War II era, Chrysler astounded the technical world with its "Superfinish" process (actually a liquid honing procedure) that was used on the brass sealing bellows in their fluid drive clutches. Transmissions have come a long way since then.

This discussion of the restoration aspects of transmissions must, necessarily, be very general in scope. Actual repair procedures are so varied and specific in nature that it would take a library of books (or a shelving unit of CDs or DVDs) to cover them adequately. Every distinctive transmission, automatic or manual, comes apart differently and needs specific procedures to effect adjustments and repairs. Most of this is best left to experienced transmission mechanics with the requisite special tools and knowledge. The simpler transmissions—early planetary, sliding gear, constant mesh and automatically shifted constant mesh— will yield complete success to amateur repair in many cases. Some generalities regarding these units are covered here. Fault diagnosis and maintenance are also discussed.

Maintenance for Standard Transmissions

Standard transmissions are usually trouble free for long periods and great distances if they are operated properly and if they receive good lubrication. If, on the other hand, they are regularly shifted in a violent manner, or operated with a dragging clutch, or require, but don't have, a working clutch brake (sliding gear type), they will suffer severe damage. If they run dry, or their lubricants are contaminated with water, debris or dirt, they will inevitably suffer failure.

Transmissions are difficult enough and expensive

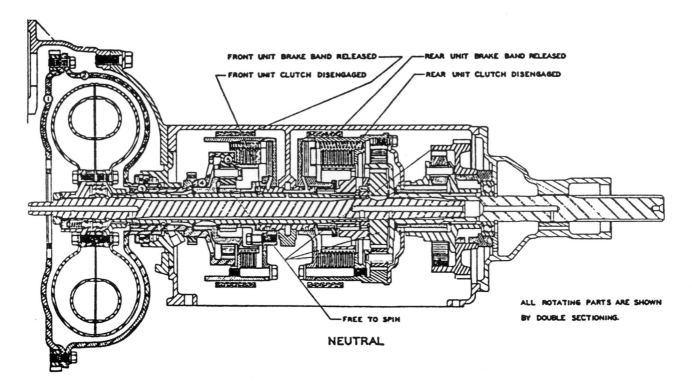

FRONT UNIT BRAKE BAND RELEASED — REAR UNIT BRAKE BAND RELEASED
FRONT UNIT CLUTCH DISENGAGED — REAR UNIT CLUTCH DISENGAGED

FREE TO SPIN

ALL ROTATING PARTS ARE SHOWN BY DOUBLE SECTIONING.

NEUTRAL

Just before World War II, General Motors developed a fully automatic transmission (Hydramatic) which utilized a torque converter and hydraulically shifted planetary gearsets. In this arrangement, the torque converter has a "stator" with variable pitch blades. This makes it possible to multiply engine torque and provide the effect of small gearing changes. Larger changes are achieved by coupling and uncoupling different ratio planetary gearsets by applying hydraulic pressure to tighten or loosen bands applied over the planet drums.

enough to rebuild to make it good sense to attend carefully to their maintenance. While there are numerous "quick fixes" for specific transmission faults, all of them evade the real issues, though some of them will work for a while. Who amongst us has not owned a car with a synchronized transmission that someone treated for failing synchros with a handful of sawdust in its lubricant? The old handful-of-sawdust or rosin trick will work to fix a malfunctioning gear synchronizer in the very short run. In the medium run it will severely damage a transmission that only may have needed minor repair before this kind of shoddy fix was attempted.

Likewise, a three-speed transmission that regularly slips out of second gear is often dealt with by the simple expedient of tying a short loop of rope under the dashboard so that it can be used to restrain the shifter in second gear. This evades the problem of a worn fork or rail, or a broken detente spring, or even a bad clutch pilot bearing. The repair of these items is so easy to effect that it is a waste of good rope to go the Neanderthal route. Besides, alert judges always deduct points for rope. If you experience mechanical problems with a transmission, diagnose and repair them.

The routine maintenance of standard transmissions mostly involves keeping their linkages adjusted, keeping them filled to the correct level with good quality lubricant of the right specification and keeping any external venting devices clear of clogging. It is a good idea to periodically flush standard transmissions with a good solvent and to then thoroughly dry them before refilling them with lubricant. This should be done about once or twice every

decade, depending on storage and use.

There is one retrofit transmission device that I heartily recommend. That is a magnetic drain plug. Companies like Lisle offer them in a variety of sizes. If these plugs are used in transmission (and rear end) drain plug applications, and if they are blown clean at regular lubricant change intervals, they can extend the lives of gearbox units up to two times.

Transmissions that are linked to their shifters externally (column shift) usually have provisions for linkage adjustment. In most cases these involved centering linkage on fork levers. Sometimes stay slots or pin slots are provided to get linkage into its correct positions before locking it to the shift levers on the transmission. If you have any questions about linkage adjustment procedures, consult an appropriate data source (shop manual or general car repair manual). The worst linkage problem that you are likely to encounter is worn or bent linkage in column shifters. There is no quick fix for this problem. Bushings or levers and rods may have to be replaced to restore the operation of this type of shift linkage.

Modern manual transmissions usually run in multi-grade motor oils or ATF (Automatic Transmission Fluid). I don't like the idea of using motor oil or ATF because some of the additives in such fluids are inappropriate to lubricating manual transmissions, but that's what many of today's transmission manufacturers specify. Older transmissions run on anything from 600W steam cylinder oil ("boiler grease") to modern EP (Extreme Pressure) lubricants. Some of the older lubricant designations, like "110 F.W.," can be troublesome to correlate to modern lubricant nomenclature. In this case, "F.W." stood for "Free Wheeling" and the numbers in that scale run a bit higher than the SAE (Society of Automotive Engineers) Gear Oil numbers that are currently in common use. The SAE gear oil numbers that most of us are familiar with do not correlate to the SAE numbers used for motor oils. SAE 50 motor oil, in fact, has the same viscosity as SAE 90 gear oil. To make matters even more confusing, a new system, "ISO-VG" has descended on us with a whole new viscosity scale, and cause for new confusion (or clarification, depending on your point of view).

Up to a point, when you are lubricating a slightly worn transmission, it makes sense to use a slightly heavier weight lubricant than was specified originally. However, if you are going to drive in cold temperatures, this can make shifting hard. In very cold climates, the thicker oils, like SAE 140 gear oil, will tend to channel and can damage transmissions. I keep a mixture of SAE 90 and 140 gear oil around for older cars that specify 110 F.W. or any SAE viscosity from 75 to 90. A mix of equal parts of 90 and 140 produces an actual viscosity of around 105—when you mix oils of differing viscosities the results will tend toward the lower number by some very complex factor.

Almost all modern gear oils are of the EP (Extreme Pressure) type. The designations "hypoid," "multi-purpose" and "APG" ("All Purpose Gear") mean the same thing as EP. These oils were developed to combat the high gear face pressures generated by the wiping, sliding motion of hypoid rear end gearsets and the resulting high heat that they generate. (Hypoid bevel gear applications for rear ends were first introduced by Packard in the late 1920s, and greatly popularized by Chrysler after 1934 on their Airflow series cars. The sole reason for using hypoid gears is to lower the floors in rear-wheel-drive cars.)

The EP lubricants developed for and required in hypoid rear end gearsets have phosphorus-based and sulfur-based additives in them that are designed to combine at a glacially slow rate with the steel in gear faces, and thus achieve a coating action that simple viscosity could not provide at the elevated temperatures at which hypoid gearsets run. This chemical reaction only occurs at very high temperatures. At least, that's what the lubricant companies claim. Supposedly, non-hypoid gears do not produce enough heat to cause EP lubricants to react with their steel. I'd award that proposition a big "maybe."

The problem is that gears that run in these lubricants have to be made of specially formulated steel alloys to somewhat resist their corrosive features. These alloys only came into use at the time of the introduction of hypoid gearing. Hypoid lubricants can be corrosive and can etch bronze and brass and, given enough time—usually decades—they can also pit and even weld non-hypoid gears through chemical reactions. Of course, this damage only occurs to gears in cars that were designed before hypoid gearing appeared on the scene, and before EP gear oils became the universally available automotive gear lubricants.

Since transmission gears do not produce the kinds of face pressures or oil temperatures that require EP lubricants, and since these lubricants can be very bad for such things as planetary overdrive units, I avoid using them in transmissions. This is a fine point, but fine points are what restoration is all about. Some of the manufacturers of EP/Multi-Purpose/APG/hypoid lubricants claim that the extreme pressure additives in their formulations are not activated until they reach the elevated temperatures at which hypoid gearsets run. As I said, I have my doubts about this.

OK, if you are *not* to going to continue to use the ubiquitous yellow squeeze bottles of Penzoil 80-90 EP gear oil, what are you going to use? With a little effort you could probably lay your hands on some straight mineral oil in the right viscosity range, and that would be pretty close to what a 1920s or 1930s car originally used in its rear end or transmission. But lubricant technology has come a long way since then. Modern gear lubricants have all kinds of useful anti-scuff, anti-corrosion, anti-foam, etc. additive packages. You want that good stuff. Fiske Brothers, the makers of the Lubriplate line, still manufactures 90 and 140 weight lubricants that have all of the good additives except the EP package. These are designated as products #4, #8, and SPO series gear oils. For my money they are the highest-quality non-EP lubricants available anywhere. They are optimum for use in any transmission and in any non-hypoid rear end. Never use them in hypoid rear ends because disaster will soon follow.

There is, of course, the possibility of using synthetic, non-EP lubricants in standard transmissions made after the mid 1930s. This sounds like a very attractive possibility due to the superior lubricating and viscosity stability characteristics inherent in these formulations. The trouble is that some of what is sold as "synthetic" lubricant is snake oil. Even the good synthetics may rapidly eat or swell Neoprene and some other seal compounds that are found in the transmissions of older cars. That's why they should never be used in pre 1970s cars.

A final and often overlooked aspect of routine transmission maintenance is to make sure that if an air vent is provided for your transmission, it is clear. Failure to do this can get you involved in seal replacement before it would otherwise be necessary.

Standard Transmission Fault Diagnosis and Repair

If it works, leave it alone. Clean the outside of the case, flush the inside, but don't disassemble a transmission if there is no indication of fault. It's a waste of time, and you may regret such a venture when it comes time to put the thing back together. If you encounter a problem, such as worn shift rails, a broken detente spring, or a leaking seal, satisfy yourself with repairing just the offending part or system. Resist the temptation to get out the spanners and pullers for a total disassembly. Once you remove the access plate(s) and clean things up inside a bit, you should be able to inspect a transmission completely to determine the presence of problems like chipped gear teeth, worn shafts, or rough or sloppy bearings or bushings.

Almost all standard transmission problems will manifest themselves in four simple kinds of symptoms: noise and vibration, gear clash when shifting, jumping out of gear and lubricant leaks. Except for the last symptom, any one of these can be caused by a transmission problem or a clutch defect. Over the years, untold numbers of transmissions have been ripped out and torn down to correct problems that had their causes in clutch malfunctions. Clutches are usually easier to repair than transmissions, and much more likely to cause problems. Be sure to eliminate clutch problems before proceeding with a transmission rebuild.

If diagnosis and inspection have revealed a real transmission fault, remove the transmission, as outlined in the clutch section of this chapter, and look for the fault. Clean things up and inspect gears, shafts, synchronizer cones, springs, bearings, retainers, and engager teeth. All of these should be smooth and within reasonable wear limits. If you find a broken gear, or any other broken or badly deteriorated part, you should Magnaflux every stressed component in the transmission, including the case.

Since the same people who design transmissions are also the authors of the more advanced jigsaw and other puzzles, (Rubic of cube fame was almost certainly a transmission designer), you had best have "the book" available before you attempt transmission disassembly and repair. You will need disassembly/assembly procedures and the specifications for shaft end play, shimming and adjustment, among other things, for any complex unit. A shop manual will also speed disassembly and may prevent catastrophic mistakes. Transmission disassembly sometimes requires force, but usually very little, and always in the right places. Two-pound hammers and 9-lb. slide hammers are "out" for this work. However, a good press may be a necessity.

If you do need to take the gear clusters and shafts out of a transmission, look at the bearings very critically. If they are at all deteriorated, replace them with exact duplicates. Always use new snap rings if this method is used to retain parts. If transmission parts are wired, be sure to replace the wire in an effective and correct manner. New gaskets also should be used. On later synchronized transmissions, there are lots of little parts, and sometimes special fixtures are needed to reassemble the clusters. Again, a good shop or general repair manual is invaluable in this work if you are new to it.

Automatic Transmission Maintenance and Adjustment

Until recently, almost all post-World War II era automatic transmissions were comprised of three basic systems: one or more fluid couplings or torque converters, one or more planetary or constant mesh gearsets, and an hydraulic, hydraulic/vacuum or hydraulic/electric control system. The new wrinkle in transmissions, CVTs (continuously variable transmissions), has not yet been around long enough to find its way into many collector cars.

If this sounds complicated, that is because it is. The repair of these units can be a complex proposition, and is usually best left to specialists. I have often noted that automobile repair and restoration is not nuclear physics and can be understood by most people. Automatic transmission repair may well be the exception to this.

There are not too many things that a driver can do to damage an automatic transmission without trying, but there are a few. Shifts from "park" or "neutral" into a driving ranges at high RPM, or into "park" at speed can damage a transmission. The shift into park shouldn't be a problem, but if the pawl lacking device malfunctions, great damage can occur. A more subtle way to damage some automatics is to tow a car without disconnecting its drive shaft or to push start a car for substantial distances. Some automatics can take this and some can't. It depends on whether or not they have a rear oil pump and whether both rear and front pump outputs are necessary for lubrication and drive. Consult the appropriate owner's manual or *Motor's* manual to determine if a particular automatic is susceptible to push starting or towing.

Some early automatic transmissions require a few minor adjustments on a periodic basis, but most do not. Some require periodic checks of a few critical parts. All automatics should have their hydraulic fluid checked and changed on a schedule.

Hydraulic transmission fluid nomenclature can be confusing. Such designations as "AQ Type A, Suffix A" or "Type F" or "Type M" or "Dexron" and "Dexron II" make for this confusion.

Then there are some unknown quantities, like "Chrysler Fluid Coupling Fluid." The owner's manuals for fluid coupling-equipped Chryslers suggested that light engine oil could be used in emergencies, as long as it was flushed out later. It is amazing how many owners of these cars filled their transmissions with SAE 10 weight engine oil when they couldn't find "Chrysler Fluid Coupling Fluid." If that wasn't bad enough, the actual gear boxes on these cars ran in SAE 10 engine oil because they had hydraulic plunger shifting devices that could not tolerate a thicker, more adequate gear oil in cold weather.

Some later Chryslers and DeSotos with hydraulically shifted gears actually circulated the engines' oil through their fluid couplings. That didn't work, but it did surprise a lot of service station attendants when these early 1950s V-8s absorbed 13 quarts in oil changes.

Such "unusual" engineering was not, by the way, confined to Americans. The French and British had their own strange ideas about transmission lubrication, too. On the early transverse engine cars that Alex Issigonis inspired, such as the Austin America and MG 1100, Mini Cooper and the FWD French Simcas of the 1970s, common sumps were used for engines and gearboxes. The effect of sharing lubricant between engines and transmissions was disastrous. The engines and transmissions didn't last long. A few years after the last of these cars was imported, they were hard to find on streets and highways, but very common in salvage yards.

Generally, engine oil should not be used in older transmissions, except in a few very specific cases, like the gearbox sections of Underdrive Chryslers. Even there, a good mineral oil of the right weight is probably a better bet because it more closely resembles the old engine oils than do modern engine oils.

Older automatics (Hydramatics, Torqueflites, Fordomatics, and Flashomatics) run on AQ ATF Type A, Suffix A, Dexron, or Dexron II, depending on their age. Dexron II can be substituted for the now obsolete Dexron. The latter was obsoleted because its formulation used a friction reducer derived from whale blubber, and that material became unavailable as whaling was outlawed worldwide. Dexron II should probably not be used in cars specified for ATF AQ Type A, Suffix A fluid, unless the transmission involved has been completely rebuilt. This is because the Dexron II fluids contain detergents in their additive packages that are so vigorous that they will sometimes loosen scale in a torque converter or fluid coupling that has been run for years on AQ Type A, Suffix A. The scale then plugs things up. The same is true for more recent Dexron III fluids. In fact, the detergents in Dexron ATFs are so aggressive that they are often added to motor oils by mechanics to free sticking hydraulic valve lifters. The designation "AQ-ATF" is obsolete, but applied to fluid for GM Powerglide transmissions and some others. The ATF AQ Type A, Suffix A to Dexron III range of fluids will substitute here, depending on whether the unit in question has been rebuilt.

Early Ford automatics used AQ Type A, Suffix A fluids and more recent Ford transmissions use the Dexron II and later Dexron III fluids or Mercon and Mercon V. For some years in the 1970s Ford transmissions used "Type F" fluid, which included a unique friction modifier to enhance clutch engagement. These units must get Type F, or their clutches will slip and engage roughly and at the wrong times. Some rebuild kits, it is claimed, include clutch materials that are Dexron compatible. This wrinkle further complicates servicing these Ford transmissions because, even though a transmission might normally use Type F fluid, a rebuild may have converted it to Dexron II. Due to the nature of the friction enhancers in Type F fluid, it should never be used in units that specify any of the other fluid types. The Allison "C" series fluids should not be used in passenger car automatics, and the mysterious and illusive "type B" fluid was actually an early version of Dexron and, if specified, can be replaced with Dexron II or III.

Chrysler, Honda and Toyota specify their own proprietary ATF fluids and these should be used in units of these origins.

The proper fluid change intervals for automatic transmissions are a controversial topic. It is my suggestion that on a new or rebuilt transmission, the fluid should be changed every two years or 25,000 miles. At present, manufacturers do not recommend this routine change if a car is driven in "normal service," whatever that is. Many manufacturers have not provided drain plugs in their torque converters or transmission pans for many years.

In the cases of older automatics, fluid should be evaluated for color and odor. Most transmission fluids start out with red dye in them. If they become brown or foggy looking, this indicates that burning or water contamination has occurred. When this happens, they must be changed and the causes of the discoloration or cloudiness discovered.

If transmission fluid smells burned, it must be replaced. A note of caution is required here. When you sniff a dipstick for the purpose of evaluating transmission fluid, try to do it when no one is looking. While this is a perfectly valid evaluation procedure, it can be difficult to explain to bystanders and you will invariably look dumb doing it.

In the opinion of many transmission technicians, an oil and filter change is not a good idea if a transmission has gone for decades or long mileages without either. This is because the detergents in transmission oil—unlike motor oil—are very aggressive and can loosen scale when fresh fluid is used to replace fluid with depleted detergents. If you buy a car with a 30- or 40-year-old automatic and you have reason to believe that the fluid has not been changed for decades, and that fluid looks and smells OK, I suggest that you leave it alone. Some people will disagree with this recommendation, but it has the support of three of the four best transmission techs that I know. In particular, the Dexron series fluids are fortified with aggressive detergents, so be careful about putting them in old, potentially scaled, units. Torque converters tend to collect scale. Releasing it into transmissions can cause all kinds of problems.

All of this boils down to a gamble and, while I don't like to toss the dice in any aspect of automotive maintenance or restoration, that kind of risk seems built into the fluid change decision with old automatics.

If you decide to replace old, additive depleted transmission fluid, you can mitigate some of the risk by removing the transmission and having its torque converter flushed on a flushing machine. Then drop the transmission's pan and replace its filter and fluid.

Another important aspect of automatic transmission maintenance is that fluid must be kept at the correct level. You can severely damage the bearings and seals in a transmission by overfilling it, because its fluid will tend to aerate and foam as the transmission operates. Underfilling will also cause problems, but not as quickly or dramatically, unless several quarts are involved. The best bet is to follow instructions and to allow for the expansion of the fluid that will occur as it is heated in operation and for the amount of fluid that is retained in the transmission's servo plungers as it is shifted through its ranges. All of this is covered in shop manuals and in general repair manuals.

A large number of automatic transmission problems turn out really to be engine problems. If an automatic does

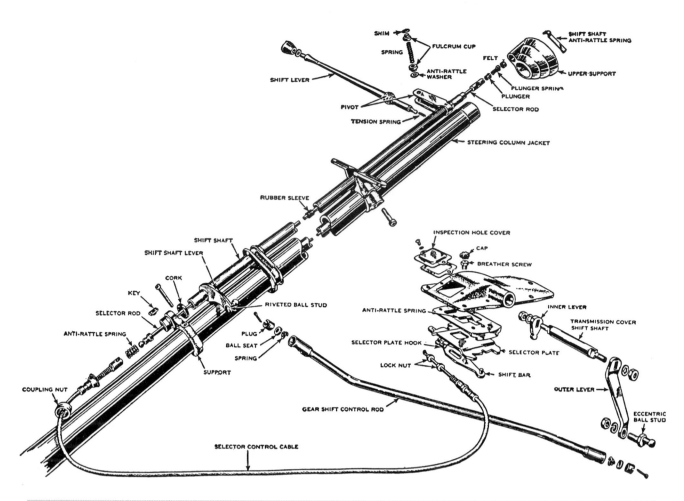

Steering column-mounted shift linkage on older cars can be a problem in terms of wear and proper adjustment. The worst of it applies to standard transmission linkage, like that pictured here, but automatic linkage can also become worn and get out of adjustment. Note the use of both a cable and linkage rods in the unit pictured here.

not get adequate torque from the engine coupled to it, it will appear to malfunction. If an engine has weak vacuum for any of several possible reasons, a vacuum modulated automatic attached to it will not shift correctly. Before any diagnosis of an automatic transmission is attempted, be sure that the engine that runs it is in good working order and performing up to specifications. Many automatics have been treated for problems that were really engine problems. Avoid this error.

Proper adjustment of automatic transmission shift and T.V. linkage (if used) is essential and must be done by the book. Some of these adjustments are complex and require the use of jigs or gauging rods and points. Get a book that covers the unit that you are working on and follow it rigorously. Vacuum modulators are easy to replace, inexpensive, and often defective. Isn't that nice? Beyond that, it is usually possible to externally adjust the bands on transmissions that have them. These adjustments are sometimes based on torque, sometimes on dimensions and sometimes on oil pressure. You have to go by the book on this one, too.

Any time that you deal with an automatic tranny, either from the bottom through its pan, or just to add fluid at its top, it is essential to keep things almost medically clean.

Automatic transmissions are precise dimension units and have very little tolerance for contamination of any kind.

Automatic Transmission Diagnosis and Repair

Any good shop manual for a car with an automatic transmission has a large section devoted to diagnosis and repair of the tranny. This usually includes a sequence schematic and a troubleshooting guide. You may need both, because there are numerous maladies that afflict automatics and cause them to run hot, or to vibrate, or to fail to shift smoothly, or to slip in gear, etc. Each of these maladies has one or more specific potential causes. Some of them can be definitively diagnosed without disassembly. If there are no gross defects in a transmission's performance, and the only problem seems to be a lack of crispness in its shifts, or some slippage in these shifts, a band adjustment will often cure the problem, providing that it is a band-controlled, or partially band-controlled, transmission. Other "good news" maladies are such things as case leaks due to porosity—these will frequently yield to an external epoxy repair.

Even the trouble-prone governors on many automatics

are accessible with a minimum of disassembly and can be replaced without having to remove and disassemble them. Neutral safety switches are always external and easy to get at. Much diagnosis can be accomplished by road testing, stall testing or the use of oil pressure gauges. Beyond that, using air pressure to operate the bands and clutches with the valve body off will accomplish a great deal towards analysis of a malfunctioning unit. All of this is very specific to each transmission type, and restorers must go by the book.

Some transmission problems involve scaled converters, or coolers that cause transmission fluid to mix with radiator coolant. These problems can be remedied without disassembling a transmission. A scaled converter will have to be replaced or can sometimes be flushed on a converter flushing machine. Leaking coolers can usually be repaired.

Most other problems will require transmission disassembly. These, and the converter flushing routine, require transmission removal. Again, go by the book. One important hint regarding automatic transmission removal is that the flex plates that connect most torque converters or fluid couplings to their engines' flywheels are fragile and should not be pried against. Never turn an automatic over to access its flex plate fasteners by prying its engine's starter teeth, or flex plate damage can occur. The best bet on most of these transmissions is to pry against the nuts where flex plates mount to the converters, or to use their starter motors to turn them over.

When you remove an automatic, remember that its converter is not held on its shaft once the transmission is pulled back from the engine. It must be restrained by a chain, bar, or strap so that it will not go "thunk" on the floor as the transmission is removed.

Actual disassembly and repair of automatics is something best left to professionals. This can be a real problem because there are probably more shady characters in the transmission repair business than in any other single aspect of automotive repair. The inherent complexity of automatics and the fact that the majority of general mechanics have no real familiarity with them creates a situation that is ripe for skilled con men. Many of them have established lucrative operations. The abuses can be flagrant, and I am not just talking about local felons. One major national chain that specializes in transmission repair has been repeatedly indicted by local authorities and by the FTC for patterns of grossly fraudulent activities.

Here's a classic example of what can happen: Most automatics produce a certain amount of clutch, band, and bushing debris and deposit this, over time, in their pans, right under their filters. A knowledgeable transmission mechanic knows this, and if the amount of debris found in a pan is within reasonable limits, attributes its existence

Small mistakes in transmission work can lead to large disasters, like the one shown here. Be meticulous and careful when you work on transmissions!

there to normal wear and to the deterioration of frictional components.

However, crooked transmission service outfits will routinely point this stuff out to gullible customers and suggest that a $1,500 to $3,500 rebuilding program is necessary. This can occur when a customer only came in for a fluid and filter change. If this bit of deception and larceny doesn't get them well into a customer's wallet, transmission crooks have been known to radically overfill customers' transmissions, knowing that this will blow out their seals after a few miles. That's right, the people who are supposed to repair transmissions have been known to sabotage them. Of course, when a customer has his car towed back after this sequence of events, the gents at the transmission shop shake their heads wisely and remind him of their predictions of impending disaster. The evidence of what they did is spread out on the road a few miles away and can no longer be used as proof of their misdeeds.

So, there is a dilemma. Special knowledge, special tools, and some real hazards in the form of very compressed clutch springs tend to make automatic transmission repair something beyond the competence of the novice to intermediate restorer. Larceny makes many repair shops an almost equally uncertain option. The best advice that I can give for dealing with automatic transmissions that need repair or restoration is to shop carefully for an experienced and honest repairer and demand a reasonable guarantee for the work that you commission.

Getting the Drive
Back to the Wheels

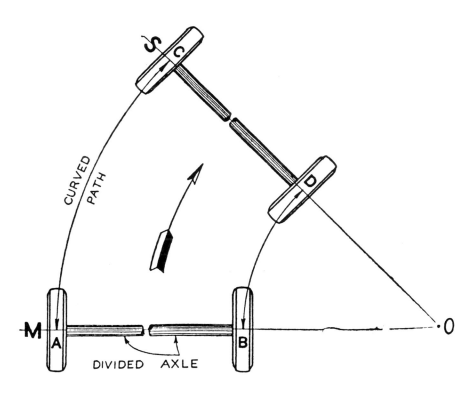

In addition to other problems that had to be solved in early automobiles, there was the need to adapt some sort of device that would allow the outboard drive wheel to turn farther and faster than the inboard wheel, while keeping both of them linked to power, when a car rounded a turn. The answer was the "differential."

VERY EARLY MOTORIZED VEHICLES either drove their wheels directly, as was the case with electric cars, or through some cumbersome arrangement of belts, sprocket chains, or friction discs. There were really two problems that had to be solved in designing the "drive lines" for these cars. One was to transmit the drive the distance from the engine to the rear wheels—after all, very few early collector cars are front-wheel drive.

Another major problem was to provide some basis for

a vehicle's powered wheels to turn at different speeds. This was, and is, necessary because when a car rounds a corner, the outboard wheel must turn farther and faster than the inboard wheel.

In addition to these major problems, the development of final drives also encompassed a gear reduction between roughly 3:1 and 4:1. Also required was the connection of an engine to a car's driving axle in a way that allows the engine to be mounted for-and-aft in the front of a car and connected to drive wheels placed at the back of the car facing fore-and-aft. A right angle gearing mechanism (rear end) is necessary to accomplish power delivery with this layout.

These issues required the development of a great deal of hardware that then had to be refined considerably before we could have the Hotchkiss drive/live axle system that has been used in most rear-wheel drive cars from the first decade of the 20th century until the advent and eventual dominance of front-wheel drive in the last twenty years. Of course, pioneer cars tended to have their engines mounted in the rear, or amidships, and the distance to the driving axles was only a matter of a few feet, or less. Then, too, the power output of early engines was so limited that the drive hardware didn't have to withstand the extreme stress and friction put on these parts in the later stages of their automotive development.

By the end of the first decade of the 20th century, monsters like the Simplex 90 and several upper echelon Mercedes used massive one- or two-stage sprocket chain systems to transmit their driving power to their rear wheels and to reduce their overall drive gear ratios. Such systems were dangerous, noisy, inefficient, trouble-prone and messy. Other than that, they were fine. What was clearly needed was some form of drive system that was compact, quiet, efficient and easy to maintain.

Enter Hotchkiss and the torque tube drive systems. Both systems employ a rigid driveshaft connected by one or more universal joints to a rear ring-and-pinion/differential gearing device. The rear end arrangement associated with these drive systems uses an internal differential gear system that is bolted or riveted to the ring gear. It transmits drive to the axles through differential side and pinion gearsets. The whole system runs in an oil bath and is contained in a heavy casing that is bolted directly to an automobile's leaf springs, or positioned by leading and/or trailing arms under coil springs.

This "conventional" drive system has dominated automobile construction from early in the last century until recently. It is a marvel of simplicity and durability—particularly when you consider what preceded it.

The torque tube drive system, which was primarily used on medium priced and expensive cars, was very common in the 1920s and died out in the 1960s—when Buick finally abandoned it. This system uses a hollow driveshaft casing that bolts firmly between the rear axle housing and a floating ball socket at the back of the transmission. In this system, only one universal joint is used—at the front end of the driveshaft. The rear axle uses the common RWD ring-and-pinion gearset with a differential case and gears attached directly to the ring gear. The torque tube system is very strong and prevents axle windup during acceleration or movement from a standstill. However, it is a heavy and expensive system to build, and this construction necessitates removal of the entire rear axle and disconnection of the rear braking system for U-joint service or transmission or clutch removal.

Hotchkiss drive, favored by car builders from the 1930s on, is similar to torque tube drive, except that the driveshaft is in the open and two or more universal joints are used to account for the deflection of the drive line angle that occurs as a rear axle moves up and down over or on its springs. This system was used very early in the last century, but was avoided by many manufacturers due to its inherent tendencies towards axle windup when power is applied. On non-leaf spring applications, some addition of trailing or leading arms, or other devices, is used in conjunction with Hotchkiss drive to locate the axle and to overcome its windup tendencies.

There are, of course, many substantial variations on these themes; for example, the worm gear rear ends favored by Ford on its trucks for many years, or the three-universal-joint open-drive-shafts-with-center-support-bearings used on trucks, limousines, and in other applications where very long driveshaft distances dictated this design.

Even within the standard Hotchkiss and torque tube designs, there is enormous variation in axle construction and universal joint type. Before any disassembly and repair or restoration work is attempted, it is important to understand what you are dealing with and what the appropriate renovation procedures will be. In many cases, special tools and gauging devices are necessary to repair driveline components.

Such items as pinion depth gauges and companion flange holders are sometimes difficult to "fudge." Other tools, like rear end spreaders, can be fabricated from your scrap steel bin if you know what you are doing.

Universal Joints

Most universal joints in rear-wheel-drive cars are simple and very perishable parts. Newer versions of cross-and-yoke type joints often do not allow for maintenance lubrication and seem to fail predictably at the end of their "design lives." Older U-joints of this type either run in an oil bath (some torque tube installations), or are greasable through zerk or needle fittings, or are filled with heavy gear oil through a small central filler plug.

For some older U-joints that are greasable there are replacement joints that are not greasable. This is a normal situation and you should not be alarmed if a new joint that replaces an old greasable joint has no provision for greasing. I prefer the greasable types because they seem to last longer if they are maintained. When greasing the greasable-type joints it is not necessary to use the hard-to-find short fiber and sodium soap greases that were originally specified for this application. Good-quality general purpose lithium or aluminum complex grease, like Lubriplate 1200-2, will work well.

It is important that these joints, and the driveshaft slip joints that are frequently located next to front U- joints, be greased carefully or with a pressure-limiting gun. Don't over-grease these joints, and don't pump them up quickly with a conventional grease gun (10,000-20,000 PSI) because

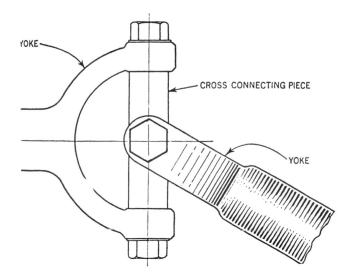

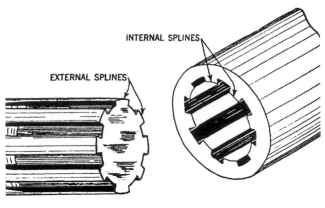

Universal joints of the yoke type are easily understood from visual inspection. They allow drive to be transmitted through an angle – but not too large an angle. That is because if they are deflected to too large an angle, their output speed varies in a sine wave pattern, inducing noise, vibration and chatter into their power transmission. This is hard on vehicle occupants and on powertrains.

On rear-wheel-drive cars, as the axle bounces up and down, the drive shaft length has to change slightly to accommodate these changes in distance from the transmission output shaft to the rear end input shaft. A splined slip joint, such as the one shown here, is how this is accomplished.

you will blow the seals out of them and hasten their failures. Blown seals will quickly produce a grease slick six inches wide on the bottom of a car in the area of the joint. As with any greasing operation, wipe off the fittings before and after injecting grease into them.

For many years, Chrysler used special roller-and-trunion U-joints that are a bit more complex than the conventional cross-and-yoke type. Follow the instructions in a shop manual or other information source when dealing with these and be sure to get the roller pin centered when you reassemble this type of joint. Another odd variation on the normal cross-and-yoke type U-joint is one formed by two back-to-back cross-and-yoke units. This is a "C.V.," or "constant velocity," joint and is designed to cancel the output speed variation that is inherent in a deflected cross-and-yoke type joint.

U-joint repair involves disassembly, cleaning and replacement of worn or suspect parts. Removal of most U-joints is accomplished by unbolting the rear joint from the rear end pinion companion flange and removing the driveshaft, front U-joint and slip joint from a car. Always tape or rubber band the bearing caps of an unattached U-joint, so that you will not have to chase the teeny-weeny little needle bearings that can fall out of the caps if they fall off and end up all over your garage floor. Also, be sure when you unbolt rear U-joint caps or straps that the driveshaft doesn't fall onto your anatomy or onto the floor. One will damage you and the other can damage the joint or possibly the driveshaft.

Further disassembly of U-joints usually involves removing bolts, locking clips, or snap rings. The latter can be removed with needle nose pliers or snap ring pliers. The

joint's caps can then be forced out of their yokes in a joint press or a vise. If you use a vise, place a small socket (smaller diameter than the cap's outside diameter) against one U-joint cap and use a larger socket (larger than the cap's outer diameter) outside of the yoke to receive the opposite cap. Now close the vise jaws to press the U-joint caps and spider out of the yoke. At this point, you can pull the spider out of its remaining cap and push the opposite cap out.

This procedure is crude but effective. Never hammer on a U-joint to remove it, and never use a pneumatic "zip" gun for that purpose. Either of these approaches will usually remove the joint, but only at the expense of a bent yoke or damaged cap seat—if you slip. Never grasp a driveshaft in a bench vise with anything but minimum pressure and soft jaws, and be sure to support the opposite end of a shaft when you are working on a U-joint yoke. Never hold a driveshaft yoke in a common bench vise, since the vise has enough mechanical advantage to bend a yoke or deform the driveshaft tube.

Universal joints need repair when they emit noise or rumble, or when you can sense that the joint has play in it when hand pressure is applied. When U-joint failure occurs, you will find worn or corroded needle bearings, worn bearing caps and/or worn cross shafts.

On most joints, repair of these parts is futile, making replacement necessary. Some very early joints use bushings that can be replaced, and some later joints allow the replacement of parts of the cross-and-yoke system. Total replacement is always best. Bad seals that allow lubricant to leak out and water to get in are a main cause of U-joint failure. A certain amount of care is necessary to avoid seal damage when installing new U-joints. It is also critical that

A dedicated U-joint removing tool, like the one shown here, is very handy for removing U-joint spiders and caps from their yokes, but you can accomplish the same job in a shop vise with some assorted sockets, if you are careful.

the yoke bore surfaces are free of burrs and other defects for joints to install and work properly.

When reinstalling U-joints, be sure that they are "phased" correctly (the yokes are almost always set in the same plane and not at 90 degrees to each other) and don't over-tighten the bolts or straps that secure rear U-joints to their companion flanges. If lock washers or other locking devices are used to secure U-joint bearing caps or straps, be sure to continue that tradition. Many joints are susceptible to incorrect phasing by misassembling the slip joint behind the front U-joint. Some have arrows or other markings stamped on the parts to make correct phasing easy. A few have blind or missing splines to make misassembly impossible. What a great idea!

The most intriguing U-joint that I ever saw had two yokes bolted at 90 degrees to opposite sides of a piece of 1/2-inch thick rubberized fabric. This was on an MG model "M" from the early 1930s. It was "factory." Other designs go in the opposite direction, towards complexity, with double cardan joints and center support bearings. All of them require precision and considerate handling if they are to move power to the rear end of a car without excessive vibration and failure.

Driveshafts

Most driveshafts are relatively simple and crude-

looking devices that appear to be innocent of any charges that could be leveled against them. However, this is not the case. For one thing, driveshafts and their universal joints are very bad at transmitting power if they are asked to drive through angles that are beyond their design limits. Then, too, driveshafts are susceptible to warping, denting and imbalance—all of which will produce a rumble under your feet and premature failure of other driveline components. As rugged as they look, driveshafts are surprisingly delicate, and must be maintained within very close dimensional and balance tolerances if they are to operate without simulating the San Andreas Fault zone during an earthquake.

The first item to check on a driveshaft is the integrity of its slip joint. The splines should be tight and free to allow driveshaft length variations as the rear springs compress and release, which causes the shaft-to-transmission output coupling distance to shorten and lengthen. The slip joint will be found in front of or behind the front universal joint on Hotchkiss drive cars, and near the rear axle or torque ball on torque tube drive cars.

The second item to check is driveshaft straightness and balance. Straightness is initially checked by rotating one rear wheel with the other blocked and the transmission in neutral. Any movement of the shaft surface laterally by more than a tenth of an inch or so may indicate a bent shaft. This can most accurately be checked in a large lathe. Driveshaft imbalance is also a common problem that usually occurs because something got added to the shaft (like undercoating) or something got subtracted from it (like a welded balance weight that fell off when its spot weld succumbed to corrosion). Again, this has to be checked in a lathe with a balancing attachment or on a specially designed balancing machine.

Unbalanced driveshafts can be repaired by rebalancing, but warped or bent shafts should be replaced entirely or have their yokes rewelded to new shaft tubes. This may sound extreme, but my experience with "straightened" driveshafts has been uniformly unsatisfactory.

One little trick that mechanics often use when shaft imbalance is suspected is trial-and-error balancing with a screw-type hose clamp applied to various locations and at various radial positions on the suspect driveshaft. If the vibration situation can be improved this way, diagnosis of an out-of-balance shaft is confirmed. This "little trick" should never be considered a final repair, as it is not precise enough for that purpose. Over the years, I have encountered several automobiles with hose clamps on their driveshafts—apparent attempts to mask a problem for the purpose of selling a car.

Long, two-piece driveshafts with center support bearings frequently suffer defects in their center support bearings, or in the rubber cushions that locate those bearings. Always check for this on cars equipped with driveshafts with center support bearings.

Some driveshafts have external vibration damper systems that are easy to find and sometimes require replacement. A sneakier system was one used by Chrysler

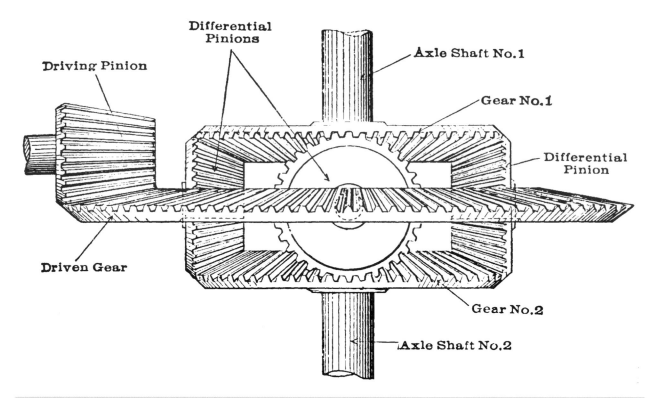

Driving Pinion

Differential Pinions

Axle Shaft No.1

Gear No.1

Differential Pinion

Driven Gear

Gear No.2

Axle Shaft No.2

Differential gearing is easy enough to understand if you have a unit in your hands and can watch it work. Try staring at this nice diagram of a ring and pinion gear and a differential gearset and see if the notion of its operation doesn't just "fly into your head."

that located a rubber damper inside the shaft itself. These can go bad and result in permanent imbalance of the shaft.

One thing that Hotchkiss drive systems do badly is driving through excessive angles. When a car is restored, and the engine or rear axle has been removed, it is a good idea to check the driveshaft angle with a spirit level/protractor and compare the drive-shaft-to-rear-axle-angular-deviation with that allowed by the manufacturer. If this angle is in excess, it is unlikely that the U-joints will be able to perform their function without audible complaint and rapid wear. Angular correction is accomplished by shimming either the transmission on its rear mounting surface or the rear axle housing where it attaches to the springs. If you find any shims in these areas at the time of disassembly, keep track of them or your reassembly will probably fail.

Automotive Rear Ends

Most automobile rear ends will outlast several engines if they are properly set up and reasonably well maintained. They are among the most trouble-free assemblies in automobiles. There are, of course, some exceptions, such as certain E-type Jaguars and a few other cars.

That's the "good news." The "bad news" is that when a rear end needs repair, beyond something simple like a pinion shaft seal replacement or a wheel bearing replacement, it can be pretty tough going. There are usually some special tools, fixtures, and measuring devices associated with rear end disassembly and setup. The need for precision is enormous.

However, rear end repair is something that a talented amateur can handle if he has access to the necessary tools, equipment, and information.

With all of this in mind, and given the rarity of the need for major rear end repairs, it is usually preferable to substitute a functioning rear end for one that is damaged, unless, of course, the damaged unit is very rare and/or expensive. In terms of labor, probable service life and cost of repair, a rear end transplant almost always comes out ahead of "going in" to repair a malfunctioning unit.

When you do go in, you will find a device that is very tough in some respects and very delicate in others. There is always the need for great precision in rear end work. Worn or broken differential parts are unusual because differentials are only activated when a car rounds a corner or spins one wheel. Bent and broken axles and leaking seals are common, but can usually be repaired without resorting to major rear end disassembly. Worn or chipped-out ring and pinion gearsets are a common cause of serious rear end problems.

Axle nomenclature is important because the type of axle that you are dealing with will determine, in large part, the correct repair approaches and procedures. Gear-driven rear axles and their parts are described by the following broad terms and categories.

LIMITED SLIP or "POSITRACTION": These units, available from around the 1960s on, use clutching devices to overcome some of the tendency of differential gear Positraction-equipped cars to allow the wheel with the least

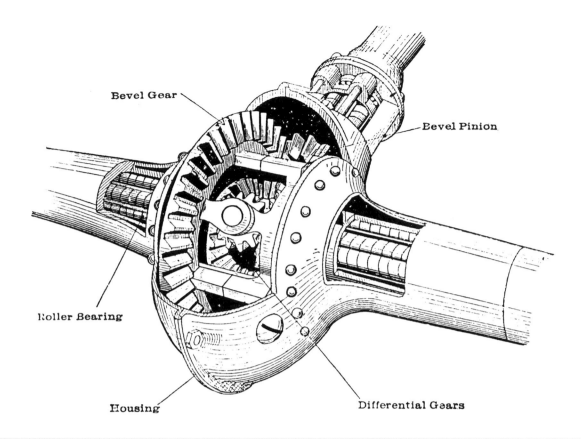

Bevel Gear

Bevel Pinion

Roller Bearing

Housing

Differential Gears

This Ford axle setup doesn't have a center section; its halves bolt directly together.

traction to spin. A "posi car will climb the side of a barn in a sleet storm. However, it can be difficult to repair these units when they malfunction. It is almost always easier and cheaper to transplant a whole rear end assembly when axles of this type go bad. When you add lubricant to them, be sure to use the special lubricants that they require to keep their clutches holding.

More recent Torsen traction-enhancing devices do not require special lubricants because they do not have clutches. They are much more reliable than the older clutched units.

INTEGRAL, REMOVABLE CARRIER, AND BANJO AXLES: These terms describe the basic construction of axle housings. The most common one in collector cars is the integral axle, which has the guts of its ring and pinion set and their bearings bolted to the major housing that includes the axle tubes. On these units, you will find a cover plate at the back of the axle housing that allows access to the gears and bearings. It is usually better to service integral setups with the axle removed from a car.

Removable carrier-type axles are set up so that the ring, pinion and differential gears and their bearings can be removed from the axle housing in one, separate subassembly. This makes them easy to work on, as you can pull the "pumpkin" and leave the axle housing under the car. This construction has no removable back plate.

The banjo-type axle is constructed in two lateral halves that bolt to a central casting, or to each other, or both. Banjo axles are unnerving to work on because about the only final adjustment that you can make on them with certainty is ring

and pinion backlash; and that leaves a great deal unknown.

FLOATING AND SEMI-FLOATING AXLES: These terms apply to axle outer end bearing construction. The semi-floating construction (there is also a "three-quarter floating") has the axle end bearings inside the axle tubes, so that the axle shaft ends both bear a vehicle's weight and transmit drive power to its wheels. In the full-floating design—still used on many trucks, heavy-duty three-quarter-ton capacity and over—the bearings that support the wheel hubs are mounted on the outsides of the axle tubes, and the axle shafts bear none of the vehicle's weight. In a full-floating axle setup, the shafts are usually retained by a snap wire and can be removed with the wheels and hubs left behind. Some older cars used full-floating axles, although this practice is only applied on fairly heavy-duty trucks today.

FLANGED AND REMOVABLE-HUB AXLE SHAFTS: Older axles were made in two pieces with a straight shaft and a splined or keyed hub nutted to it. After World War II, through the 1960s, manufacturers switched to a one-piece axle construction, with the flange/hub and shaft forged in one unit. On a very few of the removable hub type axles, the hub has unfinished splines that are conformed by nutting the hub to the axle shaft. On this type, the hubs are not reusable and must be discarded after separation from their axle shafts.

OTHER AXLE DISTINCTIONS: There are some other axle types and distinctions out there, such as the worm drive assemblies favored by Ford for their early trucks,

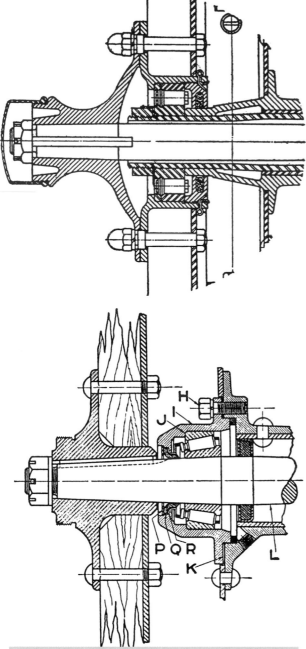

The "full floating" axle design (top) puts a vehicle's weight on the wheel bearing and outside aspect of the axle tube, so the axle shaft only transmits power. In the "semi-floating" axle design (bottom) the axle's wheel bearing and axle end bear the weight of the vehicle and transmit drive to the wheel. This puts much more stress on the end of the axle shaft.

chapter on transmissions. Please refer to that chapter for details. In general, there are three types of lubricants that you should be aware of: EP (extreme pressure), non-EP, and "posi." In modern hypoid gear axles, that is, axles with the pinion gear entering the ring gear below its centerline, you must use a hypoid type lubricant. Lubricants in this class counter the very high temperatures generated by the extremely high face pressures and wiping actions of hypoid configured gear teeth. The correct lubricants for this application are designated as EP (Extreme Pressure) hypoid, multipurpose or APG (All Purpose Gear).

For axles that are not hypoid type, you should probably use a non-hypoid lubricant of the correct weight. Lubriplate still makes 90 and 140 weight lubricants that have all of the additives that good gear oils should have (anti-scuff, anti-foam, anti-corrosion, etc.) but none of the EP additives (phosphorous and sulfur based chemicals) that can corrode non-hypoid gears. The metallurgy of pre-hypoid units, in some cases, may not be able to withstand the assault of hypoid additives over long periods. Etching of brass and bronze by these lubricants is a certainty, and pitting and welding of ferrous gear teeth with non-hypoid metallurgy is a distinct possibility.

Positraction type axles require the use of lubricants with friction modifying additives to ensure that their clutches will grip. This class of lubricants must be used in these units, but should never be used in non-locking type axles. Basically, hypoid gear oils are a compromise and are not very good lubricants for general purposes. That is probably one of the reasons that this type of axle has a comparatively high failure rate.

Rear axles run in gear oil, generally SAE 90 to 140 on the gear oil scale. The older ones used 140 and the newer ones use 90, or even 75W-90. I have seen people try to use the old, original specification 600W boiler grease to quiet a noisy rear end or to compensate for excessive ring and pinion backlash. This will not work, and unless a very early car specifies this kind of heavy grease, its use should be avoided. Modern SAE 140 gear oils are the same viscosity as the old 600W oils and are much better lubricants. I have run a good grade of 140 in rear ends that specified 600W with excellent results.

Rear End Diagnosis

Rear end symptoms divide into two classes: noises and leaks. Beyond dealing with those symptoms and making a simple check for gear backlash or for a bent or broken axle, there is not too much that can be determined without disassembly. That is probably why about half of the rear ends that are disassembled suffer this fate for no valid reason. Unfortunately, it is not unusual for a mechanic with more enthusiasm for wrench work than analytical ability to disassemble a rear axle to seek the source of a noise that is, in reality, being generated by an entirely different part of a car—such as tires or front wheel bearings.

Before you go down this glory path, please remember

and a few obscure planetary differential units. The two-speed Columbia unit, fitted primarily to Ford products, is another interesting variation. 98 percent or more of all axles ever built will conform to one or more of the above descriptions.

Rear Axle Lubrication

Many of the important distinctions regarding the gear lubricants used in rear axles were covered in the previous

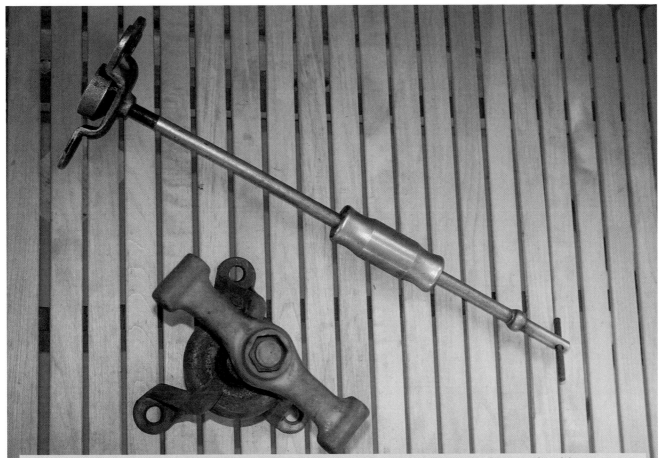

The slide hammer axle puller (right, rear) will usually remove a stuck axle. It bolts to the hub and delivers impact when its weight is slid against its stop. The striking hub puller (left, front) is designed to remove hubs from axles, and should be used gently. Pounding the ram screw striking arm delivers enormous force and shock to the hub and axle end, enough to separate them, or if overdone, to endanger both.

this: Rear axles don't often malfunction. They are very durable, and are good candidates for being left alone. Car noises, like leaks in a house roof, seldom originate where they *seem* to come from. If you do take a rear end apart for no good reason—like a noise that really has its origins elsewhere—it is more likely to fail than if you had shown the restraint and good sense to leave it alone. This is because it will be virtually impossible to get the bearing preloads and unit dimensions to exactly what they were before disassembly, and what they were when the parts wore in. "For goo'ness sake, if it ain't broke, don't fix it."

Rear axle leaks are usually simple to correct. Leaking casting gaskets may yield to some careful and even tightening, or they may need replacement. Pinion seals and axle seals are relatively easy to replace.

Noises and vibrations from rear ends are more complex to analyze. Books could be, and probably have been, written about them. Here, a few paragraphs will have to do.

Rear end noise symptoms are best heard from the back seat of a car with the rear windows open or, in the cases of convertibles, with their tops down and the audio system switches in the unaccustomed "off" position. These noises can have timbres varying from rumbles, to screams, to clickings, to roars. Be sure that you eliminate common symptomatic noises, often mistaken for rear end noises, before you tear into a rear end. Tire noises should disappear

when the tires are over inflated, at least the pitch of their noises will change. U-joint and seal noises can be confirmed by close inspection. True rear end noises will almost always change radically as you go from acceleration, to coast, and back to throttle. If the noise that you are hearing doesn't do this, it is probably a tire noise or a transmission noise. Clicking noises in rear wheel drive vehicles that are heard as you round corners are very likely to be differential related. In any case, before disassembling a rear end to correct a noise or vibration problem, get someone with rear end experience to listen and render an opinion.

Rear Axle Shafts and Wheel Bearings

Most axle work involves the axle shafts, their outer bearings, and their oil or grease seals. Such work usually does not involve the center section of the axle housing, and is accomplished entirely from the outer ends of the housing. The exception to this is some General Motors products from the 1930s, and long after, which required removal of "C" washers from the inner ends of the axle shafts for shaft removal. Chevrolet was famous for this system.

Flanged axles are removed by loosening the nuts or bolts that secure their retaining plates, just behind their flanges.

Usually, there is a hole in the flange that allows access to the retainer fastener heads by rotating the axle around to access them. Once the retaining plate and seal behind it are free, the axle should slide out with its bearing. A little persuasion with an axle slide hammer may be necessary.

Removable hub-type axles usually don't allow easy access to the fasteners securing their bearings, seals and retaining plates. Their hubs usually have to be removed to permit retainer and bearing removal. The removal of splined or keyed hubs from axles is one of life's little annoyances because they frequently don't want to separate with persuasion of less magnitude than a small nuclear detonation.

The first attempts to remove these hubs, after the securing cotter keys and axle end nuts have been removed, should involve using a threaded puller. If this fails, it is common procedure to escalate things to the use of a barbaric device called a "striking hub puller." This is a puller that is struck to generate enormous force and substantial shock on its ram threads. It is capable of inflicting great damage by warping an axle hub or splitting the end of an axle, without actually accomplishing removal of the hub from the axle shaft.

The alternative to using this kind of brute force is disarmingly simple. Loosen the axle hub retaining nuts about half to three-quarters of a turn from finger-tight and replace their cotter keys. Now drive the car a mile or two on a bumpy road. Usually, the hubs will come off in your hands when the nuts are backed off the rest of the way. Of course, if a car isn't running, this won't work and you may have to use pullers, and even mild heat, on the hubs to remove them. If heat is used, it should be kept under 350 degrees F. to avoid changing the temper of the axle and hub. It helps to strike the hub with a brass hammer while applying force and heat.

When separated, the axle's tapered end and hub center hole should be inspected for damage to the keyways or splines. Axle shafts and their bearings are removed by hand, or with a puller, after retaining plates and seals have been removed.

Chevrolet, and a few other GM cars, used "C" washers to retain their axles, as well as retainer plates. This is like wearing a belt and suspenders, but as long as you know about it, it shouldn't cause problems. These axles are removed as above, except that the rear end case cover has to be removed, the differential pinion shaft locking screw loosened and the pinion shaft removed. Then, the axle ends can be pushed in from their recesses in the differential side gears and the "C" lock washers that retain them can be removed with a magnet.

Chrysler had a nasty little trick in the 1960s of drilling holes in the inner ends of its axles and inserting a flanged pin-spacer-doohicky, with the pin ends entered into each axle end. Be careful not to lose that pin in the soup when you remove this type of axle shaft. It is particularly easy to do this if you are using a slide hammer to remove an axle on one of these installations.

Broken axles are in a department all by themselves because removing their inner ends can be a study in frustration. Magnets sometimes do the trick, and there are several different types of stub removers made to deal with this situation. Some of them may even work.

Any time that an axle is removed, it should be checked for twisting and straightness. Twisting can usually be seen on the surface of the axle shaft, and straightness can be determined by placing the machined ends of an axle on V-blocks or chucking them in a lathe. The axle splines, squares, or hexes that engage differential side gears should be inspected for chipping, cracking, or other damage, while axle seal bosses should be looked at for erosion.

Bent axles theoretically can be straightened, but if they are twisted, there is little that can be done to prevent their failure, so they should be replaced. Damaged seal areas can be spray or MIG welded and remachined, or sleeves, such as Chicago Rawhide's "Speedi-Sleeve" product, can be found for many shaft diameters and easily and inexpensively installed. It is always a good idea to Magnaflux axles and hubs when they are out for any reason.

Axle outer bearings are driven or pressed off their shafts. Considerable force is usually required to do this. If an axle bearing is retained by a small, ring-like piece driven against its side, this collar can be removed by supporting its bottom and striking it hard in three places on its circumference with a cold chisel. After this assault the ring should slide off its axle boss easily. Never try to drive an axle bearing and a ring retainer off an axle at the same time. The best way to remove press fit axle bearings is to use a press. Whatever method you use, protect the splined ends of axles from damage, and protect the threaded ends of removable hub type axles. Also, be sure to protect the oil seal surfaces on axles from accidental damage when you are removing bearings and their retainers.

Some axles have their bearings located so close to their bearing seal retaining plates that there isn't room for a bearing pulling cage behind them. On these, the outer races have to be ground away until individual rollers can be removed and then the whole outer race. This will allow the inboard edge of the inner race to be held for the purpose of pulling it off the shaft.

Never attempt to reuse a bearing that has been removed from an axle. This can be tempting when the object of a repair is to replace a $3.50 seal, but you have to destroy the $35 axle bearing to get to it. Resist the temptation. Axle bearings can be expensive, but they are not reusable after removal because the removal process destroys them. Also, be sure to mark the right and left axles if both are removed. It's easy to forget to do this, but it is important to get it right.

When reassembling an axle shaft, its seals, retaining plate, bearing and bearing retainer ring, be sure to get the parts in the right sequence and orientation. It is surprisingly easy to put a roller bearing in backwards, or to forget a seal until after the bearing is on an axle. This often causes restorers to strike their foreheads with their palms, and can

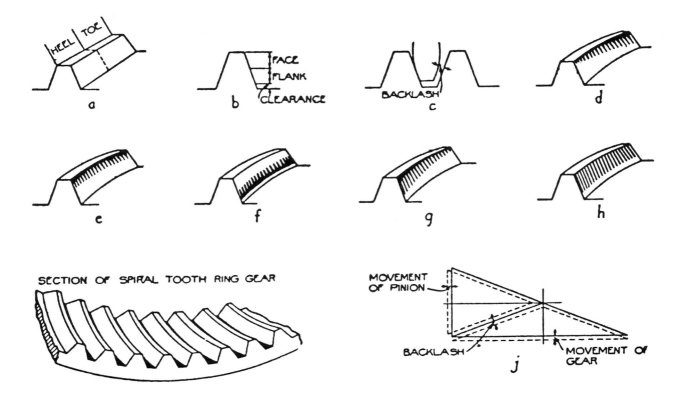

Ring and pinion gear tooth contact pattern can be read in white or red lead. This gives a good visual indication of ring and pinion mesh. While red and white lead are difficult to find these days, small amounts of them still reside in the tool boxes of a few seasoned old mechanics. Many manufacturers provided graphic data on correct mesh patterns in their shop manuals.

lead to headaches and, in extreme and repeated cases, to badly sloping foreheads.

When ring retainers are used to secure bearings to axles, never drive them on in the same operation as installing the bearings. First drive or press the bearings home. Then, drive the retainers against the bearings.

When pressing or driving bearings and retainers on, it is essential that most of their circumferences be supported. Don't try to drive a bearing on with a cold chisel. Bearings can only be driven or pressed on shafts by their inner races. Force applied to the outer race of a bearing will destroy it. When installing or removing bearings and their retainers from axle shafts, it is very good practice to use some kind of protective sleeve to prevent damage to adjacent sealing surfaces.

Always wear good eye protection when working with bearing press fits on axles. Flying chips are a very real possibility. Bearing races can "explode" when they are forced off or into place.

After an axle shaft, its bearings, seal(s) and retainer have been assembled, it can be installed in the axle housing. There are several points to note here. If shims are used behind the retainer to provide for axle shaft end float adjustment, these should be reinstalled as they were found when the axle was removed, and the end float should be checked with a dial indicator. The shims can then be adjusted to provide for the correct combined axle end float values.

In some axle designs, a threaded adjuster is used to control end float. In either case, this factor must be attended

to, or the wheel bearings can be destroyed in service. Always use new gaskets behind axle retainer plates, and be sure that they are made from material that will compress to roughly the same thickness as the original gaskets when they were compressed.

A few rear axles had a second set of grease seals at the inner ends of their tubes. These were more to control lubricant outflow than to stop it and do not require replacement unless they are very badly damaged.

Be sure that if retainer plates can be installed in more than one position on their bolts, they are installed with their drain holes down. This allows for the escape of any axle lubricant that gets past the seals and that might otherwise threaten brakes. Be sure that when you slip axles into their tubes that the oil seals in the tubes' outer ends (if used) are not contacted by (and possibly cut by) the axles' inner end splines as they are passed through them during installation. If such seals exist in axle tubes, they should be changed when axles are removed and replaced. These seals are hammered into axle housing ends with special installing drivers and should be coated on their outer diameters with a non-hardening sealer before they are installed. Their lips should be greased lightly before axles are inserted through them.

With the axles and retainers installed, the retainers can be tightened. Always be sure to reestablish whatever method was used to secure the retainer fasteners—cotter keys, wire, aircraft nuts, bend tabs and the like. Tightening axle retainers is an acceptable method of seating axle bearing outer races in axle tubes, as long as excessive force is not applied to do this.

On removable hub-type axles, the hub inner surfaces and the axles' tapered mating surfaces should be cleaned and deburred. The hubs can then be installed on the shafts with a very light coating of grease on both surfaces of that interface. The hub nuts then can be tightened to the correct torque—usually a very high (grunt eliciting) value. The hubs should then be rapped with a brass hummer a couple of times and the end nuts retorqued to specification, and then advanced to the first available cotter key hole. Never slacken these nuts to align cotter key holes. If necessary, to avoid having to use excessive force to align cotter key holes, you can remove the axle end nuts and lightly file their bottom surfaces to advance their fully tightened and key aligned positions into coincidence.

A final check of axle end float should then be made and compared to the manufacturer's specification. The axle case can then be topped with the correct lubricant be put into service. Always make sure that axle venting port(s) are clear, so that pressure does not build up in the housing and blow lubricant past the tube end seals and towards your brakes.

Rear End Disassembly, Repair, and Installation: When You Have To Go In

Only the foolhardy (or possibly, "Only the lonely…") would consider going into an engine without some bare minimum of knowledge of repair procedure and specification information. Ring/pinion/differential assemblies represent a similar situation. These are highly evolved units that require exact and precise setup. You can't just feel your way around in there and hope for the best, with any realistic expectation of success. Rear end inner bearings, unlike wheel bearings, usually operate on the principle of pre-load. This means that two bearings work in opposition to each other with a small but specific loading on the shaft between them. In most rear ends, preload is used on the shaft that carries the pinion gear and on the bearing set that supports the ring gear/differential assembly. Preload involves a critical adjustment and allows for no "fudge" factor.

Similarly, the ring and pinion gear dimensional relationship is susceptible to four types of adjustment movement: pinion depth (pinion in and out) and ring gear position (to one side or the other). These adjustments use shims or threaded adjusting rings and must be made exactly by the book. One of the final outcomes of these adjustments is ring and pinion gear "backlash," which should be read for confirmation of what has been done to adjust these gearsets.

Precision and cleanliness are essential in rear end work. Due to the relatively enormous pressures to which these parts are subjected in normal service, chips, burrs, and the like pose real threats to the entire assemblies. Everything must be meticulously clean where this work is performed. Always use new keys, pins, tab washers, and other locking devices. Check fasteners for cracks, distortion and worn threads. If adjusting shims are damaged during removal, replace them with new ones.

When you go into a rear end, the first step is to drain the lubricant and to remove the axle shafts, as outlined previously. If you are working on a removable carrier type unit, the "pumpkin" can then be removed from the axle housing and installed in a holding fixture on your bench. For integral axle types, you will have to work on the parts assembled in the axle housing. Banjo axles are separated either before or after removing the pinion gear carrier, depending on construction.

It is always a good idea to get any measurements and mesh indications that are possible before you change the relationships of the parts in an axle by disassembling it. On banjo axles this will mean determining gear backlash before any disassembly occurs. On integral and removable carrier type axles, it is a good idea to measure backlash, pinion depth, preload and tooth contact pattern (explained later) before disassembly. This will give you data for comparison purposes, after your reassembly is complete.

All loaded bearing parts in a rear end should be Magnafluxed and checked for burrs, chips, warping, run-out, pitting and any other relevant defects that occur to you. Gear teeth should be checked for excessive scuffing and wear. Bearings must be in perfect condition, and any scoring, spalling, or indications of burning or pitting will mandate their replacement.

Ring gear and differential case removal is accomplished with the axle shafts out and by removing the bolts holding the bearing caps on the differential side bearings. These caps should be labeled and/or marked for location and orientation. The ring gear and differential unit can then be removed, but it may take a special slide hammer or pry bars to persuade it out of the axle housing. Sometimes, an axle case spreader has to be used to free a ring gear and differential case from its axle housing. If this type of device is used, it must be used with restraint, and never for more than a 0.020 inch spread of the axle case. If shims are the method of adjustment for a ring gear's position, they should be saved and noted for location.

Differential cases are bolted or riveted to the ring gears. The manner of this attachment is extremely important. Special hardened, shouldered bolts or rivets are used to precisely locate these parts. Differential cases, themselves, should be labeled for position in ring gears and the relative positions of the case halves must also be labeled so that reassembly will return these parts to their original orientations.

Pinion gears are usually removed from axle housings or carriers by holding their companion flanges or yokes with special holding fixtures and removing the nuts securing the flanges or yokes to their pinion gear shafts. The flanges or yokes are then removed with special pullers. Then pinion gears and shafts can be removed by pressing them into the axle housing after their ring gears have been removed. Some pinion shafts are secured to axle housings on separate carriers that can be removed as units.

On some rear ends, collapsible pinion spacer/preload bushings are used. These parts are designed to achieve specified preloads by deformation, as their flange holding nuts are tightened. Never try to reuse one of these spacers. They must be replaced.

The gears in ring and pinion sets and in differential gearsets should be inspected for defects. If either of these sets has defective gears, the complete sets will have to be replaced. You can never replace either just a ring or just a pinion gear, or one gear in a differential set. While differential gears and shafts rarely wear, if you do find worn differential shafts or gears, they must be replaced. Rear ends are one of the places where a bad or mismatched part will quickly ruin the other parts with which it works. Half measures don't succeed here.

When everything is spotlessly clean, and all defective parts have been replaced, a rear end can be reassembled and set up. As suggested earlier, a manual and the wisdom to follow it are musts at this point. It is also essential that any new gears that are used are in matched sets and their bearings are the correct grade for this application. Just finding a bearing or pinion gear that "sort of" fits will not work. Most ring and pinion gears are numbered to indicate the status of twins in a common heritage.

They are also frequently marked for pinion depth setting. Some are marked for tooth mesh point, particularly those without a "hunting tooth." That is a tooth that creates an odd gear ratio and insures that the same teeth do not have to mesh in each revolution of the pinion with the ring gear. Hunting tooth design results in odd gear ratios, like 3.23, but greatly reduces gear wear.

Rear end bearings should be matched by number and by application, not by dimension only. Extreme care should be taken in installing rear end bearings on their shafts and in their seats. Pressing a well supported bearing is correct; hammering a bearing home is a "definite no no."

Ring gears should be bolted into differential cases at the right torque values and with their halves in the correct relationship to each other and to their ring gears. All parts that assemble should be checked for burrs and other defects, and defects in them must be corrected before installation. Shims should be installed as they were removed, with final shim adjustment left for later. Threaded adjusters that locate ring gear bearings should be put in their original positions and the bearing caps tightened to the correct torques. At this point, the manual must be followed for correct pinion gear depth and preload and for correct ring gear lateral position and preload. In some cases, special measuring jigs will be required to measure the critical pinion depth dimension. In other cases, dial indicators and other fairly common tools will suffice for rear end setup work.

While I have the greatest admiration for people who improvise tools and measuring jigs, rear ends are one place where this kind of endeavor is often inappropriate. There is a rumor abroad in the land that if a pinion gear has its outer edge brought exactly flush with the inner edge of its ring gear, it will be in adjustment. This rumor is false and, if followed, will promote failure. Many pinions are marked for depth over-standard and under-standard, so simply bringing a pinion flush with the inner edge of a mating ring gear will not work, except in a few pre-1930s cars that specified this primitive form of adjustment. Whatever adjustment technique is used, there are two sources of information about ring and pinion mesh that are always available and that should be compared to known specifications.

The first is backlash. When all dimensional adjustments have been made to ring and pinion gears, backlash must be within specification, or something is wrong. The second general indication is gear tooth contact pattern. Some manufacturers used gear tooth contact pattern as the primary specification for their entire rear end setup procedure and did not rely on dimensional data.

Gear tooth contact pattern is read by painting the ring gear with white or red lead paste. White lead works best. The ring gear is then turned by rotating the pinion gear. A little drag should be applied to the ring gear as it is turned by applying the hand brake or by pressing a pry bar against the edge of the ring gear. A clear mesh pattern will appear on the lead paste on the ring gear teeth. Each rear end application will have a slightly different "ideal" tooth contact pattern.

A final check of tooth contact pattern with lead paste is so important that no matter what primary adjustment technique was employed, this method should be used for confirmation of a rear end setup. When lead paste is used, remember that red lead residue must be cleaned up because its contamination degrades rear end lubricants. White lead, on the other hand, should be left on the ring and pinion gears because it tends to improve the performance of rear end lubricants.

Until the early 1980s, when the EPA banned lead additives in gear oils, many of them contained sulfur-lead-chlorine ("SLC") additive packages, or a lead napthanate additive, to improve gear oil performance.

When all of this work is completed, and a new pinion shaft seal is installed, and the carrier or access cover is bolted back in place, you can refill the rear end with an appropriate lubricant and put it into service. It's a good idea to listen to a freshly rebuilt rear end for a while, or at least to listen for it. If you are inclined toward prayer, this might be a good time to apply some of it.

Chapter 16

Front Wheel Bearings and Drum Brake Friction Systems

Brake and front end environments require careful and meticulous work. The grease in this spindle and hub must be protected from dirt and water, and must also be kept separate from the brake friction surfaces, just a few inches away. That protection and separation are provided by one seal and one dust cap. You can see why you have to be careful when you work on brakes and front wheel bearings.

AUTOMOTIVE FRONT WHEEL BEARINGS have changed less and are subject to less design variation than just about any other complex, stress-laden system in automobiles with the possible exception of the lowly Schroeder valve (tire air valve). Even the widespread adoption of disc brakes and front-wheel, drive a quarter of a century ago, has made little significant difference in the principles of front wheel bearing design.

All front wheel bearing systems with which I am familiar utilize anti-friction bearings of either tapered roller or ball configuration. Most of the differences in design involve details such as grease seal placement or provisions

Most brake environments end up looking pretty sad by the time you restore a car. The brake disc in this photo is obviously corroded from sitting for a long time and shows minor grooving. The hub dust cap is obviously leaking grease.

for external greasing. The front spindle bearings on rear-wheel-drive vehicles and older front-wheel-drive vehicles tended to be disassembleable, while newer spindle bearing sets on front-wheel-drive cars are not.

Another important distinction is between systems using tapered roller bearings and ball bearings. Both of these approaches use two thrust bearings working in opposition to each other to support a car's weight, to transmit its power to its wheels (FWD) and to align its wheels. The tapered roller type, which has pretty much dominated the field since the beginning, runs with a small but essential amount of side play to allow for bearing expansion and to let the inner bearing races "creep" or march around their spindles. The ball bearing type, which involves an annular thrust design, usually operates under a small amount of preload.

If wheel bearings are set up correctly, and if their seals perform adequately to keep grease in and water and dirt out, they will require very little attention. Under most conditions, good wheel bearing grease will last the better part of a decade, and inspection and repacking can safely be left to intervals of 25,000 miles or more. When these bearings are disassembled and repacked, they become vulnerable to maladjustment and subsequent failure. I have probably seen more front wheel bearings fail shortly after repacking than at any other time, including after intervals and mileages of extended service. I believe that this is due to improper installation and/or adjustment.

Front wheel bearings probably are victimized by receiving more attention than they merit. While they do not often fail, they are easy to inspect, and their failure symptoms (mostly noises) are easily confused with those

Front wheel bearings are pretty simple items, but they have to work right or they will scream, howl or rumble. Many people don't realize that the inner race of a wheel bearing marches slowly around the spindle that it is mounted on as the wheel turns mostly on the bearing itself.

of other, less accessible parts of cars, such as transmissions and universal joints. They can also affect the performance of other systems, such as steering and braking—resulting in false diagnoses and unnecessary disassembly of those systems, when it is really wheel bearings that are at fault. Try to avoid this pitfall. Remember, too, that just jacking up a car and rotating a wheel by hand will almost never result in detection of a bad front wheel bearing. These faults are

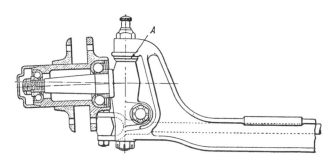

The front wheel bearing setups on rear wheel drive cars haven't changed much since this king pin front end was manufactured early in the century. Most modern applications use tapered roller bearings instead of the annular ball bearings shown on this spindle.

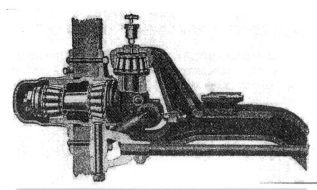

Spindles with tapered roller bearings will go a long way if they are kept dry and clean and have adequate, but not excessive, lubricant packed into them.

The 85-year-old spindle flange shown here is suspect for cracks. Dry magnetic particle inspection showed possible cracks, so a more sensitive wet magnetic particle inspection, shown here, was performed with a black light. No cracks were found.

Sometimes you have to make tools when you lack the special tools that were used for special procedures when cars were current. This wrench was made to remove a hub nut from a spindle by welding some angle iron and a nut to a flat piece of scrap steel. It's crude, but it worked.

usually only evident with load applied.

Front wheel bearing failure is relatively easy to diagnose. Like rear wheel bearings, front wheel bearings indicate failure by emitting noises anywhere from howls to screams to rumbles. Also, like rear wheel bearings, front wheel bearings will change the tone of their complaints as a vehicle takes a curve. This is because the load on and speed of the wheel bearings change differently, side-to-side, in a curve. The noise produced by a defective front wheel bearing will be different or absent in a left or right turn.

So far, all of the indications of trouble are the same for front and for rear wheel bearings. The diagnostic difference between them is that in a rear-wheel-drive vehicles, defective rear wheel bearings will change their tonal output as the operation of a vehicle is changed from power to back-throttle (coast). This change in operation should not affect the noises made by bad front wheel bearings.

Disassembly and reassembly of front wheel bearings is simple but exacting work. Whether disassembly is being pursued to correct a diagnosed defect or for time-and-mileage maintenance considerations, careful inspection of the system's parts is essential. These are safety-related systems. Their integrity can be a matter of life and death.

The 20- to 100-year-old metal found in the front spindles of collector cars is always suspect and can fail suddenly, and with catastrophic results. These parts should always be checked with a crack detection system like Zyglo, Spotcheck or Magnaflux when they are exposed by any work in this area. When these parts are off a car, or if there is any reason to doubt their integrity, a full magnetic particle inspection regimen should be applied to them.

Front Wheel Bearing Disassembly and Inspection

Front wheel bearing work should always be done with tires and wheels removed from a vehicle's hubs. If a brake disc or drum can be separated easily from its hub, this should be done before the hub is removed. To remove the hub, gently unscrew or pry off its dust cap. Pry-off type hubs are nudged off by working around their circumferences. Once this type of cap is pried or tapped out enough to loosen it, a pair of large slip-joint pliers can be used to complete its removal.

By the way, these small tin press-on caps, and caps that screw on wheel hubs in older cars, are the only proper recipients for the term "hub cap." The steel, plastic and aluminum decorative devices that snap onto wheels to cover their bolting accesses are properly called "wheel covers."

From here on, it's important that you note the relative positions and orientations of the parts that you take off a spindle. It's surprisingly easy to install a bearing cup backwards on some cars, and the results will be disastrous. It is also important to keep the parts from one side of a car unmixed with those from the other side.

With the front axle cap off, you will encounter a cotter key or, sometimes, a bend-tab washer. Remove and discard these locking devices; never try to reuse them. When one considers the pain and suffering that has afflicted humankind since the advent of the automobile age because some people have tried to reuse cotter keys and other retainers rather than spending a few cents for new ones, you sometimes wonder how, as a species, we have survived. Behind the cotter key, you will sometimes find a nut retainer and always a spindle nut. Remove these. Under this there is a nibbed thrust washer, which can be removed easily with a hooked wire.

At this point, pull the hub out an inch or so from its spindle, and then push it back while supporting its outer aspect. Now, the outer wheel bearing's inner race, cage, and balls or rollers can be removed with one hand, while the other continues to support and center the hub assembly.

Now, with both hands, withdraw the hub assembly from the spindle. The inside wheel bearing and its seal will come out with the hub. The grease seal can now be removed from the hub by prying. With the seal out, the inside bearing can be removed.

At this point, all of the parts that you have removed should be washed in solvent and completely cleansed of old grease. If, in this process, the brake drum or disc rotor is contaminated with solvent or grease, it should be rewashed in alcohol or in one of the chlorinated solvents designed for cleaning brake parts or in one of the biodegradable detergent-type solvents that are being sold for this purpose.

Inspect the bearings (balls or rollers, cages and races) for rust, pitting, galling, burning fretting and cracking. If any of the bearing components are bad, the whole bearing will have to be replaced. To remove the bearing races from a hub, you will need a special puller or press attachment, or

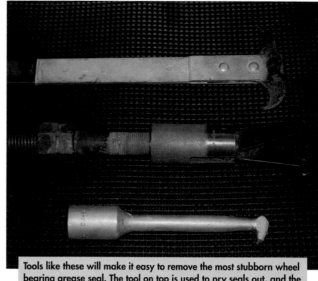

Tools like these will make it easy to remove the most stubborn wheel bearing grease seal. The tool on top is used to pry seals out, and the ones on the bottom attach to a slide hammer and whack seals out with impact. No matter how you remove wheel bearing seals, never try to reuse them.

you can use a soft steel drift punch. In all cases, wear eye protection while performing outer bearing race removal procedures, and if a punch is used, be sure to use it evenly around the circumference of the bearing race that you are working on. Never allow the race to become cocked or tipped in its bore during removal, as this will damage the hub bore. The same considerations apply to the installation of wheel bearing races.

The spindle should now be cleaned thoroughly and inspected for cracks, burrs, and other damage. Since the inner races of wheel bearings are designed to "creep" slowly around their spindles, to distribute wear evenly over their bearing surfaces, any roughness on spindles must be repaired or the spindles must be replaced. Of course, the discovery of any spindle cracks mandates replacement of this critical safety component.

Front Wheel Bearing Reassembly

When the bearings, hub, and spindle are thoroughly clean and dry, they should be repacked and reassembled. Older practice was to use short fiber greases, but modern high-temperature greases without fiber are much better. Never mix greases or add grease to existing lubricant if its type is unknown. The three grease types available for wheel bearing applications, lithium, sodium soap, and synthetic, are not compatible. Each bearing should be lubricated by smearing its outer race with grease and using a needle fitting or pressure cone to lubricate its inner race and balls or rollers. Packing by hand rubbing is possible but messy and slow.

The grease recess in the hub should be filled level with the sides of the hub, and a thin coating of grease should be brushed onto the spindle locking parts and on the inside of

You can rub grease into wheel bearing cups, rollers and outer races with your hands, but it's a messy job. The cone pictured here makes this a much neater job. The needle greasers, shown in front of the greasing cone, can be used with a grease gun to inject grease between wheel bearing rollers or balls.

This seal driver has just enough adapters to drive almost any wheel bearing seal that a restorer will ever encounter. If you don't have a seal driver in a needed size, it is easy enough to make one.

the axle dust cap. Do not over-fill the hub or pack it solid, as this can result in seal leakage and possible damage to brakes.

After the inside bearing inner race, cage, and rollers have been inserted in the hub, the grease retaining seal can be installed. Its outer press fit surface should be coated with a non-hardening sealer, like Permatex High Tack, and it should be inserted with a seal driver only. Do not try to install any grease seal with a punch or hammer, as you will probably warp the seal and render it useless. Always install grease seals with their lips facing toward the lubricant reserve, and always coat the seal lips with a little grease. If NOS leather or felt seals are used, they should be soaked in heavy oil for at least 30 minutes prior to installation. Always check seal mating surfaces for burrs, scratches or other defects, and remove these with a machinist's knife or with a file and sandpaper, or solve the problem by replacing the spindle. Coat seal wiping surfaces with a smear of grease. Some installations utilize a removable hub spacer; be sure to include this in reassembly if it is used.

Being very careful not to damage the seal lip on the spindle threads, the hub can now be lifted and placed back on the spindle, and the seal engaged with its mating surface. While supporting the outer end of the hub with one hand, insert the outside bearing inner race and rollers (or balls) and place the bearing thrust washer, spindle nut, and spindle nut lock (if used) in position. Much older installations used a second nut and lock plate here. The wheel bearings can now be "adjusted" for preload or end play. Don't forget to install the cotter key after adjustment.

Ball bearing-type front wheel bearings either use some specified preload, or a zero clearance setting. Preload is set with a torque wrench to manufacturers' specifications. If it is specified, zero clearance is best checked with a dial indicator attached to some convenient part of the hub and indicated off the spindle's end. Generally, the specified

clearance for older cars will be in the 0.002- to 0.005-inch range for tapered roller bearings, and about 0.001-inch for cars equipped with disc brakes. These clearances are best determined by using a torque wrench to tighten the spindle nut as the hub is turned in the direction of its forward rotation. A torque of 10 or 15 lbs.-ft. will seat a wheel bearing. Its spindle nut is then backed off and retightened, finger tight. It is then backed off a specified number of nut castellations—usually from one to three—and secured with a cotter key.

Do not overtighten the spindle nut during the initial seating procedure, as the small points of contact of the bearing races and balls or rollers make damage to these parts a very real possibility. Do not put too much faith in the dial indicator method of checking clearance, as the grease in bearings will tend to interfere with any precise measurement of endplay. Always check the final assembly of a wheel bearing for play by shaking the wheel with your hands, but be sure not to confuse ball joint or king pin play with wheel bearing movement. With a wheel and tire mounted, you should feel barely perceptible wheel bearing play in roller bearing equipped front spindles.

While too much play will damage the bearing components and possibly cause a steering shimmy or brake vibration, wheel bearings that are too tight will overheat quickly, causing scoring, brinelling and self-destruction. Remember, there must be room for roller bearing parts to expand as they get hot, and the inner races must remain loose enough to be able to creep around their spindles. After you have disassembled and reassembled enough of them, you get a feel for front wheel bearings that will allow you to confirm proper adjustments.

The final step in wheel bearing replacement (or "repacking") is to coat the sealing edge of the axle cap with a non-hardening sealer and tap it evenly into place. If the cap contains a funny-looking copper wafer spring, that is part of the car's radio static suppression system. It should be stretched enough so that it contacts the end of the spindle and reinstalled.

Drum Brake Friction Systems

My first recollection of brakes dates from the early 1950s, when all of the kids in my town were deeply involved in the Soap Box Derby competition. The year that I began to notice such things, the "brakes" on these kid gravity carts consisted of a pedal which, when pushed by the operator, rubbed directly on the road's surface, thus breaking the cart's momentum-derived speed. It was primitive, but it worked. I remember wondering why automobiles didn't use the same kind of apparatus to stop.

Shortly after that, the official Soap Box Derby rules changed and required brakes that bore directly on the vehicles' "tires." This system consisted of a board that was positioned on a pivot and moved by cables and pulleys. When the brakes were applied, the snubber board rubbed against the front surfaces of the rear wheels to slow the racing cart. Of course, this was a much more difficult system to construct than the road snubber system that it replaced, and there was a good deal of grumbling about that. But it did stop the carts more certainly and with less sideways deviation than the old system. I remember thinking that this was the height of engineering sophistication—the ultimate in vehicle braking.

Again, I wondered why automobiles didn't operate their brakes with similar hardware. While I now understand the drawbacks of these two types of primitive braking systems, I still find their simplicity alluring—particularly when I find myself involved in repairing one of the more complex modern hydraulic drum or disc systems.

What all braking systems have in common, whether they are Soap Box Derby style or the latest four wheel floating caliper disc setups, is the function of exchanging mechanical motion for friction that produces heat, and dissipating that heat into the environment—or, in the cases of recent hybrid vehicles, for regenerated energy.

Automobile engines burn gasoline or other fuels to produce heat—which is energy. This energy, through the medium of expanding air, or water vapor, drives pistons or rotors that are linked in some fashion to the vehicle's wheels to produce mechanical motion. Braking reverses this process by using mechanical pressure to create massive friction to counter a car's forward or rearward momentum.

This applied friction produces sudden and massive heat buildups, which the braking system must then dissipate into the environment. When you consider that the average city-driven car in these United States has its brakes applied more than 50,000 times a year, and exchanges roughly 30 percent of its kinetic energy for the heat resulting from braking, it all seems awfully wasteful.

In fact, it is so wasteful that generations of inventors

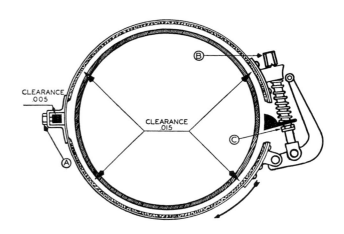

You can eyeball external contracting brakes and figure out how they work and how they are adjusted. Their advantages end there.

and tinkerers have tried to recapture some of the energy extravagantly dissipated in braking and store it in some form, such as compressed air or electricity, so that it can be put to purposeful use. Until the recent advent of hybrid gasoline-electric vehicles with battery storage and regenerative braking systems, these efforts failed due to the logistics of the situation and the weight and complexity of the hardware that was proposed to effect the recapture of this energy. New breakthroughs make it possible to accomplish this, but the number of vehicles produced with regenerative braking is miniscule small, to date.

Brake design is the business of creating compact, reliable and convenient mechanical packages that will create friction and dissipate the resulting heat. Early automobile innovators were more concerned with making their machinery go than with stopping it, and they initially followed carriage practice with "spoon" brakes or levers that acted directly on hard tires, much like the improved Soap Box Derby brake design mentioned previously. By the time of the epochal 1885 Benz, a crude transmission brake had become popular among the then nascent automobile builders of the world, and this system remained popular as late as the 1920s, as evidenced by the Model T Ford.

Other popular early braking systems included driveshaft brakes that brought contracting brake shoes to bear against a drum mounted on a car's driveshaft, and rim brakes that acted on wheel rims, much as modern bicycle hand brakes do. There were oddball variants of these primitive systems, like cable brakes that wrapped around wheel drums, and the delightful system used on early Lanchesters (always different) that activated a braking cone opposed to the clutch cone to brake the car's motion when the clutch was depressed beyond its point of disengagement.

After 1900, the convention of rear drum brakes had been adopted by most manufacturers, although transmission brakes continued to be popular on cars with planetary (epicyclical) gearsets. These drum brakes were usually external contracting systems. Sometimes, external contracting bands were combined on the same drums with internal expanding shoe systems to provide separate foot and hand brakes. Compared to what had gone before, these systems were very effective, reliable, and compact.

By 1920, internal expanding drum brakes had become the convention, and by the middle of that decade, hydraulic activation was beginning to appear. The self-servo principle, which uses the rotary motion of a wheel to transfer a small part of a car's kinetic energy to one or both ("single servo" or "dual servo") brake shoes, and thus to assist the operator's foot-applied braking effort, was being perfected; as were better lining materials and better brake drum constructions. The 1930s saw the continued evolution of the hardware for self-servo brakes, the common use of vacuum power assist units on heavier cars and the universal acceptance of hydraulic brakes. (Ford was, of course, the last major manufacturer to adopt hydraulic activation systems. Seems Henry didn't like things that he couldn't understand.)

From the late 1930s until the introduction of full disc brakes by Chrysler in the early 1950s, brake design, and even actual brake hardware, changed little. There was continuous improvement in friction materials for shoes, but design advances encompassed mostly short-lived, minor innovations like pressed steel brake drums, steel-lined aluminum brake drums and miscellaneous hardware to make brakes "self-adjusting."

Gradually, aircraft-derived caliper disc brake systems evolved from Chrysler's wonderful, but cumbersome, full disc system of the early 1950s. Caliper disc brakes then evolved into the now common floating ("slider") caliper systems that grace the front axles of almost every car made today, and the rear axles of many contemporary cars and trucks.

Some General Working Considerations

The balance of this chapter will deal mostly with the internal expanding drum brake systems that dominated the field from the 1920s until the 1970s, after which disc brakes began to replace them, at least in front applications. External contracting brakes and transmission or drive shaft brakes were so specialized to each manufacturer that they are best dealt with using specific manufacturers' instructions and data. Disc brakes are not covered in detail here because readily available modern repair information deals with them extensively.

The first consideration in brake work is that these are precise systems that must operate reliably under very demanding conditions. Brake temperatures of 300-400 degrees F. are common and sporadic temperatures as high as 600, or even 700 degrees, can occur in heavy braking situations. On the average car in heavy braking, forces involving literally hundreds of horsepower may come into play.

All of this means that the critical parts in brake systems can be highly stressed and require the most exacting work

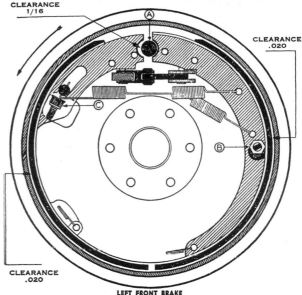

MIDLAND STEELDRAULIC BRAKE

CLEARANCE 1/16
CLEARANCE .020
CLEARANCE .020
LEFT FRONT BRAKE

The Midland Steeldraulic brake was a mechanical internal expanding brake that was favored by Ford long after the competition had gone to hydraulic brakes.

in repair and restoration. If, for example, grease is allowed to get on brake friction surfaces, it will modify their friction characteristics to the point of rendering the brakes useless.

Brake work should be backed up with good, specific information regarding the system that you are working on. Shop manuals, *Motor's* and *Chilton* manuals, and other sources of information should be used extensively. You should understand the function and environment of every part in a system that you are restoring.

Raybestos Manhattan—a major brake parts supplier—published a particularly good series of general instruction and data manuals on braking systems that had specific information on current and older cars (titles vary: *Passenger Car Brake Service Manual*, *Grey-Rock Brake Service Manual*, etc.). Brake component manuals go back to the 1930s under various authorships and sponsorships and are prime sources of good brake restoration information. Older automobile owners' manuals usually contain extensive information on brake adjustment procedures; many of them even deal with relining procedures. Automobile shop manuals always contain extensive data on the braking systems for the cars that they cover.

When you work on any aspect of a braking system, it is necessary to consider the whole system. Repairs to friction system parts must always be performed on pairs of brakes, front or back. My preference is to go through every aspect of the hydraulic, mechanical and friction systems of any braking system that I work on, no matter what the original complaint may have been. It is, for example, dangerous to work on just the friction parts of a braking system without inspecting its hydraulic system for bad hoses, leaking cylinders and deteriorating lines.

Or consider a system that has worn friction parts but a perfectly operating hydraulic system. However, when you

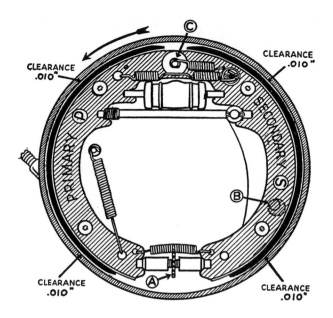

The principle on which "servo" brakes operate is simple enough, but you absolutely have to know which shoe is primary and which is secondary when you rebuild one of these systems. The primary shoe will always be the first shoe from the anchor pin in the direction of rotation of the brake drum. It is often shorter than the secondary shoe and may have a different friction facing material from the secondary shoe.

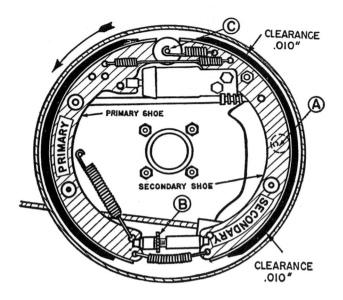

This single acting hydraulic brake is of the servo type and uses a single acting hydraulic piston. By the time you add self-adjusting hardware to a brake like this, it gets pretty complex. This one is manually adjusted and is relatively simple.

install new shoes or pads, the hydraulic pistons are pushed back into areas in their cylinder bores where they have not been working, and where pitting and deposits may cause rapid failure of the piston seals and result in system leaks and failures. This will be a particularly likely outcome with drum-type brakes because they are at the end of a one-way hydraulic systems and their boots—unlike the very positive dust seals on caliper disc brakes—are notoriously ineffective in sealing out moisture. If you just install new shoes on drum brakes without refurbishing the hydraulics, the new shoe facings will probably be ruined by leaking fluid in short order, and the whole job will have to be redone. Worse, the system will be dangerous to operate after the first, incomplete, repair.

As I said, the expense and time involved in renovating *whole braking systems* pays off in the long run. Complete brake rebuilds produce a degree of certainty that is wholly appropriate to a safety system that is as critical as are brakes. Remember, old hydraulic braking systems do not have the redundancy that modern systems do (dual hydraulic circuits) so one small area of failure can cause them not to operate.

New grease seals are a must when front brakes are restored. Rear brakes should at least get new outer seals if a two seal system is used and new seals if a one seal system is provided. You just don't want to sacrifice the time and money involved in brake work—not to mention personal safety—to the probability that a $4 seal that has not been replaced will ruin your job.

Because brake work involves new linings and grinding, cutting or replacing drums, it will modify system friction characteristics (coefficients of friction). It is essential, therefore, that brake work encompass both brakes at either end of a car. Never work on just one brake, or you will almost inevitably produce a car that swerves in braking. I have seen people take spray cans of chlorinated solvent and air blowguns to "clean up" oil soaked brake linings with the misconception that they have effected a repair. This can become a doubly deadly misconception because, in the long run, the asbestos that they blow around may get them, even if the grabbing, uneven brake system that they have created doesn't do them (as well as others who have the misfortune to share the roads with them) in. When seals leak, replace them in axle pairs, and replace the oil-soaked linings that they have contaminated in axle pairs, as well.

Virtually all collector car brakes will have shoes made from asbestos compounds that are either molded with resin or woven. This stuff is dangerous and is virtually impossible to handle safely. Asbestos fibers are exceedingly short and thin—that's part of the hazard that they pose—and you should never attempt to vacuum them up with a shop vac because they will go right through its filter and into the shop air, on the way to your lungs. Never, never blow brake system parts off with compressed air before they have been soaked with water or solvent and cleaned that way. Even after that, it is best not to blow off asbestos-laden brake parts. Exposure to this stuff can kill you in one or more of several slow and painful ways. The safest way to deal with the asbestos-laden debris found around, behind and in brake drums is to wet them down with water and remove debris while they are wet.

This certainly isn't a completely satisfactory hazard

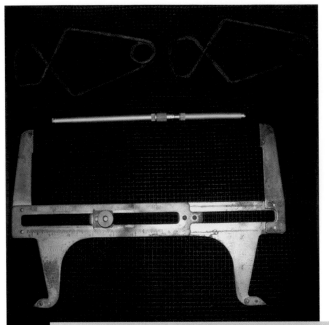

The brake gauge in the front of the photo measures both drum diameters and installed brake shoe diameters. It is a very handy item to have when you are assembling drum brakes. The tubular micrometer behind it allows precise measurements of brake drum diameters. The two spring clips in the back of the photo are used to hold drum brake pistons into their cylinders against their springs and are useful when you are working on brakes that do not have plates for this purpose. Also shown are close-ups of the calibrations on the tubular micrometer and brake gauge. The micrometer is much more accurate than the brake gauge.

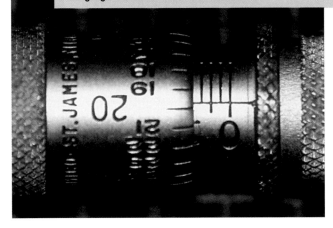

precaution but, for the present, it will have to do. By now, non-asbestos synthetic brake lining materials (Kevlar and other trade names for aramid fibers) are available in the aftermarket and have applications as replacement brake friction materials for the asbestos linings in our collector cars. The stuff to be wary of is what gets sold in this category as NOS parts at swap meets and from small mail-order vendors. It almost certainly contains asbestos.

The synthetic replacements for asbestos content brake linings may be too abrasive for the metallurgy of some old drums, and it will be difficult or impossible to find molded linings in some diameters required by older cars. Worse, legislation prohibits commercial stripping of asbestos content linings from brake shoes, and it may be very difficult to find providers for some relined shoes. All of this is stated in the nature of describing a range of problems for those who rebuild the brakes on old cars.

Those of us who work on older cars should be ever mindful of asbestos hazards. Some assessments of these

hazards have claimed that the dangers of working with automotive friction surface parts have been overstated because automotive applications of these fibers tend to result in grinding off the "hooks" that bond them to human tissues. This may be true, but I have not seen much independent evidence (independent of the brake manufacturing companies' defense efforts in the massive litigation lodged against them) that suggests that asbestos brake debris is not dangerous to human health. I suggest that if you work with old brakes regularly, or even occasionally, you treat asbestos debris like "the Black Death," and consult relevant authorities on state-of-the-art approaches to working safely with this stuff.

Drum brake systems can contain a fair number of springs, washers, pins, levers, cables, and other parts that can go "plink" on the floor when brakes are taken apart. This is particularly true in the more complex, self-energizing (servo), self-adjusting brake systems that came into use after the mid-1950s. Make sure that you keep track of where and how parts go, and be sure to draw diagrams, take pictures, or refer to appropriate manuals if you have any doubts.

Brakes can be misassembled and work, but they will not work properly if "only a little bit" is wrong. When I first worked on brakes, I often found it useful to take one side of an axle pair apart and reassemble it before I did the other side. This approach made the opposite end of the axle available as a model for reassembly of the side that I was working on. The availability and convenience of digital cameras today makes this practice unnecessary. I recommend snapping lots of digital photos as you go along with any brake disassembly. Small mistakes of misassembly are easy to make, and will always cause problems, but there are some big mistakes available, too.

For example, modern systems of the single-servo, fixed anchor-type use a "primary" and a "secondary" shoe system. In this system, the primary shoe has a shorter lining and does comparatively little braking. Instead, it uses a little of the kinetic energy that the passing drum surface imparts to it to wrap or pivot the two shoes around the anchor pin and force the secondary shoe into the drum surface. It's a neat trick to use a car's motion to produce an enhancement of braking force to stop the car.

The rebuilder's problem is that since the primary and secondary shoes often differ only in lining length, or sometimes only in lining material, it is very easy to mix up these shoes at the time of installation. The result is a braking system that mostly tends to be ineffective, or which overheats the primary shoe that is misplaced in the secondary shoe position. Mixing the two shoes also may tend to cause brakes to lock up or grab violently in stops from high speeds.

In this case, careful notation at the time of disassembly, keeping an opposite axle brake assembly in tact for comparison, a good reference manual or some theoretical knowledge will help. In fact, you should already have the necessary theoretical knowledge from reading the preceding sentences to sort out primary and secondary shoe positions in servo brake systems. The primary shoe, with the shorter lining, will always be the first one in the direction of forward wheel rotation from the anchor pin. Think about it!

Brake reconditioning tools, like shoe arc grinders and drum lathes and grinders, are complex, expensive and potentially dangerous sources of airborne asbestos particles and fibers; so this work will almost certainly have to be sent out. There are a few relatively inexpensive hand tools and gauging devices that are necessary to work on brakes. Good brake pliers, hold-down spring tools, and piston retainers are on the "necessary" list. A drum/shoe diameter caliper gauge will be very helpful, but is not essential.

Drum Brake Fault Diagnosis

The main symptom of brake malfunction is pretty obvious and pretty deadly—a vehicle fails to stop in a straight line in a reasonable distance. Precursors to this symptom can be odd noises and vibrations that accompany brake applications. Any of these symptom clusters will require brake inspection. The causes of the symptoms usually will be evident in conditions like leaking fluid or worn, warped or scored parts. A low brake pedal is usually caused by actuating system faults, but it can also have its origin in the friction system. This is particularly true in disc brake systems where maladjustment of the rear brakes combines with pad wear in the front brakes to produce low pedal. The failure of a drum brake's self-adjusting mechanism can also cause this problem.

Obscure problems, such as a loose backing plate or wrong or incorrectly installed parts from a previous rebuild, also can promote brake problems. Sometimes, brake symptoms have their origins in defects in other, related systems. Bad wheel alignment will frequently be very evident in braking situations, causing swerving that is mistakenly blamed on brakes. A loose wheel bearing can do a very good imitation of a defective brake shoe.

Drum and Shoe System Disassembly and Inspection

Brake drum removal is accomplished by removing wheel nuts or lugs and wheels, after which brake drums usually can be removed. In a few cases, retaining screws or clips must also be removed to unsecure drums from their hubs. Some rear brakes and many front brakes have integral drums and will require hub removal to get drums off. This procedure was covered previously in this chapter, under the front wheel bearing topic, and in the last chapter in reference to rear axle shafts and wheel bearings.

Always be sure that the parking bake is not engaged when removing rear brake drums, and if the shoes offer any resistance to removal, back off their adjusting mechanisms—with particular care to raise the star wheel locking levers or wires on self-adjusting mechanisms—before making any attempt to back the star wheels off. After cars sit for long periods, their brake drums can get pretty well frozen to their hubs, and a drum puller should be used, within reason, to free them. Heat applied around the studs and on the center boss may aid removal, but it must be very moderate heat to avoid damaging these parts.

For particularly stubborn drums that won't yield to heat and mild shock or to a puller and judicious tapping with a brass hammer, there is a trick. It is to drive one or more of thc wheel studs back into the drum—be careful not to force the stud into any part of the brake mechanism—with a hammer, and to insinuate the end of a small, "cheap" (OK, 78 cents or less) screwdriver between the drum and the hub in the removed stud's hole. A little wedging with the screwdriver and a hammer will free the most recalcitrant, stuck brake drums. You may have to drive several studs in (they are almost always held by friction, but if they aren't, don't use this trick) to get enough positions to make this wedging maneuver to work.

After performing this trick, you probably will have to repair burrs that you raised on the drum and hub, and you will certainly "total" the screwdrivers that you used for this purpose (small loss). While you can warp a drum doing this, the alternative may be to cut it off with a torch, so it would have been "toast," anyway. On the good side, not only does this trick usually work, but it also provides an appropriate fate for those 78-cent (or less) screwdrivers that you see in bins in the middle of supermarket aisles—I know of no other

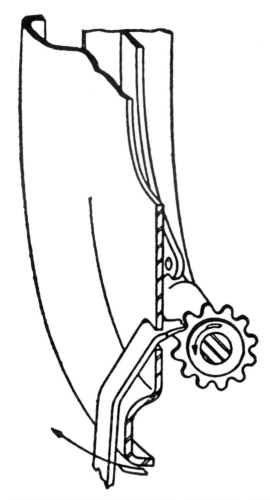

You'll need a special, curved tool to adjust the star wheels on drum brakes. Most of these adjusters have a locking wire that has to be lifted and kept off the wheel while you adjust it.

Brake spring removal can be a clumsy job. It sometimes involves the use of the plier end of a pair of brake pliers applied between a spring end and the brake lining material. Sometimes, the cupped end of the pliers handle is rotated around an anchor pin to lift a spring end off of it. Conventional swear words are legitimate here, but always check for the presence of small children before using them.

With all of the hardware off a brake backing plate, clean it thoroughly and check for damage to it and for its tight attachment to the axle or spindle boss. Brake drums should be checked for cracks, scores, taper ("bell mouthing"), out-of-round, glazing and rust pitting. If any of these conditions is found, drums must be reconditioned or replaced. A good bore gauge, tubular micrometer, or other similar device should be used to measure several drum positions vertically and radially. If a drum is off by more than 0.005 inch in any dimension, it must be turned, ground or replaced. Make sure that drums are not ground and/or worn beyond their wear limits. This is 0.060 inch over standard for most drums, but a few can go to 0.080 inch—a tolerance against which I strongly recommend.

Drums that are worn or turned beyond their wear limits lack the rigidity and thermal absorption capabilities to deal with strong braking forces and high temperatures. They can distort or break in heavy braking in an emergency, when you can least afford it and with potentially dire consequences.

Shoes should be inspected for lining thickness and uneven wear. Glazing, oil contamination, cracking, and lining adhesion to shoe metal should also be inspected. Wear within 1/16 inch of rivet heads on riveted shoes, and less than roughly 1/4 inch of lining on metallic or on bonded shoes, will mandate relining. Metal shoe parts should be inspected for deformation, weld integrity, and worn ends or elongated pivot points. Defective shoe metal means replacement in most cases, since repair is usually impractical.

Other brake hardware should be evaluated critically. Hold down and retracting springs are usually easy to get and inexpensive. They should be replaced almost routinely whenever you have occasion to remove them. Certainly, stretched or distorted springs or springs that are discolored from heat or from rust must be replaced, and it is generally a good idea to replace all springs if one of them is found to be defective. Brake shoe push rods can bend or wear. If you find them in either of these conditions, replace them. Other adjuster parts can wear or acquire burrs. These should be cleaned completely, deburred and sparingly lubricated or, if there is any doubt, they should be replaced. While the cost of replacing all of the minor hardware in a brake system adds up, it is frequently a good investment to go this route. Complete hardware sets that greatly reduce the cost of individual hardware items are available for some brake applications. A sticking adjuster wire or stretched retracting spring that is tolerated in a rebuild can cause all sorts of trouble later.

legitimate or illegitimate use for them; so taking one out of circulation this way is a small service to humanity.

When brake drums have been removed, the debris behind them should be flushed away with water or another suitable solvent. Oil should be removed with a solvent-saturated rag. Then throw the rag away. Water, alcohol, and chlorinated brake solvents are the only solvents that should ever be used on brake friction surfaces.

Petroleum-based solvents must never come into contact with brake linings or drums. If very minor grease or oil residues must be removed from these parts, this should be done with special chlorinated solvents that are designed for brake work. Badly soaked brake linings cannot be adequately cleansed and should be scrapped.

Brake shoes are removed by first clamping their activating hydraulic pistons with a piston clamp (if they are not restrained by a resident sheet metal device) and removing the shoe retracting springs with brake pliers. The shoe hold-down springs can now be removed with a special tool and the shoes and their push rods will then come free. Parking brake parts and self-adjuster parts should be accessible for removal now.

Reconditioning Brake Drums and Shoes

Brake drums can be cut or ground on special drum turning equipment. Some people prefer the theoretical precision of drum grinding. Steel drums should only be ground, not cut. Cutting allows the lathe operator to hear the hard spots in a drum (heat hardened areas) and know when he has cut below them. Grinding does not allow this certainty. In any case, be sure not to cut or grind a drum beyond its diametral limit and, if cutting is used, be sure to employ a slightly rounded cutting tool to avoid "threading" or grooving the drum.

A turned drum should be deburred with 80-grit sandpaper and washed in soap and water. Since drum friction surfaces will rust very quickly after they are cut or ground, drums should not be reconditioned until the time of their installation is at hand, unless they are immediately treated with a special brake friction surface preservative.

Brake shoe linings are either adhesive bonded or riveted to their metal shoes. Modern bonding techniques, which use a baked adhesive, are so wonderfully effective that many restorers now have all of their relined shoes secured by this method. However, I strongly recommend using both bonding and rivets on restored brake shoes. Retaining brake linings to shoes with rivets only can be tricky because you never really know how tight they are, and shoes that are just riveted and not bonded do not provide the level of heat transfer from linings to the metal shoes that bonded shoes do. Rivets can work loose under lining stress conditions, but the newer bonding adhesives seem to perform so well that they prevent this situation. Of course, external contracting shoes and transmission brake shoes require relatively soft friction materials. These have to be riveted in place in almost all cases. The more common internal expanding brake systems use molded shoes that are compatible with adhesive bonding, whether or not this was the original attaching technique. I stress that using both bonding and riveting approaches is the best practice—yes, it's yet another of those belt-and-suspenders propositions, but I bet that you never heard of anyone who held his pants up that way losing them.

For many years, brake shoes were available in oversizes in increments of 0.010 inch, designated X, XX, XXX, and XXXX. Shoes were then matched to drum diameter requirements after drums were turned or ground. Then, shoes were "arc ground" ("arced") or cam ground to specification. On non-servo brakes, this grind was from 0.010 inch to as much as 0.025 inch under final drum diameter, which would allow about 0.005 inch clearance between the ends of the shoes and the drum, with the centers of the shoes in contact. Servo brakes worked on 0.040 inch, or more, diametral difference between the shoes and the drums for 0.010 inch, or more, of shoe end clearance.

Unfortunately, arc grinding shoes—which is the only proper way to replace brake shoes—involved the use of grinders that made little or no provision for dealing with asbestos hazards. People died from operating these machines and strict regulatory action followed. The current crop of "safe" arc grinders is so expensive to buy and insure that few concerns do arc grinding anymore. Providers of the exacting "cam grinds" that many collector car brake shoes require can be very hard to find.

Yet reconditioning brakes without the benefit of an arc grind is poor practice. Shoe contact can be so slight or so improperly positioned as to glaze and crack linings very quickly after reconditioning. For the work in this area that I do, I have found a supplier who will bond shoes with new linings of the correct thicknesses for oversizes or, at least, shim new linings to the correct dimensions, and arc grind them for a proper drum fit. There are still several regional suppliers, and a few local suppliers, who offer this service. It is well worth the effort to seek them out.

One practice that should be avoided is using metalized linings in applications that originally called for nonmetallic lining materials. Metalized linings should be used where they are provided for in original designs, but never used in unauthorized applications. These linings require a rigorously controlled 20-micron drum finish that can be difficult to achieve with some of the drum finishing equipment out there.

Reassembly of Drum-Type Brakes

Drum brakes reassemble in the reverse order of their disassembly. The raised riding pads on brake backing plates should be *lightly* smeared with high temperature grease before remounting the shoes. Pushrods and shoe engaging ends should get the same treatment, as should the parking brake strut ends and anchor pins. The shoes can now be engaged with the various pieces of hardware of the parking brake and self-adjuster system, and held in place by installing their hold-down springs. Be sure to sparingly lubricate the self-adjuster parts with a dry lubricant, such as graphite, and check to make sure that they are very free to move to allow for their self-adjusting feature to work.

The retracting springs can now be installed, using either brake pliers hooking ends or the spring anchor installing tool that is formed out of the sharp end of most brake pliers handles. Be careful not to overstretch retracting springs during installation, and be sure to use photos, notes, manuals, or the model of the opposite brake to get them in the right places and correct orientations. Some springs that are seemingly identical differ only in tension. These are usually identified by color codes that must be followed for brakes to work properly.

A final check of the common single, fixed anchor pin brake system operation can be made by moving the bottom of the shoe/adjuster assembly fore-and-aft an inch or so to check for freedom of motion. Throughout brake shoe and hardware installation, try to avoid touching the linings and

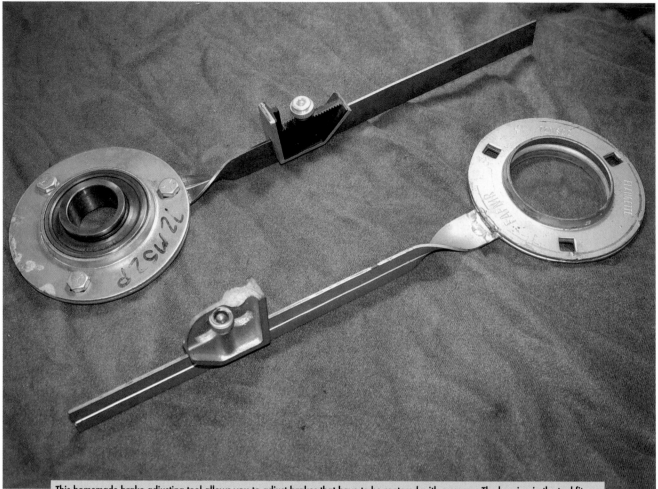

This homemade brake-adjusting tool allows you to adjust brakes that have to be centered with a gauge. The bearing in the tool fits on a wheel spindle and the gauge arm stop is set to the correct diameter. Then, the brake shoes are adjusted until the tool can be swung around them with a consistent clearance from the tool arm stop to the brake linings.

drum surfaces. If any contamination has gotten on them, remove it with repeated applications of a chlorinated brake solvent and a very clean rag or towel. The shoe adjuster should now be backed off sufficiently for the drums to be remounted and secured in place.

"Major" and "Minor" Brake Adjustments

Drum brake systems that have an adjustable anchor pin or, in the case of dual activation systems, two adjustable anchor pins, must have their shoes centralized on their backing plates after a rebuild has disturbed this relationship. In some cases, this adjustment is made by turning an anchor pin cam after its locking nut has been loosened. In other cases, the anchor pin is moved up and down by tapping it with a hammer. In either case, the object of this "major adjustment" is to center the shoes in the drum. Various procedures are specified for making this setting, from hit-and-miss methods to using brake activation to center shoes. The best method is almost always to use a brake centering gauge that describes a circle from the spindle at the linings'

edges. If such a gauge is not available, one can usually be fabricated easily.

"Minor brake adjustments" are often necessitated by wear, but must always be made after relining brakes. It is essential that the parking brake be completely released before attempting either major or minor adjustments. Minor adjustments are typically affected by either turning cam adjusters on the backing plate, or by adjusting a star wheel adjuster behind the drum. The object of these adjustments is to bring brake shoes as close as possible to the brake drum surfaces without actually touching them. With both types of adjusters, the shoes are brought into hard contact with drums via the adjusting mechanism and then backed off a specified number of notches or flats (or by dimension) to the point where no contact exists.

The amount of back-off is specified for each type of brake and must always be the same on all wheel pairs. It is critically important that brake shoes be brought into an initial hard contact with their drums before they are backed off and that there is no drag when this adjustment is completed. In the case of self-adjusting brakes, a rough adjustment should be made at the time of shoe installation. The self-adjuster lock lever or wire must be held off its star

Brakes have come a long way since this early Packard external contracting drum brake setup was new in the early part of the 20th century. Although brakes like this will never perform very well, they must be restored to perfect operating condition, just because they are so marginal.

wheel during adjustment. Failure to do this can damage the self-adjusting mechanism. In the case of cam-adjusted brakes (minor adjustment), be sure that the adjusting nut is locked by friction or a locking nut so that it can't vibrate out of adjustment after the adjustment is made.

You must reinstall any rubber covers or hole plugs that you remove from brake backing plates to gain access to cam adjusters or to star wheel adjusters. Failure to reinstall or replace these covers can result in corrosion damage to brake parts and, if the brakes get excessively wet, in poor braking.

After self-adjusting brakes are repaired, a car should be driven backward and stopped in reverse several times to allow the self-adjusters to do their jobs and set running brake shoe clearances. I always make a final check of brake adjustment by making a hard stop on gravel. During this stop, I check to see if the steering wheel pulls to one side or the other and to note any tendency of the car to swerve. I then inspect the gravel for roughly equal length "skid marks" in it.

Chapter 17

Brake Actuating Systems

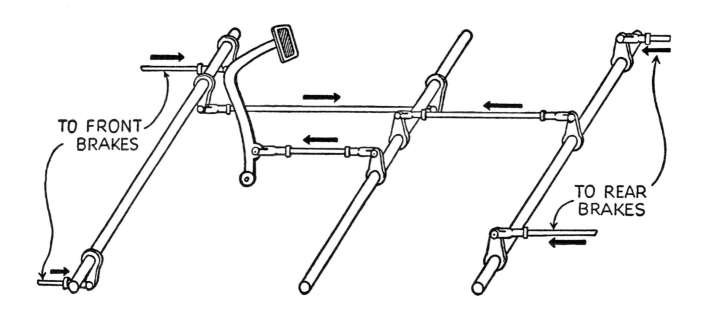

TO FRONT BRAKES

TO REAR BRAKES

O F COURSE, THE MOST IMPORTANT PROPOSITION with the earliest automobiles was to make them go. Little attention was devoted to the business of stopping them. Such crude braking devices as had been used on horse drawn vehicles more than sufficed to stop cars in the early motoring age. However, these devices were not adequate for the task of slowing and stopping the multi-cylinder automobiles that began to appear at the turn of the century, and various expanding and contracting drum brake devices and combinations came into use.

In every case, these drum brakes were activated mechanically by the application of levers, cams, rods, cables and the like. In almost every case, braking was accomplished by applying friction to slow the motion of the rear wheels, only, either directly via drum brakes mounted on them, or indirectly, via driveshaft or transmission mounted drum brakes. Wheel braked systems employed an equalizing bar pivoted off a central point, much like the equalizer system used on contemporary parking brakes to even braking force applied to the two wheels on an axle.

Even with that addition, these systems remained remarkably simple to construct and easy to maintain. The few four-wheel brake systems that appeared in this era, such as were used by Mercedes on some of their powerful behemoths, were cumbersome, complex and finicky. It was generally assumed at this time that braking the front wheels of an automobile would cause it to flip end-over-end. Besides, no one had yet devised a practical and inexpensive mechanism for activating front brakes that would maintain independence when the front wheels were turned. In any case, equalizing such a system to the rear brakes was beyond the imagination of most pioneer automobile designers.

By the mid-1920s, and in some cases before that, the increasing power-to-weight ratios of automobiles made it necessary to find braking systems that were more aggressive than the prevalent two-wheel systems. The earliest of the four-wheel brake systems in this era used complex arrangements of cables and pulleys to activate front wheel drum brakes, with lots of hardware to allow for steering, equalization and proportioning of force between the front and rear brakes. This quickly gave way to Perrot rod activation (universal-jointed, rod-activated devices). This system was wonderfully complex and precise, and Bowden cables were wonderfully simple, but unwonderfully prone to binding. The (sheathed) Bowden cable was, at least, simple and relatively inexpensive to construct. It quickly became the standard of front wheel brake activation. Later, it was replaced by hydraulic activation.

The use of hydraulics in brake activation had its origins before the turn of the century in bicycle brakes and is still used in some very deluxe bicycle applications. By the teens of the 20th century, some European carmakers were experimenting with this form of brake activation. It was introduced in this country on the 1921 Model A Deusenberg—a car which sported truly "hydraulic brakes" in the most real sense of the word. The working fluid in the system was actually radiator coolant, water. A more satisfactory hydraulic system was brought out by Chrysler in 1924, and by the 1930s, most car manufacturers had adopted this type of brake activation.

The advantages of hydraulic brakes are numerous and substantial when compared to the various devices for mechanical activation that preceded them. Perhaps, most important, you can pipe and hose hydraulic fluid anywhere without having to provide straight paths and large clearances, as you would for mechanical activation devices like levers and rods. The most complex accesses and positions become easy to accommodate when you don't have to arrange room for mechanical motion. Then, too, hydraulic systems go a long way towards equalizing all four brakes—as long as the shoe mechanisms are not grossly out of adjustment. Pliant hydraulic hoses solve the problem of supplying brake force to front wheels and rear axles when they deflect during steering maneuvers and axle deflections.

This is a far cry from the constant meddling that is necessary with the rods, bushings, collars, levers, pulleys and the like in mechanical brake systems. Where these devices are prone to binding and distortion, hydraulic fluid does not suffer these faults. The proportioning of brake application between front and rear brakes—as front wheel brakes were adapted, it was soon discovered that because front wheels bear most of a vehicle's weight in braking situations, they must do most of the braking—became simply a matter of selecting proper dimensions for the hydraulic cylinders and pistons in a system and, perhaps, providing a limiting valve, or valves, to control rear cylinder peak pressures. Finally, hydraulic systems are relatively cheap to construct and are relatively easy to maintain.

OK, with all of these advantages there has to be something wrong—certainly Henry Ford thought that there was because he resisted hydraulic brakes into the late 1930s. What was wrong with hydraulic systems, for all of their great advantages, was, and is, that they are grievously vulnerable to complete and catastrophic failure.

We're talking about an emergency in front of you, and your foot pushes almost effortlessly to the floor with no braking effect on your vehicle. Any breach in a single hydraulic system—leaking fittings, ruptured piston seals, rusted through or fatigued tubing, rotted hoses—any of these, and you will lose all four brakes. This applies to most collector cars. To counter this problem, Saab and Jaguar provided dual hydraulic systems on their cars, starting in the 1950s. These dual systems were required by law on new vehicles sold in the United States after 1966.

Mechanically activated brakes may work badly when they are not properly maintained, but they do work. Neglect the inspection and maintenance of hydraulic brakes, and you will likely get a far more intimate view of another automobile, feature of the landscape, local architecture or fellow human being than you had ever cared to. And hydraulic systems deteriorate from their day of manufacture. Often they do so internally, and thus, invisibly.

The vulnerability of hydraulic brakes has been recognized since their inception. A hydraulic system does, of course, have mechanical backup in the service brake system, but this hardly provides adequate braking to stop a vehicle at speed in an emergency. On their premier car in 1950, Saab recognized this hazard and introduced "dual diagonal" hydraulic circuitry on their cars. It relied on two separate hydraulic systems to activate separate pairs of brakes on a vehicle. At about that time, Jaguar offered a similar system, "tandem brakes," that used separate hydraulic systems for front and rear brakes. In either system, if a hose ruptured or a line burst, you still had the benefit of one front and one rear brake on opposite sides of the car, or of a front or rear pair of brakes, to stop the car. In 1966, the Federal government made the requirement of separate and redundant hydraulic systems one of the first "safety" rules applied to passenger cars sold here. As these systems have evolved since the 1960s, proportioning valves and pressure limiting valves have become accustomed parts of them, as well as warning lights that indicate a failure in one of the two hydraulic circuits.

While hydraulic brakes represent a usable and compact system that can be activated with reasonable pedal pressure and travel, without mechanical assistance, they may not apply enough braking pressure to stop a heavy vehicle within a suitable distance. The use of self-energizing ("servo" and

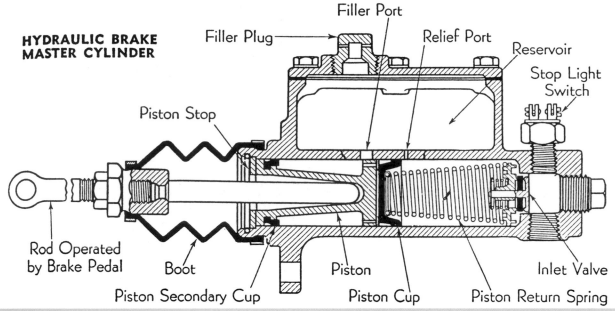

HYDRAULIC BRAKE MASTER CYLINDER

Filler Plug — Filler Port — Relief Port — Reservoir — Stop Light Switch — Piston Stop — Rod Operated by Brake Pedal — Boot — Piston Secondary Cup — Piston — Piston Cup — Piston Return Spring — Inlet Valve

Hydraulic brakes had many advantages over mechanically operated brakes. One disadvantage of hydraulic brakes is that they can fail for causes that are not apparent from an external inspection.

"dual servo") shoe devices helps to solve this problem up to a point, but if you go too far down the self-energizing road, you get brakes that can lock up violently when applied at high speed. The infamous Midland "Steeldraulic" brakes of the 1930s are an example of this.

The inherent performance limits of simple hydraulic brakes, taken together with the American public's assumed preference for "feather touch" braking, has resulted in the development of various mechanisms to provide "power assist" for braking purposes. Such efforts go back to Rolls Royce in the 1920s, when that firm used clutched mechanical power from a transmission driven disc to enhance brake output. The French, always fascinated with the use of hydraulics, used engine pumped hydraulic fluid to activate their brakes on some cars, like the Citroen DS-19, DS-21 and SM—with the brake pedal being little more than a variable aperture hydraulic valve. The most common of these assist devices was, and remains, the "HydroVac" type, that uses a vacuum reserve tank evacuated by engine manifold vacuum to activate a piston or diaphragm that enhances applied brake pressure. This works either directly on brake activating rods or through hydraulic fluid.

By the early 1930s, such systems by Bendix and others were in use on heavy American classics in the form of piston-in-canister units attached by linkage rods between the car frames and their mechanical brake linkage. As hydraulic brakes came into widespread use, vacuum assists were either mounted directly behind master cylinders and physically linked to them and valved by their push rods, or mounted remotely and hydraulically valved to provide amplification of hydraulic pressure. This latter practice was very common on large limousines and trucks of the 1950s.

While there have been many detail changes in hydraulic activation systems since their introduction in the 1920s, the basic concepts of their operation have changed little. Such additions as dual systems and the use of proportioning valves between front and rear brakes are more matters of elaboration than of basic changes in principles.

There have been vast improvements in such things as hydraulic fluids, lines and hoses. The introduction of optional ABS (anti-lock braking systems) to American cars in the late 1960s and their subsequent digitalization and widespread use by the 1990s represents a major improvement in braking effectiveness and safety. This innovation involves pulsing or modulating the hydraulic pressure to any wheel (or wheels) that decelerate(s) suddenly enough to skid. It produces both shorter straight-line stopping distances and increased steering control in most braking situations, and is probably the most basic change in automotive hydraulic braking systems in the last 60 years.

Stability control takes this concept further, using complex algorithms to deprive skids of their pivot points by selectively braking or releasing inboard or outboard wheels in oversteer and understeer conditions.

However, collector cars with hydraulic brake activation do not often have these elaborations and share a refreshingly high degree of sameness from car to car and decade to decade.

Mechanical Brakes

The operation and repair of mechanical brake activating systems is easy to understand but sometimes difficult to accomplish. The simple, two-wheel systems that operate only rear brakes involve single and double ("push-pull") rods, levers, cross-shafts, and clevis or bearing joints. All of these items can be understood from inspection.

Usually, most of this linkage is keyed, splined, or flat-shafted into arbitrary relationships. Where adjustments to the activating linkage of mechanical brakes are possible,

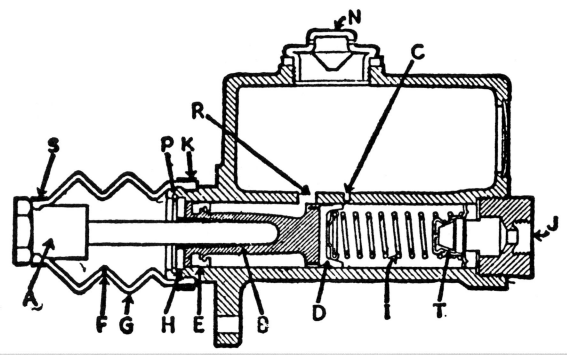

The compensating port ("C" in this diagram) is the key to master cylinder operation. It precisely controls the volume of the fluid in the system and makes up for hydraulic fluid's expansion and contraction. Be sure that this port is clear; they sometimes plug up.

they should be attempted only when a problem is known to exist. There can be many variables in these systems, and each has an effect on the rest of the system. It is never advisable to dismantle one of these systems unless it is necessary to correct wear or maladjustment. If disassembly is attempted in the course of general restoration work or for cosmetic or other reasons, the relationships of shafts to levers and clevis joints and to rods must be noted and reestablished. Adjusting the position of a lever on a shaft will affect the ratio of movement and applied force. It will also create specific dimensional change. Where levers, rods, or clevises are adjustable and have gotten out of calibration, it is a general rule to reset them in the positions that will give the maximum mechanical advantage while providing the correct movement dimensions for the system to work. Of course, when two sides of a system are not equalized automatically, it is critically important to set them up in identical ratios and dimensions.

Brake equalization is most commonly provided for by a floating, equalizing lever/shaft, or with adjustments at the brake shoes or bands themselves. Never attempt to equalize brakes at any point farther toward the foot or hand activator than is necessary.

Perrot rod brake hardware is very precise and complex and must be dealt with by the book. It should be checked for wear and deformation and repaired as necessary. Once set up, this type of linkage will function until it wears, is physically damaged, or is molested by someone attempting to service it.

Sheathed cable activation is much more common and much easier to deal with. Service brakes that use this type of hardware are still common, and rarely cause problems. Of course, equalizer bars have to be free and must be lubricated

to this end. If a sheathed cable system does not have a provision for lubrication, it can and should be lubricated by spraying the cable entrance and the outside of the sheath with a good penetrating cable oil. This will keep it free and prevent internal corrosion that can cause seizure. Cable systems that operate on pulleys require cleaning, lubrication of the pulleys and cables and dimensional adjustment on a routine basis. Cable systems that terminate in levers and shafts, with the shafts entering the brake backing plates, frequently have a provision for greasing these shafts. Be very careful here to use a minimum of grease because any excess can easily get on the brake shoe facings.

When front brakes are cable operated, it is imperative that interference between the cable sheaths and the front tires be made impossible. Sometimes, large circular rubber bumpers are attached to cable sheaths at potential points of contact with tires to accomplish this. Most older cable systems can be greased directly with a fitting or by use of a cable-lubricating device. Be sure to use a good-quality grease with a rust inhibitor additive for this purpose. When new sheath cables are fabricated from bulk, it's a good idea to assemble or to inject them with anti-seize lubricant, as this will provide almost eternal lubrication and protection from corrosion.

The adjustment of cable systems is usually pretty straightforward. In most applications there is only one adjustment for shoe wear and cable stretch, and this adjustment usually has a self-locking nut or a double nut. A few systems that don't have an equalizing bar allow for individual adjustment of the cables on each side.

Hydraulic Brake Operation

The operation of hydraulic brakes is based on the simple fact that when you exert pressure in one place on an incompressible fluid that is contained in a closed system, it will almost instantly create an elevated and equal pressure in all parts of the system. In practice, this means that a piston (or pistons) in a "master cylinder" is pressed by a brake pedal via linkage and compresses the fluid in the master cylinder. The master cylinder is connected by brake lines and hoses to "wheel cylinders." Pressure applied at the master cylinder immediately becomes increased fluid pressure at the wheel cylinders. Pistons in the wheel cylinders are the only other parts of this closed system designed to move, so the pressure exerted on them causes them to move out in their bores.

Thus, as a master cylinder piston moves and displaces the brake fluid in its bore, there is a corresponding movement of the wheel cylinder pistons in their bores. Since they bear indirectly on the ends of the brake shoes, the shoes move. That movement brings them into contact with their brake drums.

Not only can a hydraulic system transmit and equalize fluid pressures, it can also proportion them. If, for example, a master cylinder pressurizes a system with front wheel cylinders that have twice the cross-sectional area of the rear wheel cylinders, there will be twice as much mechanical energy available at the front pistons than at the rear ones for application to the brake shoes. Further fine-tuning of hydraulic systems can be accomplished with in-line metering, proportioning, and pressure limiting devices. These can limit, time and sequence the operation of individual parts of the system. In a few rare applications, a restricting baffle is used between the two pistons in wheel cylinders so that one brake shoe gets full hydraulic activation before the other. When you get a feeling for hydraulic theory, you can figure out the reasons behind and functions of these kinds of fine tuning devices.

All but the earliest hydraulic brake systems use a "compensating port" design. This is necessary because the volume of fluid in a brake system changes minutely as the hydraulic fluid expands and contracts with temperature changes. If, for example, a closed hydraulic system made no provision for this change in fluid volume, an increase in temperature and a corresponding increase in fluid volume from its expansion might tend to apply the brakes by displacing wheel cylinder or caliper pistons. In the compensating port design, the brake pedal bears on a push rod that, in turn, bears on a double piston in the master cylinder. This piston has two soft sealing surfaces associated with it—the "primary cup" and the "secondary cup." The primary cup is responsible for pressurizing the closed hydraulic activation system, and the secondary cup seals the whole system from the atmosphere. The compensating port opens the hydraulic pressure system to the fluid reservoir at the completion of each braking cycle, and thus allows fluid adjustments that automatically accommodate changes in fluid volume.

When a brake pedal is released, the forward edge of the primary cup comes to rest just behind the compensating port, which is a small hole in the top of the cylinder that leads to the fluid reservoir. When the brake is activated, the piston pushes the primary cup forward, displacing fluid through the compensating port until the primary cup has moved past the compensating port and the system is thus closed. Further movement of the pedal/piston/primary cup compresses the fluid in the master cylinder bore and exerts pressure through the lines and hoses on the other activating parts of the system. Each time the primary cup returns to rest and uncovers the compensating port, fluid flows to or from the reservoir to provide the correct volume in the working master cylinder bore. If the fluid expands or contracts, it can enter or leave that bore through the compensating port, as necessary. Both ambient temperature changes and engine heating changes are addressed this way.

There are a couple of other wrinkles necessary to make hydraulic brake systems work. One is that as brakes are released, the master cylinder piston is forced back rapidly by the spring that positions it, and it has the potential of creating excessive negative pressure behind it in the system as it recedes. This would create a vacuum bubble that would invite air and moisture to enter. To prevent this, an intake port between the master cylinder bore and the fluid reservoir is provided just behind the rearmost position of the primary cup when it is at rest. The part of the piston that bears against the primary cup has several small holes drilled lengthwise around its periphery. When, as the primary cup and piston return rapidly to rest, the pressure ahead of the primary cup and piston goes below atmospheric pressure, fluid from the reservoir enters the master cylinder bore through the intake port and passes through the holes in the piston, around the primary cup, and into the area in front of the primary cup. This fluid is able to get past the primary cup to fill any vacuum because it is traveling in the opposite direction from the direction in which the cup seals pressure. This ability to prevent the buildup of excessive negative pressure in the hydraulics maintains the integrity of the system.

A second important wrinkle in all but the earliest hydraulic braking designs is the matter of residual pressure. This involves a spring-loaded or cup-type check valve at the output end of the master cylinder bore which maintains a constant pressure of about 12 psi in the plumbing and hardware beyond the master cylinder. This pressure keeps the wheel cylinder cups expanded and in a state of readiness for brake application. The small pressure that this check valve retains in the entire hydraulic system beyond the master cylinder prevents anything from entering the system through the plumbing connections or wheel cylinder seals. On dual master cylinder units, the residual pressure check valves are positioned on the sides of the cylinders rather than in the ends of their bores.

The secondary cup, which is mounted on the back of the master cylinder piston, serves to align the piston and to seal the system from the outside. It plays no part in pressurizing the brake fluid in the hydraulic system.

The master cylinder reservoir is usually part of the cylinder casting, but in some designs it is mounted above the cylinder and connected by a pipe or other means. In any case, the fluid reservoir must have the ability to give up and take on fluid without air locking as the operation of the master cylinder piston and its seals causes fluid to enter and exit through the intake and compensating ports. In older designs, this was a venting function and took place through a small hole drilled in the reservoir cap. More recent applications use a flexible diaphragm under the master cylinder filler cap that can move in and out easily to accommodate volume changes in the reservoir.

A major variation in the compensating port design was used by the British for several years after World War II. It employed a mechanically tripped valve that unseated and opened the system to the reservoir at the beginning of each stroke. In this funky system, the master cylinder reservoir is at the end of the cylinder and the output port is in the middle.

Wheel cylinders or calipers—a.k.a. "slave cylinders"—simply respond to the pressure produced by master cylinders. Most wheel cylinders have two opposed pistons with seals ahead of them and a spring to keep the pistons positioned against their brake shoe push rods. Some older designs use blind wheel cylinders with only one piston. This design is called "single acting." A few obscure systems use pairs of single acting cylinders, often on rear wheel brakes with a lever between the pistons to allow for hand brake operation. There are many other obscure variations on the main hydraulic braking theme.

Dual circuit master cylinders have more parts but operate on exactly the same principles as the single master cylinders, outlined above. In most of these "tandem" designs, two separate pistons work in the same master cylinder bore, with the rear one bearing against the front one through the medium of a stiff coil spring. One or more seals are used to separate the two pistons. If one of the separate hydraulic subsystems loses integrity, the brake push rod can still activate the other one.

Hydraulic System Diagnosis

Because older hydraulic brake systems are single systems and have no backup in the event of failure—a hand or foot service brake is hardly an adequate backup—their operation must be perfect, and any questions of deterioration must be addressed in servicing them. When brakes work only after they are "pumped up" or require regular additions of brake fluid to keep them functioning, they must be reconditioned.

It has been the general tone and philosophy of this book that "if it ain't broke, don't fix it." That is not to say that you shouldn't attend to an item's cosmetics for restoration purposes but, generally, it is best to leave things that work alone, beyond cosmetic restoration. In the case of hydraulic braking systems and components, exceptions can and should be made. Any time that any part of a hydraulic system is repaired, the entire system should be inspected, with a strong prejudice towards repairing or replacing many parts in the whole thing. If one hose or one line or one wheel cylinder is leaking, then all hoses, all lines, and all wheel cylinders become suspect and should be dealt with.

Personally, I tend to go further than this. I don't believe in repairing or replacing the individual components in hydraulic systems; I believe in restoring entire systems. The usual cause of deterioration of any part is corrosion or corrosion and wear in combination. This factor will affect all parts in any system at different rates. However, if a wheel cylinder is leaking, it is a pretty good bet that the same corrosion or wear that afflicts it has attacked the other wheel cylinders to varying degrees, the master cylinder and the lines, and even the metal reinforcing strands in the hoses.

If you don't want to go the route of a complete overhaul when any single defect in hydraulics is encountered, at least inspect every component. But remember that dangerous deterioration of hydraulic systems is as likely to be internal as external; so even the most thorough inspection will probably miss critical faults. These faults can be deadly. Keep that in mind when you deal with hydraulics in braking systems.

Inspection of braking hydraulics should begin with the fluid in the master cylinder reservoir and at the slave cylinder bleeder nipples.

If brake fluid is cloudy or brownish, it is a safe bet that it has been contaminated with moisture and that internal corrosion in the system is underway. The master cylinder itself should be inspected for leaks, with particular attention to any fluid leakage or corrosion that is concealed by the push rod boot. This leakage usually will have a granular appearance.

Brake operation should be checked for low pedal, spongy pedal, very high pedal, and sinking pedal. These faults indicate, respectively, fluid leaks in the system or leakage of the primary cup in the master cylinder, air in the system, improper push rod adjustment or assembly, or a bad primary cup seal or cylinder surface.

Hoses and joints should be inspected for cracks and seeping. Brake lines should be checked for external corrosion and for kinking. Either mandates replacement. Finally, wheel cylinder boots should be pulled back and the cylinder ends inspected for fluid leakage and visible corrosion. Any of the above defects mandates a local repair of the problem area at the very least, and probably reworking the entire system.

I realize that my suggestion, that any corrosion defect in a hydraulic system should be construed as grounds for refurbishing the whole system, sounds fanatical. Over the years, a couple of rapid approaches toward relatively fixed objects has bred this fanaticism, and this is one of the few forms of that condition that is healthy.

Some General Considerations in Hydraulic Brake Service

In addition to thoroughly inspecting hydraulic braking system components and having a general inclination to restore whole systems when a defect or defects is discovered in any component, you will do well to remember that any change in a friction system can affect hydraulics. Installing new pads in disc calipers or new linings on shoes will force pistons back into their bores where they are likely to have their seals in contact with pitted or otherwise deteriorated cylinder surfaces. This creates a tremendous tendency for calipers and wheel cylinders to leak a few thousand miles after new pad installation or relining. Consider this when you do work on a brake friction system. The advantages of reconditioning entire braking systems at one time are so great that piecemeal reconditioning should be viewed as substandard.

Before hydraulic parts are removed, it is a good idea to label them. Wheel cylinder assemblies should be marked in a way that identifies them as to location on a car. A numbering system will also serve you by making it possible to be sure that if you send cylinders out for sleeving, you can identify the ones that are returned as yours.

Several years ago, I had a problem with a major supplier of this service in this regard, and my numbering system made it possible to get my parts back from the location to which they had been returned erroneously by the service provider.

There is no place in automotive restoration or repair that requires more cleanliness than hydraulic brake work. This, of course, means that precautions must be taken to keep chips, abrasive grit, and flying smut off hydraulic parts prior to assembly. It also means that great care must be taken to avoid contamination by petroleum-based lubricants and solvents. Under no circumstances should metal or rubber parts be washed in petroleum-based solvents, and if contamination has already occurred, a thorough cleaning in methanol, ethanol, isopropyl alcohol, or in a chlorinated brake solvent is necessary. Petroleum-based products cause hydraulic seals to swell and malfunction; very small amounts of contamination can do great damage. Sometimes, this contamination is difficult to avoid, as is the case in one method of freeing stuck pistons from wheel cylinders, detailed later in this chapter. But these instances should be kept to a minimum, and complete follow-up cleaning with appropriate solvents must be performed.

A very few automobiles used OEM copper brake lines, so these lines are, in a strict sense, "authentic." Well, this is one place where authenticity should take a back seat to some sense of the preservation of human life. NEVER USE COPPER TUBING FOR BRAKE LINES. I don't know why some manufacturers saw fit to use copper lines as recently as the late 1940s and early 1950s for some parts of their braking systems, but I do know that the practice was dangerous.

Even super-strength copper alloys lack the toughness to withstand the repeated surges of hydraulic pressure that are common in braking systems. Copper line material will not flare properly for the mandatory "double flare" used in brake hydraulics, and it "work hardens" severely from road vibration over any long period. I have seen brake failures attributable to the use of copper lines, and this resulted in accidents that should not have occurred.

Many parts in automobiles are simply incapable of being misassembled. Suspension parts usually don't fit if you try to assemble them incorrectly, and if you hook up wiring incorrectly, the electrical components that it connects probably won't work. But the hydraulic components in brake systems are both subtly and endlessly susceptible to misassembly.

Reversing wheel cylinder cups or getting the parts in a master cylinder out-of-order can be easy to do. The real problem is that a misassembled component may seem to work for a while, before the inevitable problems occur. There are three ways to confirm the order and orientation of parts in a master cylinder or in wheel cylinders. The logic of operation will make it clear why, for example, the flat side of a wheel cylinder seal always goes against the piston, or why the end of the master cylinder piston with peripheral holes drilled through it always faces the cylinder output end. A good diagram of the component that you are working on will also provide necessary assembly information. Finally, noting how assemblies came apart can usually be relied on to provide the key to reassembly, though this is the least certain of the three methods, due to the possibility of misassembly in a previous rebuild.

Hydraulic systems are containment systems that are under continuous attack by corrosion from the inside and from the outside. Every sealing part has its own logic and every junction has a reason that it seals. Think about this when you are reassembling a brake hydraulic system. If tapered pipe threads are used to create a seal, then nothing is needed to insure a seal beyond undamaged threads and adequate tightening. If, however, the threads at a junction are not tapered and there is no contact seat visible, it is likely that a seal is achieved by the use of a copper-sealing washer. Never try to improvise or freelance a new sealing system.

Flares, pipe threads, deformable seats, and copper washers seal because they become slightly deformed and compressed when they are tightly assembled. Any visible physical damage to the contacting surfaces of these parts will probably cause a leak. It is a good idea to routinely replace copper sealing washers, and to check all pipe threads for defects. Some copper sealing washers have raised serrations. These are deformed in use and should not be reused.

To check joint seals effectively means that you must understand the nature of each seal that is used in a system. Checking for leaks, after completing assembly, is also a good idea, but it is no substitute for considering seal integrity at each junction when you assemble and tighten it.

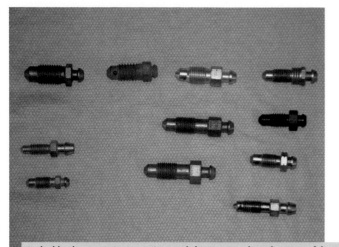

Brake bleeders come in many sizes and shapes. One thing that most of them have in common is that they are easy to snap off when they corrode into the threads that they screw into. A little PTFE ("Teflon") tape applied to their threads helps to prevent them from seizing and seals them to make vacuum bleeding easier.

Master and Wheel Cylinder Disassembly and Inspection

Master cylinders disassemble in a variety of ways. Some have one blind end and others have threaded end plugs and/or snap ring retained washers to keep everything inside. A few master cylinders and some wheel cylinders have stepped bores and use two cylinder diameters for proportioning purposes. A good diagram and/or some experience will tell you how to get most of these apart. It helps to remember that the internal parts of master cylinders, and of some wheel cylinders, are under considerable spring pressure; so a means must be found of compressing their internal springs, while threaded plugs or snap rings are removed.

Usually, on master cylinders, a dull Phillips screwdriver will perform this function admirably when it is pressed against the back end of the piston where the push rod would normally rest. Be sure to note the location and condition of sealing washers where threaded plugs are used to terminate master cylinders. Many tandem or dual master cylinders use small threaded stop plugs in their sides to limit movement of the front piston. Be sure to remove such plugs before beginning disassembly. On single systems, the residual pressure check valve will be found at the front end of the cylinder bore and should come out easily. On tandem cylinders these check valves are pressed or threaded into the cylinder output ports on the sides of the bores. If they are pressed in, they will have to be removed by catching them with the threads of a sheet metal screw and prying the head of the screw out. A slide hammer fitted with a hardened sheet metal screw will do this job, too.

Wheel cylinder pistons sometimes get stuck in their bores and can be very difficult to remove. When this situation is encountered, it is usually possible to blow them out into a bunched rag with air pressure. Be careful when you do this. You have to contain the pistons. Never eject them in a line where they can hit your body or wedge your fingers against something. They tend to pop out with enormous force. When air pressure is not enough, a car's hydraulic system can be used to force pistons out, as long as the other cylinders are still in place and restrained or their lines capped. In extreme cases, I have used a grease gun to provide hydraulic force to remove badly stuck wheel cylinder pistons, but this is a last resort because it creates a petroleum contamination problem, and extensive cleanup must follow this procedure. Of course, any of these pressure methods will only release one piston. That solves the problem in single-piston systems. For dual piston wheel cylinders, removal of one piston will allow you to remove the internal cylinder parts: cups, spreaders (if used) and springs. The piston opposite the one that was removed by pressure can then be carefully tapped out of its bore with a brass drift or shaft that is padded on its sides to avoid hard contact with the cylinder walls.

Many master and wheel cylinder kits contain new pistons. If the old pistons are scored, new pistons should be used, even if you have to procure them separately. If new pistons are not available, scored pistons can usually be successfully dressed with silica carbide sandpaper (400 to 600 grit) or, preferably, with fine glass bead (AH series).

Brake cylinder walls may suffer from scores or pits or both. These can sometimes be removed by honing with a brake cylinder hone. Generally, if a cylinder can be cleaned up and a piston-to-cylinder clearance of no more than 0.005 inch maintained, honing is an acceptable repair approach. Honing should be held to the minimum material removal necessary to accomplish the job. A good soap and water wash-up should follow honing. Always lubricate hone stones with the type of brake fluid that will be installed in the finished system, and always use a very low-speed drill motor to run the hone (800 to 1200 RPM). It is a good idea to follow up the material removal aspect of the honing procedure with a polishing operation. This is accomplished by wrapping your hone stones with a strip of 320-grit abrasive cloth and running the hone in and out of the bore several times. Do not use a finer grit abrasive cloth than

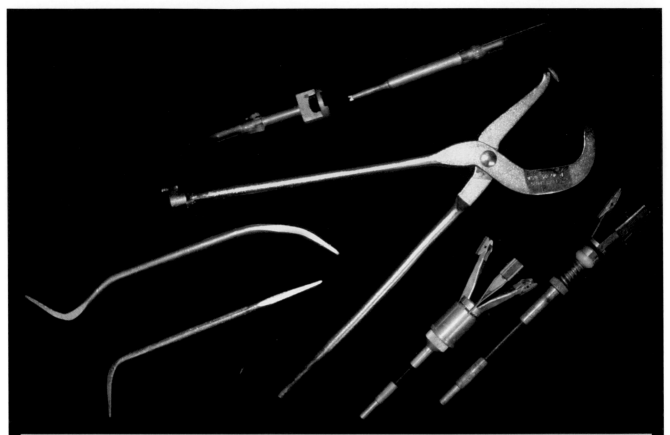

The brake "tool kit" pictured here has many items that you will need to work on collector car drum brakes. Top left and right are two types of hold down spring tools. The big pliers below them is used to remove and install many different kinds of brake springs. To the left of the brake spring pliers are two star wheel adjusting tools. Below the pliers are brake cylinder hones; the one on top is for disc caliper cylinders and the one below it is for regular slave cylinders.

320, as some cylinder wall texture is necessary to maintain seal lubrication.

Cleanup follows this step. Avoid a mirror-like cylinder finish, as it will deprive seal lips of adequate lubrication. Also, always make sure that the master cylinder intake and compensating ports have no projecting burrs that will damage delicate seal lips during subsequent installation or operation.

All honing operations should be followed by rigorous inspection of cylinder bores with an inspection light. If any pits or scores are left, or if there is more than 0.005-inch clearance between a cylinder and its piston(s), sleeving or replacement of the cylinder will be necessary because the seals will not work effectively in these situations.

Cylinder sleeving is often cheaper than cylinder replacement. If it is done with brass or stainless steel, it will produce an almost eternal working surface if the hydraulic fluid that is used is kept in good shape. This is because these materials, unlike original cast iron and aluminum cylinder surfaces, are not subject to the kinds of corrosion that will cause leakage. Brass is the most common sleeving material, and although this might seem a poor choice because of this metal's relative softness, it works very well if pistons are properly deburred.

Remember, master cylinder pistons run on a film of brake fluid and should never touch cylinder walls. If they are properly deburred and lubed for assembly, and if brake fluid is not allowed to transmit corrosion particles from other parts of the system into master and wheel cylinders, cylinder-to-piston contact and wear will not occur for many years.

Wheel cylinder pistons do not run on a film of lubricant or fluid other than what is put on them at the time of assembly. This is because their seals are on their inside ends. Always be sure to use a good film of brake assembly lubricant on these items when you install them. It is the only lubrication that they will ever get.

The problem with honing brake cylinders is that it tends to not work in the long run. By the time you get visible pitting in brake cylinder walls, there are probably invisible corrosion risers running into each pit's base through the intergranular structure of the casting metal. This is an ideal location for corrosion to restart after honing, and it frequently does. I vastly prefer properly sleeved master and wheel cylinders to honed items, or even to new ones because the cylinder bores are made corrosion resistant by this process.

A final area of disassembly problems that you may encounter when you get into hydraulic systems is the business of stuck line jam nuts and bleeder nipples. If jam nut surfaces round or split, they can be removed and replaced with minimal difficulty. Bleeder nipples can sometimes be persuaded out with an air/impact wrench at a low setting. If an air wrench doesn't work, sometimes "tapping sockets"

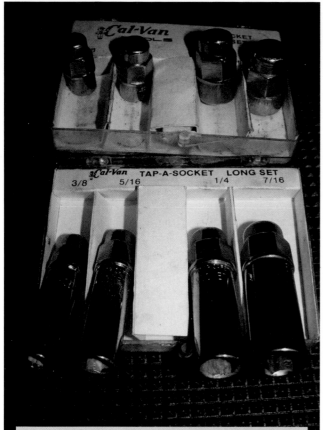

These "tapping sockets" sometimes help to remove stubborn hydraulic bleeder nipples without breaking them. The socket fits over the nipple, and you hammer on the socket's end as you turn the nipple and socket with a wrench. Sometimes the shock of hammering dislodges a stuck nipple. Other times, you break the nipple off anyway.

These handy little repair nipples can sometimes be tapped and threaded into wheel cylinder and caliper bosses when you break off a nipple. You have to drill and re-tap to install these parts, and there isn't always enough material to allow this installation.

Always use a good assembly lubricant when you assemble hydraulic components that will run in a hydraulic fluid environment. Never use brake fluid to assemble them because it is hygroscopic and will cause rusting in open air.

will work, but frequently a nipple will break, and removal will have to be pursued by drilling it out. There are some nifty brass nipple seats available that thread into an oversize hole and contain their own nipples. Don't depend on these, however, because sometimes there isn't enough material in a bleeder screw boss area to allow for drilling and tapping the oversize threaded holes that are necessary for the installation of these repair items. Sometimes, a new wheel cylinder is the only workable answer.

Master and Wheel Cylinder Assembly

When you have reconditioned or new master and wheel cylinders and pistons are in hand, and new seals and other soft parts have been procured, reassembly can begin. There are two imperatives; to get the parts in the right order, and to keep everything scrupulously clean. Be sure to provide a clean working surface, and be careful of things like the contamination that can fall out of your hair (if any) or off your clothing (always present).

Never store disassembled hydraulic brake parts out in the open where they can become contaminated with dust and abrasive residues. All parts should be coated with brake assembly lubricant (for non-silicone fluid intended use) or at least with brake fluid prior to assembly. Cups must be started in their bores carefully to avoid lip damage. A blunt plastic probe, such as the handle of an artist's paintbrush is

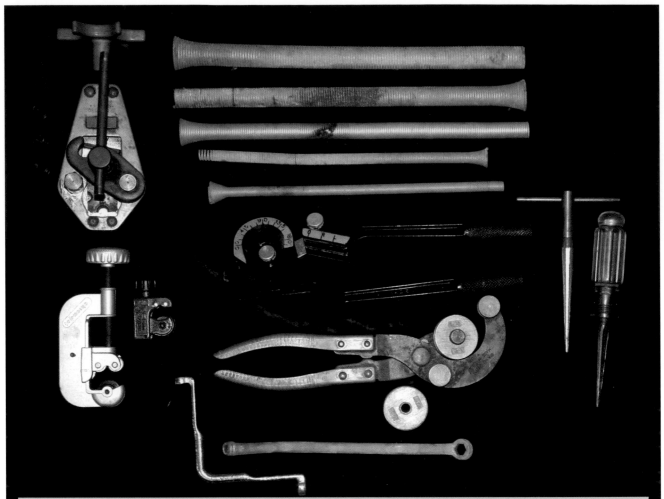

The "brake hydraulic tool kit" shown here is about what you will need to fabricate new brake lines from bulk. Shown on the top left is a tool for making double flare terminations on brake lines. Several different-sized mandrels for double flaring different diameter brake lines are shown to its left. On the far right are two line reamers. Two tubing cutters are shown at the bottom left. The smaller (red) one is great for working in tight quarters. In the center are three different devices for bending curves into brake lines. The spring sleeves on top work pretty well, but the rolling benders below them usually work better. Bending tools work by preventing lines from collapsing as you bend them. At the bottom are two special bleeder wrenches to help you bleed a hydraulic system after you have made and installed new lines.

handy for this purpose.

When a master cylinder is fully assembled, it should be "bench bled" by mounting the cylinder casting in a vise and running a line or hose from its output port(s) into its reservoir(s) and pumping fluid through it by depressing the piston with a metal rod. Later, this will make bleeding the system in the car much easier. The master cylinder boot should be examined for the presence of a small drain hole, and if one is found, it should be positioned downward when the boot is installed.

If a master cylinder on which you are working has a vented reservoir cap, be sure that its vent is clear. If a diaphragm is used to seal the top of a reservoir, check it for tears, pinholes, or other defects. When the master cylinder is in place, its push rod should be adjusted for a little bit of clearance to its piston. If you don't provide some clearance here, the primary cup lip may cover the compensating port, resulting in possible hydraulic lock up. Too much clearance will produce low brake pedal. About 1/8 inch to 1/4 inch is usually ideal, but check manufacturers' specifications for exact dimensions for this factor. Wheel cylinders assemble

in a straightforward way. Be sure to tighten them adequately but not excessively to their brake backing plates.

Hydraulic Hoses and Tubing

If brake hoses are replaced, hydraulic hoses must be selected that are the right length and end configuration. Hoses that are too long can get mixed up with a car's tires when the wheels are turned to extreme angles or when axles rebound. The input ends of hydraulic hoses are secured by clips, nuts, or other devices to their chassis perches. These fasteners can be reused, or preferably replaced with new hardware when hydraulic hoses are removed and replaced.

Brake lines can be purchased in prefabricated lengths with nuts and flares already assembled. They can also be fabricated from bulk materials. The latter will make a neater job because you can cut lines to correct lengths with no compromises and use it without resorting to the extra couplings that sometimes become necessary with prefab lengths when runs are very long.

Whether reusing old lines (usually a bad practice), using prefab lines or making your own lines, be sure to carefully inspect any line that you are installing for damage to the double flares at its ends. Cracks here are common, so beware. If you do your own double flaring, be sure to ream and wire brush the naked end of the line before applying the first flare to it. A little brake fluid or hydraulic assembly lubricant applied to your flaring mandrel will lubricate it during deformation and give you a much better job. Also, be sure to get the jam nuts in place before making your flares; they're easy to forget.

Always blow brake lines out with compressed air before you install them. This removes all debris left by cutting and forming operations. If you have to thread a line through a chassis and/or components, you should temporarily tape the end that is being maneuvered past obstructions to prevent contamination from entering it. Always locate brake lines away from hot engine and exhaust parts. Radiant heat can sometimes overheat brake fluid in lines and help cause it to boil. Installed lines should be inspected for kinks, damage to their anti-corrosion plating, nicks, and possible interference with any moving chassis parts. A line that nests on a sharp chassis feature can be cut over time by vibration. Any of these defects will require replacing or rerouting the lines. Long runs of brake line must be clamped down to chasses to prevent excessive vibration and work hardening. Parts houses can often supply chassis clips for this purpose, when the originals have rusted and broken (almost always).

While brake lines can sometimes be bent by hand, it is better to use bending tools for this purpose. These tools are designed to prevent line kinking and collapse. It is usually easier to form brake lines prior to installing them, using the old lines for patterns. Sometimes, however, this is not possible, as the lines must be bent-in-place to get past obstructions. If you are replacing factory brake lines, it is best to follow the original pattern, and not get too innovative about improving on the factory engineering.

A Word About Brake Fluids

Brake fluids have been made out of all sorts of things over the years, from fish oils to phosphated diesters. Until recently, almost all of them have been hygroscopic, which means that they aggressively seek moisture from the atmosphere. Then, contaminated fluid corrodes the internal parts of brake hydraulic systems. Most brake fluids have a disastrous effect on automotive finishes when they are spilled on them.

For many years, the English had a predilection for using natural rubber seals and cups in their hydraulic braking systems. The conventional brake fluids available in the United States will swell and destroy these parts. American fluids used in English cars with old rubber seals must be designated as compatible with the English OEM fluids: Girling "amber," "crimson," or "green." Fluids sold in this country are typically designated by their boiling points, and

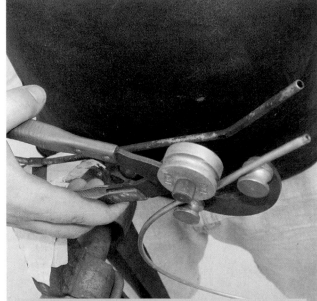

When you custom bend brake lines, it helps if you get the curves just right. This is easier to do if you hold the original line gently in a vise as you bend the new line to its contours.

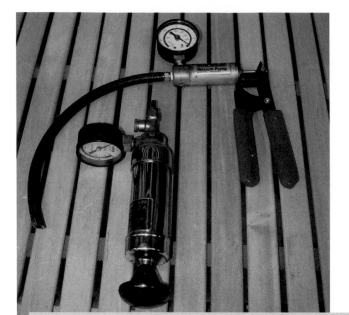

Vacuum bleeding can be accomplished with a hand pump and a receiving jar. The jar is plumbed to the bleeder nipple and then evacuated with the vacuum pump. Brake fluid flows into the jar. This is a one-man operation. Two types of pump are shown in this photograph. The one on the right is a one-hand pump that frees your other hand to loosen and tighten the bleeder nipple as you work.

were formerly described by an SAE grading system. More recently, DOT (Department of Transportation) numbers have become the prevalent standard for designating brake fluids. Presently, DOT 3 and DOT 4 conventional fluids are available, with DOT 4 having higher (about 60 degrees F.) dry and wet boiling points.

Silicone fluids are definitely an improvement on the older hydraulic fluids. They are designated DOT 5, and have very high boiling points (wet, 500 degrees F.). They also resist thickening at low temperatures, which is one of the biggest problems with conventional brake fluids.

Silicone fluids also provide superior lip lubrication for seals and are compatible with all seal compositions, including those in the troublesome English seals of the past. Best of all, the silicone based fluids are not hygroscopic, which means that they don't absorb moisture and lose their boiling resistance or become corrosive. They also don't damage automotive finishes.

With all of these advantages, and only the disadvantage of a substantially higher price, I don't know why the purveyors of silicone fluids have frequently insisted on misrepresenting their capabilities. While these capabilities are great, silicone fluids cannot, as some sellers have suggested, be put in a system and forgotten forever. While they are not hygroscopic, they do shed moisture, and this will tend to pit and corrode brake parts internally, particularly in their systems' lowest regions. In relatively new systems this is not much of a problem because master cylinder reservoirs are separated from atmospheric moisture by diaphragms.

However, in older systems with vent holes to the atmosphere, minute amounts of moisture enter and are deposited in brake systems every time that brakes are operated. For this reason, silicone fluids installed in older cars must be changed every three or four years under normal conditions, and more often in very damp areas.

While this falls short of the oft-made promise of eternal service life for these fluids, you will find that at the change interval mentioned above, there will be very little damage or deterioration of brake components.

When silicone fluid is installed, it is necessary to use an alcohol flush to completely remove all conventional brake fluid residues from a system that is to receive the fresh silicone fluid. Pushing the old, conventional fluid out with new silicone fluid applied through the master cylinder is, in my opinion, sloppy and dangerous—despite the fact that some sellers of silicone fluids endorse this shoddy practice.

Silicone fluids are not made primarily of silicone, but are a silicone hydrocarbon composition with only a few percent silicone content by weight. When people refer to "synthetic brake fluid" they apparently are referring to silicone brake fluid, because I know of no synthetic brake fluids in the sense that they are "synthetic lubricants."

Bleeding Hydraulic Brake Systems

Brake bleeding can be frustrating work. Bleeder nipples tend to stick and break, trapped air can be difficult to liberate, and spilled brake fluid can ruin body finishes. Still, it's essential that this frustrating operation be done carefully and completely. Vehicles with ABS systems can require a handheld scan tool to cycle the ABS pump to remove air from these systems. This is definitely work best left to people with experience in it and the equipment and know-how to perform it properly.

Brakes can be pressure bled by forcing brake fluid into a master cylinder reservoir under pressure and opening wheel cylinder bleeders, one at a time, until all air has been expelled from the system. The pressure tank needed to accomplish this is relatively cheap and simple, but so many different master cylinder filling configurations exist that having on hand the various adapters necessary to bleed the brakes on a variety of cars can be a problem.

Two-person bleeding is the old way. In this operation, one person pumps the brake pedal slowly and the other cracks the bleeder nipples open slightly during the pedal down strokes. This pushes air out of the system via a hose placed tightly over each bleeder nipple at one end and routed into a jar with its other end submerged in brake fluid. A bleeder hose with an automatic check valve ("one-man bleeder") can sometimes be used to replace the second person. Some garages vacuum bleed brakes with hand or electric pumps. In this process, air, then fluid is sucked through bleeder nipples successively until clean, unaerated fluid emerges.

Some people bleed brakes by using a second person or a "one-man bleeder hose" at the wheel cylinders while they inject fluid into the master cylinder through the large fluid port in its reservoir with a special syringe that is sold for that purpose. This is certainly a valid approach to performing this job. It addresses a major issue in brake bleeding—not letting the fluid in the reservoir fall below the cylinder's bottom while you are bleeding a system.

All of the brake bleeding methods described above work, and all of them require two cautions. One is not to attempt to reuse any fluid that you have purged from a system. No matter how clean such fluid may look, it is contaminated and should be discarded. The other caution is to keep the fluid in the master cylinder reservoir at a high enough level during bleeding to prevent emptying the reservoir and allowing air to reenter the system as you bleed it.

Some manufacturers recommend beginning the bleeding procedure with the wheel cylinder that is farthest from the master cylinder and working to the closest one. Others recommend the opposite approach. I have always started with the farthest one.

The hardest air to get rid of in a system is often the air that stands in a vertical section of the brake pipe below a master cylinder. Persistence will help solve this problem, as will a few raps on that pipe to dislodge air bubbles adhered to its sides as you bleed the brakes. Disc calipers also tend to retain air bubbles and should be tapped lightly while they are being bled. If you encounter frozen bleeder nipples, do not attempt to bleed a system by cracking the line nuts that feed the slave cylinders. This is sloppy and dangerous.

Always be sure to top off master cylinders after bleeding brake systems. If silicone fluid has been installed, do something to alert mechanics and others to this fact so that they will not accidentally top a converted silicone fluid system with conventional fluid. When using silicone fluids, be sure to pour them into master cylinder reservoirs slowly because if they are agitated excessively they tend to retain air bubbles that can then be pumped into a brake system. Adding fluid by pouring it down a clean rod will prevent this aeration. It is a nice touch to install rubber or plastic

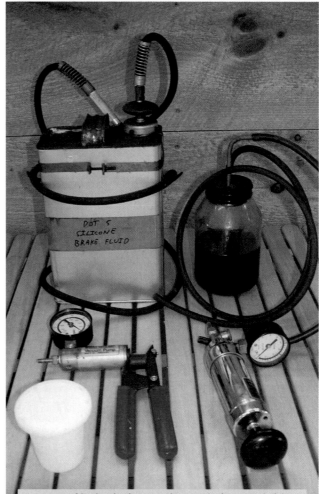

Two vacuum bleeding hookups are shown in the foreground of this photo. On the left is a one-hand fluid pump and receiving canister. On the right is a two-hand pump and a jar with plumbing for vacuum extraction of brake fluid. In the background is a one-gallon container of brake fluid and a fluid dispenser. This type of pump should not be used because it allows the fluid in the can to become contaminated with atmospheric moisture. Unless you go through a gallon of fluid a day, stick with 1-pint cans, and keep their lids tightly secured when you are not pouring fluid out of them.

nipple caps over the bleeder nipple ends after bleeding a brake system.

The completed brake system should be strongly activated by one person, while another looks for leaks at all junctions and connections. Be particularly careful to inspect areas where flared pipes go into junctions, as defects in the flares and/or junction seats are common and will cause leaks. The hydraulic line-connecting block, mounted on most rear axles, is one such place. If everything is right, the pedal will achieve a hard stop midway to the floor and will not sink further under continued foot pressure.

Brake Booster Operation and Service

The earliest brake boosters used leather-sealed vacuum pistons with crude valving to assist mechanical brake systems. Some of these vacuum cylinders required

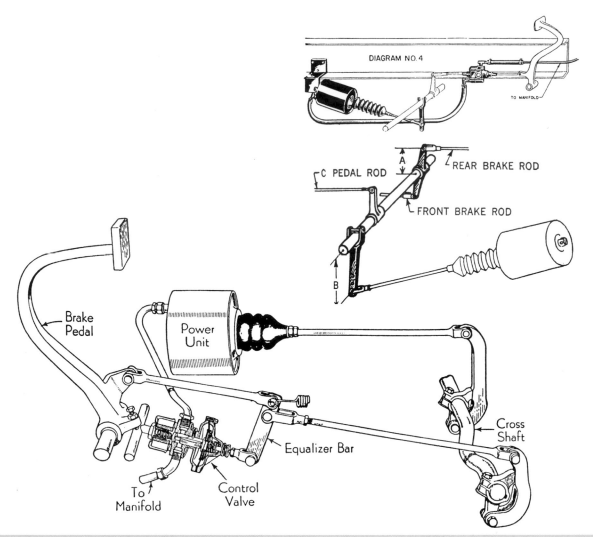

DIAGRAM NO. 4

TO MANIFOLD

A

C PEDAL ROD

REAR BRAKE ROD

FRONT BRAKE ROD

B

Brake
Pedal

Power
Unit

Equalizer Bar

Cross
Shaft

To
Manifold

Control
Valve

Early brake vacuum booster devices were connected to brake and valve linkage in a variety of ways. Some of these units are rebuildable and some are sealed and cannot be disassembled for restoration.

lubrication and some could be disassembled for repair. Many of these early units were sealed in a way that precludes repair. Later boosters used diaphragms that were acted on by engine vacuum. These boosters were mounted directly behind master cylinders. This type of unit often can be disassembled. Then, its valves can be serviced and/or its diaphragms replaced. Many of these units are available on an exchange basis and there are specialty rebuilders out there who will do custom rebuilds. Owner rebuilds are also possible if you can procure the necessary parts.

In service, brake boosters seldom fail. Usually what is taken for their failure is leaking vacuum plumbing leading to them or engine problems that result in low vacuum—

vacuum that is too low to operate these units properly. When simple vacuum boosters do fail, the fault is usually in their valving, seals or diaphragms. Many boosters have replaceable air inlet filters. These should be checked and replaced periodically.

The simplest test of vacuum booster operation is to depress the brake pedal with steady pressure and then start a car's engine. If the pedal sinks farther to the floor and then stops well before reaching the floor under steady foot pressure when the engine is started, it means that the booster is doing its job.

Never, for any reason, disassemble a working booster.

Chapter 18

Chassis, Suspension and Steering

EARLY AUTOMOTIVE PRACTICE IN CHASSIS, suspension, and steering greatly resembled that in horse-drawn vehicles, bicycles, and steam traction engines—some of the progenitors of automobiles. In the very earliest days, this meant a wood, steel channel, or platform (leaf spring) chassis, full-elliptic springing and either a steerable front axle or a king pin/tie rod steered pair of front spindles. It is important to note that none of the forerunners of the automobile really provided the basis for automotive construction in these areas, yet each had something to contribute to the concepts of automotive steering, suspension and chassis construction.

Horse-drawn vehicles provided the concept of a frame supporting a body, and since the body design of some early automobiles was very similar to that of horse-drawn vehicles, these frames were somewhat appropriate to early automotive practice. The problem was that this concept of framing was not intended to support and align the power drive components of automobiles. The springing of buggies and coaches did not allow for the increased speeds available with automobiles and, while these very early vehicles' center pivoted axles worked well with a team of horses, they were inadequate to the steering needs of double-digit horsepower self-propelled vehicles.

Bicycle frames provided an example of light, tubular construction, but this was mostly wasted on early automotive efforts because there was no simple technology for affixing the other components of an automobile to a tubular framework. While bicycles did not incorporate much in the way of springing, they did provide the example of an inclined king pin steering system. With a little imagination

and a lot of trial-and-error, automotive pioneers were able to join these two systems into the tie rod-steered systems that still prevail in many of today's heavier duty trucks.

Steam traction engines—really road-going locomotives without the need of tracks—provided the idea of a frame that could contain and align the power components necessary for self-propulsion. These cumbersome—and lovely—beasts operated at very low speeds, required a city block of planning to execute a turn or stop and tended to be operated by individuals who could press 400 lbs. without producing more than a minor puddle of sweat. Many of them had chain steering linkage that employed log chains.

Taken altogether, then, the horse-drawn vehicle, bicycle and steam traction engine provided the conceptual bits and pieces for automotive frames, suspensions, and steering systems. But, of course, it took a lot of development to begin to make these bits and pieces fit into a working whole.

Frames

After evolving their frame designs from horse-drawn vehicles and traction engines, early American automobile manufacturers quickly settled on the use of ladder type steel channel frames. These remained the standard, with a few variations, until the advent of the unitized body/chassis systems that were in low production by the 1930s and on the way to dominance after the 1960s. Engineering advances tended to modify the ladder frame into the X-frame and then modified the X-frame back into the ladder format.

There was also some experimentation with welding frames instead of riveting them. A few manufacturers, like

"Return with us now to those thrilling days of yesteryear... " It's all here, in two flavors and in a glorious mishmash of the old and the new, DELCO and Armstrong lever action shocks, coil springs, and recircuating ball and rack and pinion steering. What more could any car collector want?

Franklin in this country and Morgan in England, continued to champion anachronistic wood frames well after their obsolescence was obvious to everyone else. For the most part, channel formed, riveted ladder and X-frames had become standard practice by the 1930s. In addition to benefiting from years of development, these frames could be manufactured easily and efficiently by companies like A.O. Smith, and were both durable and relatively inexpensive to fabricate. Lighter frame forms, such as backbone frames and boxed frames, found very little acceptance in the United States.

Some of the big classics of the 1930s have frames with channels a foot deep and weights over 600 lbs. These units resemble battleship bulkheads and bridge girders and can operate with minimal flexing. Most frames, however, allow for a certain amount of controlled flexing and are not designed to be absolutely rigid. The Model T Ford frame, for example, is a flimsy looking affair that has the appearance of tremendous inadequacy to rough roads and heavy loads. But that is only an appearance. The metallurgy and simple design of the Model T frame are so good that few of these frames ever fractured in reasonable use. The battleship-style frames, on the other hand, can fracture easily after several years of operation. The problem of frame cracking was so prevalent in early cars that Marmon even advertised that after delivering thousands of their Model 34 cars, only seven had been returned to the factory with cracked frames.

The structural defects that a restorer is likely to encounter in frames include: sagging, fracture, twisting, impact bending and weld or fastener failure. In extreme cases, channel frames, and more frequently welded box frames, may evidence corrosion damage so severe that it destroys their structural integrity. This problem also afflicts the box-formed front and/or rear stub sections of several early unitized chasses.

Sagging primarily afflicts trucks that have been overloaded and passenger cars suffering advanced corrosion damage. There have been cars, like some early '50s Studebakers and some '50s Chevrolets and '60s Fords, that routinely succumb to frame sag when they reach high mileages. If the sag was produced by overloading, it can be removed by applying counter-force on a frame straightening rack and "sistering" the sagged area(s) with added structure. Corrosion-caused sags, and those in inherently weak frames, can be dealt with by removal of damaged areas and splicing in new material.

This is difficult work that requires careful measurement and a good deal of knowledge of the strains that act on a frame. For example, it does no good to splice a light piece into a frame and then to weld it to the area of greatest stress. The weld will weaken the piece that you have added, and it will probably fail in the same way as the original frame did. It takes some careful analysis of the causes of the initial failure and some good, practical strategy to put strength where the failure originally occurred. It is frequently easier to find a replacement frame when sagging has occurred, or at least to replace side rails completely.

Welded box frames, favored by the British for many years, tend to corrode, weaken and bend in critical areas. It is not uncommon to see some skillfully placed angle iron used to correct this problem on these cars.

Some British car specialists think that the inherent corrosion weakening problems of welded box frame cars are best dealt with by the quaint practice of forcing oil into frame box sections and then draining it out, as routine seasonal maintenance. If this sounds Druidic and extreme, try the experience of welding patches to rapidly disappearing metal on this type of construction. You may come to advocate the chassis oiling regimen after that experience.

Twisted frames can usually be straightened on a frame rack. This involves using hydraulic pressure to force the

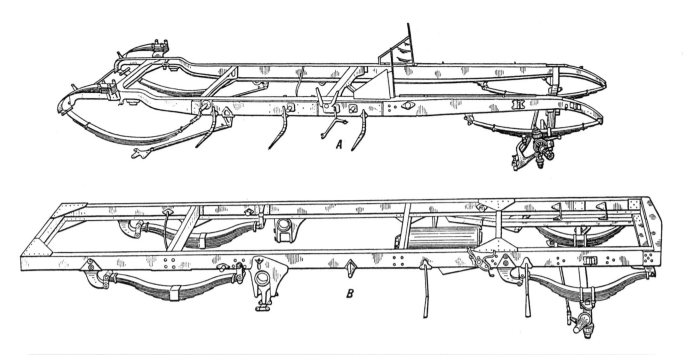

First there were ladder frames (above) and then there were X-frames (below). Some of them were quite massive, but this didn't always stop them from

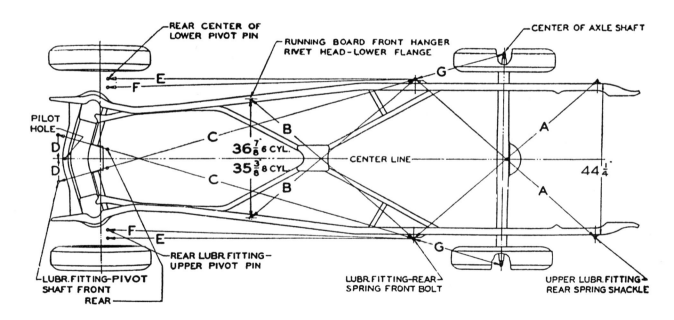

Frames are bilateral, and diagonal measurements across them should be consistent, as should the elevation of similar points.

components of the frame back into a semblance of their original alignment. When this is done to relieve twists or even to repair impact damage, any welds, rivets, or bolts that fasten the frame members together must be rigorously inspected for cracking, stretching and hole deformation. It is generally a good idea to straighten frames cold when possible. Certainly, most twisting, bending and minor impact damage can be dealt with in this way. When more severe impact damage is encountered, it is permissible to use mild heat (1200 degrees F. or less) in conjunction with hammering and force to get things back to where they should be.

Any frame straightening operation should be guided by the fact that automobiles are constructed in a bilateral fashion. This suggests that the left and right sides are mirror images of each other in all important respects. In practice, this means that diagonal measurements from distinctive symmetrical points on frames should match. Altitude measurements to a (very flat) floor from similar points on each side should also be the same. Straight sections should, of course, be straight. A piece of string or a good laser can help enormously in this work.

Thus, unlike the situation with modern unibody constructed cars that require complex and expensive

Chassis damage can occur in unexpected places. The frame crack shown here is in a high stress area that is also subject to corrosion under the vehicle body.

Here is some simple frame corrosion damage. It is very common in 1960s and 1970s frame cars, and considerably less common in older cars that have received good care.

"body machines" and fixtures to correct damage, older frames can be checked and put back to true with little more than a flat floor, a tape measure and some long pieces of string—provided that you have the means of securing the frame and applying significant force where it is needed to straighten it. If you want to get fancy, a laser level on an indexed mounting on a tripod—particularly one equipped with spirit and/or bulls eye levels—can be used to produce results with terrific precision.

Frames are held together with welds, bolts or rivets, or with combinations of these fastening techniques. Bolted frames are rare under collector cars, while riveted frames are most common. I'm not fond of rivets because there is no simple and certain way to determine how tight they have remained in service. In fact, some rivets were loose right after they were applied and they often loosen further in service. In any case, rivets should be checked for discernible looseness and frame members should be examined to see if they have left marks indicating a change in relationship to each other. With some experience, you can get an indication of a rivet's tightness by tapping on its head and listening carefully to the sounds that it makes.

Rivets can be tightened or replaced. When replacement is necessary, I prefer to use bolts and a thread-locking compound. Bolt heads can be disguised to look like rivets if appearance is an issue. Cold riveting is possible but lacks the certainty of factory hot riveting. Bolts, of course, can be replaced easily, but be sure to use Grade 5 (or higher) bolts to fasten frame members in any critical areas. Old factory frame welding usually has the uncraftsman-like appearance of work done by Genghis Kahn's humblest minion. It may well be the worst welding that you will ever see, and the older it is, the more primitive the applied technology and resulting welds are likely to be. Even if frame welds show poor penetration, inclusions, and cracking (short of complete separation), they should not be repaired. However, if structural integrity is in question, rewelding is necessary. Such welding should always be done by stick or MIG methods and never with a torch. Do not over-weld a frame. Where welding was done in inch-long beads, alternating with gaps, there was a reason for this, and repair should follow the same pattern, or new weaknesses can be introduced.

One common error that can produce frame fractures is to drill holes in a frame for what seem to be good reasons at the time. Avoid this practice because it can weaken a frame severely. If holes must be drilled, consider the problems

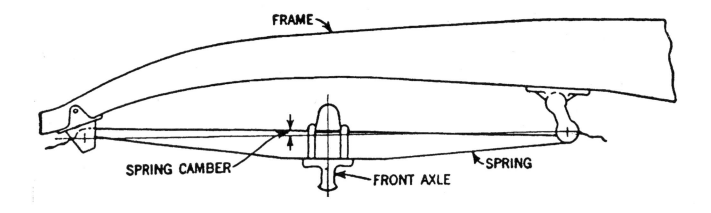

FRAME

SPRING CAMBER

FRONT AXLE

SPRING

Rubber bumpers, like the one shown mounted on top of the axle in this drawing, were the first attempt to control spring rebound. These devices are still used today and are called, "jounce bumpers." They are important, and you should make sure that they are in place on any car that you own. Modern materials, like urethanes, make them much more effective than the old rubber bumpers.

of stress before you drill them in ways that may weaken a frame in a critical area or areas. To restore a frame properly, you will have to get it very clean and examine it for fracture cracks. If any are found, repair them by welding.

In this case, drilling holes just beyond the ends of visible cracks *before* you weld them will help to prevent their propagation.

Suspension Springs

There were a few unfortunate self-propelled vehicles built without springs, but the practice of springing had been firmly established in carriage and railroad usage before the advent of the automobile. Early automobile springing tended to follow buggy practice and consisted of two full-elliptic transverse springs.

Gradually, this practice gave way to the use of four springs with two mounted fore-and-aft on each axle. Later, full-elliptics were replaced by three-quarter-elliptics, and then by semi-elliptics. Henry Ford and a few others persisted in using transverse springs (Why use four springs when two would do the job?), and the Ford and Lincoln lines were stuck with this archaic practice until two years after Henry's death. Some sophisticated transverse applications, such as the rear ends of modern Corvettes, have persisted to the present.

By the mid 1930s, independent front suspensions that used front coil springs had evolved into common use. Some manufacturers, like Buick, also applied coil/link systems to their rear suspensions. By the 1960s, Chrysler had introduced torsion bars (unwound coil springs) in this country in their front-end suspensions. This practice gained popularity until the advent of Earl S. McPherson's wonderfully compact and efficient struts. McPherson was an engineer at Ford of England who invented his strut

around 1950. By the 1960s its use was common.

By the 1970s, McPherson's invention was widely applied to rear suspensions (called Chapman struts after Colin Chapman, who first applied them to rear suspensions). The McPherson/Chapman setup is by now one of the most common forms of suspension in use.

Most collector cars have leaf springs in the rear and either coil or leaf springs in front. In most cases where leaf springs are used, a chassis is supported above its axles, but in a few American cars and many British cars, it was common practice to hang the chassis under the springs ("underslung").

Springs succumb to breakage and loss of height or "arc." In either case, the best remedy is spring replacement. Certainly a broken or sagged coil spring must be replaced because there is no repair or adjustment available. Sagged or broken leaf springs theoretically can be welded and recambered. I say "theoretically" because in actual practice such repairs tend to be short-lived.

An even worse repair practice is to substitute a coil spring or leaf spring that "sort of fits" for a damaged item. This is frequently done by people with a surplus of good intentions, optimism and enthusiasm, but a notable lack of knowledge of and/or experience in these matters. In its worst form, this practice involves finding a leaf to replace a broken leaf in a multiple-element spring. With a little cutting and grinding, something can usually be made to fit. At best, this practice will result in unmatched springs with inconsistent rates. Such a condition produces a car with a suspension that is at war with itself. At worst, the replacement of one leaf of a spring with the wrong item will simply cause breakage of other leaves in short order.

Installing incorrect coil springs or torsion bars (beware of the difference between left and right torsion bars) will produce equally disastrous results. This is also true

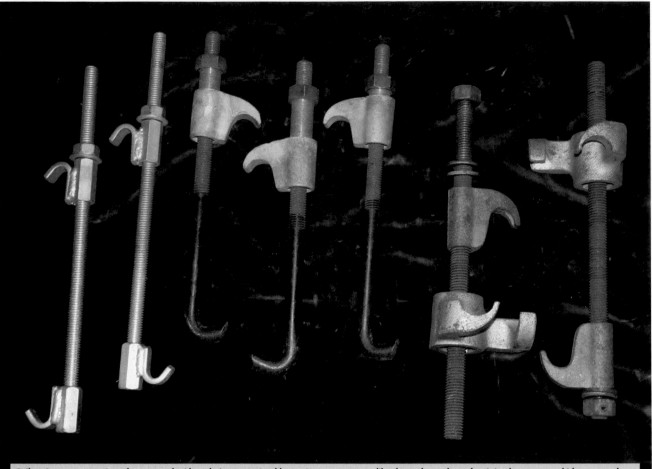

Coil springs can sometimes be removed without being restrained by spring compressors, like those shown here, but it is always a good idea to use them for safety.

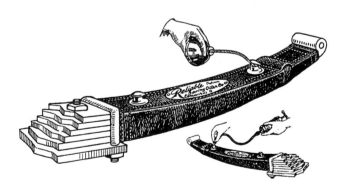

Most spring gaiters, whether leather or metal, tend to keep dirt and water in and lubrication out, the very opposite of what they are supposed to accomplish! The early gaiter pictured here provided for lubrication.

of installing spring "lifts" between the sagged coils of a spring. While this remedy may raise a vehicle back up to an approximation of its correct height, it will render the suspension ineffective and the steering dangerous. Spring breakage is the likely final outcome of this bad practice.

Sagged springs cause cars to ride too low and produce changes in steering geometry and general handling characteristics. New springs are really the only sound answer

for sagged springs. If these are not available, it is frequently possible to have them made, if data on the characteristics of the correct springs is available. Shop manuals usually give a method of measuring correct spring height in terms of measurements from distinctive features of a vehicle to the ground. There should also be a tolerance for allowable spring sag, but if this is not stated, an inch is generally too much deviation in body height from original.

Spring removal is always a dangerous business if it is attended to casually. This is particularly true in the case of coil springs. Not only must a car be well supported for this operation to be performed safely, but the energy in the springs must be released carefully. Leaf springs can usually be taken out of a car with a good set of jack stands, a good floor jack and a clearheaded understanding of what you are doing. Coil springs also can usually be dismantled this way but, if possible, it is always best to use a good-quality set of spring compressors. Some coil springs and all McPherson struts *must* be removed with a spring compressor.

Leaf springs require lubrication, or they will squeak and eventually bind up badly enough to deform or break. Over the years, this lubrication has been provided for by a wide variety of methods. Early cars used heavy grease or oil impregnated canvas between their leaves. Later, Oilite buttons and rubber buttons were used. Plastics, like polypropylene and Mylar, have also been employed

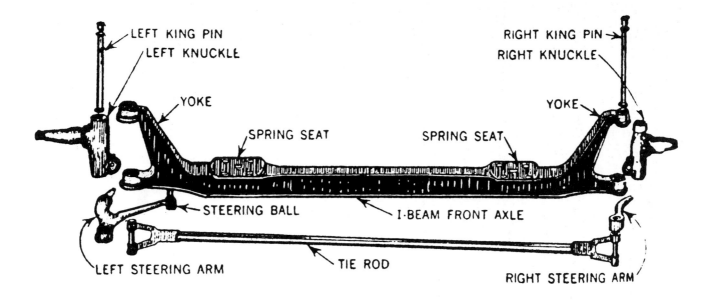

Front beam axles don't cause much trouble if they don't get bent. You can adjust camber by using shims under the springs that mount to them, but any other adjustments require bending the axle.

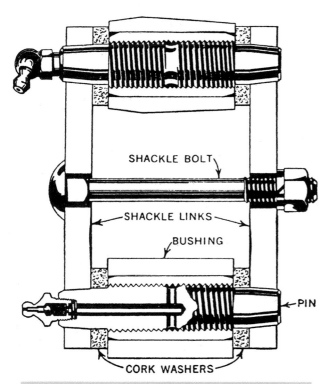

This spring shackle uses the "threaded" bushing design that was very popular for many years. This system works well, as long as its gaskets seal out water.

to separate and lubricate spring leaves. One of the best separators is zinc strips, which are, I think, still used by some truck manufacturers.

Many collector cars have spring "gaiters," covers fashioned from anything from canvas and rubber to leather and sheet metal. These covers were designed to keep dirt and grit out and lubricants in, but in practice they seem to keep dirt and water in and to make it between difficult and

impossible to get fresh lubricant in.

My basic approach to leaf spring lubrication is to remove any covers, disassemble the springs, and spray them with a heavily graphited lubricant like SlipPlate. This lubricant is designed primarily for agricultural chains, sprockets, machine glides and gravity boxes, but it also works admirably on automotive springs. It inhibits rust and sticks tenaciously to spring surfaces without any undue affinity for dirt. Its appearance is charcoal gray.

One of the areas where I tend to diverge from the strict observance of authenticity is in the matter of metal covers or permanently stitched leather gaiters for springs. Many metal covers have provisions for using a C-clamp-like lubricator tool to force out lubricant between the springs' leaves. This, however, does not force out the water that may have lodged under these covers. This water tends to rust springs and to make them squeak. In my estimation, most metal covers and stitched leather gaiters were removed soon after the cars equipped with them were delivered, and it is, therefore, not particularly inauthentic to do without them. Laced leather covers are a different matter because they can be removed for "spring cleaning" and lubrication.

Leaf spring shackles and attachment points have been constructed over the years from everything from threaded bronze bushings to rubber or plastic insulators and on to no bushings at all. Where hard metal bushings are used, it is important that they be lubricated regularly with a good-quality chassis grease and that new bushings and shackle bolts be fitted if damage or wear has caused excessive clearance. Where rubber or plastic bushings are used, replacement is also the remedy for wear, damage or deterioration. It is important that rubber and plastic spring shackle and attachment bushings not be lubricated with petroleum-based lubricants because these can soften and damage them. In fact, don't lubricate these bushings unless they squeak, and then

Replacement king pins and bushings used to come in nice steel boxes like this one. If you see a box like this with the front end parts for your car, don't be bashful, buy it!

only with a soap-based rubber lubricant or dressing.

Suspension Diagnosis and Repair

Rear suspensions on collector cars are usually based on live, solid axles and leaf springs. Such systems are almost endlessly durable. Some of these suspensions use Panhard rods to control lateral axle movement, or stabilizer bars to control sway. Rear coil spring/link suspensions are less common but there are still plenty of them out there.

About the only vulnerable points in these suspensions, other than their springs and their shackles, are any bushed pivot points. These are usually easily repaired with new bushings and bolts. A few collector cars have swing axle systems or fully independent rear suspensions. These are more difficult to maintain and restore, since they use power transmission joints (universal and constant velocity types) and more complex locating hardware than do simple live axles. Chapman strut rear ends also present special restoration problems, as struts contain "cartridges" or other internal components that must be repaired or exchanged when they wear out. Modern independent rear suspensions (IRS) have constant velocity joints and may require extensive parts replacement when these joints wear. For that reason their boots should be eased back and they should be relubricated after long intervals in service.

Front suspensions can be very simple or very complicated. The beam axle front-ends that prevailed into the mid-1930s are simple and straightforward. Their chief maladies are king pin wear and beam distortion—the latter affects wheel alignment and will be discussed in the next chapter. King pin replacement procedures vary with type—ball, roller or bushing, among others—but essentially involve replacing king pins and their bushings or bearings in sets. This work usually requires the use of such specialized tools as a press and large reamers. It should probably be left to someone with experience in this field. Correct shimming of king pin joints is something that you have to do by the book.

What anyone can accomplish is to check for king pin wear. This is done by jacking up the front end of a car until the wheels are off the ground and shaking them vertically. If there is discernible movement that is not in the wheel bearings, the king pins are worn to the point of needing replacement. Always observe appropriate safety precautions for a jacked car when you perform this test. Remember, too, that the early "Knee Action" or "unequal A-arm" front-ends still used king pins that were and are susceptible to wear.

Beam axles are remarkably free of problems unless, of course, they get "bent out of shape." When this happens, they must be forced back into correct alignment—caster, camber and king pin inclination—but that is also an issue for the next chapter of this book, the one on the topic of steering and wheel alignment.

In the 1950s and 1960s, the venerable king pin was replaced by two ball joints. This simplified front-end construction by allowing for both vertical suspension travel and steering deflection in the same joint. Ball joints are either bolted, riveted, pressed or welded to their suspension arms, and are very susceptible to wear that necessitates replacement. These joints are frequently checked by the shaking procedure described for king pins—particularly when their lack of soundness is being demonstrated by someone who is trying to sell you a repair. This test will work on some suspensions, where the coil spring is located between two A-arms, or where torsion bars are used and the jacking is done on the lower A-arm and not the frame.

However, when a coil spring is located in a "tower," above the top A-arm, a special wedging fixture must be placed between the upper A-arm and the chassis, and the car must then be jacked up from the frame or body pan for this check to work.

The object of all this is to "unload" the ball joint under inspection so that it can be checked for wear. Some systems tolerate more ball joint wear than others. Check the manufacturer's specifications for the car that you are working on in this regard. Many recently manufactured ball joints include wear indicators, which are pins that extend out of, or recede into, the ball joints when they are beyond their wear limits. Again, check a manual for the car that you are working on. Remember that in any ball joint system, one joint bears the car's weight (the "load" joint) and the other does not, the "follower" joint. The load joint will almost invariably wear out first, but be sure to check both joints because they are both susceptible to wear.

Ball joint replacement involves substantial disassembly of a front end, and it also involves releasing potentially lethal spring forces. In the cases of pressed-in joints, riveted joints and welded joints, some skill, experience and special

Different ball joint and suspension designs have different checking procedures. A pry bar against the bottom of the unloaded tire is used to check the style used on this car.

equipment are necessary to effect replacement. While this work is not the most specialized area of front end repair and renovation, it is specialized enough so that it should be left to front end shops, or at least to those who are experienced in this work. In some cases, bolted joints or joints that were originally riveted but have been replaced with bolted joints, can be changed by generalists. Remember that ball joint work must be followed by a complete wheel alignment.

In most cases, A-arms will have to be removed for ball joint replacement. When this is done, it is a good idea to check and replace the inner A-arm bushings. These bushings are generally inexpensive and this is a good time to replace them because you can get at them easily.

Many coil spring front ends have brake reaction rods and sway or "stabilizer" bars as part of their design. These frequently require bushing replacement. This is just a matter of bolting and unbolting rods and removing and replacing their old, worn rubber or plastic bushing parts. The parts involved are almost always remarkably inexpensive and the improvement in steering control and ride stability that results from replacing these parts when they are worn is enormous.

Snubbers, Shock Absorbers, and Other Things That Prevent "Bumps in the Night"

Shortly after someone noticed the advantages of springing automobile chasses from their axles, it was also noticed that without some added control, chasses tended to rebound violently and repeatedly when bumps in the road were encountered. The first attempt to limit this excessive and undesirable spring deflection involved rubber stop bumpers mounted between springs and their axles. This not only prevented hard metal collisions when the springs fully compressed, it also limited spring compression and, thus, rebound. Rubber stop bumpers became standard parts of all suspensions and contributed mightily to chassis stability. However, the problem of excessive and unnecessary rebound was still there.

Early attempts to limit or damp this rebound included the Hartford patent friction shock, the Watson reel snubber and various air-oil damping devices, among others measures. By the late 1920s, hydraulic lever-type shocks were gaining popularity, and by the late 1930s, the telescoping, hydraulic shock absorber had become common. There were, of course, variations on these themes, such as the complex Westinghouse air shock system and General Motors' Knee-Action design. The latter incorporated a hydraulic rebound-limiting device in the A-arm of that particular suspension layout.

Early friction shocks were temperamental when they got hot, wet or wore, and they proved to be generally inadequate. Various reel-type shocks, configured like

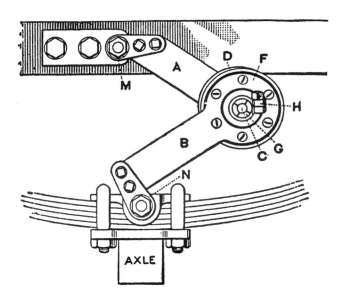

Friction shocks were very prone to failure and really didn't work well when they did work. This design was quickly dropped in the early years of this century.

of some hydraulic "jack oils." Never use brake fluid or transmission fluid in this application. Permatex still makes a jack oil that works admirably in most American Knee-Action and rotary hydraulic shocks. The same fluid can be used in the very few telescoping shocks that are refillable (Chryslers right after the war, for example).

Shocks should always be bench bled before installation. This almost invariably involves working the shock to its travel extremes in an upright position. A very small number of telescoping shocks are bled upside down. Check manufacturers' repair and replacement data on this point.

Chassis Lubrication

It is amazing how far suspension components will go if they are properly lubricated. Current practice is to specify molydisulfide, lithium, or aluminum complex-based greases for ball joints and a very high quality lithium-based grease for just about everything else. It is imperative that a high-quality grease be used in these applications. The cumulative cost of such grease is far less than the cost of a premature front-end rebuild. I have used Lubriplate MoLith and 1200-2 greases in chassis applications for years, and have found that these greases stand up to age, water and pressure. There are other good greases, but whatever you load in your grease gun, this is no place to economize. Avoid using the price leader grease from your local discount house; it won't perform well, and the repair costs that may result from using it can be significant.

On older cars that specified heavy gear oils for chassis lubrication and used Alemite pin fittings, it is permissible and desirable to use modern greases. Of course, chasses that were lubed through oil cups must get oil of the specified weight. I would advise following manufacturers' recommendations on greasing intervals, but under no circumstances would I let these intervals exceed 2,000 miles or one year. Some collector cars have "grease bags" to contain grease around areas like ball joints and tie rod ends. These sometimes have threaded plugs fitted where grease fittings install.

There is some mythology about not over-greasing these units to the point of running them almost dry. That may have been sound practice when they were new and the bags were intact, but by the time these cars enter the collector realm, it's a good idea to grease them sparingly but regularly. At least, that keeps grease in the joints. The bags, which are really balloon seals, should be replaced when other work is done that requires their removal.

When I was taught to use a grease gun—yes, someone actually gave me instruction—it was alleged that grease should be applied only until you could see old grease begin to come out of a joint. Later, I figured out that this advice, given by the owner of the gas station where I worked, was incorrect. It probably saved some grease, but at a cost to the customers whose cars were put on this regimen.

You should grease joints until a substantial amount of old grease is expelled and you see new grease escaping.

window shades, by the likes of Watson, Gabriel, and Lincoln (properly called "snubbers") only prevented springs from unloading too rapidly because they only worked in one direction. True, effective, double acting shock absorption (in both directions) had to wait for the hydraulic units of the 1930s and after. Modern shocks of the tubular telescoping type are marvels of valving and temperature compensation and perform far better and more reliably than did their predecessors.

Almost all early shocks are susceptible to rebuilding. The friction variety usually need new flat springs and friction discs. The reel-type almost invariably need new canvas strapping and friction shoes. Sometimes, they also need new graphite lubricators.

Early hydraulic lever shocks and more recent Armstrong (British) lever shocks sometimes need little more restoration than topping up with fluid, but sometimes they require extensive rebuilding to restore seals and piston or rotor clearances. All hydraulic shocks are prone to valve failure and, in the case of some of the later Knee-Action shocks, this can involve three or more separate valving systems. Rebuild kits and instructions are available for some older shocks, but many will have to be sent to specialty rebuilders when their original performance is to be restored.

British shocks must be filled with the correct fluid. This is almost invariably Armstrong Super Thin Shock Oil. Attempts to replace this fluid with its rumored equivalent, SAE 20 cycle fork oil, are to be discouraged. The original fluid is readily available from foreign car parts specialists and is relatively inexpensive. However, if you need much of it, the shocks that you are filling probably need rebuilding. American lever action shocks should be filled with special shock or Knee-Action fluids, which are the equivalent

You spray 3M Body Schutz and Rocker Schutz right out of the can with one of the special guns pictured here. It produces a rough but resilient surface, and you can paint over it with body paint. Body Schutz is very resilient and will repel attacks by gravel and other flying road debris.

propane torch to free them is barbaric and futile.

Refinishing Chassis and Suspension Parts

Chassis and suspension parts are among the few parts on automobiles that can benefit from the use of all of the sandblasting equipment that they sell out there. These components are heavy enough not to warp under abrasive blasts, and they are so irregular and thus difficult to clean that abrasive blasting is an attractive way to cleanse them before painting. However, this only works when these parts are disassembled and when sensitive areas, such as tie rod ends and king pin joints, are protected from abrasive particles. All abrasive media residues must be removed prior to reassembly.

If you are going the route of a total restoration and everything is apart, abrasive blasting or dip stripping are very appropriate cleaning methods for whole chasses and for chassis and suspension parts. Dipping should be followed quickly by priming and painting. A good enamel is the best paint choice. Avoid using the old asphaltic "chassis paints" because they tend to oxidize badly. Enamels have almost equal chip resistance and will maintain their luster far longer.

For many years, there has been a movement abroad in the land to paint chassis and other parts of cars with Imron and other polyurethane enamels. This certainly gives them a beautifully shiny and totally inauthentic appearance, but these paints are tough and can withstand chassis duty easily. I object to these paints on car bodies because they are totally inauthentic, and look it. On the other hand, if you must go "high tech" in the area of paint, chassis and suspension parts are the best places to do it. The problem with using polyurethane finishes in these areas it that it is difficult to remove them, and you may be creating a major problem for the next restorer.

When abrasive blasting is employed to clean a disassembled chassis or suspension parts, they must be primed within hours and painted within days. Priming alone will not prevent rusting. Blasted surfaces begin to rust immediately. This problem is not as severe with dip-cleaned parts because any good dip process involves a rust-preventative phosphate coating as part of its final rinse.

Now, this may come as something of a shock to some people out there driving around in cars with enough primer spots to qualify them for measles clinics, but conventional primers are not waterproof. There are some epoxy primers on the market that are waterproof, but the sandable gray and red oxide primers that we all know and love are not. Point that out to the next vendor you see at a swap meet with stacks of freshly primed NOS or NORS (New Old Restored Stock) sheet metal parts splayed out in the open on the grass.

When a car is not going to be disassembled for total restoration but there is a need to make everything look

This is because you really want to purge the old, hardening grease out of joints. This advice should provide mirth for the fellows who manufacture, distribute and sell grease. Nonetheless, it is sound. However, having given this advice, I hasten to add that the old grease that is exuded from joints should be wiped off carefully and completely and removed from the area before it becomes a dirty mess. Grease fittings should always be wiped clean before a pressure gun is applied to them, or contamination from road grime will be forced into joints or bushings, possibly promoting rapid wear and/or failure. They should also be wiped off after greasing. It is not a bad idea to use the inexpensive little grease fitting caps that can be purchased for Zerk fittings. On Alemite or pin-type fittings, metal covers must always be installed.

Grease joints that won't take grease at the 10,000 to 20,000 PSI that most grease guns generate can sometimes be freed with an oil ram. This is an inexpensive tool that is configured as a piston in a cylinder. The other end of the piston is a hammer ram that extends out of the cylinder. You fill the cylinder with light oil, place its open end against any Zerk fitting (except 45- and 90-degree Zerks that are easily broken by applying side force), and hammer the piston against the oil. The force of the hammer blow seals the fitting to the end of the cylinder for an instant and forces the oil into the fitting under enormous, instantaneous pressure. If this doesn't free a fitting or joint, the next and only step is disassembly. Heating fittings and joints with a blowtorch or

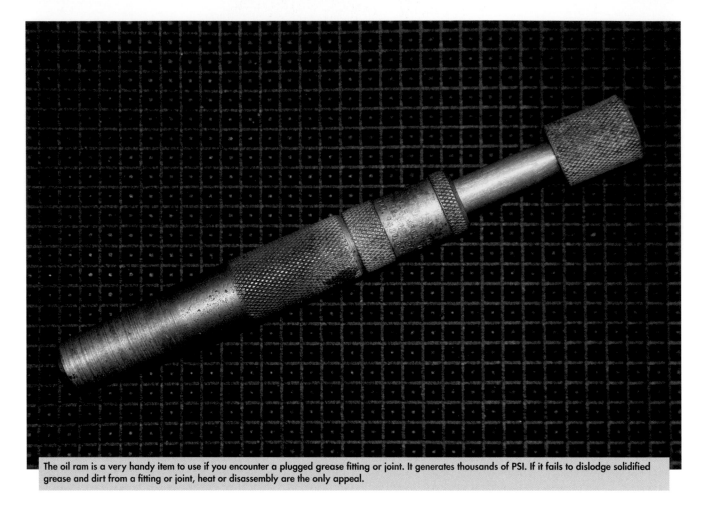

The oil ram is a very handy item to use if you encounter a plugged grease fitting or joint. It generates thousands of PSI. If it fails to dislodge solidified grease and dirt from a fitting or joint, heat or disassembly are the only appeal.

presentable, there are some half measures that will work on chassis and suspension parts. The first step is to totally degrease the area(s) to be dealt with. This can be done with a steam cleaner or high-pressure washer and detergent. If a heavy-duty detergent is used in either of these devices, most of the paint will come off, along with all grease. Degreasing should be followed with scraping and wire brushing any badly rusted spots and manually or power sanding deeply rusted areas.

It is not necessary to remove all rust residues. You should then wipe everything down with a grease-removing solvent cleaner such as PrepSol (DuPont 3919S) or Pre Kleano 1000. A medium enamel reducer will also work for this step, but be careful with whatever you use so that you don't spread grease around the surfaces that you are cleaning.

The areas to be painted should then be scuffed lightly with a 400-grit sandpaper or a fine Scotchbrite pad and blown off with compressed air. You can then coat them with a pre-primer, primer, or conversion coating. If a pre-primer such as R-M's Eurofill is used, the paint adhesion will be superior, but it will also be necessary to remove all traces of original paint and most rust before application. If R-M's Metal Conditioner (M-C 801) is used, you cannot use an etching or pre-primer, and you must use a conventional or epoxy primer before top coating.

It is also possible to go directly from the scuffing stage to priming without using metal conditioner or pre-primer, but the paint adhesion will not be as good. The priming step should be followed by application of a good acrylic enamel, preferably with a hardener or curing agent. In areas of known and extreme road abrasion you can use a rubberized undercoating, such as 3M Body Schutz or Rocker Schutz, between the primer and the paint topcoats. This will give a wrinkled appearance, but will also produce a very resilient finish that will tend to repel gravel bits and flying smut without chipping.

When cleaning, priming, and painting operations on undercarriage components are completed, it is always good practice to grease all fittings and drive out any water that may have become lodged in the joints during steam cleaning or pressure washing.

Chapter 19

The Mysteries of Front Ends Made Almost Simple

I SHOWED THE FIRST DRAFT of this chapter to my favorite front end and frame man. He kept it for a couple of days. When I stopped in to see him and discover his reaction to it, he looked at me with his head slightly cocked and said very slowly and purposefully, "I read 'er, and guess I didn't know half of that stuff. Ya know, it isn't really that complicated. All you gotta do is make the front wheels stand up straight."

It isn't quite that simple, but his point is well taken. The theory that governs front wheel alignment and steering geometry is pretty dense stuff. If you try to get into it too quickly it will make your head hurt. You can know shockingly little of this abstruse theoretical stuff and still diagnose and correct many of the possible problems in front end alignment and steering systems. I don't recommend do-it-yourself front end restoration and alignment, but understanding the basic underlying theory of front end alignment and steering will help you to commission this work effectively when the need arises.

In the normal course of events, the average car restorer will never have to do his own front end alignment and steering restoration work, beyond replacing worn bushings and joints, and maybe setting toe-in. Front end alignment should be left to specialists who have the equipment, theoretical knowledge and experience to do the job. While there is some old, portable front end equipment out there that can often be purchased for seductively low prices, I think that this capability makes little sense for individuals and shops operating at a level much below the Jay Leno collection. However, it can be important for restorers to understand front end alignment and steering basics. This understanding will help them to make decisions about

some of the available options in this work.

Front end alignment is fussy work. It involves eight or more interrelated factors. It requires both experience and a feel for the theoretical aspects of the situation. I have seen inexperienced practitioners spend literally days trying to do something that a seasoned front end technician can accomplish in an hour.

The example to which I am referring involved an attempt by a dealership to align the front end of a 1971 Saab that I owned. A whole day was spent on one of John Bean's newest optical racks. The problem (a persistent leftward pull) got better and worse, but never disappeared. On the second day, after the service foreman embarrassingly failed to get the original complaint fixed without adding three or four other problems, and in complete frustration, the car was taken out on the road and shims were added and subtracted to get a "running fix." That didn't work either.

Of course, the then "new" front-wheel-drive cars, like Saab, had much more critical alignment requirements than other (rear-wheel-drive) cars, and the combination of an inexperienced technician and a misaligned rack produced repeated failures.

Success was attained in the way that success in alignment is almost always attained. The car was taken to a shop that was exclusively devoted to wheel alignment and frame work —every small to medium-sized city has one or more such shops—and the problem was solved routinely. That is because for such specialty shops, these problems are routine, and because it is a good bet that technicians who work exclusively on front end and frame alignment problems pretty well know this field and how to apply its solutions to the problems afflicting your car.

Remember, on old cars, front end alignment is not an exact science. There is an element of judgment that mandates the use of the powers of observation, experience and theory. If you find that a provider of this service is treating your problem like a big production, go somewhere else where it is treated as a routine matter.

When you find one of the shops that specializes in alignment (they will typically have from two to 15 racks) you may be in for a great surprise. Some of the equipment that they use is likely to be ancient (Bee-line, Bear, Hunter, and Bean are among the favorites) and is incredibly simple. You will almost never see the cumbersome optical equipment of the 1950s through the 1970s in use in these shops, but most of them have installed a lot of the new digitalized laser and diode stuff. The place where you will find a lot of the fanciest stuff is at the dealerships.

Unfortunately, you usually, but not always, will find the least competent front end technicians there, as well. The older equipment is without buttons and whistles and derives its readings from turntables and spirit levels on magnetic or clamp bases. These, in turn, derive their authority from gravity and from immutable laws of physics and geometry. This simple equipment requires the simplest calibration—namely a vertical post—and a flat floor to produce readings that are easily good to 1/10th of a degree in the hands of a skilled alignment practitioner. The fancy stuff bounces signals off fixtures on a car's rear wheels to align its front wheels needs constant and tricky calibration, among other things. The only advantage to using it on older cars is that it usually informs a mechanic where and how much to change shim and cam adjustments—something that any good front end technician will figure out and/or intuit without that specific advice.

One concession to modernity that most of the good front end shops that I know have made is to install a very simple and inexpensive optical device to read toe-in. This device has replaced the more original and quaint 1930s scribe markers in almost all shops. On the other hand, the up-to-date, computerized/laser/diode front end paraphernalia is often designed to be operated by very low paid recruits, fresh out of vocational schools. What it saves dealerships in wages, it probably returns tenfold in owner frustration with cars that don't track right, or that scrub the edges off their tires.

Where the fancy computerized consoles excel is in producing a maze of mostly useless information about a car's alignment condition. I say "useless" because there aren't that many adjustments available on most cars. The few that there are tend to affect each other as they are made.

There are, in the nature of the thing, five angles and three factors that affect handling, steering, and tire wear patterns on older cars. Information beyond these factors is mostly useless, and often confusing.

Admittedly, the theory and practice underlying modern front-wheel-drive and all-wheel-drive—not to mention those few exotic four-wheel-steer vehicles of the 1990s—and swing axle and IRS rear-wheel-drive cars have become incredibly complex in the war to gain perfectly neutral steering at all speeds, and to eliminate the dreaded "torque steer." As a result, they may actually benefit from alignment on the computerized racks. Frankly, I don't pretend to understand these modern suspension and steering systems—and neither do many of the best front end technicians whom I know.

But old car restorers are lucky. The cars that we collect, nurture, restore and love tend to have beam axles or unequal A-arm ("double wishbone") front ends. If your tastes run to the modern, they might include cars with some early McPherson strut front ends, but not the new, tricky stuff. (You find that on "new cars.") The steering systems that point most collector cars where you want them to go respond favorably to no more than five alignment angle adjustments and three vehicle factors. This is the stuff that you were always vaguely aware of but didn't dare ask about for fear that someone might try to explain it to you. Tighten your seat belts. Here we go.

The "How" and "Why" of Alignment Factors

All alignment theory and practice flows from one simple purpose—to keep a vehicle's four wheels rotating with a minimum of slipping, scuffing and dragging, no matter what amount of lock (turn) is applied to its front wheels. While it is impossible to completely eliminate slip, scuff and drag in all driving situations, they can be reduced to low and acceptable levels.

Alignment theory, after the turn of the 20th century, and up to the recent past, concentrated on five basic angles of the front wheel spindles and king pins to achieve this desired purpose. These are camber, caster, king pin inclination (KPI), toe-in, and toe-out-on-turns. We'll go into some details of these angles later but here is a rough description of them. Picture an axle with king pins attached to its ends in perfectly vertical positions and with its wheels attached to spindles pointing straight ahead.

CAMBER involves leaning the wheels in toward each other at the bottom (positive) or out at the bottom (negative).

CASTER involves inclining the tops of the king pins back, towards the rear of the car (positive) or forward (negative).

King pin inclination (KPI) involves angling the king pin tops toward each other. This, of course, would cause the camber to go negative unless the KPI were accounted for in the construction of the spindle. KPI is a fact of front end construction. It is never adjustable and is rarely even measured. In double A-arm suspensions it is considered as a line between the centers of the two ball joints, or the angle of the king pin, if a king pin is used. If KPI is out-of-specification, it means that something is deformed or bent.

TOE-IN involves angling the front or forward edges of

the wheels toward each other—sort of pigeon toed or knock kneed.

TOE-OUT is the opposite, with the front edges of the wheels inclined away from each other.

TOE-OUT-ON-TURNS is a non-adjustable feature that is built into the geometry of front end parallelogram and center steering linkage. It causes the inside wheel in a turn to move a few degrees more than the outboard wheel. The reason for this will be explained shortly.

It is clear that there is a direct relationship between KPI and camber, but the other angles are also very interrelated. Any solution to a front end problem must take into account the fact that manipulation of any one of the five angles may require intervention in one or more of the adjustments for the others. The whole thing is a system and the parts are interrelated. That is where the application of experience and theory become necessary to do good front end work.

Numerous ways have been devised to make front end adjustments. Some of them are truly obscure. The most common involve threaded sleeves, shims, cams, bolts-in slots, and adjustable struts. In the nature of the thing, it is common for manipulation of one adjustment to affect others. For example, shim adjusted double A-arm suspensions frequently utilize the same shim packs to adjust camber and caster. A change in one will affect the other, unless this tendency is accounted for in the first adjustment.

A Brief History of Alignment. In the Beginning...

The earliest suspensions under steerable wheeled vehicles employed center pivot axles. These axles pivoted off only single king pins at their centers. They physically moved both front wheels in fore-and-aft arcs in the act of steering. While this practice was perfectly acceptable for light, horsedrawn vehicles and the buggy-like automobiles derived from them, it had some pretty obvious drawbacks. One was that the dimensions and layouts of automobiles developed in ways that did not allow for the intrusion of wheels being moved fore-and-aft a foot or two to steer them.

Another serious drawback was that the long expanse of front axle from a center king pin to a wheel spindle acted like a lever when the wheel hit a bump or rut, transmitting an enormous jounce back to the steering wheel or tiller.

This problem was solved in the second decade of the 19th century—in the early dawn of the automobile age—by a German mechanic, George Lenkensperger. Lenkensperger's solution was to fix the axle under the vehicle on springs near its ends. This amounted to most of its crosswise length. Then king pins were provided at each of the axle's ends for the wheels to turn on. The motion of the wheels being steered was, then, almost entirely sideways as they pivoted on short spindles around their king pins. There were two problems with this setup—one trivial, and the other serious and in need of an immediate solution.

The trivial problem was that Lenkensperger sold the British rights to his invention to a London publisher and book merchant, Rudolph Ackermann. It has been known as the "Ackermann axle" in the English-speaking world ever since. This, of course, was only a problem for Lenkensperger.

The other, more serious problem was that the uncorrected dual king pin axle produced a scrubbing situation because the two front wheels did not pivot around a common center. This Lenkensperger problem is, of course, known as "Ackermann effect."

The Lenkensperger solution was parallelogram steering linkage. You guessed it—most people attribute the solution to Ackermann . Yes, it's called the "Ackermann axle."

Remember, the purpose of front end wheel angles and steering geometry is to minimize scrub, slip, and drag. This means that as a car rounds a curve, all of its four wheels must be positioned as close as possible to exactly 90 degrees to the direction of their travel and oriented on circles radiating from a common center. Until fairly recently, this center was assumed to emanate from a line drawn through the rear wheel centers. To achieve such a common center, the inboard wheel in a turn must turn further—on the radius of a smaller circle—than the outboard wheel, or slipping will occur.

In practice, this is achieved in the Ackermann axle by the use of steering geometry that automatically advances the inside wheel in a turn further than the outside wheel. With this provision, both front wheels are turned on radii that have a common center on a line drawn through the hubs of the rear wheels.

As a point of interest, it is now known that the ideal common center is actually somewhat forward of the rear axle, due to certain phenomena involving centrifugal forces as a car rounds a turn. That's a fine point that neither Lenkensperger nor Ackermann appreciated.

While the calculation of toe-out-on-turns to compensate for Ackermann effect is complex, the actual hardware is very simple. By arranging the steering linkage in a parallelogram format with the fore and aft connecting links canted in at the rear, the angular characteristics of turning levers can be used to advance inside wheels farther than outside wheels in a turn.

Unfortunately, the adoption of the Ackermann axle did not completely eliminate the problems that produce tire scrub and sideways slip in vehicles at speed. There still remained a "scrub radius," which is the distance between lines projecting a vehicle's weight onto the road and the actual contact patches of its tires. This "evil" radius tends to cause steering spindles to act like levers and to transmit road shock back through the steering linkage. It also tends to put enormous force on king pins and cause binding and hard steering.

An American auto inventor and manufacturer, C. E. Duryea, considered these problems at the turn of the century and conjured up the idea of inclining king pins, but not wheels, outward at their tops to project a vehicle's weight closer to the center of the tire contact patch, and

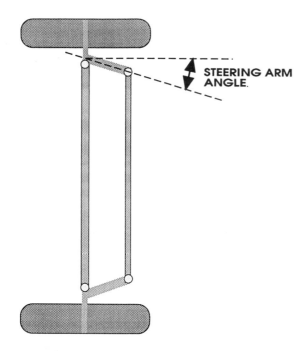

STEERING ARM ANGLE.

STEERING ARMS

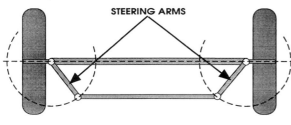

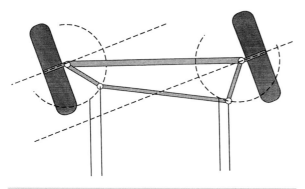

These three schematics show how Ackermann effect steering linkage works. The key is in the parallelogram structure of this system and the inclined side links.

wheel brakes, particularly non-hydraulic types that may have problems with perfect force application equalization, require a scrub radius of nearly zero. Other innovations, like positive caster in combination with mild toe-in, help to reduce scrub radius and its effects.

Ackermann steering linkage and various measures to eliminate scrub radius have come a long way towards reducing slip, scrub, and drag in automobile steering, but they have by no means completely eliminated these adverse factors.

Despite theoretical perfection on paper, real world suspensions are subjected to a myriad of complex variables, like changing tire shape under varying loads and steering angles, vehicle wind resistance effects, varied road crown and bank and so forth. It is hard to believe that these problems could ever be completely solved, though the advent of four-wheel-steered cars with variable rear camber suggests that solutions to some of the classic suspension/ steering dilemmas are "just around the corner," albeit, at the cost of great complexity in hardware and software.

There are several obvious symptoms of a car's wheels being out of alignment, and a few that are subtle. The obvious ones are: excessive and uneven tire wear or deformation ("cupping"), the tendency for a car to pull to one side or the other when driven on a flat road surface, a lack of stability that causes a car to "wander" about on the road, lunging into turns, failure of the steering wheel to return to center after a turn, or a tendency for it to snap back violently, etc.

More subtle symptoms of misalignment sometimes involve a handling feel that is just "not right." I have owned cars that seemed to handle adequately until I drove other examples of the same cars and found their handling much better or worse than the example that I owned or was testing. The change of half of a degree of caster can make this kind of difference in a car's handling feel, and there is generally some room in making front end settings to accommodate factors like: individual preferences, different tires, driving styles and running conditions. For example, a car that is likely to be heavily loaded may need a bit of extra positive camber to compensate for the fact that running load can reduce actual camber. It is very important that car owners communicate clearly and exactly to alignment service providers what the problem(s) with their cars are and the kinds of conditions in which they are driven. When I have alignment work done, I stay with the car while the work is being performed so that I can "bug" the person doing the work and make sure that it addresses all of my concerns.

No amount of alignment skill can compensate for worn or deformed suspension and steering parts. In any case, the level of hazard posed by these defects is intolerable. Sure, I know that the expedient of a bit of extra toe-in will seem to tighten up a front end with worn tie rod ends, but this a very temporary and unreliable fix. Certainly, before alignment work is attempted, things like worn or bent linkage, a sloppy steering box, bad ball joints, bad shocks, worn king pins, worn A-arm bushings, sagged front springs, etc. should be checked out and corrected as necessary. Unevenly worn

thus to reduce the undesirable scrub radius. A more common solution was to camber wheels out at their tops (positive camber) to bring their contact patches closer to the line of projected vehicle weight. As time went on, both of these ploys were used, along with wheels that offset a car's weight inward and increasingly shorter spindles. Wider tires (balloon type) also helped in this effort to cancel scrub radius and made possible the successful application of four-wheel brakes.

The problem here was that when brakes are added to the front wheels of a vehicle, the existence of any scrub radius will cause the vehicle to pull violently sideways if the brakes are even slightly out of adjustment. Four-

tires will throw alignment settings off and make adjustment useless. Small suspension defects, like worn sway bar bushings or binding caused by excessive friction in some part of a suspension, can create handling characteristics that may be taken to have their origins in the suspension settings, but really do not. If the true causes of handling problems are not precisely determined, what follows will be a great deal of chasing after one's own tail, adjusting and readjusting things to no useful end.

In any alignment proposition there are three issues that are as important as the wheel alignment angles themselves and that must be settled before any measurement or adjustment of angles takes place. These are: frame straightness, side-to-side wheelbase equality, and vehicle or spring height.

If there is any evidence of frame misalignment or distortion, a frame must be measured laterally by taking diagonal measurements from similar points and comparing them. This is most easily done with fancy optical/laser/computerized/Captain Video equipment, but can also be done just as appropriately by dropping a plumb bob to a floor—it has to be a very level and smooth floor—and making chalk marks to represent the desired measurement points on the frame.

A second critical pre-alignment check is to make sure that the distance between the front and rear wheels on both sides of a car are the same. Recambered or mismatched springs, or incorrect spring or axle mounting, can create dimensional errors here that for all of the world will seem like alignment problems.

Most important, the height of coil springs must be measured at either the spring ends or by vehicle height and compared to data on correct dimensions. This is so important that some manufacturers recommend using temporary alignment struts or braces to bring vehicles up to correct height when alignment angles are set. If coil springs are sagged, most of the alignment settings that you make will be incorrect.

A final and often overlooked pre-alignment check involves drag link misalignment. On older cars with beam-type front axles, it is surprisingly common for a bent steering knuckle arm or sagged springs to cause drag link misalignment. This, in turn, can cause excessive and unpleasant road shock to be transmitted back from the suspension to the steering wheel. When drag link alignment is correct, the drag link shaft (or a line from the center of the pitman arm ball to the center of the steering knuckle arm ball) will intersect the front spring's front eyebolt at its center.

On the few cars that have their front spring eyebolts at the backs of their springs and their shackles in front, the drag link should be aligned with the middle of the shackle. The steering knuckle ball end should be positioned roughly over the middle of the back of the width of the axle with the wheels pointed straight ahead, and the straight line distance from one end of this curved part to the other should be the same as from the pitman arm shaft center to ball center.

Variation here means a bent steering knuckle arm—which is not all that uncommon on older cars. Because modern independently suspended cars don't have the drag link setups used on older beam axle cars, many younger front end men don't have experience looking for problems in this area—you may want to keep this potential problem in mind when having a beam axle system checked for wheel alignment.

Camber and King Pin Inclination

Historically, camber was the first alignment angle that received serious consideration. It was particularly important in early cars because no one had discovered the possibilities of KPI. Positive camber was the only known way to reduce scrub radius. While modern cars utilize very little positive camber, they still carry enough to keep a vehicle's weight predominantly on the larger inner wheel bearings. In the days of leaf springs and beam axles, positive camber was included in front end designs, partially to offset the tendency of loaded axles to sag and produce the effect of negative camber. After the mid-1930s, the adoption of double A-arm front ends based on parallelogram geometry tended to keep load from affecting camber, and thus limited this factor. These modern suspensions often run on very little positive camber, and even zero camber under running load.

Camber is measured with the wheels pointed straight ahead on a flat floor or on alignment rack turntables. It is commonly measured off the machined surfaces of spindle hubs, but can also be measured from fixtures attached to a car's wheels. In either case, a spirit level device was the traditional method of measuring camber. Since camber and KPI are directly related, modern front end practice is sometimes to combine them into a single measurement called "included steering axis angle." But because KPI cannot be adjusted, the term "included steering axis angle" really denotes what was traditionally referred to as camber in the sense of what is actually adjusted.

On cars with beam axles, camber is not adjustable, except by the extreme expedient of bending an axle. Any shop that did much work on the older Ford Twin-I-Beam light truck and van front ends will have a nifty little hydraulic fixture for making this kind of adjustment. [Later Twin-I-Beam units were heavier than the early ones and were not supposed to be "adjusted" that way.]

Both front wheels should have equal camber, except in some independent front ends where slight extra positive camber is provided on the left wheel to compensate for the tendency of crowned roads to steer a car to the right, off the crown. A car will always pull to the side with more positive camber, so building some extra positive camber into the left wheel suspension adjustment helps it to climb road crowns and keep going straight down the road.

Early A-arm suspensions used a variety of means to

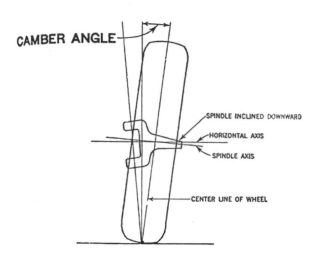

CAMBER ANGLE

SPINDLE INCLINED DOWNWARD
HORIZONTAL AXIS
SPINDLE AXIS

CENTER LINE OF WHEEL

The CAMBER angle of a suspension is the deviation from vertical of a wheel with respect to the side of the car. Positive camber in a right side wheel is shown here. Negative camber would have its top leaning in and its bottom out.

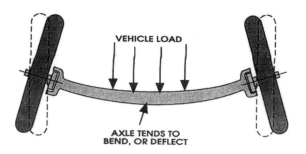

VEHICLE LOAD

AXLE TENDS TO
BEND, OR DEFLECT

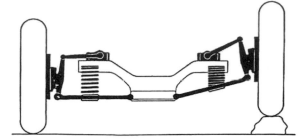

Overloading a beam axle will produce a dramatic camber change and really destroy a car's handling characteristic, often permanently. Double A-arm suspensions employ geometry that is designed to maintain relatively consistent camber throughout their travel, but some deviation occurs. That's why sagged springs can cause handling problems in cars with this suspension design.

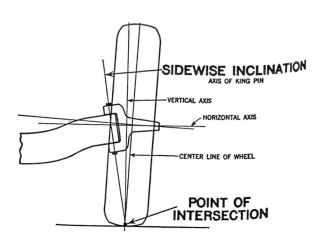

SIDEWISE INCLINATION
AXIS OF KING PIN

VERTICAL AXIS

HORIZONTAL AXIS

CENTER LINE OF WHEEL

POINT OF
INTERSECTION

KING PIN INCLINATION (KPI) is the angle of the king pin or other axis on which a wheel turns from true vertical: KPI relates to camber, except that KPI is not adjustable, while camber is.

adjust camber. Shims behind the top A-arm mounting brackets and eccentric adjusters at the king pin ends were the most common approaches. Later, when ball joint suspensions came into common use, shims and bolts-in-slots, among other means, became the methods of choice for adjusting camber.

KPI is usually in the range of 4 to 9 degrees and can be measured using special equipment, but will never be incorrect unless a spindle or other major component is deformed. When this is suspected, KPI should be measured and appropriate action taken to replace bent parts if KPI is out-of-specification.

It should be noted that although KPI cannot be adjusted, it does perform two important functions in front end design. I have already mentioned that the adoption of KPI added greatly to reducing the scrub radii of early automobiles and helped to make possible the adoption of four-wheel-brakes. Another desirable effect of KPI is that it causes a steering wheel to self-center in the straight-ahead position. This is because by including KPI in suspension design, steering the wheels off center causes the steering knuckles to raise the car slightly. While this rise is very slight, it does mean that the weight of the car bears—albeit at a tremendous mechanical disadvantage—to bring the wheels back to center position when they are turned out of that position. This produces directional stability and is one of the purposely employed design factors that keeps cars going straight.

Caster

Caster is the factor of tilting the tops of king pins back (positive) or forward (negative) from a vertical axis. In the case of double A-arm suspensions, the king pin pivots, or a line through the ball joints is inclined forward (negative) or backward (positive) to produce caster. What all of this accomplishes is to project a vehicle's weight forward of, or behind, its tire contact patch. Projecting it forward produces a tire contact patch that is heavier in the direction that the wheels are turned. This, in turn, produces a factor called "self-aligning torque," which tends to straighten a wheel from the direction in which it has been turned.

Boiled down to its nugget, this means that positive caster (king pin top or axis back at the top) produces a tendency for the wheels to come back to center automatically. Bicycles

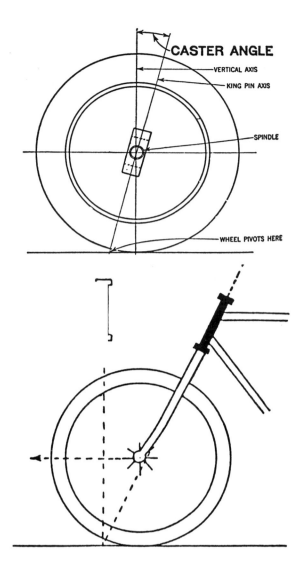

CASTER ANGLE

VERTICAL AXIS

KING PIN AXIS

SPINDLE

WHEEL PIVOTS HERE

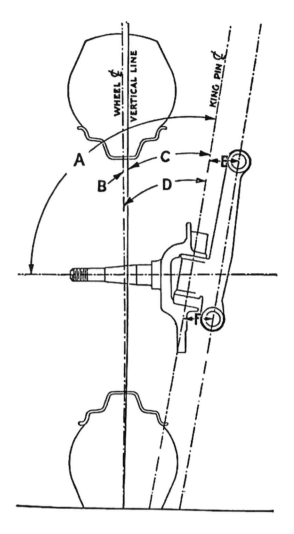

WHEEL ℄
VERTICAL LINE

KING PIN ℄

A B C D E

F

KING PIN ANGLE

WEIGHT CARRIED ON LARGE BEARING

The CASTER angle of a suspension is the fore-and-aft deviation of the king pin, or axis on which the wheel turns from vertical. If the top of the king pin or axis is inclined forward from vertical, the suspension is said to have positive caster. If negative caster (rare) is the design, the top of the wheel axis leans back from vertical.

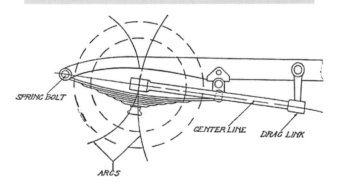

SPRING BOLT

CENTER LINE   DRAG LINK

ARCS

Drag link alignment is important in older collector cars. Misalignment can cause severe bump steer. This situation is found fairly often.

With the advent of independent front suspensions based on double-wishbone hardware, after the mid-1930s, cars were designed with just enough KPI to load their weight mostly on their (larger) inner wheel bearings. These diagrams show how it is possible to design KPI and camber to project a car's weight on a line near the center of the tire tread. This greatly reduces the undesirable scrub radius that would otherwise cause "bump steer."

use extreme positive caster to achieve self-centering. That is how brave and coordinated kids can go down the road on bicycles without touching the handlebars.

If too much positive caster is cranked into suspension settings, the wheels will tend to snap back too hard after making a turn, and the steering wheel will do the same. In some front end designs, king pin inclination has already been set to create directional stability and little or no positive caster is needed to bring the steering wheel back to its center position after a turn. This approach has the advantage of reducing any tendency for a wheel to self-center too violently. There are even some modern designs that use negative caster to reduce self-centering tendencies when KPI has been employed for this purpose.

Caster settings must be made correctly, or alignment problems from road wander and wheel snap-back, to the horrendous "caster shimmy" may result. Generally, the caster settings of both front wheels must be equal, although sometimes a slight variation of less than one half of one degree may be used to offset the tendency of cars to fall away from the crowns of roads. Beam axles often used as much as 9 degrees of positive caster to keep wheels self-centered. Independent suspensions use much less caster than that.

If there is variation in caster between the wheels on a beam axle, the axle is bent and must be straightened. If both sides deviate from specification by the same amount, tapered shims can be used between the axle and spring mountings to increase or reduce caster.

Early double A-arm suspensions usually provided for caster adjustment via shims behind the upper control arm mountings, strut adjusters, pivot cams, etc. Some ball joint suspensions don't provide for caster adjustment at all, but require hydraulic ram tools placed against the platform (unitized body structure) sheet metal to make these adjustments.

Caster is measured by turning wheels through a total arc of 40 degrees (20 degrees in either direction off center) and measuring the difference in the deviation from vertical in that sweep. It is important to note that older equipment tended to work by measuring a greater arc, up to 60 degrees in some cases, and this equipment will not give correct readings for the now-conventional 40-degree arc in which caster is measured. Minor variations in caster greatly affect the feel of steering systems and the directional stability of cars.

Toe-in

Toe-in was once thought to be related to camber, and manufacturers specified relatively large amounts of toe-in for that reason. Later, it was discovered that this relationship does not really exist. Present theory holds that when a vehicle is steered straight ahead, toe-in or toe-out will produce tire scrub. This reasoning appeals to common sense. A very small amount of toe-in, like 1/16 inch, is still specified for some modern vehicles because this insures that the wheels will not toe out. The reasoning behind this is that any looseness or wear in steering linkage will be put under compression by toe-in and therefore will not result in toe-out. While toe-in produces tire scrub, toe-out will make for something worse—scrubbing, wander and instability in a vehicle. On that basis, a little bit of toe-in is a good insurance policy against toe-out and its unpleasant consequences.

Toe is usually adjusted by means of two clamp sleeves on steering linkage tie rods. These should always be set in equal amounts in opposite directions to achieve correct adjustment. On some cars, the steering wheel is centered by moving both of the toe adjusting sleeves in the same direction, but this adjustment factor is more usually accomplished by repositioning the steering wheel on its

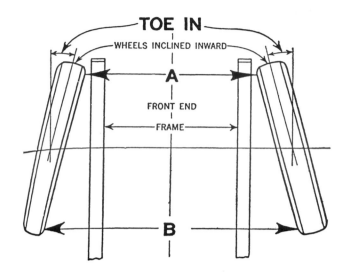

TOE-IN is the deviation from perfect horizontal parallelism of the front wheels. If the wheels point slightly towards each other in front, this is called toe-in, but if they point out from each they are described as having toe-out. Most suspensions call for a very slight amount of toe-in to keep steering linkage under a little tension.

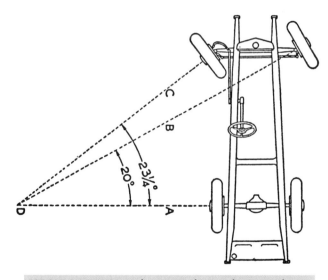

TOE-OUT-ON-TURNS is made necessary because the inner and outer front wheels in a turn describe different arcs with different radii. The inside wheel has to turn farther to avoid dragging and scrubbing. Modern rack-and-pinion suspension designs omit this factor because modern tires are capable of dealing with the resulting scrub.

splines. Cars with "center steering" linkage setups have only one sleeve. Where a range of adjustment is shown for toe-in, it is probably best to use the lesser figure.

Since the early days of automobiles, toe-in was measured with some sort of scribe marker instrument that measured the distance from wheel to wheel or from similarly positioned tire treads. Presently, this determination is usually made with a simple optical projecting device that makes for more accurate adjustment.

Toe-out-on-turns is built into the geometry of the parallelogram or center steering linkage. It is measurable on the turntables of front end racks, but is not adjustable. If toe-out-on-turns does not meet specifications, something is badly worn or bent. Bent steering linkage must be replaced. It is impractical and dangerous to attempt to straighten it.

Steering Box Adjustment, Lubrication, and Repair

There are probably a dozen variations on basic steering box design. All of them involve redirecting the plane of steering shaft motion into another plane and the imposition of some ratio or ratios on the input/output of the steering wheel and pitman arm. Steering boxes are also designed to be "irreversible," which means that they attempt to minimize the extent to which bumping forces on wheels can transmit shock and movement ("bump steer") back to steering wheels.

Almost all steering boxes allow for two or more adjustments. This is true of common boxes, like rack and pinion, recirculating ball, worm and nut, worm and sector, worm and roller and many other configurations. Both adjustments position and snug each of the moving parts in the box for the purpose of eliminating any play or clearance that would result in lost motion between the steering wheel and rack or pitman arm. The two common adjustment systems must be adjusted in the correct sequence and often require the use of a small, accurate torque wrench to create a very mild preload on the bearings supporting the driving steering gear, or to measure small amounts of drag.

The second stage of adjustment usually involves snugging the driven member of the system against the driving member and checking the system for binding throughout its range of motion. It is critical that during this adjustment, the pitman arm be disconnected from the steering linkage so that the mesh of the steering gears can be sensed without interference. If the connection of the pitman arm must be broken at a splined joint to make this adjustment, the relative positions of the components should be noted and marked so that it can be reestablished.

Excepting modern rack-and-pinion setups, power steering systems on collector cars are divided into two types—the self-contained rotary type and the linkage type. Again, there is tremendous variation in the design of these units, from the early units pioneered by Pierce-Arrow and Revere, to modern systems that are still used on some heavy-duty light trucks. All of them use a torsion, or spool, valving device that operates pumped hydraulic pressure against a piston or baffle to assist steering. The pumps and steering units used to affect power steering are often rebuildable. When failure occurs, it is usually from bad seals and valving components. Scored hydraulic parts are also a possibility. Power steering fluid should be periodically flushed and replaced, and all hydraulic hoses in steering systems should be checked for signs of leakage and deterioration. If this occurs, replacement with new hoses is necessary.

Rotary and linkage power steering systems should only be replenished with power steering fluid. Some of them will tolerate automatic transmission fluid, but many will not. It is always best to use a specially formulated power steering fluid. Some linkage systems are externally valved and still need separate lubrication for their steering gear boxes. This lubrication is accomplished with SAE 90 gear oil, the same lubricant used in conventional steering boxes. Modern steering boxes will tolerate EP ("Extreme Pressure") lubricants, but older ones should be lubed with a non-EP mineral oil. Some of these older units have felt seals that EP additives will destroy. It is almost never a good idea to use cup or chassis grease in a steering box. It will tend to channel and fail to lubricate the pressure bearing surfaces of gears and bearings. When you find grease in a steering box, it will usually have to be removed by disassembly. Sometimes, if it isn't caked too densely, it can be thinned and siphoned out of the box by adding warmed SAE 80 gear oil to dissolve it.

The exception to this involves a very few cars that had steering boxes that did not provide seals to retain oil. These boxes should be lubricated with an NGLI 1 chassis grease. Early Dodge Brothers cars, and a few others, were built this way—with steering boxes that didn't have seals.

An Overview: The Physical Restoration and Refinishing of Collector Car Bodies

PLEASE INDULGE ME FOR A FEW PAGES while I tell a story. Many years ago, when I was old enough to have had my driver's license for a few years and had begun to take some of my father's classic cars to meets near our home in Bennington, Vermont, I had a startling experience. I took our 1932 Lincoln Dietrich Convertible sedan to a meet that was combined with a parade and other festivities celebrating the bicentennial of a town in northeastern Massachusetts.

The meet was poorly organized—things involving old cars were very informal in those days—and the bicentennial oversight committee had decided that there should be awards for the old cars that attended. Unfortunately, they had no clear idea how to judge the cars. First, they procured the awards: a drop light from a local hardware store, a towrope from an auto parts store, a soldering iron from an electrical shop, and a hundred bucks from somewhere. Then they hit on a unique "communitarian" scheme for judging the participating cars.

After the parade, the cars were driven onto a huge field in the random order in which they had arrived and parked side-by-side. Then, the cars were counted off in groups of three.

The owners in each group of three cars judged the cars in that group. The winners of this elimination were driven forward two car lengths, and new groups of three were counted off from among them. Winners in this elimination were then driven forward, and so on, until my Lincoln and I reached the "finals." There were three cars in the final elimination. The other cars in that group were a very badly restored Franklin Olympic 6 and a very nice Durant.

As I remember it, the mathematics of the thing worked out so that only the Franklin and my Lincoln arrived at the final selection. However, to make the finals a decision of three—and thus reduce the possibility of a tie and an unseemly fistfight—the Durant had been selected by all of the residents of the next-to-last row and promoted from there to the final selection.

The Durant was a nice job by the standards of that time and represented what we used to call "a good owner restoration." The Franklin was another matter. About the kindest thing that could be said about it was that its water pump was not leaking, and that was only because it had an air-cooled engine.

The Franklin was a complete mess in every detail. The upholstery was beastly, crooked seams, stuffing bulging out, lumps and so forth. The engine, when it finally started, belched out a cacophony of moans, knocks, wraps, and other noises of imminent self-destruction. The plating? There wasn't any; aluminum paint had replaced it. In addition, the body and fenders had been hammered and filled with plastic to the point that it was hard to recognize that the thing was an automobile, much less a Franklin. Things were missing, obviously wrong parts were everywhere, and lubricant seemed to be dripping from everywhere, even from places that do not normally contain it. Perhaps I exaggerate, but not by much.

I had to wonder if this poor vehicle had crossed the line of an age-old question. Was this car a mess or was this mess a car? Two related questions coursed through my mind. How had this thing, the Franklin, gotten to the meet under its own faltering power, and why had it gotten to the finals of the judging competition?

That latter question involved considerable self-interest on my part because in those days, and particularly at my young age in those days, the hundred bucks part of the prize represented serious money, enough money to plan any manner of frivolous fun, or even to contemplate a substantial automotive acquisition.

It was the Durant that had me mildly worried. Of course, it was absurd to be judging my mighty, custombodied 12-cylinder Lincoln in the same competition class with a Model A-like Durant. However, the meet's oversight committee had overlooked that kind of possible outcome in the rush to "have some old cars at the celebration." Still, the fine points of the conceptual defects in the judging scheme seemed less important to me than the hundred bucks cash prize.

Although I was young, I understood that one of the niceties of being a gentleman was not to vote for yourself in a competition, particularly with the voting so open to view. Since I had the best-restored car of the three and far-and-away the most interesting and impressive, I considered the pleasant fate of selection by my colleagues to be all but inevitable. Confidence was definitely high. Since only gross misjudgment by my colleagues could result in any outcome other than my car winning, I pretty much settled into the pleasant exercise of deciding between the several delightful alternatives that my newly acquired hundred bucks would make possible.

The only cloud on the horizon was a nagging uneasiness that the poor judgment that had promoted the Franklin to the final elimination might be repeated and deny me the prize. It was but a fleeting thought. The justice of my cause was too obvious. I dismissed my sense of nagging uneasiness and faint apprehension. Isn't it funny how easy it was for me to be overconfident in my father's car?

Of course, this story would not be worth telling if my fortunes had not taken a severe turn for the worse at this point. That is just what happened.

A woman of about 30, who had been hovering around the Franklin all afternoon, came over to the Durant owner and me and very earnestly asked for a moment in private with us. Her story was simple and compelling. Her father had begun to restore the Franklin years earlier, but had since contracted some terrible disease of the nervous system. He had lost his job as a machinist, his sight was badly impaired, and his hand-eye coordination was all but nonexistent. Still, he persisted in trying to restore his Franklin. It had become the most meaningful entity in his shattered life. He had come to derive his sense of self-worth as a human being from his engagement with this car. Due to his deteriorated senses, he had no idea what a botch he had made of it, and thought that he had done magnificent work. For reasons that are self-evident, no one had informed him otherwise.

The afternoon of the competition his daughter had told this sad story to her father's competitors at each rung of the competition. Because winning had become so important to

him, he had voted for himself and had unanimously won each round of the competition up to that point. After she left, the Durant owner—who turned out to be something of a jerk—suggested that her story might be a clever deception; a ruse to grab the brass ring and $100 for her dad. He said that it should be "each man for himself."

I told him that I would certainly vote for the Franklin and that he would inevitably lose by a 2-to-1 decision. I suggested that he stifle his greed and vote for the inevitable winner.

Part of the strange judging format that we were using that day called for the members of each three-car group of owner-judges to examine the other cars in each group together and to discuss their fine points. We started with the Franklin, and soon there was no doubt in my mind that the owner's daughter had been telling the truth about her father's condition and about the central role of the Franklin in his life. The poor fellow blindly and lovingly called our attention to each butchered detail of that miserable automobile. Almost nothing was missed. In addition to his other problems, the Franklin owner had very little knowledge of Franklins or of automobile restoration. During the tour of his car, he managed to point out several atrocities that he had committed against it that might have slipped past my cursory inspection. Of course, to him these atrocities were ingenious implementations of breathtaking new restoration techniques.

What a miserable mess. Muttering obscenities at fate, the Durant owner joined me and the Franklin owner and the award was unanimous to the Franklin.

There is a point to all of this. Different people see restoration, and particularly body restoration, differently, and the high standards that we are about to discuss are lost on many, if not most, people. I have seen the most miserable excuses for sheet metal work under paint applications that border on the criminal, which are held by the owners and craftsmen involved to be forms of perfection. And these people have no diagnosable maladies of perception. I also have seen—and this is important—work done to a standard that I cannot presently hope to duplicate. That is important because it is only when one recognizes one's present limits that improvements are possible.

Expectations

Stepping back from the gross and slovenly that are all too common in "commercial" autobody and refinishing work, there are gradations of workmanship, up to and including the truly excellent. The distinctions can be subtle. The art of metal finishing involves, in its final stages, manipulations of surfaces by two or three thousandths of an inch. That may sound like precision beyond the necessities of utility, but the human eye can distinguish dimensional surface deviations in these amounts in small expanses of sheet metal. Under certain conditions, a failure to hold surfaces to this fine standard can produce visibly devastating results in the final product.

Take the example of new cars, and this includes cars

from the lowliest Toyota to the lordliest BMW. Have you ever noticed that the finishes on new cars are often terrible? There is a reason for that, and it is instructive to examine it.

New cars are painted under conditions that are impossible to duplicate in refinish situations. The metal being painted is, or should be, completely free of defects and contamination. We are talking about pickled, freshly stamped, degreased and often galvanized metal. The air supply, primer and paint are provided or manufactured to standards of consistency and purity that are unattainable in aftermarket refinishing situations. The paint application is often done by laser-guided robots, with a precision that no human being can hope to match. Ambient air in the paint area and in the air lines is absolutely clean and dry. The paint itself is usually a "reflow" type that literally flows again after its initial set, when it is subjected to oven temperatures of 160 degrees F., or more, in huge bake ovens.

This is completely different from the air dry finishes that are used in the aftermarket, where "what you see" can be "what you get" after the first wet paint applications dry, except, of course, for the option of color sanding and "wheeling" a rough finish flat. Even though high-heat drying would be desirable with air-dry enamels, it is only possible to a limited extent because trimmed, upholstered and wired interiors will not take much heat in a refinish situation. So with all of its inherent advantages, why is some contemporary factory paint so often so terrible? Why does it always contain levels of orange peel that no restorer would tolerate?

The answer is simple. Today's car manufacturers have eliminated as much labor as possible from their production regimens. This means that die stamping has been reduced almost entirely to single (or at the extreme, double) draw operations. This helps to contain skilled labor costs, but limits both panel design and panel quality. It means that panels and the dies that stamp them are designed to reduce expensive die maintenance. Finally, it means that there is little opportunity for handwork in modern production painting processes. Inaccurately formed sheet metal somehow has to be made to look acceptable and to hide defects.

The answer is orange peel, purposely induced orange peel, to hide badly stamped sheet metal panels. This orange peel is guaranteed either in the basic paint chemistry that is used or by employing application standards that purposely will cause it—like running spray gun head pressures of 70 lbs. or more. The latter will guarantee ample orange peel to hide any manner of wavy panel stamping.

Sadly, the car-buying public has come to accept these citrus skin surfaces and little notice is taken of their essential ugliness. It was only in the early 1990s that new paints and new application technologies have combined with more accurate tolerances in sheet metal fit and higher finish standards to produce finishes that sometimes look almost as good as the old hand-rubbed factory finishes of many years ago. They call that "progress!"

Body and Refinish Standards Are Higher for Old Cars

The factory finishes on many of our collector cars were applied to very high standards. Early varnish finishes were laid down with brushes, and then sanded and pumiced by hand to perfection. These finishes involved incredibly cumbersome sequences of application, baking and sanding. Unfortunately, they often achieved the thickness of a dime. They were very expensive to apply. In fact, the old varnish, lacquer and baked enamel systems created bottlenecks in auto production that had to be removed before the massive volume figures of the late 1920s could become reality.

The answer was the invention of nitro-cellulose lacquer ("Duco") by DuPont in 1923, and synthetic (alkyd) enamel in 1929. These early synthesized finishes were more durable than their predecessors and were sprayable. The bottleneck was eliminated, and good, durable finishes became common on both cheap and expensive automobiles.

The bodies of middle-priced and upscale cars made in what we now think of as "the collector car era" were more robustly constructed than are the bodies of many cars today. Panel thickness was once commonly 18 gauge or more, as opposed to the present practice of 22 and 23 gauge or less. Stampings were often performed with multiple draws and levels of perfection were possible that are only beginning to reappear on a few high-end cars in the last decade.

One of the effects of having cars leave the factory with good-quality sheet metal and nearly perfectly applied finishes was to maintain good quality in the repair sector. The quality of repair has always tended to rise or fall to match production quality. In the "old days," body men pounded out dents, welded tears, and generally dealt with metal in ways that involved skills and care different from and way beyond what occurs in contemporary body shops. In part, this was because bodies were easier to work on, due to this thicker, softer metal in them and better access to the backs of panels. Fenders were most often bolted on, rather than welded on. This made types of repairs possible that are unthinkable today. Specialists, skilled in metal finishing and shrinking, were commonly available, whereas they are hard to find in today's body shops. On the other hand, modern equipment and materials for repairing autobodies and painting them have begun to close the quality gap in recent years.

In the 1950s, the development of polyester ("plastic") body fillers ushered in an age of unskilled and shoddy work in place of the craftsmanship that had, in many cases, gone before. The "rough 'em out, smooth 'em up" school of Bondo artists came to dominate the field of crash repair. Gradually, but certainly, the public came to accept low-quality sheet metal repair under badly applied finishes that happened to match the basic appearances of OEM sheet metal and finishes. Is it any wonder that it remains difficult to find commercial body shops capable of doing work to

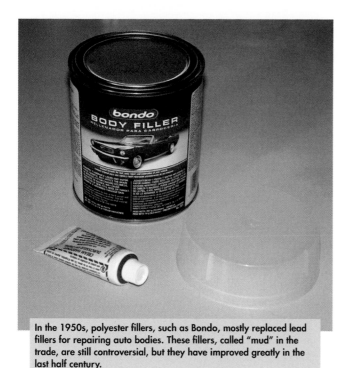

In the 1950s, polyester fillers, such as Bondo, mostly replaced lead fillers for repairing auto bodies. These fillers, called "mud" in the trade, are still controversial, but they have improved greatly in the last half century.

Old Crafts and New Technologies

It is almost amusing that Detroit, following the lead of European and Japanese manufacturers, is suddenly in a frenzy to improve "fit and finish," and to make (as the ad said) "Quality [is] Job #1." On all but the very cheapest American cars, fit and finish was always an important aspect of producing and marketing automobiles, and of repairing them. Lapses from high standards began in the 1950s. However, the new or reborn emphasis on fit and finish has one radically different aspect from what used to be called "quality."

Whereas quality formerly was in large part achieved by numerous manual operations requiring judgment, skill, coordination and experience, the new emphasis on fit and finish is largely an outgrowth of statistical analysis and digital manipulation. It's all numbers.

Take an example. Doors on cars used to fit because they were adjusted, either crudely or delicately, so that the jams and edges were even. Someone manually made them fit. Now, they fit because the basic forming, jigging and welding of the components involved is done by incredibly accurate machines, robots.

An avalanche of numerical data is crunched by computers and used to control complex and versatile machines that employ feedback to monitor and correct errors and mistakes. The result looks like craftsmanship in the old sense, but there is little skill or judgment involved at the production level. Now, the skill and knowledge are applied almost solely in engineering and specification.

A revolution of sorts also has been taking place in the repair sector. The crude old frame racks are being replaced by three-dimensional body/frame machines that can take a unitized body that is twisted like a pretzel and move its distorted structure until everything fits precisely. And all of that is done without a single hammer blow.

Take another example: GMAW (Gas Metal Arc Welding, usually, and incorrectly called "MIG") welding. With one of these machines—which now can be bought for less than $500—and a good grade of 0.023-inch wire, a virtually inexperienced operator can produce stronger and better looking welds than could formerly be done by a master craftsman with the arcane art of "hammer welding."

Skill in applying finishes has pretty much gone the way of chivalry, since it is possible to apply modern finishes, like catalyzed enamels and urethanes, and then color sand them and polish them. The results are not always restoration quality, but it can be frighteningly good.

The field of autobody restoration cannot ignore the new technologies, but must constantly evaluate them and their applications to restoration work. New cleaning techniques, like plastic media blasting (PMB) and new finishes, like powder coating, must be considered in restoration work.

However, it is not desirable to embrace all of the new products and procedures that come along as, for example, several restorers found out when they tried a "revolutionary

restoration standards?

Let me cite an example of this problem. Several years ago, I was invited to a very major paint manufacturer's local unveiling of a new automotive paint product line. I and several other guests at the event were shocked at the amount of orange peel in the examples of this product that the manufacturer proudly displayed. In the course of the unveiling, the manufacturer's representative demonstrated the application of this isocyanate hardened acrylic enamel system. He achieved the same orange peel results in his application that were evident in the samples on display.

I noted that his indicated spray gun pressure was 85 PSI at the wall regulator and 70 PSI at his gun's tailstock. When I suggested that this might be causing the orange peel, he laughed at me and said something to the effect of, "If you're so smart, let's see you do better." I took the challenge and reduced the air pressure to 45 PSI at the tailstock, after increasing the paint reduction from 125 percent to 180 percent. The result was far from great, but it was certainly a flatter paint application than the factory "rep" had been able to make. Most people know that too low gun pressure will produce orange peel. Fewer people know that too high gun pressure will produce the same result by pounding each coat into the coat under it. I had him. Right?

Wrong. He agreed that my application was flatter and looked better, but added that his application was far closer to new car factory standards. His point was that unless you were painting an entire car (a "complete") he had a better match to the rest of the OEM panels in the average contemporary car than I did. Unfortunately, he was right. My smoother, flatter paint was a likely mismatch with the average new car. The standards of modern manufacture and aftermarket work affect restoration in the very materials that are available—and sometimes unavailable—and in their recommended applications.

new" sprayable filler material several years ago. It fell out and lawsuits followed.

The sweet spot is to find appropriate levels of technology and to master their applications. Some tools and skills haven't changed much for thousands of years. The dollies, spoons, picks and hammers used by metal men have their origins in the hand tools used by coppersmiths in the Middle East thousands of years ago to form pots, pans and pitchers. This early tool repertoire was refined and expanded by tinsmiths and applied to the bodies of animal-drawn carriages in recent centuries.

At first, autobody construction involved tacking sheet metal to a wooden framework and hammering it smooth. The technologies for such refinements as welding, filling and painting evolved gradually, as did the expectation that the results of these crafts should look nice.

To my knowledge, the basis of good sheet metal work, metal finishing, has not changed in basic outline or in many particulars since the beginning of the age of the automobile. What has changed is our willingness to take the time to develop the skills to accomplish metal finishing.

A few developments, like the arrival power hammers (Yoder and Pettingell) in the 20th century have improved efficiency and productivity at the high end of custom sheet metal fabrication, but the bulk of metal shaping endeavors is little changed in the last 100 years.

Without going into the fine details, metal finishing is the business of conforming sheet metal surfaces to their correct shapes by dollying, bumping, picking and filing them. Occasionally, shrinking is required, and sometimes filling low spots with lead is necessary. Properly, most of this work is done with simple body hammers and dollies, and with a very clear understanding of the limits and capabilities of the material on which the work is being performed—sheet metal.

Sadly, contemporary body practice is too often to pound out dents crudely, often doing additional damage to the metal, and then to glob the results over with polyester body filler. Such repairs lack permanence and are usually visible to an experienced eye, even under skillfully applied paint. Our discussion of sheet metal work in this book will not consider the "rough 'em out, smooth 'em up" variety of auto bodywork. It will also skip the easy option of panel replacement that exists in modern body repair, because that option usually is not available to restorers.

Goals and Necessities

The need for safety is nowhere more crucial than in bodywork and refinishing. Like other aspects of automotive restoration, bodywork is laden with both obvious and hidden hazards. Eye, ear, lung and skin protection fit into this obvious category, but there are also hazards that are subtle.

The tin/lead filler used in bodywork tends to produce lead oxides at elevated temperatures that are deadly to breathe. The lead filings and dust that are generated in bodywork can penetrate human skin and produce lead poisoning. Some of the automotive finishes that are on the market are significantly more toxic than the older ones that they have replaced although none of the solvents in solvent-based finishes are particularly safe to breathe or to get on your skin. When you get into isocyanate-hardened paints, you should take label cautions *very* seriously.

One bodywork and refinishing restoration goal that is often botched is to adopt a logical sequence of attack. My shop once worked on a Jaguar XK 150 on which another restoration shop had already spent a fortune of time and money with no good result. This car arrived with all panels painted and repaired, and a nice white enamel finish in place. The only problem was that it still had to be rewired, its interior had to be removed and replaced and a complete mechanical restoration had to be performed.

After our mechanical, electrical and (subcontracted) upholstery work was finished, we stripped the paint, repaired some body defects and refinished the car's exterior panels. The time and money that had been spent painting the car's body the first time were wasted. Clearly, the sequence in which this car's original restorer had attempted to do the work was inefficient.

While there is debate over whether to refurbish a car's interior before or after painting its panels, it is generally most effective to make refinishing the last step in a restoration. Certainly, mechanical work should be completed before finish top coats are applied. The nature of what you are attempting to accomplish will dictate a logical sequence of attack, so figure out an approach. Don't just proceed at random.

Judgment in the abstract is easy to cultivate. The question "what do you do when..." is always easier to answer as an exercise than when you have the stuff in your hands and you want to do something...quick. You have to work at developing judgment, and you must be vigilant to maintain the authority of that judgment. It is amazing what atrocities are committed with body tools and refinish materials in the late hours of the night and wee hours of the morning.

Work habits fall into the same category as judgment—they only have value when they are not suspended in emergencies. Usually, lapses of these two essentials of good work go together. In the end, good work habits controlled by sure judgment produce craftsmanship results. There is no place in this proposition for luck, good or bad. When the time and trouble are taken to learn to do something right, it should become an inalienable possession. At the very least, don't alienate it yourself.

Permanence is the unseen component of high-quality body restoration. Of course, what is seen immediately is important, but durability is really the main issue.

Of particular importance is corrosion resistance. Here, impeccable habits, such as neutralizing soldering fluxes and killing tallow residues (from leading) become paramount. Both gross and subtle errors in judgment, such as using lap welds instead of butt welds or brazing body joints instead of welding them, will limit durability and ruin your

Of all the hazards in body restoration work, lung hazards are among the most subtle and deadly. The foam and paper breathing masks shown on the right have very specific and limited uses—to filter out airborne dust and sanding particles. They will not filter out evaporating solvents and should only be used for sanding operations and never for breathing protection when you are painting. The two masks on the left will adequately protect your lungs with some paints, but others will require an outside, pumped air supply. Be sure to consult manufacturers' recommendations on this issue. No protective filter will work when it is dirty or contaminated. It is important to change filters and pre-filters regularly on these devices. Old and new pre-filters and filters are shown in front of the double canister breathing apparatus on the far left.

efforts before their time. Auto body paint is an unforgiving medium. It can magnify small mistakes in what was done to the metal that lies below it. Small mistakes can come back and haunt you years later. Have you ever seen paint check, blister, peel, dull or crow's foot? Somewhere in the chains of events that led to these kinds of defects, you will find one or more mistakes.

Up to this point, this discussion of bodywork and refinishing sounds pretty goody-goody, including, as it has, topics like safety, judgment, cleanliness, etc.

I'm here to tell you that bodywork and refinishing are distinctly not goody-goody. Somewhere in good bodywork, you usually will find evidence of larceny, fraud and deception. That's right, while bodywork is a matter of fine judgments and subtle appearances, it necessarily is performed with materials and skills that rarely yield absolute perfection without a little bit of help. There is often need for trickery—real smoke and mirrors stuff. Here are some examples.

It can be difficult or impossible to match paint color exactly. If fenders and doors are assembled with a mismatch of "half a shade," (there really is no exact definition of a "shade") or more, the careful eye will sight along a body panel end, like a door seam, and the mouth that is attached to the same brain as the eye will mumble, "mismatch." The

eye can make that distinction, and the mouth is frequently impossible to shut up.

Of course, the eye finds the mismatch exactly where it expects to see it, at the edge of a panel. It is easy to see it there, so long experience has taught the eye to look for a mismatch there. By now, a parallel expanse of slightly mismatched panel edges will show it up like Rudolph the Red-Nosed Reindeer's schnaz at a New Jersey garden party.

If, on the other hand, a slight mismatch is blended into the middle of a door or fender in a wavy line, the eye is less likely to spot it there because it will be mistaken for a phenomenon of varying light—maybe for a reflection off the ground or a projection of sunlight through clouds. The eye pretty much sees what it expects to see. That fact can be used to advantage to trick it into seeing what the metal man/painter/magician wants it to see. Judgment enters in when you restrain yourself from trying to hide a "two-shade mismatch" with the "tricks of the trade."

OK, the fewer tricks, the better, but some are necessary. While it is important to shrink body metal into an approximation of its original lateral dimensions, some excess metal can be hidden in the high crown areas of body panels. If this kind of thing is not done, body work becomes endless.

There are certain realities of automobile construction

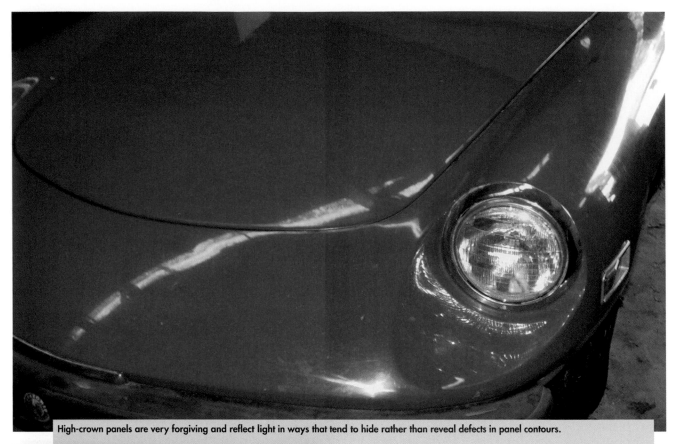

High-crown panels are very forgiving and reflect light in ways that tend to hide rather than reveal defects in panel contours.

that will both encourage and limit how much Houdini you can bring to what you are doing. Automobiles are bilateral, which means that for the most part their right and left sides are mirror opposites of each other. This would limit the variation that you could engage in from one side of a car to the other but for the important fact that cars are rarely parked in front of mirrors, and no one I know has perfected the business of seeing both sides of a car at once. Bodywork on both sides of a car should create a great similarity of

features and dimensions, but absolute mirror image fidelity is beyond what is necessary and was rarely achieved on the premises of factories or custom body builders, anyway. Remember some of this before you go all out to measure and jig for the perfection of a panel contour that no one will ever notice because the only points of comparison are to the other side of a car.

Pitfalls and Worse

Here are a few of the thousands of things to avoid in this work.

The first is buying a car that has had its bodywork butchered. While it can be difficult to tell how much Bondo and how many pop rivets and bits of roofing tin lurk under shiny paint, some determinations are possible. I would advise spending as much time as is necessary to discover this kind of concealed damage, because there is nothing worse than the queasy feeling that you get when you discover it, "... Oh no! Someone's been here before."

Most auto body butchers will work in ways that tend to thicken panels, but they must contour their unauthorized dimensional additions back where the ends of their butchery meet adjacent panels. When you see a panel that seems to fall away in the last few centimeters before its edge, watch out. Often, when a door panel has been built up excessively with filler, you will see the thickness at its edges, or you will see the panel fall away towards its repaired edges in its final

It doesn't take much experience or imagination to see that filler has been used excessively to hide damage in the two situations that are shown here. The panel contours are very uneven. The panels certainly did not leave the factory that way. Creeping rust is the final indication and result of "gobbing it on."

few centimeters.

Closely related to that kind of butcher-work is the artistry that is sometimes practiced in creating modified and inauthentic bodies. Usually, these are easy to spot—touring cars don't often look exactly like sedans below their beltlines—but some of this work is subtle. The fellows selling examples of it tend to have one thing in common—they sweat a lot.

Obviously, some materials, such as fiberglass bandages and pop rivets, should never be used in restoration work, but misusing proper materials can be just as destructive, and honest people sometimes do this.

Here are two general "don'ts." Never mix paint product lines, and stick with known brands of refinishing supplies. About two or three times a year, someone tries to sell me no-name, $4-a-gallon lacquer thinner in 55-gallon drums. The economics are attractive, but the results are invariably unlovely if this stuff is actually used to thin lacquer.

Always remember that a finish will suffer from, and magnify, any mistake that lurks below its outermost aspect. Bodywork is the foundation on which filler, primer and paint build. A defect underneath will probably cause any finish to unravel like a cheap sweater.

Specialties

It is possible to do credible work in the areas of

bodywork and refinishing with a minimal amount of equipment. What you attempt will depend mostly on the skills and conditions that you have acquired and created. If you are just starting out, you will find lacquer work easier than enamel work because lacquer is a very forgiving finish and is almost endlessly susceptible to repair and rework. Unless you have substantially greater skills and a very dust-free environment, I would avoid a more difficult finish, such as alkyd enamel, which tends to be very intolerant of

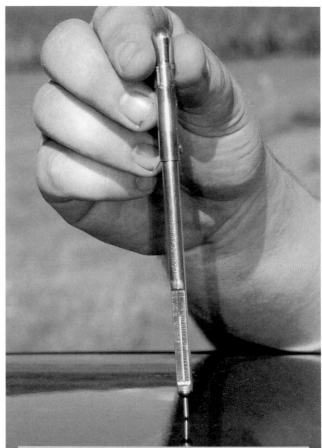

If you don 't have an eye for spotting the excessive use of plastic or lead filler, I highly recommend magnetic tools, like those shown here, to make that determination. The Tinsley gauge (above and top left) is expensive, but will indicate paint thickness accurately in mils. It will also read the use of small amounts of filler. Less accurate and much less expensive versions of magnetic paint thickness gauges are also available. The Spot Rot (at left) is inexpensive, but will reveal the use of excessive filler. I recommend magnetic coating and filler thickness tools, even if you do have a good eye for filler. More accurate ultrasonic coating thickness gauges are nice instruments, but are probably overkill for investigating overly thick paint and filler applications.

substandard application or poor application conditions.

If you subcontract your body or paint work, you will find very few practitioners in the commercial repair sector who are capable of doing quality restoration work. You will also find restoration shops to be very expensive for this sort of work—they have to be to maintain quality. Materials, supplies and equipment overhead are major expenses, as is the labor of skilled craftsmen. For example, a set of air intake filters for our spray booth now costs over $200, and a set will only last for two or three cars.

Some specialty work, such as striping—never with a wheel—has to go to specialists. I couldn't begin to develop these skills if my life depended on it, and I don't know many people who could. Other specialties, such as panel fabrication and welding, may involve combinations of skills

and equipment that are impractical for the amateur restorer to acquire. On the other hand, they may not. I have learned to do "amazing things" with a small sheet metal brake, rawhide mallets, a shot bag and a gas welding setup. The level of satisfaction that comes from some mastery of this work is enormous.

I have suggested that there are times when a smoke-and-mirrors approach to bodywork and refinishing is necessary, but there is also a basic, enforced honesty in bodywork. Even with the aid of a $49.95 hammer and dolly starter kit, complete with full instructions for metalworking, an inexperienced metalworker will not accomplish Michelangelo-like metal finishing his or her first time out. With some practice, he or she may get acceptable results. Your basic Sears paint spray outfit, used in a dusty garage, will not produce good quality refinish work. However, if you clean and vacuum that garage carefully, and use the Sears sprayer with skill, the results can be surprisingly good, but always short of great.

Chapter 21

Sheet Metal Basics

The three books shown here are the most basic and important texts for the metal man. The one on the left evolved from a tool catalog and was the first systematic guide to auto body sheet metal work. The two on the right are really the same book in different issues. They offer a comprehensive understanding of auto body sheet metal work.

SHEET METAL WORK FALLS INTO TWO REALMS, manual arts and technical skills. The strategies for and operations of removing complex deformations (a.k.a. "dents") from sheet metal body parts are so variable as to make choosing between them an art in itself.

There is usually no single correct approach to such a complex task, and various approaches may produce virtually equal results. Of course, there are also numerous substandard or incorrect approaches to this work that can hide original damage while actually producing further, hidden damage.

Because elements of judgment, efficiency, experience and even inspiration are possible in sheet metal work, it borders on being an art. However, other aspects of sheet metal work, such as hammering, welding and knowing the effects of heat on this material, are highly technical and require a clear understanding of cause and effect before you can understand and perform them successfully. These are really technical areas that can be demonstrated scientifically. The result of all of this is that good sheet metal work requires a study of basic technical factors, experience in the actual work and imagination and ingenuity in approaching some of the more difficult problems posed by sheet metal repair.

There are several textbooks that deal with automotive

sheet metal and refinish work, in particular, and that devote one or more chapters to sheet metal repair, in general. Some of these books are fairly useful for beginners, but many of them are designed for use in conjunction with classroom instruction. The latter really don't work very well without it.

While it is possible to approach some mechanical repair operations with "the book open" on a fender, this will never do for body restoration and refinishing. As well, classroom guides will tend to tell you just enough to make you dangerous, and will often overlook much that is basic. That's the best of them. The worst of them tend to describe procedures, operations and materials in ways that are completely and perfectly understandable, as long as you understood these things *before* you read the descriptions of how to do them.

There are two books that I think really do provide useful insights into how to deal with various aspects of steel sheet metal repair. Unfortunately, one of them is too cursory for most people and the other is too detailed. However, if you are new to this work, you should have a look at both of them.

The Key to Metal Bumping by Frank T. Sargent was first issued in the late 1930s and was basically a user's guide to the body tools made by the Fairmont Forge Company. Various revisions and editions followed the original issue, and by the third edition (1953) this book had become a pretty good treatise on the "Fairmont Method" of dealing with sheet metal repair. The third edition also included all sorts of helpful hints regarding welding and other skills. The basic premise of the book is that you must employ a specific method to straightening sheet metal. You cannot just go in with a hammer and start banging out things that seem to be in, or vice versa.

The method proposed in *The Key...* involves distinguishing between permanently deformed metal and metal held out of place by permanently deformed metal. The prescription for repair is to analyze the order in which damage occurred during the impact that caused it, and to remove it in the reverse order. *The Key...* is a short book and leaves a lot unsaid, but it is a good basic guide to the field of dinging out and metal finishing sheet metal.

At the times of its issue and revisions, *The Key...* was almost revolutionary in proposing a method of analysis and plan of attack to confront sheet metal repair work. I would suggest that the proposed plan is useful, but not the only way to approach these problems. In any case, *The Key...* is a good place to start the study of sheet metal work. It is also readily available from a number of old car hobby booksellers and from suppliers of autobody tools and supplies.

Automobile Sheet Metal Repair, by Robert L. Sargent (Chilton), and its newest revision, *Chilton's Mechanics Handbook, Volume 3: Autobody Sheet Metal Repair* is the most comprehensive general book that I know of on this subject. Whereas *The Key...* makes this work sound wonderfully easy and simple, Sargent confounds the reader with the full complexity of every aspect of the analysis

and remedial operations involved. This sure isn't bedtime reading if you want to sleep at night, but if you take the time to read it and understand it, you will gain a good grasp on the theory and the practice of this work. I recommend it highly for those dedicated to learning how to perform this craft.

One thing that you will get from reading these books, or the rest of this chapter, is the concept that sheet metal repair involves more than just beating or pushing out a dent. Beyond that, there are approaches that will efficiently yield a repair that looks good, is permanent, uses no or very little filler and restores the basic integrity of a damaged panel. That, of course, is the object. However, no matter how many articles, books, pamphlets, videotapes, CDs, DVDs and seminars you absorb on this topic, experience is still essential to perfecting your sheet metal technique.

NEVER attempt to do work like this solely based on book knowledge. The best approach is to find some old body panels: doors, fenders, hoods, etc., and damage and repair them yourself to get the feel of the thing. Armed with a basic knowledge of the craft, you will learn more in five or six hours of experimentation with real sheet metal parts than you would have thought possible. I stress this point because I have seen body panels and whole cars ruined by people who thought that body work was as simple as skilled practitioners or glossy tool sales pamphlets make it look. It isn't. Scrap panels are cheap, but the repair of the damage you can do to a treasured car will be expensive.

In addition to practicing your technique on scrap panels during your early learning, you can often try new or alternative strategies out on them. Sometimes, it's easy to duplicate in scrap approximately the actual damage in something that you are working on. Then, you can experiment to determine what the most effective repair strategy will be. Scrap panels also provide a wonderful inventory of formed metal sections for repair purposes. It's amazing how often you can find an area or part of a scrap panel that can be modified for a specific place or purpose that you have. This can save hours of work with rawhide mallets and shot bags.

There are many neat tricks in bodywork that can save time and promote quality, but there are also some very bad "dirty tricks." In each case, it is important to know why something is supposed to work rather than just taking someone's word for it. Over the years, manufacturers have come up with many tools and materials that don't work at all, or that work only to a limited extent or in limited situations. Take, for example, panel flanging tools. There are very few applications where these tools can be used appropriately and to advantage. Mostly, they are used to save time and to reduce the skill levels that otherwise would have been required to fit panels properly for butt-welding. When used improperly, these tools stop being neat tricks and become devices of destruction. In these cases, either experience or common sense, or both, should guide you away from such misuses.

Then, there are the really dirty approaches that should

The following sequence of photographs describes a basic work hardening experiment in sheet metal. It illustrates how work hardening occurs, and what its effects are. The factor of work hardening is critical to auto bodywork and restoration because it limits how far you can move metal without annealing it. The experiment involves a strip of 22-gauge sheet metal. It will be deformed and straightened with a pair of sheet metal pliers, and then with a low-crown body hammer on an anvil.

The metal is placed in the pliers and bent by hand as close to the pliers Jaws as possible.

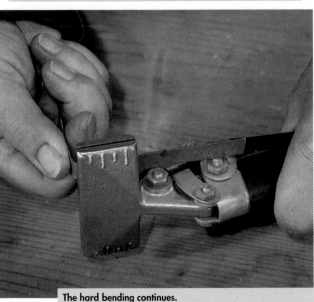

The hard bending continues.

never (as opposed to "almost never") be used. Drilling holes and using body hooks or welding studs to sheet metal to pull it when it could have been pounded out from behind come readily to mind. I realize that you will see so-called "professionals" doing this stuff and, in fact, I see several examples of these and other barbaric "techniques" on display at automotive trade shows every year. They may work well enough to meet the needs of low-end commercial work. That doesn't make them right for restoration work. Intuition and common sense should tell you which approaches are damaging and which are in the interests of the preservation of old automobiles.

One of the nice things about sheet metal work is that simple tools and simple approaches are often best suited to the needs of repair and restoration. Seemingly complex problems can often be subdivided into a series of simpler problems and tasks, and solved simply. While fancy clamping, pulling, pushing, and bumping tools are available, a few good hammers and dollies, along with the skill to use them properly, will almost always provide the best basis for restoration repair work on sheet metal.

This is not to argue against some of the sophisticated equipment and techniques out there, but just to state that knowledge and experience are always the starting points in this work, and that much of what passes for sophistication in the modern repair sector has very little application to old car restoration.

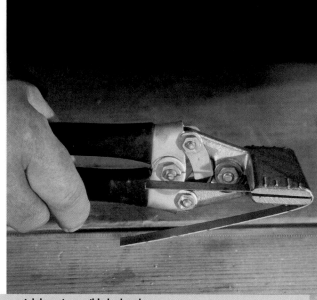

The bending continues until the sheet metal is bent back around the pliers' jaws as tightly as is possible by hand.

Sheet Metal: Composition, Fabrication and Basic Characteristics

The sheet metal used for automobile panel fabrication, and for some panel support structures, is a highly evolved and complex series of alloys based in the steel family. Sheet steel uses several alloying components to achieve desirable characteristics. The most important of these is carbon, which is added to steel in concentrations of between 1/4 and 3/4 of 1 percent, (usually near 1/4 percent for automotive sheet metal). Because many operations are involved in converting a basic slab of raw steel into what we call "sheet metal," the choice of characteristics that alloying is designed to accomplish must begin with these transformations in mind. Beyond that, automotive sheet metal has to be die-formed into complex shapes, trimmed and sometimes flanged. In many cases, it also has to be weldable for attachment purposes. These needs dictate the specific constitution of the steel used in automobiles.

Numerous technical terms define the physical characteristics of steels. These include elasticity, hardness, ductility, plasticity, yield strength, toughness and so forth. Each of these terms, and several others, has a specific meaning when used to describe steel.

The descriptive terms that are of most interest to us are plasticity and elasticity. The first, plasticity, describes the ability of steel to be formed by pressure (dies) without tearing, cracking or otherwise failing. The second term, elasticity, involves the ability of steel to deform and subsequently spring back to its original shape without any change in that shape.

In both cases, the key phenomenon is the presence or absence of something called "work hardening." This phenomenon is of crucial interest to those who work with sheet metal. It involves the fact that as sheet steel is deformed (by die stamping, accidental impact or a repairman's hammer), its crystalline structure changes with the effect that it becomes harder and thus more resistant to further change. The classic example of this is a demonstration with a paper clip, which begins life as a piece of straight wire and is then bent into its customary shape.

Yet, if you attempt to straighten one of the bends in a paper clip by grasping its straight sections 1/2 inch back from a bend and applying force in the reverse direction from which it was applied to make the bend, the wire will not straighten completely. Instead, the metal on either side of the original bend will ultimately deform before the bend is completely removed. Photos that accompany this chapter make this point with regard to a 1/2-inch-wide strip of 22-gauge body steel.

What has happened in this example is that the original bend that I put in the strip of mild steel has work hardened it to the point that when I apply counter-pressure to it to remove the bend, I create two more deformations on either side of the original one. It is easier for the metal adjacent to the original bend to yield than it is for the metal in the original bend to yield because that metal has been work hardened by its original deformation.

The phenomenon of work hardening is critical in the design and fabrication of sheet metal automobile panels. It is both a problem for, and an asset to, anyone who has to repair sheet metal. The asset is that the areas where dies have deformed sheet metal from its original flat state provide much of the necessary panel strength in body design. The problem is that when a panel must be straightened due to impact damage, it will have hardened in several places and in ways that may make it difficult to straighten it without inducing additional deformations.

It was hardened in the original stamping process of its manufacture. It has been further hardened by road

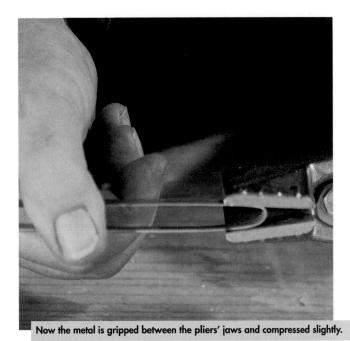

Now the metal is gripped between the pliers' jaws and compressed slightly.

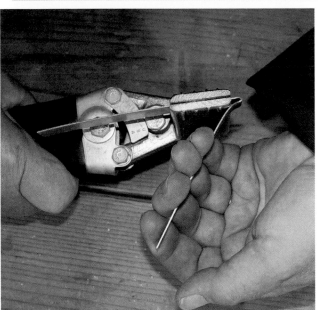

The metal strip is now gripped in the pliers as close to the bend as possible, and an attempt is made to bend it back straight by hand.

vibration, which is particularly prevalent in configurations like pontoon fenders. Finally, impact damage has further hardened it. Now, it may be difficult or impossible to get the panel bumped back into shape without dealing with the work hardening of the metal that is holding it in its deformed shape.

Sometimes, you can work around work hardening by adopting a repair strategy that forces things back into place in spite of it. In the case of the infamous paper clip, it is possible to bend it almost back into a straight wire if the work-hardened legs of the bend are supported close enough to the center of the bend during the reforming operation. It is also possible to hammer it flat on a vise or anvil. In other cases, the effects of work hardening are so severe that the metal involved will readily fracture before it can be

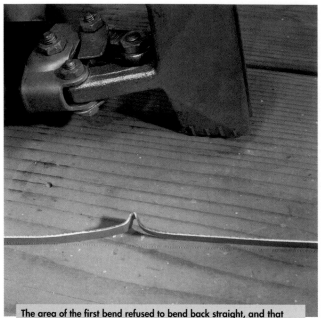

The area of the first bend refused to bend back straight, and that the metal on either side of it has yielded to the reverse bending pressure first. This is because the metal in the original bend was work hardened and provided more resistance to bending than the unbent metal on either side of it. Without some further intervention, this is as straight as the author's wife can get the steel strip with her hands and a pair of sheet metal pliers. This is a visibly dramatic demonstration of the work hardening phenomenon. It also is very similar to what happens when you attempt to hammer a crease out of a fender by hammering directly on the crease.

hammered or forced back into its original shape.

In these cases, heating the affected area to its "transformation temperature" is usually the best solution. This process is called "annealing." Auto body sheet metal will lose the effects of work hardening if it is heated to temperatures of about 1,600 degrees F. and air cooled. The application of such heat allows the crystalline structure of the metal to rearrange itself in ways that undo work hardening effects. The problem is that this solution may produce a panel, or areas of a panel, that have little of the hardness that was stamped into them originally. Since the original stamping was probably designed to induce work hardening into the panel's critical areas as an element of its structural strength, annealing can create structural weaknesses. Heating followed by water quenching (rapid cooling) is the most common solution to selectively re-hardening metal in ways that maintain some of the original hardness of the die stamped panel.

The die-stamping process is a wonderful thing to behold in an automobile stamping plant. When you see it, you can appreciate the enormous forces at work when automobile panels are manufactured. In the stamping operation, huge dies (108 inches long dies are pretty standard for large panels) that weigh many tons are forced together under enormous pressure with sheet metal between them. The dies are often lubricated if they are the "deep draw" variety. The first action of their closing is for "binder rings" to clamp the metal at its edges before the dies deform it. If this were not done, metal would be pulled into the die and would wrinkle under the pressure of the closing die faces.

More recent stamping technology employs even more massive and complex tri-axle transfer presses that literally roll shapes into metal.

Following the stamping process, trimming operations and (sometimes) flanging operations occur. In almost every case, the areas of high deformation, such as creases that run the length of a panel, are put there to give the metal strength by purposely work hardening areas that will bear stress or load in service.

The sculpted and ridged sides of automobiles are usually as much accommodations to the needs of structural design as to the whimsies of styling. Of course, some areas of great deformation are there for the necessities of function, as, for example, the formed ends of panels on a car that wrap around so that the car can end!

The die stamping operation produces three types of panel area, and infinite combinations of these three. The three basic types are: high crown, low crown and reverse crown. It is critical to distinguish between them when you repair damaged automobile panels.

High crown panels are those with a great deal of curvature in all directions. They have a rounded appearance and fall away from a point both north and south, east and west. These are, of course, panels that have been substantially deformed in the die stamping process. They usually are much easier to work with than low crown panels because they have fewer tendencies to buckle under heat or when they are hammered on after they have been deformed or mildly stretched by impact or by previous repair. When high crown panels are properly finished, they tend to reflect light in a way that is forgiving, even if their exact original curvatures are not retained in repair.

In contrast, low crown panels are quite flat and have very little curvature north, south, east and west. They may have curvature in one direction, like the top of a door or fender, where the format is usually a simple bend in one direction. The slab-sided doors on Lincoln Continentals in the early 1960s are another example of low crown panels. Low crown panels have little of the internal strength of high crown panels because they underwent very little deformation and work hardening in their die stamping process. Strength is often added to low crown panels by adding supports, or sometimes by forming them in the pre-stressed ("monocoque") construction that is occasionally borrowed from aircraft design for advanced automobile design.

Low crown panels can be very hard to work with because, if they are large, any stretching will make them buckle when they are returned to their correct shapes, unless the stretched extra lateral dimensions of the panels can be chased to their edges or hidden in high crown areas somewhere else. Otherwise, they have to be shrunk accurately when they have been stretched. This can be a very difficult repair procedure.

A particularly common variant of this problem occurs in restoration work when cars with very flat doors have had those doors fill with water and rust out for several inches

To really straighten this strip and to overcome the work hardening in its bend, would take mechanical force, as is shown here. This will tend to stretch the metal, unless it is done very gently. Keep these characteristics of sheet metal in mind when you go to straighten out a ridge, V-channel or buckle in a mild steel panel.

along their bottoms. Any welding process that is used to section in new metal will produce some degree of heat distortion in the door skin. This must be painstakingly eliminated.

In four-door cars, the back doors usually must have contours that match the front doors, thus continuing the body lines. The door pairs on each side of the car will have to reflect light in a way that indicates that the panel match is uniform and continuous. If this cannot be done, I would suggest that the car always be parked in the middle of a large field or unlined parking lot, and away from anything distinctive that may reflect light off of its sides and indicate the problem! Good luck.

Reverse crown panels are simply high crown panels in concave configurations. Reverse crown areas are sometimes found between fenders and trunks, among other places.

Like high crown panels, they are usually easier to work with than low crown panels, but they often present unique access problems.

Obviously, most old car body panels are combinations of high and low crown areas with an occasional reverse crown thrown in. When a choice is available as to where to weld a patch seam or where small amounts of stretched metal should be relocated, high and reverse crown areas are good bets, as long as they are not weakened by annealing or by changes in curvature in the process.

A final characteristic of auto body sheet metal that should be considered is its basic gauge or thickness. There are half a dozen gauge wire and sheet steel gauge standards running around out there, but automotive material is generally described by the "Manufacturers Standard Gauge for Sheet Steel" standard. In this system, the gauge number

Many collector cars exhibit combinations of high and low crown panels. This Cord's fenders are very high crowned in many areas but the doors, sides, cowl and hood are very low crown panels.

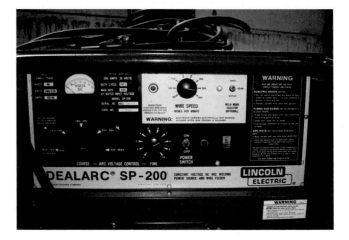

"MIG" welding has revolutionized some aspects of auto body work. The unit above cost nearly $2,000 in the early 1980s and is big and bulky. While it had all of the features of a modern MIG welder, it lacked a solid state contactor and was somewhat cumbersome to use. Units like these were sold only by specialty welding shops and suppliers.

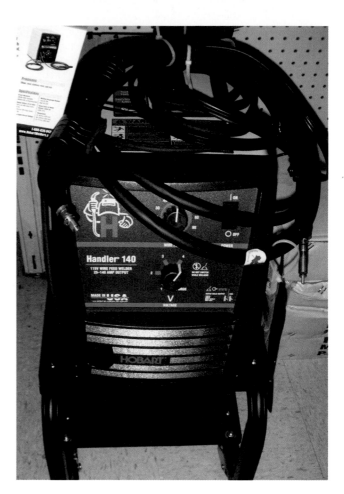

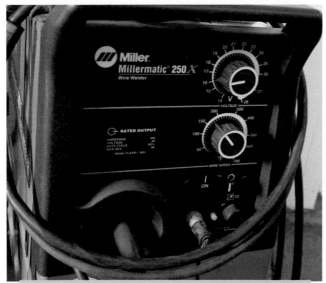

Modern MIG welders, like these, are easy to use, precise and inexpensive. You can buy them in many retail stores these days.

is the number of pieces of steel of a specific thickness that can be fit into an inch. Thus, 2-gauge would be 1/2 inch thick; 4-gauge would 1/4 inch thick, and so forth.

Automotive sheet metal once ran in the range of 18-gauge, which was 48 thousandths of an inch thick (actually 0.0478 inch). 20-gauge became common in more recent times, and this meant 0.0359-inch-thick metal—still a lot to work with in bumping and metal finishing. However, more recently, 22-gauge (0.0299-inch) has become common, and now 23- and 24-gauge (0.0269- and 0.0239-inch, respectively) have appeared on the scene under the euphemistic name, "high-strength steel." This dreaded (by real metal men) and miserable stuff contributes slightly, I suppose, to lightening automobiles, but carries with it a host of problems. The first is that the alloys used to make it are difficult to form in repair situations because they are relatively hard (high carbon) and have very little elasticity. Check out the decklids on some modern minivans and hatchbacks in any parking lot and note the dents and creases

left by people's hands when they have been overly energetic in slamming them shut.

The high-strength steels are also so thin that in areas where salt and moisture are a problem, they exhibit rust perforation alarmingly soon after their manufacture. The elaborate, much ballyhooed and highly advertised anti-corrosion treatments being applied to them are, in fact, necessitated by the thinness of the material from which cars are fabricated. There is some hope, however, because some manufacturers have begun to increase panel thickness slightly on some of their newest cars.

The gauge of the metal with which you are working may determine, in large part, the best repair approach. If, for example, at some future date people decide to restore some of the econoboxes that graced our streets and roads as new cars in recent years, they had better locate a good supply of NOS body panels before they undertake such projects. Many contemporary panels are too thin and too hard to hammer straight when they are seriously deformed. Traditional metal finishing techniques are out of the question because files tend to skate over their high carbon metal or, if they do cut, they weaken the panels grievously or cut right through them. Even disk sanding them can be a hair-raising experience if you are not super careful.

The good news is that the thick, relatively soft metal in most collector car bodies is very susceptible to straightening, welding and metal finishing. When some of the newer technologies, such as MIG (properly GMAW) welding, are

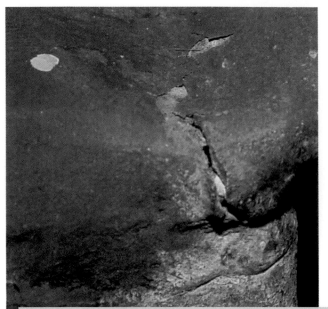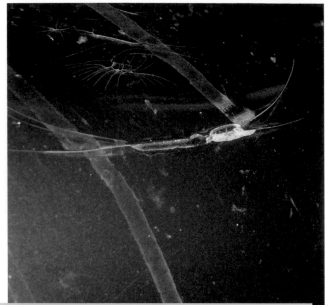

In the fenders in these two photos stress cycles, and probably minor impact, have combined to cause damage. Corrosion has begun under fractured paint and added to the problems. The first photo is of the front of a steel fender. The second shows the side of an aluminum alloy fender.

applied to them, repair becomes so easy that it is permissible to listen to the radio while you are working.

Basic hammer and dolly work, shrinking operations and welding operations applied to old cars are attainable skills, not the impossible dreams that they sometimes seem to be when you attempt to apply them to most contemporary autobody sheet metal.

Acquired Characteristics in Old and Damaged Sheet Metal

The types of damages that can occur to collector car sheet metal are just about unlimited. The most common, by far, are corrosion damage and impact damage. Beyond this, each car that you work on is likely to exhibit some daring innovations in the field of possible sheet metal defects. Stress cracking occurs routinely in some areas of some cars. Wood-framed bodies often exhibit structural shifting that deforms sheet metal, while swelled framing wood can bulge sheet metal in ways that are difficult to resolve. In cars with welded and spot welded attachments, a combination of vibration and corrosion can cause things to break loose and move in ways that produce major messes.

Yet with all of these possibilities, the damage that I most dread is that done by people armed with minimum knowledge, bad attitudes, heavy hammers and the misconception that they are in the body repair business. When these types and their minions add acetylene torches, plasma arc cutters and pop rivet guns to their basic repertoire of chipped hammers and hardened-screw-tipped slide hammers, they become a definite menace to the welfare of sheet metal everywhere.

It is sometimes difficult to fathom the degree of

imbecility and the resulting destruction that some of these Bondo artists have done to the panels of the poor automobiles that have had the misfortune to come under their hammers. Instead of carefully analyzing the nature of the panel damage that confronts them and repairing it in non-destructive ways, these minor thinkers apply the heaviest hammers or biggest pry bars that they can wield against damaged areas of metal, literally bashing things back toward their right places. In that barbaric process, they produce stretching, further deformation and work hardening that are difficult to correct later.

When confronted with rust or torn metal, sectioning and butt-welding are usually beyond their limited skill levels, so out come the flanging tools, brazing rods, and pop rivet tools. More damage inevitably follows.

These guys buy plastic filler by the 55-gallon drum and the only apparent limit to their use of this stuff seems to be that they never allow the weight of the filler to exceed the weight of the original automobile. Aside from the fact that this kind of work has a life expectancy of between 6 months to 2 years, it always produces severe problems when it has to be reworked by someone who wants to do it right. OK, you've been warned. Also, as always, avoid seeing things in stereotypes.

The two most common forms of sheet metal damage, corrosion and impact, should be dealt with in very specific ways. Corrosion damage must be detected by investigation that employs physically picking and probing, in addition to visual inspection. This may seem brutal, but all kinds of corrosion can be lurking under seemingly sound paint. Certainly, where paint has bubbled and/or blistered, there is good cause to suspect underlying corrosion. A scratch awl is your best guide to its extent. Where body contours appear to be modified, or where panels are 1/8 inch thick, or more, you will often find rust, fiberglass bandages, pop riveted roofing tin and any manner of other mischief underneath

The damage here is corrosion damage, with maybe a little stress damage thrown in. This rust-through was probably initiated by gravel and road debris chipping the paint. Rust then began in small areas and lifted more paint, causing more rusting.

the surface.

Flanged and brazed panel patches are also frequently found under bubbling paint. Sometimes, and this is almost a pleasant surprise, filler will be used to cover dents and other impact damage because the attempted repair involved difficult access to the back of a panel or the individual making the repair lacked the skill and/or commitment to bump the panel into correct its contours. Alas, more often than not in these cases, a slide hammer and hardened screw, body hooks, or welded studs were used to pull dents out crudely, and what lurks under the Bondo is serious corrosion damage, made worse by this kind of attempted repair.

The drift of all of this is that the only proper way to repair corrosion damage that perforates sheet metal is to weld in new metal, and the only proper way to deal with impact deformation is to beat it back out in ways that produce the least stretching and buckling of the metal.

Sometimes, small amounts of filler are necessary. When this is the case, body lead (actually an alloy of tin and lead that is now commonly available in a 30/70 ratio) is really the only way to go in restoration work.

In addition to the work hardening that occurs in body panels when they are stamped and later subjected to road vibration and flexing forces, there are several other changes in autobody sheet metal that occur when there is impact damage and the attempt to repair it. The most important of these is stretching. When a panel is severely deformed in an accident, it is sometimes stretched. This means that the pressure exerted on it has caused it to become longer or wider, or both. When this happens, it also has become thinner somewhere. Unfortunately, the act of straightening a deformed and stretched panel involves hammering on its ridges and channels, either directly over a dolly block or adjacent to one. This often results in further stretching the metal because metal is made thinner when it is hammered on. Bad repairs often work harden and stretch metal. This

can create a difficult combination of defects to address with proper repairs.

The opposite of stretching is "upsetting," which sometimes occurs in impact damage but more often is the result of bad repair strategy. This phenomenon involves making an area or areas of the metal in a panel thicker and laterally smaller than it or they were originally. Hammering down a bad buckle directly over a dolly block can produce an upset because the metal may have no lateral place to go. The result is that the upset part of the panel becomes thicker and laterally smaller than it was. This defect must be corrected for the metal to assume its correct original contours. Upsetting can be dealt with in a repair situation and is, in fact, sometimes purposely induced to overcome the effects of stretching. In that case, it is called "shrinking."

Impact Repair Approaches

Impact and corrosion damage are sometimes so severe that it is necessary to find replacement panels or to fabricate and section new metal into damaged areas. An example of a small panel fabrication and of section welding are shown and described in the photos and captions that accompany the text of the next chapter. Much of the bodywork that a restorer is likely to encounter involves minor crash damage—dents, scores and the like. It is the complete removal of such damage that can distinguish a very well restored car from one that looks like a near miss.

The most important aspect of repairing this kind of damage is to understand the material with which you are working—sheet metal—and to have some general and specific notions of how it got deformed and what kinds of actions will be necessary to return it to its original shape with a minimum of distortion, stretching and upsetting. Remember, a dolly block and hammer used the wrong way can be as destructive as the events that caused the damage that you are trying to repair.

Proceed in these matters with a very definite plan of attack. Part of that plan should be based on the known sheet metal theory that is described in this book and in the books mentioned at the beginning of this chapter. Another part of your plan will come from your experience, gained from experimentation with scrap panels. The point is, when you swing a body hammer, or decide where to begin to remove a dent, or whether to work "on dolly" or "off dolly," your knowledge will guide you and your experience will give you an intuitive sense of what the results of a given action will be.

Prior to the publication of Fairmont Forge's *The Key to Metal Bumping* in 1939, such texts that existed in the field of body repair tended to be vague and to stress the black magic aspects of the craft. Sheet metal skills tended to be passed on by oral tradition, which meant that there were some awfully good practitioners and some who were pretty bad. *The Key…* was a major contribution to the craft because it proposed a simple and very understandable format for sheet metal defect analysis and repair.

The nugget of the "Fairmont Method" was to logically distinguish between "direct" and "indirect" damage. Direct damage includes areas that have come into direct contact with an impacting object or objects. Indirect damage describes areas that are deformed and locked in by the results of the direct damage, but which were not actually directly impacted.

Most indirectly damaged areas will spring pretty much back into proper shape if the adjacent areas of direct damage are removed and the forces holding the indirectly damaged areas are thus released. Stamped steel has a memory that promotes this return to original format. Typically, briefcase-sized dents involve mostly indirect damage in terms of the amount of effected surface area. The Fairmont Method prescribes unlocking large expanses in sheet metal that are not deformed beyond their elastic limits by working only on those areas that are. A small "key" unlocks a big puzzle. The revelation of the Fairmont Method is that you don't have to get a big hammer and pound mindlessly on everything that seems to be pushed in or out in a process that inevitably stretches and work hardens metal unnecessarily and counter-productively.

Instead, inspection and analysis will indicate which areas involve direct damage and therefore should be dealt with first. In addition to inspection, the application of logic will yield an understanding of the sequence in which direct and indirect damage occurred. If direct damage is repaired in the reverse order that it occurred, most of the indirect damage will be released as you go along.

It all sounds simple, but in 1939 it probably had all of the impact of a major revelation because much of what had gone before in the official explanations of how to perform bodywork had involved incantation and witchcraft. Unfortunately, it turns out that bodywork isn't all that simple because trying to determine exactly what order damage occurred in can be a proposition that will make your head hurt. It is always possible to construct a theory of the order in which damage occurred, but it is frequently the case that alternative theories are as good or almost as good as your preferred theory.

That's why more recent approaches to body damage analysis and repair strategy tend to pay more attention to what is there and less to exactly how it got there. I tend to side with the latter approach but hasten to add that if you can determine the order of deformation of a particular damaged area, removing the constituents of the damage in the reverse order of their creation is always a good approach. It is not, however, a good idea to waste half a day theorizing about the order of creation of damage, since this is not absolutely necessary information to have in-head before you proceed with corrective measures.

In any theory of damage analysis and repair strategy, the damage itself is reduced to one or a combination of three possible constituent parts. These are V-channels, ridges and buckles (also called "rolled buckles"). These three categories, and their almost infinite combinations, cover the field. Ridges, as the name implies, are areas of raised metal, which stand out in a linear formation. V-channels are depressed areas formed into lines, the opposite of ridges. Buckles are areas that are forced and locked into the metal by the waveform created in the metal by the original impact.

Unlike ridges and V-channels, which are either results of direct damage or fairly gentle extensions from it, buckles are formed by the collapse of the metal when it is under pressure and literally has no alternative other than to collapse. Buckles often involve substantial upsetting, which is not the case with ridges and V-channels.

When you recognize and understand the genesis of these three components of damage, you will be in a position to execute an effective strategy for their removal. In large part, your actions should unlock what are usually large areas of indirect damage.

In a sense, the test of a good strategy is how little hammer and dolly work is necessary to remove damage. The analysis method works because breaking damage into components, and attacking those components logically represents an efficient attack on the causes of the problem. The alternative, to mindlessly attack the symptoms of damage, ends up as the "bigger hammer" approach and usually fails to recognize even such obvious components of damage as bent substructure. It substitutes damaging counter-force for intellect and skill. For that reason, it usually fails.

Sometimes new, NOS, and reproduction sheet metal parts can be found to replace collector car panels that are damaged beyond practical repair. Unfortunately, the replacements often require a great deal of rework to make them usable.

The Repair of Minor Impact Damage

THE EMPHASIS IN THIS CHAPTER is on the words "repair" and "minor." I emphasize repair because much that passes for repair is actually further damage, done in such a way that after it is covered up with "mud," it will give the short-term appearance of being repair.

The proper object of restoration, of course, is to work for the long term and to create restorations that use a minimum of filler—preferably lead. Hopefully, they look as though no repair has ever been made and continue to look that way for a very long time. This means that the repaired area or areas must resist corrosion and metal displacement due to vibration as well, or better than, the rest of the panel that was repaired.

The term "minor" in this chapter's title is emphasized for two reasons. When damage has progressed to the point where it is classed as "major impact damage" and a panel is buckled and distorted from several directions, it is beyond the competence of most shops to make effective repairs. Shops that employ specialists to do this sort of work can accomplish wonders, but the economics of these situations and the nature of the construction of most cars tend to work against this approach in most restoration projects. Certainly, damage that was repaired fairly routinely in the past is presently handled by panel replacement or by "totaling" a car.

Unless a car has very great value, the commercial proposition of building up a wreck for restoration purposes is almost always a bad proposition. An unwrecked car is a more expensive entry into car collecting, but the end result will almost always be more economically feasible and satisfying. I have seen many fenders that could theoretically be straightened, but that would require so much bumping, sectioning, shrinking and other handwork that it was impractical to restore them when the cost and availability of replacement fenders in good condition was considered.

This is not only true for panels that are badly crumpled from impact, but is also the case for those that are badly rusted or that have been hammered, welded and brazed to the point that there isn't much usable metal left to work with.

The second reason that I emphasize "minor repair" in this chapter is that this is the most common damage that you will encounter in collector cars. The usual proposition is to remove a simple ding, dent, crease or gouge. Such work is within the competence of many shops and, very probably, within the competence of many, or most, of the people reading this book. If, on the other hand, the damage in question is going to require the use of tensioning, heat or portable frame straightening equipment, it should only be attempted by those experienced in this work and equipped to do it.

If your restoration proposition is to turn a pretzel back into an automobile, you should consider buying new panels or employing a very advanced shop. As in so many other areas of automobile restoration, wisdom may be in knowing when to quit and what *not* to attempt.

If someone wants to explore the limits of the art of resurrecting sheet metal, it is best to let him do so on someone else's car and with his own or someone else's money.

Body hammers come in many sizes and shapes for many purposes. In front is a high crown/flat pick combination hammer. Behind it is a fender dinging hammer used to push out damage from behind. The next hammer back is an automatic shrinking hammer that is designed to pull metal in. Behind it is a low crown bumping hammer with large and small round faces. In the far back is a combination low crown/flat pick hammer.

Strategy for Removing Minor Damage

In the previous chapter, reference was made to the "Fairmont Method" of sheet metal damage correction. This method involves careful analysis of specific damage and its categorization into one or more of three distinct configurations: ridges, V-channels or buckles and rolled buckles. As well, in this approach all areas of displaced metal are separated into "direct" and "indirect" damage, with the aim of working out direct damage in ways that release indirect damage that may be locked by it into sheet metal.

The "nugget" of the Fairmont Method is to remove damage in the reverse order in which it occurred. Most of the later damage removal theories are not as focused on the reverse order format and allow for other reasonable sequences of removal, as long as they fit the logic of the situation.

The main item to remember is that there is nothing terribly mysterious about the business of straightening damaged sheet metal. A logical and orderly approach will cover most situations. Whatever approach to damage repair is pursued, the key will be careful analysis and adoption of a well-thought-out strategy to correct damage. In a very few cases, genius is useful in this work, but I don't know much about that. The main point is that you must *think before you strike.*

When simple damage is caused by impact, its removal can almost always be accomplished by the use of carefully chosen counter impact. Damage requiring tension, heat and other extraordinary measures to rectify it is no longer "simple." When you strike metal with a hammer, dolly or both, you must have reason to believe that your chosen action can and will move metal in the direction(s) that you want it to, and that it will not worsen the situation.

If your strategy for getting rid of a severe ridge is to pound it mindlessly down with a hammer or dolly face, the result will be an uncontrolled upset, which amounts to further damage. Sheet metal is somewhat forgiving of mistakes, but it tends to get harder and less tractable the more that you work it.

If you make too many mistakes, it can become a very unforgiving medium. So, before you hit a hammer blow, be sure that what you want to happen can and will happen. At first, you will think a lot and hammer very little. That's fine. Later, your experience will enable you to know, almost intuitively, what will work and what will not work. Even the most experienced sheet metal man, and certainly the novice, will need more than a good plan of attack. He will need to exercise powers of observation to see that the original plan is working, or sometimes not working.

The pick end of the combination hammer on top left is a handy size for raising small areas of sunken metal, but it takes some pretty good room to swing that hammer. The devices shown below it may solve the headroom problem. The next hammer is designed for picking metal in very tight spaces. It requires a very small swing. To the right are two different automatic pneumatic pick hammers. These require no swing and are operated off compressed air. The tool shown on the far right is a percussion hammer that also is driven by air and can be used like a pick hammer to raise or lower metal in some situations.

Auto Body Hand Tools and Their Basic Uses

HAMMERS. Body hammers are specialized tools that have very specific uses. The most common body hammers are classified as bumping hammers, picking hammers or combination hammers. The latter have one crowned bumping face and one relatively sharp picking surface. Body hammer bumping faces are designed to move small areas of metal with overlapping impacts, either in conjunction with dolly blocks held on the other sides of panels or without them. These hammers typically weigh from 12 to 16 ounces and have a crowned face or faces that measure from 3/8 to 1 1/4 inch across.

Hammer bumping faces are usually round, but there are some square faced hammers available for working evenly up to bends, creases and edges. Small bumping hammer faces may be highly crowned and are used primarily for dinging off-dolly (just beyond the edge of a dolly held under and against the metal that you are hammering) or without a dolly. Larger, less crowned faces are generally used for dinging on-dolly. When you strike a reverse crown panel or hammer from the back of a crowned one, the hammer face

Shown here are the "business ends" of these pick hammers and devices.

must have slightly more crown than the area of the panel that is being struck.

The key to using bumping hammers effectively is in knowing which one to use, where, and in what combination with or without dollies. It is also critical to know how hard a blow to strike and the proper manner in which to strike it in the widely varying situations presented by bodywork.

Generally, the best autobody hammer blow is soft compared to that used in other fields, like carpentry or blacksmithing. Multiple, adjacent or overlapping hammer blows are best in most situations. These blows are the opposite of the dead (no rebound) blows common to almost every other endeavor that involves using a hammer. For most situations, the correct sheet metal blow is a rebounding, glancing slap that is generated primarily from the wrist, with the hammer held loosely enough to rebound smartly from each blow. In this work, forget what your father told you when he taught you to drive nails. There is no single, powerful master-strike that will straighten a panel or remove a ridge.

There are two simple cautions about the selection and care of body hammers. Buy good ones in the first place, and never use them for anything but striking sheet metal. A good body hammer has a balance that allows it to be swung easily and to rebound crisply. Its face(s) must be kept polished and free of gouges or deep scratches; otherwise, it will damage sheet metal when it strikes it. I always do a little "custom contouring" with a grinder on the new hammers that I buy. This allows me to get their crowns just the way that I want them. Hammers should be polished with fine sandpaper to maintain the smoothness of their surfaces.

The selection of face size and crown is particularly important when you hammer directly on sheet metal. A small bumping hammer face with a lot of crown will generate much higher local impact pressures than a large, less

This photograph illustrates the different configurations of low crown and high crown hammer faces. Never use a hammer that has less crown than the metal that you are striking.

Dollies are really very complex and highly evolved tools. Each surface on a dolly has a specific use and purpose. The dolly in the bottom of this photo is a "shrinking" dolly.

crowned hammer. When working on-dolly (striking metal with a dolly directly under the area that you are striking) or under a buckled area, a large, low crown hammer will be more forgiving than a small one because it will be less likely to compress and laterally stretch or upset the metal. Some body men still use wooden, rawhide, or plastic mallets in situations like this.

Pick hammer faces are, as the name implies, radically pointed hammer faces. They are used to "lift" small areas of metal in the size range between a 25 cent piece and the dimensionally smaller change that you can get for it. Very sharp pick hammers are intended for use on high crown panel areas. My experience is that the sharper ones are more useful if you use them with a lot of restraint. This is especially true when you use them on high crown panels. I find them much easier to control for fine work, but this is a matter of personal preference. The basis for using pick hammers effectively is not to try to do too much with them in single blows and not to use them with too much force. An improper (usually overenthusiastic) pick hammer blow can make a real mess by creating reverse dimples and worse. On combination hammers that have one bumping face and one pick end, be ever vigilant not to allow the rebound of an enthusiastic bumping stroke to drive the pick end of the hammer back into some part of your anatomy. It hurts.

DOLLIES. Dollies are the workhorses of metal moving. They are really hammers without handles, or hand-held anvils, depending on how you choose to use them. While to the inexperienced eye a dolly block may look like a hunk of pig iron, it is really a carefully evolved and highly complex tool. Dollies have several faces and working surfaces. These may involve several different crowns and combinations of crowns called "transitions." The variety of working surfaces on a dolly is crucially important because in many applications you will have to match the crown of the dolly to

the part of a panel on which you are working.

Like hammers, dollies will work best when they have a balance that allows you to strike easily with them or to use them as rebound tools. Both dollies and hammers reach their highest potential as tools when they are used in ways that allow their balance to create a natural rhythm as a worker manipulates them. In fact, there can be something wonderfully musical about the sight and sound of a good metal practitioner working this craft.

Dollies are often used as short, handleless hammers for roughing metal out in places where hammers would be impossible to swing. They also are used to back up metal that is being hammered on from the other side. In this application, the dolly is sometimes held directly under the area where hammer blows are being directed (hammering "on-dolly") or, more often, held adjacent to it. In this second mode ("off-dolly"), the dolly block is used in conjunction with a hammer to smooth out metal by knocking ridges down or bringing V-channels up. The tension of the dolly against the metal in the off-dolly mode is translated almost instantaneously into sharp rebound impacts after hammer blows are struck on the other side.

This combination of impacts is highly effective in moving metal back into the shapes that it lost under the impacts of accidents. While hammer on-dolly work is sometimes essential, the most impressive results in releasing indirectly damaged metal are usually achieved working off-dolly.

SPOONS. This class of body tools sometimes seems to include any impacting or anvil tool that isn't a hammer or a dolly. Flat spoons are used to spread the impact of hammer blows in such applications as hammering down bad ridges or buckles. Other types of spoons are small dolly-like anvils on handles, while still others have gentle curvatures that can be used to pry with or to back up hammer blows in

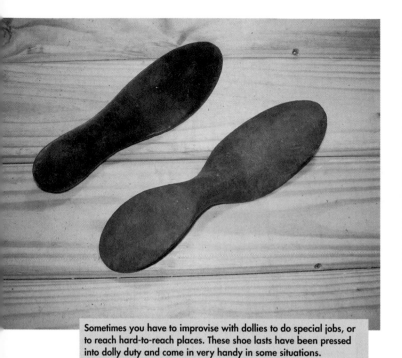

Sometimes you have to improvise with dollies to do special jobs, or to reach hard-to-reach places. These shoe lasts have been pressed into dolly duty and come in very handy in some situations.

Dollies are often used in combination with body hammers, but sometimes they are used alone.

Dollies are really just hand-held anvils when you use them to back up hammer work. You won't hand hold the item shown here, but it can be very useful in some phases of bodywork.

hard-to-reach places.

BODY FILES. These specialized files are used in the final stages of metal finishing to level surfaces and to indicate low spots so that they can be "lifted" with a pick hammer or by other means. Minor high spots will be indicated or removed by filing. The use of body files requires experience and coordination. Used properly, a body file is pushed evenly and smoothly away from the operator in a mildly diagonal direction. It is also gently rocked from its front to its heel during the stroke. Never use a body file with the same rationale or motion that you use a wood rasp or bastard file—that is to remove a lot of material quickly. To do so would cause binding and gouging and would serve no

useful purpose. You can use a body file and pick hammers to perform the final stages of panel leveling. This can be done with surprisingly little material removal. When lead filler is used, body files are the preferred method of shaping and removing excess material.

DISC SANDERS. These hand-held grinders are used to remove rust and paint and, like body files, for grinding metal to level it or to indicate where it has to be raised or lowered. The key to using a disc sander is to hold the disc as flat to the workpiece as is practical—a 15-degree angle is about right, but this will take some practice—and to keep it constantly moving over a panel in slightly overlapping strokes. If the sander is kept in one place too long, it will remove too much material and become part of the problem, rather than the solution. In addition, it is easy to over-heat a spot with a disc sander. This will become evident when a spot in the area that you are sanding turns red or a scorched hue of blue, by which time damage will have occurred.

On a 7- or 9-inch disc, at least 1 inch of cutting surface should be flexed into contact with the work piece. Small disc sanders (4 and 4 1/4 inches) have smaller contact rims with sheet metal. While all sanders should be moved fast enough on material to prevent gouging and overheating, they should not be skated over surfaces too quickly or insufficient cutting will take place and the result will be an uneven surface.

Many body shops begin sanding operations with a 24-grit abrasive (mountain boulders) and work up to finer grades. I have generally avoided using very course discs for paint removal. A DA (dual action) sander is slower but safer for this work. I prefer to use a 50-grit abrasive for leveling work. Many shops use a 36-grit abrasive for this purpose, but I find 50-grit comfortably slow.

Always use closed coat abrasives when grinding, not paint removal, is your purpose. Generally, overlapping

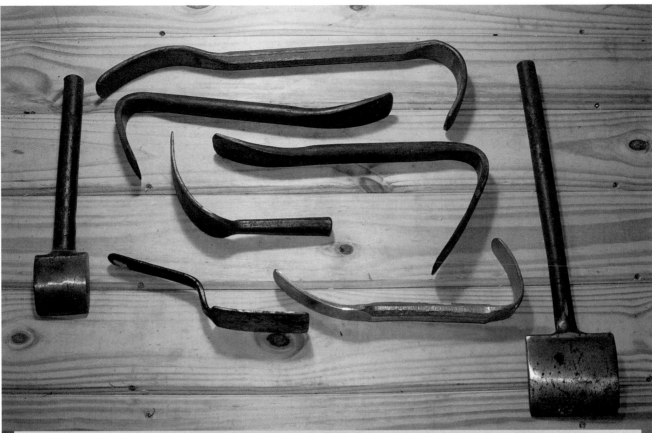

Body spoons are used to back up metal (like dollies), but will insert where dollies won 't fit), to pry out metal, and to spread hammer blows when they are hit against metal with hammers.

Body files come in a wide variety of shapes, sizes, and tooth patterns. These are among the most important tools in bodywork because they will help you to finely shape metal and to find high and low spots in it.

Disc sanders cut metal faster than files do, but they are neither as accurate nor as controllable for fine work. The two sanders on the left in the first photograph are electric, and the two on the right are pneumatic. Always use disc sanders very carefully. You can do an enormous amount of damage with them if you don't.

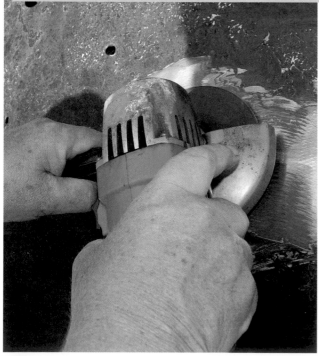

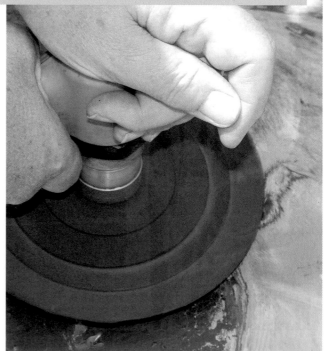

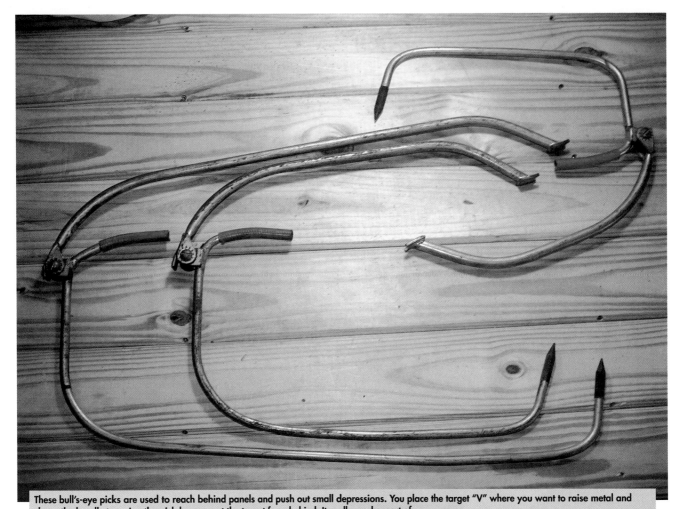

These bull's-eye picks are used to reach behind panels and push out small depressions. You place the target "V" where you want to raise metal and clamp the handle to swing the pick hammer at the target from behind. It really works, sort of.

horizontal strokes will accommodate most work best, but it is permissible to use a vertical pattern for some grinding and indicating purposes. A disc sander is much faster and easier to use than a body file, but a properly used body file offers precision and control that I could never develop with a disc sander. Some body men use a disc sander to remove excess plastic and even lead filler, but I think that this is poor practice in the case of plastic filler, and deadly one in the case of lead. Fillers are simply too soft, compared to the surrounding sheet metal, to be leveled effectively with a disc sander.

In the case of lead filler, this practice is extremely dangerous because it puts a potentially lethal spray of minute lead particles into the air. These particles can be breathed, ingested and absorbed through exposed skin. They will not kill you immediately, but their cumulative effect tends in that direction.

OTHER BODYWORK TOOLS. As in almost every area of restoration, there is an almost endless assortment of neat and wonderful tools and devices that may have substantial usefulness when it comes to bodywork. Even if they don't, they have an enormous potential for impressing everyone but your spouse, being borrowed endlessly by everyone in sight and, finally, leading to financial rack and ruin.

Bull's Eye picks have an enormous appeal, and

These air-driven hammers are pretty violent, but they can be used to drive ridges out of severely damaged metal if you have enough room to operate them.

pneumatically operated "power hammers" are terrifically useful for smoothing metal. If you get into sectioning and fabricating work, your tool *modus operandi* will soon outgrow using someone else's sheet metal brake, so your

Soft hammers, like these polypropylene and rawhide mallets, work very well for straightening slightly deformed metal without stretching it. The more bodywork you do, the more you will come to use mallets instead of hammers.

over others that are theoretically possible. One unifying theme will be that any appropriate procedure in metalwork will aim to work with the damaged metal in ways that unlock as much indirect damage as possible by working on or near the direct damage. Thus, buckles are worked on directly and early in any proper scheme of repair, while hammer off-dolly work is used extensively to level V-channels.

In every case, as the metal is struck, it is given a place to go that tends toward the desired final result. This is different from the all-too-common body shop practice of reaching behind a severe dent and just bashing it out with a dolly along the line of the lowest V-channel. People who follow that misguided course of action create situations with so many distortions, stretches, and upsets in a panel that after they are done it would take expert applications of stretching, shrinking and sectioning, among other ploys, to bring the panel back to its correct, original contours. Of course, people who would commit the first error are usually far from bashful about using torrents of "mud" to hide the results of their defective approaches to basic sheet metal work.

When used correctly and within their limits, the tools described here, and in later chapters in this book, will aid greatly in effectively repairing the minor sheet metal damage that is often encountered in restoration projects. Like all tools, there are always possibilities for misusing them and creating additional damage.

While good and appropriate tools are important to performing high quality body restoration work, it is the skills and judgment of those who wield them that are most critical to getting the best possible results.

tool "wish list" will come to include a brake. Fabrication work will also require an assortment of rawhide, wood, or plastic mallets and a good shot bag. As you get further into this work, you will doubtless want an English wheel, a bead roller, and a shrinker-stretcher. All of this stuff can be useful if you have the skill to use it, but most restoration projects can be accomplished with simple hand tools like hammers, dollies, spoons, files, and a good disc sander.

Every example of damage that you encounter will present its own unique circumstances and dictate a preference for some particular strategies and procedures

These English wheels form and stretch metal and are incredibly versatile tools. They are not as dramatic as power hammers but can do great long runs of smooth work. Custom body builders used English wheels to form the panels in many collector cars. English wheels are fairly expensive and require considerable skill and experience to use effectively.

Some Final Thoughts on Acquiring Bodywork Skills

Sheet metal work is not a mysterious black art. There are probably hundreds of thousands of people in this country who have learned to use body tools properly and who can produce excellent results. It takes basic knowledge, patience, imagination and coordination. Most of this can be obtained with experience and with a bit of reading on, or instruction in, the basics. Practice is the critical element in acquiring necessary experience and good habits. Almost anyone who seriously attempts to learn this craft will begin by using hammers too hard and too rigidly. Spend a day with some scrap panels from a salvage yard, and your hammer blows, your placement of dollies and your picking and leveling techniques will improve almost miraculously. In the course of weeks, months, and years, many amateurs can become skilled practitioners of the sheet metal arts, even though this work is not the main pursuit of their lives.

Have at it, and good luck.

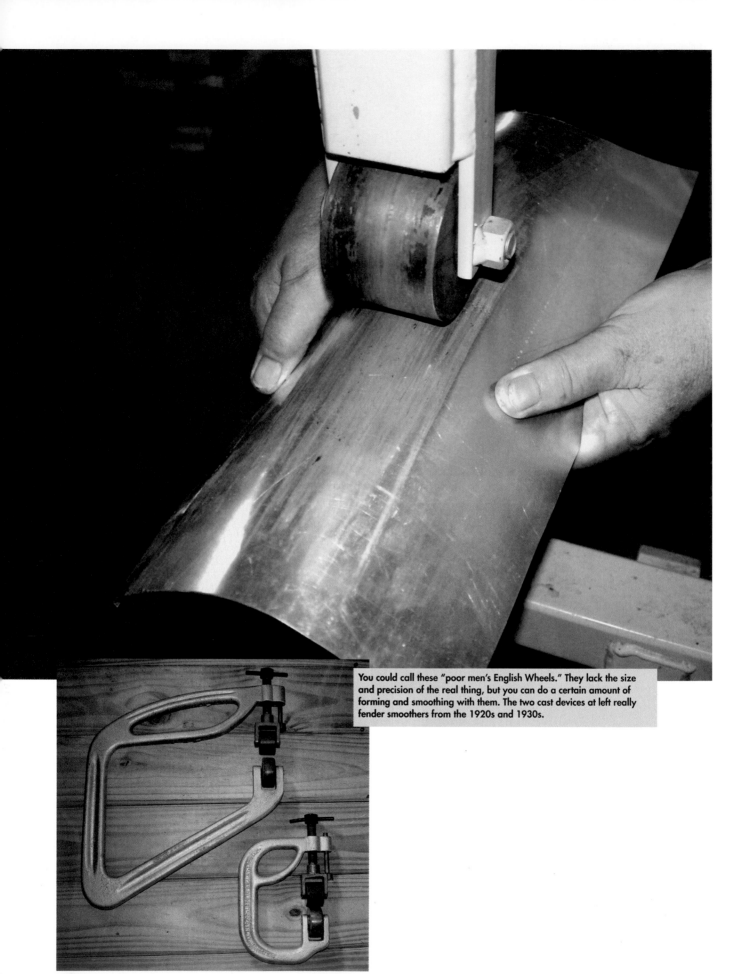

You could call these "poor men's English Wheels." They lack the size and precision of the real thing, but you can do a certain amount of forming and smoothing with them. The two cast devices at left really fender smoothers from the 1920s and 1930s.

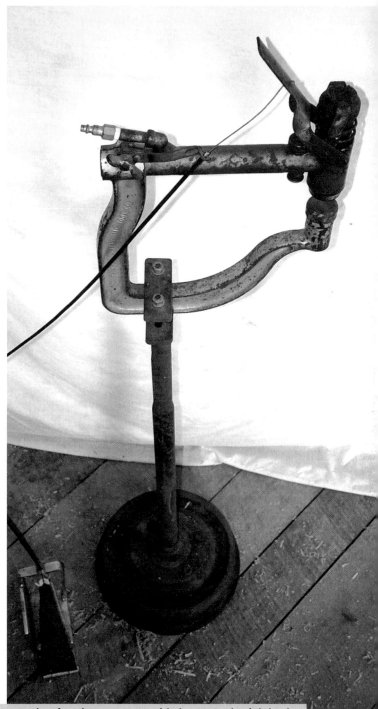

The planishing hammers pictured here were designed to be hand held and to remove dents from the turret top cars of the late 1930s. They failed at that task because they stretched metal mercilessly. However, they are very useful for forming and smoothing metal. When mounted on stands, they also are useful in panel fabrication and repair.

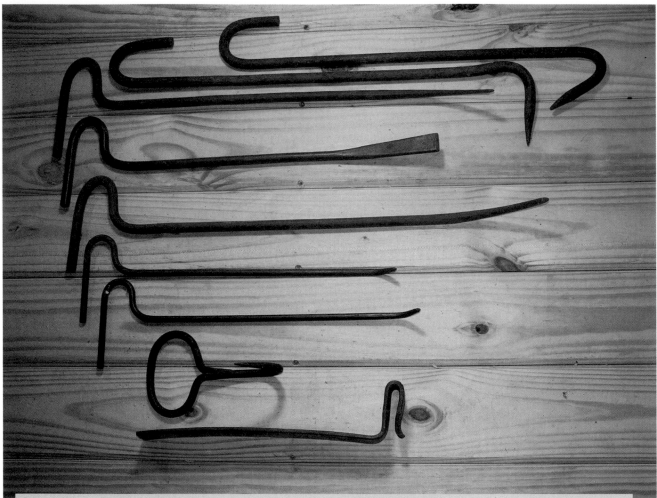

These pry bars are incredibly handy in bodywork. I haven 't seen bars like these sold in this country for years, so if you see a set, make haste to buy it for your body tool collection.

If you plan to do much sheet metal work and can't justify buying and storing a 4-foot finger brake, like this one, find a sheet metal shop or restorer who will let you use theirs.

These bead rollers are about the only effective way to put raised beads in sheet metal parts and are very useful for that. The larger one shown is outfitted with a hard rubber lower wheel and can be used to do some very interesting and useful forming operations.

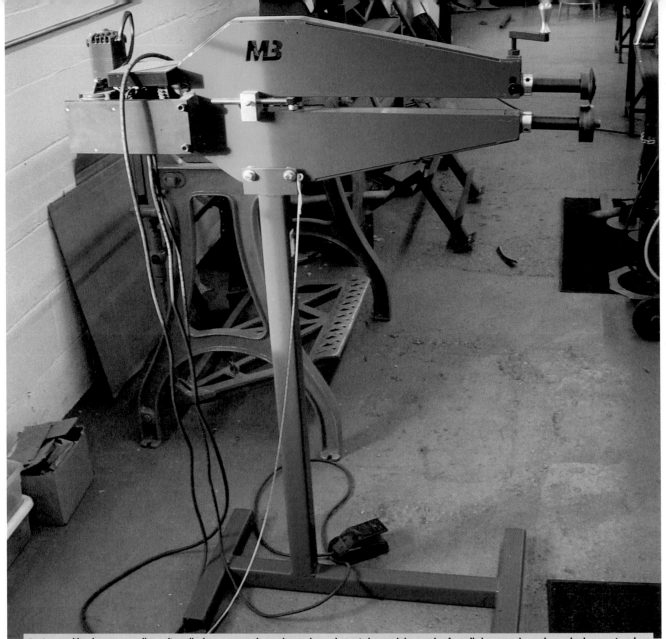

Equipment like the power rollers, slip-rolls, hammers and stretchers, shown here, is beyond the needs of small shops or shops that only do occasional sheet metal forming.

These power hammers do speed up forming work greatly, but you can usually find other, slower ways to do what they do.

This combination sheet metal brake/slip roll/sheer works well for small projects in light-gauge metal. The finger brake feature is particularly useful but the brake is limited to 90-degree bends.

Tools like this slide hammer "dent puller" (center) and the body hooks (around it) are readily available in body shop supply stores and in hardware stores. I wouldn't say that they have no place in auto bodywork, but I will say that that place is not in restoration work. Using devices like these to pull out dents means drilling holes in sheet metal, and in restoration work that should never be done just to pull out dents. It falls into the category of "quick and dirty" work. It is always better to find access to the back of a panel and pry or pound out that kind of damage.

This shrinker/stretcher setup will allow you to make many items that are necessary in restoration sheet metal work. Items like window surrounds are hard to make without it.

This stud-gun puller kit has some use in restoration but, like the slide hammer puller and hooks, you can usually find a better way to do what it does. Some welded studs and examples of three stud sizes are shown here.

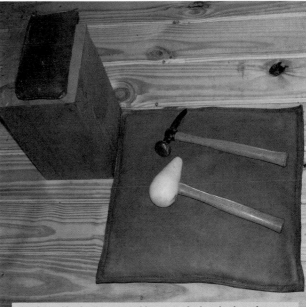

Shot bags, like the two pictured here, are the best backups for most panel forming operations that you will have occasion to perform with hammers and mallets.

Shrinking and Stretching, Welding and Sectioning

N AN AGE WHEN IT IS NOT UNUSUAL FOR BODY MEN to substitute efficiency for skill and to fill small dents with polyester dumdum, it never ceases to amaze me that there is still a great interest in the demanding and arcane techniques of metal shrinking.

The interest seems disproportionate to the need for this technique, but when metal is stretched, it is often necessary to shrink it. It is always desirable to do so in preference to other measures that are taken to hide stretched metal.

I have seen bodies in restoration that looked as if they had some rare form of metal measles from the 200 or 300 shrink spots that graced their sheet metal exteriors. Such applications are often done in excess. In the 1980s, one seller of restoration aids began retailing serrated shrinking hammers, serrated shrinking dollies, mechanically activated shrinking hammers, slapping (shrinking) files, and finally, a rotary "shrinking disc." The retailer quickly discontinued the latter item when its potential hazards became known. In any case, it seems that restorers are interested in shrinking.

What perplexes me about all of the paraphernalia and printed dither on this topic is that the basic technique of shrinking with an oxy-acetylene torch is simple, well known and relatively easy to master. I cannot imagine why anyone would want to perform this procedure any other way, unless, of course, he didn't have a torch. In that case, it might be best to leave shrinking to someone who does have this equipment and the requisite knowledge to use it for that purpose.

None of this, of course, rules out the possibility that some of the profusion of cold shrinking tools may even work. However, because the good old torch shrinking technique works so well, it should be the first choice for this operation.

Shrinking involves "upsetting" metal that has been stretched. That means, in practice, that the metal will be made dimensionally thicker and laterally smaller (less long and wide) in a small area around the shrink spot. The actual operation of creating this upset involves heating a small area of metal until it bulges slightly and hammering that bulge back down.

Because the colder metal at the boundaries of the heated area is harder than the metal in it, a hammer blow will force the heated area down and out. When it meets the unyielding boundary areas of surrounding cold metal, it will have no choice but to thicken. Surface area will be exchanged for thickness and a "shrink" will be accomplished in a very small local area—say 1/4 to 1/2 inch across.

The purpose of shrinking is to restore original contours to metal that has been deformed and stretched, either by impact in an accident or, as often, by the impact of a body man's hammer-on-dolly in a misguided straightening operation. Identifying which bulges are stretched and which are simple deformations is part of the art or skill of metal shrinking. It is possible to over-shrink metal and to leave it under tension that is as counter-productive to restoring original contours as was the original stretching that was the object of remedy.

One common mistake is to attempt to shrink all visible bulges in a panel. When a bulge that is simply metal locked in a rolled buckle is shrunk in a mistaken effort to put things right, it would have to be classified as further damage—although stretching it back will usually present few problems. All of this makes it imperative that any panel that is suspected of being stretched should be straightened before any shrinking operations are attempted. That is the only way to distinguish between real stretches, and bulges that are not stretched. If you try to guess where the stretches are, and then to shrink them before you rough out and

The most common reason for sectioning in new metal is rust. The rust shown here is probably not bad enough to require the removal of metal, but if it progresses much further that can change. Water dripping off the car's roof trim has helped to cause this problem.

No question about it. New metal will have to be welded in, to repair this damage. The probable cause of this damage is a water trap inside the cowl, probably a welded body support.

bump a panel, you are unlikely to be correct more than half of the time. Why gamble against those dismal odds?

Another reason to straighten metal before you do any shrinking is that while the basic shrinking operation draws metal from all directions into an upset, the placement that you choose for your shrink spots can very precisely draw metal mostly and specifically from two directions.

For example, if a gouge has stretched the metal in a panel, it is desirable to shrink metal at right angles to the gouge and not to draw the gouge in lengthwise. In practice, shrink zones of 3/8 inch to 1/2 inch in width by about 2 inches in length will prove adequate for shrinking most deep gouges. Note that gouges rarely produce stretching for their entire length. This is dictated by the natures of the kinds of impacts that create them and the crowns of the panels where they usually occur. All of this depends, of course, on the severity of the impact, on the final configuration of the metal and on damage to any substructure that supports the damaged metal.

Before any shrink operation is undertaken, the optimum location for shrink spots or zones must be determined. This is the most difficult part of the shrinking process. In almost all cases, the center of the stretched area should be the place to apply the shrink(s), but this is not always the case. As with any metal moving procedure, you have to determine what you want to accomplish and then construct a theory, or rely on experience or intuition, to determine that the action that you take will, in fact, cause the desired result. If you just "sort of" shrink somewhere in the vicinity of a stretch, and hope for the best, the results will, at best, be inconsistent and at worst counter-productive.

The actual shrinking operation is remarkably uncomplicated. You simply heat a spot of 3/8 to 1/2 inch (larger spots are sometimes used) to bright red with a small tip on an oxy-acetylene torch. Always use a small tip. Somewhere between blue and bright red, the spot that you are heating will bulge out because local expansion of the heated metal is stopped by the unheated metal that surrounds it. All that the heated metal can do to expand is to bulge out.

Put the torch safely aside, and with or without a dolly behind the spot, hit it flat against the surrounding metal with a large-faced, low crown body hammer. Usually, after you complete this part of the shrinking operation, you will find a slightly depressed center and raised metal at the periphery of the heated and hammered spot. Now, the area should be worked flat to the level of its terrain with a hammer-on-dolly. You do this by lowering the raised area that surrounds the depressed area of the shrink spot. Then you bring the depressed area up. Be sure to use a dolly with a crown that will allow you to flatten the metal around the shrink spot without interference from other areas of the surrounding panel.

At this point in the metal shrinking operation, experience and judgment will dictate your next move. If it is apparent that over-shrinking has occurred, or will occur, as the panel further cools, it is possible to use the hammer and dolly to restretch the area slightly to prevent a final condition of over-shrink. It is also possible to reduce the shrinking effect by quenching the shrunk area with a wet sponge while it is still hot. This "quenching" operation tends to reverse the shrink effect slightly. The point is, you can fine tune the shrink to get the desired result at this time.

That's all that there is to it. Shrinking isn't one of the black arts, but it does take some practice and experience to get a feel for when and where to shrink and how far to go with it. Mastery of conventional, oxy-acetylene shrinking should be a useful procedure for about as long as automobile

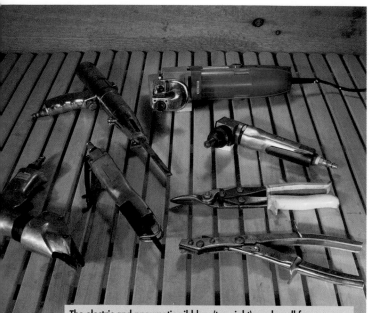

The electric and pneumatic nibblers (top right) work well for removing damaged sheet metal from some panels. Both are fairly usable in close quarters. The hand nibbler (bottom right) is easier to control. The pneumatic and hand shears (bottom left and second up from the bottom on the right) can also do this work effectively. The pneumatic hacksaws (center vertical row) are hard to turn, but work for some straight cuts into panels.

In some situations, hacksaws are very handy for cutting out parts of panels. Note the three hacksaws shown in the bottom of this photo. They extend their blades so that you don't need much access to the back of a panel to use them.

bodies are constructed from sheet metal.

Sectioning: Cutting and Forming

At some point in many restorations, it is possible that body renovation will require the removal of parts of panels and the fabrication and attachment of replacement metal. This is necessary when parts of a panel are so damaged by rust or impact, or both, that the existing metal in the panel cannot be salvaged. Cutting out the old metal is usually easy enough, and some simple shapes for "patch panels" are not difficult to fabricate. Others are. Complex panel fabrication is a highly specialized endeavor and should be left to those with experience in this field.

There are many ways to cut damaged sheet metal out of panels. You have a choice of shears, nibblers, saws, snips, grinders and, most recently, plasma arc cutters. Never use an oxy-acetylene cutting torch for this purpose as it is much too hot and can massively distort areas where you make such cuts. Shears and nibblers are fast and easy to control, but because of the width of the cuts that nibblers produce, they can be difficult to use effectively in this situation. They present operational problems in close quarters because they are often bulky and they are not good for making sharp radius cuts.

My preferences in panel cutting tools are saber saws outfitted with sheet metal blades and plasma arc cutters. The saber saw approach is slow, and sometimes presents access problems. A saber saw makes a very narrow and precise cut, so the sacrifice in speed is probably worth it.

Plasma arc cutters cut metal with a narrow stream of super-heated air. Good plasma cutters are quite expensive, however, they cut very quickly and precisely and cause very little distortion in the metal adjacent to the cuts that they make. They are also capable of making very precise cuts. If you can afford one of these devices, it is often the premium way to cut out damaged sheet metal for sectioning. Some plasma cutters have available "extended arc" tips that allow you to cut without keeping the torch in contact with the piece that you are cutting. Used properly, these tips can produce extremely precise outline cuts along markings on the target metal. However, this takes very precise torch manipulation that is usually beyond the accuracy needs of patch panel cutting work.

When you cut metal out for sectioning, remember that you will have to fit new metal very closely to your cut line. For most welding techniques, the butt edges of the new and the old metal should be separated by about the thickness of between a dime and a nickel, about 7 1/2 cents, you might call it. This means that you should design your removal of old metal to accommodate this close fit-up, insofar as this is possible. The usual reason for metal removal is either very severe local impact damage or, more often, rust perforation. In either case, be sure to remove as much metal as is necessary to get past the damage and into good metal, but no more.

New metal for replacement purposes should have excellent fit-up in all dimensions, including thickness. Not only should a patch piece fit well into its lateral boundaries and third-dimensional contours, it should not have to be tacked into place under tension to make it match the contours of the panel to which it is welded. If patch pieces

Suspicious areas, where rust-through may have occurred, should be probed with a scribe and/or a pick hammer to see if they go completely through the metal.

are fitted under tension with the surrounding metal that holds them in place, it is likely that with time, vibration and work hardening the whole panel will warp. Generally, a few extra minutes spent in perfecting fit-up and contour match will save both time and quality in the final result.

Panel fabrication shaping can be accomplished with simple tools, such as shot bags and wooden, rawhide or plastic mallets, or it may require more substantial tools, such as a sheet metal brake, a shrinker/stretcher, a slip roll set, special anvils, a power hammer or an English wheel. Most of this stuff is beyond the sophistication of all but a few restoration shops. Yet, many of us have such tools as: a sheet metal brake, a shot bag, set of mallets and small wheeling machine. An amazing amount of metal forming can be done with just this simple equipment, and with very good results.

Even sophisticated shops frequently have to build complex shapes from small pieces that they weld together. Such fabricated shapes aren't very pleasing to look at in the raw, but when they are metal finished, filled and painted the results are quite acceptable. It is important to realize that it will be difficult or impossible for most of us to form complex shapes in metal without the expedient of welding subassemblies together. With a little planning and ingenuity, you can replace a lot of expensive equipment this way, particularly when your need is only occasional. After some years of experimenting with and acquiring sheet metal forming skills, I am often amazed at the fabrications of complex shapes that I am able to accomplish.

The next 18 pages detail a sectioning repair to the cowl of an early Jaguar XK-E. This repair is typical of sectioning work that is often required to restore old car bodies and fenders. The damage was caused by impact and made worse by a bad previous repair. The photographs are arranged in the following categories and order:

- Discovering the extent of the damage
- Laying out and cutting the new panel
- Shaping and forming the new metal
- Removing the damaged metal

- Discovering hidden structural damage and remedying it
- Fitting the new panel
- Welding in the new metal
- Finishing the welds and the panel repair

Discovering the extent of the damage

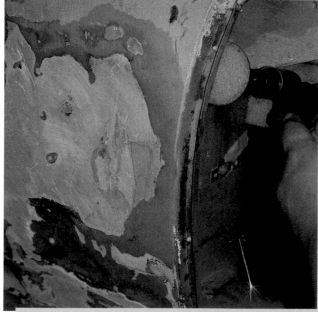

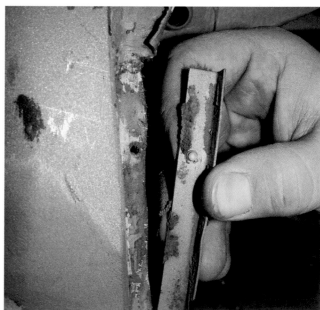

The damaged area is examined, cleaned for further inspection and easily removed metal is excised.

The lead filler that was used to hide damaged metal and a crude weld was burned and brushed away, revealing a crudely welded seam.

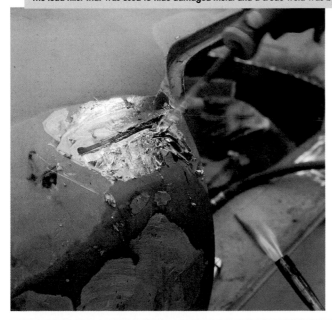

Laying out and cutting the new panel

The area that will be replaced is now patterned in a three-dimensional representation on poster board using visual, measuring and even pressure impression techniques. Later, the pattern will be transferred to a metal patch panel.

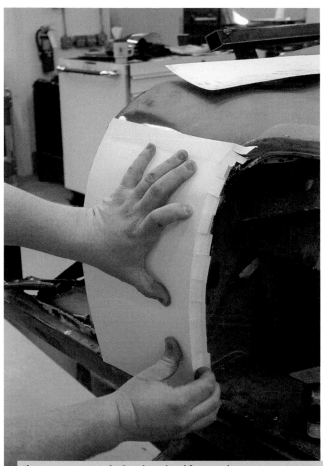

The paper pattern is further shaped and fine tuned into an accurate 3-D representation of the panel that is being sectioned. Then, the rough dimensions of the pattern are transferred to a piece of new sheet metal.

The metal is then cut and checked and rechecked against the pattern and trimmed to shape.

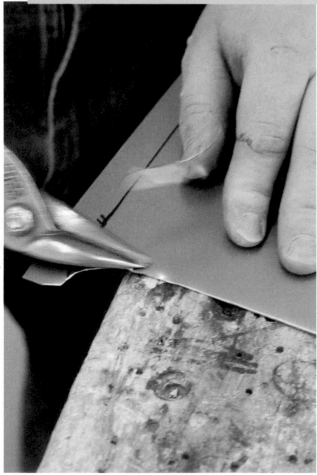

More measuring, dimensioning and fine tuning is done to assure a perfect fit of the new patch panel into the Jaguar's cowl metal. A large sheet metal brake is often used to flatten one edge of the repair panel (bottom right).

Shaping and forming the new metal

The front edge of the metal is now formed on a Pexto rolling machine with a steel wheel die against a hard rubber wheel die.

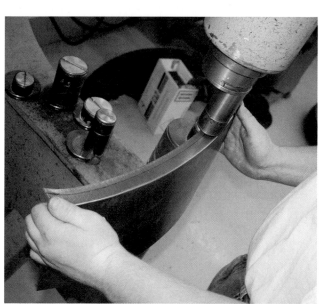

More forming is performed on the patch panel by hammering on it and with a power shrinking head. The patch panel is repeatedly checked against the place where it will be fitted.

The panel is fine tuned by hammering on it on an anvil and on a soft surface. Excess metal is trimmed away with shears. Note that the shrinking operation is fine tuned with a manual shrinking device.

Removing the damaged metal

The bad metal is now cut out of the cowl with an abrasive wheel and pneumatic hacksaw. It is then pried away until it can be removed.

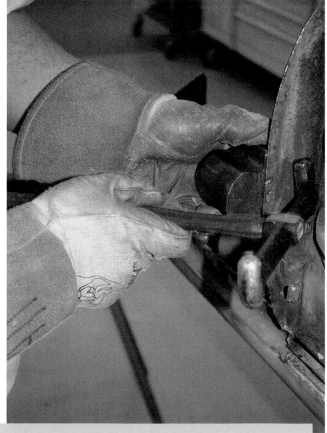

Some straightening and further cleanup of the damaged area is performed.

Discovering hidden structural damage and remedying it

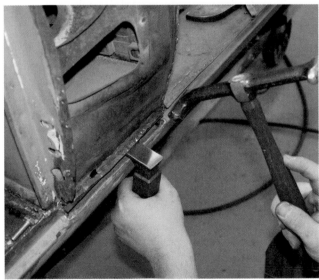

The newly discovered damaged area is structural. It is reformed, cleaned and welded back to structural integrity. Metal Inert Gas ("MIG") welding is used for this operation.

Fitting the new panel

The repaired structural area is now trimmed with power abrasive devices to accept the formed patch panel.

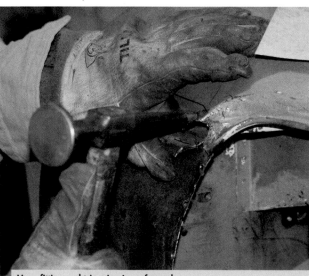

More fitting and trimming is performed.

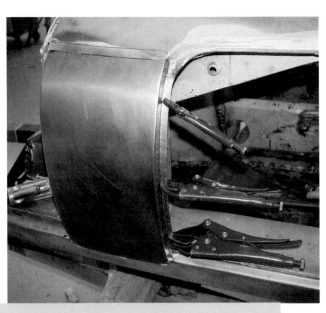

Note how much better the panel fits its space as the work progresses.

The area where the new panel will be welded to the old metal is cleaned and the new panel is drilled for button-hole welds that will look like the original factory spot welds. The drilled holes are deburred and the panel is fitted. Additional holes are drilled to fasten the Cleco fasteners that will temporarily hold the panel in place during the welding operation. The Clecos are installed.

Welding in the new metal

The new panel is now tack welded into place against the old metal with a Tungsten Inert Gas ("TIG") welder. Then, the metal fit and contour are fine tuned and more tack welds are made. Note the operation with a small screwdriver to adjust the butted edges of the top of the panel. Finally, the patch panel is welded into place with button-hole and more tack TIG welds.

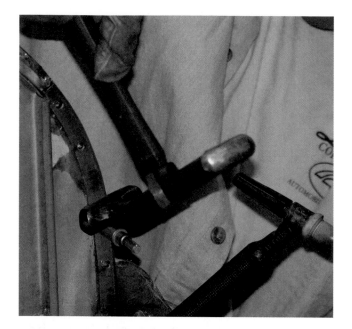

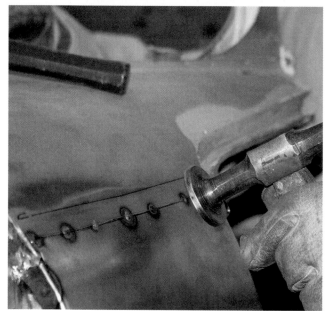

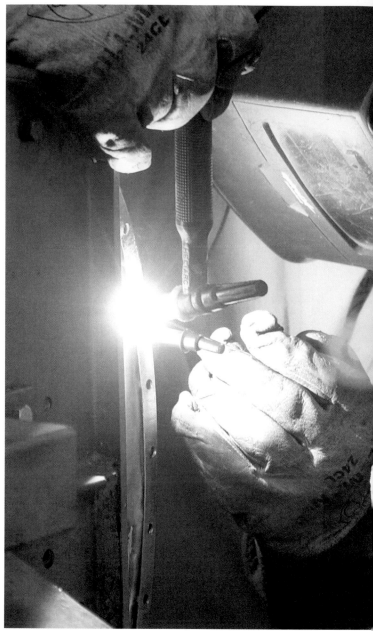

A similar procedure is applied to the bottom welds on the panel.

Finishing the welds and the panel repair

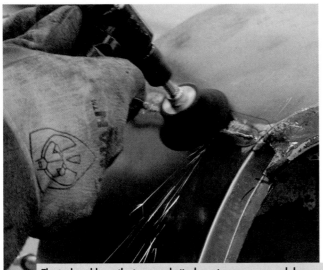

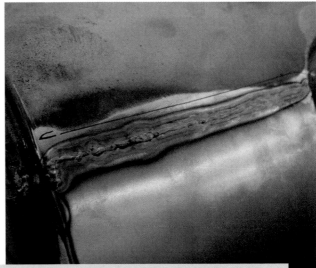

The tack welds on the top panel attachment are now ground down and a continuous bead welded over them. Then, the continuous bead is ground flat to the panel. A similar approach is used on the bottom panel attachment.

The finished panel repair looks like this.

The finished top weld looks like this.

Some General Thoughts on Panel Attachment (Welding)

Welding is really the only effective way to attach panel patches. Over the years, everything from brazing to pop rivets and sheet metal screws has been used for this purpose, and over the years everything from brazing to pop rivets and sheet metal screws has failed in this application.

For several decades, spot welding (resistance welding) has enjoyed some popularity for panel patch attachment and has been one of the most dismal failures of all, except where it is used to replace attachments that were originally made in this manner. The problem common to all of these non-butt welding attachment methods is that is that they employ lap joints. This means that the repair must then hide the lap joint, unless it is done in an area like a door jamb that was originally fabricated that way.

When lap joints are used to attach metal patches in areas that are flat and that originally had no joints, a counterfeit contour must be created to replace the original contour of the panel in the area of its new attachment. The expedient of using a panel flanger to offset and hide a lap joint produces other problems that are worse than any problems that it solves.

No other method of attachment will have the strength that welding exhibits, and none of them are strong enough for the kind of service that should be inherent in restoration work. Finally, for various reasons, methods of panel attachment other than butt welding usually provide excellent places for corrosion to start, or restart, and from which to progress.

The main problem with welding sheet metal is that as a prerequisite you have to know how to weld in general. In addition, sheet metal is quirky and likes to warp and burn through when welding temperatures are applied to it, particularly at its edges.

Hammer welding, which is welding followed by a stress relieving application of hammer-on-dolly impact, requires knowledge, experience, coordination and planning. It is an attainable skill for many restorers, but not everybody. The expedient of brazing panel attachments has been used by some people because the heat involved is much less than is employed in welding, and the attendant problems of metal distortion are greatly reduced. The trouble is that braze-welded joints lack sufficient strength for panel attachment. Besides, capillary brazing in this application necessarily involves use of the despised lap joint. When you encounter a brazed joint in sheet metal you may have a real problem because unless all traces of the braze are removed, you will never get a conventional fusion weld to work properly.

If you don't want to invest the time and effort necessary to learn to hammer weld, you might consider joining the "MIG Welding Revolution." While MIG welding (properly, GMAW "Gas Metal Arc Welding") has some small disadvantages when it is compared to hammer welding,

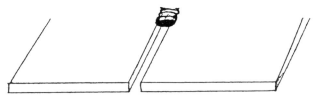

Butt welded joints, like the one in this illustration, are really the only way to go in restoration sheet metal work.

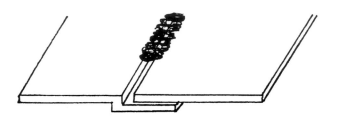

Sheet metal lap joints and offset lap joints (bottom) have several drawbacks. They thicken the metal in the joint area, and this must be hidden in an inauthentic contour, or behind the panel. They are also difficult to seal, and very subject to attack by moisture from behind. As sheet metal vibrates in service, lap joints often end up as visible creases because they can't flex with the sheet metal surrounding them. Butt welded joints (top) are really the only way to go in restoration sheet metal work.

they are minor and there are some very great advantages to MIG welding panel joints. This is because the heat involved is comparatively local, and distortion—a major enemy in panel welding—is reduced to a minor problem. Not the least of the advantages of MIG welding is that it is easy to learn and master—about half a day will do nicely to get most people started—and it is not absolutely necessary for someone to have the kind of metallurgical knowledge that is virtually required of a good gas weld practitioner. Then, too, the price of usable wire feed (MIG) welders has come down a thousand of dollars to as little as $500.

Most MIG welds don't have the nice, rippled appearance of really good gas welds, but the strength is there and usually the distortion isn't. When a finished MIG weld is ground level and refinished, it will hold its own against any skillfully made gas weld. In the early days of MIG welding, some people claimed that MIG welds were inherently hard and prone to cracking in service. Improved welding wires have pretty much answered that complaint.

There are several general rules for panel welding that apply equally to electric and gas weldments. One is that long reach Vise Grip type tools, clamps, Clecos, welding magnets, and the like, should be used to position pieces precisely before making the tack welds that will hold them in place prior to final welding. Do not use sheet metal screws, pop rivets and all the other substandard stuff that they sell for this purpose. With any welding technique, be sure to limit the distance that you attempt to weld at one time, so that heat buildup can be minimized and distortion reduced. A "stitch weld timer" feature on your MIG welder will take care of this for you automatically.

Sheet metal welds should be much flatter than the

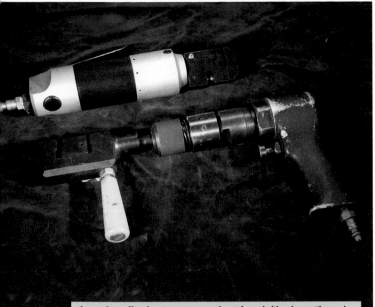

Flanged or offset lap joints are made with tools like these. The tool on the top is an air-over-hydraulic device that pinches and flanges the sheet metal at the edge of a panel. The flanging tool on the bottom is run directly off an air "zip" gun. Flanged offset joints have the same drawbacks as plain lap joints and, like lap joints, they are easy to fabricate.

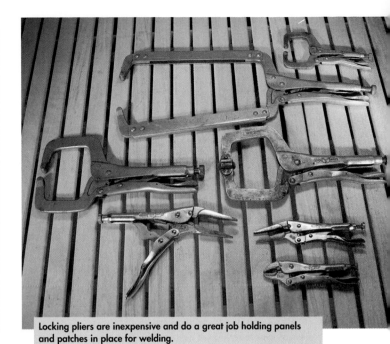

Locking pliers are inexpensive and do a great job holding panels and patches in place for welding.

welds used to join thicker materials. Near-flush weld beads are usually best because welds that stand high above sheet metal surfaces will have to be ground almost flat, anyway. You will always have to do some grinding, but it should be held to a minimum.

You will find that with MIG welding, a little practice goes a long way.

Gas Welding and Brazing

The invention of the portable oxy-acetylene welding torch apparatus at the turn of the century provided a compact, reliable and reasonably safe source of very high heat for cutting, forming, and joining metals. The flame produced by a "neutral" mixture of these two gasses is roughly 5,850 degrees F., with temperatures as high as 6,300 degrees F. possible with an oxygen-rich flame. One of the outstandingly useful characteristics of this flame involves its outer "envelope," which provides a relatively neutral or inert environment in which the rapid corrosion associated with ferrous metals at these temperatures does not take place. This envelope acts to shield intensely heated weld metal from atmospheric oxygen.

As the techniques of welding developed, practitioners learned to move oxy-acetylene flames along the seams of metals to be joined in a way that causes a "puddle" to flow along this joint. This puddle can be enhanced by the addition of filler rod to form a very strong joint of fused metals. For this reason, it is sometimes called a "fusion" weld, in distinction to soldering and brazing, which occur at much lower temperatures (typically under 800 degrees and 1100 to 1500 degrees F., respectively) and involve some

molecular commingling, but not actual fusion. The puddle used in gas welding is kept in the inert outer flame envelope with the hottest part of the flame, its inner cone, held a short distance from the surface of the puddle. The outer flame envelope prevents immediate oxidation (corrosion) of the weld and of the area immediately adjacent to it.

Unfortunately, gas welding produces considerable heat buildup in the areas next to welds, and distortion can easily be induced into the work. This distortion has to be worked out later in a time-consuming process. For this and other reasons, the technique of hammer or "forge" welding was developed for use on sheet metal, among other applications.

Using this technique, an operator welds a small length of a seam, between 1/2 inch and 1 inch, and lays the torch aside. Very quickly, he hammers the hot weld between a hammer and a dolly, then quenches it with a wet rag or sponge. The effect is to relieve some of the stress that is inherent in the weld and surrounding area, and to limit the heat buildup and resulting distortion. It sounds simple, but involves moving very swiftly and certainly and with a minimum of confusion. If you try this technique, you will find that such simple issues as finding a place to hang your still burning torch become critical due to the lack of time available to perform the whole operation before a weld cools.

Good hammer-welded sheet metal joints can be things of great beauty. The time needed to correct the distortion resulting from using this welding technique may be worth the extra effort. However, I am not sure that MIG welding isn't a better bet if you haven't already mastered hammer welding. It's a matter of temperament, choice and preference.

If you do decide to go the gas welding route, you will have to learn the basics of welding before you ever get

Although electric welding has almost completely replaced oxy-acetylene welding in commercial body shops in recent years, restoration work still benefits from gas welding in some situations.

A "GasSaver" type valve is very useful when you do hammer welding. When you hang the torch up on the valve hook, the gas flow is stopped and the flame goes out. When you remove the torch handle from the hook, the gas flow is reestablished and the torch can be lit from the device's pilot light. Without one of these valves, you will have trouble quickly finding a place to safely stash your torch during the hammering and quenching phases of hammer welding.

near sheet metal. Foremost among these considerations is safety. Acetylene is inherently unstable and capable of violent spontaneous combustion. It must be treated with great caution and respect. Pressurized oxygen can burn explosively in the presence of something as innocuous as engine oil, and must also be treated with considerable respect. The oxy-acetylene flame is almost unearthly hot and will do as good a job on your flesh as most of the exotic weaponry in the latest Steven Spielberg sci-fi thriller.

There are a few things about gas welding that are subject to myth, rumor and misconception. The first is that virtually any welding should be done with anything but a neutral flame. The neutral flame is the sharp, focused, unfeathered flame that you can adjust your torch to. The feathery flame is acetylene rich (carburizing) and the hissing pale blue one is oxygen rich (oxidizing). Always use a neutral flame when you weld sheet metal. The proponents of using a mild carburizing flame for sheet metal welding tend to eat goulash before breakfast and wear combat boots.

Most people who are inexperienced at gas welding sheet metal tend to use torch tips that are grossly oversized for the job at hand. The result is burn-through and distortion. The tips supplied with most welding outfits go from the mildly useful to the kinds of tips that would best be used on bridge girders and ship bulkheads. Before you attack sheet metal, be sure that you are using a sufficiently small tip. The key in this work is keeping the heat very local to your weld. That avoids heat buildup and distortion.

When you torch weld sheet metal, be sure to use plenty of tack welds to hold things in place before you run your bead because surfaces will start to move as they get hot. Learn the technique of using the end of your filler rod to block heat from reaching sensitive edges. The key to success is torch technique and, in the case of sheet metal, this means forehand welding with tip angle, rate of travel, torch distance

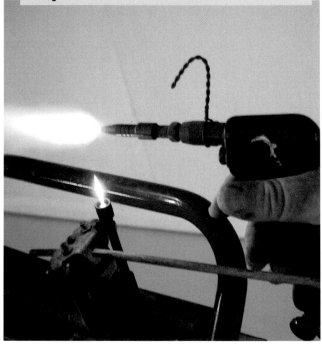

and torch manipulation (weaving) techniques appropriate to the special requirements of sheet metal welding. Only practice will give you mastery of these critical aspects of this work.

One very good habit to acquire in working with flame-generated heat is to control heat applications by moving the flame in and out from your work, not sideways. This is critical in some soldering applications, but is also a good habit in welding. Unfortunately, it seems that most people's reflexes don't work this way, and you will have to cultivate

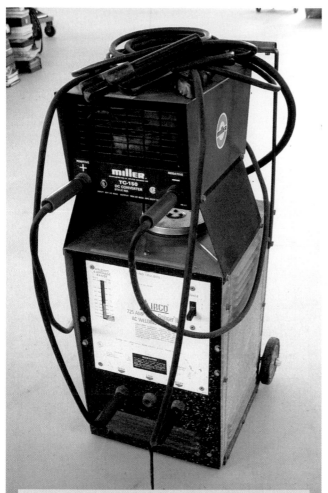

This stick welder has been fitted with a DC converter (top box) and is extremely useful for general purpose welding. Although sheet metal rod is still sold for welders like this one, the results with it are far inferior to what can be accomplished with a MIG welding system.

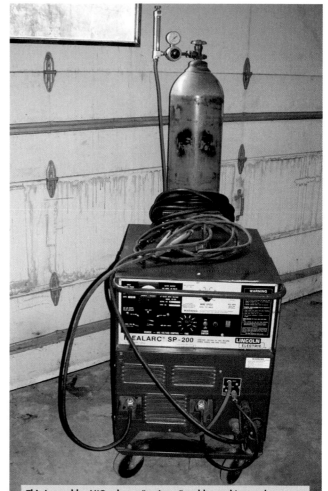

This is an older MIG, almost "antique," welder and is very heavy and bulky by today's standards. In MIG welding, wire speed is somewhat comparable to the amperage or "heat" setting on a stick welder, and the voltage adjustment is comparable to arc length in stick welding.

Modern MIG welders are relatively inexpensive and are sold in many different kinds of stores, from welding suppliers, to lumber and hardware stores and farm stores.

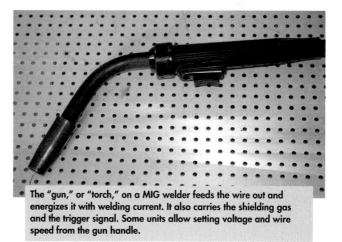

The "gun," or "torch," on a MIG welder feeds the wire out and energizes it with welding current. It also carries the shielding gas and the trigger signal. Some units allow setting voltage and wire speed from the gun handle.

this approach if you want to make it yours. Remember, when things look too hot, pull back, then adjust your rate of travel.

Finally, do not attempt to do too much welding with small oxy-acetylene tanks. Miniature acetylene tanks are OK for very small jobs, but if you attempt to withdraw gas from an acetylene cylinder at a rate of more than 1/7 of its

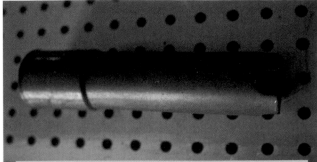

This "spot" attachment allows a MIG welder to make a button-hole or through weld. MIG welders don't do real resistance welding, but they can approximate that appearance by melting a spot in one layer of metal through and into the layer below it.

Some MIG welders allow you to set "burnback," and have settings for "stitch on" and "stitch off" timer control. The second knob down on this control panel is for setting a timer to make spot type welds.

0.023-inch welding wire is very fine, as you can see in this disassembled end of a MIG gun.

Spot welding was used in the production of many collectible cars. Modern unibody cars have upwards of 4,000 spot welds holding them together. The clamp-type spot welder, shown here, does very nice work if you can gain access for its jaws.

capacity per hour, you will find that the tank will discharge the acetone in which its acetylene is dissolved, and you will have an awfully messy weld. For the same reason, when an acetylene tank is laid on its side in transit or for some other reason, it must be stood upright before it is used for at least the same amount of time (up to 24 hours) that it sat on its side. Otherwise, it will discharge acetone.

Electric Welding

At about the same time that portable oxy-acetylene welding equipment was being perfected, electric welding became practical. In this technique, an electric arc (either AC or DC) is used to heat the area of a weld. Some electric techniques like TIG (Tungsten Inert Gas), carbon arc and

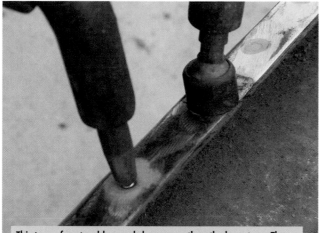

This type of spot welder needs less access than the lever type. The blunt contact energizes the base metal, and the sharp contact makes the weld. You have to press hard with both contacts to make this kind of welding work. More modern versions use computer controls.

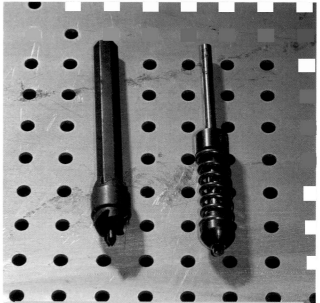

The spot weld cutter on the left, and the pilot drill on the right, are used together to remove old spot welds. First, you drill a pilot hole in the center of the spot weld that you want to remove, and then you drill the weld out with the cutter. This type of cutter comes in two or three sizes.

resistance ("spot") welding use non-consumable electrodes and either weld by heat or heat and pressure. Some of these techniques require the addition of filler material from a rod. Other techniques, such as MIG and "stick," (shielded arc) welding always use a consumable electrode to add metal to welds.

From the 1920s on, stick welding became increasingly important in structural welding and was applied to sheet metal with some degree of success. While people did weld sheet metal with stick electrodes, and even did this with AC equipment, the results were often pretty terrible, while the skill required was enormous. Massive improvements in alloys and fluxes in the decades immediately before and after World War II made stick welding a little more usable on sheet metal, but gas welding always seemed to be a better way to go.

Enter the MIG welder.

Originally, wire feed welders were proposed only as a way to save the expense of wasted electrode stubs in conventional shielded arc welding. The idea was to feed a continuous wire into a weld and avoid creating the stubs that occur as welding rods are consumed to points near to their ends. Craftsmen tended to throw away very long stubs to avoid getting caught changing rods in the middles of welds. Feeding a wire electrode also made changing sticks in the middles of welds unnecessary. The only problem was fluxing the weld.

Stick welding relies on the powdered flux that surrounds metal electrodes. This flux vaporizes at welding temperatures and, in part, turns into a shielding gas that protects welds as they are being made and when they cool from atmospheric corrosion. A protective layer of slag, formed from elements in the flux, protects welds during final cooling.

Several products called "weld through primers" are available. They are used to protect spot and MIG welds. You spray them on a weld area between and on pieces BEFORE you weld them together. This is very useful in protecting the overlaps in welded lap joints, where protection cannot be added effectively after a weld is made because there is no access to the area. In this situation, conventional rust-proofing agents would interfere with the electrical conductivity that is necessary to make MIG and spot welds. Weld through primers survive the heat of welding and provide excellent protection.

Using a spot abrasive blaster allows you to see spot welds before you consider what to do with them. Note how it has removed paint from the recesses of spot welds that a disc sander could not get.

Automatic, self-dimming welding lenses, like this one, allow you to see what you are doing through an undarkened lens. When you start an arc, the lens automatically dims in 1/5000th of a second, or less. Both beginners and pros have given rave reviews to automatic lenses.

With a continuous feed of wire welding material, fluxing did not seem possible because a coated wire could not be fed smoothly and without shedding its flux as it was fed. The first solution was to use flux-cored wire, but this was expensive and hard to work with. A better solution was to feed a relatively inert shielding gas, like helium (and later argon and carbon dioxide blends, and later still just carbon dioxide) from the torch tip (properly, "electrode handle" or "gun") into the weld area to shield the weld.

Very quickly, the application of wire feed gas shielded welding technology was applied to sheet metal fabrication and repair. Refinements in wire composition, gas blends and wire feeding mechanisms occurred early in the development of MIG welding. Improvements in the electrical characteristics of the MIG welding machine transformers quickly followed. Solid state controls and circuitry greatly reduced the sizes and weights of later MIG machines, and prices fell, accordingly. Features like "stitch timers," which turn the arc on and off automatically to reduce heat buildup in welded areas, became standard features on many MIG welders, instead of expensive add-ons.

In sum, the rapid development of MIG welders and consumables in the last three decades has literally revolutionized body shop practice. Virtually every body shop has one or more of these welders, while the old oxy-acetylene torches are relegated to dusty corners in many

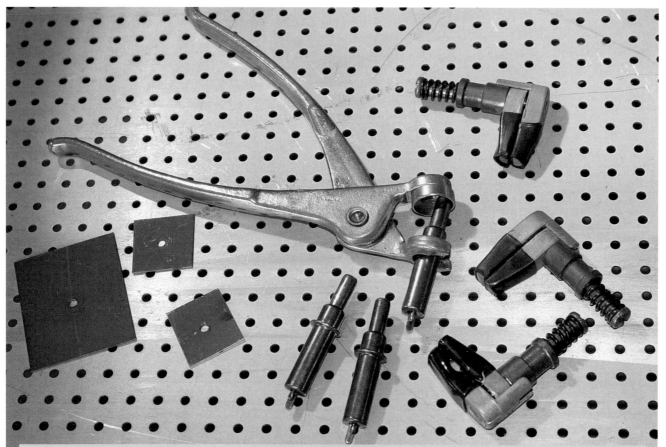

Holding pieces in place to weld them is critical to good patch welding. Welding magnets and Cleco spring fastener devices are endlessly useful for doing this.

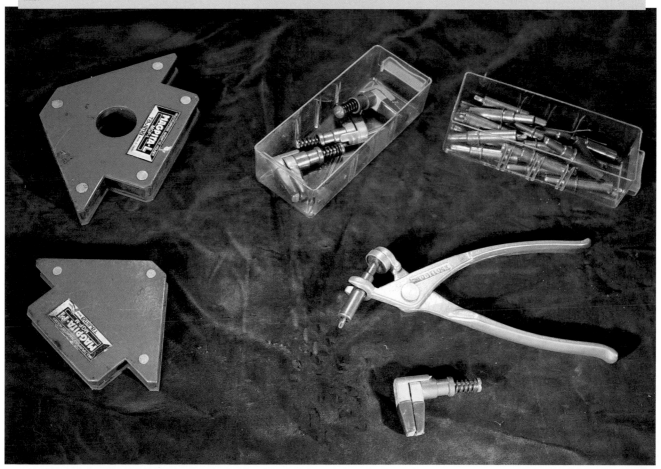

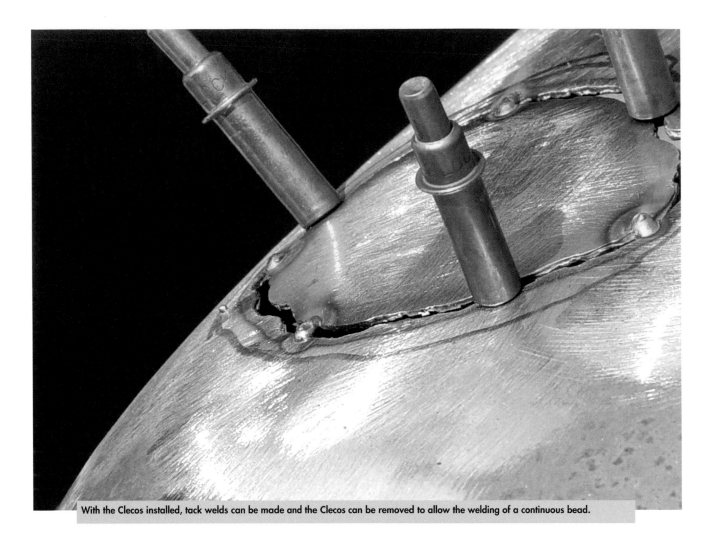

With the Clecos installed, tack welds can be made and the Clecos can be removed to allow the welding of a continuous bead.

of these shops. MIG welding is cheap, fast, and effective. It requires far less skill than gas welding when sheet metal is involved. In recent decades, minimum wire sizes available for these units have been reduced from 0.035 inch to 0.030 inch and to 0.023 inch/0.025 inch. This thinner wire makes MIG welders capable of welding with even less heat and distortion. If you are contemplating getting involved in sheet metal welding, MIG is the best way to go.

The specific MIG format used on sheet metal is called "short arc," which involves burning off the end of the wire electrode in a cycle of "shorts" and then reestablishing the shorts as the wire feeds out of the gun and into the weld puddle. The cycle is repeated roughly 200 times a second.

Other possible MIG welding modes are globular transfer—globs of metal are transferred—and spray arc welding, which is a molecular transfer of metal. These last two formats are not used in sheet metal work. Wire speed and voltage in MIG welding are adjusted to achieve a desirable arc. These adjustments are often made primarily from the sound of the arc as it occurs. An arc with a "frying egg" sound is usually ideal.

Control of the MIG welding arc is accomplished by adjusting voltage, which basically affects weld penetration and height and wire speed, which basically relates to amperage and arc cycle frequency. Some of the newer MIG

units automatically adjust their voltages when wire speed is set, and many MIG welders have a "burnback" control that times the period that the electrode wire is energized after the gun trigger is released and the wire feed stops. This last adjustment is used to prevent the wire from sticking in the puddle when it freezes at the end of a welding application. "On" and "off" times can be set on welders with stitch controls. All MIG welders operate with direct current (DC).

Many MIG welders come with a spot attachment and spot timer. This setup allows you to make welds by heating through a hole in the top layer of metal into an underlying layer. This isn't as neat in appearance as a real resistance weld, but it can be very useful in restoration work.

Resistance, or "spot," welders create a joint by applying very high amperages and fairly high pressures to the small spot being welded. All of these involve mechanically or manually activated electrodes that are closed by levers or pneumatic devices. No filler materials are added. Resistance welding is extremely useful in reestablishing broken or corroded welds that were originally made with this technique.

Some welding modes, such as carbon arc welding, have become pretty much obsolete because other techniques outperform them in almost every application. Others,

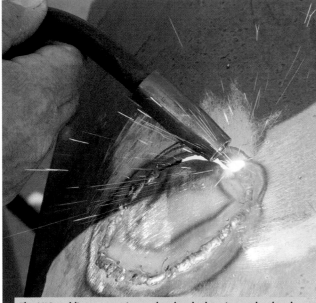

The MIG welding process is very hot, but the heat is very local and confined. This limits distortion of metal in the weld area.

The final step in section welding in metal is to grind the weld bead down almost level with the surrounding metal.

such as TIG welding, (properly called GTAW for "Gas Tungsten Arc Welding") still excel in specific applications such as stainless steel and aluminum weldments. In these applications, they outperform other approaches, such as the use of spool guns with MIG welding, but they have little general application beyond a few specialties.

While TIG welding produces very neat, low distortion welds in sheet steel, it is slow, the equipment for it is expensive and it requires great skill to perform. MIG welding is, by the way, replacing TIG in many situations where aluminum must be welded.

One big caution that applies to all electric welding on automobiles is to be sure to disconnect the battery and alternator from a car before welding commences. Welding current surges can destroy alternator diodes and other sensitive solid state devices. They can also cause battery explosions, at least theoretically. For obvious reasons, never weld near gasoline tanks, hoses, lines, or other places where gasoline liquid or fumes can be ignited.

A recent development in arc welding has been the invention inexpensive, safe and effective automatic self-dimming welding lenses. This type of device makes it much easier to weld than with a conventional helmet and lens. I would recommend these automatic lenses to anyone who plans to do much electric welding. They greatly simplify and aid this work.

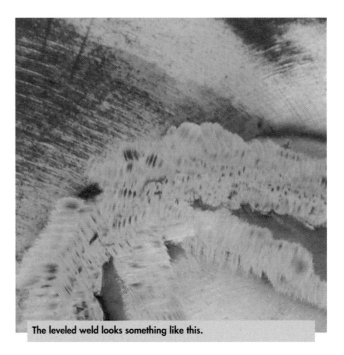

The leveled weld looks something like this.

Chapter 24

Auto Body Metal Preparation and Filling

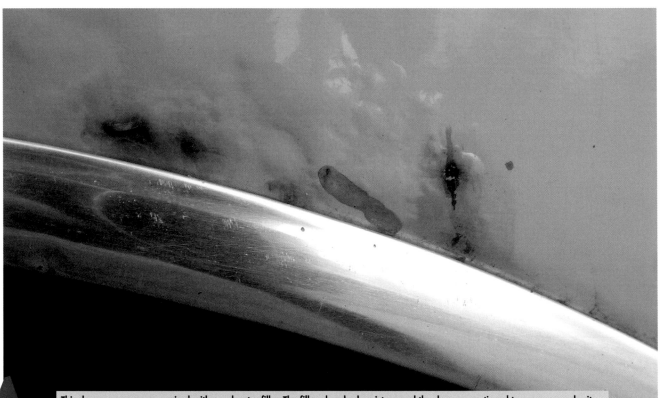

This damage was once repaired with a polyester filler. The filler absorbed moisture and the damage continued to progress under it. Newer polyester fillers are said not to have this problem. Note that this filler was used near panel edges where it had little chance of succeeding. A lead repair would have been a better bet.

AUTO BODY REPAIR AND REFINISHING is a process that involves building a surface step by step to a final result. If, at any step, there is a defect, this defect will often be carried into the final result. There are some available fixes as you go along, but these frequently involve compromising quality.

For example, both body lead and polyester fillers are susceptible to pinholing. In either case, pinholes are usually a result of poor application technique. In both cases, the pinholes can be filled with spot or glazing putty. This solves the immediate problem, but frequently creates more problems down the line. Putties have a tendency to shrink and to trap solvents that later cause paint to bubble, unless they are allowed to dry for extended periods.

Since raw enthusiasm or a production schedule usually gets in the way of these extended drying times, the putty used to fill pinholes frequently lifts paint, or paint falls into it and creates small but noticeable depressions in the final refinished surface. This sequence can take months, but it is all too common. The point is, any mistake in building up to a final finish will usually come back to haunt you, so there is a premium on not making mistakes as you are building a finish. Body finishing may not have the precision look of machine shop work, but it is definitely precision work, nonetheless.

Concepts in Body Filling

Ideally, there would never be any need to use body filler because metal would be bumped and metal finished into perfect contours without the use of any filling material. However, this usually is not practical. There are some dents that, because of their locations, defy bumping out. Usually, this involves a lack of rear access. In other cases, welding and bumping repairs have left minor lowered areas that cannot be readily metal finished by picking and filing. On newer cars, the sheet metal is so thin that there is literally not enough of it to file to a finish without weakening panels or actually cutting through them. In these cases, a little fill is an appropriate remedy.

It should be emphasized that the use of a little filler may be appropriate, but no matter what type of filler is used—lead or plastic—it is never appropriate to pile it up in 1/2-inch-thick globs. There is always an alternative available to straighten the underlying metal better than that.

There are basically two classes of filler in common use, as well as a few uncommon fillers. The only appropriate filler for most restoration work is lead. That may seem a flatfooted statement, but it is made on behalf of a flatfooted fact. Restoration work aims at preservation, authenticity and permanence. Lead is the authentic repair for the period before the mid-1950s, and it is the only permanent repair filler.

Plastic fillers were introduced in the mid-1950s and quickly gained almost universal acceptance in the repair field. This was because they are cheap, fast to do and require only minor skill in application. They are also capable of producing repairs that are the equal of lead in finished appearance but not in durability or permanence.

The problem is that every generation of plastic fillers has come with the promise that, unlike its predecessors, it is permanent and won't fall out or allow corrosion to start behind filled areas. And with nearly perfect regularity, each generation of polyester fillers has failed in both regards. While there has been general improvement in these fillers over the years, and while some of them are better than others, none seem to have the adhesive strength, inherent strength or moisture sealing capabilities that body-filling lead alloys do.

Some polyester fillers are just plain junk, such as those that are thickened with talc. These will start to self-destruct shortly after application. Others are formulated more carefully and use non-absorbing thickeners, such as granite spheres. If these are applied properly over well-cleaned surfaces, they will last long enough to make respectable repairs. I doubt if any of them will last long enough for restoration work, and when plastic filler fails, it usually has allowed the original damage to progress to a much worse state than when the repair with it was made.

It is interesting to note that as recently as 30 years ago, the automobile companies still used lead to seal the seams on some top-quality models, and they often used lead to repair body damage that occurred on their assembly lines. In part, this reflected the inherent quality of lead repairs and, in part, it was because the time required for plastic filler to cure is not readily available in manufacturing production schedules. Large reductions in the damage done to cars during their manufacturing made this a non-issue by the late 1980s. In any case, environmental objections to lead caused its abandonment in production situations about 30 years ago.

I cannot imagine a basis for claiming that plastic filler repairs are superior to lead in quality. The usual claims made for them involve material cost, overall labor cost and the skill level required to apply them. None of these claims recommend them for restoration. It is true that virtually anyone can use plastic filler with little more instruction than is printed on the can, while lead work is nowhere near that easy. Yet, lead work is an attainable skill for almost anyone who takes the time to understand the principles underlying its use and to practice with the materials and processes involved. Unfortunately, the health and environmental issues that attend the use of lead body fillers are both valid and serious.

There are some fillers that are neither lead nor conventional polyester-based plastics. Some of these are epoxy resins that are filled with materials like aluminum powder. Most of these are comparatively expensive and, from what I have seen, they are no more than marginally better than conventional polyester-based fillers. Ditzler's highly regarded Alum-A-Lead, for example, used to fall out after five or more years of service, just like the cheaper polyesters did. Then there are the real exotics in the world of fillers, the sprayable polyesters. These achieved some unsavory notoriety decades ago and again just a few years ago, when several restoration shops filed suits against one of the companies that manufactured this stuff. They came back, recently, even with their dismal record.

I have met people who swear by sprayable fillers, and I have met really good body practitioners who use them in restoration work. Still, based on my personal knowledge of these materials, I would not recommend them or anything but lead alloys for body repair filling in almost all situations. For limited use in restoration work, the environmental and health objections to lead filler are minimal.

There are a few places where plastic fillers should be used in preference to lead. These must always be places where very little filler thickness is needed and where buildup can be kept to a minimum. The usual reason that plastic filler must be used is that framing wood, upholstery, wiring or something else that will not tolerate the heat associated with tinning and leading is so close to a repair area as to make lead filling repairs impossible. In these cases, plastic

Abrasive blasting is very effective in removing paint, corrosion and, particularly, deep rust pits. It works well on small parts like these, but can cause warping in large panels unless special plastic beads (PMB for Plastic Media Blasting) or very fine mineral abrasives at high pressures are used.

can be used sparingly. However, plastic should never be used on edges or corners of panels because it lacks the necessary adhesion and structural strength for this kind of service.

Plastic also must never be used where it is not or cannot be sealed from behind because all plastics are, to some degree, susceptible to absorbing moisture, resulting in rust and loss of adhesion. The barbaric practice of drilling holes in a panel and pushing polyester filler through them, to give it mechanical adhesion to a repair, will cause all kinds of problems unless the backside of such a repair is sealed against moisture. Even then, this is a sloppy, destructive and substandard practice.

Surface Preparation for Fillers

Whatever type of filler you use, surface preparation will be critical to achieving a successful bond. Welds in areas where fillers will be used must be ground almost flat. Do not attempt to pile filler over welds to hide them.

The most critical aspect of surface preparation involves getting the underlying metal absolutely clean. This means that all paint, rust, oil, silicone, loose galvanizing, flying smut, etc. must be removed. If any of these contaminants are left on a sheet metal surface, the adhesion of coatings or fillers will be adversely affected and corrosion is likely to start.

The best way to clean panels in preparation for coating them or applying filler to them is to sand them, wire brush them or very carefully blast them with abrasives in deeply pitted areas. Metal that has been cleaned by dipping it in chemicals still needs to be recleaned before coating or filling it. Since abrasive blasting has a great potential for

warping sheet metal, it must be used very sparingly and very carefully. Blasting is very effective in dealing with porous areas, such as welds that will not yield their scale to wire brushing or sanding.

If you do use blasting in areas where access prohibits the use of other cleaning methods, be careful not to use aluminum oxide blasting media if lead application is to follow—it will interfere with proper tinning. For some reason, aluminum oxide sandpaper does not cause this problem as badly as blasting with aluminum oxide media.

One useful old practice was to use muriatic acid (HCL) to clean and etch metal in preparation for painting and as a tinning flux. This is a practice that has slipped into disuse, and properly so. It is difficult to clean metal after that kind of an etch, and the acid fumes are dangerous. While there is something quaint about cutting the acid with zinc and all that ancient flapdoodle, this is one "lost art" that should remain among the missing.

Silicone is one of the deadly enemies of filler and coating adhesion. Since this is a component in most auto waxes and many lubricants (as an anti-foam agent, in the latter), it has to be removed from panels very thoroughly before they are filled or coated. Silicone and wax removers, such as Pre-Kleeno (R-M) and PrepSol (DuPont), should be used before paint is sanded off. Otherwise, sanding will push silicone residues into the metal. It is also good practice to wipe down sanded bare metal with a silicone and wax remover before you tin for lead application or apply plastic filler.

A 36- or 50-grit sandpaper will do nicely to provide a surface for good filler adhesion. It is best to extend filler about 2 inches, or more, beyond an actual repair area, so that it can be blended smoothly into the underlying and surrounding metal. Always design your filling for minimum

A spot blaster is great for removing small pitted areas from a panel before you strip it with a disc sander or by other means.

Body lead comes in many sizes, alloys and shapes. Not all lead alloys are suitable for bodywork.

height. The glob-it-on-grind-it-off-later school has several obvious drawbacks.

The Theory of Lead

The quality of tin/lead alloys—other alloying elements, such as bismuth are sometimes used to supplement or to replace tin—that makes them suitable for body filler is that they enjoy a "plastic" state for about 100 to 150 degrees F., depending on their proportions of tin and lead. In this plastic state, they are neither liquid nor solid, but have a paste consistency. Auto body tin/lead alloys typically begin to soften at 361 degrees F. and go liquid in the 450 to 500-degree range, depending on their alloying proportions. These proportions in tin/lead body alloys vary from 10 to 60 percent tin, with greater tin content resulting in lower melting points.

Interestingly, alloys of tin and lead melt at lower temperatures than do either of these metals in their pure form. The best general-purpose body fill alloy is composed of 30 percent tin and 70 percent lead. Alloys with more lead tend to be stronger, but have more limited plastic ranges and are, therefore, more difficult to work with. When structural strength is not the prime consideration, 30/70 body lead is the best bet. It is important to note that not all "lead" is suitable for bodywork as, for example, plumber's lead, which is nearly pure lead. The 20/80 and 10/90 tin/lead alloys that are used to seal body seams and for other specialized purposes are not particularly suitable for general body filling.

Lead filling technology has been around for literally hundreds of years. The paraphernalia for applying body lead is simple and relatively inexpensive to acquire. It consists of a low-temperature flame source (air/propane and air/acetylene work best) and assorted hardwood paddles, and paddle lubricant (mutton tallow works best). While more exotic application methods such as "lead guns" have been

These old "lead guns" shoot molten lead. They were used with a "cold tinning" process to apply lead to body panels at very low temperatures. Modern body technicians would never use tools like these because the lead dust that they generate can be deadly.

used, and innovations such as "cold tinning" once found considerable favor, these techniques have generally fallen into disuse because they are inherently dangerous and require great skill to achieve favorable results.

Success in applying body lead involves a certain amount of dexterity in torch and paddle manipulation, but above all, it involves close observation. If you carefully watch the lead with which you are working, you will have ample indications of its changes of state from solid to paste to liquid. While lead doesn't give the obvious color change and sparking signals that steel does when it is heated, it does give discernible indications that can be used to effectively

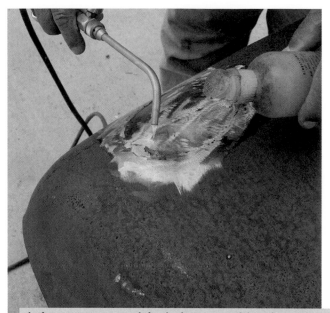

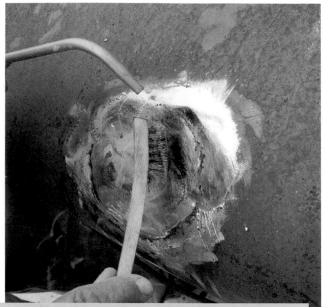

The first step in tinning panels for "leading" is to sand them clean and to apply a good flux. The flux should fizzle and sputter off the heated panel, leaving a thin brown residue. Always use a flux that is designed for tinning under body lead. Sometimes, it helps to brush flux into the metal with a stainless steel bristled hand brush.

This air/acetylene torch is ideal for tinning for lead and for applying lead.

This natural gas/air torch is used in factory production to apply lead to exotic sports cars and other custom-built auto bodies.

gauge its state and to avoid working it too cold or too hot. You have to watch carefully. A lead surface will sag and shine when it is hot and frost as it cools.

Tinning for Lead

Tinning means depositing a small amount (thickness) of solder on a surface to create an initial bond. When this has been done, lead can be built up over the tinned area. Tinning involves the use of a flux to allow solder to bond to steel or aluminum without corrosion. In this case, the flux acts as a cleaner to keep the metal from oxidizing at the temperatures that are needed for initial bonding. Once the

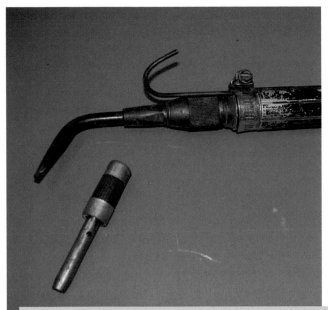
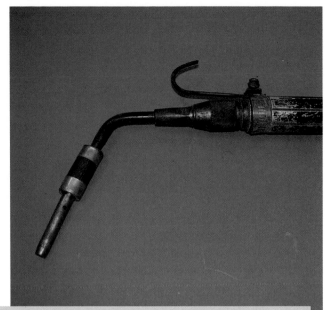

An inexpensive approach to getting an air/acetylene torch is the push-on tip shown in these photographs. You simply push it onto the end of n conventional acetylene torch and fire it with acetylene (only) from your torch outfit's tank.

metal is tinned, there is no need for further fluxing because the solder coating from the tinning shields the underlying metal and prevents corrosion.

The key to tinning is to start with absolutely clean metal. It is tempting to try to bridge over a speck of hard-to-clean corrosion here and there, but it won't work. The object is not to remove most of the rust on a surface; it is to remove all of it. When a surface to be tinned is completely clean, it can be heated and fluxed. Only a flux designed for use under body lead should be used. There are many kinds of body lead flux available; the most common are fluids with zinc chloride dissolved in them and pastes that contain tiny bits of solder. Some of the older flux powders and pastes are still available.

Fluxing fluids are applied to hot metal—hot enough to fizzle them as they are brushed on with a solder brush or wiped on with a rag. Then, a flame is played over the metal until 50/50 coil solder can be melted onto the fluxed surface. When the solder melts, a thin coating is deposited and wiped gently over the surface.

The wiping is done to spread the solder and to remove the flux debris and residues from it. The wiped, tinned area will have a clean and shiny appearance. If any more than a trace of flux is left at this point, it will embed in the lead that is applied over it and cause problems later.

Soldering pastes contain minute bits of solder in a flux matrix. These pastes are applied much as the fluids are, except that they are heated after application and until they turn brown and melt on the surface that is being tinned. Then, they are wiped. Pastes have the advantage of keeping surfaces cleaner than flux fluids because they bond solder to them just as the flux is cleaning them, without having to go to a second step to apply solder. Tinning pastes tend to be quite expensive.

The wiping operation in tinning must be vigorous

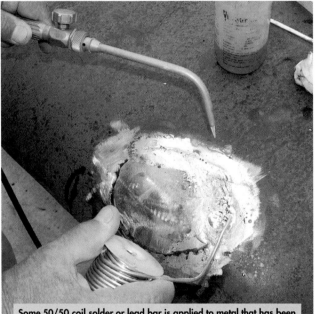

Some 50/50 coil solder or lead bar is applied to metal that has been heated with a flame hot enough to melt the solder on its surface.

enough to remove almost all flux residues, but not so vigorous as to remove the tinning solder itself and uncover the base metal. This would defeat the purpose of the tinning operation. While there are many theories and individual preferences regarding what solder to use for tinning, 50/50 has proven best for this purpose.

Never make the mistake of tinning with 50/50 acid core solder. This malpractice was advocated at one time by trolls and gremlins who operated body shops under drawbridges. It is a terrible practice that causes all sorts of problems because the corrosive acid flux continues to eat away at the base metal and solder after you complete your work.

The flame used in tinning and lead application has to

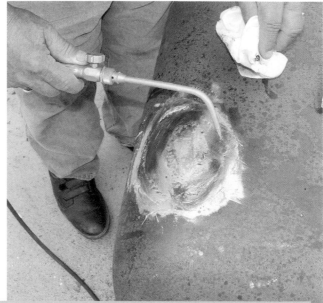

After tinning, the solder should be wiped gently off the metal to reveal any breaches in its adhesion to, and coverage of, the base metal. This step also removes excess flux. Do not wipe very hard, or you will remove too much solder. It is very easy to make that mistake.

be a fairly mild, soft flame with good neutral characteristics. Some people even use infrared heat lamps for this purpose; others use propane torches. I prefer to use an "air-acetylene" torch, which is relatively inexpensive and provides a calm, long, clean flame with very nice temperature gradations through its length. You can generate this flame either with a special torch that you run directly off an acetylene tank (often called a "plumber's torch"), or with an inexpensive air-acetylene adapter tip that you slip over a regular oxy-acetylene torch tip. In the latter case, only acetylene gas is used.

Tinning and leading with an oxyacetylene torch and a carburizing (carbon or fuel gas rich) flame is something like going after a house fly with a rowboat oar—it can be made to work after a fashion, but good results are difficult to achieve. The oxy-acetylene flame is simply too intensely hot, small and closely graduated for lead work. Its use is likely to cause local overheating and alloy separation. Also, it requires your complete attention just to manage the flame. In lead work, there is plenty to do besides controlling the flame, so stick with a cooler, softer flame that is easier to direct and control.

The Practice of Applying Lead

After tinning, body lead is applied and shaped with a lubricated hardwood paddle. The same kind of torch that you used for tinning is used to supply the heat for lead application. Some lead men skip tinning with 50/50 coil solder or paste, and use 30/70 body lead to wipe a tin coat on base metal. This practice saves very little time and will not produce the bond strength that tinning with 50/50 will. It's a practice that should be avoided.

Experience with lead is essential to gaining proficiency in this work, as leading is a matter of fine coordination and precise judgment. There are a few rules that the beginner should note. It is much easier to apply lead to a horizontal surface than to a vertical one. Beginners, who usually have problems with overheating the lead and causing it to run and even to separate into its constituent metals, will find that applying lead to vertical surfaces is like trying to make water run uphill. For this reason, it is best to perform leading when surfaces are horizontal. Sometimes it is not possible, but if it can be arranged, it is all to the good.

Cleanliness is essential in leading. Any contamination that gets into the lead will cause problems later. The practice of working with charred or dirty paddles or in the presence of sanding debris should to be avoided. Always make sure that the lead bar that you are applying is as free from contamination as possible.

The most crucial element in applying body lead is to control surface temperature. If you overheat body lead, it will turn to liquid, separate into its tin and lead constituents, and run out or become unworkable. Separated lead has little plastic state so it's virtually impossible to form it with a paddle, after you peel and scrape it off of your shoes.

At the other extreme, if you attempt to work lead too cold, it becomes grainy and crystallized, and ultimately yields a result that is porous and weak. And, if all of that isn't enough, lead also tends to get funky if it is overworked; so you have to get things into shape quickly after you start to paddle your lead.

Temperature control is achieved by watching the lead surface carefully for the indications of the solid/paste/liquid change-of-state mentioned above. The trick is to cycle the torch flame over the area that you are working every 5 seconds or so and to do your paddle forming between these flame applications. Remember, your paddle will tend to cool the lead, and it is bad practice to work it right up to the point that it goes solid. If you work too long and allow

Good lead paddles, such as the three shown at the bottom left, are inexpensive. The tin of refined mutton tallow (bottom right) will last a car restoration hobbyist for many years. The paddle on the top of the photo is about 75 years old. It's a metal paddle with a wooden handle. You were supposed to grease the paddle with chassis grease from a gun until the hollow handle was full. Then the grease dripped out of a hole in the heal of the paddle and lubricated your work. It is a terrible idea to use chassis grease to lubricate a paddle for lead work.

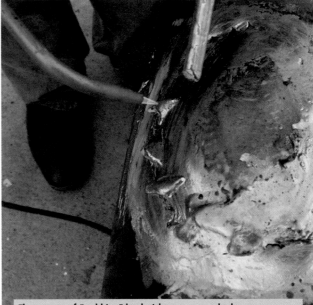

The process of "stubbing" lead sticks onto a panel takes some practice, but it is not difficult to master. You play your torch flame on the panel to keep it warm and on the bottom 1/2 inch of your lead bar to separate a stub from the it and deposit it on the panel.

As you paddle lead, you have to keep your paddle lubricated with melted tallow. From time to time, use your torch to melt a puddle of tallow and dip the working surface of your paddle in it.

too much cooling between flame applications, it will be difficult to heat the lead throughout its thickness without overheating the material close to the surface where the torch is played. Keep things well into a mushy state in the area on which you are working. Of course, lead applications that are too thick exacerbate this problem.

The best torch manipulation for temperature control is in-and-out. Human reflexes tend to cause one to move a torch to one side or the other when overheating in an area occurs, but this only causes a "meltdown" someplace adjacent. Learn to withdraw the torch from your work when heat buildup is excessive, and to bring it in when more heat is needed. The best situation when you apply lead is to keep it in a state like cold peanut butter and to spread it at about that consistency.

Lead is usually sold in 1/4-lb. and 1/2-lb. sticks, and in 1- and 1 1/4-lb. bars. There are also some odd shapes out there, like the wonderful "star bars" (they handle heat more evenly). I have found the 1/4-lb. sticks far easier to work with than the heavier bars. In practice, a stick is held in contact with the tinned panel to which it will be applied and teased with a flame that is played just above its contact with the panel, until the bar softens. The object is to heat about the bottom 3/4 inch of the stick until it goes plastic and sticks to the tinned panel. Then, it can be twisted off ("stubbed"), leaving its stub adhered to the panel. When you see the stick begin to soften, push it in and give it a twist. Perfecting the timing of this sequence will take a little practice. Several of these 3/4-inch-long deposits may be required to get enough lead in place to paddle into, and fill depressions in, the area on which you are working.

The tool used to form lead is a hardwood (usually maple) paddle that has been treated with a lubricant. The lubricant allows the paddle to glide over the lead without sticking or excessive charring. The paddle should be relubricated during use with refined mutton tallow or bee's wax. This is done by playing your torch flame over the solid lubricant and dipping the paddle's working surface into the liquid lubricant that is melted. Tallow works far better than bee's wax because it is easier to remove it later from the leaded panel.

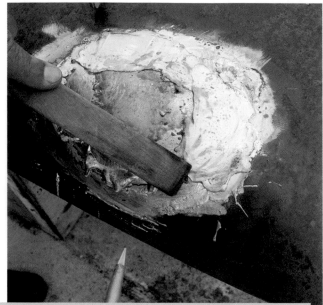

You play your, flame over the lead as you paddle it. Temperature control is the key to successful lead work. If you underheat your lead, it will be grainy, porous and weak. If you overheat it, it will vacate its alloy form, separating into its tin and lead constituents. It will then drop out of the repair area and decorate your shoes.

A mush pot is the best way to apply lead when you have to apply it thickly. You adjust your heat to keep the lead in the pot at peanut butter-like consistency and paddle it right out of the pot and onto your work. You can also make a mush pot out of sheet metal with a ramped side for easy lead removal. Always remember that applying lead too thick is never a good idea.

The same trolls and gremlins who used to tin sheet metal with acid core solder also used to use motor oil as a lubricant for leading paddles. That was "way back when," at which time motor oils didn't have the detergent and other additive packages that they contain today. Even then, motor oil was a poor choice for paddle lubrication because it was hard to cleanse ("kill" in the terminology of lead work). Given the content of the present detergent additive packages used in motor oils, it is impossible to kill this stuff. Refined mutton tallow is inexpensive and has advantages over all other possible lead lubricants that I have encountered.

One trick that you may find handy in lead work is to fabricate special paddles for working with special panel shapes. Commercially available paddles tend to be flat or convex. These are fine for work on flat, crowned, and mildly reverse crowned panels. However, if you are working with some odd configuration, like a small diameter cylindrical shape, you will find a nearly matching concave paddle invaluable. Good, dry maple board, about 1 x 2-inch, can be filed and sanded into a variety of special shapes. Its working surfaces should be dipped or boiled in melted tallow before you use it to form lead.

If, for some reason, you are working with a fairly thick lead application—a practice that should generally be avoided—you will find it difficult to make your torch heat penetrate the entire lead thickness. Sometimes, even careful torch control won't accomplish this. When this happens, the lead can be grooved with the side edge of a paddle, heated, and then paddled back flat, as necessary. This is not a good situation because it usually involves overworking the lead, but it is sometimes necessary. A better approach to thick lead is to keep the lead in its plastic state in a mush pot or ladle, and spoon it into place with your paddle. The use of a mush pot or ladle requires good manual skills and judgment, but it's sometimes the best approach.

While it is not necessary to quench lead, this is a good practice if the heat used in the tinning and lead application has caused any panel distortion. Quenching will tend to relieve this distortion and does no harm to the lead.

Some Body Solder "Don'ts"

Over the years the gremlins and trolls who had these body shops under the drawbridges developed some approaches to lead work that have not entirely disappeared from common usage. We can learn from their example how *not* to do things.

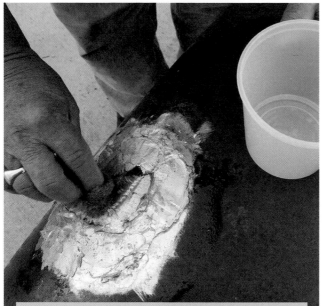

After you have completed applying body lead, you should "kill" it with a good metal conditioner. Do this both before and after you file the lead, otherwise you may put contaminants (flux and tallow residues) into the pores of the lead. That can cause paint to lift later. Ammonia and vinegar can also be used to kill lead.

In my opinion, lead is superior to plastic filler. However, when it is mindlessly piled into dents or over very rough bodywork, its inherent superiority becomes meaningless. Don't feel that just because you are using lead instead of plastic there is no limit to its usable depth.

Unlike plastic, which is best applied in progressive, thin layers, you should try to do all of your leading in one shot. Don't depress the center of a leaded area or gouge it to the point that more lead has to be added.

Don't work lead too hot or too cold. If you overheat it, you will probably lose the lead anyway. It will run off the panel and onto the floor. If you work it too cold, the lead will become granular and have poor strength and vibration resistance.

Don't overwork lead filler. It's like concrete; if you overwork it, it becomes brittle and funky.

Don't ever disc sand a leaded repair. This won't work because even though lead is a metal, it is far too soft to disc sand, and you will gouge and depress it. The fact that it is a metal makes it easy to file because it is similar to the steel that it is adhered to and that borders it, but this advantage does not extend to disc sanding. More important, lead dust is highly toxic and can be absorbed through the skin or aspirated and ingested with saliva. The body eliminates lead at such a slow rate that its effects tend to be cumulative. Lead poisoning is very unpleasant and/or deadly. There is no reason to disc sand lead; if you do, you will probably disappear, like those gremlins and trolls.

Finishing Lead

Finishing lead is relatively easy, particularly because it is a metal like the underlying panels that it is used to fill. It should be shaped with a Vixen-type body file of six, seven

or eight teeth-per-inch configuration, then finished with a finer Vixen-type file. A mill file can also be used. Body files should be slid away from you and sideways in a smooth, sweeping motion. They should always be lifted for the return stroke, never dragged back across your work.

It is best to work from the toe of the file to its heel with a gentle rocking motion, and the file should always be glided lightly over the lead and steel, not pushed into it. Always file from the outside of a leaded repair area toward its center to avoid depressing the center. Vixen-type files are expensive, but they can be resharpened several times with a liquid hone (wet abrasive blast). A slightly dull file seems to work better than a fresh, sharp one because it has less tendency to gouge the lead. If you coat new, freshly sharpened files with a light application of turpentine, they will glide nicely until they are dull enough not to gouge. Turpentine is also an excellent preservative for body files.

The final contouring and smoothing of lead should be done with 50- and 80-grit open coat sandpaper mounted on a sanding board or wrapped around a body file or a flat paint stick. I prefer to use paint sticks for this work because, if you operate them with your fingertips, they give a very precise feel for the contours of the surfaces under them. Think about and feel what you are shaping while you file and sand lead filler, because the feel that comes back to you is really a status report on the contour of the surface under your file or sanding board.

The final step in lead finishing is to remove contaminants that can ruin the finish that you will build on top of your lead work. Tallow residues can be killed by scrubbing with Pre-Kleeno, PrepSol, and other similar solvents. Flux residues that may have worked up through the lead when it was being paddled can be neutralized with vinegar, an ammonia and water solution, or a sodium bicarbonate and water mix. In the latter two cases, mixing proportions are not critical. Killing the paddle lubricant and neutralizing flux residues may seem a fine point, but if these steps are not taken, you will probably regret it.

One way to effectively neutralize both flux and tallow residues in the same operation is to treat leaded areas with a good etching metal conditioner. This type of product still is offered by some major paint system manufacturers.

Plastic Fillers

Plastic filler is remarkably easy to use. Careful attention to the instructions on the can will tell you about all that you will need to know to carry you through. There are a few tricks to using plastic filler that I know, and there probably are several more that I don't know.

One potential pitfall with plastic filler is that the plastic tends to separate in its can. It should be stirred vigorously before the hardener (catalyst) is added to it. If this is not done, large wet spots that never fully cure may form in the catalyzed filler. Plastic filler should be mixed with its catalyst pretty much according to its manufacturer's recommended proportions. Exact analytical balance/

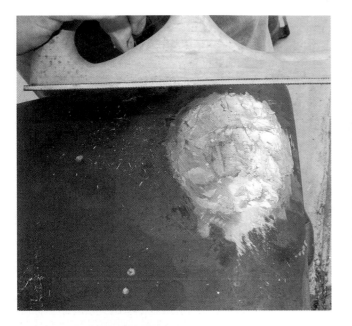

Successfully shaping lead with a body file takes a knack, but most people can develop this skill fairly quickly. The filing motion used is a rocking, sliding motion away from you and sideways. You should shift the weight on the file from its toe to its heel as you make your sweep. The small, one-hand file shown in the last photo is usually used to file against edges, but can also be used in final finishing of open areas.

micrometer measurements are not necessary, but if you get the mixing ratios too far off, the filler will never set or will set too fast.

Mix this stuff well, as the tendency is not to mix it well enough. However, try to avoid too vigorous a mixing regimen that will trap air bubbles in the plastic. This will cause pinholing and other mischief later. It is important that plastic fillers be mixed on clean, non-contaminated surfaces. Glass and sheet metal are preferred for this purpose. Some people mix their plastic filler and catalyst on waxed cardboard, only to find that the wax gets into the filler and causes all sorts of problems. Others have found that unwaxed cardboard absorbs the polyester catalyst and throws off the mixing proportions.

Plastic is applied to panels with a putty knife or squeegee. It should be pushed into and along panels to insure mechanical adhesion and to force air bubbles out of it. Several thin layers of plastic are always preferable to one thick one. It is a good idea to lay down one very thin final coat, extra carefully, as a kind of seal coat. At normal room temperatures, plastic filler can be shaped with a "cheese grater" file after about 20 minutes, or less, and it is best to accept this fact rather than to try to shorten the cure time by over-catalyzing or by applying heat to curing filler.

After plastic is grated into rough shape, it can be coated immediately with additional plastic filler to fill depressions or gouges from the first shaping operation. After a few hours—depending on temperature—the plastic can be finished with abrasive paper to bring it to proper final contour and smoothness before painting it. Pneumatic "air files" work very well for this operation, as do orbital "jitterbug" sanders. Final sanding is done by hand with sanding blocks.

These sanding boards can be used to do very fine shaping, smoothing and blending on panels that you have repaired with lead.

Turpentine is an excellent lubricant and preservative for body files.

After you have finished shaping a lead repair, "kill" it again with metal conditioner. The first "kill" should be before you file the lead.

It should be remembered that because plastic fillers usually are not waterproof, they must be sealed on both sides of a repair soon after they are applied. People who drive around with their Bondo showing will find that it will absorb enough moisture to cause corrosion of the metal under the plastic. That rust then expands and pushes the filler off the metal. This process can start before the filler is primed and painted. At some later date, the whole repair can fall off the car. The same reasoning applies to plastic filler that is gobbed over holes drilled through a panel. Moisture can be absorbed through the holes and into the filler. Then, rust will begin and deteriorate the repair.

And now a word about the use of fiberglass patches ("bandages") to cover rusted-out sheet metal: *"Don't!"*

Various Other Surface Preparation and Filling Issues

There is a certain logic involved in doing good body surface preparation and filling work. When this logic is followed and buttressed with careful observation, good results should follow. For example, at every stage of this work, it is best to ask whether moisture will be able to

Disc sanding lead falls squarely and heavily into the "don't" category. It's dangerous because it creates airborne lead particles that are toxic. It also tends to gouge soft lead surfaces. Lead should only be shaped manually with files and sanding boards.

somehow get at the underlying repair after it is finished. If the answer is "yes," something will have to be done to prevent this. Be careful not to inadvertently cause problems, such as plugging drainage holes in the bottoms of doors. Don't take actions that require corrections later, when you can avoid this. The best way to deal with gouges in filler is not to make them in the first place. Don't count on the limited abilities of glazing and spot putties to get you out of trouble that you shouldn't have gotten into in the first place.

Always be ready to experiment with new techniques and new materials, but confine most of your experimentation to your spouse's "everyday car" and save the "tried and true" stuff for your restoration work. Some great ideas pan out and some don't.

For example, many years ago, I experimented injecting a "non-shrinking, closed cell" urethane foam under and behind the headlight brows and rocker panels of a car. I applied this foam in these body cavities after these rusted areas had already been repaired once before I got there. I reasoned that since the foam had a very minor shrink factor (0.5 percent), and could be injected into these areas, it might displace moisture that would otherwise condense there. The fact that this foam was closed cell and non-absorbing in nature made the proposition look even better. So far it has worked in my test application. In fact, it has become a standard procedure both in restoration and in some new car factory applications.

If you have a potentially good idea for improving some aspect of restoration, and if that idea has low potential for doing future damage, give it a try. That is one of the ways that restoration has improved and advanced over the years. People tried out both good and bad ideas. Some of the good ones stuck.

Chapter 25

Automotive Refinishing, Part I

Modern paint chemistry is extremely complex. Unless you do a lot of painting, you should stick with one product line to insure compatibility. We use BASF's R-M paints because we like the product and we like the local distributor.

PAINT USED TO BE SIMPLE; we even called it "paint," and the act of applying it was simply called "painting." Now, it's called "finish" and "refinishing," (These, of course, cost more than "painting.") and you sometimes seem to need knowledge approaching the depth of a Ph.D. in organic chemistry to weave your way through the ever-increasing and confusing array of products recommended and mandated for successful results in refinishing. In the old days, DuPont, R-M and Ditzler pretty much covered the refinishing systems and products waterfront. Today, there are many more brands and house brands than the old "big 3." European systems, in particular, have added numerous new types of products to the refinishing world.

Perhaps the most distressing aspect of the new finishes is that I find myself speaking authoritatively about the differences between acrylics and epoxies, or the effects of polyisocyanate hardeners or urethane cross-linkers. Other people probably have the same problem. In point of fact, I have not the slightest idea of what these words really mean, but only some small sense of the observed characteristics of the different products that are described by these names. When you get into the intricacies of applying finishes with the newer products, and the inevitable "either/or" decisions that have to be made, it all becomes mind numbing.

How much simpler it was in the "old days." There was lacquer and there was enamel, and there were only a few very specific additives for these two paints. There were few or no problems of compatibility when these additives were used. Such application monstrosities as metallics and basecoat/clearcoat systems were pretty much reserved for the hot rod set. You simply did not encounter the difficult or impossible repair situations that "advances" in paint technology have made common today.

The old nitrocellulose lacquers are a case in point. They were almost absurdly easy to apply, and you could tolerate contamination in spraying them up to, and possibly including, walking on a freshly sprayed car. The trick was that the old lacquers were exceedingly hard and brittle and almost endlessly susceptible to being feathered out, spotted in, sanded level and compounded smooth. Virtually any mistake, or disaster, could be repaired easily, or even compounded out without really repairing it at all.

The old, alkyd enamels, like Dulux and Super Max—they were often called "synthetic enamels"—were comparatively soft finishes. They were not difficult to apply, but it was understood that when they came out of tack (dried to the point of no longer being vulnerable to landing dust contamination) what you saw was what you got. They could be repaired with some difficulty with lacquer, but, because they "gassed" (unless they were baked at the time of application) it was difficult to recoat them until they had cured for six months to a year. These were very shiny and beautiful finishes. Their inherent softness gave them a great ruggedness, compared to the harder lacquers of those times.

The trouble was that they required a very clean spraying environment because if contamination landed in them before they came out of tack, it tended to produce large craters in a finish. The idea of buffing (it was called "wheeling") enamel, or "color sanding" it, was virtually inconceivable. These enamels had to be applied in relatively wet coats, and they had a malignant tendency to "fish eye" if there was any grease contamination under them. An early DuPont additive, FEE (Fish Eye Eliminator) gave some resistance to the dreaded fish eyes. Later, when silicone waxes became common, adding FEE to paint became a standard part of painting in some shops. FEE, by the way, was a concoction of silicone hydrocarbon that simply contaminated the paint that you sprayed to the point that the varying surface tension created by grease or silicone contamination on your target ceased to exist.

Both nitrocellulose lacquer and synthetic enamel are still slightly available through a diminishing number of specialty finishing products suppliers, and there is a very small school of restoration purists that insists that cars painted in these finishes originally must be restored in them for the purposes of authenticity. These same purists will tend to wax lyrical about the "depth" of nitrocellulose lacquer, which is, indeed, one it its more desirable traits. The synthetic enamels are a bit harder to defend from the authenticity perspective because most cars that were painted in enamel were painted in stoving enamels— paints that were "reflowed" by oven baking shortly after their factory application.

This is virtually impossible to do in restoration. Still, contemporary aftermarket synthetic enamels do approximate the appearances of these factory-baked enamels and were a standard in the repair sector until the 1960s. They were used until fairly recently in commercial repair as "economy finishes," and in some restorations.

It should be noted that, in their day, these older finishes were miracle finishes; much as the acrylics and urethanes were later to achieve this status. It is safe to say that if nitrocellulose lacquer had not been invented, automobile mass production as it came to exist in the 1920s, and as it exists today, would have been impossible.

Prior to the introduction of nitrocellulose lacquer in automobile production in 1924, there were no sprayable finishes. The old varnishes had to be painstakingly applied by hand with varnish brushes or by dipping panels or flowing ("hosing") paint over them. It was common for a factory varnish job to entail 40 or 50 labor-intensive steps, and to require more than a month for complete application. The old varnishes were truly beautiful, but the time and skill involved in applying them, smoothing them with sandpaper and pumice and baking each coat made them expensive to apply. Worse still, they had to be applied very thick because they lacked durability factors like chip and ultraviolet resistance. This meant that in many climates their life expectancy in service was little more than a year. The tendency for these thick finishes to crack, along with an equally disastrous tendency for them to oxidize ("chalk" in paint lingo), meant that about three years was the most that you could expect from such a finish. Add to all this a lack of resistance to chemical and petroleum stains, the fact that these varnished surfaces were very hard and brittle, and thus not very resistant to scratching and abrasion, and you can see why, by the 1920s, the auto industry was looking for something better.

Enter Duco, the first sprayable finish, in 1924. It revolutionized the business of painting and repainting cars. By today's standards it was an absurdly simple paint to compound because its binder basically involved dissolving cellulose (cotton fiber) in a solvent like acetone or toluene. Of course, there was more to it than that, and the production process for manufacturing nitrocellulose lacquers remains one that involves a considerable hazard of fire and explosion, unless it is carried out under very rigorously controlled conditions.

The new nitrocellulose finishes of the mid-1920s could be sprayed on and dried in a few hours, instead of a few weeks. This greatly reduced the cost of finishing cars and opened the bottleneck that the old varnishing operations had created in the logistics of mass-producing automobiles. By today's standards, nitrocellulose lacquer is a very fragile and non-durable finish, but compared to the varnishes that preceded it, it was a miracle of durability.

Synthetic or alkyd resin enamels were introduced at the end of the 1920s and represented much more durable finishes than nitrocellulose lacquers. They were also sprayable, and thus practical for production and repair. These enamels did not have the depth of lacquers, but they had greater gloss and did not have to be compounded to achieve their final gloss. In fact, they could not be compounded until they had cured for months. The good side of that proposition was that they did not show the buffing ("swirl") marks that are almost always present in buffed lacquer finishes.

One distinction that should be emphasized is that the synthetic enamels were softer than the nitrocellulose lacquers and, as a consequence, they were more durable. It somewhat confounds common sense that a softer finish would be more durable than a harder one, but it is true. Nitrocellulose lacquer, which is among the hardest of finishes, is, for that reason, brittle and susceptible to chipping, cracking and scratching. Softer paints, such as synthetic enamels (and later the acrylic lacquers and enamels, and later still, the urethanes and polyurethanes), are much more resistant to any kind of flexing or abrasion damage, due to their inherent softness. Softer, tougher paints are also less susceptible to being buffed or rubbed out because they tend to smear and burn when they are "wheeled." The newer "hardened" or "catalyzed" enamels can be buffed, if anyone wants to do this.

By the mid-1950s, lacquers based on acrylic resins began to replace the more fragile nitrocellulose lacquers. These new lacquers were not only more durable than the older ones, they also had less tendency to oxidize and to suffer abrasion damage. Part of this derived from the fact that they were softer than their predecessors, and part of it came from their improved resistance to the sun's ultraviolet rays. The first acrylic lacquers were sold by DuPont under the name "Lucite," but the other major automotive paint suppliers, Rinshed-Mason (R-M), Ditzler (Pittsburgh Paints) and Sherwin Williams, quickly followed with similar products of their own.

A few years later, in the early 1960s, acrylic-based enamels pioneered by Sherwin Williams began to replace the traditional alkyd enamels and provided the same kinds of advantages as acrylics had in the field of lacquers.

Up to this point, the new acrylic products tended to resemble the older products in overall appearance, but were vastly superior in durability. True, the nitrocellulose lacquers had more "depth" than the acrylics, and some of the more translucent hues of the alkyd enamels seemed to have deeper gloss than their acrylic replacements, but, all told, these differences in appearance were minor.

This comparison is made only between nonmetallic colors, as modern metallic paints are greatly different from earlier nonmetallic paints in appearance. This is not to say that the older paints could not be mixed in metallic formats.

What we today call "metallic" was called, "Pearl Essence" at the time of its invention in the 1930s. Early Pearl Essence paints used a reflective component manufactured from fish scales, but aluminum flakes quickly replaced this quaint additive. Today, metallic effects are achieved by adding the likes of aluminum or titanium flakes to finishes to create the metallic effect that is seen in almost every modern automotive finish. Whereas factory metallic finishes are the standard today, most of the old paints were nonmetallic, particularly where nitrocellulose lacquers and alkyd enamels were involved.

Paint developments after the 1960s included finishes that in no way resembled the older paints, except that they, too, were designed to cover metal. The aircraft and trucking industries provided the basis for the development of the super shiny, super tough (soft) polyurethane finishes, and for a myriad of urethane and isocyanate additives (called "cross-linkers" and "catalysts," respectively) to enhance the gloss and toughness of acrylic enamels, and even of acrylic lacquers. The straight polyurethane enamels, such as Imron ("The Wet Look") and Durethane, have little chemical or physical resemblance to any previous finishes, and are, in my opinion, unauthentically shiny. The myriad of cross-linker, hardener, and gloss additive products that is presently available can also be used to make enamels buffable. Of course, buffed enamel is an anomaly in restoration work because the traditional synthetic enamels could not be buffed out; they were too soft.

One trend that becomes obvious to anyone who follows the modern paint scene is that the enamels and their additive packages produce finishes that are harder and harder, while lacquers have gotten softer and softer. In Europe, and to a lesser extent the U.S., manufacturers such as Kosmoski House of Kolor have developed super finishes, like epoxy-acrylics, that are difficult to classify in their characteristics in terms of the traditional distinction between enamels and lacquers.

The "official" distinction between enamels and lacquers is that lacquers form their films by simple evaporation of the solvents in them—the carriers (also called "vehicles" or "volatiles") that give them liquid form. Enamels, on the other hand, dry ("cure" or "set" in paint terminology) in a two-stage process. First, the volatiles in their solvents evaporate, and then their "binders" oxidize or set through some other chemical reaction, which almost always involves oxidation of their binders by oxygen in the air. Lacquers can generally be dissolved in their solvents after they have dried. Enamels, on the other hand, cannot be dissolved with lacquer thinner or with the less aggressive enamel reducers after they have cured. This is the basis of a test to determine the nature of paint if it is unknown. If lacquer thinner will dissolve a dried finish, it is almost certainly a lacquer. If lacquer thinner will not dissolve a dried finish, it is probably an enamel. That test applies only to the older nitro-cellulose lacquers and alkyd enamels.

Choosing Restoration Paint

In the past few years, the development of finishes has taken on a complexity that is almost awesome. It is not just new products that relate to the new exterior plastic automobile components, like bumper fascia, or the new super durable finishes and clear coats. There are also so many systems of, and additives for, finishes that it is virtually impossible to keep up with them. There are dozens of systems out there.

An example of this proliferation and complexity is RM's old standby enamel, Super Max. This paint had been on the market long before I began painting cars 35 years ago, and was an alkyd enamel. Over the years, R-M developed about half a dozen additives for Super Max. These imparted isocynate and urethane characteristics to this paint. Later, the label on Super Max indicated that it "contains acrylics," while a new R-M paint line, Limco, was sold as an alkyd enamel. Since then, R-M has developed two new acrylic "super" enamels, Miracryl 2 and Diamont At the same time, their parent company, BASF, which owns the Glasurit line, began selling its super enamels in this country and elsewhere. Other major product developments and changes in these lines continued after that. See what I mean about paint line proliferation and confusion?

A reasonable question that a restorer might ask is, "What is the best paint or line of paint products?" I don't know the answer. This topic has become something like asking, "What is the best religion?" Feelings run high on many options.

I used to be familiar with the DuPont and R-M lines. Ditzler finish systems were too complicated for my tastes, and I didn't like the service at the local Sherwin Williams' jobber. In recent years, it has been all that I can do to keep up with R-M finishes, and my familiarity with DuPont has slipped to a mild acquaintance. R-M, in turn, has exploded with new products since its sale by United Technologies to BASF of Germany.

At this point, I would advise anyone who works occasionally with automotive finishes to find a good line of paint, with a good local jobber behind it, and become as familiar with it as possible. There is an ongoing revolution in automotive finishes with the introduction of products like flex agents, elastomeric finishes, water borne primers and paints, latex based paints, etc.

It is also common wisdom in most cases not to mix paint product lines in the same job because the complexity of the chemical reactions in modern paint products makes this risky. Finally, avoid the clever fads that come along, like using lacquer thinner to reduce enamel. The long-term results of such ersatz innovations are generally pretty bad.

The Constituents of Automotive Finishes

Whatever the complexity of modern finishes, all paints and primers are still derived from three basic classes of components, pigments, binders, and solvents. Pigments are ground powders that, by their hues, particle sizes, and particle shapes, impart characteristic colors and substratum textures to paints. Some paint experts believe that the pigment particles in paint tend to reinforce its film and make it stronger—much as gravel increases the strength of concrete aggregate. Metal flake additions are often noted as being desirable in this regard. Pigment engineering in paints has improved in recent years with the introduction of more stable pigments and the use of ultraviolet shields (blue tints) to protect such traditionally vulnerable colors, such as reds.

The binders in paints are liquids that form paint films and bind the pigments in the film surfaces. Originally, the binders were made from natural entities, and particularly from rosins and natural oils, such as tongue and linseed. Later, synthetic binders formed the basis of the alkyd enamels. More recently, man-made plastics, such as acrylics, polyurethanes, PVCs (polyvinylchlorides) and latexes have been used as the basis of paint binders. Most of the "improvement" in paint has come from the development of binders with improved adhesion, gloss and durability characteristics.

The final component of all paints is some sort of vehicle or solvent that dissolves the binders (which have already suspended the pigments) and allows them to be sprayed in atomized form from liquids. After spraying, the solvents evaporate and the paint film is formed. In the cases of lacquers, the evaporation of the solvent (thinner) usually leaves a fully developed paint film and completes the process. I say, "usually," because the advent of cross-linked lacquers was an important exception to this rule.

In the case of enamels, the evaporation of the solvent (reducer) triggers an oxidation or other reaction of the binders in the paint, which produces the final film. Of course, enamel takes much longer to dry than lacquer, and its reduction must be controlled more precisely than the thinning of lacquer.

There are exceptions to the simple paint componentry described above. Some of the new finishes use catalysts which cause their binders to set up almost completely, thus replacing oxidation by atmospheric air. Simple color pigments have now been supplemented with aluminum powder particles of different sizes, configurations and coarsenesses to produce the metallics that prevail in contemporary automotive finishes. Finally, additives that the painter adds, or that the factory has already added to paint, are used for a myriad of purposes, such as improving gloss, reducing tack time, improving chemical resistance, improving flow out, etc.

Needless to say, the original sprayable finishes—nitrocellulose lacquers—were marvels of simplicity because their binders were little more than cotton dissolved in solvents, and the solvents and pigments were also simple. After that, paint chemistry started to get much more complicated!

The Choice of Paint for Restoration

The choice of finishes for restoration work usually involves some level of compromise between authenticity and practicality. Early cars that were painted with varnish are not refinished in this material because cost, lack of availability and extremely limited durability combine to make the use of original varnishes impossible. Instead, these cars are refinished in acrylic lacquers, which somewhat approximate the appearances of the original varnishes.

Cars originally finished in nitrocellulose lacquers are sometimes restored in these finishes. Although nitrocellulose lacquers came off the shelves of the major line automotive paint jobbers more than three decades ago, they are still available from a few reputable specialty suppliers. The problem with using nitrocellulose paints is that their durability is very inferior to that of modern acrylic lacquers, and their need for maintenance is constant. They scratch easily, and their surfaces oxidize quickly. On the good side, they are easy to feather sand and spot in—if you can match colors. That's a big "if," because some of the mixing colors for these paints have shelf lives of about six months, and the mixed paints tend to darken substantially after that. Saving some repair paint for a future emergency after you spray a car is usually futile, particularly if reds or browns are involved. And trying to match the presently available nitrocellulose paints by formula usually doesn't work; there just isn't that much control in their manufacture anymore. Hand or spectrometer matches are usually the best that you can do The latter *can* produce very satisfactory results.

Some people, myself included, advocate using acrylic lacquers to replace original nitrocellulose finishes. I feel that the appearance of the acrylics is very close to that of original nitrocellulose finishes, and durability is much better. The repairability of acrylic lacquer finishes is also very good.

If you can find a paint chip for a standard color in a modern paint that is close to the original color that you are trying to duplicate, you are assured of being able to secure additional matching paint for repair or respray for years to come. And the major manufacturers control their color consistency rigorously, so a match should be easy. Remember, if you start with a nitrocellulose paint, there is no conversion possible of the formula for that paint to a modern acrylic finish.

The availability of synthetic (alkyd) enamels is limited and will doubtless end in the near future because there is a decreasing market for alkyd enamels. I have no particular objection to refinishing cars that were originally finished in synthetic enamels with acrylic enamels, and I have no objection to adding the best gloss and durability additives available for modern acrylic enamels to make them even better finishes. But I think that it is an act of barbarism to color sand and buff out acrylic enamels in restoration work. There is something so totally wrong about the appearance of the resulting finish that it makes me shiver. This is because the older enamels could not be buffed The whole point of using them was the gloss that they imparted without wheel marks. Their appearances are thing of simple and great beauty

The fact that the hardeners available for acrylic enamels make it possible to buff them out does not mean that you must or should do this. The ultimate horror in this regard is the combination of orange peel and wheel marks that can be seen in many examples of contemporary body shop practice and, sadly, some restoration work. That's OK on new cars, but it looks awful on old ones, where this situation could never have existed when they were new. It should also be pointed out that when catalyzed acrylic enamels, such as Centari, Delstar, Acrylyd, Diamont, Ultra Base 7, etc. are used in conjunction with appropriate gloss additives, they produce beautiful finishes that air dry to an appearance that is very much like that of the old synthetic enamels. They are much easier to apply than the old finishes because they flow out more easily and they come out of tack faster.

Finally, we come to modern finishes such as basecoat/clearcoat systems, epoxy-acrylics, and polyurethanes. No one would argue that these are not inherently beautiful finishes, but they are totally and visibly inauthentic for most restoration purposes. They can be difficult to repair, and the problems of removing some of them will plague future restorers. All of this will probably rule out their use when the authentic restoration of old vehicle bodies, chassis, and suspension parts are the issue.

If you have trouble distinguishing what the finish on your car is, or was originally, you may be able to determine this from the paint plate on the car, by reference to the appropriate shop manual, or by consultation with a paint jobber who still has the manufacturer's color books for the period when the car was built. Generally, the finishes on lacquer painted cars can be dissolved in lacquer thinner. Thinner or reducer will not dissolve cured, air dried or baked enamel. Before the mid-1950s, most cars, including Fords and Chryslers, were painted in baked enamel. The exceptions were GM brands, and some of the independent automakers, who used nitrocellulose lacquer finishes on their cars. After the mid-1950s, acrylic lacquers steadily replaced nitrocellulose lacquers—you actually had to pay considerable extra for the option of a "Lucite" finish on a GM car in the mid to late 1950s. Ford, Chrysler and some others experimented with "super" enamels in the late 1950s and early 1960s but generally went to acrylic enamels by the 1970s.

To sum up: In most restoration cases, it is best to find a modern, nonmetallic color that closely approximates the original color that you want to use. If the original finish was a lacquer, an acrylic lacquer can be used, and if it was a synthetic enamel, an acrylic enamel can be used. If you want to go the route of absolute authenticity, nitrocellulose lacquers and alkyd enamels can be used, but durability will be sacrificed if this is done. And, of course, if one of the old enamels is used, don't attempt to buff it out unless it has been fortified with additives and cross-linkers that make this possible. Even then, it is much better *not* to use these finishes if your spray conditions will require color sanding and buffing an enamel finish The results look awful! I would advise against using clearcoat/basecoat systems in restoration work. They can be very beautiful, but they are inauthentic to all but the most recent collector cars, and they can be very difficult to repair.

No matter how "high-tech" modern finishes get, careful surface preparation and contour sanding will probably always be the basis for achieving great results with sprayed automotive finishes.

You can remove top coats from old baked primers and preserve the primers by gently using the DA and orbital action sanders shown here to selectively strip the top coats off them. It's slow work, but it's usually worth the effort to preserve original primers if they are in good shape.

The Great "Bare Metal" Debate

"Of course, we went down to bare metal before we painted it." Sound familiar? It is always said with such commanding authority and such calm self-assurance that it makes you wonder why anyone would do anything else. But other approaches are possible, and they are not necessarily "substandard." I have no objection to going down to bare metal. You have to when certain conditions are present. When substantial areas of a finish are breached and rust is coming through, it is necessary to take the whole finish to bare metal because the corrosion that can be seen is probably about to spring up in other places where it cannot yet be seen. When a finish is flaking and peeling, or has defects like crow's feet that penetrate it, it is necessary to go down to bare metal before you refinish. But when a tough finish, such as factory baked enamel, has adhered to a car's panels for 25 or more years and shows no signs of defect or failure, it is not necessary to go down to bare metal, unless, of course, you like the sound of hearing yourself say, "Of course, we went down to bare metal before we painted it."

The point is, the adhesion achieved by some of the baked primers on factory fresh metal will be hard to equal if you take your car to bare metal and start over. When factory paint has been recoated one or more times in subsequent refinishings, it is a good idea to strip some or all of the later top coats away with a good DA sander or plastic media blasting to avoid ending up with a paint film that is too thick after you recoat. If you are using one of the new paints over an original factory primer or top coats, and particularly when you are using one of the new finishes with additives, it is often a good idea to use a sealer or sealing primer-surfacer as a barrier coat to prevent lifting and bleeding through, etc. Water-born barrier coating

primers are particularly useful for this purpose because they are incredibly neutral and will not lift any type of underlying paint or primer. Up to a point, they can also be used over air dry enamel that is still gassing.

What I think should be avoided is the business of sanding to bare metal just so you can say that you've been there. Any method of complete paint removal involves some hazards for a car's panels. Disc sanding can unnecessarily remove good metal if it is not done very carefully, and abrasive blasting often results in panel warping and other mischief if it is attempted without the benefit of one of the new plastic (type III) abrasives or the more exotic mineral abrasives. Chemical paint removers frequently leave residues in crevices that later cause paint to bubble and lift. They can be messy to use. If paint must be completely removed to neutralize rust or to correct poor adhesion, then there is no other choice than to use one of the common paint removal methods. Where a choice exists, evaluate the condition of the underlying primer on its merits and consider salvaging it if it still has integrity.

Primers—The Foundation of Any Refinishing Endeavor

The old air-dry primers used in body shops for refinishing were made with nitrocellulose binders and were wonderfully sandable, due to their inherent hardness. They weren't very durable because they were brittle and lacked adhesion to base metals, but if their application thickness was kept to reasonable levels, they soldiered on under paint for extended tours of duty. They did not have the "fast build" of modern primer-surfacers because they were blended with fairly low levels of solids. At recommended thinning, they were comparatively watery, which is probably why they were such good primers.

There are only two ways that a primer can bond to a base metal: mechanically and chemically. The old primers, with the exception of the (then) exotic zinc-chromate based primers, achieved adhesion purely by mechanical bonding. What this means is that primer infiltrates the nooks, crannies and crevices of sanded base metal in ways that mechanically lock the primer to that jagged terrain.

The trouble with the old primers—from a modern body shop practice perspective—is that they were sprayed thin and didn't build fast enough to do much filling without many applications and a lot of dry ("flash") time between applications. With the introduction of modern acrylic paints, a revolution in primers occurred. It gave us "fast build" or "high solid content" primers (now called "primer-surfacers") based on acrylic binders. These primers saved time, while the less brittle acrylic binders added durability to them. I have never thought that the mechanical adhesion of these thicker primers is as good as that of the older, thinner primers. Their very thickness prevents them from interlocking effectively with the topography of base metals. Read on; this story has a happy ending.

In the last 20 years, the major paint companies have introduced "etching" primers (usually based on zinc phosphate additives and one-part or two-part epoxy binders). These are truly miraculous primers that bond to base metal like nothing available before ever did. The secret is that they are thin, tough and chemically reactive with steel, aluminum and galvanizing. This produces both chemical and mechanical bonding. My experience these primers leads me to believe that their bonds to metal will probably survive anything short of a nuclear detonation at ground zero. This class of primers (I would tend to call them "pre-primers" because they are distinctly not sandable and should have conventional acrylic based primer-surfacers applied over them for filling and sanding purposes) is so good on steel, aluminum, and galvanizing that it is foolish to paint a car in restoration without using them when a bare metal substratum surface is involved.

Unlike the old zinc chromate primers, which were available for aluminum and steel, the new zinc phosphate primers are relatively inexpensive and are very easy to apply. It is best to apply them thinly, and you must not cut into them when you sand or you will have a terrible mess. But the adhesion of these new etching primers is out of this world. Because these reactive primers are designed to react with base metals, you must not use one of the old conversion ("phosphatizing") coatings or metal conditioner systems under them. I give them five stars on a four-star scale. They are that good. They are also very waterproof, so the problem of moisture getting through primer before you can apply your top coats is eliminated.

You should use a good, sandable acrylic primer-surfacer over etching primers. This will give you a good surface to sand. It is also a good idea to change primer colors (red to gray, or gray to red) after the first coat of primer-surfacer has been sprayed on an etching primer. That first "guide coat" of primer-surfacer will warn you to back off when you get near to cutting into the etching primer as you sand the primer-surfacer. Avoid using the "quick and dirty" non-sanding primers, because restoration work will always involve sanding primer coats to get a good, smooth, properly contoured surface for top coats to build on.

Facilities and Equipment

The facilities and equipment required for refinishing are pretty straightforward. You will need a good environment in which to spray, a good source of clean, dry, non-pulsating air and a good spray gun. Depending on the climate where you live and the nature of the construction of your workplace, and maybe your skill in negotiating, this setup will cost you anywhere from about $1,200 to $40,000. Let's take the components of a good spraying environment and setup, one at a time.

An adequate environment for spraying means a clean area where you can severely curtail or eliminate dust fall, and where you can force enough air through to provide a minimum of one air change every minute or so. This means matching the cubic air capacity of your exhaust fan to the volume of your spray room

Such an area must be well lighted and absolutely separated from any open flame or source of ignition spark. Temperature control must be reasonably constant, and humidity control is highly desirable. Most of this suggests a spray booth or something very close to it. Yet, very credible spraying can be done in a clean, force-ventilated area of a garage if dust can be kept out of it and if the floor can be kept wet to suppress dust. In some climates, winter spraying means the use of a huge furnace ("air makeup unit") to provide ignition free, warm incoming air to replace the air that is extracted by ventilating fans.

Take heart because there are some body shops that do credible work and have spray booths (mandated by state and local regulations), but they tend *not* to use them because of the difficult logistics of moving cars in and out of them. Instead, at about 4:00 p.m. every day, they hose down the floor, check for lurking government inspectors, and spray everything in sight. What they don't directly spray, they usually hit with enough overspray so that they might as well have sprayed it directly. There's a lot of cleanup in these propositions! Anyway, this reality points to the possibility of spraying without a spray booth and saving between the $1,200 and $40,000 that a contemporary spray booth costs.

An important item that some good spray booths provide is adequate lighting. This is critically important, as it is impossible to do good work when you can't see what you are doing. Any spray environment needs adequate light.

You'll need a minimum of six or seven SCFM (Standard

A good spray booth needs to be sealed from dust, well lit and able to produce a complete air change in between 20 seconds and a minute. Some of the new high-tech, down-draft spray booths with conditioned air and baking units go for more than $100,000. But that's production-painting stuff. Old car restorers can easily make do with much less sophisticated facilities.

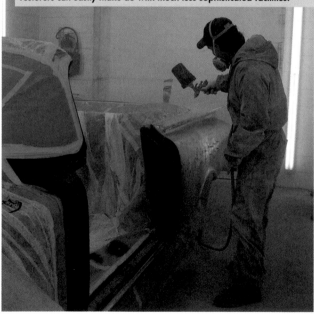

Cubic Feet Per Minute) of clean, dry, compressed air to spray cars—more if you choose to use a modern, low overspray HVLP (High Volume Low Pressure) spray gun. For conventional spray equipment, this translates into at least a two-horsepower compressor with at least a 20-gallon tank. A five-horse, two-stage job with a 60- or 80-gallon tank will serve you much better, and will comfortably handle HVLP spray guns. Don't try to spray restoration finishes with a

1-horsepower compressor with a 12-gallon air tank. It will probably add so much oil, water, grunge and air pulsation to your spray air that it will be all but impossible to do high quality work.

Modern HVLP units use multi-stage turbines to supply air. These tend to cost much less than comparable compressors for spraying.

Compressors used for painting should have their

For many professional painters, the Binks 7 spray gun (right) was the reigning champion of lacquer guns. The (counterfeit) Eclipse touch-up gun on the left was preferred by many painters for spotting in finishes to repair damage. More modern spray guns have replaced these old standbys, but they are still very good and very usable guns.

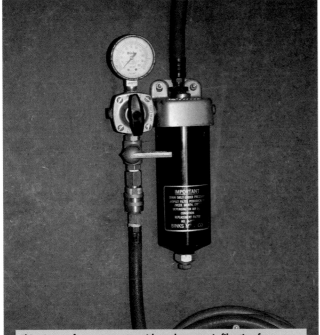

This air transformer setup provides adequate air filtration for spraying the old paints. Modern finishes are much less tolerant of air contamination and moisture, and you should figure on a desiccant, deliquescent or refrigeration air purifying system if you expect to do really top-quality work. Adding a coalescing filter upstream of the transformer can only help.

tanks drained daily, and they should be connected to one or more air filters or "transformers." The "coalescing" filters offered by Hankenson, LeMan, Balston, Van Air and other manufacturers are highly recommended Desiccant, deliquescent, membrane and refrigeration type dryers are costly but do terrific work cleaning and drying air.

Since silicone contamination is a particularly deadly enemy of good refinishing—it causes fish eyes to form in freshly sprayed paint—it is highly recommended that a compressor oil be used that is free of silicones. Most industrial grade compressor oils use silicone foam suppressants, which accounts for a lot of the trouble that body shops have with fish eyes—they come in with the spray air. Be sure to use a compressor oil that does not include a silicone foam suppressant, because some compressor oil will inevitably get past any compressor's rings and into your air. Even the best filters may not be able to completely remove this silicone contamination.

In addition to clean and dry air, adequate and consistent pressure is critically important in the application of modern paint systems. Air pressure that is too low will cause inadequate atomization of paint, which results in

The immediate future of spray guns is supposed to be HVLP (High Volume Low Pressure). However, many very good "shooters" I know don't partake of that future and still use the old standbys, Binks and DeVilbiss lacquer and enamel guns. The guns in this photo (front row, left to right) are DeVilbiss, Binks and Sharpe HVLP guns. They are as good as many of the older, non-HVLP guns, and some of those were very good. HVLP guns use a lot of compressed air but they do a great job atomizing paint, and they produce much less overspray than conventional guns. That means a healthier spray environment and less pollution from painting, not to mention using less paint.

Five-horsepower compressors, like those shown here, are about the minimum air pump size that will give you really good spray air, and about the largest pump that can reasonably be run on split-phase current. Smaller compressors can be made to do the job, but the results are sometimes ragged.

Whether you locate your compressor inside or outside, be sure to check its oil, belts, valves and water trap regularly.

An inexpensive tailstock air pressure regulator can be very helpful in maintaining consistent air pressure. These "cheater" valves help to address the issue of air pressure drop in the long hoses that feed air to spray guns.

Here's an important painting tip: No matter how well you apply pre-primers, primers and top coats, your sheet metal will always be vulnerable to attack from its backside. Always use the best products that you can find to protect these areas, or nasty rust will come right through your panels.

orange peel and other paint problems. Air pressure that is too high will cause solvents to evaporate too rapidly, before the paint hits the target. In enamels this can cause orange peel, as the high-velocity air and solvent aimed at fresh and uncured paint can disrupt the curing process of the coats under the one that you are spraying. Never rely on your compressor's air pressure gauge or on your transformer air pressure gauge for accurate indications of the air pressure at your gun. An inexpensive tailstock regulator and gauge will tell you exactly what the air pressure that is entering your gun is and allow you to regulate it effectively.

Air pressure used for spraying should be kept within paint manufacturers' recommended limits. Good painters generally favor the low to middle range of these recommended spray pressures.

Painters used to be divided on the merits of Binks (models 7 and 62) and DeVilbiss spray guns. A few favored Marsten, Sharpe, and the wonderful but strange Bendix Sicmo (now greatly improved and sold under the Croix name) guns. In recent years, Japanese and Taiwanese copies of the Binks 7 and other "classic" guns have proliferated. I have used the copies and I own examples of the originals. I think that the originals are better, but hardly enough better to justify the price difference between as little as $25 for the copies, and more than $250 for the originals. If your use is only occasional, the copies should do nicely.

The wonderful new HVLP spray guns by Binks, DeVillbis, Mattson, Croix, Accuspray, Sharpe, Sata, Iwata and a few others will set you back between $500 and more than $1,500 a copy.

Until a few years ago, almost all good automotive refinishing spray guns used a siphon principle to draw paint into their air streams. More recently, many painters have been using gravity-fed guns and pressure-fed guns (HVLP, with two-quart, belt-hung pressure-feed pots to feed conventional guns. I think that all of these innovations offer advantages to painters—in some cases, major advantages.

Air-driven stirring attachments for spray gun paint cups are nice if you are going to spray a lot of cars, but are hardly necessary for occasional, general automotive painting. Gun heaters and the use of "hot" lacquer and enamel should be discouraged for safety reasons. By "hot," I refer to the old technique of spraying lacquer and enamel at 160 degrees F. to reduce overspray and to economize on the use of thinner and reducer. HVLP equipment will accomplish the same purpose and will not involve the fire and health hazards that are inherent in spraying finishes at elevated temperatures. It is acceptable to raise the temperature of the paint that you spray from 20 to 30 degrees Fahrenheit above the ambient temperature in your spray environment because this is the range of the drop in spray temperature that occurs from atomization and evaporation of the solvents between your gun and your target with conventional equipment. Heating paint beyond this point is hazardous and is ill-advised,

One of the latest things in industrial painting is electrostatic attraction. Surely, some high-buck restoration shop will advertise this innovation in the near future, but it is beyond what is necessary to do very good work with conventional spray equipment.

Chapter 26

Automotive Refinishing,
Part II

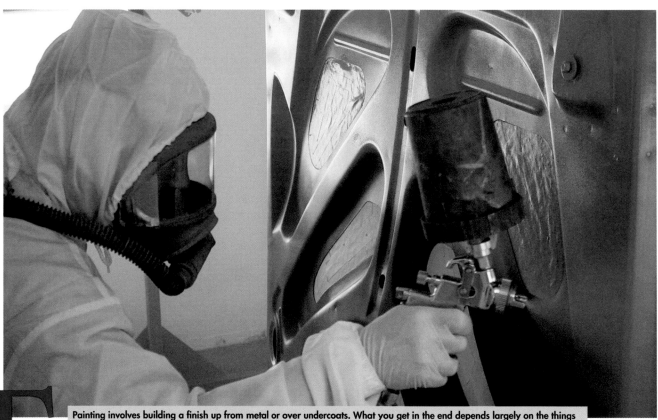

Painting involves building a finish up from metal or over undercoats. What you get in the end depends largely on the things that you did before you applied the top coats.

THERE IS SOMETHING ALMOST ATHLETIC about automotive refinishing when it is compared to most other aspects of restoration work. It's not only that you have to be alert to move smartly around a car when you paint it, you will also have to call up knowledge, skill, coordination and experience to do this work well. Unlike mechanical restoration work, where you can sort of poke away at things at your own pace, painting tends to impose its own strict imperatives and schedules on you.

Frequently, several things have to happen at the same time or in a very close sequence for a finish system to work. With today's complex painting systems, the need for precision is great. There can be times when you may want to push the "panic button" as sags, runs, contamination or other disasters occur. This is normal for beginners, but when you get the gist of the thing, the disasters should be relatively small and infrequent. Painting simply requires a disciplined approach to the work and the ability to deal with special problems as they arise. The more you paint and the more different materials and systems you use, the easier it gets. When it becomes natural, you can go after perfection.

The simplest prescription against panic is to attend to the details as you go along. This doesn't entirely preclude the possibility of local disasters, such as contamination getting into a freshly painted area, but at least it raises the odds in your favor and helps to rule out careless mistakes—the ones that you can avoid. In painting, the trouble that you don't get into is the trouble that you don't have to get out of.

Various and Assorted Matters of Strategy

The war of restoration refinishing is won or lost on the battlefield of small details. Small early mistakes can mushroom into catastrophic events if you don't perspire over the small details.

Take, for example, the matter of paint contamination rising from the surface below it. It is always best to wash a whole car or repair area with detergent and water, and to rinse it thoroughly with water before you paint it. You should follow this wash by wiping down the surface with a special wax and silicone remover before sanding and painting it. Finally, after sanding, and before priming or painting, you should do a final wipe-down with wax and silicone remover.

If this regimen is followed, and each step is invested with an adequate amount of washing and the use of clean wiping rags or towels, there should be no contamination problem in your priming and painting. If, however, contaminants, like silicone, are not removed in the initial wipe-down with solvent, they will be sanded into the old finish, or into bare metal. Then, they can come back to cause fish eyes in the primer and in topcoats. This can be a very difficult problem to deal with when you are spraying a car. Certainly, it would have been better to have prevented the problem from occurring with a thorough initial washing, so that it could qualify as "the trouble that you didn't get into."

Solvent cleaners such as PrepSol (Dupont) and PreKleeno (R-M) are designed to remove all of the contaminants that tend to disrupt paint. They also soften underlying finishes to promote the adhesion of succeeding coats of finish or primer. They should always be used when you recoat any surface that has sat for more than 24 hours since the previous coat of primer or paint was applied to it.

Sometimes, you will have occasion to refinish a surface that has numerous chips, rust spots, and other defects. Often, the number of these areas will dictate sanding the whole panel or car to bare metal. If you do not, you must feather edge sand each defect. There can be a great temptation to try to talk yourself out of dealing properly with a few minor spots ('it'll never show'), but this will come back to haunt you later. At best, the applied finish will look terrible because defects that looked minor will come through and show in your finished work; at worst, the new

coats will tend to lift off underlying finish areas that are not properly sanded, primed and leveled.

Or take the matter of cut-throughs. Sometimes, the best of us on the best of days sands through primer and down to shiny metal. "Oh, c'mon, how can a little spot like that hurt? Eh what? Huh? Dirty a clean spray gun just to prime that little spot? And then have to wait and wait for the primer to dry. And then sand it. Then, clean the gun. Then, you are back where you started. How much can it hurt to paint over it? After all, there's primer all around it."

Well, you will always lose in the long run if you try to paint over cut-throughs without repriming. The deities of painting know where every cut-through is, and they always couple with the demons of rust to make sure that the most innocent of these raises a rust bubble no smaller than your thumb nail. Don't mess with the paint deities and the rust demons, or "you'll be sorry."

And while we are on the unpleasant topic of cut-throughs, it should be mentioned that whenever you encounter a rust spot or nick, it must be sanded to bare metal. Whenever you encounter a cut-through, it must be sanded to a feather edge. Both of these defects should be treated with a one-part or two-part metal conditioner/conversion coating system and primed before painting.

Do fenders really have to come off a car to paint it? Isn't there a strategy to avoid this? Well, if the paint on a car is in basically good condition and the fender seams are factory filled (almost always associated with welded-on fenders), you can sometimes get away with not removing fenders. But fender seams are always suspect and must be inspected closely for pending trouble there. If, on the other hand, the construction of a car involves the use of fender welting on fenders that are bolted to body panels, you must remove the fenders before you paint. There is no way to paint up to fender welting, nor should you waste much time trying to find one. Great minds have already tried. By the time paint is defective, the welting will be defective, either where it is visible or deeper in the seam where it can't be seen. It must be replaced when a car is refinished.

It is possible to paint up to trim, and there are some tricks to accomplish this that are noted later in this chapter. However, if it is at all practical to remove trim before you paint, it is always desirable to do this. All kinds of contamination, not to mention rust, lurk behind/under old trim. The only time that you shouldn't remove trim before you paint is when trim cannot be replaced, and removal entails the likelihood of destroying it.

Sometimes, restoration maintenance involves spot repair. This, of course, only applies if you are lucky enough to have a collector car with only one, or a few spots or areas, that require attention. Some colors and some paints are so difficult to match that refinishing a whole car becomes necessary just to repair a single spot or panel. More often, you can make a spot or panel repair that will be indistinguishable from the rest of the car. But you need a good underlying strategy and a whole lot of skill to pull this off.

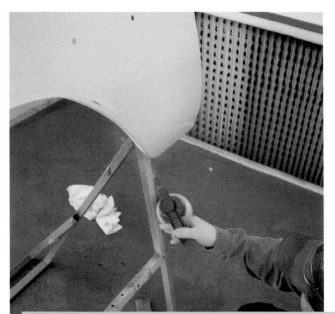

Whether you are painting a small item, a full panel, spotting in a fender or painting a whole car, be sure to wipe down the areas that you will paint with a good cleaning solvent just before you spray.

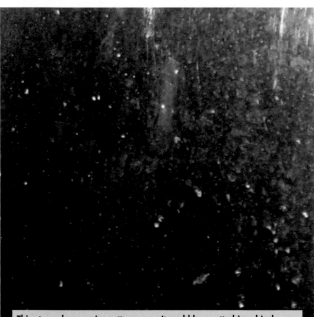

This stone damage is pretty severe. It could be spotted in, chip-by-chip, but it is easier and better to paint the whole panel, or probably, the whole car.

The most obvious gremlin lurking in these situations is the matter of color match. There are so many reasons that paint can mismatch that it sometimes amazes me that it ever actually matches. The paint that you are trying to match by formula may have been from a batch that was off in the first place, or the paint that you are matching it with may be off-color. This is usually the result of mixing error. Then, too, the existing paint probably has faded since the car was painted. When formula matching fails, or cannot be attempted for lack of a valid, original formula or materials, you go to spectrometer matching or hand matching (limited availability). Matches attempted with the handy-dandy little "tint" kits that are offered by paint manufacturers usually

produce a color that is, well, recognizable as the one that you are trying to match—no better. Real hand matches are the province of strange old men who live in the back rooms of a very few paint supply stores. I think that these individuals are kept under lock and key because their talents are so rare and useful that they dare not be let out into the sunlight. I know that our own favorite little-old-can-match-any-color-perfectly-for-thirty-five-bucks-plus-the-cost-of-the-paint-man lives in a city almost 100 miles from here, and I am glad to drive the distance and pay the $35 every time I need a color match. He seems to do better than the spectrometer match equipment that I have employed.

One sure way to miss a color match is to buy your paint at some joint that uses apes for counter people and lets the apes mix the paint. You can usually spot these joints in advance of buying badly mixed paint from them. It's easy. They are the ones with the messy mixing equipment and the counter-people who say, "ya know, ya know," a lot.

When you are trying to spot paint, or to paint only one panel on a car, the best strategy is to make your blend where the eye doesn't expect to see it. This is because, for the most part, the human eye sees what it anticipates seeing, or wants to see.

Have you ever seen lightning strike up? Of course not. Things fall out of the sky; so you expect that. Lightning strikes down from the heavens, right? Wrong! Ninety-plus percent of all visible lightning strikes upward from the ground to the sky, and, in any case, it all happens so fast that the unaided human eye could not possibly determine the direction of travel of lightning. But it always seems to strike down because that's the way it *should* go and that's what you expect to see.

Let's apply this concept of expectation and perception to auto bodywork. If your idea of panel painting is to paint only a door, a hood or a fender, then your color match will have to be absolutely perfect—an unlikely event. If the door,

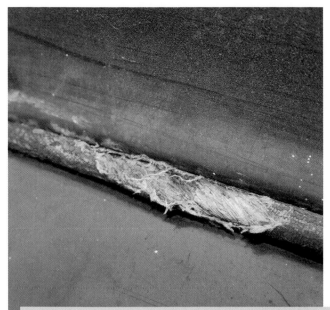

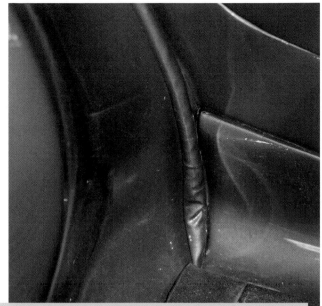

No appeal here; the fender welting in the first photo is completely destroyed and the welting in the second photo is probably "shot." That is likely why someone painted over it. The strip under the visible bead of welting secures it to a body and insulates fenders from the body. The painted welting in the second photo is probably porous and will absorb moisture and deteriorate the paint and then the metal that it is supposed to protect. The fenders on this car should have come off when it was painted. Now, they will have to come off to deal with the welting.

Stripping a car to bare metal is something that most restorers would like to avoid, but sometimes it is necessary.

Sometimes, painting involves "tricking the eye." I wouldn't blend a spot repair at the vertical panel edges of this car, but the horizontal/vertical lines separating the hood panels and the cowl would be good places to hide a slight color mismatch if it occurred.

hood or fender that you paint is just a little bit off the shade that it has to match in the surrounding panels, your eye will instantly detect the problem at the panel edges because that is where it expects to see a mismatch. Experience has conditioned it to expect that.

The best bet for hiding slight color mismatches in side panels is to use wavy blend lines that are in from the panel edges.

If you run your blend line in an irregular fashion into adjacent panels, your eye (any eye) is less likely to notice it because a color change of that sort could be caused by any number of optical and lighting variations—the clouds,

reflections off a lawn or your own shadow. In the same vein, if you blend paint near a point where a panel has a near 90-degree bend, or intersects trim, your eye will have trouble detecting the blend and mismatch because it expects lighting variations to produce color change in these kinds of areas. All of this amounts to a necessary kind of trickery that can be employed to hide slight color mismatches. This approach is a good insurance policy, even if you achieve a near-perfect match.

That is because no match is or will ever remain perfect. Remember, even if old paint and fresh paint initially match, they will tend towards a mismatch as they age. This is because

Sanding backups and abrasives come in very wide variety. Some work better than others for specific jobs. The paint stick in the foreground makes a terrific sanding backup when it is wrapped in abrasive paper. Its shape is terrific for verifying the flatness of panels.

Sanding

Sanding is a subtle art. If it is not done correctly, the deficit will show through any amount of good paint that you may apply. Mostly, good sanding involves good manual techniques, attention to detail and clean habits.

The choice of abrasive is important. Silica carbide sandpaper is best for sanding paint and primer, and aluminum oxide-based papers are best for sanding metal. When paint is sanded, a wet technique with a "wet-or-dry" type paper is usually best—though some painters advocate dry sanding in most situations. Never sand with your bare fingers or the pressure points on them will put ridges into what you are sanding. Machine sanding is OK for rough work, such as scuffing with a DA sander, but finishing work must be done by hand.

If you try to strip paint with such boulder-type abrasives as 24-grit or 36-grit, you will have scratches to fill that require excessive effort or filler. It's OK to use this stuff where you know that you will be using filler over it—in fact, it gives the filler something to hang onto—but I wouldn't use it on sheet metal that is only going to be primed and painted.

To strip paint in that situation, 80- and 100-grit abrasives are plenty rough enough. Because good restoration work is not as vitally concerned with production schedules as is commercial work, it is best to use sanding grits for rough work in the 80 to 100 range; certainly never less than 50. At each sanding stage, a grit must be chosen that is capable of removing the scratches caused by the last grit that was used. This removal must be complete and efficient. It may take three or four grits to get from 80 or 100 to 400 or 600. If you try to abbreviate this process, you will either take more time than necessary to produce a satisfactory result, or you will produce an unsatisfactory result.

Make sure that your sanding patterns are random.

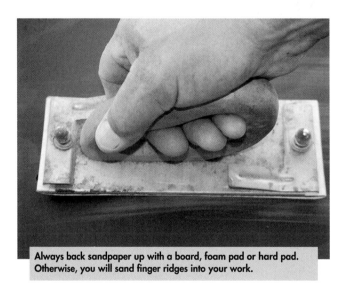

Always back sandpaper up with a board, foam pad or hard pad. Otherwise, you will sand finger ridges into your work.

they are aging from different starting points and lack perfect chemical identities and environmental histories.

One sure tip-off to a spot repair is a failure to level the repair area. Remember, when you spot in paint, you have to bring the area that you have sanded and feather edged back up level with the rest of the panel, or it will stand out like the proverbial "sore thumb." Panel surface variations of as little as 0.003 or 0.004 inch can be seen easily, particularly if they occur in a small enough area.

A very good strategy in blending a panel or spot repair is to use a mist coating of uniforming finish to melt overspray into the underlying paint. This involves a very fast shuffle or the use of two spray guns. It sounds like a real potato race, but with some practice it will come naturally. Major paint manufacturers provide detailed instructions and materials for employing this technique.

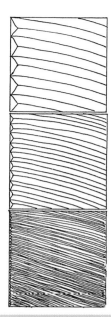

No doubt about it, sanding involves scratching, but as the scratches become finer, a surface becomes smoother. That's why you work from coarse abrasives to fine abrasives when you sand.

This 24-grit sanding disc will remove finishes fast, but you can do a lot of damage to metal with it. I prefer tamer grits for paint removal, say in the 80 to 100 range.

Straight line sanding is best, but be sure to vary the contact patch of sandpaper and panel to avoid ridging paint or primer. Use a foam or hard rubber sanding block or pad to back your abrasive paper. Inspect your work regularly by wiping it clean with a damp rag or sponge, and then go on to the next (finer) grit. When you change grits, be sure to change backing pads and sanding water, and be sure to clean up completely after each grit. Failure to do this will produce abrasive cross-contamination, and you will put isolated scratches of the previous, coarser grit into the work that you are now doing with a finer grit.

Parallel, lengthwise strokes work best for most sanding. Circular strokes have some application in feather edging, but generally should be avoided when you do general sanding. An occasional wipe of Ivory soap across your wet-or-dry sandpaper will make it last much longer and will give you a better feel for the surface that you are wet sanding. Never use white gas or any other volatile solvent to wet sand.

Raised edges or corners are a particular hazard when you are sanding—they like to cut through. You can avoid this by spending less time on these troublesome areas and more on flatter areas. Ultimately, the best leveling with sandpaper is done in the early stages of sanding with a board sander. One neat trick in the final stages of leveling the primer under a finish is to wrap a paint mixing stick in abrasive paper and run it down the surface under three fingers. This will give you a very fine feel for what is underneath. Never try to determine surface level with your bare hand on any painted surface. If you do this on primer, you will contaminate it and, in any case, you will not get a good idea of surface condition because of the friction drag of your fingers. A rag under your fingers tips changes the whole picture and will expose every defect in a surface that you are feeling.

"Stick" with good tape and always use fresh masking tape. The two rolls of tape in front are 3M's Fine Line and Plastic Tape, in 1/8-inch widths. They are great for masking around sharp corners.

One way to determine primer film thickness and how close you are to cut-through disaster as you sand is to use a "guide coat" of primer. This involves changing primer colors after the first or second coat. When your sanding takes you into the color change, you know how close you are to what is under the primer that you are sanding.

Masking

Masking a car does not involve the subtlety that sanding does, but errors in masking tend to be obvious and ugly. The first issue is tape. There must be 50 or more manufacturers of masking tape, and the major supplier of the stuff, 3M,

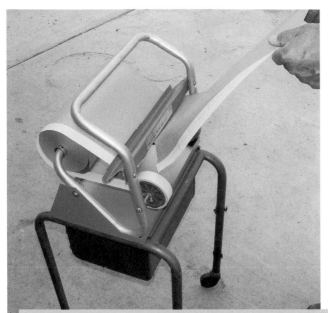

These "maskers" automatically apply tape to the edges of masking paper. They save time and are inexpensive to own.

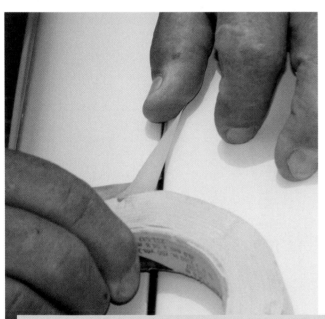

One of the secrets of masking is to pull tape with the fingers of one hand and conform it to panels with the fingers of the other.

must have 50 different grades of it. It is important to use a good grade of masking tape, one that is intended for body masking. Stick with known brands of tape.

Masking paper comes in many variations of quality and effectiveness. You tend to get what you pay for. Cheap masking paper or, heaven forbid, newspaper used for masking, tends to let paint bleed through—this is particularly true when the paper lays down flat against the surface of the masked area. When acrylic lacquer is used, newspaper will shed its ink just from the solvent vapors that contact it.

For masking tricky, curved areas, 3M and others offer special, flexible plastic masking tapes. These will flex far more than conventional masking tape, and can be bent in very sharp radius turns. They are just great for precision masking finicky trim. Typically, they come in widths from

1/16 to 3/4 inch. They are quite expensive. The trick in applying any masking tape is to pull it under tension around curves and force it into conformity smoothly. Don't pull tape too tight or it will fight its way back by losing adhesion.

When you mask rubber parts, be sure to clean them first with a suitable solvent, as adhesion to their surfaces is uncertain if this is not done. If trim cannot be removed and you have to mask it, be sure to leave about a 1/32-inch gap in the tape from the base of the trim to the panel. This allows for paint to flow in and avoids some rather "sticky" tape removal problems later.

On occasion, you will find a 3/4-inch bristle brush, with the bristles cut back to about 1/2-inch length, useful to force masking tape against the thing that you are masking. Toothpicks and clothespin ends also come in handy for this purpose. Really intricate work can sometimes be

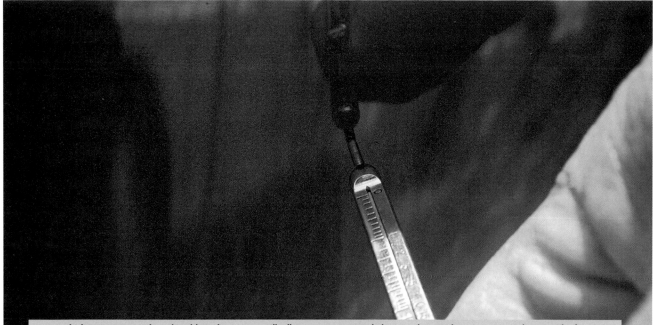

A paint thickness gauge, such as this old Tinsley gauge, will tell you pretty accurately how much paint there is on a panel. It's good information to have before you plan your strategy for refinishing. Of course, if you can afford one of the new ultrasonic paint thickness gauges, go for it. They are much more accurate than the spring tension type gauge, shown here, but probably represent expensive overkill for restoration work.

accomplished with spray-on masking compounds, some of which can be scored and peeled off when they dry. This marvelous stuff is water soluble, and masked areas can be coaxed clean with water spray when things are dry.

One interesting wrinkle in masking is "crease line" masking. This involves bending tape and paper back along the edge of a panel to create a small pocket. As spray reaches the pocket, it tends to eddy and produce a very nice blend that can be mist-coated or compounded into a panel. This trick is particularly usable if you are painting to a metal edge that bends very sharply.

The removal of masking tape has likely caused the expression of more profanity than many other and more difficult aspects of restoration painting. If you pull tape when the paint on a panel is too wet, the paint will string and creep and you will get a rough edge. If you pull it too late, you are likely to peel paint back with the tape and get a ragged edge. Tape should be removed from panels painted with lacquers and acrylic lacquers an hour after spraying and from panels painted in alkyd and acrylic enamels after six hours.

The Great "24 Hand Rubbed Coats of Lacquer" Fallacy— Paint Film Thickness

For some reason, mostly ignorance, there is a notion abroad in the land that a pile of paint half an inch thick is somehow desirable in restoration painting. It is supposed to have visible "depth." While it is technically possible to

stack 20 or more coats of paint onto an auto body, it is most clearly and distinctly not desirable to do so. It doesn't add to the appearance of the poor car that has to burden under this load, and it produces a finish that is not long destined for this world. One of the main causes of paint failure involves the thermal expansion characteristics of paint and its limited ductility. These characteristics combine to cause

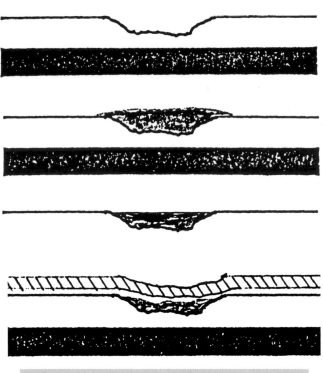

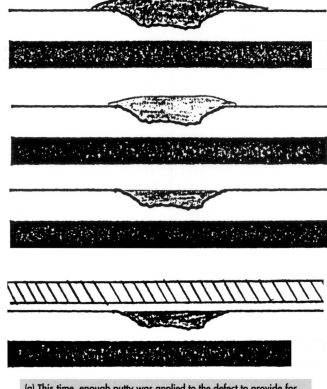

paint to fracture over extended periods. The thicker paint is, the greater the chances of thermal cycle failure. As paints get older and harder, they become increasingly vulnerable to this kind of breakdown.

In the days of the old nitrocellulose lacquers, there was a factor of abrasion and chalking that meant that these paints had to be compounded fairly regularly to remove surface scratches and oxidized material. Each compounding or polishing removed some paint and, eventually, you would cut through the finish. This situation suggested to some that a thick initial finish would be serviceable for a longer time. This was marginally true—up to the point that the paint cracked from its overly thick application.

In any case, modern acrylic-based paints, and particularly modern catalyzed enamels, are so tough and resistant to oxidation that it is hardly necessary to polish or compound them to maintain their luster. This means that a more durable, thinner application will survive the environment better than a thick one.

There is no reason to pile up acrylics and there is every reason not to. Modern catalyzed enamel systems will produce good results with as little as two coats, and there are painters who advocate holding their application of just two coats. Acrylic lacquers can be held to four or five coats with very acceptable results. Because restoration involves a

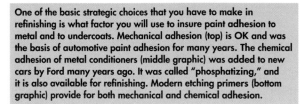

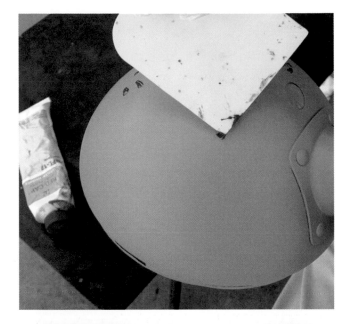

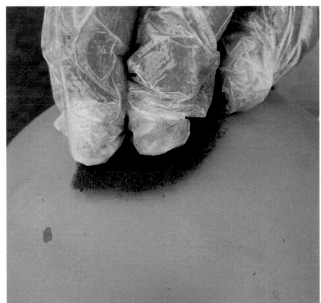

This sequence of photographs shows the application of glazing putty to fill some minor sand scratches and pits in the primer on a driving light housing. In this case, the putty was applied and wet sanded. Then the part was sprayed with a sealer and "denubbed" with a Scotchbrite pad. Sealing is one way to guarantee that there will be no sand scratches in a finish. Note the use of plastic gloves to protect the primer from skin oils.

more permanent proposition than simple repair, I would suggest spraying enamel in four or five coat applications and spraying acrylic lacquers in six to eight single-coat thicknesses, or three or four double coats. In the case of enamels, the coats should be full and wet after the first coat, which is usually medium.

In any case, the total thickness of paint on a car should not exceed 0.007 inch to 0.009 inch (seven to nine "mils"), and less than this may be desirable. It is important that the total film thickness is considered in observing this limit. This includes underlying paint and primer, sealers, primer surfacers, and, of course, the paint that you add to what already exists.

Spray guns come in an astounding variety of sizes, designs, and qualities. A general purpose gun (right) and a spotting gun (left) are shown here.

The latest thing in car spraying is HVLP (High Volume Low Pressure) guns—particularly gravity HVLP devices. They use low atomizing pressure and produce very little overspray. The gun on the left is the HVLP type, and the one on the left is conventional. Note the huge 'fan "holes in the air cap on the HVLP gun.

The nonsense about "24 hand rubbed coats of lacquer" means that time and money have been wasted and quality has been compromised. At best, it means that paint has been used where lead or primer-surfacer should have been used for filling. At worst, it means that a very fragile and short-lived finish has been produced.

One place where unnecessary paint often accumulates is in priming. I have seen primer applied in such thick accumulations that it must have taken 10 wet coats to produce such piles of the stuff. Primer is not a substitute for bodywork. Rather than pile it up, use a guide coat to keep it honest.

You remember in high school there were some people who seemed OK, but who had "bad reputations" for cutting up. Sometimes, they reformed their ways but their bad reputations lingered. Spot and glazing putties are like that. They have terrible reputations and are often assumed to be guilty of causing any problem that occurs in a finish. Actually, these materials are not bad in themselves. It is just that they are endlessly misused, and get blamed, even when it is the practitioner on the other end of the squeegee who should take the rap.

Putty has its obvious limitations. It is not body filler and is much too brittle and shrinkable to use for that purpose. It also has very little "holdout," which means that top coat finishes tend to sink into it. Still, it can be used effectively to fill deep scratches and pinholes up to about 0.040-inch, provided that two cautions are observed. First, putty must be allowed to dry completely before it is coated over, or it will gas and shrink in ways that destroy anything that you try to apply over it. Second, its holdout is so poor that it requires covering with a sealer or primer-sealer before you can attempt to paint color coats over it. Dry times with putty can be up to a day or two if you elect the maximum depth

of 0.040 inch. Glazing putty differs from spot putty only in that the former is compounded with 80 percent solids and the latter contains 90 percent solids. Putties are designed to dry as rapidly as possible, given their thickness. A few of them are still compounded in the format of nitrocellulose lacquers with extremely high solids content.

Spray Guns

The choice of spray gun is an important aspect of finishing. Some guns are of questionable quality, and some are very good. Different guns have different characteristics that make them work better or worse in varying situations. The nozzle and air cap setup for a good enamel gun will probably not work well with lacquer. Guns with sharp cutoff patterns have applications where guns with softer pattern edges do not, and *vice versa*. Ultimately, you will need different guns for different applications, but, in the interim, the different specification fluid tips and air caps that are available from most manufacturers for their guns will cover a range of applications with a single gun. Always use fluid tips and air caps that are designed for the purposes that you are pursuing.

In the hierarchy of spray guns, the lowly primer gun is the bottom feeder. Primer is highly abrasive to the insides of spray guns and very difficult to clean completely out of them. It is good practice to demote your worst gun to this fate and, when it is too shabby for even that, to bury it decently.

The wings on a spray gun air cap are generally used in a horizontal position, which produces a spray pattern that is vertical. However, for some jobs it is very advantageous to turn the wings to a vertical position and to use a horizontal pattern. One problem that used to routinely afflict spray

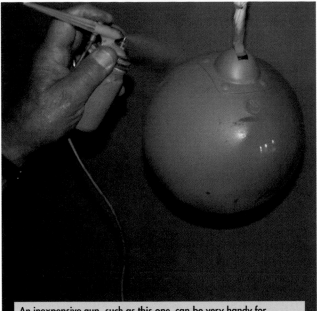

An inexpensive gun, such as this one, can be very handy for spraying the intricacies of small parts. The only trouble is it has a round spray pattern, and that can take some getting used to.

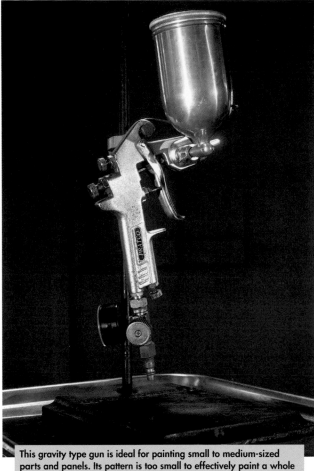

This gravity type gun is ideal for painting small to medium-sized parts and panels. Its pattern is too small to effectively paint a whole car.

guns was that their cup vents dripped. Every siphon gun has to have an air vent in its lid that allows air in to replace the paint that is evacuated from the gun cup. This, of course, only pertains to siphon-fed guns. Air vents used to be an ever-present hazard to good painting because when you tilted a gun down to paint a horizontal surface, such as a hood or roof, paint dripped out of the vent onto the surface that you were painting. About 25 years ago dripless cups by Binks and Marsten arrived on the scene. This type of cup has pretty much replaced the old "drippers." That is almost entirely good, except that the dripless air vents require a little extra attention when you clean a gun. Extra attention should also be paid to the cup gasket when you clean a gun because any paint that lurks there can ruin color matches. Guns should never be stored with the cup lid secured tightly on the cup gasket. Leave the lid-securing handle or lever just slightly tightened beyond contact. This saves lid gaskets.

It is important that spray guns be cleaned scrupulously and thoroughly after each use. Never put off cleaning a gun that has been used until the next day. Acrylic lacquer thinner or gun cleaner is the best solvent for this purpose, and repeated shaking, wiping, and spraying of solvent are the best ways to clean a gun, short of using an expensive gun cleaning cabinet/machine. When your gun is almost completely clean, you can loosen its air cap a few threads and hold a rag over the gun tip. Then spray out some solvent to force air and solvent back down through the gun.

Never immerse a gun in solvent, and avoid the automatic gun cleaning devices that tend to do this unless you have a modern gun with packings that are designed for this kind of cleaning. The problem with immersion is that the gun packings will be wetted and dried out to the point where they won't work. The outside of a gun can be cleaned with a bristle brush and solvent. After cleaning, the packings on a gun's air and material needles should be lubricated with a

drop of light oil and tightened only finger tight. Finally, it is important not to lay a gun on its side before it is cleaned. This can cause paint to run back into air passages and plug your gun. Be particularly careful if you are using catalyzed enamels or polyurethane paints because they have the potential of setting up and ruining a gun if they are not cleaned out of it during the period of their "pot lives."

Spray Guns: Adjustment and Technique

It is important always to remember the goals of spray painting and to create conditions that naturally lead to the fulfillment of these goals. They are to spray in a way that causes paint to flow out in a uniform coat that has no runs or sags and that has minimum effects from overspray. Part of success in the attainment of these goals involves the choice of paint, thinner, retarder and additives. Part of it involves gun adjustment and technique. What you do with your spray gun can usually make the products you are using work, or not work.

There are basically five factors that you can control on a conventional gun. These affect the amount of paint deposited, its format, and the shape of the deposit pattern. The first factor is air pressure, which controls the degree to

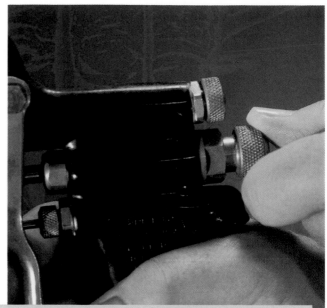

Adjusting a spray gun takes some practice. First you set the pattern (top knob), then you set the material flow to fill the pattern that you have set (bottom knob).

After you finish using and cleaning a spray gun, always lubricate its needle shafts with light oil where they enter packings.

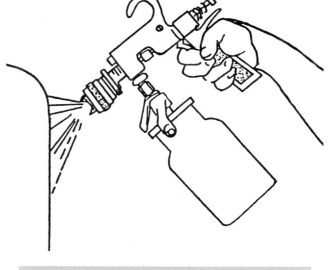

Never hold a gun like this. It's not perpendicular to the panel and will produce very thick paint at the top of its pattern and very thin paint at the bottom.

which a gun atomizes paint. The thicker the paint is, the more air pressure you will need for complete atomization. Yet the more air pressure you use, the more likely it is that the most volatile fractions of the paint/solvent mix will evaporate before paint reaches a panel. This can result in several problems because the paint mix becomes unbalanced. Orange peel is among the problems that can be caused by excessive spray air pressure. Every manufacturer recommends a pressure range for each of its products, and it pays to follow these recommendations rigorously. Generally, the lowest pressure that will adequately atomize a paint is best. Gun air pressure should always be measured and fine-tuned with a tailstock gauge and adjustment.

The second gun adjustment is the "fan" pattern, or "spreader." This controls the amount of free air routed through a gun's air cap wings to squash the pattern from a round into an oblong shape. The adjustment of this factor changes the spray pattern from a circle to an increasingly long, thin shape. A full-bodied oval shape is best. When fan pressure is too high, you begin to get a pattern that looks like two circles. The best way to set the fan is to "flood" a test sheet with paint by triggering your gun until paint runs out of the pattern that you are spraying. This is done with the pattern set horizontally. The paint should run out of the pattern evenly and not more strongly at the ends or in the middle. With sufficient experience, it is possible to skip this test and set your gun's fan air adjustment by the achieved shape of the pattern on a test sheet.

Always spray a test pattern with your gun before you attempt to spray a part or panel. And always remember that if you spray your test pattern on paper, you will have to allow for the difference between paper and a panel and account for that difference in your settings. Paper absorbs the solvents in paint, so paint is less likely to sag or run on paper than on a panel.

All of these test spray patterns are usable for particular purposes. The one on the top, right is very balanced and will produce a smooth finish.

A "flooding test" is the best way for beginners to balance the pattern (fan) and material adjustments on spray guns. In the graphic, at right, the adjustment that sprayed the bottom flooding test pattern is the right one to use. The bottom pattern in the photograph is a bit center heavy with paint but still the best of the three shown.

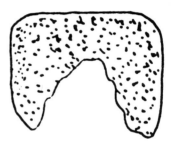

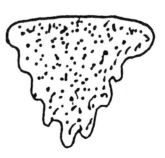

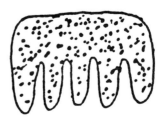

When the desired spray pattern has been tuned in, the material control adjustment (which is really a trigger stop) is manipulated to "fill the pattern." This simply means that you adjust the rate of material flow until paint is deposited at the rate that you want when the gun is moved at the speed and distance from the panel that you are going to use. Most guns will operate best when moved at a speed of roughly 1 foot per second and is held at a distance of 6 to 10 inches from a panel. Lacquers work best with a gun distance of 6

Sometimes you have to adjust your paint thinning or reduction after you mix paint. You cannot cover all contingencies with spray gun and air pressure adjustments. Just mixing to manufacturers' guidelines does not always work. Keep things on the thick side until your are sure of your mixture.

to 8 inches, and enamels are generally sprayed at distances of 8 to 10 inches. HVLP spray guns reduce these distances somewhat.

Clearly, these adjustments are closely interrelated. Air pressure, material flow, gun speed and gun distance all affect the amount of paint deposited in one place. Pattern format and paint reduction also affect this, as does the amount of overlap between succeeding gun strokes. Always remember the goal of spraying—to achieve flow-out without runs or sags and with minimum overspray. The interrelated factors affecting paint deposit are all aimed at this relatively simple purpose. Your experience is the only guide that you have.

To some extent, lacquers, and to a great extent enamels, require a bit of faith to achieve flow out. Paints do not land on panels in a flowed out condition. Some enamels may take minutes to achieve this; others take only seconds. You have to spray with enough faith in your paint to know that flow-out will occur. Of course, if you spray too dry, you will not get paint to flow out, but if you try to spray wet enough to get instant flow-out, you will get sags and runs in your finish. Experience and faith are necessary.

Lacquers are less of a problem in this regard than enamels because they are sprayed very thin (125 percent reduction is pretty much standard) and are harder to make run or sag. Lacquer solvents are also much more volatile than those used with enamels, so when you are spraying lacquer, what you see while you are spraying is pretty much what you will get when the paint dries.

Paint manufacturers like to specify the kinds of coats that are best for the applications of their various products.

Mixing to exact recommended proportions by volume, a viscometer test and the old standby of visually checking paint run off the end of a mixing stick can be used. Each method has its place.

Such terms as, "dust coat, dry coat, fog coat, mist coat, medium coat, light coat, heavy coat, full coat," etc. abound on paint cans and on paint data sheets. For the most part, these terms are self-explanatory, and advice of this type from a manufacturer should always be followed.

There are a few terms that are not obvious. "Double coats" involve a rapid application of two coats. These are frequently achieved by repeating each gun stroke. "Cross coating" means applying a second coat—usually immediately—at right angles to the first coat. This is one of the times that you will want to adjust the air cap wings on your gun for a pattern at right angles to the one used in applying the previous coat. "Mist" coats and "fog" coats are very light coats with minimum deposits. "Fog coats" usually involve very high atomization with abnormally high gun air pressures and large gun-to-panel distances. These coats are used to lay a base for some enamels and sometimes to spray special primers such as zinc phosphate and zinc chromate. "Mist" coating can be used to melt-in overspray from lacquer and acrylic enamels that are used in spot and in some panel repairs. In this approach, you use over-thinned or over-reduced materials.

The use of "banding" coats is an old trick. This involves gun passes that outline a panel at its edges before it is sprayed in the usual half overlap, horizontal strokes. "Triggering" is the business of stopping the paint and air flow from your gun at the end of each stroke, and then starting it again on the reverse pass. If this is not done, you will tend to get excessive paint buildup at the ends of your gun strokes as you reverse your guns direction, and will promote unnecessary overspray.

One of the most pervasive errors made by novice painters is to "fan" a spray gun or to move it with a combination of arm travel and wrist twist that varies its distance to the target at the beginnings and ends of your strokes. Good, steady arm travel is fine. You should hold your spray gun as perpendicular as possible to panels. Excessive wrist twist or "fanning" a gun changes its angle to a panel. As the angle goes to either side of 90 degrees, the effective distance from the gun to the panel increases and uneven paint application results. I have a tendency to fan a spray gun, and I have to periodically cure it with an Ace-type bandage around my wrist when I spray.

Never try to paint by continuing gun strokes into areas that you can't see, in the vain hope that if you don't change any gun factors (speed, overlap, target distance, etc.), the paint will flow out all right. This is a gamble that you can easily lose.

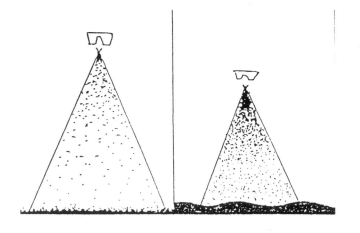

If you hold a spray gun too far from a panel (left) you will get dry, flaky paint (lacquer) or orange peel (enamel). If you hold the gun too close to a panel (right), you will get thick, sagging, running paint.

For most spraying with automotive finishes, a 50-percent overlap left-to-right and return right-to-left spray pattern is used. The gun should be untriggered and retriggered at the end of each stroke to avoid paint build-up at panel edges.

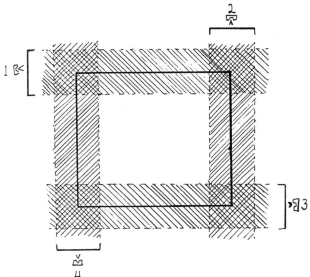

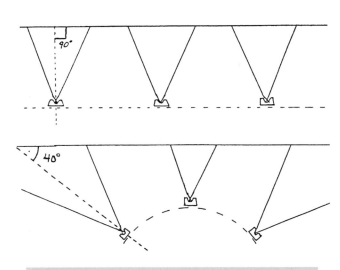

"Banding" a panel means applying coats of paint around its edges before you fill it in.. It's an old trick and a good one. After the banding coats are sprayed, you spray the panel in a conventional 50 percent overlap, left-to-right, etc., way, being sure to untrigger and retrigger at panel edges.

Always keep your spray gun at 90 degrees to a panel as you move it along. That way, you will deposit paint evenly on the panel (top graphic). If you "fan your gun," you will deposit paint unevenly and make a terrible mess. Fanning a gun can be a difficult habit to break. It is very easy to lose this essential configuration in the task of spraying. Concentrate on it.

Those Dreaded Sand Scratches

Sand scratch swelling can be a very persistent problem for some painters—you certainly see enough of it on restored cars! Unlike defects such as blushing and fish eying, which are easily preventable with good habits and judgments, sand scratch swelling is a problem that sometimes seems to defy the exercise of good paint practice. It is caused by solvent residues and vapors lingering in the bases of scratches in underlying coats and coming back to swell top coats. The cheap and easy solution to this problem is to use sealers over primers or over sanded finishes that are being recoated. Sometimes, sealers are necessary, but the most effective sealers are the non-sanding types, and these produce an inferior base for the application of top coats.

Correctly sanded primer is always the best base upon which to build a finish.

The good alternative to sealers is to prevent sand scratch swelling by eliminating the scratches themselves. This is done by avoiding sandpaper grit cross contamination and by using carefully graduated sandpaper grits up to 600. Some people advocate using some of the "ultra" type sandpapers (1200-, 1500-, 1800-grit and higher), or even compounding primer to guarantee removal of all scratches that could cause sand scratch swelling. Compounding is advocated particularly for use around feather edges, where sand scratches can lurk and are hard to see in primer. I think that compounding is beyond the needs of these situations. If oil-based compounds are used for this purpose, the cleanup presents problems. Adequately sanded primer, say 600 grit, should not produce sand scratch swelling and usually

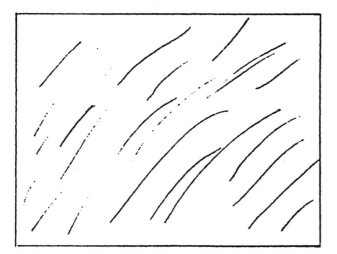

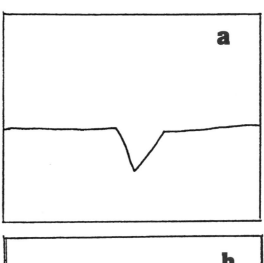

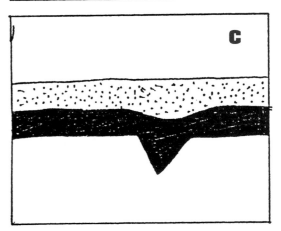

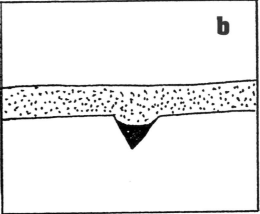

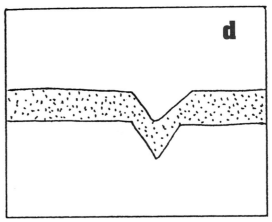

Sand scratches above are those fine, scratch-like depressions that can sometimes be seen in finishes.
(a) A scratch is left in an undercoat.
(b) The solvent from a top coat lingers in the bottom of the scratch and is trapped there when the top coat dries.
(c) The solvent works through the top coat, and the top coat falls into the depression left by it.
(d) When the solvent completely evaporates, the top coat follows the contour of the scratch as it fills it.

should not need sealing.

Some painters argue that compounding or the use of ultra-fine sandpaper grits guarantees that there will be no sand scratches that can swell. Others, me included, believe that these practices leave surfaces with too little "tooth" for the adequate adhesion of top coats. I have never seen sand scratch swelling where primer was carefully and completely sanded with uncontaminated 600-grit paper. Sanding with finer grits, or the use of sealers, seems unnecessary to me if you are top coating fresh primers. You can do a lot to prevent sand scratch swelling when you paint by making your first gun passes with fog coats and by allowing adequate drying times, flash times, or setup times between coats throughout the priming and painting processes.

Special Situations, Problems of Compatibility and Sealers

Beginning painters often ask, "Is it lacquer that you can't paint over enamel, or the other way around?" In fact, things aren't quite that simple. I wish that they were. The rules of paint compatibility are complex, and as the variety of paints and additives has increased, these rules have become more complex. There are a few simple statements that can be made about paint compatibility.

Fresh, uncatalyzed enamels that were not force dried cannot be recoated for a year after they are sprayed, unless some exotic coating, such as water-born primer/barrier coat, is used over them. The same can be true of uncatalyzed acrylic enamel. Paint that is chalked, cracked or crumbly cannot be made the basis of any top coat system, no matter

This is how sand scratch swelling occurs.

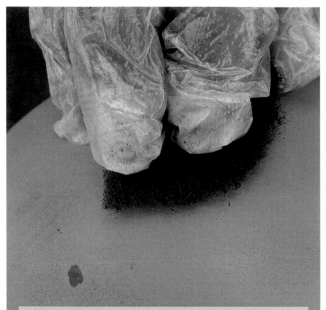

This item was sealed to prevent sand scratch swelling. A fine Scotchbrite® pad can be used to knock the nubs off the sealer, but you cannot sand it. That's a problem with most sealers—you have to live with the surfaces that they leave.

what "miracle" sealer is used. Such defective paint must be removed and a new base built up before you paint.

Almost any kind of paint can be applied over any other, but it is almost always best to use a sealer when color coats are sprayed over anything but a primer, primer-surfacer, or primer-sealer. In the case of acrylic lacquers over enamels, a sealer will enhance adhesion. In the case of painting over nitrocellulose and acrylic lacquers, it will promote holdout and prevent fading or sinking in. There are sealers designed for top coating with lacquer and sealers designed for top coating with enamel. This distinction must be observed. It is also critical that an enamel-based sealer or primer never be "sandwiched" between a lacquer base and lacquer top coats. Virtually any other combination can be made to work well if an appropriate sealer is used. Of course, all of this requires that the final, combined film thickness of the old paint and the new paint is kept at a reasonable level; 0.007 inch to 0.009 inch is about as much paint as you should have in a finish.

When sealers are used, it turns out that the most effective of them tend to be the "non-sanding" types, and the best that you can do to smooth them out after spraying is to knock the "nubs" off them with a fine Scotchbrite pad. Never try to sand these sealers. The advantage of non-sanding sealers is that they are more certain to promote holdout, and they accomplish this with far less film thickness than sandable sealers. If overall film thickness is a problem on a particular job, you may want to use one of the non-sanding sealers. Some primer-surfacers have limited sealing abilities; this depends on their type: acrylic lacquer-based or synthetic enamel-based. Always be sure to use the right sealer for a job.

The advent of such additives as flex agents has added to compatibility problems, or at least to the possible questions that a painter will have about them. The best solution is to deal with a good jobber who has the information that you are likely to need, or who can talk to someone in the manufacturer's home office or regional office to get this information. Most of the major paint companies provide very good technical support for their products.

General Admonitions

There are some general warnings and recommendations that are contained in or on virtually every refinishing shop manual, paint data sheet and paint can label. I think the reason these warnings are repeated so often is because there are people out there who still ignore them. Let's sample a few.

Mix paint thoroughly. To do less is to cause color match problems or even film problems. Paints that have sat for a long time should be stirred with a paddle and then shaken on a paint shaker. This will free the "glup" that has settled on the bottom of the can so that it can be shaken into solution. Never use paint if everything in the can cannot be mixed into solution. Paints should also be mixed thoroughly with their thinners and reducers. You can't overmix solvents and paints, but it is easy to undermix them. Paint will settle in a spray gun cup as you spray, so be sure to swirl it periodically, or mix it with a stick if it has sat in your gun for very long. An automatic stirring cup eliminates this problem. Some paints cannot be shaken due to aeration, and this prohibition must be observed when it is stated in instructions. Other paints need to have their additives poured into them slowly and with minimum air inclusions. Always observe instructions regarding minimum "gel" times for some paint additives, and never spray catalyzed or two-part paint systems after, or even near, the ends of their "pot lives."

Paint must be handled in a clean environment. Be careful at every stage of handling paint to avoid contaminating it. Always blow off the jambs on paint can friction lids before you open them, so that contaminants lodged there don't fall into your paint. Always use clean vessels to receive paints and to mix them in, and always use clean spray equipment. Paint should be strained through a gauze filter on its way to your gun cup, and your gun should be outfitted with an in-cup filter, if possible.

Don't touch primed surfaces with your bare hands. Skin oils can never be sufficiently removed from your hands to avoid contamination. The best policy is to clean an about-to-be-painted surface with a cleaning solvent or with fast enamel reducer. The surface then should be wiped with a tack rag and blown off with the air-only trigger-position on your gun. If cracks or crevices, such as door seams, are involved in the area that you are painting, always blow them out with an air gun before painting.

Don't let your enthusiasm or boredom get in the way of allowing adequate flash times (lacquer) or setup times (enamel) between succeeding coats that you spray. Lacquers benefit from intervals between coats that are a bit longer than their apparent flash times, and enamels need

Paints and primers settle, even the ones that aren't supposed to. Always mix them thoroughly, first with a stick and then in a mechanical shaker, like the electric and pneumatic ones shown here. You can check paint for sediment by probing the bottom of the can with a mixing stick. After paints are thinned or reduced, you still need to be stirred to keep their solids in suspension. Keep mixing things as you paint by swirling your gun occasionally.

from 10 to 30 minutes of setup time before recoating. If you abbreviate these times, you are likely to have problems with trapped solvents in lacquer and runs, sags, or excessive orange peel in enamels. Primers are best sprayed in fairly wet coats for maximum adhesion, but this means that they need decent flash times, and then some, between coats.

Follow manufacturers' recommended mixing ratios for thinners and reducers for specified shop conditions. You can't make "medium" reducer or thinner work in all shop conditions and it is foolish to try. In very hot and humid conditions, retarders may allow you to spray lacquers and acrylic enamels without blushing and other defects, but don't count on it!

Tricks of the Trade

There must be hundreds or thousands of little tricks that make painting easier and better. There are also plenty

First, filter your paint or primer when you pour it out of the can. Then filter it again after you have thinned or reduced it, when you pour it into your paint cup. Then, if possible, fit the pickup tube on your spray gun with a small filter to add a final guarantee of paint purity. This last step is not possible with many gravity-type guns.

of pretty bad tricks, but these usually look like what they are—unacceptable short cuts. Just watching an experienced painter (best done with one's mouth firmly set in a closed position) can provide a wealth of ideas on good ways to do things.

When complete cars are being painted, it is crucial that you adopt an approach to proceed from panel to panel in a way that minimizes overspray problems. There are three or more panel sequences that experienced painters use. The adoption of a particular pattern depends on the venting characteristics of the spray booth or area that you are working in and the nature of the car that you are painting.

Just working from front to back, or *vice versa*, is almost never the best approach. This is a situation that requires some thought and planning.

When you work with a new paint, and particularly with some of the new enamels, it's a good idea to experiment on a primed panel. You can't get a good sense of how paint will flow if all you do is spray it on the paper that you use to set your gun pattern. Paper tends to absorb the solvents in paint spray and it will give you a false indication of the potential for sags and runs with a new paint.

Color matching, and particularly metallic color matching, depends mostly on the paint tint. It also depends on gun air pressure, speed of travel, material setting, fluid tip and air cap choice, paint thinning and coat wetness and overlap.

A surprising amount of color adjustment can be accomplished by varying the factors that affect the wetness of the coat that you are applying.

When you spray paint to fill and level a feather-edged area, the practice of "feathering" the gun trigger can be invaluable. This involves working the gun trigger deeper where you want more paint and backing it off as you come to the feather edge. This will give you more paint where you want it, in the low spots. Feathering a gun takes some practice, but it is a skill worth developing.

Sometimes, despite your best efforts, an area catches

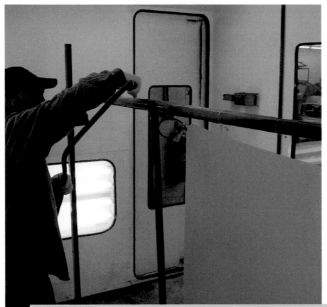

Always blow off surfaces in your spray area that might collect dust or contamination, as well as parts and panels, in your final approach to spraying them. This will drive sanding residues out of crevices so they won't end up in your paint.

too much paint and you get a sag or run. Keep a cool head and don't despair...yet. Your pinky, thumb or forefinger can be educated to make a quick cleanup repair stab. Later, when the paint has set up, some pretty dry gun passes, followed by some wet ones, will make the damage done by your finger virtually disappear. When you use an "educated finger" for this maneuver, you still have to be careful of overspray and careful not to get the paint film too thick in the repaired area.

Melting in overspray can save a lot of hand work on lacquers and enamels. To do this, a uniforming solvent or a retarder mixed with thinner or reducer is used in a mist coat. The mist coat is radically over-thinned, with only about 10 percent paint in the mix. Different manufacturers have different approaches to mist coating for blending, and these should be followed. This kind of operation can make quite a difference in the overall results that you get in a "paint job."

Some "tricks of the trade" are little habits that promote cleanliness in handling paint and equipment. The practice of blowing out the lid interfaces of friction cans has already been mentioned. It is a little habit that prevents a lot of contamination. It isn't a bad idea to tape paint can lids with masking tape when you store paint to keep dirt out. Taping the inside of a paint can rim to form a pouring spout that keeps paint out of the can top groove is another good practice.

Surgical gloves are great for protecting your hands from paint and solvents and for protecting panels from the oils in your skin.

One trick that is always a benefit is to know the complete line or system that you are painting with. Additives like retarder that are designed to correct painting problems should not be used just because they are there. It is always better not to use them if possible. If conditions call

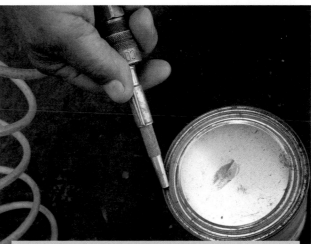

Paint must be kept clean at every stage of handling it. Blowing out friction can lid seams before you open paint cans is just common sense.

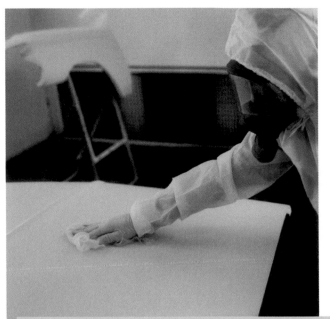

Finally, always gently wipe parts and panels with a tack rag before you spray them.

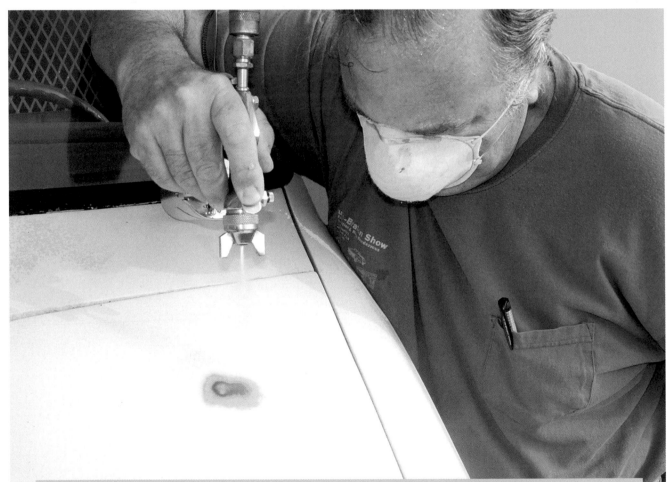

Feathering your paint gun trigger is a real plus when you have to level paint in areas like this feather-edged spot repair.

for them, you have to know about their potential for solving problems. On the other hand, performance additives, such as gloss additives, often improve painting results.

Always remember that proficiency in refinishing includes dealing with the unexpected quickly and effectively—as if you expected it.

Chapter 27

Automotive Refinishing Part III, After the Paint Dries

This equipment buffs and polishes finishes. It can be used to bring out the best in the paint that you spray, or on old finishes, but there are limits to what you can do with buffing and polishing. The products in the background are for polishing fresh paint without sealing it in ways that will interfere with its curing process.

MOST OF OUR EXPERIENCE IS, OF COURSE, with dried or cured paint. Refinishing an old car is a complex, time-consuming and expensive proposition, and most of our efforts are necessarily directed to making existing paint work. Sometimes this is paint that we have recently sprayed and that needs further work to produce an acceptable finish. At

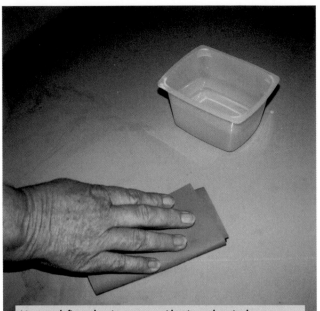

New, much finer abrasive papers, with grit numbers in the thousands, and catalyzed enamels have made it possible to do something that you never could do in the past—polish and buff enamel. I'm not sure that restorers of early cars painted in baked enamel want to use this option because it creates the look of finishes that did not exist until the 1970s. That is, combinations of orange peel and buffing swirl marks.

other times, it is possible to work with an older, existing finish in a way that allows us to improve its appearance to the point that it becomes acceptable.

Occasionally, the problems of an existing finish or of a new finish are so great that the only practical approach is to refinish. All of these situations differ from those discussed in the previous two chapters because they involve existing finishes. Finally, after a finish has dried, it must be maintained and sometimes repaired if it is to have a reasonable service life.

Compounding and Polishing

Old, oxidized or stained finishes and new, unleveled rough ones require polishing to achieve a smooth and attractive luster. Compounding and polishing are essentially the same operation, except that compounding involves coarser abrasives. Both compounding and polishing level painted surfaces by abrading or "scratching" them very minutely. While it may sound strange to consider scratching a surface to polish it, this is the nugget of virtually all polishing processes. The key is in the size of the abrasives that are used and the sizes of the scratches that they impart. Just as 300- or 400-grit abrasives will visibly scratch and dull a finish, abrasives in the 1500-grit and above range will polish it. In the latter case, the scratches are so fine and closely spaced that they produce the optical effect of gloss and luster. That is, until you look at them under a microscope; then they look like what they are—scratches!

Compounding is the first step, and polishing is the second step in bringing full luster to a rough finish. Finishes that are already pretty level do not need to be compounded, and you can go directly to polishing. Both of these processes can be accomplished either by hand or with a machine. Hand compounding and polishing have the advantages of vastly reducing the risk of cutting through a finish on edges or at styling reliefs. Hand compounding and polishing often produce fewer objectionable swirl marks than machine compounding and polishing because they can be performed in relatively straight lines, as opposed to the circular motions characteristic of machine polishing.

The main problem that some people have with hand compounding is that it represents a variant of the human experience known as "WORK," and even "hard, dull WORK." Machine compounding and polishing are also "work," but never "WORK." While I prefer the appearance of a hand-compounded and polished finish, the amount of effort required to level and polish lacquer or catalyzed enamel finishes by hand can be considerable in some cases. It all depends on what you start with.

Not all finishes can be compounded or even polished. Lacquers and acrylic lacquers dry in a way that invariably leaves a surface that will be improved by polishing and/or compounding and polishing. Catalyzed urethane and cured or hardened alkyd enamels can be polished with fine abrasives, and this should give them an added gloss. Alkyd enamels cannot be polished until they have aged for six months or a year.

I consider polishing any kind of enamel an to be an unnecessary and inappropriate step in restoration work. This is, of course, a personal opinion and goes against a lot of modern restoration practice. I think that if these enamels are properly applied in an appropriately dust-free environment, they will achieve a natural gloss that I find far more attractive and authentic than the one which includes the swirl marks that accompany polishing.

The abrasives used in compound and polish are made from anything from Tripoli to pumice, talc and synthetic abrasives. Hand polishes and compounds generally use oils for their bases, while machine compounds and polishes are usually water-based. You can get compounds and polishes in different grades, depending on how aggressively you need to remove surface films and decayed paint to clean and/or level a finish, and how fine you want the abrasives for your final polishing to be. As in any abrasive finishing operation, you move to progressively finer grits to produce a glossier and shinier result. When working with enamels, you begin with finer abrasives than those used initially on lacquers. Both machine and hand abrasives are designed to break up into ever finer particles as polishing with them progresses and the final stages of shine are achieved. Abrasives designed for machine application tend to break up faster than those designed for hand application. Machine compounds also tend to dry (evaporate their solvents) faster than hand compounds because of their different bases. In general, use hand abrasives for hand compounding and polishing and machine abrasives when you use a machine for this work.

It should also be noted that there is a tremendous difference in the quality of various brands of compounds

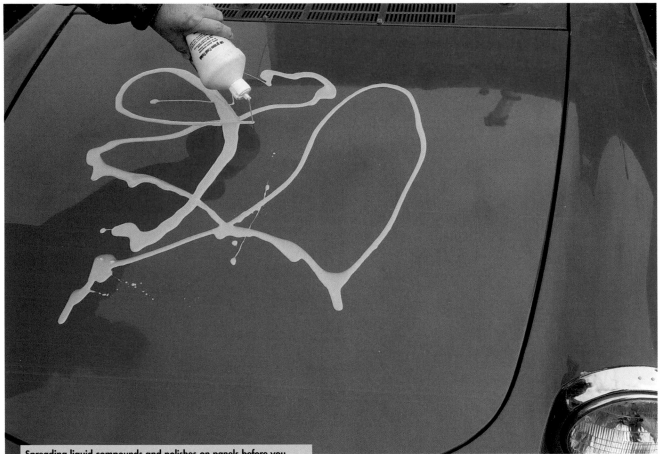

Spreading liquid compounds and polishes on panels before you power buff them is easy ... and sort of fun, but the actual buffing operation has to be done very carefully or you will burn or cut through a finish. Buffing with power equipment is not the time to show your "wild side."

As a bonnet gets clogged with paint and spent abrasives, you can clean it with this kind of tool.

and polishes. The ones sold in body shop supply stores and marked "for professional use" invariably produce better results than the cut-rate stuff sold in discount stores. The professional stuff doesn't come in neat little $1.29 tins, so if you want good quality compounds and polishes, be prepared to spend more than that. In working with

polishes and compounds, employ the least abrasion and surface removal that will get the job done. In the case of old finishes with deep scratches, or of new ones with excessive orange peel, a fairly course grade of compound or even a preliminary "color sanding" with a 600-grit abrasive paper, followed by smoothing with 1200-, 1500-, 1800- or even

You have to protect edges and styling lines when you power compound or polish, otherwise you may cut through the paint at these vulnerable points. One way to protect these areas is to tape over them and then hand compound and/or polish them later.

2200-grit abrasive paper, may be necessary for the initial leveling. Developments in coated abrasive technology have produced papers that are much finer than those that were available a decade ago. Some of these are consistently higher than the old 1200-grit papers, and are not just made up of particles that average to a stated grade. While these new papers can be used to do terrific leveling work, they should only be used when it is absolutely necessary to remove quite a bit of material for leveling purposes. They also tend to be quite expensive.

One unfortunate tendency that has crept into the practice of some body shops, and even of some restoration shops, is the business of applying finishes, particularly catalyzed enamels, badly and in grossly contaminated environments. This dirty application is then routinely followed by color sanding to level and clean up the finish, and then by machine compounding and polishing to give it gloss. This approach produces superficially attractive results, but close inspection will indicate the sins of unevenness and contamination in the original paint. The options of color sanding and wheeling a finish can be valuable, but they should never become a routine part of refinishing with any material, particularly catalyzed enamel.

It is also important to understand that, just as some finishes, such as uncatalyzed acrylic enamel, cannot really be effectively polished right after they are applied, there are other limits to what can be done after the fact with abrasives and finishes. Acrylic lacquers, for example, require some form of polishing after application, but if you attempt to do this too soon, you will dull and ruin the surface on which you are working. Sometimes, older finishes that have chalked (oxidized) can be saved with compounds and/or polishes, but other times they are deteriorated to the point that they can no longer be polished.

Whether a hand or machine application of compound or polish is being attempted, it is important to mix the compound thoroughly before you begin using it. In hand compounding and polishing operations, the abrasive is applied to a soft damp pad or wad of rag and the surface is rubbed in straight lines. Apply only enough compound to do the area that you are working on, and confine this area to about the size of a car door, or less. As the surface begins to polish and the abrasive breaks up, your rubbing strokes will encounter less resistance; you will feel this happen. At this point, you can ease up the pressure on your applicator. Finally, the mostly dried compound should be buffed with a clean cloth and very little pressure. A second clean cloth can be used to advantage for a final buff.

While it is much more difficult to cut through a finish in a hand operation than in a machine operation, it

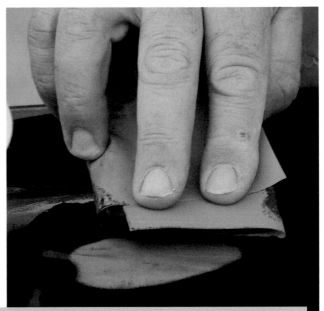

Feather edges can be machine sanded or hand sanded. I like to start with a DA sander and then finish by hand with fine abrasive paper on a foam backup pad. Note that the primer under this 70 year-old factory paint is roughly the same color as the topcoats. You can only see a little difference in color in the feather edge ring. Using primer that is the same color as topcoats has the advantage of hiding chips in topcoats when they occur. The downside of this trick is that you get little or no warning when you are about to cut through a finish to bare metal.

is possible. This is particularly true when you employ the rougher grades of compound. Course compound is also a hazard when it is used on older finishes where you really don't know how much color coat there is left to compound or polish.

When you compound or polish, be particularly careful of raised edges, crease lines and other places where a panel bends sharply. Not only does the pressure from hand, and particularly from machine, polishing tend to concentrate in such places, but the finish is thinner there to begin with, and consequently, it is easier to cut through it. Be careful.

Machine compounding and polishing are much faster than comparable hand operations. A tufted wheel or a "bonnet" is used with paste type abrasives, and a lamb's wool bonnet is used with liquid polishes or with very fine paste type abrasives. There are several other new polishing head configurations on the market. Effective polishing machines operate at around 2,000 RPM, or less, so you should avoid using the faster hand-held machines that are really designed for grinding. Excessive speed or pressure will either cut through paint, or burn it. Good wheel polishing is done with only moderate pressure, and you must keep the wheel moving at all times to avoid burning or cutting through a finish. As you polish, your bonnet will tend to clog with paint and spent abrasive, and it must be cleaned periodically by running a cleaning tool over it to remove the clogs.

In machine polishing, abrasive is applied to a surface that is being polished and the machine is moved first horizontally back and forth with overlapping strokes over a small area. The machine is then moved vertically up and down with overlapping strokes over the same area. The edge of the pad or bonnet should be lifted slightly, about 1/2 inch, in the direction that the wheel is being moved, either horizontally or vertically. Do not continue to polish after the liquid lubricant in your abrasive has evaporated

or you will damage the finish. Also, do not attempt to work too large an area at one time. A door or fender will be about right.

Machine compounding and polishing can produce dramatically favorable results, but it is also very possible to produce burns, scorches and cut-throughs with surprising ease. Edges and bends in panels exacerbate these problems, and such areas should be avoided when you wheel panels. If it is difficult to avoid these areas with your wheel, it is best to tape them with masking tape to prevent problems. After machine polishing is complete, you can remove the tape and do the vulnerable areas by hand. It is almost never possible to get safely into every painted surface on a car with a wheel, so some hand work is generally necessary. Caution is the byword here, because it is a terrible feeling to have to repair a new finish that has been damaged by cutting through it, or burning its surface, with a polishing wheel.

It should also be noted that polishing wheels throw off fine airborne abrasives in considerable quantity and with great velocity. It is necessary to wear goggles and a respirator or dust shield when operating one of these machines.

Spot Repairs to Damaged Finishes

The ability to spot repair a finish is often utilized in restoration practice when damage is confined to one, or to a few, small areas. The objectives of spot repair are to produce a finish that blends into the panel being repaired and that matches it in gloss, color, texture and level. While spot repairs can be made with finishes other than acrylic lacquer, this is certainly the easiest modern finish to work with in this way, and it usually produces very acceptable results in spot refinishing.

This feather edge spot repair revealed clean metal. Sometimes sanding a defect in a panel will expose rust, which then has to be dealt with.

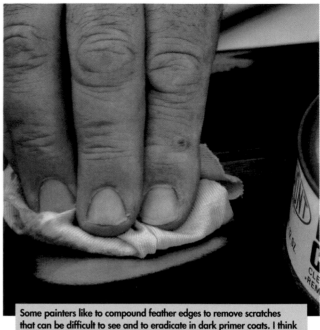

Some painters like to compound feather edges to remove scratches that can be difficult to see and to eradicate in dark primer coats. I think that this practice is unnecessary and that the same purpose can be accomplished with fine abrasive paper and wet sanding.

Spot refinishing generally follows the outline given for panel and overall refinishing, stated in the last two chapters on refinishing in this book, except, of course, that there is the additional problem of blending the edges of the repair area into the old finish. The first step in spotting in work is to wash the panel where the repair will be made. Do this well beyond the edges of the repair area. Wash with water and mild detergent, and then rinse thoroughly with clean water. This should be followed by a solvent wash with a silicone and oil removing solvent. The repair area should then be sanded down as far as is necessary.

If a paint defect was the reason for the repair, it must be sanded to bare metal or to the primer, if it is still in tact. If there is rust, or if metal repair was necessary, the sanding must go to bare metal in the repair area. When bare metal is exposed, it should be treated with metal conditioner. Then, the excess conditioner must be wiped off the surrounding finish with a damp cloth. If you are simply repairing a scratch or similar superficial defect, you should sand far enough to prevent excessive film thickness when the color coats are applied. The total thickness of paint and primer should not exceed 8 or 9 mils, in any case. There are various devices for measuring paint thickness, such as the magnetic Tinsley Gauges or some very fancy electronic (ultrasonic) gear. Generally, with some experience, you can tell by sight and feel how much paint is on a panel when you sand through it to bare metal in one spot. Come to think of it, those paint thickness gauges are not a bad idea.

Whether bare metal or primer remains after sanding, the edge of any repair area must be feather sanded so that it *gradually* comes up to the level of the areas beyond the repair area. There are wiping "lacquer dissolving" solvents available to feather lacquer finished surfaces for this purpose, but these tend to produce an inferior result to hand sanding feather edges and should only be used on very small spots,

if at all.

Surfaces well beyond a feather edge sanded area should be masked to avoid deposits of overspray. If there is bare metal in the repair area, it should be primed. Then, a primer surfacer with good holdout characteristics should be used to fill and level the entire repair area. The technique of feathering a spray gun—releasing the trigger partially and applying less paint on the feathered edges of a repair area—can be utilized to great advantage in this work. Be sure to allow adequate flash times for primer-surfacers and for the color coats that come later. Remember, drying paint shrinks roughly 50 percent from its wet state.

Some refinishing practitioners advocate compounding the feathered edges of a repair area before spraying primer-surfacer. Hand compounding is best if this procedure is followed, but machine compounding can be used and is advocated by some painters. I have never found compounding necessary at this point, but prefer to do careful sanding with uncontaminated 600-grit paper.

In either case, the area should be cleaned with water and then with solvent prior to applying primer-surfacer to it. It is generally recommended that a cleaning solvent be used for this purpose, but I have found that these solvents tend to soften the primer and can produce several problems later. A fast enamel reducer is almost ideal for this kind of solvent cleanup operation. After the primer-surfacer that was applied to the repair area has dried adequately, the area should be block sanded or board sanded to level the repair area with the surrounding panel surface. This area should be cleaned with a solvent cleaner or fast enamel reducer after it has been washed down with water. You are now ready to apply color coats.

If the repair is to be made with acrylic lacquer, a two-gun technique will serve best. The basic proposition here is to cover the repair area with as many color coats as are

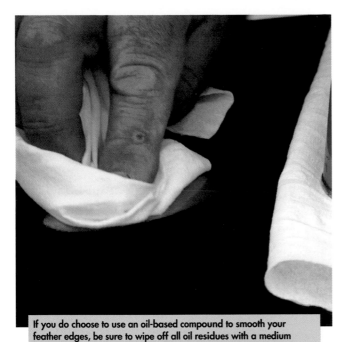

If you do choose to use an oil-based compound to smooth your feather edges, be sure to wipe off all oil residues with a medium enamel reducer before you apply any other treatment or coating.

When you have sanded to bare metal, always treat the exposed metal in feather edged spot repairs with a good metal conditioner.

necessary to achieve hiding of the primer and to blend the edges of the repaired area into the existing finish. When hiding is achieved, a mist coat of highly thinned color (5 percent) is applied with the second gun to the edges of the repair area. This mist coat will blend those edges into the surrounding finish. A product like DuPont's Uniforming Finish is ideal for this purpose, but, of course, this should only be used with DuPont systems. Other manufacturers have special products or special procedures with conventional thinners and reducers to accomplish the same result. While it is generally effective to follow color coating with a blender coat, sometimes more than one blender coat is necessary, and sometimes it is necessary to alternate color coats with blender coats around the edges of paint that is spotted in after applying a second color coat.

It is much more difficult to effect spot repairs with enamels, but it is possible, and with some finishes it is necessary to do this to get a texture and gloss match. Enamels are used in roughly the same way that lacquers are for spotting in, except that straight retarder is usually the solvent used in the blender (mist) coat. The blender coat is sprayed over the edges of the repair and it is sprayed very dry, and only after the color coats, never between them. The blending process with enamels is almost a fog coating process.

When the repaired finish is thoroughly dry, it should be compounded well beyond the repair area to remove any overspray and to blend it into adjacent areas that were masked during the repair. If everything was done properly, a repair can be made that is indistinguishable from its surroundings.

Remember, body shops accomplish such repairs with metallic colors every day, and compared to the problems encountered in that proposition, spotting in solid colors can be kid's stuff.

You will note that I have not discussed how to effect spot repairs in clearcoat/basecoat systems. That is because I do not know how to do this and doubt tat it can be done with results that are acceptable for restoration work. I have talked to about a dozen painters who say that they can do it without leaving the telltale dull ring around the repair area in the clearcoat. But I have not yet seen anyone accomplish it.

There are some points that will help you to make successful spot repairs. The first is that this is demanding work, and it is important to strenuously observe all of the general cautions of good paint practice regarding cleanliness, paint mixing, solvent choice, gun technique and the like. It is also important to choose the boundaries of your spot repair area carefully so that the contours of panels will work to your advantage and not against you. If, for example, your chosen boundaries end at panel edges, it will be much more difficult to make a repair that does not show.

It is also important to remember that while it is possible, by rigorous attention to detail, to control the leveling of a repair area, its gloss and the quality of its blend into surrounding areas, you will have great difficulty controlling its color match. Good paint mixing and careful attention to gun technique will help you achieve a good color match, but if the repair paint does not match the surrounding panel, there is very little adjustment possible with gun technique alone that will save the situation. The use of a factory tinting kit *may* help.

Another useful technique is to raise your masking barrier and check the color match after you have sprayed two or three color coats. Color adjustment can be made at this point with the final color coats, as necessary.

One of the surest ways to ruin a spot repair is to neglect to provide adequate flash times with primer and color coats as you go along. This factor should be watched carefully.

Very Minor (Brush) Repairs

Automobile manufacturers sell and people buy little bottles of "repair" or "touch-up" paint that allegedly can be used to repair modern automotive finishes. This has been going on for at least 60 years. Business must be pretty brisk because all kinds of aftermarket manufacturers also sell little bottles of this stuff. Actually, there isn't anything particularly wrong with what is in the bottles, but it is what is not printed on the bottles that can get you into trouble. Remember that these are small bottles, about the size of a Magic Marker, and there isn't room to print much on their sides. Generally, the instructions suggest that it is important to shake the bottle until the agitator ball can be heard, and for some discreet period after that. Then, the instructions often seem to trail off into vagueness and only generally hint at application technique.

Armed with these bottles, people sally forth and attempt to cover little rust spots and nicks with the handy-dandy little nail polish-type brushes that are included in the lids of the little bottles. You see people performing this repair ritual in their driveways with every expectation that they have preserved the finishes of their cars. Often, the touch-up paint is applied over rust and even over the moisture that is left from washing the cars. The prime time for such repairs is in the fall to protect finishes from the ravages of on-coming winter.

Of course, rust just continues to fester under this kind of ill-conceived repair. Apparently, the well-meaning people who indulge in this fix-up-fantasy don't realize that the thumb nail-sized bubbles in the paint on their cars often originate in tiny nicks that were repaired this way. They just go on buying the bottles of touch-up paint and performing their touch-up rituals every year.

It is possible to make quick and reasonably effective brush repairs to small (1/4 inch in diameter or less) breaches in finishes, but it takes more than a dab of paint out of a bottle to do this.

Proper brush repairs can be an effective temporary repair technique. To make them durable and of satisfactory appearance, you still must follow the logic and sequences of proper refinishing. This begins with removing *all* rust from the area to be repaired.

A dental pick can be very handy for this purpose, particularly where rust has gotten into the pores of metal and produced pitting. Spot blasters also work well for this application. The repair area should then be sanded and feather edged. Since the object of brush repairs is to keep the repair area small, the feathering can be done with a lacquer dissolving feather edging solvent if lacquer is the finish being applied. Otherwise, you can rotate a piece of 320- or 400-grit sandpaper under the tip of your finger to produce shiny metal and a feather edge at the repair site. The bare metal should then be treated with metal conditioner and the excess wiped off the surrounding paint with a damp cloth. Next, the repair area should be primed and filled by lightly brushing in coats of primer-surfacer until it is roughly level with the rest of the finish.

The primer-surfacer can be applied with either a small artist's brush or a striping brush. It can also be air brushed through a 1/8-inch round aperture in a 3 x 5-inch card. The air brush and card technique produces the best repair, but you have to vibrate the card mask slightly as you shoot to blur the edges of the spray. This can be something like patting your head and rubbing your tummy at the same time; some people can do it naturally and other people have trouble with it.

Whatever technique is used to apply the primer-surfacer, it should be allowed to dry thoroughly between coats. The characteristic shrink of primer-surfacer, 50 percent from a wet condition to a dry one, should leave room for color coats and keep them roughly level with the panel when they dry.

When the primer-surfacer has flashed and dried, it should be sanded lightly with 600-grit sandpaper. This type of repair will rarely produce perfect leveling and is really a stopgap measure to arrest corrosion and further deterioration of a finish and to produce a reasonably attractive surface. If you try to achieve a perfect level, you can easily sand through the primer-surfacer, so settle for a reasonably level surface with a little depth left for filling with the color coats.

The next step is to brush the color onto the repair in about four coats. It should then be allowed to dry thoroughly. Then the repair area is compounded to blend it into the surrounding paint. Acrylic lacquer works best for this type of repair and should be mixed relatively thin with about 5 to 10 percent retarder included to help it flow out. Don't try to brush more paint in when preceding coats are tacky and stringy.

While brush repair is far from a perfect repair technique, it is a reasonable maintenance measure for finishes that would otherwise deteriorate from stone chips and other paint film defects. It has the integrity to confront corrosion, and if this kind of repair is carefully leveled, it will have a reasonably attractive appearance.

Paint Defects— What Went Wrong?

Back in the 1950s, when new and aftermarket automotive finishes were applied in either nitrocellulose lacquer or alkyd enamel, there were very few special problems in normal painting situations. One defect that constantly plague painters was the problem of fish eyes.

Fish eyes come from oil or silicone on the surface that you are painting. It can be there when you start painting, or it can be sprayed in with the air coming from your spray gun. Remember, in those days, many shops still were using war surplus and prewar vintage equipment, and some of the compressors in those shops had to have their oil checked very regularly because their rings were tired and leaked oil. Since rebuilding a compressor was a bothersome prospect

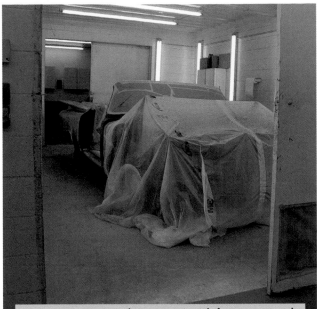

Keeping your spray area clean, vacuuming it before you spray and wetting its floor to suppress dust will help keep contamination out of your finished paint.

and the down time was a real problem, some other solution seemed desirable.

In response to the epidemic of fish eyes, DuPont introduced what may well have been the first paint film additive. It was supposed to suppress fish eyes and was called FEE (fish eye eliminator). It came in a squirt bottle. One squirt per pint paint cup seemed to smooth out paint almost miraculously—like oil on troubled water. Of course, miracles were simpler in those days. Some of those compressors were fuming oil pretty badly, and one squirt of FEE seemed to help, but it didn't always do the job. Now, it seemed that if one squirt would help, two squirts would be twice as good. Three, four and five squirts followed, as we got used to those miracles of the postwar world.

The trouble was that finishes that were applied with gobs of FEE—the other manufacturers quickly marketed their own versions of the stuff—tended to craze and crack paint a year-and-a-half down the road. Of course, you had yourself to blame for this problem because it was caused by purposely disregarding the instructions that came with this product. Worse yet, since FEE and its clones were designed to suppress fish eyes by literally saturating the paint with silicone hydrocarbon (to change its surface tension characteristics), it became very difficult to refinish cars that had had all of this free silicone embedded in their finishes. And this was exactly what happened when massive amounts of the stuff were squirted into paint.

In today's world of numerous and complex paint additives, the chances of additive-induced defects are infinitely greater. I suppose that is part of the price that has to be paid for finishes that are inherently better than the finishes of 40 or 50 years ago.

The surprising thing is that most defects in paint can be traced to fairly basic application problems and errors. There is an enormous commonality of causes for a varied

list of paint defects, and it is not often necessary to look for exotic causes. Such simple problems as contamination, inappropriate gun technique and failure to allow adequate flash times and setup times for finishes can cause a multitude of paint defects. The list that follows is not an exhaustive list of defects, nor do the causes given for each defect constitute a complete list of possible causes. I have concentrated on the most prevalent and obvious paint defects and the most common and correctable causes for them. Various refinishing textbooks and manufacturers' paint shop manuals can be referred to, as needed, for some of the more exotic paint defects and their causes.

In the following discussion of paint problems, the corrective measure to be taken for each problem should be assumed to be to reverse the cause of the problem. If, for example, the cause of a problem is stated to be inadequate air pressure, the appropriate correction is to increase the air pressure. Where the corrective action required for a problem involves a factor other than reversing the cause, for example, the use of a sealer to prevent bleeding, the

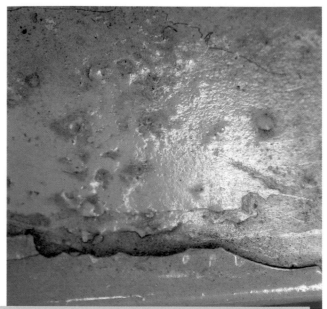

Lifting is one of the ugliest of all paint failures because it is highly visible and usually relatively easy to avoid. The first photo shows lifting caused by adhesion failure due to the undercoat gassing and pushing off a topcoat that was applied over it too soon. The above right photo shows lifting caused by applying new paint over an unsound, failing substrate.

appropriate corrective action will be stated specifically. Finally, where the factor of "gun technique" is stated as a possible cause of a problem, this is meant to include gun fan and material adjustments, tailstock air pressure regulation, distance from the panel, speed of the pass and correct gun stroke technique.

RUNS AND SAGS. This problem afflicts novice painters as they attempt to find the territory between causing this defect and spraying too dry. The most usual causes of runs and sags are gun technique and a failure to allow sufficient flash (lacquer) and setup (enamel) times for underlying paint coats. The use of solvents that are too slow for shop conditions and of air pressure that is too low are also often implicated in runs and sags. Be particularly careful when you spray very dark colors that you can see what you are spraying and adjust your gun pass speed appropriately to avoid runs and sags.

COLOR MATCHING PROBLEMS. The paint itself is the usual culprit in color match problems, and it is a good idea to spray a sample of any paint that you have to color match, so that adjustments to the paint itself can be made before you commit to a bad match. The factors involved in gun technique can make a difference in paint color, even with solid colors. Finally, a failure of top coats to completely hide underlying paint coats can result in color match problems. Complete hiding may require more paint, or the use of a sealer under top coats.

BLEEDING. This problem can involve any color, but it is most pronounced when some red undercoats are being over-coated. It involves a top coat solvent penetrating underlying paint and causing the color to bleed through. When bleeding is a problem, an appropriate sealer has to be used.

CONTAMINATION. This is an ever-present threat. Contamination on the surface that you are painting, of the

room in which you are painting or of the air or the paint that you are spraying can cause a whole range of problems, from cratering to fish eying and lifting. Surfaces to be painted should be solvent cleaned, blown off and tack wiped before coating. The spray area should be cleaned with a vacuum cleaner and the floor watered down to suppress dust. A painting area must have adequate ventilation, but such ventilation must not draw dust and grit into the area where painting is done.

The air supply for painting must be filtered clean of solid and liquid contaminants. Paint must be handled carefully and filtered into clean vessels when it is measured and mixed. Spray equipment must be kept completely clean and should always be cleaned up immediately after use. Be sure to clean spray gun lid gaskets and anti-drip tubes completely.

ORANGE PEEL. Some orange peel is normal in enamels and it is somewhat inherent in the nature of how enamels dry. The equivalent of orange peel in lacquer is a roughness that can be compounded out and, in fact, lacquers are compounded and polished level and glossy as standard operating procedure. Orange peel in enamels can be limited by using the correct solvent for shop conditions, sticking to manufacturers' recommended levels of reduction, and following recommendations on air pressure.

Correct air pressure is essential to spraying enamels, as very low air pressure produces orange peel by producing inadequate atomization of paint, and excessive air pressure tends to disrupt underlying coats and to evaporate solvents before paint can hit a panel. Good gun technique and adequate setup times also greatly influence the occurrence of orange peel. Remember that some cars were factory finished with large amounts of orange peel, and it is not desirable to eliminate this defect to the point that you create a mismatch with OEM paint in the process. Of course, if you are painting an entire car, you have a chance to improve on the OEM finish.

BLUSHING. This defect is manifested as a cloudiness in color coats and is caused by moisture (humidity) getting into a paint film. The use of solvent that is too fast for conditions can cause blushing. This is particularly true on humid days. If it is possible to schedule painting at times that allow you to avoid very humid conditions, try to do so. Using appropriately slow solvents, and even additions of retarder for hot, humid shop conditions, should prevent blushing. Sometimes, a mist coating with a slow solvent heavily laced with retarder will reverse blushing if you get to it quickly, before it dries completely.

FISH EYES. These are small defects where newly applied paint pulls away from small areas and refuses to adhere to them and coat them. They are always caused by wax, oil or silicone contamination. The best insurance against fish eyes is to carefully wash the area to be painted with mild detergent and water and then to wipe it down with an oil and silicone removing solvent before sanding it. It should be rewiped with solvent after it is sanded and just before it is painted. Fish eye-eliminating additives will suppress fish eyes, but because they do this by saturating paint with silicone, they can cause problems later when another refinish is attempted. In fact, the fish eye problems that you encounter on a previously refinished car may well be due to the excessive use of this additive at the time of a previous refinish.

In some shops, airborne silicone can be pulled into a paint area by ventilation fans that pick up wax debris from cars waxed with silicone waxes in adjacent areas. Some silicones get into painting air supplies because this substance is used as a foam suppressant in most industrial oils, and these oils are commonly used to lubricate air compressors. Most, or all, synthetic compressor oils do not use silicone anti-foam additives because they have less tendency to foam than conventional industrial oils.

SAND SCRATCH SWELLING. This defect produces very small scratch patterns in fresh paint and results from solvent trapped in the bottoms and sides of the grooves left by abrasives. Careful washing between the use of different grits of sandpaper, to avoid abrasive cross-contamination, and final sanding with grits in the range of 600 should eliminate most of this problem. The use of ultra grades of sandpaper or rubbing compound on vulnerable areas, like feather edges, is also highly effective. However, this last practice may produce long-range adhesion problems by not leaving enough tooth in the primer for really good adhesion. A final protection against sand scratch swelling involves using an appropriate sealer to prevent the solvent in top coats from penetrating what lies is under them.

ADHESION PROBLEMS—PEELING AND LIFTING. This type of problem may not manifest itself immediately, but it is pretty common because there are so many possible causes for it. Painting over uncured enamel is a common cause of paint lifting and peeling, as are compatibility problems between top coats and their basecoats.

Even when sealers are used, if they are the wrong types for the top coats involved, they will not prevent lifting. Too thick an application or accumulation of paint will cause adhesion problems in the long run, as will the use of incompatible solvents for the paint systems that you are using. Painting over an unscuffed surface can produce topcoat lifting, and painting over oil and other contamination, such as rust, will quickly cause paint to lift. Sandwiching an enamel primer or color coat between lacquer coats will produce lifting at a later date, and failure to provide adequate flash times for lacquers can cause lifting.

Sometimes, softening an underlying finish with a pre-clean solvent will allow top coat solvents to slightly penetrate it and will provide for better adhesion. Condensation trapped under top coats or primer can expand in warm conditions and cause a finish to lift and peel. This usually first shows up as blisters. Additive incompatibility is also a cause of adhesion problems.

DULLING. This condition involves a gradual loss of gloss or luster in a finish. It is frequently caused by compounding or polishing a finish too soon after application. Inadequate flash times can also produce this defect, as can the use of incorrect additives or incorrect dosages of appropriate additives. Improper reduction and thinning can result in dulling, and sometimes these problems are caused by a "holdout" failure in which the color coats sink into underlying paint. This last problem can be solved with the use of a correct sealer.

WRINKLING. This defect involves enamels and can have many of the same causes as adhesion problems. It can also be caused by a rapid change in shop temperature conditions in the early cure stage of enamel, or by the use of the wrong solvents for shop conditions. Wrinkling often results from additive incompatibility, piling on too many thick, wet coats or force drying a finish too soon after application and while solvents are still very present. Low air pressure and surface contamination of underlying surfaces can also cause wrinkling.

CHECKING, CRAZING AND CRACKING. This kind of stress defect in paint surfaces usually takes some time to show up and is frequently brought out by extreme temperatures. Paint films that are too thick are frequently the cause of cracking defects, and compatibility problems of top coats and undercoats also are often implicated. Additive compatibility problems can cause this type of defect, as can inadequate flash times and incompletely mixed paint. Sometimes, cracking occurs in a paint surface due to underlying surface cracks that transmit the defect to the overlaying topcoats.

BLISTERS. These nasty little pinhead-sized bumps are usually caused by humidity or moisture trapped under a paint surface. Blisters can be a result of weather conditions (high humidity) at the time the paint was applied. Moisture in your air supply or moisture residues from wet sanding that were not removed prior to color coating also can cause blisters.

OVERSPRAY. This defect, of course, can be controlled

Areas like this inner fender should be taken to bare metal, painted, and undercoated. Note that the factory was kind enough to leave this area in raw metal below the horizontal paint line that is visible. It is completely unprotected. While restoration aims at authenticity, this is one place were it is OK to deviate from that ideal and give this metal some protection.

with proper masking. It also can be compounded out. In enamels, excessive overspray can result from the use of the wrong reducer. Gun technique is also an issue in overspray defects. The new HVLP spray equipment pretty much eliminates any overspray problems.

DRY SPRAY. This problem can afflict lacquers and enamels and results from the use of the wrong solvent or of an inappropriate gun technique. Any gun technique and air pressure combination should be chosen to atomize a finish and apply it without runs or sags but also in a way that will cause it to flow out smoothly.

SINKING TOP COAT AROUND A FEATHER EDGE. This is the tendency for paint to sink into a feather edged area around a repair and to produce a dull halo effect. The use of a primer-surfacer with good hold-out characteristics should prevent this problem from occurring.

PINHOLING. These little pin-sized rascals in top coats are caused by inadequate flash times with lacquers, by spraying with your gun too close to a panel, or by piling paint on too thick and too wet. This type of defect is caused by trapped solvents under paint that was applied too fast or too thick or both.

SINKING. This problem involves the application of paint over incompletely cured body filler or over incompletely dried putty. Both of these substances shrink as they dry, and if they are painted over before they have fully

cured or dried, a finish will tend to sink with them.

DRY SPOTS. This is a problem that is usually created by the use of under-thinned or under-reduced paints or by the use of poorly manufactured solvents. Air pressure that is too high will also cause this defect, particularly in lacquers.

WET SPOTS. This defect involves paint that never dries but always remains tacky. It can be caused by paint contamination, surface contamination, incompatible paint and thinner or reducer or cold or poorly ventilated drying conditions. Failure to allow undercoats to dry before recoating can also cause this problem.

Finish Maintenance

Automotive finishes are under constant and vicious attack by road dirt, acid rain, industrial soot, flying stones, road salt, humidity, insects, pesticides, and sunlight—to name just a few of the hazards out there. The question naturally arises, "What can be done to protect finishes and prolong their service lives?"

The simplest maintenance of automotive finishes is to wash them regularly with a mild detergent and cold or lukewarm water. Avoid washing a car in direct sunlight and be sure to flush off loose grit with a hose before sponging or wiping a finish. If you don't do this, you will abrade a car's finish when you wash it. Always flush the underside of a car with water when you wash it.

If at all possible, try to use soft water when you wash a car to avoid spotting its paint with the minerals dissolved in hard water. Never wash a car with hot water—it stresses its paint. Always dry a car with a chamois or soft towel after it is washed, and never allow it to air dry without wiping. Any washing process involves rubbing the finish of a car and removes some paint in that process. There is always a very real possibility of scratching a finish when it is being washed. Be sure that sponges, brushes, and towels used in washing and drying are free from grit that could scratch a finish. Belt buckles can be real finish destroyers when you are washing a car.

Proper maintenance of automotive finishes requires that small breaches in paint be repaired, as outlined earlier in this chapter, and this should be done as quickly as possible, certainly before corrosion can penetrate deeply into the metal. Modern paints tend to be very resistant to oxidation, compared to their predecessors, but at some point any finish will chalk and the appearance of oxidation—usually visible as a slight clouding and roughening of a finish's surface in its initial stages—should be compounded and/or polished out.

There are two schools of thought about waxes and about the new super "sealants" that have been on the market for two or three decades. One school holds that waxes do little to protect finishes and, because most modern waxes contain abrasives and chemical paint softeners, they tend to deteriorate a finish in the long run. Almost all modern waxes, and particularly the sealants, contain silicones. These can get into crevices and later make refinishing difficult. The anti-wax school holds that modern finishes are so inherently tough that they do not benefit from the application of waxes, and that while the appearance of water beading on a freshly waxed hood is an intrinsically satisfying sight, wax does little to protect finishes. The other school of thought holds that waxes seal and protect paint and even enhance its ability to resist scratching and chemical damage.

I have attended to this question with almost incessant meditation and prayer—it requires no less—and have come to the conclusion that waxing a properly applied modern finish is pointless, at best. There is no significant protection available from waxing, and the abrasion and softening of finishes caused by most waxes is undeniable. If you enjoy waxing a car, I think that you should continue to enjoy this activity, but the probability is that you are doing it for yourself and not for your car. The gloss-enhancing effects of wax are very temporary, at best. Certainly, wax should not be applied over fresh finishes as it will interfere with their "breathing" and, thus, with their complete drying or curing. Sometimes, cars are waxed after refinishing to remove swirl marks that were induced by hand or machine polishing. There are several products on the market, such as Liquid Ebony and Final Finish, that give freshly painted cars a gloss and temporarily subdue swirl marks without interfering with the drying or curing of a fresh paint. Every

This approved safety can is a good place to deposit used paint towels and rags because, under certain conditions, they can spontaneously combust. I hope that your restoration efforts proceed on "full" as you enjoy this great pursuit.

time I feel the urge to wax a car, freshly painted or not, I reach for one of these pseudo waxes instead.

On cars finished with nitrocellulose lacquers, or in cases of deteriorated acrylic finishes, waxing probably does help. In these cases, a wax system should be used that has an abrasive polish as a first step and a pure carnauba wax for the second part. This avoids the chemical softeners and silicones that are common to the one-step waxes that are the basis of the waxing controversy. Of course, there are few nitro-cellulose finished cars left on the planet, but you sometimes encounter this type of finish on dashboards and other interior panels on very old cars.

Since much of the rust that deteriorates finishes originates from the undersides of panels, there is the idea that sealing a car with undercoating and sealing its trim with paraffin-based sprays will retard body deterioration. I think that this is true if the application of undercoating is very carefully done and if a non-hardening, paraffin-based undercoating is used. The old, asphaltic undercoatings rusted many cars because they hardened and cracked. In that state, they tended to attract moisture to metal by capillary action. They then held moisture against metal. That helped to rust the metal.

Similarly, I have seen modern paraffin-based undercoatings that were so casually applied that rust that might not have otherwise started occurred at the edge of the application. I have yet to see undercoating stick to the undersides or backsides of panels on a car that was not relatively new when it was undercoated.

Steam cleaning an old car will not help in this regard. Undercoating a rusting surface is probably pointless and even may be counterproductive. It is also critical that if undercoating is used in car doors and other areas that have drainage holes, those holes not be plugged with the undercoating.

One of the greatest contributions that you can make to the survival of the finish on a collector car is good storage. Storage outside in the sun is, of course, bad for paint, upholstery, rubber etc. Yet, storage in a musty, dank garage is just as damaging in other ways. The height of bad storage is to put a car under a plastic sheet so that the plastic (usually polypropylene) can scratch and abrade the finish that it contacts. Plastic sheets also tend to trap moisture and keep cars in near rain forest conditions if they are used to cover cars sitting on unsealed floors. Car covers, tarps, and the like usually do more harm than good by trapping moisture. I have seen cars ruined over prolonged periods by this kind of storage. I use simple bed sheets to cover cars in storage.

Any covers used over collector cars should be at least "breathable," or should keep moisture entirely away from a car. The Omnibag storage system and other similar products completely seal cars from moisture in heavy plastic bags and use a desiccant that can be periodically oven dried to keep the moisture level in the bag at desert levels. This system works.

Concrete floors look as if they should be waterproof, but in an untreated state, concrete is a substance that constantly passes and releases moisture that can attack the underside of a car. Putting foamed styrene sheets or polypropylene sheets under concrete before it is poured can help limit this problem. There are also sealants that can be applied over clean concrete that will greatly reduce its ability to release moisture. Putting a four or six mil polypropylene sheet, such as Visqueen, under a car in storage can help a lot, but, of course, moisture that the concrete releases still comes around the sides of the car. Good ventilation is your best bet, and this can be arranged in most storage buildings without having to resort to forced-draft ventilation.